Managing Retailing

SECOND EDITION

PIYUSH KUMAR SINHA

Professor, Marketing, and
Chairperson, Centre for Retailing
Indian Institute of Management Ahmedabad

DWARIKA PRASAD UNIYAL

Associate Professor (Marketing)
Indian Institute of Management (IIM) Kashipur

UNIVERSITY PRESS

OXFORD
UNIVERSITY PRESS

Oxford University Press is a department of the University of Oxford.
It furthers the University's objective of excellence in research, scholarship,
and education by publishing worldwide. Oxford is a registered trademark of
Oxford University Press in the UK and in certain other countries.

Published in India by
Oxford University Press
YMCA Library Building, 1 Jai Singh Road, New Delhi 110001, India

© Oxford University Press 2007, 2012

First Edition published in 2007
Second Edition published in 2012
Fourth impression 2014

ISBN-13: 978-0-19-807594-3
ISBN-10: 0-19-807594-4

Typeset in Garamond
by Le Studio Graphique
Printed in India by Yash Printographics, Noida 201 301

Dedicated to my parents,
Mr Mithileshkumar Dwarkaprasad Sinha and Mrs Shail Sinha

Piyush Kumar Sinha

Dedicated to my parents,
Mr B.P. Uniyal and Mrs Usha Uniyal
My wife Sneha Uniyal and son Rudraksh Uniyal

Dwarika Prasad Uniyal

Preface to the Second Edition

Retailing is the set of business activities that adds value to the products and services sold to consumers for their personal or family use. It is the final link between the manufacturer or producer of goods and the direct consumers of those goods. In other words, it is the last link of supply chain management. Retailing involves all the activities in the sale of goods or services to the final consumers for personal or direct consumption, through a fixed location. Thus, retailing in its most simplified form may be defined as *an activity that involves the sale of merchandise from a fixed location, such as a store, for direct consumption by the customer.* It can also be defined as *an activity that ensures that customers derive maximum value from the buying process.*

The dictionary definition of a retailer is 'a dealer or trader who sells goods in small quantities'. The most important job of a retailer is to present *the right goods, in the right quantity, at the right time, in the right condition, and at the right price.* This is a function that provides the 'last mile connectivity' between an organization and its customers and its nature keeps changing with time and place.

Retailing is a very evolving business. It has been a challenge keeping pace with these changes, especially in India and several emerging economies. It has also attracted researchers from across the world seeking new insights into the phenomenon. Updation of information is a warranted change, which has been our motivation to present this second edition.

New to the Second Edition
- New chapter on retail marketing
- New case studies
- Updated data
- New sections including rural marketing, foreign direct investment (FDI) in retail, retail inventory management, negotiations in retail, and fairness in pricing

Extended and New Chapter Material

Chapter 1: The Domain of Retailing Updated data and tables

Chapter 2: Indian Retail Industry
- A new section on rural marketing, citing examples of innovative rural retail initiatives, such as Hariyali Kissan Bazaar and Project Shakti; another new section
- A new section on FDI in retail detailing experience of FDI in retail trade in China and of Thailand in opening their retail sector to FDI
- A new case study on Nirantar Agrasar Retail and updated data and tables

Chapter 3: Retailing in Other Countries
- New sections describing the retailing scenario in Brazil, Russia, and Chile
- Updated data, tables, and annexure

Chapter 4: Understanding Shopping and Shoppers Updated data and tables

Chapter 5: Delivering Value through Retail Formats
- New sections added to expand the discussion on non-traditional retailing formats—catalogue stores, shopping strips, rural marts, flower markets, and cattle fairs

- New section discussing an attitude-based model for store format choice
- Updated data

Chapter 6: Deciding Location
- New section on Converse's Breaking-point Model, as a method of estimating demand
- New section on determining location for online retailers

Chapter 7: Category Management New tables depicting the importance of shelf presentation and indices for category performance

Chapter 8: Supply Chain Management
- New sections on retail inventory management, retail logistics management, and electronic data interchange in supply chain management
- New case study on Woolworths Limited, Australia

Chapter 9: Retail Buying
- New sections on negotiations and contracts in retail
- New annexure exhibiting snapshots of contract agreements used by retailers

Chapter 10: Store Layout and Design New section on layout for e-tailers discussing the entertainment, organization, and informativeness elements of retailer websites

Chapter 11: Retail Marketing Strategy This new chapter highlights the decisions that retailers take to compete in the marketplace. It dwells on building strong retail brands. It takes a research-based consumer attitude route to explain the process. The role of attitude, cognition, and affect has been highlighted in the process. The activity of sales enhancements has been approached through a strategic as well as tactical route, for retailers to adopt them very easily. It also highlights the role of social media and how retailers across the world are using them strategically. The use of a balanced scorecard for enhancing retail performance and customer service has also been explained.

Chapter 13: Establishing a Pricing Strategy New sections on fairness in pricing and impact of pricing strategy on formats, which presents a price-based classification of store formats.

Chapter 14: Building Store Loyalty General revision by expanding the existing discussions

Chapter 15: The Shop as a Social Entity Expanded discussion on the link between the external elements of the retail environment and shopper behaviour

Chapter 16: Technology in Retailing A new section on the technology–human interface

Glossary Many new terms have been added.

Acknowledgements

Several individuals and organizations have contributed significantly to the second edition of the book. We are grateful to Sujo Thomas, who provided the research assistance for this book. Sudhakar, of indiaplaza.com, needs special mention for providing the case on Fabmall.

The publishers have made every attempt to preserve the quality and suitability of the book for students of retailing in management schools. We acknowledge their initiative and commitment.

Readers can send their suggestions and feedback at pksinha@iimahd.ernet.in and uniyal.dwarika @gmail.com.

PIYUSH KUMAR SINHA

DWARIKA PRASAD UNIYAL

Preface to the First Edition

Retailing is an integral part of the value chain in an organization. It is a function that provides the 'last mile connectivity' between an organization and its customers. In many parts of the world, retailers have emerged as one of the most potent forces in influencing the performance of the value chain.

Retailing is undergoing unprecedented change in developing economies. In India, this change is very perceptible. Fuelled by the growth in consumer income and changes in their spending patterns, the retail industry is growing at a rapid pace. The economic liberalization of the country has not only facilitated the entry of international retailers but also provided Indian retailers the opportunity to adopt the best practices and formats of some of these successful international retailers. This is a phenomenon that is being witnessed in all parts of Asia.

Retailers in Asia face issues that are unique to the continent. Traditional stores exist in the same space as new format stores. Retailers have been small in size and several in number. In India alone, there are more that 15 million retailers and, with the advent of new format retailers such as Shoppers Stop, Big Bazaar, and Crossword, their number is rising. However, the share of organized retailing, including that of online retailing, has remained the same throughout the last decade. This poses a problem for the manufacturers as they need a different set of skills and competencies to sell through different formats.

With the emergence of large retail chains and malls, retailing is fast emerging as an important area of study in business schools. Today, there is growing interest in retailing among MBA students as it has opened up several new avenues of employment. An understanding of the developments in the world of retailing, especially from a localized perspective, would help all those involved in the management of retailing as a business as well as a function. A study of retail operations, store location, shopper behaviour, pricing and communication strategies, and the functioning of the supply chain would help students and practitioners understand the management of store operations.

About the Book

Managing Retailing is designed to meet the needs of management students for a comprehensive textbook on retail management. It provides an in-depth coverage of retail theory based on original research. The book presents concepts that are clearly explained through illustrations, examples, exhibits, tables, and figures. With its problem-solving approach, the book will also be useful for practitioners involved in retail businesses.

Some chapters are unique to this book. The chapter on category management provides a different perspective from the conventional merchandise planning described in most available textbooks. The chapter on store loyalty would help students and practitioners understand how loyalty programmes can be managed successfully. A new dimension to retailing has been added in the chapter on shop as a social entity. The chapter on technology discusses recent developments in retail technology, with special emphasis on in-store technologies.

The end-chapter case studies have been selected to suit the learning requirements of the readers for each chapter. These cases cover different aspects of developing retail markets. With their focus on decision-making, the cases illustrate the application of concepts discussed in the book in actual situations. The cases on FoodWorld and Planet Health bring out the challenges faced by a first mover and highlight how retailers can carve a niche for themselves by providing enhanced customer value. The case study on Akaash Book Depot has been provided to illustrate the process of deciding the store location. Girish Food Store is a case that would help readers gain an insight into the strategic and minute detailing required for category management. The case study on Crossword has been discussed to highlight the strategic role played by loyalty programmes in enhancing the performance of a store.

Coverage and Structure

This book has been structured along the retailing decision process. The world of retailing has been explored in Chapter 1. The chapter describes retailing as a value creation and delivery process, indicating that retailers need to create utilities for the customers. The chapter outlines the history of retailing and discusses various theories that have been propounded to describe the evolution of retailing. It also discusses various decisions that retailers need to take in order to make their operations efficient and their business sustainable.

Chapters 2 and 3 describe the retailing industry in India and some other Asian countries. The retailing scenario in the US and some European countries has been described as a reference point. These chapters provide an insight into the world of retailing in developing nations and highlight the opportunities and challenges faced by retailers in these nations.

Chapter 4 is aimed at understanding shoppers and the phenomenon of shopping. The chapter views shopping from different dimensions to provide a holistic view of the phenomenon. It describes the demographic, psychographic, and values and lifestyle (VALS) profiles of Indian shoppers.

Chapter 5 discusses the formats available to retailers in the current scenario. The retail format is a tangible aspect of the value proposition of a retailer. The format of a store is the face of the retailer. It helps retailers realize their objectives. The chapter classifies retail formats into store-based and non-store-based retail formats. It delves into the benefits and limitations of each of these formats. It also discusses emerging formats such as Internet retailing and supercentres. It discusses electronic retailing, or e-tailing, in detail and provides a comprehensive view of the e-tailing business. The chapter suggests a process for deciding on a format that would best suit the retailer's objectives, resources, and target market.

Chapter 6 explains the process of identifying a location that would be most suitable to the retailer. It describes the process in terms of two broad steps: (i) deciding the trading area, and (ii) identifying a site for the store. It also discusses various models that are utilized for this purpose.

Chapter 7 discusses how category management helps retailers provide the right mix of products, at the right price, with the right promotions, at the right time, and at the right place. Category management, as a cornerstone of efficient consumer response (ECR) initiatives, is designed to devise suitable merchandise offers.

Chapter 8 discusses supply chain management, which is another important aspect of ECR. It describes the supply chain as a system of adding value to the business. While the focus is on managing cost and continuous supply, it also highlights the importance of forecasting demand. In addition, the chapter deals with the phenomenon of private branding, which has seemingly emerged out of the vacuum left in the supply chain when manufacturers fail to consider the requirements of every retailer. The chapter discusses how retailers can use the supply chain to develop competitive advantage.

Chapter 9 is devoted to the buying function of a retailer. It focuses on the criticality of the purchasing activity to retail businesses. The chapter describes the role of the buyer and the characteristics that retailers look for in such a person. It goes on to describe the process efficient retailers would follow in developing a buying plan. This involves demand forecasting and detailing down to the stock keeping unit (SKU) level so that the store has the lowest inventory cost and is never out of stock.

Chapter 10 discusses store layout. The emphasis of the chapter is on arriving at a layout that reduces the stress experienced by customers while shopping. The chapter describes several plans available to the retailer for managing the circulation. It discusses the elements of store layout, such as planning and circulation, storefronts and entrances, merchandise display, materials and finishes, and graphics and signage. It also delves into the role of factors such as scent, music, and lighting.

Chapter 11 discusses the role of external and internal communication in building store image, with special focus on point of purchase (PoP) communication. It discusses the various tools of external communication in terms of their advantages and limitations. The chapter discusses the role and packaging and the considerations involved in designing a product pack. It provides a framework for developing appropriate strategies for PoP communication and suggests the right tool of communication in a given condition. The conditions are described on the basis of the level of customer involvement and the value proposition that the store provides to the customers. Further, the chapter provides a 3 × 3 matrix to suggest options for PoP communication in various situations.

Chapter 12 elaborates the process of developing pricing strategies and policies. It also highlights the impact of pricing on other elements of the retail mix. The chapter discusses the bases of pricing, such as demand-oriented pricing, cost-oriented pricing, and competition-oriented pricing. It also discusses the options available to retailers in implementing a pricing strategy, such as everyday low pricing (EDLP) and high–low pricing. In addition, the chapter discusses the phenomenon of reference price in detail and explores various studies on the impact of reference prices on shoppers' behaviour with regard to store and merchandise choice.

Chapter 13 deals with the management of customer loyalty. The chapter first delineates the factors affecting the store choice behaviour of customers. It goes on to discuss the store choice behaviour of Indian customers. It then explains how loyalty is different from patronage. The chapter also provides a framework for managing shopper loyalty.

Chapter 14 looks at the shop as a social entity. Shoppers have been found to modify their behaviour on the basis of the type of store environment they are in. They tend to alter their behaviour as they move from one store to the other. The chapter attempts to explain this phenomenon by exploring the various tangible and intangible aspects of this 'society'. It views the store as a world with its own code of conduct, language, and norms. With the customers at the centre of activity, the chapter explores the world of retailing.

Chapter 15 discusses the role of technology. Retailing has witnessed the adoption of several technologies that help in managing the supply chain and product displays and make shopping an enjoyable activity.

A common thread that runs along all the chapters in the book is the process of delivering value to the customer, where manufacturers and retailers are strategic partners. The book has been designed to aid prospective retailers and manufacturers in taking effective retailing decisions. In order to develop a holistic understanding of various aspects of retailing, it is suggested that the text be used along with the cases. Readers are requested to read this book with an eye to understand and implement the best practices of new format businesses as well as traditional retailers.

Acknowledgements

Several individuals and organizations have contributed significantly to this book. It has been supported financially by Research and Publication, Indian Institute of Management Ahmedabad (IIMA). The research assistance for this book was provided by Vandana Sood. She also helped in coordinating with other organizations and individuals. We are thankful to the reviewers of this book for providing useful insights. The tedious task of editing was undertaken by Mark Parkinson, whose feedback on the language and consistency of the book was very helpful. Several organizations helped in bringing out the book. We would like to thank the Media Research User's Council (MRUC) for providing the IRS data used in the book. We are grateful to our colleagues at IIMA and MICA for providing encouragement and support in so many different ways. We also thank Mani Nagasubramanian, RD & M, Bangalore, for providing a large stock of photographs.

The publishers have made every attempt to ensure the quality and suitability of the book for students of retailing in management schools. We acknowledge their initiative and commitment.

Readers can send their suggestions and feedback at pksinha@iimahd.ernet.in and uniyal.dwarika@gmail.com.

PIYUSH KUMAR SINHA

DWARIKA PRASAD UNIYAL

Brief Contents

Detailed Contents

10. Store Layout and Design   355

11. Retail Marketing Strategy   405

1 The Domain of Retailing

LEARNING OBJECTIVES

After studying this chapter, you will be able to
- understand the concept of retailing
- understand the history of retailing
- discuss the utilities and dis-utilities provided by retailing
- elucidate the theories of retail development
- gain an insight into the retail management process

INTRODUCTION

Retailing as an activity can be traced back to the times when human beings stopped producing all their requirements by themselves and trading came into being. Communities such as potters, blacksmiths, and fishmongers sold their products to households. This was different from wholesale trade that led to spice routes from Malabar (Kerala) to Europe and beyond through Afghanistan and to silk routes in India and China. Retailers have now become an integral part of society.

RETAILING DEFINED

Retailing involves the sale of merchandise from a fixed location, such as a store, for direct consumption by the customer. It can be defined as an activity that ensures that customers derive maximum value from the buying process. This involves activities and steps needed to place the merchandise made elsewhere into the hands of customers or to provide services to the customers.[1] Retailers organize the availability of merchandise on a large scale and supply them to consumers on a relatively small scale. In the process, they provide the accessibility of the location and convenience of timing, size, information, and lifestyle support. When retailers perform these activities, they create value for their customers, who pay for these services. These values are created continuously through a combination of service, price, accessibility, and experience.[2]

One of the major roles played by retailers is to enable the adoption of products and services. Unless the product is made available at the store and is adopted by the retailers themselves, it is difficult to derive high values out of the marketing expenditure. The phenomenon, known as *dual adoption*, states that when a product is launched, customers adopt it symbolically, the actual adoption happens only when the retailers put forth the product in the right perspective.[3]

With more and more customers making purchase decisions at the store, retailing has gone beyond being a part of distribution function. It merits an independent marketing activity that is a combination of distribution and communication. Moreover, the changing canvasses of marketing, where physical products and the physical space of activity are also being joined by services and non-store retailing formats, pose new realities for retailers. They need to re-orient their perspective. There has to be a clear shift from a *distribution-oriented perspective*, where the physical aspects of merchandise availability and supply chain play an important role, to a more *consumer-value-oriented perspective* for attaining sustainable competitive advantages.

RETAILING AND DEVELOPMENT

Retailing has always played an integral part in economic development. Nations with strong retail activity have enjoyed greater economic and social progress. Retail activity provides a clear indication of the spending pattern of the consumers of a country. Retailing contributes to development by making the goods/services from the producers and suppliers of merchandise available to the population, catering to their individual requirement. By bringing the product to the customers, retailers help create demand for new offers, leading to the expansion of markets. Some of the benefits of a thriving retailing sector are

- access to products,
- better merchandise,
- not having to settle for a second or third choice when shopping for a particular product, and
- greater customer satisfaction and higher levels of customer service.[4]

Retailing symbolizes consumerism. The East European countries experienced a low rate of growth when they were under the Communist regime. After these countries opened up to the market forces and became part of the emerging economies, retailing became one of the forces driving consumption. Many international retailers gained instant popularity as they provided the customers a different shopping experience. A similar situation is now being witnessed in India, where new format stores, such as Shoppers Stop, Big Bazaar, and Crossword, have become places to see and be seen in, and customers are deriving a significant hedonic utility out of shopping. Shopping is taking on a new meaning in many categories. It now occupies a major part of the customers' leisure time.[5]

UTILITIES OF RETAILING

Retailing provides several utilities to customers. These utilities have been described as *distribution service outputs* by Louis P. Bucklin. Bucklin classified the utilities provided by retail decentralization into better product availability, waiting time, lot size, and variety. This implies that retailing ensures wider product availability to customers, reduced waiting time, provides them the desired lot size, and enhances variety, that is, the merchandise mix available to customers.[6] These service outputs evolve around the utilities of form, place, time, and size that a customer wants to optimize. Bucklin's classification was further refined into accessibility, product assortment, assurance of product delivery at the desired time and in the desired form, and availability of information and ambience.[7]

The discussion so far indicates that manufacturers are not the only agencies that add value to the product through production and communication. Retailers convert the merchandise received from manufactures into desired forms and also get involved in the communication function by providing information about availability and delivery of merchandise. In addition, retailers also communicate through store ambience and point of purchase communication. Thus, retailers play an important role in adding value to the merchandise produced by manufacturers. Through ambience, retailers also add a new dimension of non-economic output.

A framework for channel selection suggested by Rangan et al. indicated that customers tend to choose a particular channel based on eight attributes: (i) product information, (ii) product customization, (iii) product quality assurance, (iv) lot size, (v) assortment, (vi) availability, (vii) after-sales service, and (viii) logistics.[8] Thus, customers base their channel selection on the presence of these utilities. A similar classification of distribution services by Oi groups them into exchange, product line, convenience, auxiliary services, and production.[9] The performance of some of the distribution services by retailers instead of manufacturers has been referred to as the postponement of the manufacturing function so that the value to customers is delivered in the best possible manner. Thus, it is evident that retailing is not just about storing and distributing products. It is an extension of all the functions that would be carried out by the manufacturer, though in a different form. A retail store can be considered as a separate entity that is an integral part of the value delivery system that ensures that customers are satisfied with the promises made by the members of the channel. Retailers, therefore, provide the last mile connectivity of the brands with their customers.

Managing Values

Distribution services create utilities as well as dis-utilities, that is, negative (perceived) values for the customers. Several authors have attempted to classify these values.[10] The most acceptable description has been provided by Sheth, who states that consumer choice is a function of multiple values, including values that extend beyond economic utilities. The five values are (i) functional (in perceived terms, economic), (ii) emotional, (iii) social, (iv) epistemic, and (v) conditional. Functional values are related to economic needs; emotional values address psychological needs; social values satisfy the need for a sense of belonging; epistemic values address the need for novelty and ego satisfaction; and conditional values satisfy the needs arising out of a particular condition.

A combination of positive and negative values, as shown in Table 1.1, brings out several dimensions of retail business that affect value design and delivery to customers.

HISTORY OF RETAILING

Retailing as an occupation came into existence when farmers started producing more food than they required. Trading was an important part of daily life in the ancient world. Different people had different skill sets, and people who had a surplus of one good desired the goods they did not have or could not produce.[11]

In India, the existence of the current *kirana* format and other shops can be traced to the *Manusmriti* and Kautilya's *Arthshastra*. These texts provided guidelines for dealing with customers, after-sales service, and quality and price guarantees. Such scholarly works provided the equivalence for exchange in case of barter. They also defined the tax structure for retail and wholesale transactions. Kautilya commented on the location of stores dealing in specific products in a city. He also discussed the manner in which funds and investments could be managed for better results. Memoirs of traders who came from Europe indicate that Indian merchants carried out business with low margins in order to enhance sales. Indian history and archeology record the existence of markets during the Harappan civilization also. Elaborate descriptions of local and periodic *haats* have also been found.

TABLE 1.1 A Generic Perceived Customer Value Grid

	Positive Functional Values	Positive Social Values	Positive Emotional Values	Positive Epistemic Values	Positive Conditional Values
Negative Functional Values	Convenient opening hours, but expensive	Place to be, but expensive	My late father's favourite supplier, but too expensive	Newly opened store, but inconvenient location	Extreme cheapness of available produce because of glut, but too narrow range
Negative Social Values	Good merchandise, but 'not-my-kind-store'	Many habituals who are good acquaintances, but also the opposite	My late father's favourite supplier, but many dubious clients these days	Newly opened store, but 'not-my-kind-store'	Extreme cheapness of available produce because of glut, but 'not-my-kind-store'
Negative Emotional Values	Good prices, but unpleasant salespeople	Lifestyle store, but unpleasant sales personnel	My late father's favourite supplier, but unpleasant sales representatives	New interactive kiosk at store, but unpleasant visitors	Extreme cheapness of available produce because of glut, but unpleasant visitors
Negative Epistemic Values	Good prices, but never any new item	Lifestyle store, but never any new item	My late father's favourite supplier, but no innovative items at all	Always has lots of new items, but not accessible for inspection	Extreme cheapness of available produce because of glut, but never any new item
Negative Conditional Values	Good merchandise, but air conditioner out of order	Place to be, but music system out of order	Touching opera performance, but air conditioner out of order	Winter fashion show, but music system out of order	Extreme cheapness of available produce because of glut, but electrical doors out of order

Source: van Waterschoot, Walter, Piyush Kumar Sinha, Joeri de Haes, Annouk Lievens, and Steve Burt, 'Revisiting the Concept and Classification of Distribution Service Outputs', Working Paper No. 2004–12–02, IIMA.

These were the places where commodity exchange was carried out and people congregated and derived several non-economic values.

The new retail formats that are now seen in India have their genesis in Europe. The earliest traders were believed to be the Cretans who sailed across the Mediterranean and carried on trade with the people of the area. They flourished for 2,000 years, and their culture influenced other great trading civilizations. The Phoenicians followed the Cretans as civilization's major traders. They distributed the goods of Egypt and Babylonia. Tyre, Sidon, and Carthage were the principal trading cities of this empire. After the Phoenicians, came the Romans. The Romans established a different form of retailing. They set up numerous small shops with centres. In fact, ancient ruins indicate that the world's first department store was in Rome. With the fall of this empire, retailing disintegrated.

During the period after the fall of the Roman empire, independent peddlers were the only retailers. They carried their merchandise around on their back. They went from village to village selling their wares. By the twelfth century, artisans and traders began to organize into 'guilds' and opened up small shops. These guilds helped them gain social and economic advantages. During the thirteenth century, fairs and markets flourished. Early fairs often had a religious foundation. People would gather at churches and exchange goods on feast days. People travelled long distances to participate in larger markets called fairs. Tea centres run by Lipton were the first chain of stores.

At the start of the twentieth century, markets were witnessing the precursors to the present-day retailing scenario:[12]

1. The retailer, and not the products he/she sold, was the brand.
2. Family-owned retail units dominated the market, but large retail corporations were also emerging in the form of corporate and cooperative stores.
3. Small retailers were resisting the entry of large retailers.
4. Many retailers and manufacturers had direct relationships.
5. New technologies in transport and construction were influencing store decisions.
6. International sourcing by retailers was also witnessed.
7. City centres were becoming major points for comparison buying.
8. Shopping centres were coming up at city centres and railway stations.

These developments were also witnessed in other countries, especially in North America. Large corporations were entering into retailing in the USA and Canada in the early twentieth century. The history of American retailing can be traced back to shops located near ports where merchants from Europe would dock their ships and sell the merchandise. Many American retailing institutions originated after 1850. Prior to that, most Americans lived on farms and were self-sufficient. During this time, peddlers and general stores were the only retailers in the country. Department stores started gaining prominence after 1850. As department stores grew in cities, rural citizens used the first form of direct catalogue/mail order marketing. This allowed them to get the goods they needed without the hassle of travelling long distances into the city.[13]

The development of railroad systems and refrigeration between 1890 and 1920 enabled shoppers to travel more widely and choose from a greater assortment of merchandise. The first set of department stores opened during this time. They offered more convenient and consolidated locations, longer hours, and better prices. American retailing witnessed the proliferation of other formats such as supermarket chains and shopping malls between the two World Wars. National brands such as Wonder Bread and Hostess were introduced in the market during this time. The first convenience store, 7–11 (Texas), and the first McDonald's (Illinois) also opened.

The time between 1950 and 1970 witnessed the emergence of major players and formats. The first indoor regional mall was set up by Southdale. The next big retail shift came when Sam Walton opened the first Walmart and discounters, such as Kmart and Target, opened their stores. These stores used low costs and high turnovers to provide customers with lower prices. Kroger installed the first retail bar code scanner and the first GAP store opened in San Francisco. Walmart integrated computer systems to its operation. These mass retailers also set up independent distribution systems to gain the volume necessary for negotiating with suppliers, track inventory, and allow for just-in-time (JIT) replenishment. In the next decade (1970–1980), the retail industry witnessed the emergence of category killers and wholesale club stores such as Toys "R"Us, Home Depot, Circuit City, and Sam's Club. The industry started getting consolidated at this time.

During the 1980s, superstores and retail category killers made up about one-third of the US retail revenues. In response to these price players, other formats such as malls, speciality stores, and grocery stores started stressing on 'retailtainment'. Mall of America—one of the largest malls in the world—opened in Minneapolis. Sears exited its general merchandise catalogue business. This was the time when the retailers started focusing on the 'store as brand' strategy. The 1990s can be termed as the times of the Internet. Amazon.com launched its book retailing business using e-commerce. This period also witnessed major internalization efforts by large retailers. The 1990s witnessed a lot of turbulence in the American retail industry. Retailers turned into multi-format entities, especially with the help of the Internet. The focus has now shifted to the emerging economies and retailers are searching for a different business model to succeed in these markets ruled by small retailers.

From the year 2000 onwards, the pace at which traditional retailing is getting transformed into modern retailing is incredible. This is evident from the straggling shopping centres, multi-storey malls, and huge complexes that offer shopping, entertainment, and food all under one roof. Along with the striking transformation in the demographics of the Indian population, we are also experiencing the advent of large corporate houses and superior IT management in the retail sector. This sector has grown at a compound annual growth rate (CAGR) of 11.2 per cent during the period 2007–09, with food and grocery accounting for the major share. The Indian industry is dominated by unorganized retailers, but the organized retailing revenues have also increased at a CAGR of 19.5 per cent during the period 2007–09, with the apparel and footwear segments accounting for the major share.[14]

THEORIES OF RETAIL DEVELOPMENT

The retail scenario keeps changing continuously. These changes are brought by ever-changing customer requirements, economic development of the nation, falling borders, new technologies, and by entrepreneurs. Countries like India and many other Asian and East European countries are witnessing unforeseen changes in the landscape of retailing. The traditional retailers, recognized as mom-and-pop stores, are now sharing the canvas with malls, departmental stores, and large price format stores. Several theories have been propounded to explain such developments. We shall now discuss some of these theories.

Wheel of Retailing

The wheel of retailing theory is one of the oldest and most acceptable theories of the development of retailing. It postulates that retailers enter the business at a fairly low status, low prices, and with low price operation. This helps them compete against the established retailers. With time, when such retailers succeed, they acquire more sophisticated and elaborate facilities. Finally, they mature as high-cost, high-price retailers who become vulnerable to new entrants, who, in turn, go through the same process.[15] This happens because these stores are usually established by entrepreneurs who are aggressive and cost conscious and do not want unprofitable frills. However, they tend to lose the control over cost as they acquire age and wealth. Their successors turn out to be less competent. Either the innovators or their successors fail to adapt to the changed environment and the laxity in management lead them along the wheel.[16] Figure 1.1 shows the wheel of retailing.

The Retail Accordion

Retail development is linked to human habitation. It expands or contracts in line with the geographical expansion of the society. When a new area or location is developed and customers start living in that area, the early stores deal in almost all products needed by these customers. Few stores that come up match the offerings of these early retailers. Most of them attract customers due to convenience, as the travel and search costs from other localities are more. In most cases, these stores deal with consumer non-durable products and several emergency or infrequently purchased products such as hardware and electrical products. However, as the locality evolves, a set of stores starts and offers merchandise that does not necessarily overlap with that of the existing retailers. These stores also specialize in a particular category. In most cases, these are consumer durable and household appliances. Petrol pumps, restaurants,

Low-priced merchandise;
high value store

High-priced merchandise;
top range store

Trading up mid-priced merchandise;
mid-range store

FIG. 1.1 The Wheel of Retailing

shops selling gifts and other lifestyle products, and beauty salons are some of the retailers that emerge. This trend continues till the trading area witnesses a good growth. As the growth tapers, the retailers turn their attention from acquiring more customers to maximizing the value per customer. This starts a phenomenon where retailers start adding unrelated merchandise to their offering and slowly a large number of them become 'general' merchants.[17] The cycle continues, and after some time, 'specialist' retailers emerge, which add significant value to one category of merchandise and attract clientele on the basis of either range or value added products. Some of them become price players and some emerge as category killers.

Melting Pot Theory

According to this theory, a new value proposition by one retailer gives rise to two new retailers with the same proposition.[18] This theory, also called the *dialectic process*, suggests that retail firms adapt mutually to the emerging competition and tend to adopt the plans and strategies of the opposition.[19] This was epitomized in the earlier *avatar* of Tesco, where it would simply match what Sainsbury would offer. Their policies became similar in terms of facilities, offerings, supplementary services, prices, and even the loyalty programme rewards.[20] It took almost ten years for Tesco to recover from this and become the most respected retailer. This phenomenon of melting pot is also very evident in the white goods sector, catalogue stores, and petrol pumps. This gives rise to a process where a successful retail 'formula' catches like wildfire and many retailers adopt it without really finding out the key success factors. Thus, after some time, the mortality rate increases and many of them are not sure of the reason for its failure. In the grocery sector, India is facing a price-led dialectic process. The instant success of the model attracted several retailers and just buying in bulk and selling it cheaper than the current retailers has not led to many facing closure.

Polarization Theory

This theory suggests that, in a longer term, the industry consists of mostly large and small-sized retailers. The medium-sized becomes unviable. This is called polarization. The large-sized retailers take advantage of large and direct purchases from the manufacturers and offer a large range at very competitive prices. This phenomenon has led to an increase in the size of retailers and reaction in their numbers. Larger stores offer one-stop shopping. The smaller retailers tend to offer a limited range of products, but add value to their offers with other services, or tend to specialize. It is found that firms tend to be more profitable when they are either smaller in size or they are big. The mid-size firms fall into the Bermuda Triangle.[21]

The *Bermuda Triangle Effect* refers to the phenomenon where the performance of mid-sized firms suffers if big mid-sized firms continue to 'act small', or small mid-sized firms set up costly big-firm practices. Informally organized firms have low fixed costs. Small firms that are informally organized have low operating costs, but as size increases, the need for coordination within the organization increases, and informal organization often leads to errors and confusion. Thus, the cost of operating informally increases as a convex function of scale. Conversely, formal organizations incur fixed costs such as the cost of running an information system. For a small firm, this fixed cost is distributed over a small output, so that the cost per unit of revenue is high. However, as the firm increases in size, the fixed cost is distributed over a larger volume, thus lowering operating cost as a fraction of revenue.

Ideally, small organizations should be managed informally and large organizations should be managed formally. As a firm grows in size, it should have a transition at the cost cross-over point from informal to formal management. However, organizations do not have a transition at the optimal point. Some move from informal to formal too early, others wait too long before making the transition. The result is that mid-sized firms face higher costs and lower profitability. This leads to the Bermuda Triangle of management—many firms enter it, not all get out of it from the other end. There is plenty of evidence to suggest that small independent retailers have been affected by large retailers. However, it is expected that specialized stores would grow to and fill the mid-size segment.[22]

India is witnessing a peculiar phenomenon where both independent and large format stores are increasing by leaps and bounds. However, it is too early to predict whether polarization would occur in India as well.

RETAIL MANAGEMENT PROCESS

Retailing is a complex business. The complexity comes not out of the activities involved, but out of the detailing and precision involved in implementing each of the decisions. It is about every customer that visits the store and about every transaction that the customer gets involved in. While most retailing businesses involve products, the act of retailing is essentially a service that the manufacturer asks the retailers to perform. The product, which is the centre of activity for most of the manufacturers, becomes just one of the elements in the delivery of retailing service to the customers. In this business, the customer is always present during the process of delivery of the service. The presence of customers in the premises or during the process makes retailing a very involving business.

Compared to manufacturers, retailers have to take much better care of their customers because, unlike manufacturers of brands, the trading area of a retail store is limited. There is a high likelihood of exhausting the store's potential faster. Thus, the business has to depend far more on repeat purchase. Manufacturers are generally concerned about the market share arising out of the number of customers or the rate of usage. Retailers are more concerned about deriving more value out of their limited customer base. This makes it imperative that opportunities are assessed more accurately and customers are well cared for.

The retailing process involves several decisions. Figure 1.2 provides a framework for retailing decisions. At the core of the framework is the *retail value proposition*. The proposition is derived keeping in mind the market profile and expectations, opportunities present in the market, competitive stances and activities, and the retailer's objectives and resources. Based on the proposition, retailers decide on the formats, merchandise, location, supply chain, pricing, promotion, and other aspects of the retailing mix.

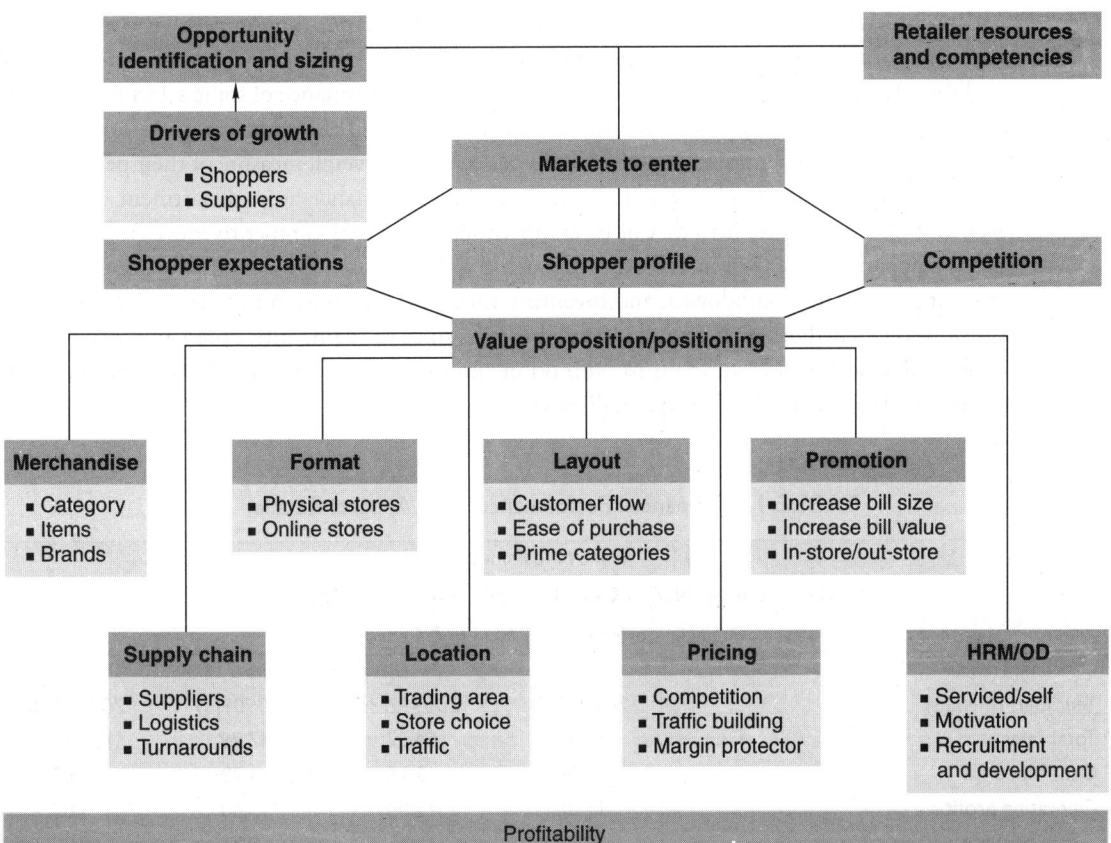

FIG. 1.2 Retailing Decisions

Retail Performance and Profitability

The profitability of a retailer is based on a judicious use of its three main resources of inventory, space, and people. A good management of inventory and efficient consumer response by a retailer would help not only in getting better markups due to the right merchandise, but also higher sales at full price and lower markdowns. A higher inventory turnover benefits the customers by providing them merchandise that is fresh and as per their requirements in terms of stock-keeping units (SKUs) and items. For the retailer, it translates into a higher return on inventory. The return on the investments on the store, called the real estate, is determined on the basis of the sales or return per square or cubic feet of space. This reflects the usage of the space in a way that allows shoppers to feel comfortable while shopping as well as to find the required merchandise easily. It involves not only the amount of space allocated to a department or a category, but also the way the space is being utilized for stocking, displays, promotions, creating the right ambience, and administrative offices.

The third major resource of a retailer is the people and the investments in technology. People in the store are the ambassadors of the store. They play a very crucial role in delivering the desired experience to the customer and provide a human touch to the operations. In consonance with technology, they help in achieving efficiency as well as effectiveness in the operations of the store. In several formats that are chosen primarily on service, people and technology become the competitive weapon to win over other formats that use price or merchandise as key choice criteria for the customers.

Tables 1.2 and 1.3 provide a glimpse into the financial performance of some select retailers. The key performance parameters are the operating profit margin (OPM) per cent, gross profit margin (GPM) per cent, and net profit margin (NPM) per cent as an overall measure of their performance. In addition to these, a retailer would also look at the performance at its department or category level, and would compare it to that of its competitors to assess its competitiveness. An example of such a comparison is shown in Table 1.4. In such a scenario, it would evaluate the performance in terms of its markups, markdowns, and inventory turnover contribution to assess its efficiency. The contribution earned becomes critical in retail business since the competitive pressure forces retailers to take quick decisions with regard to promotion and pricing, and the contribution represents the money that the retailer has at its quick disposal.

TABLE 1.2   Financial Performance of an Apparel Retailer

Trent (Westside)			
Current price (NSE): 1,043.50 Mkt cap: ₹2,092.94 Crore			
Financial performance [Value in ₹ Crore]			
Quarterly Trends	*Last Four Quarters*		
Year Ends (Months)	201003(3)	200912(3)	200909(3)	200906(3)
Total sales	162.54	154.67	147.98	122.30
Other income	7.94	3.16	4.79	6.62
Operating profit	12.38	12.04	5.60	3.83
Gross profit	18.42	13.25	8.71	9.95
Reported PAT	13.98	15.86	5.26	5.11
Equity capital	20.04	19.53	19.53	19.53
OPM (%)	7.61	7.78	3.78	3.13
GPM (%)	10.80	8.39	5.69	7.71
NPM (%)	8.20	10.05	3.44	3.96
Annual Trends			
Year Ends (Months)	200903(12)	200803(12)	200703(12)	200603(12)
Operating income	511.73	514.16	452.00	346.44
Operating profit	8.76	18.30	33.07	35.22
Other recurring income	25.97	23.61	14.31	9.42
Adjusted PBT	21.17	28.76	35.49	33.34
Reported PAT	25.21	32.58	31.58	24.38
Equity dividend (%)	55.00	70.00	70.00	65.00
Balance Sheet			
Year Ends (Months)	200903(12)	200803(12)	200703(12)	200603(12)
Equity capital	19.53	19.53	15.76	14.43
Preference capital	0.00	0.00	0.00	0.00

(Contd)

(Table 1.2 Contd)

Reserves and surplus	587.23	586.30	371.73	255.17
Loan funds	165.55	65.61	65.67	65.72
Current liabilities	150.80	143.63	109.85	112.89
Net block	94.86	102.57	72.51	66.53
Investments	395.85	469.34	308.22	232.97
Total current assets	414.60	216.62	172.70	142.80

Ratios				
Year Ends (Months)	200903(12)	200803(12)	200703(12)	200603(12)
OPM (%)	1.71	3.55	7.31	10.16
NPM (%)	4.68	6.05	6.77	6.85
Reported EPS	12.90	16.68	20.04	16.90
Return on net worth	4.15	5.37	8.14	9.04
Debt/Equity	0.27	0.10	0.16	0.24
Financial charges coverage ratio	8.03	9.77	11.91	15.16
Current ratio	2.75	1.51	1.57	1.26
Dividend per share	5.50	7.00	7.00	6.50

Source: http://www.tata.com/0_invetor_desk/trent.asp, accessed on 6 July 2010.

TABLE 1.3 Performance of a Multi-format Retailer

	Pantaloon Retail			
Particulars	2008–09	2007–08	2006–07	2005–06
Income	NA	NA	NA	NA
Gross sales	NA	NA	NA	NA
Net sales	6,341.70	5,048.91	3,236.74	1,867.77
Other income	6.06	3.76	92.03	4.20
Expenditure	6,131.53	4,857.05	3,147.76	1,725.73
Cost of goods sold	4,429.95	3,512.19	2,209.48	1,476.89
Operating margin	1,911.75	1,536.72	1,027.26	390.88
Personnel	274.26	274.07	206.09	112.07
Other expenditure	969.05	802.13	570.00	370.23
Increase in stock	NA	NA	NA	233.46
Gross profit	216.23	195.62	181.01	91.89
Net profit	140.58	125.97	119.99	64.15
Equity capital	NA	NA	NA	268.84
EPS	8.04	8.34	8.71	25.30
Reserves	NA	NA	NA	500.01
GPM (%)	NA	NA	NA	4.90
NPM (%)	NA	NA	NA	3.40

Source: www.pantaloon.com, accessed on 6 July 2010.

TABLE 1.4   Department-wise Comparison of a Retailer's Performance: An Example

Particulars	Store	Benchmark Competition	Comparison of Financial Performance (Figures in ₹ Crore)							
			Department A	Benchmark Competition	Department B	Benchmark Competition	Department C	Benchmark Competition	Department D	Benchmark Competition
Net sales	270	300	27	30	25	22	18	24	40	35
Percentage of total store sales (%)	100	100	10.00	10.00	9.26	7.33	6.67	8.00	14.81	11.67
Markup (%)	40	39	39	37	36	38	28	27	33	33
Markdown (%)	25	23	22	25	21	22	25	23	11	12
Gross profit (%)	22	20	40	35	18	17	20	20	23	22
Cash discount (%)	2	1.87	2	1.9	2	2	2	1.9	2	1.8
Marketing promotion expenditure	5.4	7.5	0.5	0.75	0.3	0.35	0.2	0.3	0.7	0.9
Manpower expense	17.55	18	1.755	1.8	1.625	1.32	1.17	1.44	2.6	2.1
Inventory turnover	2.5	2.1	3	2.8	1.2	1.6	1.8	1.6	4.2	4
Interest on inventory (%)	11.50	11.50	11.50	11.50	11.50	11.50	11.50	11.50	11.50	11.50
Inventory carrying cost	10.8	12.99	1.08	1.299	1.0	0.88	0.72	0.96	1.6	1.4
Contribution (%)	18	16	22	21	20	20	14	16	23	19

SUMMARY

Retailing is a crucial function that marketers perform in order to deliver the promised offer to their customers. In most cases, it is performed by firms called retailers. These entities make the suitable product available to the customers through packaging, stocking, and other distribution outputs described as 'decentralization', 'waiting time', 'lot size', and 'variety'. Retailing is an integral function of marketing that creates utilities in terms of economic, social, emotional, conditional, and epistemic values sought by customers.

Retailing has been linked to the economic development of a society. It represents a consumption-oriented economy.

Shopping has been regarded as a chore as well as an enjoyable experience. Some have used terms such as 'shopping therapy' to signify relief from monotony. A customer seeks different values from shopping, based on the motive of purchase. Retailers use different value propositions to remain competitive in the market and design strategies for delivering these values through a judicious mix of the retail management elements. The unique value proposition is derived on the basis of the target market and shoppers' profile and expectations. It takes the shape of merchandise, location, format, service, ambience, and other elements that help the customer choose a retailer and decide on patronizing it.

Several theories have been posited to explain how retailing develops. One of the most prominent among them is the wheel of retailing theory. It postulates that retailing serves a very utilitarian and basic function of availability in the beginning and slowly develops to deliver hedonic experiences, and then again gets into the loop of being utilitarian till some retailers redefine the business again.

A retailer uses three main resources—inventory, real estate, and people—to deliver value to its customers and to remain competitive. A retailer should assess its performance at the corporate level, store level, and also at the department or category level. It is also advised that it carries out a comparison of its performance with competitors to find out whether it has been efficient in it operations, and whether the strategies have been effective in providing the desired results.

NOTES

1. Dunne, P.M., R.F. Luch, and D.A. Griffith 2002, *Retailing*, Thomson South Western, 4th edn, p. 7.

2. Newman, A.J. and P. Cullen 2002, *Retailing: Environment and Operations*, Thomson Learning, 1st edn, pp. 14, 15.

3. Parthasarthy, M., R. Sohi, and R.D. Hampton 1994, 'Dual Diffusion: Analysis and Implications for Sales Force Management', *Journal of Marketing Theory and Practice*, Summer, pp. 1–14.

4. Reibstein, David and Paul Farris 1995, 'Do Marketing Expenditures Leverage Cost to Customers', *European Management Journal*, March, pp. 31–8.

5. Sinha, Piyush Kumar 2003, 'Shopping Orientation in the Evolving Indian Market', *Vikalpa*, Vol. 28 (2), April–June, pp. 13–22.

6. Bucklin, L.P. 1966, *A Theory of Distribution Channel Structure*, IBER Special Publications, Berkeley; and Bucklin, L.P. 1972, *Competition and Evolution in the Distributive Trades*, Prentice Hall, Englewood Cliffs, New Jersey.

7. Betancourt, R.R. and D.A. Gautschi 1990, 'Demand Complementarities, Household Production, and Retail Assortments', *Marketing Science*, 9 (Spring), pp. 146–61; Betancourt, R.R. and D.A. Gautschi 1998, 'Distribution Services and Economic Power in a Channel', *Journal of Retailing*, Vol. 74 (1), pp. 37–60; Hean Tat Keh 1997, 'The Classification of Distribution Channel Output: A Review', *The International Review of Retail, Distribution and Consumer Research*, Vol. 7 (2), pp. 145–56.

8. Rangan, V.K., M.A.J. Menezes, and E.P. Maier 1992, 'Channel Selection for New Industrial Products: A Framework, Method and Application', *Journal of Marketing*, Vol. 56, July, pp. 69–82.

9. Oi, W.Y. 1992, 'Productivity in the Distributive Trades: The Shopper and the Economies of Massed Reserves', in Griliches, Z. (ed.), *Output Measurement in the Services Sectors,* University of Chicago Press, Chicago, pp. 161–91.

10. Lambin, J.J. 2000, *Market-driven Management: Strategic and Operational Marketing*, Macmillan Press, London, pp. 105–11.
11. Byrd, Rodney, 'A Brief History of Retailing', htttp://www.suite101.com/article.cfm/retailing_shopping/65949, accessed on 16 February 2007.
12. Dawson, John A. 2000, 'Retailing at the End of the Century: Some Challenges for Management and Research', *The International Review of Retail Distribution and Consumer Research*, Vol. 10, Issue 2, April, pp. 119–48.
13. 'Time-line of American Retailing', http://www.kelley.indiana.edu/retail/timeline/printable/htm, accessed on 16 February 2007.
14. Sathish, D. and D. VenkatramaRaju 2010, 'Growth of Indian Retail Industry', *Advances in Management*, Vol. 3, Issue 7, July, pp. 15–19.
15. McNair, M.P. 1958, 'Significant Trends and Development in the Post-war Period', in A.B. Smith (ed.), *Competitive Distribution in a Free High-level Economy and Its Implications for the University*, University of Pittsburgh Press, Pittsburgh.
16. Converse, P.D. 1959, 'Mediocrity in Retailing', *Journal of Marketing*, Vol. 23, pp. 419–20.
17. Davies, Gary 1999, 'The Evolution of Marks and Spencer', *The Service Industries Journal*, Vol. 19 (3), pp. 60–73.
18. Newman, A.J. and P. Cullen 2002, *Retailing: Environment and Operations*, Thomson Learning, 1st edn, pp. 14, 15.
19. Luch, R.F., P.M. Dunne, and R. Gebhardt 1993, *Retail Marketing*, South Western Publishing, Cincinnati, p. 115.
20. Bell, D.E. 2002, 'Tesco Plc.', *Harvard Business Review*.
21. Nanda, Ashish 2004, 'Profitability Drivers of Professional Service Firms', *Harvard Business Review*.
22. Newman, A.J. and P. Cullen 2002, *Retailing: Environment and Operations*, Thomson Learning, 1st edn, pp. 14, 15.

CONCEPT REVIEW QUESTIONS

1. Define retailing. What services does a retailer provide?
2. Describe the theories of retail development. Which do you think describes Indian retailing in the most appropriate manner?
3. Describe the retail management framework given in Fig. 1.2. What is the fulcrum of the business of retailing?
4. How can a utility become a dis-utility? Using the framework given in Table 1.1, describe the net value that a customer would get.
5. What are the main performance criteria for a retailer? Do they remain the same at the store as well as category level?

CRITICAL THINKING QUESTION

Critically examine the retail management framework given in Fig. 1.2. Divide the model into strategic and operational decisions and provide your logic for the same. Would this be applicable to small retailers?

PROJECTS

1. Meet a retailer/store manager and find out the decisions made by the enterprise. Fit them in the model given in Fig. 1.2. Find out who makes each of these decisions in the organization and build a hierarchy of decisions.
2. Visit a place that has a cluster of retail outlets. Figure out the bases of the formation of the cluster using one or a combination of the theories of retail development.

CASE STUDY

FoodWorld-A[1]—Market Entry Strategy

Pradipta K. Mohapatra, President and Chief Executive, Retail Business Sector of RPG Enterprises, was reviewing the performance of the retail chain stores launched under the brand name 'FoodWorld'. It was three years since the first FoodWorld retail store was established. The first FoodWorld store had a modest beginning in R.A. Puram in Chennai on 9 May 1996. By November 1998, however, the total number of FoodWorld retail outlets reached 19, spread over three large cities of South India, namely Chennai (six), Bangalore[2] (eight), and Hyderabad (five). The turnover during the first year (1996–97) was ₹210 million and this was doubled in the next year. The projected turnover for 1998–99 was ₹870 million and, by November 1998, a turnover of ₹520 million had already been achieved.

RPG Enterprises' foray into retail business, in one sense, was a bold step. It was one of the first serious players in India to get into organized retailing in a major way. There were not many in the country from whom the company could learn about the nuances of modern retailing. Several initiatives undertaken by the company, therefore, were pioneering in nature. Hence, it was important to undertake a review of operations so that the company could learn from the past and view the future with greater knowledge and confidence. Was the strategy in consonance with the realities of supply and demand conditions? Was the strategy adequately focused? Was the target segment sharply identified? Was the positioning strategy appropriate? Was the design of the 'offer'—the concept that was being marketed and the retailing format and services offered—in synchronization with customer needs and expectations? Were the marketing mix elements aligned properly? Were the customers satisfied? What indeed were the 'good and the bad' that this whole new experience had taught? Mr Mohapatra knew that a comprehensive review would be required to take the company to greater heights.

Company Background

FoodWorld was a division of Spencer's, the retailing company under RPG Enterprises. RPG was one of the top five business houses in India, with a sales turnover of ₹65 billion in 1996–97 and an asset base of ₹75 billion as of 1997. RPG's business interests spanned several sectors, including power, automobile tyre, agri-business, telecommunications, retailing, and financial services. The company had a large number of partnerships with international companies, including some Fortune 500 companies. RPG's entry into retailing was through the acquisition of Spencer & Company in 1989.

Spencer & Company was founded in Madras (now renamed as Chennai) in 1865 with the objective of offering imported items to a large British expatriate and military population. By 1897, it had grown to become the largest store in India with 65,000 square feet of shopping space. At the peak of its performance in 1940, Spencer's had 50 retail shops in most of the major cities in India. The company had also integrated backwards into making some of the products that is sold, such as soft drinks, cosmetics, etc. After India's independence from the British in 1947, sales through Spencer's dropped significantly, though the company somehow survived and continued to offer food, clothing, cosmetics, and other highpriced speciality items, mainly to the expatriate community and to economically well-off Indians.

Because of deteriorating performance and poor sales, Spencer & Company was open for acquisition. The ownership changed once in early 1970. In 1989, RPG purchased Spencer's and established it as a separate division under the leadership of P.K. Mohapatra, a senior RPG executive. A major attraction of the transaction was the undervalued real estate owned by Spencer & Company.

---

1. Case prepared by Professor Abraham Koshy, G. Raghuram, and Bibek Banerjee, Indian Institute of Management Ahmedabad. Research assistance of Parvathy Raman and Anitha Basalingappa is acknowledged. The case is prepared as a basis of class discussion rather than to illustrate either effective or ineffective handling of an administrative situation.

The authors thank Mr P.K. Mohapatra, Mr Ganesh Chella, and other top managers of FoodWorld for their generous cooperation and financial support in preparing this case.

Copyright © 1999 by the Indian Institute of Management Ahmedabad.

2. Bangalore has been renamed as Bengaluru.

At the time of acquisition, Spencer's had nine retail stores—the largest retail chain in India at that time. One of the options at the time of acquisition was to focus on the development of the real estate owned by Spencer's. However, the RPG executives who were managing Spencer's felt that the potential of retail business should not be given up easily. Therefore, it was decided to experiment with one store to test the potential. If the experiment failed, then RPG would close down the retail operations. In line with this decision, the departmental store in Bangalore was modernized in 1991, retaining its product profile of hardware, food, kitchen appliances, and clothing. When the store opened, sales increased to four times the previous levels and made a healthy contribution. This settled the issue in favour of continuing with the more important activities of Spencer's, which included retailing, airline general sales agency, and pharmaceutical retailing. The total turnover of Spencer's increased from ₹250 million at the time of acquisition to nearly ₹1000 million by 1994 through a careful process of nurturing the three activities while eliminating over 20 other less vital activities. The airline general sales agency contributed more than 80 per cent of the turnover at that time.

During 1994–95, the RPG group, with the help of a large multinational consulting firm, went through a re-assessment of its portfolio of activities. A major recommendation was that the retail business development along with telecommunications and financial services should be one of the major thrust areas of the company as these businesses offered considerable growth potential. The emerging middle class had barely got a glimpse of modern retailing as retailing had traditionally been in the 'non-formal' sector and had remained unchanged for over a century in India.

RPG's Retail Focus

Based on the decision to focus on the retail sector, senior executives studied various retail formats and retailers world over and discussed issues with experts in the field. These insights provided three directions: First, that the company should not get into niche retailing; instead, they should focus on the mass market. Second, that organized retailing would evolve faster in the country as retailing format was closely related to economic development of countries. Third, that they should focus on daily necessities of households—food, clothing, and health. However, clothing was eliminated, since the company had no prior experience in the fashion industry or in textile manufacturing, which was considered essential for success in this product line, Therefore, food was decided as the entry product line followed by health care.

Yet another issue to be resolved was whether the retail business should build on Spencer's image or it should adopt a fresh approach. Leveraging on Spencer's image for retail business had its risks. While the brand name 'Spencer's' was widely associated with quality, it also had the connotation of high prices. This sentiment was reflected in the expression, 'paying the Spencer price', which commonly suggested payment of high prices. It was decided to resolve the issue of whether or not to leverage Spencer's name after obtaining market research inputs. However, one important decision was made at this juncture—to follow a supermarket format for the retailing business.

Retail Market Scenario in India

As per the 1991 population census, the total population of India was 846 million. About one fourth of this population lived in 3768 towns and the remaining in 627,000 villages.[3] In order to reach such a large population spread over a vast geographical area, India had evolved a complex retailing institutional structure that varied in size, economics, and scope of activities. Unlike developed countries, distribution in India was highly fragmented. Retail trade was largely in the hands of private independent owners and the distribution structure for fast moving consumer goods consisted of multiple layers such as carrying and forwarding agents, distributors, stockists, wholesalers, and retailers.

The retailing system in India operated at three parallel levels: the formal sector, informal sector, and the fair price shops under the government's public distribution system. The formal retail sector consisted of shops with ongoing businesses and fixed premises registered with the appropriate government agency under the Shops and Establishment Act. This included the traditional small retail shops as well as the newer forms of retail establishments. The informal retail sector comprised essentially of enterprises without any fixed premises. The hawker is the leading institution in this category and he/she represents an important link in the distribution system for merchandise such as fruits, vegetables, bread, and other low-value household goods. The total number of hawkers in India was not known. However, as the

---

3. Paper prepared on the Indian retail market by Mr Amit Roy, President, Tracking Division, ORG-MARG, India, and Mr Sujit Das, Director, Indian Research and Information Services, India.

TABLE CS1.1 Number of Retail Outlets

Number of Outlets ('000)							
Area	1993	1996	1997	1998	1999	2000	2001
Urban	2,693	3,074	3,200	3,400	3,500	3,700	3,800
Rural	5,364	6,633	7,200	7,200	8,400	9,000	9,800
Total	**8,057**	**9,707**	**10,400**	**11,100**	**11,900**	**12,700**	**13,600**

Source: Euromonitor, based on ORG and AIMS estimates

estimate in one city indicated that there were almost 20,000 hawkers engaged in retail trade, whereas the number of formal retail establishments in that city was about 36,800. The fair price shops constituted the third set of retail institutions in India. These shops, mostly owned by private individuals, sold a limited assortment of products, such as rice, wheat, sugar, edible oil, and kerosene, to consumers whose entitlement quantities of different commodities were specified in 'ration cards' (or identification cards). The government fixed the prices of items sold through this system and usually these prices were lower than open market prices. Lower prices were possible due to the fact that products sold through this system carried subsidy.

The total number of retail outlets under the formal system in the country in 1993 was estimated to be about 8.06 million and in 1998, it was about 11.1 million. It was estimated that, by the year 2001, the total number of retail outlets in the country would be about 13.6 million. Approximately 30 per cent of these outlets were located in urban areas. About 27 per cent of urban retail outlets dealt with food products, and an equal proportion dealt with non-food items. The remaining outlets carried other fast moving consumer products. Table CS1.1 shows the number of retail outlets in urban and rural areas and Table CS1.2 shows the proportion of shops carrying different products in 1996.

Small retail shops with a shopping area of 300–400 sq. ft constituted about 64 per cent of the total number of retail establishments in the country. Large and very large retail shops (shopping area of over 800 sq. ft) constituted only about 11 per cent of the total number of retail outlets. The presence of supermarkets in India was confined to larger cities and these retail institutions accounted for only about 2 per cent of the sales of fast moving consumer goods. Table CS1.3 gives the distribution of shops according to the Shop Classification Index.

TABLE CS1.2 Urban Outlets—Food/Non-food, 1996

Types of Products Sold	Number ('000)	Percentage (%)
Food	824	26.8
Other FMCG	1,430	46.5
Non-food	820	26.7
Total	**3,074**	**100.0**

Source: Euromonitor
Note: Includes only outlets stocking basic food commodities, such as rice, wheat, pulses, and spices, and includes fair price shops. Liquor stores and other food stores are included in other FMCG.

The total retail sales in India in 1997 was estimated to be about ₹6,630 billion, out of which sales for food items was ₹4,837 billion. The total retail sales represented around 53 per cent of the gross domestic product (GDP) and about 69 per cent of consumer expenditure. Per capita retail sales in 1996 was estimated to be about ₹6,297. It was estimated that the total retail sales by the year 2002 would be ₹9,236 billion and sale of food items would be ₹6,657 billion. The complexity of retail trade could also be understood by the proliferation of stock-keeping units (SKU). In 1990 there were 53 core categories of fast moving consumer goods with 7,715 SKUs. However, by 1996, the total number of SKUs increased to 15,160. In addition, by 1996, about 19 new categories of core products with another 2,579 SKUs entered the market. Competition for shelf space and limitations of small retail shops to carry a large assortment of products characterized the retail scenario in the country.

Design of the Retailing 'Offer'

In order to implement the decision to enter retailing, the company had to take four crucial decisions. These were (i) which target segment should be focused on,

(ii) what value proposition should be offered to the customers, (iii) which merchandising facilities should be offered, given the value proposition identified, and (iv) where the retail outlets should be located. The company decided to conduct detailed market research studies to obtain inputs for these decisions.

TABLE CS1.3   Distribution of Stores by Shop Classification Index

Type of Retail Outlets	Proportion (in%)
Small	64
Medium	25
Large	8
Very large	3
Total	**100**

Source: AIMS 1996.

The purpose of the first study was to understand the needs and values of customers while shopping for items of daily necessities. To achieve this purpose, a large-scale survey of consumers spread across selected metro cities, mini-metro cities, and small towns was conducted. Several useful and interesting insights emerged from this study.

Insights from Consumer Survey

The housewife was the prime decision-maker on purchase or provisions. She regarded provision shopping as a chore due to the monotony and routine nature of the purchases. Most of the consumers purchased provisions on a monthly basis, usually in the beginning of the month. In addition, they also made two or three need-based purchases during the month. On an average, they spent ₹1,000–1,500 on monthly purchases and close to ₹200 on additional purchases. About a tenth of the market consisted of ad hoc buyers for whom four or more purchase occasions a month was the norm. Their expenditure on buying provision items was similar to that of the monthly buyers. They also patronized a higher number of shops than monthly buyers. Usually, their preferred outlets were closer to home. In fact, walking to the shop was observed more among ad hoc buyers. More often than not, their purchases were less planned when compared with the monthly buyers.

A household member made the purchases. Usually, the housewife carried out this activity. On most occasions, consumers walked to the shop for making purchases. However, use of two-wheeler and automobiles was also common. On most occasions, monthly purchases were a planned activity. In fact, most shoppers went for their purchases armed with a list of items.

The survey indicated that the purchase pattern was similar across different income segments. However, the upper income households spent more on provision items, and visited supermarkets more frequently. They also used personal transportation for their shopping trips. The main sources of provisions were the grocery shops that carried a rather narrow range of products. Supermarkets as a source of regular purchase featured only in mega metros. The dominant tendency was to patronize one shop. However, in mega-metros, this tendency was less prominent. Generally, the shoppers were found to be loyal to their retail outlet. For most of them, the association dated back to over three years. For many, the preferred retail outlet was located within 10 minutes of walking distance. This was especially so in the metros. These retail shops offered basic amenities such as credit facility, goods return facility, and door delivery. These shops also sold their products at standard market prices.

It was found that those who patronized supermarkets did so essentially due to the availability of a much larger basket of products and, at times, better prices. However, no 'add-on' services were available from these shops. It was also observed that these shoppers had shorter association with supermarket outlets. In fact, the rating of these retail shops was a shade lower than that of the local grocery shops.

Buying Provisions—Customer Needs and Requirements

The consumer survey also indicated the relative importance of various attributes that a shopper was looking for in a retail outlet. For this purpose, a trade-off analysis (conjoint analysis) of the sample of respondents was made and insights obtained. The survey indicated that, although there were some differences in the relative weights for different attributes of a shop across different survey locations, attributes such as location of the shop, extra facilities (like door delivery, credit facility), and price were found to be relatively more important. Other attributes like quality of products and shop ambience were important to some extent. The other factors did not turn out to be important for the shoppers. It was also found that the relative weights for add-on facilities like door delivery and good return facility were uniformly higher across different income categories as well. Results of the survey were consistent across metro cities as well as large towns.

For the shoppers, it was important to have the shop in their own locality and even a compromise of locating the outlet in a shopping area was less preferable. Respondents preferred the prices to be lower than the standard market prices. Even a parity price was acceptable; however, they were unwilling to pay any price premium for products made available through retail outlets, irrespective of the shop's format. The superior quality of products compared to those available from the current shops would add some value. The ambience of the shops was less important to the respondents. They were only looking for basic cleanliness and neat display. Availability of additional product lines such as ready-made garments, artificial jewellery, footwear, handbags, electronic items like television, refrigerator, toaster, furniture, and furnishing materials, etc. did not add to the utility of the respondents much. What they were looking for was a shop that supplied a variety and range of grocery products, which was at least on par with the current outlet that they frequented.

The survey further obtained a comparison between respondents' current outlets and the ideal outlet that they had in mind. Analysis of data on consumer utilities suggested that there was ample scope for building competitive advantage over current near-by-location provision shops. The most important parameters on which differentiation could be made were on prices (somewhat lower than market prices), better quality than the current outlet, and better shop ambience (air conditioning).

The survey also sought inputs for deciding the type of retail outlet to be established. For this purpose, utility scores on three types of shops—discount store, value-for-money store, and department store—were obtained and analysed. This analysis indicated that the most preferred option would be a value-for-money store which was located close to the respondents' place of residence and offered extra 'add-on' facilities, with parity pricing policy, standard quality, air conditioned shop ambience, selling standard, variety/range of grocery items, and not other ranges of products like television, furniture, toasters, etc.

Insights into Customers' Awareness about Competition

The study provided a glimpse into the respondents' awareness about and shopping relationship with other supermarkets—an assessment of competition. Customers in Chennai and Bangalore knew Spencer's; but awareness levels about Spencer's were higher in Chennai. However, most respondents had not tried buying provisions from the retail outlet. Nilgiris, another supermarket, enjoyed high awareness and exposure in Chennai and Bangalore, more so in Bangalore. Availability of a wider product range was perceived to be a major strength of the retailer. However, perception of higher prices, absence of extra 'add-on' facilities, and inconveniences due to location were mentioned as their vulnerabilities when compared with their current local retailer. Almost half the respondents were aware of Nanz, another supermarket retail outlet. But less than 10 per cent of the respondents had tried this outlet. The perceptions of Chennai and Bangalore respondents about Nanz were similar to that of Nilgiris.

Customer Perception of Store Names

In addition to the first market research, a separate research was carried out to obtain inputs to decide on the appropriate name for the proposed retail chain stores. This research had three specific objectives. The first objective was to evaluate their perceptions associated with various brand name options; the second was to assess the value additions of the 'descriptor', if any; and the third was to understand the habits, attitudes, and needs of the Indian housewife related to her shopping experiences. For this research, three brand name options, namely FoodWorld, Spencer's FoodWorld, and Spencer's, were tested. The descriptor line tested was 'the right price, right choice supermarket'. The target audience for this research was housewives belonging to the monthly household income of ₹4000 to 10,000 belonging to the age group of 25 to 45 years, who might or might not be currently shopping in a supermarket. The qualitative research method of focus groups was used to generate the needed data.

When the respondents were exposed to the brand name FoodWorld, there was a spontaneous association with fast food, beverages, vegetables, snack items like idli, dosa, etc., and processed food items like instant noodles. The brand name had a positive impact on the consumer. The alphabet 'W' in the brand name was seen to connote 'two ticks' indicating a connotation of being 'very good'. The name 'FoodWorld' at a spontaneous level was perceived to be similar to Vitan and Nilgiris, two other supermarkets in Chennai, in terms of the range and quality of offer. This perception was evident not only at the organizational expectation level but also at the product/service levels. The brand name did not evoke any spontaneous association with government run retail outlets that were perceived to offer limited product and brand ranges, low prices, and reasonable quality. The product categories expected in a store with the name 'FoodWorld' was largely on the lines of respondents' planned purchase—groceries, instant foods, bakery, products, confectionery items, snacks, vegetables, toiletries, and similar items.

Consumers were not keen on frozen meat and other non-vegetarian items. Also, items like clothes, medicines, electronics, and cosmetics were not part of their product or service expectations. Service levels were expected to be similar to another supermarket in the town that was rated high by the respondents.

Respondents perceived a typical supermarket shopper to be one who was an extrovert with relatively lower budgetary constraints and yet sought a certain amount of convenience in what she did or bought for home. Projective techniques showed that a 'FoodWorld' shopper was perceived to have the following personality traits: a person who sought variety in her shopping; for whom it was important to be up to date; one who probably would have had experience in shopping in supermarkets like Vitan or Nilgiris and hence would not be overly concerned about price; one who had a small family; whose husband had a good job, earning more than ₹10,000 per month; who was likely to have a TVS Scooty for herself while her husband drove a car. A non-shopper of 'FoodWorld' was perceived to be a reserved type, frugal, independent person, not influenced by friends to spend money for shopping in a supermarket. She would most probably have monetary compulsions to take up a job, and live a closed life. A significant proportion of the focus group respondents identified themselves with 'FoodWorld' shoppers and felt that they could make friends with her in order to improve their own outlook towards life.

The study also probed the motivations and deterrents of consumers for shopping at 'FoodWorld'. At a spontaneous level, proximity of location emerged as a motivating factor. In addition, the prestige of having visited a new store motivated shoppers to try out the shop. Price, distance from home, crowding in the store, poor quality of stock (quality assessed based on visual cleanliness and neat packaging of commodity items), and poor service emerged as the major deterrents. Pleasant behaviour of store personnel was perceived to connote good service.

When exposed to the second brand name under consideration, namely Spencer's, respondents indicated spontaneous familiarity with the name. They associated it with soft drinks (a soft drink with the brand Spencer's was available in the market), shopping complexes, books, and the good times children had during a shopping trip to the shop with the name 'Spencer's'. They also associated certain traits such as modernity, quality, good location, and availability of a wide range of goods with Spencer's. Further probing indicated that Spencer's could be the name of a shop that sold consumer durables, kitchen appliances, groceries, packaged goods, etc. Despite associations of good quality, neat surrounding, and fixed prices, respondents perceived Spencer's to be more expensive than other stores by 10 to 15 per cent. They articulated apprehensions that since Spencer's was well known, it might not try to provide good service and please customers. As the association of 'fun' with shopping in Spencer's was strong, they did not perceive it to be a place for regular shopping. With respect to product expectations, they perceived Spencer's to carry all daily necessity items, gift articles, and a far larger product range and variety—they expected the shop to be much more than a supermarket.

Respondents had a different set of perceptions and associations with a Spencer's shopper. A typical Spencer's shopper was perceived to be showy, up-market in her tastes, and self-confident. An average housewife would be in awe of her. She would have two children and a servant to look after them. The family would own two vehicles; a car for the husband and a Kinetic Honda for the lady. A non-shopper of Spencer's was perceived to be one for whom economy was important. Most probably, she would be from a family with one earning member; would pride herself in being a neat and simple person; would live in a joint family; was likely to have three children, and would be apprehensive of visiting Spencer's for her regular shopping. Most of the respondents identified themselves with the non-shopper of Spencer's.

The third name that was examined was Spencer's FoodWorld. On exposing respondents to this name, the combined name seemed to suggest that FoodWorld was a section that sold food in Spencer's store. On probing, respondents perceived a store with this brand name to be a large department store that sold a wide range of products covering food, clothing, gift articles, toys, etc. The product expectations were not too different from Spencer's. A Spencer's FoodWorld shopper too was perceived to be upper middle class—a grade higher than FoodWorld shopper, but a grade lower than Spencer's shopper. Not many of the respondents identified themselves with the Spencer's FoodWorld shopper.

Shopping Habits and Benefits Sought

The research also provided some insights into consumers' shopping habits and the benefits that they were looking for from shopping. The shopper's major purchase period was the first week of the month. Shopping from supermarkets still accounted for only a small portion of all the shopping done by a housewife. Therefore, she considered going to the supermarket as a pleasure trip and an outing. Usually, she visited the supermarket with one or two friends in the later morning hours after completing her household chores. For vegetables, fruits, and meat, she preferred her traditional outlets because she believed that supermarkets were yet to offer the choice and price value she was looking for in these products. For groceries, she shopped around to check prices before she 'settled down' with the value (price, quality) that she was comfortable with. For branded items, she knew that such 'checking around' really did not matter. Buying from a popular store ensured freshness of stocks, but not necessarily low price. She preferred to buy emergency items from the friendly neighbourhood grocer.

Accuracy in the weights of the products sold was one of the basic parts of the benefits that a housewife was expecting from a supermarket. Location of the store within a certain distance, say, within a minimum auto-rickshaw fare distance, was acceptable to her. Quality of products, price, availability of a wide range of goods, and courteous service could be major differentiating benefits of a supermarket. Consumers looked for 'add-on' facilities like home delivery. However, respondents had not used this service often. Respondents also mentioned billing speed and display that facilitated purchase as other attributes that they expected.

Decisions on Marketing Strategy Elements

Based on various inputs obtained from formal market research studies and personal observations and studies carried out by senior executives, it was decided to take a major initiative in organized retailing by opening a series of retail outlets with standardized format, policy, and strategy in major cities in India.

Target Segment

The target market for the shop was decided as middle and upper middle class families. The shops were to be positioned as residential 'full service' supermarkets with limited fresh fruits and vegetables. In line with the insights from the market studies, the shops were to be highly differentiated in ambience and fitted with air conditioning, if needed from a functional point of view. The corporate fascia of the stores and signage were to be very dominant and hence the name *FoodWorld* was designed with the alphabet 'W' to appear as two tick-marks in red colour. Therefore, the shop name as the logo appeared as *Food✓✓orld*.

Positioning Strategy

FoodWorld was positioned as a full service supermarket with a limited assortment of fresh food. The main elements of differentiation were store ambience and fit-out, with a majority of shops being air conditioned. The stores also followed a functional racking system with no fancy accessories. It was decided to offer the top brands in the market across categories, supported by the FoodWorld store brand.

Site Selection

For the site selection, it was decided to identify residential high streets with a minimum of 6,000 households in a 2/3 kilometre radius, preferably in the shopping area of the locality. Only ground floors between 3,000 and 3,500 square feet with minimum 40 feet frontage would be selected. Appropriate policies for rental or lease agreements were also worked out.

Merchandising Strategy and Supply Chain Management

The merchandising strategy was to offer everything that a typical target household would shop for on a daily, weekly, or a monthly basis. This list was decided on the basis of the typical shopping list of customers as well as the budget. All the items were classified into four categories, namely destination category, strategic category, convenience category, and speciality category. Table CS1.4 gives a partial list of typical products in these different categories.

TABLE CS1.4 Categories of Products

Category Description	Typical Products
Convenience	Noodles, canned non-veg., canned fruit, canned veg., desserts, tinned milk, cigarettes, frozen foods, hardware
Destination	Cereals, pulses, flours, edible oils, diary products, vegetables
Speciality	Paper goods, pet food, batteries, miscellaneous items
Strategic	Spices, biscuits, jams, breakfast foods, baby foods, liquor, detergents, skin care, hair care, oral care, shaving needs, baby needs

It was decided that the speciality category would have medium to high range width whereas other categories would have high range width. Except the destination category, other categories would have low range width. Tactical usage of the destination category to attract shoppers would be high; strategic and convenience categories, medium; and speciality category, low. The company decided to offer top brands across different product categories, supported by FoodWorld brands in 'commodity' product categories like pulses, some cereals, etc. Maximum stock-keeping units were to be restricted to 3,000, consolidated by top best sellers by category, with high width but limited or no depth. In any category or sub-category, a minimum of two brands would be offered. Table CS1.5 gives a list of the major products, classified into different categories; number of sub-categories and total number of SKUs in each category; proportion of revenue obtained for a sample month; and the weighted average margin for the category. The chilled and frozen range of products (like soft drinks, butter, cheese, etc.) was also included in the offer. Wherever a liquor license was available, it was decided to offer this range as well.

With respect to the distribution strategy, it was decided to follow the policy of minimizing suppliers.

Since one of the key success factors in this business is effective supply chain management, careful planning and detailing of supply management policy was carried out. (For details of supply chain management issues, refer to the FoodWorld (B) in Chapter 8.) In order to manage supplies, it was decided to create regional hubs from where supplies would be coordinated to different outlets. It was decided to maximize central distribution, but follow a policy of direct-to-store supply for perishables.

Pricing Policy

Pricing was to be in line with that of the corner grocer. However, the key SKUs in the destination or 'staples' category would be discounted to match the 'cheapest' in the city, and the pricing for the balance products in the destination category was to be in line with the prevailing market prices. It was also decided to sell the top 15 branded SKUs at 3 per cent below the maximum retail price and this was highlighted in communications. For the strategic category, aggressive value added range price for protecting margins was to be followed, whereas for the convenience and speciality categories, maximum retail price was to be followed. 'Mega price offers' on at least two SKUs every month would be announced. Quantity discount savings of food SKUs was another scheme decided. It was aimed to build an image of the shop as

TABLE CS1.5   Category-wise Description of Major Products

Main Group	Total No. of Categories	Total No. of Sub-categories	Total No. of SKUs	% Revenue (Oct. '98)	Weighted Average Margin
Staples	5	35	523	28.39	14.79
Typical Categories: Cereals, pulses, flours, spices, edible oils					
Processed Foods	16	70	954	16.22	18.20
Typical Categories: Biscuits, canned non-veg., canned veg., desserts, tinned milk, breakfast foods					
Beverages	4	26	319	13.39	16.78
Typical Categories: Drinks, tea/coffee, health drinks, liquor					
Non-food	6	28	449	8.69	17.94
Typical Categories: Detergents, house cleaning agents, paper goods, cigarettes, pet food					
Health and Beauty	9	53	1069	12.10	14.97
Typical Categories: Skin care, hair care, oral care, OTC, baby needs, cosmetics, herbal products					
Perishables	4	19	310	15.79	20.18
Typical Categories: Dairy products, frozen foods, bakery, vegetables					
H/Ware and Home App.	3	33	1693	5.60	23.24
Typical Categories: Batteries, hardware, mics.					
Total	**47**	**264**	**5317**	**100.00**	**126.09**

Source: Company Records, December 1998.

a value-for-money store using this approach, supported by a 52-week continuous 'promotion' programme. For fresh vegetables, the top five items would be cheaper than the market price, and for the other vegetables the prices would be on par with the market prices. Fruits, however, would be sold at a premium quality price.

Promotion Policy

The essential focus of the marketing strategy was to drive the traffic and to increase basket and billing size. Direct mailers and shopping guides would be the main communicators. Bright prominent in-store display using posters, large shelf talkers, bulk merchandising, and floor displays would be used effectively to attract customers. Mass media would be used only to a limited extent and would be confined to announcements of store openings. Special medium-term campaigns would be undertaken as and when needed.

In line with the store image and ambience, the display policy was decided. It was decided to minimize or eliminate signage facings, and the minimum display would be for seven days, except in the case of perishables. Promotions, and special offers would be highlighted through 'gondola' ends (end space of the stocking rack). Cigarettes and other pilferage prone items would be sold through a separate counter called the 'Little Shop'.

Organization Structure and Human Resource Management

A team of experienced professional managers managed the company. The FoodWorld organization structure, regional organization structure, and the retail and entertainment organization structure of the RPG Group are given in Figs CS1.1, CS1.2, and CS1.3 respectively. Each retail shop was managed by a store manager,

assisted by an assistant manager (duty manager). In order to manage operations at the shop floor, there were customer service supervisors. Typically, the number of customer service supervisors varied between 4 and 6, depending on the size of the shop. One supervisor was in charge of cash. In addition, there were 14 to 20 customer service representatives in each shop, divided equally for two 8-hour shifts. These representatives were full-time employees of FoodWorld. Depending on requirements, part-time representatives were also employed to attend to rush hours and such additional work. Loading, cleaning, and other janitorial work as well as security was entrusted to contract employees.

The company recognized the supply of competent and trained personnel to manage different shops professionally as a potential problem area. Anticipating this requirement, the company started the RPG Institute of Retail Management in Chennai and Bangalore to train people for a career in retailing. As a first step, students who had passed XII Standard and belonged to lower income strata were encouraged to enroll for a three-month full-time course conducted by the institute. In order to attract good and needy candidates, the company visited nearby municipal schools and made presentations to potential candidates about careers in retailing and solicited their enrollment in the course. This course covered various aspects such as customer service; product knowledge; personal effectiveness, including communication, personal grooming, and hygiene; and such other relevant topics. Those who completed the course successfully were absorbed as regular employees of the shops at the level of customer service representatives. Usually, the intake for a batch was 30 participants and 6 to 7 batches were trained each year. In addition to this route, people with some work

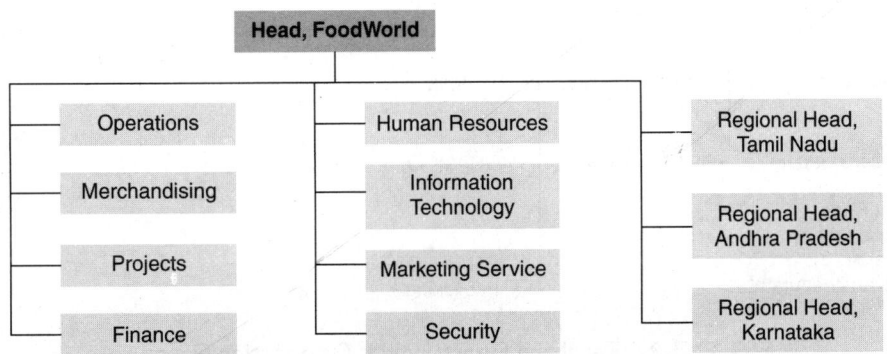

FIG. CS1.1 FoodWorld Organization Structure

Source: Company Records, December 1998

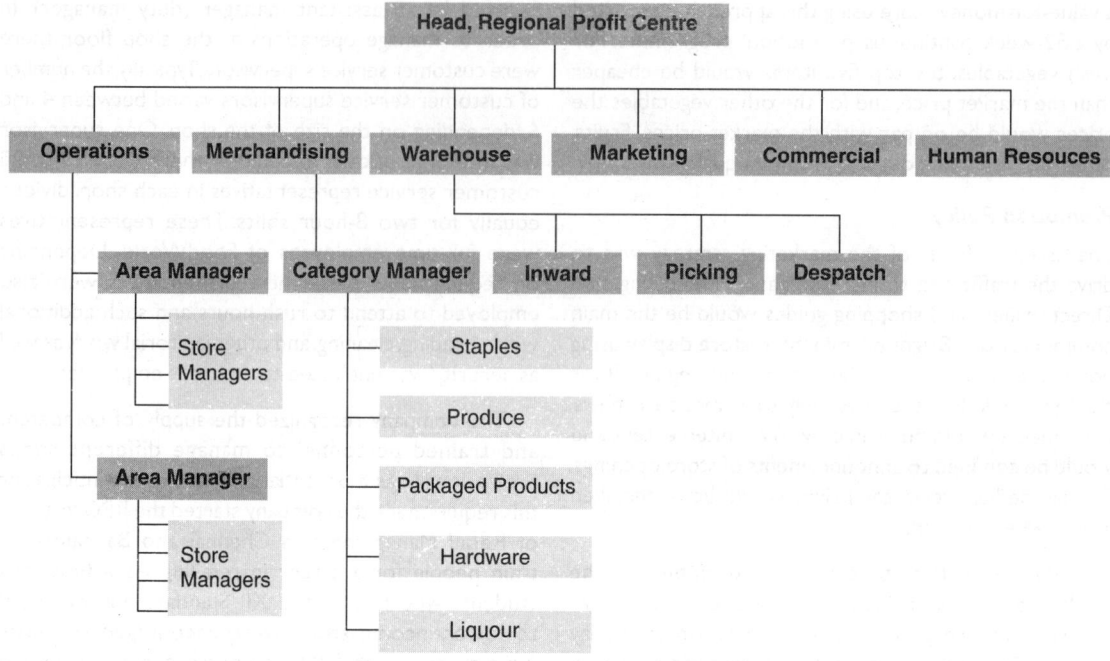

FIG. CS1.2   Regional Organization Structure

Source: Company Records, December 1998

FIG. CS1.3   Retail and Entertainment Organization Structure

Source: Company Records, December 1998

EXHIBIT CS1.1   Store Break-even

Size	:	3,500 Sq. Ft
Investment	:	₹40 Lakh—Fitout
		₹10 Lakh—Rent Deposit
Total	:	**₹50 Lakh**

Costs	₹
Rent	90,000
Salaries	80,000
Power/Fuel	50,000
Selling Exp.	15,000
Bank Charges	10,000
Security/Others	10,000
Repair/Maintenance	20,000
Adv./Promotion	15,000
Total	**3,00,000**
Depreciation	50,000
Interest on W/Cap	5,000
Total operating expenses	**3,55,000**

Source: Company Records, December 1998

experience as salespeople in retail outlets were also recruited and they were given a two-week crash course. Once a person was employed as a customer service representative, he or she was required to complete an advanced level course called the STAR programme (the acronym STAR stood for Special Training for Accomplished Retailer). This course covered topics like an overview of organization, housekeeping, security systems, etc. Only those who completed this programme were eligible for the higher post of customer service supervisor. Similarly, for becoming eligible for higher posts, a person had to pass Level II and III of the STAR programme. To a considerable degree, these initiatives eased the problem of availability of trained manpower. Moreover, detailed policies, procedures, and systems were formulated to manage the day-to-day operations of the shops.

End Results and Performance

The first store was inaugurated on 9 May 1996 at R.A. Puram in Chennai. By now, the company had opened 19 stores in the three major cities in South India. Table CS1.6 presents descriptions of these shops. At the time of planning, the store break-even was carefully calculated. Exhibit CS1.1 shows the break-even calculation for a typical store. On an overall basis, the performance of the shops was satisfactory (see Table CS1.7 for a summary of performance of different shops). However, Mr Mohapatra was aware that the challenges had just started. Improvements in performance and sustenance of success were the essential issues that the company needed to focus on. The learnings from an analysis of the past, he recognized, held the key to a bright future.

Questions

1. Draw the diagram of retailing decisions for FoodWorld as given as Fig. 1.2. Enumerate the key success factors.

2. Using the data given in the tables and figures, find out the profitability drivers for FoodWorld. What is the difference between the profitability of new and old stores? What are the reasons for this? What is your suggestion with regard to the number of stores that FoodWorld should open when it becomes a profitable store?

TABLE CS1.6 Store-wise Description

Store Location	Date of Opening	Total Area	Trading Area Sq. Ft	Store Type Based on Sq. Ft	Store Type Trading Area	Oct. 98 Sale Based on Sale (₹'000)	Oct. 98 Gross (₹'000)	Operating Expenses Margin (%)	PBIT (₹'000)	PBT (₹'000)
Chennai										
Store 1	Dec. 96	14,065	7,257	A	A	9,156	22.41	694	1358.09	1005
Store 2	09.05.96	3,000	2,404	C	B	4,415	19.43	351	506.66	428
Store 3	01.09.96	4,494	3,094	B	B	4,619	20.12	392	537.34	398
Store 4	01.09.96	4,231	3,177	B	B	5,431	20.39	399	708.33	538
Store 5	09.05.98	5,000	3,305	B	B	4,151	19.89	485	340.80	137
Store 6	23.10.98	3,500	2,700	C	B	1,269	19.89	212	40.45	-60
Bangalore										
Store 1	Dec. 96	9,500	6,492	A	A	11,487	19.04	754	1433.13	1265
Store 2	20.08.96	5,720	3,976	B	B	4,072	16.61	494	182.36	127
Store 3	05.06.98	2,565	2,472	C	B	4,910	17.18	420	423.54	285
Store 4*	29.12.96	4,362	3,729	B	B	4,242	17.40	480	258.11	61
Store 5	05.04.97	3,650	3,421	B	C	2,180	15.75	324	19.35	-44
Store 6	04.05.97	2,862	2,437	C	B	2,910	16.84	342	148.04	95
Store 7	30.07.98	3,024	2,494	C	B	4,825	16.81	388	423.08	65
Store 8*	25.04.98	3,000	2,656	C	C	2,569	16.40	324	97.32	-4
Hyderabad										
Store 1	26.09.97	4,500	2,971	C	B	3,117	16.78	349	174.033	150
Store 2	13.12.97	4,000	3,278	B	A	4,690	16.20	426	333.78	301
Store 3*	17.04.98	3,000	2,168	C	C	2,520	16.71	264	157.09	137
Store 4	01.10.98	4,084	3,500	B	B	3,445	16.63	426	146.90	120
Store 5*	31.10.98	3,500	3,000	B	B	179	14.22	143	-117.55	-190

* Some of the data are estimated.
Source: Company Records

TABLE CS1.7   Performance Trends

Year	1996–97				1997–98				YTD Apr. '98–Nov. '98			
	Budget	% of Sales	Actual	% of Sales	Budget	% of Sales	Actual	% of Sales	Budget	% of Sales	Actual	% of Sales
Stores												
New stores 96–97	8		7									
New stores 97–98					13		4					
New stores 98–98									10		8	
Total no. of Stores	8		7		20		11		21		19	
Sales												
New stores 96–97	2,577		2,088		3,366		3,654		2,830		3,148	
New stores 97–98					1,118		579		764		898	
New stores 98–98									1,241		1,106	
Subtotal	2,577		2,088		4,484		4,233		4,835		5,152	
Gross Margin												
New stores 96–97	382	14.8	349	16.7	633	18.8	671	18.4	530	18.7	587	18.6
New stores 97–98					152	13.6	107	18.5	143	18.7	147	16.4
New stores 98–98									234	18.9	212	19.2
Subtotal	382	14.8	349	16.7	785	17.5	778	18.4	907	18.7	946	18.6
Store Operation												
New stores 96–97	346	13.4	266	12.7	480	14.3	444	12.2	286	10.1	286	9.1
New stores 97–98					171	15.3	126	21.8	115	15.1	112	12.5
New stores 98–98									284	22.9	165	14.9
Subtotal	346	13.4	266	12.7	651	14.5	570	13.5	685	14.2	563	10.9
Warehouse/Regional Office												
New stores 96–97	136	5.3	134	6.4	219	6.5	268	7.3	143	5.1	167	5.3
New stores 97–98					73	6.5	42	7.3	39	5.1	48	5.3
New stores 98–98									63	5.1	58	5.2
Subtotal	136	5.3	134	6.4	292	6.5	310	7.3	245	5.1	273	5.3

Notes:
1. Figures exclude notional rent on owned properties.
2. POS Maintenance included under Maintenance.
3. Warehouse & Corporate Opex apportioned to Existing and New Stores on the basis of sales.
Source: Company Records, December 1998

2 Indian Retail Industry

LEARNING OBJECTIVES

After studying this chapter, you will be able to
- visualize the landscape and structure of Indian retailing
- understand the key sectors of retailing
- gain an insight into the drivers of retailing in India
- develop an appreciation of the key challenges faced by Indian retailers

INTRODUCTION

Whether the changes taking place in the Indian retail landscape represent evolution or revolution is a matter for conjecture. However, nobody can doubt that a dramatic transformation is under way. Due to its unorganized nature, the Indian retail industry is one of the most fragmented and challenging ones in the world. In its nature, the Indian retail market is in sharp contrast to the global situation. Retail sales in India will amount to $700 billion by 2011 and account for 22 per cent of India's GDP by 2011 as per the study conducted by Indian Council for Research on International Economic Relations (ICRIER) in 2008. The Indian retail market has over 15 million outlets and has the largest retail outlet density in the world. However, most of these outlets are basic mom-and-pop stores with very basic offerings and fixed prices, and lack good ambience. These stores are highly competitive due to lower land and labour prices. Also, these stores usually save tax as they belong to the small industry sector.

There are several challenges that Indian retailing has to face; prominent amongst these are real estate issues, capital availability, legal frameworks, human resources, and supply chain development and management. Bottlenecks in the supply chain result in limited assortments and increased costs of sourcing. The high cost of real estate owing to constrained supply is also a major factor inhibiting the growth of large format stores. New rules are required to enable retail stores to operate every day with longer hours and utilization of part-time employees, without incurring any extra cost. At present, varying sales tax and octroi tax rates in different states remain a substantial hindrance to the growth of this sector. Retailing, as a major sector of the economy, has yet to receive any overt political or bureaucratic support. Its success and growth in the future largely depend on the initiatives of the government.

In spite of these constraints, Indian retail has bright prospects, propelled by the fast lifestyle changes taking place in the Indian household. Over the nineties, India's middle- and high-income population has grown at a rapid pace of over 10 per cent per annum, even as the large low-income base has shrunk. The changing identity of Indian women and the structure of the family are driving the demand for convenience. Customers are demanding better store ambience, and are looking for solution providers and external guarantors of quality and usability. The Indian consumer is increasingly focusing on value, convenience, variety, and a better shopping experience. The increase in variety, quality, and availability of products, as well as an increase in spending power has resulted in consumers increasingly using supermarkets and hypermarkets for their personal shopping. Malls that offer shopping with entertainment are springing up in many parts of the country.

Presently, India allows 100 per cent foreign direct investment (FDI) in companies carrying out wholesale trade but prohibits the same in retail. However, there is a buzz that the Indian government is considering liberalizing its rules on FDI in multi-brand retail. A number of international retailers have, therefore, chosen to come in with cash and carry stores—the significant players being Walmart, Tesco, and Metro. According to the Department of Industrial Policy and Promotion (DIPP), FDI inflows between April 2000 and April 2010, in single-brand retail trading, stood at $194.69 million. The government has allowed single brand retailers to make direct investments. Non-store retailing now accounts for more than 15 per cent of all consumer purchases, and it may account for over one-third of all sales by the end of 2015. This chapter aims to take a closer look at the current status of the Indian retail industry and its challenges and strategies.

STRUCTURE OF INDIAN RETAIL INDUSTRY

In this section, we shall take a look at the structure of the Indian retail industry in terms of its size, food versus non-food sales, sectoral classification, infrastructure, and human resources.

Size

India's retail sector, with a compound annual growth rate (CAGR) of 10 per cent, is estimated to reach $833 billion by 2013 and $1.3 trillion by 2018. The organized Indian retail market is expected to grow at a CAGR of 40 per cent and reach $107 billion by 2013.[1]

The Indian retail market is valued at ₹19.48 trillion, as per the Indian Retail Report 2011 by IRIS. The largest category is food and grocery with a share of around 68 per cent. Only 6.5 per cent of the Indian retail market is organized, but it is growing at a CAGR of 27.69 per cent. The modern retail market share in the GDP is around 2 per cent. Table 2.1 provides a region-wise breakup of the market.

TABLE 2.1   Indian Retail Market—Region-wise Breakup

	All India (₹ Billion)	North India (₹ Billion)	East India (₹ Billion)	West India (₹ Billion)	South India (₹ Billion)
Total retail market	19,489.16	5,685.56	4,204.05	4,774.72	4,824.83
Organized	1,266.80	415.82	113.63	353.20	384.14
Unorganized	0.065	0.073	0.027	0.074	0.08
Region-wise share % (Total market)	1	0.292	0.216	0.245	0.248
Region-wise share % (Organized market)	1	0.328	0.09	0.279	0.303

Source: IRIS primary research—India Retail Report 2011

Facade of a Lifestyle Store
Source: http://www.economist.com

A Shop Cluster
Source: http://www.greatmirror.com

Fruit and Vegetable Store
Source: http://www.rvgonline.com

Dairy Product
Source: http://www.amul.com

Traditional Market

Panoramic View of Indian Retailers

A recent estimate suggests there are more than 15 million operational retail outlets in India. Thirty two per cent of these outlets are in urban areas and they are likely to grow by 1 million per annum. Fast moving consumer goods (FMCG) stores account for nearly 75 per cent of these retail outlets. Very large stores of more than 800 sq. ft area constitute only 4 per cent of all establishments. As many as 96 per cent of these outlets are small, with an average area of less than 500 sq. ft.[2] India's per capita retailing space is the lowest in the world.[3] Total retail sales area in India was estimated at 328 million sq. m. in 2001, with an average selling space of 29.4 sq. m. per outlet. It stands at about 2 sq. ft per capita compared to 16 sq. ft in the US. Unlike the earlier patterns in developed countries, India's response to economic development has been to demonstrate an increase in the number of outlets alongside a trend towards larger outlets. However, space and rentals are proving to be the largest constraints to the development of large formats in metropolitan cities, since retailers are aiming at prime locations that are already crowded. Local retailers such as Pantaloon Retail India Ltd and RPG Enterprises, in conjunction with Dairy Farm International, introduced hypermarkets during the nascent stages, leading to hypermarkets doubling their sales turnover and surface area in 2005 over the previous year. Supermarkets also expanded current value sales by expanding into smaller towns and cities, registering a 28 per cent growth in 2005 over the previous year.

According to a study by the National Council of Applied Economic Research (NCAER), almost 40 per cent of India's high-income urban population account for the 20–25 largest cities with a population of more than 1 million. Therefore, it would be a challenge for most retail formats to reach these markets during the first five years of operation.[4] Clothing stores, convenience stores, and financial services retailers aimed at high-income groups would have no need to reach beyond the 20–25 largest cities. However, basic categories such as groceries and gasoline might need to enter tier II cities, where competition is still at a nascent stage.

Food vs Non-food Distribution

The Indian food retail industry had a total revenue of $306 billion in 2009, representing a CAGR of 11.7 per cent for 2005–09. In 2014, the Indian food retail industry is forecasted to have a value of $443.7 billion, an increase of 45 per cent since 2009. The CAGR of the industry in the period 2009–14 is predicted to be 7.7 per cent.[5] The largest food retailers were the independent grocers, with a near 71.4 per cent value share. They also accounted for 66 per cent of the number of food outlets in 2001. Food retailing in India is predominantly a small-scale business. Such outlets are present in every street of India. They are mostly independent, family-owned grocery stores. These shops are abundant in urban as well as rural India. Consumer loyalty for these outlets is strong, and is built on convenience and added services such as credit and free home delivery. Wet markets also continue to be an important retail format since fresh markets are abundant in all parts of India. Fresh foods are less expensive than processed foods and are also the preferred form in most Indian households. Even in the metropolitan cities, hawkers are found selling fresh fruits and vegetables in open stalls or handcarts.

Between 1996 and 2001, sales through food retailers increased by 85 per cent to ₹7,039 billion in current terms. All food retailers recorded growth in sales. This growth could be attributed to increases in disposable incomes among the middle-class population in India. The increasing entry of women in the labour force has also led to a greater need for convenience products. This need has been met with parallel expansion in product ranges and depths, such as ready-to-eat products, ready-to-cook mixes, frozen food, instant noodles, and special condiments to make cooking simple. The proliferation of such value-added products has also increased the prices of processed foods. There has also been a rise in demand for branded value-added food. Although food sales remain the dominant retail category in the supermarkets, its share has experienced a marginal decline since 1996 as non-food lines are gradually occupying more shelf space. Grocery retailers expanded current value sales by 7 per cent in 2005 over the previous year and were ₹2,000 billion of sales, constituting about 75 per cent of the overall retail value sales.

Non-food sales in 2001 were valued at ₹4,190 billion. Average retail sales per non-food outlet reached ₹0.5 million in 2001 and department stores recorded the highest average retail sales with ₹176 million. The non-food items retailed through supermarkets generally include cosmetics, toiletries, and household cleaning products. In fact, some of the supermarkets today have crockery, household decoration items, small kitchen appliances, and kitchenware. This trend has been followed by independent grocers, discounters, and cooperatives as well. The largest non-food retailers by outlet type in 2001–05 have been general stores (29%). These outlets have high presence in the rural sector, where non-food specialists are absent. General stores carry a varied basket of goods, ranging from toiletries to hardware and, sometimes, fertilizer. With increasing affluence in the rural economy, these general stores are flourishing. Clothing, footwear, leatherwear, and accessory outlets form the next largest group of retailers, recording sales of ₹1,000 billion in 2001. Clothing retailers have the highest presence of organized retailing among this group of traders. Brand-specific stores are common in clothing and footwear. Chains of franchise stores have also developed. In 2005, non-grocery retailers accounted for ₹813 billion in sales. Although it is a smaller portion of India's retailing, it is growing rapidly. With the current value growth at 14 per cent, non-grocery retailers would benefit from the demand for premium clothing and the rising penetration of durable goods.

Sectoral Classification

Retail sectors in India can be classified into three categories, based on their future growth potential.[6] These are 'ready-to-go', 'shape/adapt', and 'wait-and-watch'.

The *ready-to-go* category comprises several sub-categories in which determined retailers can build positions immediately. This is a highly attractive sector because ease of sourcing, proliferation of products, and consumer acceptance have reached a level that permits the exploitation of size and range. These ready-to-go sectors include dry groceries (grains and cereals, packaged foods, toiletries, and household items), electronics, certain kinds of men's clothing, books, and music. In electronics, a few retailers have already begun to capture the opportunity.

Dry groceries are particularly attractive because the proliferation of brands and products has helped improve retail margins as packaged goods companies have to offer retailers better terms to obtain shelf space, and retailers can sell higher value goods to consumers. Upmarket supermarkets such as FoodWorld are attracting customers with frozen foods and a superior range of goods; discount grocers such as D'Mart attract customers on the strength of the generous discounts they can offer because of their increased margin spread. Collectively, these kinds of stores have captured nearly 20 per cent of the dry-grocery retail market since 1997.

The second category of retailing—*shape/adapt*—includes fresh groceries, women's clothing, do-it-yourself products, fast food, and furniture. It is a challenging category as retailers in these sectors must invest substantially to shape the supply chain and persuade consumers to change their buying behaviour. For example, in the case of fresh groceries, consumers prefer to buy fresh produce every day because the mobile street hawker brings fresh vegetables to the doorstep daily. Similarly, many Indian consumers prefer to choose their chicken, fish, and mutton from the meat shop. These outlets are mostly separate from produce and grocery markets as most Indian shoppers, especially vegetarians, may not be willing to shop for their food in places that sell meat. Thus, given the special characteristics of dry and fresh groceries, initially, supermarkets emphasizing dry and fresh foods may be the dominant retail format. Hypermarkets and warehouse clubs have become feasible in a few big cities as retailing gets into the second phase.

The third category of retail segments—*wait and watch*—comprises undeveloped sectors that provide no immediate opportunity for retailers. Pharmacy products and retail liquor products are examples of such sectors. Low levels of over-the-counter drug purchases and complicated regulations make pharmacy chains unattractive. Liquor retailing is not expected to take off because of the stringent and varying regulation of alcohol selling in each Indian state.

Figure 2.1 shows the state of consumer readiness and supply chain sophistication for each of the three categories—ready-to-go, shape/adapt, and wait-and-watch products. Indian retailers are venturing into all the three sectors and finding success.

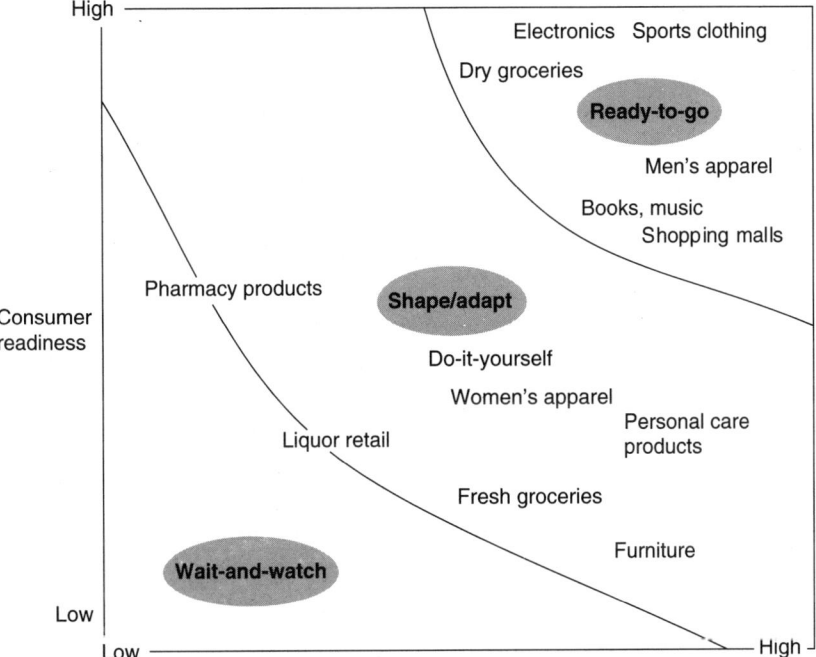

FIG. 2.1   Consumer Readiness and Supply Chain Sophistication for Three Product Categories

Source: Fernades, Michael, Chandrika Gadi, Amit Khanna, Palash Mitra, and Subbu Narayanswamy 2000.

Infrastructure

India, with a population in excess of one billion, is poised to become one of the world's largest consumer markets. Thirty per cent of these consumers live in towns and cities and the remainder in villages. Over the years, the Indian retailing scenario has been characterized by a high degree of fragmentation as compared to many developed nations. Unlike in the US, where the number of retail outlets is double that of the number of retail businesses, the ratio in India is 1:1. In 2001, it was estimated that there were 11 outlets for every 1,000 people. The average of one outlet per business clearly reveals the degree of fragmentation of the retail sector here in India. There is an increase in the number of both large and small retail formats, with each format catering to a different segment of the market.

According to a 2010 McKinsey report 'The Rise of Indian Consumer Market', the Indian consumer market is likely to grow four times by 2025. India continues to be among the most attractive countries for global retailers. The organized retail sector, which currently accounts for around 5 per cent of the Indian retail market, is all set to witness maximum number of large format malls and branded retail stores in south India, followed by the north, west, and east in the next two years. Tier II cities, such as Noida, Amritsar, Kochi, and Gurgaon, are emerging as the potential destinations for the retail sector with their huge growth potential.[7] This has already led to a significant decline in the cost of retail space in most cities, and the trend is likely to accelerate. For existing retailers as well as for new entrants, projects will become more viable as rental costs come down to more realistic and manageable levels. These new malls could bring dramatic changes in consumer buying patterns and impact the existing 'high street' retailers.

Human Resource

The retail industry in India is estimated to employ about 10 per cent of the total labour force.[8] With the retail industry witnessing high growth, job opportunities in retailing have been increasing. The Indian retail sector contributes to 8 per cent of the total employment.[9] As new retail formats and shopping outlets are coming up all over India, the number of employees going into retailing has been increasing steadily. However, the growth rate of employment has declined with the advent of IT in retailing in the larger retail formats. There is no significant presence of part-time employment. The country's employment laws do not recognize such work patterns. Most shopkeepers secure the assistance of their family members in times of need. There is no managerial part-time staff in India. Casual workers are hired for manual work and are paid daily wages. They are not on the payroll of the company. So, 90 per cent of the employees in the retail sector are full-time employees. The state governments stipulate a minimum wage for different workers in different cities, but in the unorganized sector, most sales staff are paid below this wage. In the traditional sector, wage rises have been in line with inflation, while in the organized sector, wage rises are driven by a shortage of trained staff. Turnover is also high among sales staff. Retailing has emerged as a new stream of management curriculum, providing new areas of employment. The salaries of managers in the organized sector are also relatively high.

Rural Marketing

By 2012, the rural retail market is projected to have a total of more than 50 per cent market share.[10] The rural consumer market, which grew 25 per cent in 2008, is expected to reach $425 billion by 2010–11 with 720–790 million customers, according to a white paper prepared by CII-Technopak, in November 2009. The increase in the allocation for the National Rural Employment Guarantee Act (NREGA) in the union budget has given a boost to the rural economy.[11]

Many of the FMCG products have recently witnessed a phenomenal rise in demand in rural areas when compared to urban areas. FMCG companies, such as Godrej, Hindustan Unilever (HUL), and Nestle, have significantly increased their rural employment in India looking for favourable prospects.

The high incomes in the Indian rural market along with a low cost of living make it favourable for the rural population to spend more on comparative terms. According to a McKinsey Global Index (MGI) report, rural poverty would decline significantly by 2025, which depicts the sharp turn taken by demographics in India. According to the MGI forecast, the rural market will nearly triple by 2025, creating a vast potential of $577 billion. Figure 2.2 shows that (aggregate) rural consumption growth would accelerate over the next 15 years.[12]

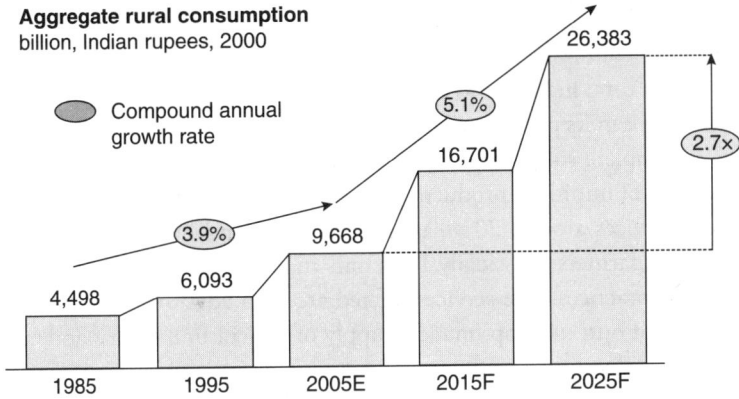

Aggregate rural consumption
billion, Indian rupees, 2000

Compound annual growth rate

4,498 — 1985
6,093 — 1995
3.9%
9,668 — 2005E
16,701 — 2015F
5.1%
26,383 — 2025F
2.7×

FIG. 2.2 Acceleration of Rural Consumption Growth over the Next 15 Years

Source: MGI India Consumer Demand Model, v1.0.

Indian retailers have an opportunity to explore the strong rural markets with an innovative retail proposition. The share of the rural market across most categories of consumption is a clear indicator of this potential opportunity and how the marketers could capitalize on the increasing mass market in India for almost all product categories. Some of the rural retail initiatives in India are described in the following sections.

Hariyali Kisaan Bazaar

Hariyali Kisaan Bazaar (HKB) is a chain of micro-level rural-initiated agricultural supermarkets set up in India in 2002 by DCM Shriram Consolidated Ltd (DSCL). The first outlet came up at Del Pandarwa (near Shahjahanpur in Uttar Pradesh) in July 2002. It gives a single-point solution to the various needs of an Indian farmer. HKB is an innovative effort aimed at offering all farming and consumer products to rural households along with financial services under one roof. Some of the main services include quality inputs such as seeds, pesticides, fertilizers, fuel, financial products, agronomic services, and knowledge information such as weather forecasts and technical support.

Each HKB centre covers around 20,000 households and caters to communities within a 25–30 km perimeter. HKB has a business model that provides services to remote regions to improve the Indian farmers' profitability and productivity.

In June 2009, DSCL announced the plan to add 300 stores to the existing 300 by 2012. The group is currently present in eight states and is India's largest rural retail chain.[13]

Hariyali Kisaan Bazaar
Source: www.farmingfirst.org

Aadhaar

Aadhaar is a service-cum-retail initiative, which was started in December 2003 by Godrej Agrovet for the development of rural India. It was established under the concept 'Everything under one roof' and its core positioning is in its punchline 'Khushiyon Ka, Khushhali Ka'.

Aadhaar, a complete solution provider for the Indian farmers, provides professional guidance with the objectives of improved productivity, higher returns, and improved cost–benefit ratio. Each Aadhaar outlet services around 20 villages in its radius and has a team of qualified agronomists who interact with farmers on a daily basis and travel to the villages in the interior to educate them on farming practices. The services offered are crop advisory services, soil and water testing services, buyback of output, crop finance, supply of agricultural inputs and animal feeds, transfer of information (weather, price, and demand–supply), door delivery of products, etc.

While the venture began by offering agricultural solutions to the farmers, based on their feedback, it has recently diversified into offering a number of other product categories including durables, FMCG, apparels, and footwear, thus catering to the complete requirement of the rural household—a one-stop shop for rural India. A number of companies are already in the process of partnering with Aadhaar for various projects, to further the initiative. The company plans to set up over 1,000 Aadhaars in 2011–2016 across the country.[14]

Aadhaar has business alliances with major corporate entities to provide services in various field of insurance, agriculture finance, healthcare, pharmacy, farm equipment, and Internet services. It helps the farmers to choose the right agricultural inputs to achieve better yields. The uniqueness of these new format stores lies in their ability to touch the lives of the Indian farmers, their families, and their communities, by offering great value propositions all under one roof. In 2010, Aadhaar became part of the Future Group.

Aadhaar
Source: www.tataagrico.com

Project Shakti

Hindustan Unilever Limited (HUL) launched Project Shakti in the year 2001 with the broad perceptive of integrating business interests with national interests. It was initiated in the Nalgonda district of Andhra Pradesh in 50 villages. The Andhra Pradesh government supported the initiative by enabling linkages with the network of the Development of Women and Children in Rural Areas (DWACRA) groups of rural women, set up for their overall upliftment. Self-help group (SHG) women strongly believe in Project Shakti as a powerful business proposition and extend their full support towards its development. It has since been extended to Bihar, Chattisgarh, Gujarat, Jharkhand, Haryana, Karnataka, Orissa, Punjab, Maharashtra, Rajasthan, Madhya Pradesh, Tamil Nadu, Uttar Pradesh, and West Bengal.

Project Shakti
Source: www.thehindubusinessline.com

Under the project, HUL offers a range of mass-market products and also imparts skills in terms of on-the-job training and support. The SHG women get micro credit facilities. While acting as direct-to-home distributors, they enjoy a better standard of living. It not only becomes a means to survive, but also brings in dignity and freedom for the women in their villages. This results in better education of their children, good health and hygiene, and overall, a better standard of living.

Choupal Sagar

ITC launched one of its first hypermarkets, Choupal Sagar, on 15 August 2004. The hypermarket is spread over five acres. It sells FMCG products, ready-made apparel, footwear, groceries, electronic durables, cosmetics, farm consumption products, and tractors, among other products. Choupal Sagar is the second layer of infrastructure, which targets multiple services under the same roof. The function of this infrastructure is to raise the overall income of the farmers and provide them good quality products and services at competitive prices. The first Choupal Sagar was located at Sehore, 38 km from Bhopal, the state capital of Madhya Pradesh. e-Choupal leverages the Internet to empower small and marginal farmers. It services about 4 million farmers and is used for bargaining as virtual buyers' cooperatives, adopting best practices, and matching up to food safety norms. Being linked to the futures market, it helps small farmers to manage risks better. ITC trains the e-choupal *sanchalak* (manager) to manage the Internet kiosk in the village. Farmers can access the daily prices of a variety of crops in India and abroad that helps them acquire the best price for their crop. Additionally, the *sanchalak* can also gather information about weather forecasts, crop insurance, and the latest farming techniques.

Choupal Sagar
Source: http://www.flickr.com/photos/cool_spark/46477776/

Tata Kisan Sansar

Tata Chemicals Limited had first started with the initiative of franchised retail outlets providing agri-inputs to farmers through the Tata Kisan Kendras (TKKs). With rural development taking place at an alarming rate, Tata as a company realized that to empower and authorize the farmers in the long run, repositioning of TKKs was essential. Hence Tata Kisan Sansar (TKS) emerged as a one-stop solution to all farmers. The TKKs were therefore re-launched and repositioned as TKS, the main focus being rendering value-added services to the farmers' overall development. In order to support the activities of TKSs, which are basically franchisee outlets, the supply chain model that evolved is a hub and spoke model.

Tata Kisan Sansar
Source: www.tatakisansansar.com

The hub acts as the resource centre to cater to the needs of the TKSs in its vicinity. Each resource centre supports primarily 20–25 TKS franchisee outlets in a radius of 50–60 km, where each TKS caters to 30–40 villages covering approximately 13 million acres. In 2010, there were 32 hubs, which catered to 681 TKSs, covering around 22,000 villages and reaching out to approximately 2.7 million farmers. The TKSs were present in 68 districts in the north zone and 20 districts in the east zone covering four and three states, respectively.[15]

Kisan Seva Kendra

Kisan Seva Kendra (KSK) is a low cost business model by Indian Oil Corporation (IOC) for meeting the needs of the rural segment. It is a one-stop shop for villagers, where along with fuel, one could purchase products for routine needs, which help to generate more income from rural markets. A wide choice of products, such as pesticides, fertilizers, grocery, stationery, banking products, auto spares, seeds, and fishing nets alongside petrol and diesel, is available in KSKs.

IOC has tied up with FMCG, financial services, and agri-input companies. It has already commissioned 1,180 KSKs.[16]

Kisan Seva Kendra
Source: www.saamco.in/farmer/farmer.htm

Rural markets have witnessed intense media exposure, rise in literacy levels, and increase in disposable incomes. The challenge for retailers lies in creating retail stores that are typically rural in nature, so that the population identifies themselves with the stores.

Foreign Direct Investment in Retail[17]

Foreign direct investment (FDI) in multi-brand retailing is prohibited in India. The FDI in single-brand retailing was, however, permitted in 2006, to the extent of 51 per cent. Since then, a total of 94 proposals have been received till May 2010. Of this, 57 proposals were approved. An FDI inflow of $194.69 million was received between April 2006 and March 2010, comprising 0.21 per cent of the total FDI inflows during the period, under the category of single-brand retailing. The proposals received and approved related to retail trading of sportswear, luxury goods, apparel, fashion clothing, jewellery, hand bags, life-style products, etc., covering high-end items. Single-brand retail outlets with FDI generally pertain to high-end products and cater to the needs of the brand conscious segment of the population, mainly attracting a brand loyal clientele, which often has a pre-set positive disposition towards a specific brand. This segment of customers is distinctly different from one that is catered to by the small retailers/*kirana* shops.

FDI in cash and carry wholesale trading was first permitted in 1997, to the extent of 100 per cent, under the government approval route. It was brought under the automatic route in 2006. Between April 2000 and March 2010, FDI inflows of $1.779 billion were received in the sector. This comprised 1.54 per cent of the total FDI inflows received during the period. It is felt that this would lead to the following effects in the long run.

- Labour displacing effects of FDI-driven modern retailing
- Job losses due to predatory pricing strategies of large retailers

- Disintegration of established supply chains by the establishment of monopoly by global retail chains, leading to their control of both ends of the supply chain
- Inability of retail to boost GDP by itself, being only an intermediate value-added process
- Disruption of the current balance of the economy by rendering millions of small retailers jobless

FDI is permitted in the retail sector in Brazil, Argentina, Singapore, Indonesia, China, and Thailand without limits on equity participation, whereas Malaysia has equity caps on FDI in the retail sector.

Experience of FDI in Retail Trade in China[18]

Foreign direct investment in retailing was permitted in China for the first time in 1992. Foreign retailers were initially permitted to trade only in six provinces and special economic zones (SEZs). Foreign ownership was initially restricted to 49 per cent. Foreign ownership restrictions have progressively been lifted and following China's accession to WTO (effective December 2004), there are no equity restrictions. Retail trade in China has been growing since 1992. Employment in retail and wholesale trade increased from about 4 per cent of the total labour force in 1992 to about 7 per cent in 2001. Between 1996 and 2001, the number of traditional retailers also increased by around 30 per cent. In 2006, the total retail sale in China amounted to $785 billion, of which the share of organized retail amounted to 20 per cent.[19] Some of the changes that have occurred in China, following the liberalization of its retail sector, include[20] the opening of over 600 hypermarkets between 1996 and 2001, the number of small outlets (equivalent to *kiranas*) increasing from 1.9 million to over 2.5 million, and employment in the retail and wholesale sectors increasing from 28 million people to 54 million people in 1992–2001.

Experience of Thailand in Opening Retail Sector to FDI

Thailand is frequently referred to as a country in which FDI has had an adverse effect on the local retailers. It permits 100 per cent foreign equity, with no limit on the number of outlets. For the retail business, it has a capital requirement of TBH100 million, and TBH20 million for each additional outlet, while it has a capital requirement of TBH100 million for each wholesale outlet. With the start of the Asian crisis in 1997, the entry ban on foreign players was removed. Within a short span of time, the foreign players expanded their operations significantly and marginalized the local retailers who were already suffering from a recessionary trend of economy. Many local players had to close down their business. The entry of foreign players in a recessionary economy adversely impacted all segments—wholesalers, manufacturers, and domestic retailers in the short run. However, it also had certain positive effects. It led to the development of organized retailing, and Thailand has now become an important shopping destination. It encouraged the growth of the agro-food processing industry and enhanced the exports of Thai-made goods through the networks of foreign retailers.

DRIVERS OF GROWTH

Indian retailing is not waiting for the size of business.[21] The challenge lies in identifying the key drivers that steer the Indian consumers' perception and shopping behaviour. The reality is that every retailer has to 'understand his customers' more discerningly than ever before and make strategic choices to pursue the right target (customer) with the right proposition.[22] According to a study, the five main values sought by shoppers are variety, value for money, product quality, fashion attributes, and time saving. The key drivers of these values are discussed here.

Spending Pattern   According to the consumer outlook study conducted by KSA Technopak (now Technopak Advisors), consumer spending is on the rise.[23] In 2002, it went up by 9.6 per cent compared to the previous year, which had shown a decline of about 2 per cent in spending. The growth implies a rise in market opportunity for retailers, estimated to be in the region of ₹150 billion among the SEC A and B categories in urban India alone. The study also revealed that savings and investments had also gone up substantially.

Customer Expectations   Consumer value expectations from markets and shops have changed dramatically in the last few years. This threw up new challenges for retailers, such as increased pressure from other product categories that are vying for a share of the same wallet of the target consumer, changing 'value' equations, and a sharper focus from retailers.

Consumer Lifestyle   With an increase in the number of educated women entering the workforce and with more two-income households with higher disposable incomes, consumer lifestyle is changing. According to KSA Technopak, the overall spending of the working woman is about 1.3 times that of an average homemaker. However, they spend much more on lifestyle products. The ratio of men to women spending in single income and double income households is 1.12:1 whereas the same is 1.05:1 in the case of double income no kids (DINK) households.

Changing Attitudes   Indian consumers are now global in their consumption pattern. They are exposed to many international and local brands and many different lifestyles that they like to adopt. The Indian consumer is adapting faster than the retailers can adapt for now. According to a study by KSA Technopak, the increased relative spending of youth, compared to elders has gone up over the past few years.[24] Teenagers are getting richer with every passing year. In fact, 90 per cent of youths get pocket money, with the average amount having increased from ₹284 in the year 2000 to ₹375 in 2001.

A study conducted jointly by Coca-Cola India and research firm NFO-MBL aimed at exploring the mindsets, media preferences, attitudes, and behaviour of youths in the marketplace. According to the study, much of their pocket money went on grooming, hanging out, indulgence, and on high-ticket items as well. Food and beverages account for the largest proportion of the teenager's pocket money (with ice-cream and soft drinks leading the category). Further, personal durable ownership has increased, with teenagers also influencing the purchase of entertainment durables at home. Also, Indian youth desperately need 'hang out' places that satisfy their notion of a 'cool' ambience.[25] The Indian yuppie consumer today reflects a strong preference for imperatives such as evaluating choices from among a large assortment of products and a pleasurable shopping experience that would provide the maximum 'value' per rupee spent. Consumer niches are beginning to drive the market and are becoming more important.

According to KSA Technopak, Indian consumers have never been more willing to experiment with products with the element of contemporary design.[26] Future trends, therefore, indicate that value equations will incorporate aesthetic considerations alongside economic and functional considerations. Before the 1980s, price was the predominant purchase determinant; some years later, quality coupled with price assumed importance. The 1990s witnessed an assortment of quality, range, and price calling the shots. Today, about 30 million Indian consumers determine their purchase decisions across diverse categories based on contemporary design coupled with quality.

In the urban markets, especially among higher income consumers, increasing 'time consciousness' is leading to higher 'shopping efficiency'.[27] Convenience, both in terms of the location of the store and in-store conveniences, is a key value. Consumers also want range, efficiency, displays, and price deals. With the increasing number of nuclear families and working women, greater work pressure, and increased commuting time, consumers are looking for convenience—convenience is defined as having everything under one roof, longer hours, and multiplicity of choice. For the same amount of grocery shopping, consumers are spending 20 per cent less time. For the same amount of eating out, consumers spend about 50 per cent less time. Irrespective of time scarcity and depressed spending, 77 per cent enjoy shopping and 61 per cent consider shopping a fun-filled activity. Therefore, as consumers are positive towards shopping at large format stores, retailers need to give them enough reason and value to shop there. The importance of price in the shopping experience has dropped to 42 per cent from 58 per cent in 1998. The importance of selection fell to 33 per cent from 65 per cent, but convenience stayed at a high 61 per cent.[28]

Indian consumers are travelling less than 1–1.5 km from their home to shop, especially in case of grocery and staples. Retailers are incentivizing non-shopping visits by creating space for young people to spend time. This is also one of the ways to hedge against any threat from 'e-tailing'.[29] Music stores, for example, are creating spaces and hosting artistes. The customer wants to pay for the total experience—from pre-purchase evaluation to use of the product.

Increased Spending of Rural Consumers   The rural market already accounts for over one-third of the durable and non-durable categories, and is growing at a faster pace than urban India. In terms of geography, retailers would need to customize their offering to tap the rural and semi-urban spending potential. Large format stores are opening in rural areas for agro-inputs. Even in non-metro urban centres, there are very good opportunities to look at starting or expanding operations.

KEY CHALLENGES

Despite the retail boom in the country, large-scale retailers seem to be having to indulge in all sorts of promotions to attract store traffic.[30] The main challenges faced by them are discussed in this section.

The *Kirana*   The *kirana* stores practice customer relationship management (CRM) diligently. The shopkeeper knows about the customers' families, their purchase history, and their needs. Consumer familiarity runs down from generation to generation. There is no major dissatisfaction with these stores. They are open for longer hours, stock most of the goods required by the residents in a given area, provide credit and home delivery, and in many cases, supply products that they do not stock without any extra cost. Consequently, a large number of customers are not willing to pay a premium for the shopping experience promised by large format retailers.

High Costs for the Organized Sector   Traditional retailing has been established in India for some centuries. It has a low cost structure, is mostly owner operated, and has negligible real estate and labour costs, and little or no taxes to pay. In contrast, players in the organized sector have high expenses to meet and yet have to keep prices low enough to be able to compete with the traditional sector. As a McKinsey report points out, Indian retailers operate on an extremely low cost base. The kiosk type of shops operate on the assumption of zero land and labour costs. For organized players, the lease alone can cost up to 6–10 per cent of sales as compared with just 3–5 per cent globally. Although manpower costs are lower at 5–6 per cent of sales as against 6–10 per cent globally, energy costs are high at 1.5–3 per cent against 1–1.5 per cent internationally, and so are the working capital costs. Capital expenses in retail business are high due to major renovations needed every 5–7 years. The rent control laws favour occupants, which limits the availability of downtown real estate.

Specialization   According to experts, the real boom in organized retailing will come once the supermarkets start selling daily need goods at 90 per cent of the regular price, as Carrefour is doing in China.[31] The key will be to plan a national scale presence, build strong sourcing networks that connect the business directly with farms, and sell fresh food at attractive prices. Subhiksha (which closed down in 2009), a Chennai-based grocer-cum-chemist, started out with low prices, proximity, quality, and range. It sold at a markdown of 7–8 per cent on the marked price. It was not a self-service store. With more than 200 stores in many cities, it sourced products directly from manufacturers, and used information technology to manage the information gaps. Although Indian consumers have started buying from other formats, they are buying mainly from store-based retailers (Table 2.2). Grocery still remains the main purchase from these stores.

Correct Merchandise Mix   Getting the right product mix is critical to retailing. FoodWorld started with 6,000 stock-keeping units (SKUs) but then cut it down to 3,500. Every retailer wants to have high-value, high margin, and fast moving products. However, this is not always possible.[32] Attention has to be paid to gross margin return on investment. One of the indices that retailers use to check volumes is 'sales density', which shows the amount of sales per sq. ft of shop space.[33] The urban Indian *kiranawalla* is estimated to sell ₹7,000 per sq. ft every year, while Indian supermarkets achieve ₹13,500. The US food–retail average is $445, while the best is Carrefour's $1,800 per sq. ft. Specifically, Shoppers Stop is reputed to have touched a sales density of ₹25,000 at one of its stores, which has become an aspiration figure for non-grocery retailers. This again could depend not only on margins but also on how briskly products move. Keeping inventory low is a challenge, and this is achieved by a good number of 'stock turns' per year. For garments, five turns is the typical figure, though this can vary from 38 times for a petrol station to two-three times for a jewellery store. Shoppers Stop turns its merchandise over an average six times. Their next year's target is seven. The Kemp Group, a toy store, rolls its toys 10 times a year. Vivek's, a household appliance retailer, has 12 rollovers a year.

Strong IT Support   The backbone of retailing is IT. It would require large investments that connect every aspect of the operations seamlessly, from suppliers to the cash counters. For instance, a store like

TABLE 2.2   Sector-wise Sales in Retailing in India (2004–09)—Value (₹ billion)

	2004	2005	2006	2007	2008	2009
Grocery retailers	4,916.80	5,227.00	5,541.10	5,837.90	6,088.00	6,240.80
Non-grocery retailers	2,122.80	2,445.70	2,824.60	3,247.90	3,578.30	3,749.60
Store-based retailing	**7,039.60**	**7,672.70**	**8,365.70**	**9,085.80**	**9,666.30**	**9,990.40**
Vending	–	–	–	–	–	–
Homeshopping (in million)	2,140.10	2,690.50	3,357.50	4,464.30	5,755.80	7,192.40
Internet retailing (in million)	3,613.10	4,743.40	7,489.30	12,475.00	19,100.50	26,288.00
Direct selling (in million)	21,625.90	24,635.20	28,474.80	33,271.40	39,611.10	46,174.00
Non-store retailing (in million)	**27,379.10**	**32,069.10**	**39,321.70**	**50,210.80**	**64,467.30**	**79,654.40**
Non-store retailing	**27.38**	**32.07**	**39.32**	**50.21**	**64.47**	**79.65**
Total retailing	**7,066.98**	**7,704.77**	**8,405.02**	**9,136.01**	**9,730.77**	**10,070.05**

Source: www.euromonitor.com, accessed on 2 September 2010.

FoodWorld generates about a million bills every month. Similarly, other stores such as Pantaloon, Piramyd, and Shoppers Stop can track sales and place orders based on scientific demand projections.

Poor Infrastructure   In India, infrastructure such as cold-chain infrastructure is primitive, affecting the modernization of the food sector. In order to succeed, supermarkets would require volumes to be cost competitive, which would require operations with hubs all over India. Indian infrastructure is not fully developed yet. Roads and rail infrastructure need to be developed. The efficiency in supply chain is far below the international benchmarks. It is also difficult to find suppliers for a large quantity as would be needed by a national chain. A strict quality control increases the prices of the merchandise and the gap between demand and supply.

Industry Status   The Indian Retail Council was formed in 2000, under the auspices of the Confederation of Indian Industry (CII). This Council is expected to serve as a group for the industry in its dealings with the government. Until then, retailing had not been considered as an industry, and there were only traders' associations at local levels. This is the first time a national association has been formed. It is a step in the right direction. It will enable the industry to ask for unified tax laws, rational octroi, and removal of other barriers and impediments. Institutional finance is not available as mall development is not understood as an industry. The existing labour laws make it difficult for shops to have flexible timings. The movement of primary sector produce is still subject to a system of middlemen, which makes low-cost sourcing difficult.

The retail business is expected to see further growth of organized retailing in both food and non-food segments in the coming years. The proportion of sales through organized retailing is estimated to increase to around 14–18 per cent by 2015. The retail sector is likely to see huge investments in the next four to five years. Newer chains will come in and present players will increase penetration. In fact, by the end of the forecast period, the established players are likely to have reached saturation levels in the metropolitan cities and will shift their focus of investments to other tier I cities. However, if the ban on foreign players holding a controlling stake is lifted, the sector could see drastic movements. On-line shopping is not likely to cannibalize the sector from other channels.

Indian retailing needs to adapt to change. The adaptation can be in terms of modification and creation of additional new formats, or in terms of adding new product categories for the same targeted customer, and very systematic and regular reviews of brands and their price points offered to the target consumer, so as to maintain the optimum value proposition demanded by customers. There is scope to create Indian versions of mass merchants such as Walmart and Carrefour. While Giant (now Spencer's) and Big Bazaar (and a few others) are already present in the market, there is room for many more to enter. Likewise, direct-to-home selling offers greater potential than what has so far been exploited by the likes of Amway and Oriflame. According to a McKinsey report, a retailer breaking into India will build e-commerce into its business plan. Retailers need to develop a plan to integrate an on-line offering with bricks and mortar operations.

SUMMARY

The Indian retailing industry is shaping up to be very different from that of other counties. It consists of a large number of small size retailers. These are traditional retailers. Only a fraction of the outlets are 'organized'. The traditional retailers are characterized by small size of operation and a very high level of service to their customers.

The retail industry can be studied from several dimensions. The industry can be segmented on the basis of the products being sold, mainly food versus non-food items. Similarly, based on the growth drivers, the industry can be classified into sectors that have rapid growth possibilities due to the preparedness of the infrastructure required for managing the business.

The industry is growing at a rapid pace due to the changes in the consumption culture of the Indian consumers. With a very young population and a rapidly growing economy, the retailing industry is witnessing the entry of Indian as well as multinational organized players. However, they face some very daunting tasks and challenges before they can achieve success. The most important of these are the changes in the attitude of the customers, their expectations, high level of value delivery by *kirana* and other traditional stores, and the state of infrastructure support.

NOTES

1. http://business.mapsofindia.com, accessed on 2 September 2010.
2. Banerjee, Arindam and Bibek Banerjee 2000, 'Effective Retail Promotion Management: Use of Point of Sales Information', *Vikalpa*, Vol. 25, No. 4, October–December, pp 51–59.
3. KSA Technopak (I) Pvt. Ltd, the Indian operation of the US-based Kurt Salmon Associates.
4. Fernandes, Michael, Chandrika Gadi, Amit Khanna, Palash Mitra, and Subbu Narayanswamy, 'India's Retailing Comes of Age', *The McKinsey Quarterly* 2000, No. 4.
5. *Food Retail in India*, Datamonitor Research Store.
6. Fernandes, Michael, Chandrika Gadi, Amit Khanna, Palash Mitra, and Subbu Narayanswamy, 'India's Retailing Comes of Age', *The McKinsey Quarterly 2000*, No. 4.
7. http://www.business.mapsofindia.com/india-retail-industry, accessed on 17 May 2010.
8. http://www.euromonitor.com, Retail Trade International 2002.
9. http://www.ibef.org/industry/retail.aspx, accessed on 29 August 2011.
10. http://www.ibef.org, accessed on 16 September 2010.
11. http://www.ibef.org/economy/ruralmarket.aspx, accessed on 16 September 2010.
12. www.slideshare.net/analysis-of-mgis-india-consumer-report-2007, accessed on 20 September 2010.
13. www.farmingfirst.com, accessed on 20 September 2010.
14. http://www.afaqs.com/news/company_briefs/index.html?id=8034_Godrej+Aadhaar+ties+up+with+Apollo+Pharmacy, accessed on 20 September 2010.
15. http:// www.tatakisansansar.com, accessed on 21 September, 2010.
16. http://www.iocl.com accessed on 21 September 2010.
17. Discussion paper on FDI in multi-brand retail trading, DIPP, GOI, http://www.dipp.nic.in/DiscussionPapers/DP_FDI_Multi-brandretailtrading_06July2010.doc, accessed on 12 April 2011.
18. FICCI-ICICI Property Service Report, February 2005.
19. 'Impact of Organized Retailing on the Unorganized Sector', ICRIER study, May 2008.
20. 'The Benefits of Modern Trade to Transitional Economies', CII–PwC study 2008.
21. Banerjee, Arindam and Bibek Banerjee 2000, 'Effective Retail Promotion Management: Use of Point of Sales Information', *Vikalpa*, Vol. 25, No. 4, October–December, pp 51–59.
22. Banerjee, Arindam and Bibek Banerjee 2000, 'Effective Retail Promotion Management: Use of Point of Sales Information', *Vikalpa*, Vol. 25, No. 4, October–December, pp 51–59.
23. KSA Technopak 5th KSA Retail Summit, New Delhi, 11 February 2003.
24. 'Thousand Malls Boom', *A&M*, 28 February 2001, pp. 34–41.
25. 'Thousand Malls Boom', *A&M*, 28 February 2001, pp. 34–41.
26. Bhushan Ratna 2003, 'Its Got to be a Mass Act', *The Hindu Business Line*, Internet edn, Thursday, 30 January.
27. Bhushan Ratna 2003, 'Its Got to be a Mass Act', *The Hindu Business Line*, Internet edn, Thursday, 30 January.
28. Consumer Outlook Study—KSA Technopak, 2002.

29. Chandran, Rina 2002, 'If Looks could Sell', *The Hindu Business Line*, Internet edn, Thursday, 29 October.
30. 'Thousand Malls Boom', *A&M*, 28 February 2001, pp. 34–41.
31. Subramanian, Nithya 2000, 'Song and Dance to Entice Customers', *The Hindu Business Line*, Internet edn, New Delhi, 13 December.
32. 'Thousand Malls Boom', *A&M*, 28 February 2001, pp. 34–41.
33. 'Thousand Malls Boom', *A&M*, 28 February 2001, pp. 34–41.

CONCEPT REVIEW QUESTIONS

1. Describe the landscape of Indian retailing.
2. What are the growth opportunities for Indian retailing? What are the drivers of growth? What are the challenges being faced by Indian retailers?
3. How would a retailer build a good business model in India?

CRITICAL THINKING QUESTIONS

1. How is Indian retailing different from international retailing in terms of costs? How would you manage in such a situation?
2. Is the rural marketing sector in India in a decline stage? Please discuss.

PROJECTS

1. Visit a marketplace. Count 100 shops and then classify them into meaningful groups to draw strategic insight.
2. What are the current key developments with regards to FDI in India?

CASE STUDY

Nirantar Agrasar Retail*

Purushottam Bhatnagar, CEO of Nirantar Agrasar Group of Industries Limited (NAGIL), was following the Indian retail growth story intently. He observed that it was interesting to see how the shopping landscape was evolving rapidly with the emergence of new opportunities for organized retailers. In 2008, India topped AT Kearney's annual Global Retail Development Index (GRDI) for the third consecutive year, maintaining its position as the most attractive market for retail investment. Exhibit CS2.1 indicates the evolution of India's retail sector across the past few years. The untapped scope of modern day retailing in India had been led by several large corporations such as Pantaloon, Tata, Aditya Birla Group, RPG, and Reliance. Several regional and local chains such as Ebony and Khadims had also emerged. While most of these developments were taking place in large cities, some companies such as Sriram, ITC, Godrej, and Tata had also ventured into rural areas. Most of the rural retailers dealt primarily in agro inputs. However, some, such as Godrej, sold non-agro products like FMCG

*Prepared by Professor Piyush Kumar Sinha and Ipshit Bhattacharya (PGP-ABM, 2007–09), IIMA.

Cases of the Indian Institute of Management Ahmedabad are prepared as a basis for class discussion. They are not designed to present illustrations of either correct or incorrect handling of administrative problems.

Authors acknowledge the support extended by Food and Agribusiness Advisory and Research Division and Yes Bank.

and consumer durables too. These companies saw value in providing products and services to more than 700 million of the population of rural India. In his observation, Purushottam was very much impressed with Sam Walton. He admired the way Walmart had started in smaller towns and slowly emerged as the largest retailer.

Triggered by these factors, Purushottam started nurturing his dream to take NAGIL to the retail sector. The company was a prominent player, especially in the Hindi belt[1]. It had already been doing well in the FMCG, leather, wind energy, and construction sectors. In the year 2006–07, FMCG accounted for about 65% of its ₹10 billion[2] turnover. Its detergent was one of the largest brands in the category with a market share of about 15%. Its leather shoe brand had established itself with middle-class office-goers. Since NAGIL had a very well established business in UP, Purushottam thought it was prudent to explore the possibility of starting the business in this state. The demography of UP indicated that it consisted mostly of small towns and cities. Only two cities, Lucknow and Kanpur, had a population of more than 1 million[3]. Headquartered at Kanpur, he wanted to explore the possibility of starting the venture from places where he had spare landholdings, such as Kannauj, Chhibramau, Bhongaon, Madhoganj, Sandila, and Bilgram (See Exhibit CS2.2). With these thoughts in mind, he called up one of his old friends, Acharya Bhatt (henceforth referred to as AB), who was an IIMA alumnus and had started retail consulting.

Puru: AB, I plan to enter the retail business. I believe that the large cities are or would very soon become very competitive. Given the very low instances of retailers entering the small towns and rural areas, I would like to explore that arena. I would be glad if you could find time to come over on Monday?

AB had just returned from Shimla from his summer break. He was still getting used to the Delhi heat when he got this call.

He called his secretary, Meghna.

AB: Meghna, see if Priyank[4] is in his cabin, I wish to see him. Get the SUV ready by evening; put two crates of Bisleri[5], one large tube of Odomos, and a dozen packs of Allout. We are going on a safari across UP. Please do keep a map of UP.

Meeting with Purushottam

AB: Puru, meet Priyank, who has been my partner in the retail consulting business for six years now.

Puru: Nice to meet you, Priyank. So AB, have you thought of what I had proposed?

AB: Puru, after talking to you the other day, we conducted a preliminary study of the six locations you have in mind. We have divided the geography into two belts, eastern and western. By our definition, three of your locations, Sandila, Bilgram, and Madhoganj, lay close to the eastern belt, i.e., the Hardoi–Sandila–Lucknow belt (east side of the river). The other three, Kannauj, Chhibramau, and Bhongaon, lay close to the western belt, i.e., the Farrukhabad–Kannauj–Kanpur belt (west side of the river). Taking into account factors such as demographic and economic profiles, political scenario, extent of commercialization, cropping pattern, area requirement, connectivity, and availability of necessary infrastructure, we feel that NAGIL should venture in the western belt. Although, for long, the western belt has been largely agrarian and the eastern belt more commercialized and industrialized, many retailers have started eyeing the western belt now. We have some news of Vishal Megamart and RPG Spencer's coming to Etawah and Farrukhabad. We find it better to enter and establish the business in the western belt before competition intensifies.

Puru: In that case, what is your opinion about a rural retail model in Kannauj?

AB: We do not know in detail yet. However, we do see considerable scope in Kannauj because it boasts of an almost half a century old perfumery industry with old established players primarily supplying to intoxicant manufacturers. As a result, it is economically stronger with respect to other locations making the possibility of a retailing venture more viable. It is also better connected by rail and road than the other two. It is about 80 km from Kanpur. You may eventually cover the other areas

---

1. Consisting of the states of UP, Bihar, MP, and Rajasthan, which account for almost a third of India's population.
2. 10 million = 1 crore
3. 1 million = 10 lakh
4. Priyank, who was also an IIMA alumnus, was Acharya's partner in the consulting firm.
5. Bisleri is a popular mineral water brand, Odomos is a mosquito repellent cream, and Allout is a mosquito repellent coil.

EXHIBIT CS2.1 India's Retail Growth Story

India Retail (₹ Billion)					
Unorganized Retail (₹ Billion)	*2003–04*	*2004–05*	*2005–06*	*2006–07*	*CAGR (%)*
Food and grocery	7,028	7,064	7,418	8,680	7.3
Beverages	212	309	373	518	34.7
Clothing and footwear	777	993	1,036	1356	20.4
Furniture, furnishing, appliances, and services	512	656	746	986	24.4
Non-institutional healthcare	950	972	1,022	1,159	6.9
Sports goods, entertainment, equipment, and books	212	272	308	395	23.0
Personal care	371	433	465	617	18.5
Jewellery, watches, etc	530	610	655	863	17.7
Total	**10,592**	**11,309**	**12023**	**14,574**	**11.2**
Organized Retail (₹ Billion)					
Food and grocery	39	44	50	61	16.5
Beverages	11	12	13	16	14.7
Clothing and footwear	168	189	212	251	14.3
Furniture, furnishing, appliances, and services	67	75	85	101	14.8
Non-institutional healthcare	14	16	19	24	20.0
Sports goods, entertainment, equipment, and books	25	33	44	63	37.0
Personal care	11	15	22	33	46.9
Jewellery, watches, etc	18	24	33	49	40.5
Total	**353**	**408**	**478**	**598**	**19.5**

Organized Retail Increase in Area ('000 sq. ft)			
	Average Size (sq. ft)	*2001*	*2006*
Supermarkets/Convenience stores	1,000	400	4,751
Hypermarkets	40,000	0	3,000
Discount stores	1,000	48	1,472
Speciality stores	800	2,121	16,490
Department stores	30,000	780	4,980

Source: 'Impact of Organized Retailing on Unorganized Sector', ICRIER Report 2008.

through smaller formats, typically a spiral expansion approach.

Priyank: I guess AB and I would move on to conduct a scenario analysis of Kannauj. We shall meet you again with our findings by the end of this fortnight.

Puru: Take one of my young associates, an MBA graduate, Vishwa, along with you for that. He maintains my distributor contacts in western UP. Using his contacts and resources, you would be able to meet people and garner information much faster and easier.

EXHIBIT CS2.2   Map Indicating Prospective Locations

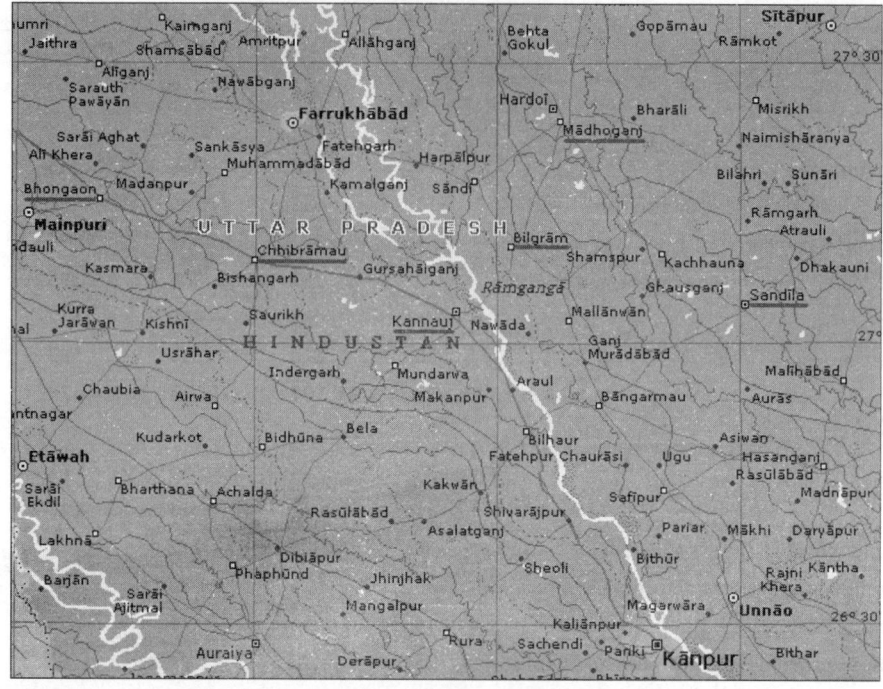

EXHIBIT CS2.3   Map of Kannauj

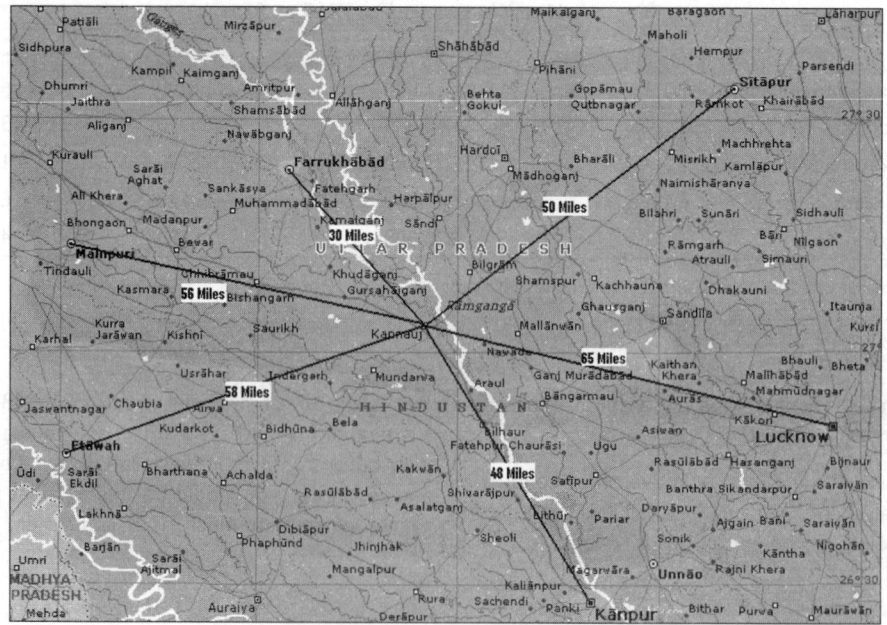

The Kannauj Block[6]

The town was located on NH91[7] on the banks of The Ganges (Exhibit CS2.3). Once in Kannauj, while Vishwa met the government officials to gather the demographic and trade data and arrange interaction with some businessmen, AB and Priyank, started exploring the terrain. They went about the place through its lanes, by-lanes, and crowded markets.

AB: Evidently retailing in Kannauj district is in its evolutionary phase. Much of it looks scattered and unorganized in terms of supply chain, quality, and reliability of costs.

Priyank: I agree. You can observe that typical of a small town market, majority of the retailing takes place in the main bazaar with shops ranging between 100 and 350 sq. ft. Most of them specialize in a particular merchandise; though some of them apparently have been at this place for long as general merchants, reminiscent of variety stores. These numerous small-sized shops and narrow roads make the market look very clustered. I also noticed that there were several shops dealing in agri-inputs and implements. On enquiry, a retailer told me that in Kannauj block, fertilizers and seeds are disbursed through 12 cooperatives and 60 private retailers, while crop protection chemicals (insecticides, fungicides, and herbicides) and plant growth regulators (PGRs) are distributed through only 12 private retailers. Very few retailers deal in liquid fertilizers. Consumer durable and farm equipment stores appear larger in size. A significant number of shoppers in most of the shops are men.

AB: Did you notice a number of general grocery, agri-input, durables, and other shops on the national highway? People say, in the past few years, as the city has expanded towards NH91, retailing has also been spreading to that region. One of the shopkeepers says that the block serves several villages within a radius of about 25 kilometers, except on the east due to the river.

Priyank: Now I see why I found so many tractors parked near the bus stand, about half a kilometre from the market.

AB: Among these small stores on the highway, I also found a larger store of TATA Kisan Kendra. I visited the store and was told that Hariyali Kisaan Bazar, the rural retail arm of the Sriram group, is located about five kilometers towards the west.

Vishwa: The government statistical department report indicates Kannauj to be a block with a population of 200,000 with a density of 585 persons per square kilometer (Exhibit CS2.4). Spread over an area of 37,800 hectares, it consists mainly (80%) of rural population. About 35% of the population is within the age of 20 and 50 and supports a literacy level of 58%; about 75% of which are educated till middle school. The main occupation of the population is farming (about 52%). Another 25% are marginal workers (Exhibit CS2.5). Depending upon the size of landholding, these farmers earn upto ₹2,00,000 per annum.

Priyank: I individually interviewed some farmers during the day. They say that a typical farmer saves about 60% of the income for the next crop. Their other primary expenditures include household consumables, apparel, education of children, and savings to buy durables and construction material. Apparently, due to a highly unreliable and seasonal income the basket size per purchase is small. However, they spend a considerable amount during festivities and special occasions amongst relatives or local community. Further, a majority of the earnings of a rural household is consumed in the year itself or is converted into assets such as housing, agricultural implements, or consumer durables such as refrigerator, television, bicycles, motorcycles, and mobile phones.

AB: What about the people related with the perfumery industry?

Priyank: This is a high margin industry with the old established players primarily supplying to intoxicant manufacturers. Businessmen, though few in number, have good income. Their spending pattern is quite similar to a tier II city consumer. Also, with better cropping patterns and higher awareness due to the high penetration of cable and satellite, especially among younger population, rural consumers are also aspiring to acquire the same status and livelihood as their urban counterparts. The role of social hierarchies, caste, religion, traditions, social norms, and customs in influencing buying behavior is also vital.

---

6. A state is divided into districts as administrative units; which in turn consist of blocks.
7. National highway linking Kanpur and Ghaziabad.

EXHIBIT CS2.4   Basic Demographic Information for Kannauj Block

Population	200,000.0	Sex ratio (females/1000 males)	862.0
Population density (persons/ sq. km)	585.0	Literacy rate (%)	58.2
Rural population (%)	80.0	Literacy rate (males)	69.0
Average family size (urban)	6.5	Literacy rate (females)	45.0
Average family size (rural)	7.0	Area (hectares)	37,800.0

Age-wise Population Distribution across Kannauj Block

Age Group	% Total	% Males	% Females
0–9	27.5	26.7	28.3
10–19	24.0	24.8	23.1
20–34	21.4	21.2	21.7
35–49	15.0	15.5	14.4
50–59	5.5	5.3	5.7
> 59	6.6	6.5	6.8

Education Scenario in Kannauj District

	< Primary	Primary	Middle School	Higher Secondary	Senior Secondary	Graduates	Others
Males	22.52	23.27	25.56	15.17	7.96	5.39	0.13
Females	22.52	29.59	29.9	9.86	5.36	2.71	0.06

Source: District statistical office, Kannauj

Consumption Pattern in Kannauj

AB: I have some information on the monthly per capita consumption expenditure (MPCE) classes (Exhibit CS2.6) of UP. If we translate this to Kannauj in the same proportion, we see that about 63% of the rural households spend more than ₹420 per month on personal consumption. This amounts to a total potential market of a ₹1 billion per annum (Exhibit CS2.7). However, this is just the government reported figure, and from what I see, I expect the number to be at least three times higher. My discussions with dealers and the manager of HKB provide a further indication of the share of food and non-food items (Exhibits CS2.8 and CS2.9). A typical household would spend about 40% of the total spending on non-food items. There has also been a recent upsurge in the consumer durable market for products such as 100cc motorcycles from Hero Honda, lubricants, 175 l. refrigerators, color televisions, and building construction materials. In view of the increasing aspirations of the local consumers, local retailers have already started to shelf products on the lines of tier II city stores.

Agricultural Scenario

Next, while Priyank and Vishwa moved out to have a look at the location and meet some government officers, AB met the district agricultural officer (DAO). He indicated that Kannauj primarily lies in the potato cultivation belt. Other important crops are wheat and maize (Exhibit CS2.10).

AB: With the help of data obtained from the officer and in conversation with various retailers and agriculturists of the region, I have prepared a molecule and product-wise usage scenario for various agricultural inputs (Exhibit CS2.11). We know the usage factors for each of these inputs. Superimposing these on the landholding scenario (Exhibit CS2.12), we arrive at the annual agricultural input requirement for the area (Exhibit CS2.13). The DAO has also provided the following scenario of the agricultural and veterinary services in the region (Exhibits CS2.14 and CS2.15). This information may help us think about some add-ons for the retailing model.

EXHIBIT CS2.5 **Economic Scenario across Various Occupational Categories in Kannauj Block**

Category		Annual Income (₹ '000)	Explanation
Farmer			
Landholding	< 2 acres	60	On an average a farmer may earn approximately ₹6,000 per *bigha*
	2–4 acres	60–120	
	4–8 acres	120–180	
	8–12 acres	180–240	
	> 12 acres	> 240	
Landless agricultural worker		15–25	150–250 days work available at established ₹100/day rate
Landless non-agricultural worker		20–35	200–350 days work available at established ₹100/day rate
Industrial workers			
Skilled		60–150	5,000–12,000 salary per month
Semi-skilled/Unskilled		20–50	2,000–4,000 salary per month
Small shop owner		50–150	Depending upon the scale of operations and type of product sold
Small business owner		300–700	Depending upon the scale of operations and type of product sold
Large business owner		> 1,000	These are usually the perfume manufacturers and cold storage owners in the area

Farmers	Agricultural Workers	Businessmen	Marginal Workers	Others	Total Workers
26,866	6,562	1,608	13,177	3,627	51,840

Source: Based on personal interview samples collected and district statistical office records

EXHIBIT CS2.6 **Percentage Distribution of UP Rural Households in Various MPCE Classes**

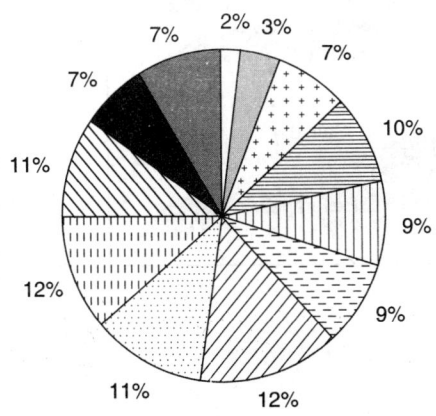

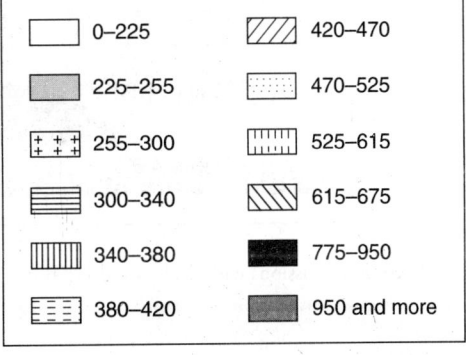

0–225	420–470
225–255	470–525
255–300	525–615
300–340	615–675
340–380	775–950
380–420	950 and more

Source: Indiastats

EXHIBIT CS2.7   Distribution of Kannauj Rural Households under MPCE Classification

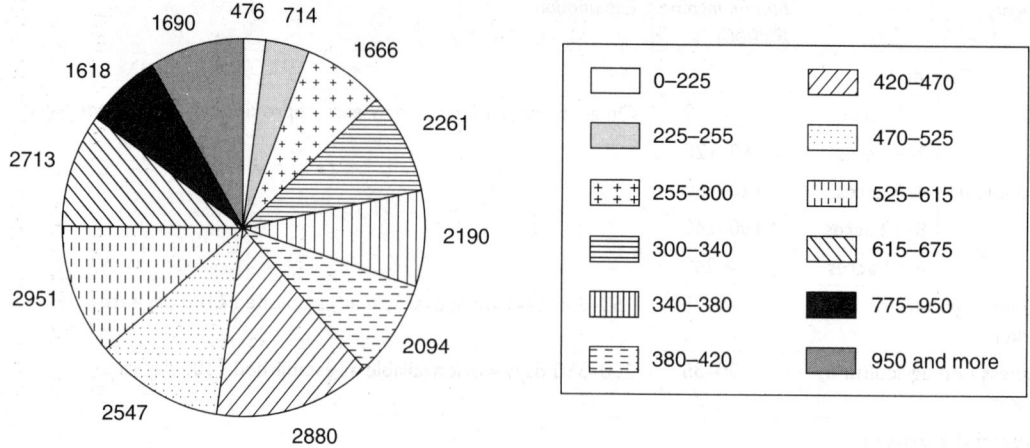

Source: Based on discussions with dealers and HKB manager.

EXHIBIT CS2.8   Spending Pattern of Kannauj Rural Households under Food Consumer Segments

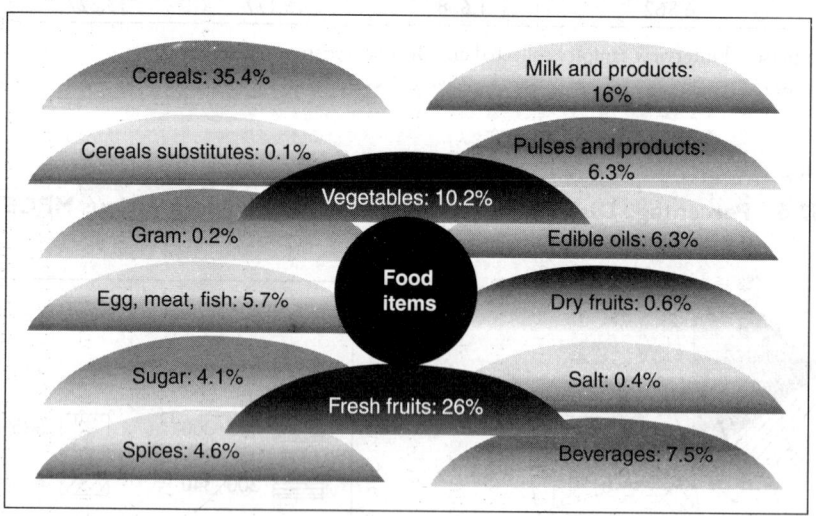

Source: Based on discussions with dealers and HKB manager.

EXHIBIT CS2.9　**Spending Pattern of Kannauj Rural Households under Non-food Consumer Segments**

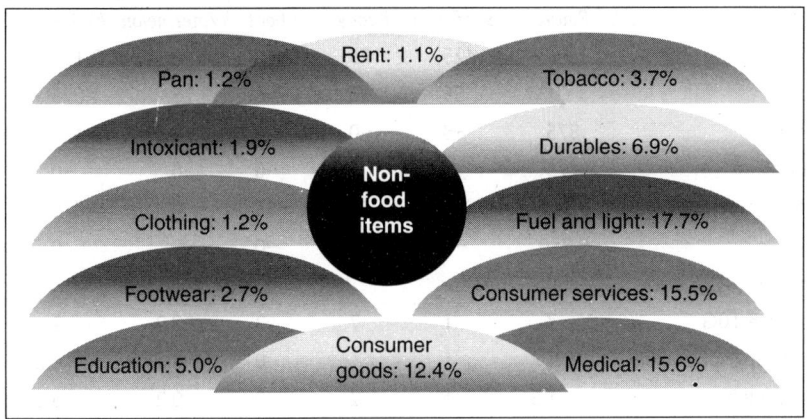

Source: Based on discussions with dealers and HKB manager.

EXHIBIT CS2.10　**Cropping Pattern in Kannauj**

Crop	Area under Cultivation (Hect)	Yield (MT/Hect)	Annual Production (MT)	Price/MT (₹ '000)
Paddy	659	2.41	1,588	10.0
Wheat	8,411	3.12	26,242	6.8
Bajra	84	0.63	53	5.2
Jowar	202	0.74	149	5.7
Maize	8,160	1.81	14,770	5.6
Barley	219	3.12	683	5.6
Urad	267	0.92	246	16.7
Moong	224	0.83	186	16.5
Chana	253	1.13	286	18.6
Peas	272	1.61	438	13.2
Arhar	265	0.96	254	16.1
Mustard	1,247	1.07	1,334	18.2
Sunflower	1,705	2.05	3,495	14.2
Potato	7,141	21.14	150,961	2.4
Other vegetables	7,341	NA		
Total	**36,619**			

Source: District Agriculture Office

EXHIBIT CS2.11   Product and Molecule-wise Usage Scenario of Various Agricultural Inputs

Various Agri-inputs		Agri-input Usage Scenario (in MT/Annum)							
		Potato	Sunflower	Paddy	Wheat	Watermelon	Maize	Flowers	Total
Fertilizers	Urea	2,625	425	175	2,075	~0	2,150	15	7,465
	DAP	3,500	85	35	996	25	1,075	15	5,731
	MOP	875	~0	~0	~0	0	430	~0	1,305
	Zinc	175	0	9.1	~0	0	~0	0	184.1
	NPK	3,500	85	35	996	0	1,075	0	5,691
	SSP	8,750	~0	~0	~0	0	0	0	8,750
	Others	50							
Insecticides	Phorate 10G	7	1	7	2	0.2	2	0	19.2
	Chloropyriphos 20EC	1	1	1	0	0	0.2	0	3.2
	Endosulphan	1.5	1	2	0	0.2	0.2	0.1	5
	Cypermethrin	1	0.5	1	0	0.1	0.2	0	2.8
	Sulphur 80WG	1	0.5	0.2	0	0	0	0	1.7
	Monochrotophan	1.5	0.5	1	0	0.1	0.3	0	3.4
	Carbofuran	2	0	0.5	0	0	1	0	3.5
	Dimetheoate	2	0	0	0	0.2	0	0.1	2.3
	Malathion	0.5	0	5	0	0	0	0	5.5
Fungicides	Mancozeb	10	0	0.2	0	0.2	0	0	10.4
	Sulphur 80WG	1	0.5	0.2	0	0	0	0	1.7
	Sulphur 80WP	2	2	0.5	0	0	0	0	4.5
	Carbendazim 50WP	1.5	0	0	0	0.05	0	0	1.55
	Metalaxyl+Mancozeb	2	0	0	0	0.01	0	0	2.01
	Copper Oxychloride	0.2	0	0.5	0	0	0	0	0.7
	Hexaconazol	0.05	0	0.2	0	0	0	0	0.25
Herbicides	Butachlor 50EC	0	0	2.5	0	0	0	0	2.5
	Pretilachlor 50EC	0	0	0.2	0	0	0	0	0.2
	2,4-D 80 WP (Na salt)	0	0	2	2	0	0	0	4
	Isoproturon 75 WP	0	0	0	2	0	0	0	2
	Metribuzin 70 WP	2	0	0	0	0	0	0	2
	Glyphosate	1	0	0	0	0	0	0	1
	Atrazine 50 WP	0	0	0	0	0	3	0	3
PGRs	Amino acid base (amino cell gold, Suryamin, Biovita, Biozyme)	4	0	0	0	0	0	0	4
Seeds		178525	8.4	9.8	1662	123.5	161.2	NA	180490

Source: Based on inputs from agri-input dealers and agronomists in the region.

EXHIBIT CS2.12   Landholding Scenario

Landholding	Area (in Hect.)	Percentage of Total	Number of Plots
< 0.5	5,461	21.2	11,774
0.5–1.0	4,268	16.6	6,475
1.0–2.0	8,140	31.6	4,353
2.0–4.0	5,592	21.7	2,300
4.0–10.0	2,128	8.3	406
> 10.0	150	0.6	12

Source: District agriculture office

EXHIBIT CS2.13   Agricultural Input Requirement in Kannauj

Landholding of Farmer (Hectare)	Number of Farmers in the Category	Total Fertilizer Requirement (MT/Hect)	Total Insecticide Requirement (MT/Hect)	Total Fungicide Requirement (MT/Hect)	Total Herbicide Requirement (MT/Hect)	Total PGR Requirement (MT/Hect)
< 0.5	11,774	3,004	10	4	3	1
0.5–1.0	6,475	2,347	8	3	3	1
1.0–2.0	4,353	4,477	15	7	5	2
2.0–4.0	2,300	3,076	10	4	3	1
4.0–10.0	406	1,170	4	2	1	0
> 10.0	12	83	0	0	0	0

EXHIBIT CS2.14   Agricultural Services Situation (2005–06)

Warehousing facilities	Cooperative	0
	Agri-dept	0
	Private	12
	Total installed capacity (MT)	2,500
Crop protection centre		0
Crop services centre	Agro	0
	Others	3
Cold storage facilities	Number	50
	Total installed capacity (MT)	247,857
Mandi Samiti		0

Source: District Agriculture Office

EXHIBIT CS2.15   Veterinary Services Situation (2003)

Buffaloes	36,454
Cows	22,754
Sheep	40
Goats	52,006
Total cattle	111,254
Veterinary hospitals	0
Veterinary pharmacies	1
Cattle service centre	2
Artificial insemination centres	3
Cattle breeding centres	0

Source: District Agriculture Office

Locational Analysis

Vishwa: Kannauj is very well connected with nearby villages via all-season roads; 25 roads connect Kannauj with villages, each having a population of more than 1,500. There are another 45 all-season roads connecting to other small villages. Government and private buses, jeeps, and shared auto-rickshaws are easily available for commuting. Due to the effective road network, most local retailers and distributors use trucks or trolleys to transport their cargo. All trading and procurement take place through these centres. Table CS2.1 provides approximate costs to transport cargo from Kannauj to various commercial centres using truckload.

TABLE CS2.1   Approximate Transport Cargo Costs from Kannauj

Kannauj to	Truck Freight Charges (in ₹)	
	Peak Season	Lean Season
Delhi	7,000–8,000	7,000
Kanpur	2,100	1,800
Farrukhabad	2,300	2,000
Lucknow	4,500	4,100

Usually, trucks are used to transport 9–15MT of cargo, whereas trolleys may help transport loads up to 7MT. GATI and XPS, two courier and cargo companies, also have good services in the region. The power supply situation is very poor and unreliable. Local retailers rely solely on diesel generator sets. During summers, one might expect an intermittent supply of electricity for only 10 hours a day, though 484 out of 693 villages in Kannauj District are electrified.

Priyank: I surveyed the location of NAGIL's plot. Apparently, we are within a radius of 80 km from major commercial centres—Kanpur and Farrukhabad. (Exhibit CS2.16 indicates an overview with respect to other major organized retail players in the region.) There is a DSCL's HKB just 3 km away from the location on the same, on the Kannauj–Tirva road. I had a look at their assortment. They seem to be targeting the villagers though they have kept certain hi-end products as well. Apparently, a new retail construction is also coming up at a distance of 5 km on the highway towards Farrukhabad. Grapevine is that it is expected to be rented to RPG Spencer's. One disadvantage, apparent to me, with the location of the plot is that it is situated across the railway line. However, most of the recent constructions, commercial as well as residential, are being developed along the highway, which runs along the railway line in Kannauj.

AB: Good you had a look at HKB's store. I too did some background research on this particular rural retail by talking to the regional dealers and the store manager. They were the first to take a step towards organized retailing in Kannauj in 2006. Spread over three acres, HKB sells all sorts of items, ranging from agri-inputs to hardware. After facing several challenges in the past two years, the number of footfalls per day has stabilized

EXHIBIT CS2.16   Overview of NAGIL's Location with Respect to Other Major Retail Players

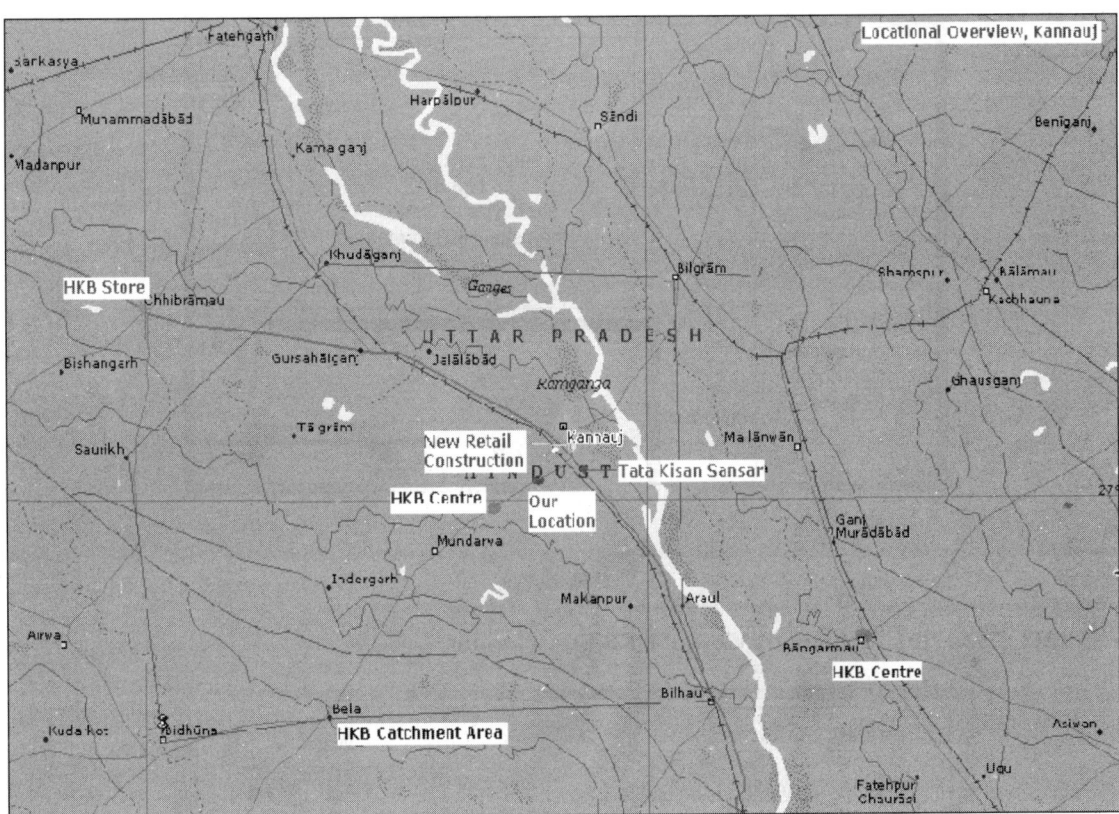

between 200 and 700. HKB operates around 25 centres and stores in western, 20 in central, and another 25 in eastern UP. Since its inception in 2006, the HKB–Kannauj centre has been able to gain considerable farmer attention through village-level campaigns. Its agronomists regularly visit farmers in its catchment area and advise them on better agricultural practices and inputs. This has helped them in developing a rapport with the local rural population. Exhibits CS2.17 (a) and (b) show the layout of the store in Kannauj.

Another important organized retail player in the area is TCL's Tata Kisaan Sansar. TCL first ventured into the rural retailing space as Tata Kisaan Kendra in 1998. These were designed to be one-stop agricultural input shops for Indian farmers. A strategic review of the business after four years led to its transformation into Tata Kisan Sansar (TKS). TKS was set up with the

objective of helping farmers to create value by improving farm productivity through better agronomic practices, availability of farm credit, and quality agricultural inputs. TKS usually operates through a franchisee which typically operates as a branded retail outlet providing agricultural inputs, farm equipments, crop advisory services, farmer credit financing, and produce buyback arrangements. A TKS operates on over 2,000–3,000 sq. ft of space and serves a catchment area of 8–10 km.

Political, Legal, and Regulatory Scenario

Priyank: I must say I am kind of surprised. Sitting over there in Delhi, and reading through national dailies' reporting of 'Reliance Shutting Shop; Putting at Bay Its ₹130 Billion Investment due to Various Kinds of Political Hindrances', I never realized there are others who have been able to do fairly well. Problems were also witnessed by Subhiksha (which has closed down) and Spencer's,

EXHIBIT CS2.17(a)   Hariyali Kisan Bazaar, Kannauj Site Layout Plan

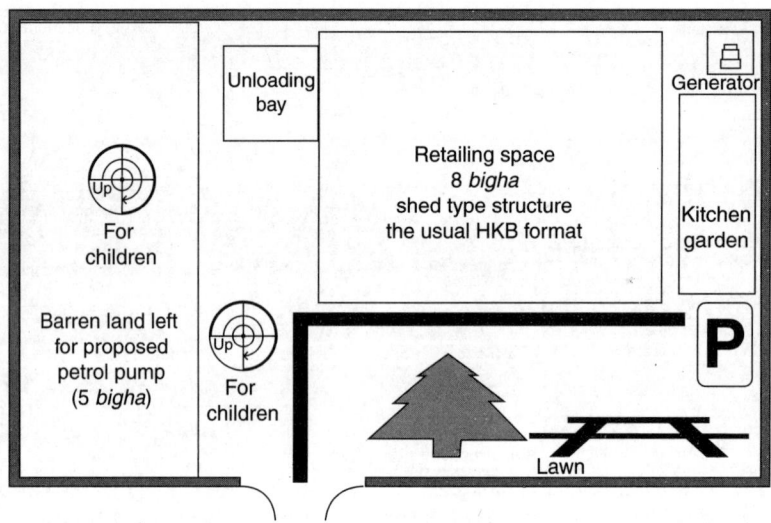

EXHIBIT CS2.17(b)   Schematic View of HKB Store Layout

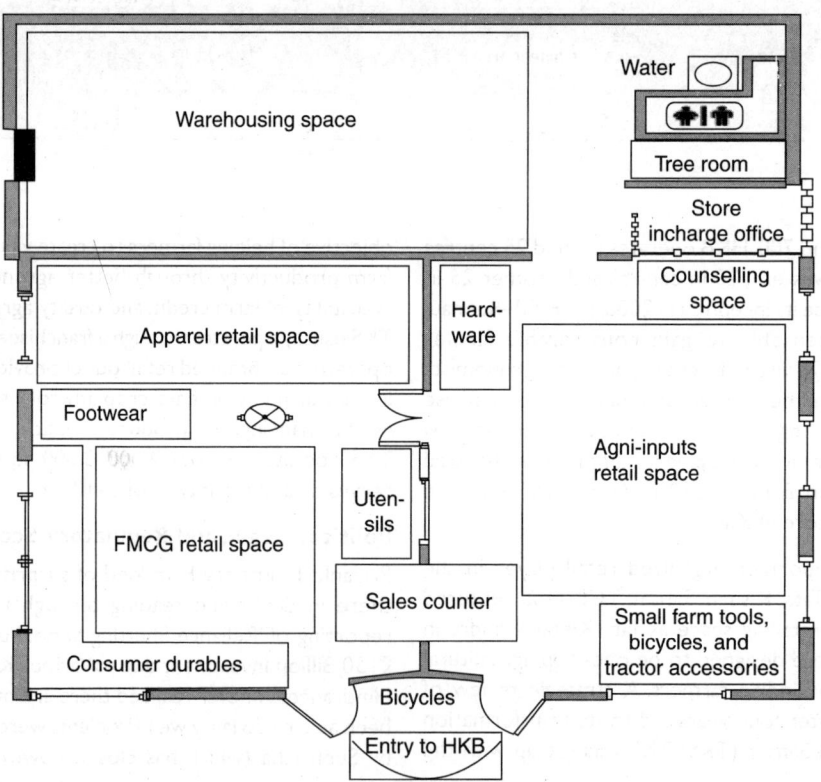

I guess. All I wonder is how are some of them able to sail smoothly while others face trouble. I always thought the UP government has not been particularly supportive of large organized retail formats because of its perceived ill-effect on small *kirana* stores. After all, which political party would play with its vote-bank by enraging the large dependent population?

Vishwa: There are two major political lobbies in UP; you emphasize on one's area, the other kills you. A retailer cannot fare well in any state without understanding the political dynamics of the state. After all, the retail and wholesale sector in UP is the second largest employer (after agriculture) in the state by providing employment to about 10% of the population.

AB: Vishwa, what did you figure out about the regulatory requirements through your discussions with district regulators?

Vishwa: Litany of licenses and enforcement of acts. Applications need to be filed to

- the district magistrate for changing the land-usage pattern from agricultural land to commercial land;
- legal metrology department with affidavit on compliance of Standard Weights and Measures Act;
- inspector—shops and establishments—with affidavit on compliance of Shops and Establishments Act;
- the municipality for operating the store 360 days a year, for extending hours of work on requirement, for storage of inflammables, for selling food items, etc.;
- the state electricity board;
- the excise and sales tax departments;
- the fire department for a no-objection certificate;
- the labour department with affidavit on compliance of Payment of Wages Act and Minimum Wages Act and I am sure there is more to it!

AB: Oh sure! That is just an indicative list. There are at least 30 licenses that I see we shall need to file. Take for example, essential commodities such as staples, food grains, and sugar. The government regulates production, supply, and distribution of these essential commodities through the Essential Commodities Act, 1955. Any retailer dealing in these products would need to obtain a license. The situation is no different for agri-inputs such as fertilizers.

Priyank: You are right, AB. However, there are certain favourable regulations in the state that NAGIL can benefit from, such as the following:

- UP was the first state to modify its Agricultural Produce Marketing Act. The Government of UP allows direct sale/purchase from the farmer's fields under the Uttar Pradesh Krishi Utpadan Mandi Adhiniyam. Cargil and ITC are procuring their produce through this mechanism. NAGIL may eventually think about developing produce buy-back arrangements with farmers.
- Besides, contract farming is being practised by reputed companies for select commodities, such as Pepsi for potato.
- The government also allows public–private partnership in financing, construction, operation, and management of agricultural markets. No fee is being levied on direct marketing of agricultural produce.

The Strategic Call

Purushottam was feeling confident with the information that AB's team had gathered. 'There seems to be potential in this place. This place is also near our headquarters and is accessible by road as well as rail. The block also seems to be a feeder town that attracts customers from all over. What about the financials?' AB provided Purushottam with a ballpark five year projection of the business and CAPEX requirements (Exhibits CS2.18 and CS2.19). He opened the envelope and started reading the report. He was into the first paragraph when his phone rang. 'I would have to leave now. It seems the meeting with the investors for this business has been advanced. In case you have some other thoughts, please mail me. I would access it on my Blackberry'.

Questions

1. Should NAGIL move into the retail sector? Please justify your answer.
2. If NAGIL goes ahead with its proposed decision of entry into organized retail, which would be the best place to start the venture?
3. Please identify the key decision areas and analyse the competitive strategies for NAGIL as an industry.

EXHIBIT CS2.18   Anticipated Financials

Capital Expenditure Requirement (₹)		Category	% of Wallet of Customer	Expected Margins
Site development costs	800,000	Apparel	6	70
Construction costs	4,500,000	Footwear	3	70
Furnishing and interiors	1,200,000	Building materials, hardware, and lubes	5	25
Electrification costs	100,000	Cosmetics	2	35
		Child products	2	60
Equipment costs		Toys and games	2	75
Generator	1,400,000	Gifts and novelties	1	75
Material handling equipment	50,000	Thermoware	1	30
Computers and peripherals	92,000	Agri-inputs	30	12
Other miscellaneous	90,000	Consumer durables	7	15
		Home furnishing	2	70
Insurance costs	1,000,000	Plastic goods	2	65
Licensing costs	600,000	Kitchen aids	1	70
Initial procurement costs	1,700,000	Glassware	1	30
Retail launch expenditure	200,000	Dress accessories	3	75
Manpower recruitment costs	50,000	FMCG	30	20
		Cleaning aids	1	70
Total	**11,782,000**	Electricals	1	75
		Average margin		**30.1**

EXHIBIT CS2.19   Proforma Income Statement

	Year 0	Year 1	Year 2	Year 3	Year 4	Year 5
	2008–09	2009–10	2010–11	2011–12	2012–13	2013–14
Total sales	0	14,000,000	15,400,000	16,940,000	18,634,000	20,497,400
Cost of sales						
Material costs	1,700,000	9,793,000	10,772,300	11,849,530	13,034,483	14,337,931
Other direct	10,500	778,000	855,800	941,380	1,035,518	1,139,070
Total cost of sales	1,710,500	10,571,000	11,628,100	12,790,910	14,070,001	15,477,001
Gross margin	(1,710,500)	3,429,000	3,771,900	4,149,090	4,563,999	5,020,399
(As a % of sales)		24	24	24	24	24

(Contd)

	Year 0	Year 1	Year 2	Year 3	Year 4	Year 5
Overhead expenses						
Selling	0	140,000	154,000	169,400	186,340	204,974
Personnel	50,000	1,590,000	1,749,000	1,706,100	1,876,710	2,064,381
General	0	68,500	75,350	82,885	91,174	100,291
Depreciation	0	718,900	718,900	718,900	718,900	718,900
Advertising costs	20,000	20,000	20,000	20,000	20,000	20,000
Insurance related costs	0	996,058	1,095,664	1,205,231	1,325,754	1,458,329
Total operating expenses	70,000	3,533,458	3,812,914	3,902,516	4,218,877	4,566,875
Net income before taxes	(1,780,500)	(104,458)	(41,014)	246,574	345,122	453,524

* *Source:* The team also indicated that the typical estimates for other established players were as follows:
  • Gross margin (% of revenue) = 10–16%
  • Fixed costs (% of revenue) = ~15%
  • Variable costs (% of revenue) = ~5%

3 Retailing in Other Countries

LEARNING OBJECTIVES

After studying this chapter, you will be able to
- develop an awareness of the happenings in the world of retailing
- take a look at the differences in retailing in various countries
- look at the prevalent and emerging formats in countries other than India
- draw out the key success factors in retailing in various countries

INTRODUCTION

Retailing is a huge and varied part of the economy. Everything from an arcade to a newspaper kiosk at the railway station retails its products. The US Department of Commerce defines retail trade as ... *selling merchandise for household consumption. In general, the stores in this sector operate at fixed places of business and take part in activities to attract the general public to make purchases.* More succinctly put, retailing links the producer of goods to the consumer.

RETAILING—THE GLOBAL SCENARIO

India is the last large Asian economy to liberalize its retail sector. In Thailand, more than 40 per cent of all consumer goods are sold through supermarkets, convenience stores, and department stores. A similar phenomenon has swept through Malaysia, Taiwan, and Indonesia. Even in China, more than a tenth of all consumer goods are sold through modern retail formats—a proportion that is growing rapidly, as shown in Fig. 3.1.

Walmart dominates the world retail market, with revenues and profits two and a half times those of its nearest rival. However, like most American firms, it operates in fewer countries and is less international in its scope than its European counterparts. Metro has a presence in 16 countries. Other well-known global retailers are Tesco, Carrefour, IKEA, Japan's *Daiei*—a drug and speciality store, Otto Versand—the German mail order giant, and Marks & Spencer—a private label retailer in the UK. North America, Western Europe, and the Asia-Pacific region account for about 85 per cent of the global retail sales. Food retailers account for about 40 per cent of retail sales. The fastest growing retailer types are health and beauty (30%), home furnishing and fixtures (19%), and mixed (19%). Latin America witnessed a de-growth in retail sales in 2006. Eastern Europe and Australasia are the regions that have the fastest growing retail markets. Ten countries, mainly from Eastern

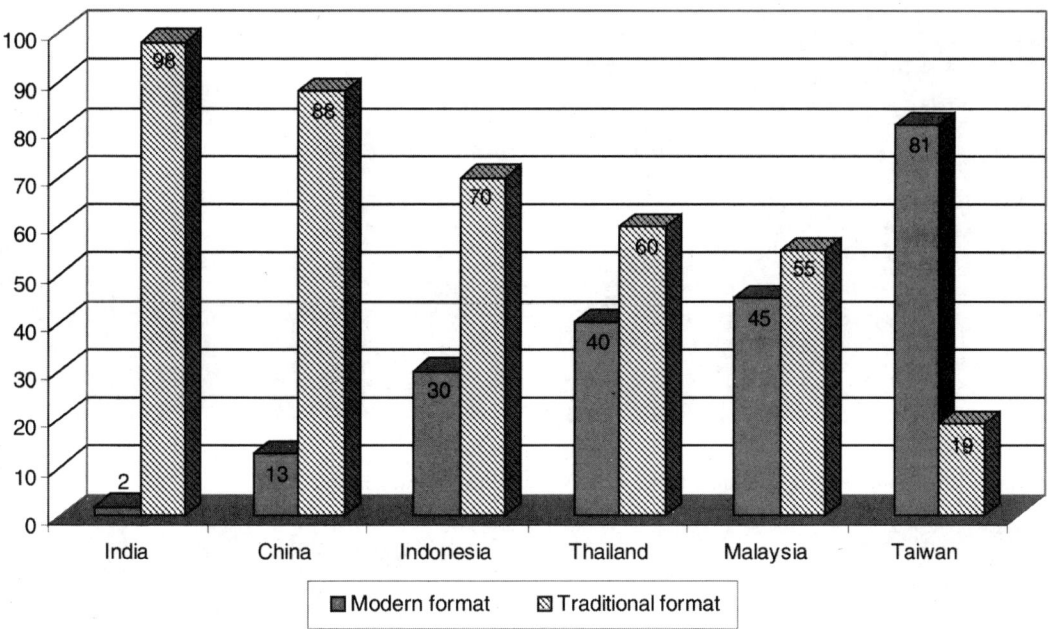

FIG. 3.1   Share of Different Formats

Source: Bell and Leamon 1998.

Europe and Asia, grew at a rate faster than 40 per cent in 2004 over that of 2005. Major global trends in retailing are given in Annexure 3.1.[1]

Let us now take a look at the retailing scenario in some specific regions of the US, Asia, and Europe.

RETAILING IN THE US

The US has the largest retail market in the world. Its retail climate is fairly open, with large plots of land available for development in most areas and relatively lenient zoning laws. Government regulations of opening hours are minimal since the demise of the 'Blue Laws' that prohibited sales on Sundays.

Retail sales in the US totalled $2,622 billion in 2006. Non-grocery retailers contributed about 70 per cent of the retail sales. About 2 million retail establishments in the country employ over 20 million people or 18 per cent of the country's workforce. While Walmart and other megafirms are also talked about, the vast majority of firms (88%) have fewer than 20 workers, and more than 75 per cent of retail establishments are single outlet, independent stores. Table 3.1 shows the sector-wise sales in the US in the period 2004–09.

Key Factors Affecting Retailing

We shall now take a look at the key factors of the retailing market in the US.

1. Time stresses have made shopping a chore rather than a source of recreation. Trips to malls are down more than 50 per cent since the early 1990s and shoppers visit fewer stores at a mall.[2]

Walmart

Source: http://shipboard.net/images/Walmart.JPG

Tesco

Source: www.igd.com

Carrefour—China

Source: http://www.carrefour.co.th

Marks & Spencer

Source: http://tre.ngfl.gov.uk

Global Retailers

TABLE 3.1   Sector-wise Sales in Retailing in the US (2004–09)—Value ($ billion)

	2004	2005	2006	2007	2008	2009
Grocery retailers	748.90	802.80	842.20	873.50	901.70	925.30
Non-grocery retailers	1,364.20	1,437.00	1,518.10	1,533.20	1,523.60	1,450.50
Store-based retailing	**2,113.10**	**2,239.80**	**2,360.30**	**2,406.70**	**2,425.30**	**2,375.80**
Vending	13.90	14.10	14.40	14.40	14.30	14.30
Homeshopping	105.30	109.40	109.80	113.30	112.40	109.90
Internet retailing	49.10	61.80	79.00	91.10	94.60	90.70
Direct selling	26.40	26.70	27.00	26.40	26.00	24.30
Non-store retailing	**194.70**	**212.10**	**230.30**	**245.10**	**247.30**	**239.10**
Total retailing	**2,307.80**	**2,451.90**	**2,590.60**	**2,651.80**	**2,672.60**	**2,614.90**

Source: www.euromonitor.com, accessed on 1 October 2010.

2. Priorities have shifted. Boomers are saving for their own retirements and their children's education. Rather than buying holiday gifts, they are going for experiences (family vacation, lessons).

3. Consumers have become more price-conscious. A Kurt Salmon survey in 1996 revealed that 84 per cent of the respondents felt that department store prices were too high. In reaction, 25 per cent said that they shopped at discounters and 70 per cent bought clothes on sale. The 1980s had seen frenetic markdown activity that has trained consumers to wait until the last minute. Swimsuits, historically full price until the fourth of July, were marked down as early as Memorial Day.

4. Value is a more complex concept than it was. Once a function of price and quality, it now includes convenience and entertainment. Thus, some warehouse stores are beginning to find that their low prices are outweighed by the inconvenience of the entire shopping experience.

5. Precision shopping has become more prevalent, reducing impulse purchases as well as random store visits. Consumers target what they need, find it, and leave to spend their time on leisure or entertainment, rather than sauntering through the store. The increasing popularity of Internet shopping allows for precision purchases as well as random information gathering.

Retail sales across all sectors slowed down in 2002. Consumers in the US began to respond to the macroeconomic factors such as unemployment, declining stock market, high personal credit card debt, and little or no growth in the overall US economy. Same store sales have been flat across all segments or have declined, with even industry leader Walmart posting a same store sales increase of only 4 per cent for the first half of 2002. The growth after that has been at a rate of about 5 per cent.

RETAILING IN ASIA

In the last 15 years, Asia has been witnessing the entry of American and European multinational retailers into its emerging markets. Global players, such as Carrefour, Royal Ahold, Tesco, and Walmart, have entered into China, Japan, Thailand, Indonesia, South Korea, Taiwan, and Malaysia.

Drivers of Growth

The key reasons for the entry of American and European multinational retailers into the emerging Asian markets are as follows.

Asian Currency Crisis   The year 1997 witnessed the Asian currency crisis. Many of the global players seized the opportunity and took over some Asian retail chains, since the crisis had weakened the local retail groups. Many Indonesian and Thai retailers became victims of takeovers by these big players. Even in Japan, Walmart acquired a 6 per cent stake in Seiyu, a department store, with an option to take majority stake in future.

Liberalization   The entry has also been triggered by the liberalization of the retail industry in some Asian countries. Japan, traditionally closed to foreign retailers, opened its borders in the light of falling property prices and the easing of local government restrictions. In China, Carrefour, Walmart, Auchan, and many other big players established themselves in big cities such as Shanghai, Beijing, and Guangzhou.

New Retail Formats   In Malaysia and even Singapore, these global retailers also made their presence felt by enticing consumers with new retail formats and offering mass merchandising, which came with economies of scale.

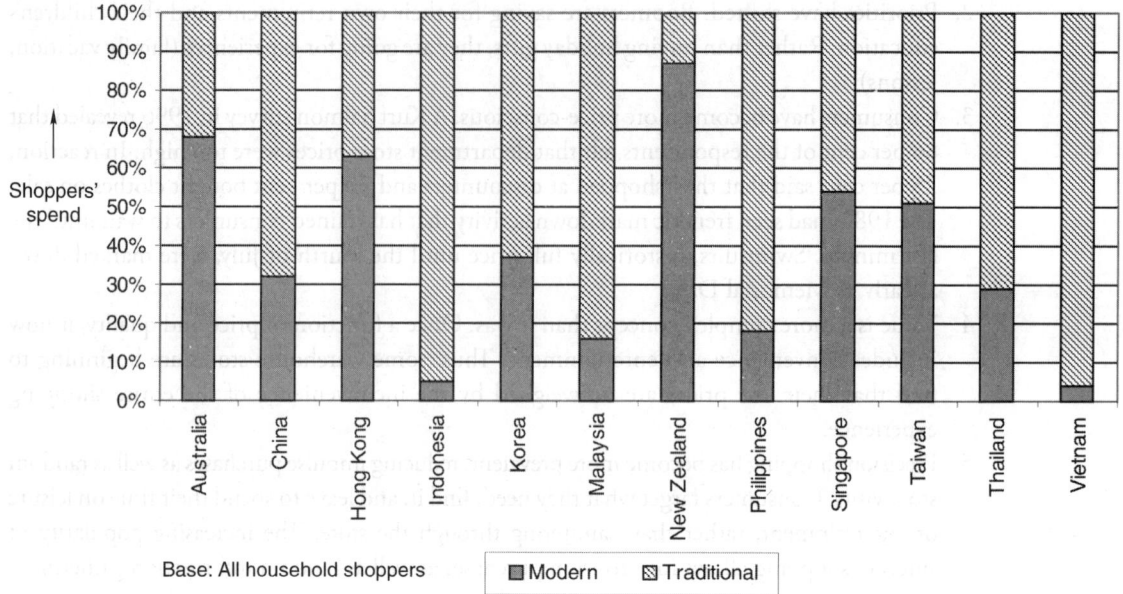

Shoppers' spend

Base: All household shoppers   ▣ Modern   ⊠ Traditional

FIG. 3.2   Split of Shopping Occasions at Modern and Traditional Outlets

Globalization   In 2005, the world's top 30 grocery retailers' consolidated sales exceeded US$2 trillion, equivalent to about 10 per cent of the global retail market. Walmart alone accounted for 2 per cent of the entire market and 17 per cent of its annual sales came from outside the US. More than 40 per cent of Carrefour's sales came from its overseas operations.

Retail sales were expected to grow in most countries in the Asia-Pacific region. Indonesia took the lead with an anticipated 16.9 per cent year-on-year growth for the first half of 2005. Faster growth was also expected from China (12.75%) and Thailand (12.3%), followed by Malaysia (8.9%), Hong Kong (8.7%), and the Philippines (8.5%).[3]

Modern grocery trade continues to expand in most Asian countries. More and more urban shoppers started going to hypermarkets and supermarkets for their grocery shopping, according to a study on shopper trends conducted by AC Nielsen across the Asia-Pacific region in 2004. Australia and New Zealand ranked highest with over 95 per cent of shoppers spending most in modern grocery outlets. Over 80 per cent of Chinese shoppers in the seven leading cities surveyed also claimed that at least half of their overall spend is now either in supermarkets or hypermarkets. As can be seen in Fig. 3.2, a number of other developing markets saw the number of shopping occasions at modern trade outlets increasing, including Thailand, Malaysia, and Indonesia.

Sector-wise Growth

In 2008, Asian grocery markets showed tremendous volume growth, led by India (+9%), China (+9%), and Vietnam (+18%), with only Taiwan (–7%) experiencing a decline in sales. The sales increased by double figures in many of these markets on the back of high inflation for key food categories. China continued to show growth throughout 2008. In account to modern retailing, there is around 53 per cent of packaged grocery sales in Asia. Over the last 12 years, more than 1,500 new stores were opened in Indonesia, taking the total to over 10,500, which shows a tremendous rise in grocery spend. The reason for this rise is that the shoppers in Indonesia prefer convenient location, relatively good service, and acceptably low prices offered at mini-markets. There have been more than 70 per cent of shoppers who claim to have become more price sensitive compared to 2008 in Asia. In Korea, the traditional store numbers dropped by 9 per cent, whereas the share of trade decreased from 15.9 to 13.9 per cent. (Nielsen's Asia Pacific Retail and Shopper Trends, 2009).

Department stores were the first form of modern retailing in Asia, and, despite all the competitive challenges of late, will remain an important part of the retail landscape. Although this format is not likely to experience strong growth in the future, it can be lucrative. There are indeed several operators in the region that have successfully re-focused their efforts and become highly profitable. Among them are Robinsons in Singapore and Thailand, Shoemart in the Philippines, and Metrojaya in Malaysia.[4]

One reason that department stores in Asia have been able to withstand the onslaught of hypermarkets is that many of the hypermarkets in the region are either fully or partially owned by the same parent companies that own the department stores. Hence, the profitability of the parent companies has not been damaged by competing formats.[5] Moreover, parent companies can afford to invest in the revitalization of department stores. In addition, many parent companies own and operate major shopping centres anchoring their department stores. Such companies often own many of the speciality concepts populating these malls, again competing with the department stores. Often, the speciality concepts are offshoots of the private labels of popular department stores. For example, both Metrojaya and Shoemart have developed strong mall-based speciality concepts that were born in their department stores. In the 1980s, many of Japan's leading department-store companies opened stores in south-east Asia and offered a similar shopping experience as other stores—with the same brands, price points, and store layouts. Although many of these Japanese operators have since exited the market, in part due to financial problems in their home market, the locals that remain cannot survive by offering the same experience.

Successful operators have altered their mix of merchandise, have become more focused on merchandising rather than cash management, and have placed greater emphasis on the development of private or exclusive brands. Metrojaya is a good example as it has a strong selection of private labels that draw customers into its stores. In addition, they have become focused on a core consumer target and attempt to develop a merchandise mix suitable for a particular lifestyle. For example, Robinsons in Bangkok has carved a niche for itself as a 'mass' department store aimed at the budget-conscious fashionable young adult.

The department stores in south-east Asia started undergoing a change in the new millenium, similar to what North America experienced in the eighties and nineties. Challenged by rapidly-growing value-seeking customers, the industry started witnessing consolidation, better merchandising, differentiation through private and exclusive brands, and clearer targeting of particular consumer groups defined by income and lifestyle. Although the industry was not expected to grow rapidly in the future, a handful of leading players in each country would survive and prosper. Some of these companies will leverage their private brands to invest in new speciality concepts. Others may use their financial strength and merchandising expertise to invest in new geographic locations such as China.[6]

Let us now take a look at the retailing scenario in some key Asian countries.

Philippines

The retail trade is witnessing a drastic change in the Philippines. The grocery retailing performance was better compared to non-grocery retailing in 2010. It was driven by the fact that non-grocery products were affected by the slowdown in 2010. The consumer spending had increased considerably, which led to a growth in retailing. It led to growth in all sections, particularly clothing and footwear, consumer electronics and home appliances, and beauty specialist retailers. The 2010 election had a positive effect on the retailers and consumers. After reporting GDP growth of 0.9 per cent in 2010, the Philippine economy recovered in 2010. The World Bank forecasts GDP growth of 4.4 per cent after the country reported 7.3 per cent first quarter growth during the year. However, growth is projected to slow down as the economic recovery of the US falters and the European debt crisis continues. The Philippines GDP is projected to expand by a CAGR of 4 per cent annually during the period of 2011–2015. According to a research, the Philippines saw a considerable improvement in Internet penetration from 27 per cent in 2009 to 30 per cent in 2010. The backbone of Philippine retailing is the huge network of small mom-and-pop stores known as *sari-sari* stores. These stores make up 90 per cent of the retail outlets and offer various advantages in terms of lower-income consumers' easy accessibility and credit terms. There are around 600 convenience stores in the Philippines. The retailers in the Philippines find the market increasingly competitive, with a lot of foreign retailers entering the market.[7]

Indonesia

After the first two years of the Asian crisis in 1997, the retail industry in Indonesia improved. Several reasons have been advanced for the country's improved economic health. Among them are the buying power in spite of increases in price, stability of the Rupiah in mid-1999 (which has since slipped following the political impasse), and the Indonesian wariness of banks that lost their credibility during the crisis. Modern retailers have benefited from the increase in spending at the cost of traditional trade. Prompted by the strong demand, retailers are investing in new facilities, especially in fast-moving consumer goods (FMCGs). Retailers have introduced marketing and promotional programmes to take advantage of the opportunity.

With the entry of foreign retailers, such as Tesco, Casino, and Giant, into the Indonesian market, the local retailers were expected to lose market share if they did not upgrade their operations, and hence they continued to invest in IT solutions despite the depressed economic situation post 1997. It is believed that retailers can reduce their inventory costs by up to 30 per cent and purchasing costs by 15 per cent if they invest in proven IT solutions.[8] The ability of some of the retailers of Indonesia to expand may, however, be constrained by the lack of space. The Indonesian government had raised fuel prices (by 3%–23%), electricity tariffs (6%), and telecommunications (15%) in 2003.[9] The increase in fuel prices, taxes, and other levies by the government was expected to affect retail sales.

Retailing in 2005 continued to grow stronger in spite of retailers' anticipation of a slowdown. Value growth strengthened to surpass 11 per cent, up slightly from 2004. The continuously accelerating growth of retailing up to 2005 can be attributed to a small extent to the expansion in the number of retailers. While modern retailers expanded at a rapid pace, the majority of retail outlets in Indonesia remained the traditional and independent ones, which grew at a steady pace in a rather low growth rate of outlets in 2005. In fact, double-digit percentage current value growth of the industry has been, to a large extent, due to the increasing revenue of retailers. Price increases of products sold in retail outlets remained common in 2005 as the rate of inflation remained high, while volume growth did not slow down too significantly. Aside from the price increases common to most retail outlets, 2005 also saw the continued expansion of big modern retail chains in a number of outlets, although the impact on the performance of the overall industry was still small.[10]

Malaysia

The Q410 BMI Malaysia Retail Report forecasts that the total retail sales will grow from MYR 153.76 billion (US$43.65 billion) in 2010 to MYR 251.63 billion (US$71.44 billion) by 2014.[11]

Specifically, total retail sales are predicted to increase at a compound annual growth rate (CAGR) of 6.5 per cent to 7.4 per cent.[12] The government is boosting consumer confidence by implementing economic stimulus programmes and lifting an unofficial freeze on the number of annual sale events. The Malaysian government had launched a five-year plan in 2001 to gear up the retail industry for the global challenges of the new millennium. The overall thrust of this policy was to increase efficiency and productivity to achieve sustainable growth and enhance consumer welfare and quality of life. This was to be achieved by strategies to boost competitiveness, providing an enabling institutional and regulatory environment, forging stronger links, and expanding e-commerce.

Consumer protection and maintenance of price stability was also to be emphasized. The retail sector was meant to assume a more prominent role in the growth of the economy and was expected to grow at an average annual rate of 7.8 per cent for the duration of the plan. In turn, retailers would have better inventory control and faster service at checkout counters. The move would also ensure effective monitoring of the prices of essential goods and see that they do not go above the ceiling. The plan had set aside a large budget for the implementation of the franchise development programme. This allocation would focus on activities such as promotions and marketing, training, financing, product development, and improvement of databases. Malaysian franchises would also be urged to export their products and services in view of the wider opportunities in global trade. On the e-commerce front, Internet start-up retailers without a physical-store presence would be encouraged as they can save costs in terms of office rentals and wages.[13]

According to the Malaysian Institute of Economic Research, the GDP in Malaysia was estimated to increase by 7 per cent year-on-year in 2010. The value sales in retailing are thus expected to increase in tandem with this growth in GDP. The gradual recovery of the economy in 2010 spurred consumers to start spending again in various retail channels. The government continues to support retailing in Malaysia. In the year 2010, the government focused on protecting and giving the best value to consumers. In August 2010, The Ministry of Domestic Trade, Co-operatives and Consumerism got the Cabinet to approve a set of new favourable rules that govern foreign hypermarkets. The government aims to create a more ideal environment for retailing in Malaysia. The grocery retailers are leading the advance of private label growth in Malaysia. The government is putting more effort into attracting foreign direct investment, after the United Nations released the World Foreign Investment Report (WIR) 2010, which showed that FDI in Malaysia plunged by 81 per cent in 2009. Hence, the government is very supportive of foreign retailers entering Malaysia.[14]

China

China's huge market-growth potential is undeniable and the opportunities are equal for all retail sectors, be it apparel, cosmetics and toiletries, department stores, fast food, or supermarkets.[15] For the retail industry, WTO membership will mean the breakdown of barriers and the opening of more investment channels. Retailers have been allowed to operate as wholly-owned companies. Shanghai, the largest and most cosmopolitan city in China, got its first Walmart store in 2005. Carrefour already has six supermarkets in Shanghai and is introducing its Champion brand of supermarket. Metro of Germany, which sees Shanghai as its China hub, currently operates 50 megastores in the country. Shanghai has an estimated 300 registered retail groups, including some of the world's leading retailers such as Carrefour of France, Aeon Group's Jusco of Japan, Taiwan's Pacific Stores, and Hong Kong's China Resources Enterprise and Kerry Group. According to industry statistics, some 70 per cent of the world's top 50 retailers are already in the Chinese market and have supplied US$30 billion worth of Chinese-made products, or 11.3 per cent of the country's entire exports.[16]

Taiwan

Historically, many small operators have characterized the Taiwanese retail market. As Taiwan became a high consumption country, its retail network evolved rapidly. The 1980s saw explosive growth in the retail industry. New outlet types slowly continued to replace traditional *bazaar* style family stores. The underlying trend was towards larger sales areas, driven mostly by the development of department stores, and more recently, supermarket and hypermarket chains. Taiwan's total retail sales in 2001 amounted to NT$1,394 billion, an increase of 30.6 per cent from 1996. The number of retail outlets in Taiwan totalled 116,403 in 2001, an increase of 33 per cent from 1996.[17] Due to the bad economic situation since 1998 and the earthquake in 1999, the annual growth rate of a number of retail outlets declined from 13 per cent in 1997 to linger between 4–5 per cent from 1998 to 2000.

In 2001, the annual growth was even lower at 3 per cent. This was primarily due to the change in consumer shopping patterns, moving from the neighbourhood stores to the one-stop shopping destinations offered by large stores. Food outlets, whose number stood at 30,538 in 2001, comprised nearly one-third of the total retail outlets. The proportion decreased steadily during the 6-year review period of 1996–2002. This was due to the closure and the less-than-average increase of food specialists and wet markets. The number of non-food outlets, on the other hand, increased rapidly over the review period, as consumers preferred well-branded specialized chain stores. Despite the unstable economic climate over the six-year period, the average annual growth was maintained at a healthy rate in both forms of retailing. However, the structure within each form changed significantly. Independent grocers lost 8.4 per cent share of total food sales while 6.2 per cent share of importance held by other non-food specialists was transferred within the same period.

The food and grocery sector accounted for 64.2 per cent of the total retail value in Taiwan in the year 2009. This sector rose at a compound annual growth rate (CAGR) of 3.9 per cent between 2004 and 2009. The economic upturn which took effect in Taiwan from the second half of 2009 continued unabated in 2010. The GDP growth in 2009 was measured at −1.9 per cent; by the end of 2010 it had reached 6.1 per cent. In 2009, the unemployment rate in Taiwan was 5.9 per cent, which fell to 5.5 per cent between January and June 2010. However, this was still much higher than 4.1 per cent recorded earlier in 2008. Internet retailing penetration has enhanced as the popularity of this form of retailing increased. Since February 2010, 73 per cent of population aged over 12 had experience of using the Internet, which was two percentage points higher than in February 2009. Sixty-seven per cent of the Taiwanese population currently has broadband access, according to government statistics. Additionally, 57 per cent of Taiwanese Internet users have engaged in Internet retailing. Consumers aged between 20 and 44 are the most frequent users of Internet retailing. The sales in the non-grocery and non-store retailing by category could be seen in Table 3.2(a) and (b).

Greater Consumer Spending   Higher consumer spending on non-food items, higher disposable incomes, and improved living standards will support moderate growth in the retail industry. The total retail sales in Taiwan was projected to reach NT$2,500 billion by 2008—an increase of more than 40 per cent from 2001. Like other Asian countries, against a backdrop of increasing disposable incomes, it is expected that consumers will allocate a larger portion of their income to non-food items. The Taiwanese are seeking to improve living standards and are thus spending more on health-care products or on furnishings to decorate and beautify their homes. In response to the changing lifestyles, many foreign retailers have entered the Taiwanese market during the review period.

Changes in Shopping Habits   The changes in the shopping habits of consumers moving from neighbourhood stores to one-stop shopping destinations offered by large stores can be seen as another

TABLE 3.2 (a) Sales in Non-grocery Retailing by Category: Value 2005–10

NT$ billion	2005	2006	2007	2008	2009	2010
Clothing and footwear specialist retailers	142.7	145.4	146.9	141.2	142.6	144.3
Electronics and appliance specialist retailers	194.1	185.4	186.5	182.2	176.7	182.4
Health and beauty specialist retailers	147.0	155.5	159.2	160.6	160.9	162.8
Home and garden specialist retailers	206.2	223.9	231.5	224.5	223.4	226.5
Leisure and personal goods specialist retailers	272.6	274.1	276.5	271.8	262.4	259.8
Mixed retailers	229.8	229.3	248.2	257.5	259.2	264.6
Other non-grocery retailers	82.0	82.5	83.0	83.4	82.2	83.8
Non-grocery retailers	1,274.3	1,296.1	1,331.8	1,321.2	1,307.4	1,324.2

(b) Sales in Non-store Retailing by Category: Value 2005–10

NT$ billion	2005	2006	2007	2008	2009	2010
Direct selling	56.2	47.4	45.2	43.5	42.0	40.7
Homeshopping	61.1	57.1	53.7	51.6	57.0	59.8
Internet retailing	35.3	38.9	54.7	62.9	70.5	76.1
Vending	3.7	3.6	3.5	3.4	3.4	3.4
Non-store retailing	156.3	147.0	157.1	161.4	172.8	180.0

Source: www.euromonitor.com, accessed on 4 October 2011.

key driver of retailing in Taiwan. Trends such as shopping in megastores and purchasing at one-stop shopping centres continued in the period 1996–2001. The education level improved upward mobility and created demand for better living standards. Megastores, in a bid to attract more customers, expanded their product offerings and offered competitive prices at the same time. All these factors will add to a very strong spirit of competition, which, in turn, will depress margins and profits for many retailers. They are being influenced by the rapid development of malls in the urban areas and changes in lifestyle. Shopping is no longer just a merchandise-driven activity. It is becoming an exercise that includes entertainment and education.

Diminishing Traditional Families and Growth of Working Women[18] By the year 1998, the traditional extended family had gradually been replaced by the nuclear family, with average family membership dropping to 4.14. The number of working women advanced by 5.8 per cent in the period 1996–2001. Most, especially urban families, became double income households. Homemakers had less time to manage household work; they sought more convenient stores and patronized new retailer types for cleanliness and convenience even when prices were higher.

High Percentage of Appliance Owners, but Low Percentage of Car Owners Most families had full home appliance sets. In 1988, 98 per cent owned refrigerators; in contrast, only 20 per cent owned cars. This low ratio made it preferable to shop at convenience stores rather than supermarkets.

Infrastructure Improvement During the 1980s, traffic and communication infrastructure improved throughout the island. As a result, new retailer types had much lower costs. Furthermore, package standardization and classification of major commodities were conducive to greater retailer efficiency.

Decrease in Relative Cost of Facilities Costs of vehicles and electrical/mechanical facilities reduced because of declining tariffs and industrialization in Taiwan. Research indicates that facility costs for more convenient retailers decreased significantly, strengthening their competitive advantage.

Recovery in Regional Economy   During the Asian financial crisis of 1997, consumer confidence was affected by the slow global economy and the tense domestic political environment. The recovery in the regional economy has encouraged retailers, especially convenience stores, to open new outlets. This is in line with the changing lifestyle needs of the Taiwanese population, which is moving towards convenience shopping. Most of these outlets are situated in close proximity to residential estates.

Japan[19]

Japan has been witnessing a slower growth in retail sales (Table 3.3). According to a preliminary report covering 102 supermarket operators comprising 8,839 outlets in Japan, clothing sales, which constitute 14.2 per cent of total supermarket sales, had dropped by 2.6 per cent to ¥167.80 billion despite increased sales in summer clothing. Although tobacco, insecticide sprays, and diet and health foods are selling well, decreased sales are reflected in other household products such as daily commodities, medical products, cosmetics, furniture, and electrical appliances—which represent 21.4 per cent of total sales—had dropped by 4.8 per cent to ¥253.44 billion. Similarly, for department stores in Japan, sales on a same-store basis have shown a downward trend. Sales data from 290 outlets operated by 99 department store operators in Japan revealed that almost all product categories have experienced a decline in sales, with 2.5 per cent for home appliances, furnitures, and other household items; 2 per cent for clothing for the fourth consecutive month; and 1.2 per cent for food sales for the third consecutive month.

Both small- and large-scale retailers are responding to the changes in consumer needs for quality and convenience. Small-scale retailers are forming independent retail street associations for governing local retail operations and fashion buildings have emerged as a newer form of speciality shopping centre with multiple small-scale retailers. The centres may be independently operated by an association, but some large-scale retailers have developed chains of such facilities which are tightly organized and marketed. The retail street associations provide the basis for the strong political voice, which speaks for the small-scale retailers. Corporate chain systems composed of shops of relatively small sizes are also being established. Most significant is the remarkable growth of convenience stores, a format patterned loosely upon American retailers by the same name, but significantly upgraded in merchandising sophistication. These stores represent a retail technology that can be implemented in the retail sector while simultaneously providing the shopping convenience that consumers demand.

Along with this development, Japan is also witnessing the appearance of corporate chains of smaller shops for speciality goods, particularly within the electrical and clothing sectors. Importantly, some of these appear in a discount format, providing lower prices and options for new suppliers.

TABLE 3.3   Sector-wise Sales in Retailing in Japan (2004–09): Value (¥ billion)

	2004	2005	2006	2007	2008	2009
Grocery retailers	35,626.30	34,886.10	34,549.20	33,948.60	33,562.50	32,582.70
Non-grocery retailers	66,669.60	66,246.60	65,283.20	65,282.10	63,348.00	59,750.10
Store-based retailing	**102,295.90**	**101,132.70**	**99,832.40**	**99,230.70**	**96,910.50**	**92,332.80**
Vending	3,681.80	3,726.50	3,758.80	3,675.80	2,694.40	2,700.50
Homeshopping	2,302.60	2,412.00	2,525.40	2,622.30	2,703.20	2,757.80
Internet retailing	1,533.00	1,786.20	2,090.80	2,393.80	2,680.00	2,959.60
Direct selling	2,204.40	2,171.80	2,111.10	2,023.30	1,942.70	1,853.30
Non-store retailing	**9,721.70**	**10,096.50**	**10,486.10**	**10,715.30**	**10,020.40**	**10,271.20**
Total retailing	**112,017.60**	**111,229.20**	**110,318.50**	**109,946.00**	**106,930.90**	**102,604.00**

Source: www.euromonitor.com, accessed on 1 October 2010.

Traditional department stores have survived because they have built a strong reputation of quality and service, which are of major importance to the Japanese consumer. They also earn good margins. During the 1980s, these stores benefited from the increased interest of Japanese consumers in brand names, service, and the status the store name provided. With the leaner times in the 1990s and with many consumers expressing a new concern for value, the department stores suffered. General merchandise store retailers are at the centre of an evolution towards conglomerate merchandising. These stores offer conveniences outside the central cities and a moderate line of merchandise with their own private labels. These systems have now exceeded the sales volume generated by the traditional department store by building large multi-store facilities on the expanding fringes of the major cities and invading the central business districts of smaller metropolitan areas. However, these stores have evolved with high cost structures. While more venturesome in importing goods and providing consumers with better discounts than traditional department stores, their impact upon price has been muted.

The strength of the general merchandisers (GM) system is derived from an expansion into other forms of retailing, such as convenience stores, supermarkets, restaurants, and speciality chains and shopping centres. The leading firms in this group have extended their position in Japan through new stores and mergers with independent operators. This would have manifestations for increasing retail competition and technological innovation, especially with the relaxation of the Large Store Law. The Law, which emerged in 1937, limits the ability of retailers to open large stores by subjecting their plans to the scrutiny and required agreement of small local retail competitors. The law has served to perpetuate the power of small-scale retailer and manufacturer. Ironically, it also served existing large retailers well since it has limited the growth of comparable competitors. Since 1990, changes in the law, made largely as a consequence of continuing pressure by the US and other nations, have diminished its strength by requiring the review process of new applications to be reduced from what was often an indefinite period to a single year. Less room is also allowed for local jurisdiction to add their own unique requirements to the new large store.

The Japanese are avid consumers of expensive retail services. They expect retailers to provide retail services in the form of convenience, quality, and prestige. The crowded road system, lengthy commutes, and a lower diffusion of automobile ownership have generated a strong need for convenience in retailing. Also, the Japanese consumer has a penchant for freshness in food, further preferring convenience. Gift giving in Japanese society accounts for as much as 7 per cent of total retail sales. The Japanese associate status and value to gift giving. Therefore, the quality of the gift and its presentation matters a lot. Most gifts have a strong obligatory element reflecting appreciation of 'favours done or anticipated' by social superiors or business benefactors. In this scenario, prestigious department stores have created a strong position by defining quality, status, and value to their customers and providing critical services such as gift-wrapping, delivery, and advice. These services are of importance to corporate as well as personal gift givers, and have preserved the position of department stores in Japan at a level significantly greater than in other developed societies.

Women make most of the decisions regarding shopping and home budgets in Japanese homes. This is because long hours of work and the need for business socializing leave Japanese men with little time for the chore of shopping. Japanese women typically leave their jobs after marriage to manage their home. After their children reach school age, they re-enter the labour force to supplement the family income, generally at relatively low-level jobs.

EUROPEAN RETAILING[20]

The top three food retailers in terms of revenue, as listed by the Fortune list, are European: Carrefour of France, Walmart of the US, and Ahold of Netherlands. Of the world's major food retailers, the Asda group of the UK holds the first position for profit in proportion to revenue. Retailing power is on the increase. However, there is an interesting divergence of experience. In the UK, where retailing is most concentrated, the buyer group share is equal to the retailer share. Retailers are the largest purchasers of groceries from producers. In contrast to this, in other countries, the buyer share is significantly more concentrated than the retailer share, reflecting the considerable importance to the industry of buying groups such as Germany's Markant Handels—the country's largest food buyer; Spain's large purchasing groups Euromadi and IFA Espanola—the top two retailers; and France's Intermache—the largest in the country in terms of turnover. There is a remarkable difference in prices for a standard food 'basket' across European countries. Hence, retailers in the UK enjoy selling power and buying power simultaneously, and are highly priced and profitable in relation to the European average.

United Kingdom

Large food retailers continue to dominate the retail market in the UK, with four of the five largest retailers being supermarket or hypermarket operators. Only Marks & Spencer, which has a large proportion of its turnover from the sales of (private label) food products, is classified as a non-food retailer. This is a reflection of the high levels of concentration in the food sector. This trend is expected to become more pronounced as consolidation increases due to tighter margins and because of the falling away of independent operators as they are unable to compete in terms of price or range. Larger operators such as supermarkets are becoming less specialized, offering a wide range of non-food products and services. Even non-food operators are increasingly following this practice. Many chain outlets now offer snacks, sandwiches, and food service.

The development of the retail industry in the UK was very rapid in the 1996–2001 period, driven largely by 'unconventional' developments. Boots, for example, was setting up in-store pharmacies and its health and beauty range within Sainsbury's stores. Marks & Spencer has launched food displays within selected WH Smith stores. Tesco and Sainsbury's are developing more city centre sites and petrol station forecourt stores in response to consumer demands for convenience. A study shows that while the retail sales would go up, the profitability may not rise proportionately.[21]

Total UK retail sales stood at approximately £297,478 million in 2009.[22] In the 1990s, the price of goods rose consistently below the overall rate of inflation. Larger retailers aimed to grow share by keeping prices low. In turn, lower prices were enabled by the economies of scale created by expanded networks. Prices in shops were increasing at a much slower rate than the prices of other goods and services, and retailers were insulating customers from the full cost pressures faced from suppliers, as well as from government costs such as increased insurance payments. Retail sales rose strongly throughout the review period and more or less withstood the recent slowdown in economic performance. Low interest rates and increase in personal borrowing sustained consumer confidence. Growth remained high at the end of the review period, with a rise in current value sales of 5 per cent between 2004 and 2005.[23]

The Internet is starting to have a strong impact on traditional high street shops and diverting a significant proportion of sales. The strongest Internet players tend to be retailers who operate online sales in tandem with a high street brand, as customer loyalty already exists and these operators already have extant logistical networks. Typically, online sales are highest in the run up and aftermath to Christmas. Consumers prefer to shop online to avoid the chaos of the high street.

Germany[24]

The retailing scenario in Germany is similar to that of the UK. The small independent specialist retail outlets that dominated the retail sector in the 1970s have almost disappeared, to be replaced by large chain stores that are able to afford the high rents in premium locations. Traditional outlet formats have been replaced by new forms of retailing such as supermarkets, hypermarkets, and discounters. In the non-food sector, promotions have become a major customer attraction in the food grocery sector. The non-food share of sales through grocery outlets continued to grow through the 2006–09 period.[25]

The retail market in Germany shows signs of polarization—the upper end consisting of branded products and exclusive goods and services, and the lower end comprising discount products and private labels. The middle and traditional retail areas have been continuously losing out in this process.

There is an upcoming trend of convenience in German grocery retailing as seen by the continued growth in forecourt retailers and convenience stores during the period of 2009 and 2010. The grocery retailing reached sales of €175.5 billion in 2010. Germany's food and beverage industry is the fourth largest industry sector in Germany, generating production value of €149.5 billion (1.2% increase on that of 2009) in 2010. The convenience stores experienced current value growth of 2 per cent in 2010, to reach sales of €365 million. The supermarkets saw the highest growth rate in 2010, of 7 per cent. Value sales in hypermarkets stagnated in 2010, reaching €33.5 billion. In 2010, the supermarket chains continued to take advantage of the organic category and low-fat products which have become increasingly popular in German supermarkets. The supermarkets in Germany majorly follow Aldi and Lidl's strategies of selling brand products at low prices; supermarkets such as Rewe and Edeka sometimes undercut the prices in discounters. In 2010, the company which led overall grocery retailing was Edeka Zentrale coming around 21 per cent share of value sales. The food, drink, and tobacco specialists are expected to see a negative growth rate in the forecast period to 2015. A large part of the turnover lost by this channel is projected to be gained by forecourt retailers. They have also advantages in terms of location, wider assortment, high frequency of transactions, and lower markups, which all will make forecourt retailers an increasingly strong competitor (www.euromonitor.com, accessed on 7 October 2011).

In the non-food sector, specialist chain stores and international companies are likely to strengthen their presence through mergers, acquisitions, or partnerships. Traditional and independent retail outlets, both in the food and non-food sectors, may continue to lose the battle for market share. Novel retailing methods including e-commerce and television shopping will gain importance, as will factory outlet centres and shopping centres. The growth of the retail sector in Germany for the period 2004–09 is shown in Table 3.4.

TABLE 3.4 Sector-wise Sales in Retailing in Germany (2004–09): Value (€ million)

	2004	2005	2006	2007	2008	2009
Grocery retailers	157,570.10	156,257.90	160,569.90	166,475.00	168,215.70	168,660.30
Non-grocery retailers	179,776.30	180,299.70	181,213.30	184,676.30	186,155.60	185,745.30
Store-based retailing	**337,346.40**	**336,557.60**	**341,783.20**	**351,151.30**	**354,371.30**	**354,405.60**
Vending	4,948.90	5,131.50	5,114.30	4,166.70	3,869.00	3,702.50
Homeshopping	12,373.80	12,034.10	11,860.60	11,720.90	11,654.40	11,264.80
Internet retailing	6,701.90	8,486.90	10,207.90	12,013.20	12,952.60	13,963.70
Direct selling	2,742.20	2,753.70	2,791.90	2,827.90	2,854.60	2,872.90
Non-store retailing	**26,766.90**	**28,406.20**	**29,974.70**	**30,728.70**	**31,330.60**	**31,804.00**
Total retailing	**364,113.30**	**364,963.80**	**371,757.90**	**381,880.00**	**385,701.90**	**386,209.60**

Source: www.euromonitor.com, accessed on 2 October 2010.

TABLE 3.5   Sector-wise Sales in Retailing in France (2004–09): Value (€ billion)

	2004	2005	2006	2007	2008	2009
Grocery retailers	191,566.40	192,100.60	195,732.80	200,040.70	206,148.30	207,636.10
Non-grocery retailers	155,841.10	159,268.40	165,660.70	169,786.90	169,632.90	168,309.60
Store-based retailing	**347,407.50**	**351,369.00**	**361,393.50**	**369,827.60**	**375,781.20**	**375,945.70**
Vending	396.10	422.20	438.30	461.70	486.00	501.00
Homeshopping	4,908.50	4,624.70	4,302.40	4,197.70	3,866.40	3,662.00
Internet retailing	2,959.80	4,096.40	5,405.50	7,262.40	9,020.10	10,839.80
Direct selling	2,608.90	2,535.80	2,475.30	2,448.00	2,460.20	2,455.30
Non-store retailing	**10,873.30**	**11,679.10**	**12,621.50**	**14,369.80**	**15,832.70**	**17,458.10**
Total retailing	**358,280.80**	**363,048.10**	**374,015.00**	**384,197.40**	**391,613.90**	**393,403.80**

Source: www.euromonitor.com, accessed on 2 October 2010.

The following sections provide an insight into the retail industry in Brazil, Russia, and Chile.

France[26]

The French retail landscape is polarized—large stores, usually located on the outskirts of towns/cities, and co-existing with smaller outlets in downtown locations. Since the 1970s, the independent owner-operated retailers witnessed the greatest fall in the number of outlets and in market shares as compared to larger stores. However, this trend has tended to stabilize in the 1990s.

In 2010, the grocery retailers accounted for more than half of value sales in store-based retailing, whereas non-grocery retailers continued to decline in France. Despite the efforts of the French government, the Consumer Confidence Index was still too low at the end of 2009 and during the first half of 2010. The fate of retailing is obviously directly linked to the health of the economy. A non-favourable GDP growth rate and Consumer Confidence Index can act as a drag on this market. The consumers tend to pay more attention to their expenditure in order to save money. The year 2009 started very poorly for retailing. However, 2010 was not too bad for retailing. The situation improved at the end of 2009 and in the first half of 2010. The overall sales increased by 1 per cent in current value terms in 2010.

Concentration is increasing through both ownership and store size. Retailers are responding to slow growth in home markets by expanding into other markets. Store chains are becoming branded in order to increase differentiation between chains for increasing store loyalty. Private labels have obtained a more dominant role within the last few years. They may be seen as a way to increase differentiation. They are also the retailers' opportunity to avoid costs of marketing incurred by the producers' brands, yielding higher gross margin. Customer satisfaction and customer loyalty are becoming increasingly important in Europe. The sales in retailing in France (2004–09) are depicted in Table 3.5.

Brazil[27]

Euromonitor International data shows that in Brazil, between the years 2002 and 2008, the number of households with annual disposable income of over US$10,000 rose by some 394 per cent to reach 26 million and those with earnings of over US$15,000 rose by 457 per cent to reach 17 million. The growth in the retail industry, which reached its highest level since 1999 in the fourth quarter of 2009, was largely due to increased consumption of durable and semi-durable goods. In 2009, grocery retailers' sales increased by 8 per cent in current value terms. Internet retailing witnessed the highest growth rate of 35 per cent constant value CAGR during 2002–08. E-commerce sales reached US$4.8 billion during the first half of 2009, which represented a 27 per cent increase over the same period in 2008. The increase in direct selling happened due to the demand from low-income consumer groups.

The cost of SMS in Brazil is among the highest in the world, and this poses a major threat to the expansion of m-commerce transactions in the future. SMS tax cuts and standardization of the service would be necessary to stimulate the continued use of these services by Brazilian consumers in the future.

Walmart has invested R$1.6 billion and opened about 90 new stores. Domestic players, such as Grupo Pão de Açúcar, continue to grow into the north and north-east markets. Specialist retailer, Mundo Verde, currently operates 150 outlets with 79 per cent of its stores located in the south, south-east, and central-west regions. Retailers such as Casas Bahia have established themselves by offering extended payment plans with no interest charges. Smaller players are exploring the less developed regions as well as small towns.

Russia[28]

Retail industry in Russia has been witnessing mixed trends. While grocery retailers increased the share of total retail sales from 54 per cent in 2008 to 59 per cent in 2009, many retailers involved in the construction of megastores, hypermarkets, and shopping malls postponed new construction projects. Despite reduction in rents, selling areas were vacant. Industry analysts expected discounters to be more active compared to other retail formats. However, Carrefour Group, which opened two outlets, quit within a very short time. Walmart's proposal to acquire the Lenta chain of hypermarkets did not fructify. Retailers had started closing unprofitable outlets. According to the company's report, Evroset Group found 800 outlets inefficient and hence candidates for closure. They have closed 600 outlets of mobile telephones and portable appliances. Some companies are trying to build their business by focusing on a few selected brands.

Although, according to Goscomstat, in 2009 foreign direct investment (FDI) into retailing in Russia declined by over 50 per cent compared to 2008, interestingly, foreign retailers with an already established strong position, such as Auchan Group, Metro AG, Stockmann OYJ Abp, and INDITEX—Industria de Diseño Textil, continued expansion in 2009. With new regulations, the government aims to support small businesses, especially manufacturers of grocery products and keep inflation rates down. Retail giants such as X5 Retail and Magnit have announced plans to strengthen their positions through acquisitions of competitors. X5 Retail added 102 new stores by 2010 in Russia. Metro AG has developed consultancy services for small independent grocery retailers. They plan to serve 35,000 independent retailers in the area of range positioning, modernization of the outlets, and retail equipment. Many store-based retailers are planning to diversify into Internet retailing. Auchan Group wants to become the largest Internet retailer in Russia and X5 Retail Group has acquired two e-shops.

Chile[29]

The Chilean economy suffered deeply as a result of the international economic crisis and in 2009 recorded its worst performance of the decade. Clothing and footwear prices declined most rapidly, dropping by almost 16 per cent in the 12 months ending September 2009. Electronics and appliance specialist retailers recorded the worst performance among non-grocery retailers, with current value sales declining by 11 per cent in 2009. Grocery retailers performed better as consumers focused on essential products, with current value sales growing by 3 per cent in current value terms in 2009. Supermarkets and hypermarkets saw a notable increase in current value sales by 7 per cent and 5 per cent, respectively. Independent grocery retailers generally performed poorly, struggling to compete due to fierce price competition among supermarkets and hypermarkets and the rapid expansion of discounters. In 2009, fairs and traditional fruit and vegetable markets also performed well due to their low prices. Shopping malls are becoming important in retailing, accounting for 21 per cent of retailing value sales. Projects worth around US$1.5 billion have been announced for 2010–2012, leading to a 56 per cent increase in overall selling space.

In December 2009, a legislation was passed requiring up-to-date display of prices for products on store shelves and for medicines sold over the counter. Chemists/pharmacies and para pharmacies/ drugstores were expected to implement this ruling in the first half of 2010. This will allow consumers to compare alternative brands and also facilitate the comparison of prices between chains.

Walmart acquired a controlling share in leading Chilean retailer Distribución y Servicios D&S in 2009 and swiftly sought to combine synergies and knowledge. New entrant Supermercados del Sur is expanding rapidly and has gained a strong regional presence targeting low- and mid-income consumers. The company aims to reach 180 outlets and to increase its sales to US$1,240 million by 2012, and with this, double its sales level of 2008. Distribución y Servicios D&S plans to invest US$280 million in smaller formats to expand its geographical reach. Falabella is planning to invest US$1.7 billion in 2010–2012 in Chile and abroad across all of its formats.

SUMMARY

The business of retailing takes different forms in different countries. These variations are caused mainly due to the consumer profile and shopping behaviour. A significant role is also played by local spatial factors such as availability of space and its costs. Most countries are witnessing multi-format retailing. Each of them has survived. Only a few have become endangered. Retailers have become global, but the act of retailing remains localized. Local resources, infrastructure, and economy play a significant role in the shaping of retailing in different countries. Successful retailers would have to respect the local traditions, customs, and shoppers' orientation and make sure that every store of the chain delivers good value to its customers.

NOTES

1. www.euromonitor.com, accessed on 16 December 2006
2. Bell, David E, and Ann Leamon 1998, 'Note on the Retailing Industry', Harvard Business School 9-598-148, 13 May.
3. http://www.asiatraveltips.com/news06/163-Retail Sales.shtml, accessed on 5 April 2004.
4. 'Asia's Grocery Shoppers Prefer Modern Formats', *Retail Asia Online Magazine*, April 2003.
5. 'Transforming Toys "R" Us across Asia', *Retail Asia Online Magazine*, August 2002.
6. 'The Evolving Role of Department Stores in China', *Retail Asia Online Magazine*, October 2002.
7. www.euromonitor.com, accessed on 4 October 2011.
8. 'Indonesian Retailers Invest More in IT Solutions', *Retail Asia Online Magazine*, August 2002.
9. 'Indonesia's Retailers Hit by Hikes in Fuel and Utilities', *Retail Asia Online Magazine*, February 2003.
10. www.euromonitor.com, accessed on 17 December 2006.
11. http://www.prlog.org/10838017-new-market-research-report-malaysia-retail-report-q4-2010.html, accessed on 1 October 2010.
12. www.euromononitor.com, accessed on 17 December 2006.
13. 'Malaysia to Boost Retail Sector under Eighth Plan', *Retail Asia Online Magazine*, May 2001.

14. www.euromonitor.com, accessed on 5 October 2011.
15. 'China's Entry into WTO will Drive Retail Business Growth', *Retail Asia Online Magazine*, November 2001.
16. 'Shanghai to Get First Walmart Store by 2005', *Retail Asia Online Magazine*, November 2001.
17. www.euromonitor.com, accessed on 17 December 2010.
18. Courbon, Pierre and Phillpe Lasserre 1988, 'Retailing in Taiwan', INSEAD, Fontainebleau.
19. Larke, R 1994, *Japanese Retailing*, Routledge, London.
20. Dobson, Paul and Michael Waterson, 'Retail Power: Recent Developments and Policy Implications', *Economic Policy*, No. 28.
21. 'UK Retail', Ernst and Young Report, http://www.ey.com/global/, accessed on 23 June 2006.
22. www.euromonitor.com, accessed on 17 December 2010.
23. www.euromonitor.com, accessed on 23 June 2011.
24. Dobson, Paul and Michael Waterson, 'Retail Power: Recent Developments and Policy Implications', *Economic Policy*, No. 28.
25. www.euromonitor.com, accessed on 23 June 2011.
26. Dobson, Paul and Michael Waterson, 'Retail Power: Recent Developments and Policy Implications', *Economic Policy*, No. 28.
27. www.euromonitor.com, Country Reports–BRAZIL, 2010, accessed on 23 June 2011.
28. www.euromonitor.com, Country Reports–RUSSIA, 2010, accessed on 23 June 2011.
29. www.euromonitor.com, Country Reports–CHILE, 2010, accessed on 23 June 2011.

CONCEPT REVIEW QUESTIONS

1. What are the key drivers of retailing in USA, Europe, and Asia? What makes them different?
2. How are the landscapes of retailing different in developing and developed countries?
3. Which formats are emerging as the drivers of growth in China, India, USA, and Australia?

CRITICAL THINKING QUESTIONS

1. In light of the different landscapes of retailing in various regions, how should a retailer build a global business?
2. How do cultural factors affect the choice of retail location in international markets?

PROJECTS

1. Visit apparel stores of three Indian retailers and three international retailers from different countries. Enumerate the differences and draw out implications.

ANNEXURE

Major Global Retail Trends

The retailing industry witnessed an unprecedented downturn in 2009 (Fig. A3.1). After a long period of value growth between 3–5 per cent since 2000, markets stagnated in 2009. The global retailing growth scenario is shown in Fig. A3.2.

Figure A3.3 shows how consumer lending as a percentage of annual disposable income surged. Figure A3.4 depicts the value growth of non-store and store-based retailing. Figure A3.5 shows the growth of grocery and non-grocery stores. The growth of store-based retailing in BRIC countries is represented in Fig. A3.6.

Figure A3.7 shows the leading retailers of the world and Fig. A3.8 shows the fastest growing retailers in various countries. Figure A3.9 shows the grocery channels value growth where the size of the bubble represents the additional sales achieved in 2009. Figure A3.10 shows the comparative growth of Internet retailing from 2004–09.

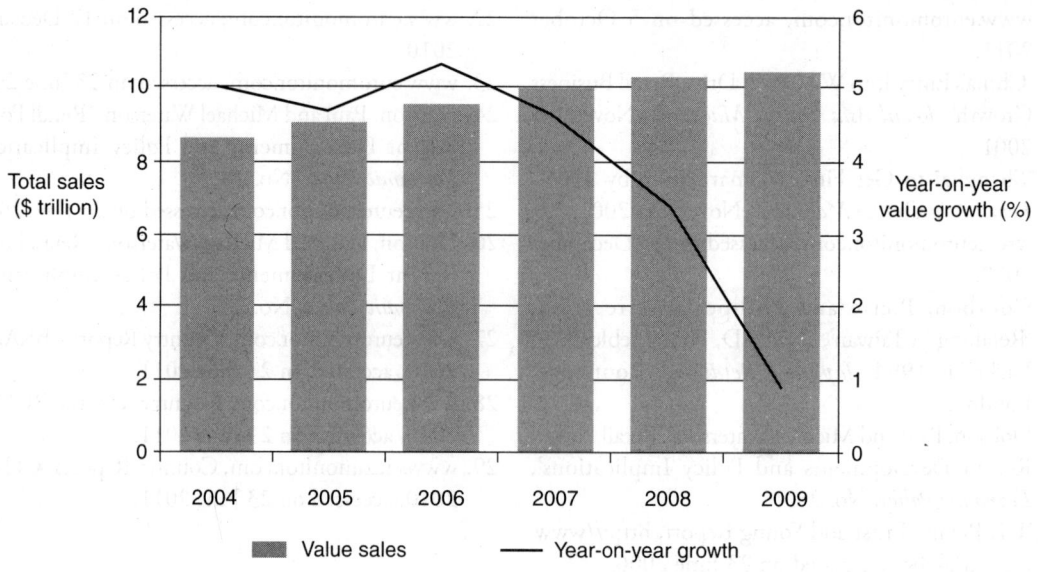

FIG. A3.1 Value Growth Crashes

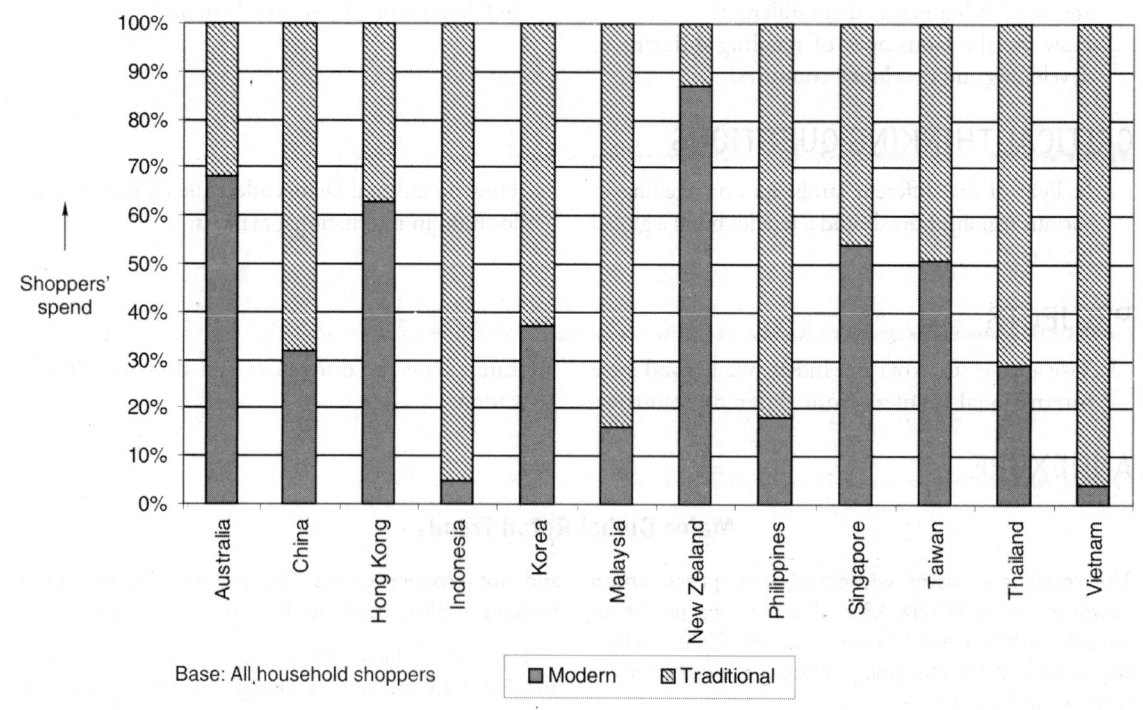

FIG. A3.2 Global Retailing Scenario

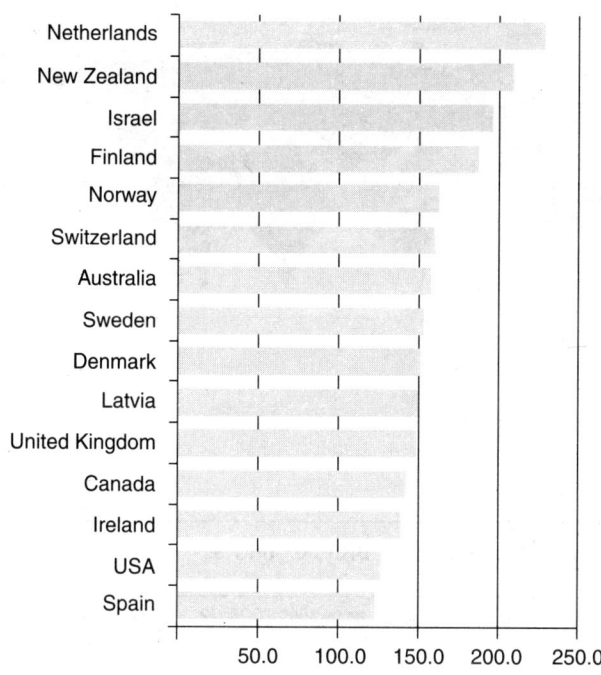

FIG. A3.3   Consumer Lending as a Percentage of Disposable Income

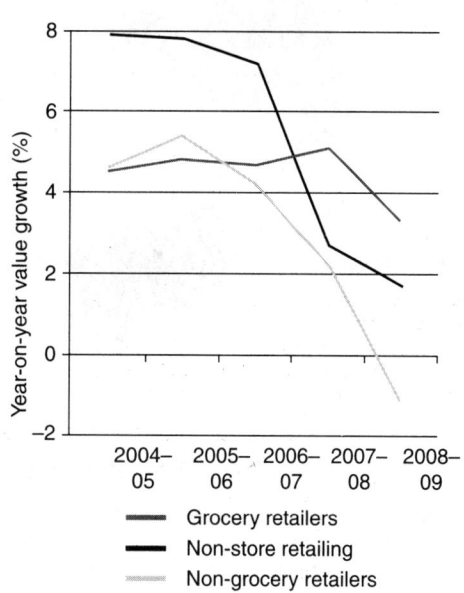

FIG. A3.4   Store-based and Non-store Retailing Value Growth

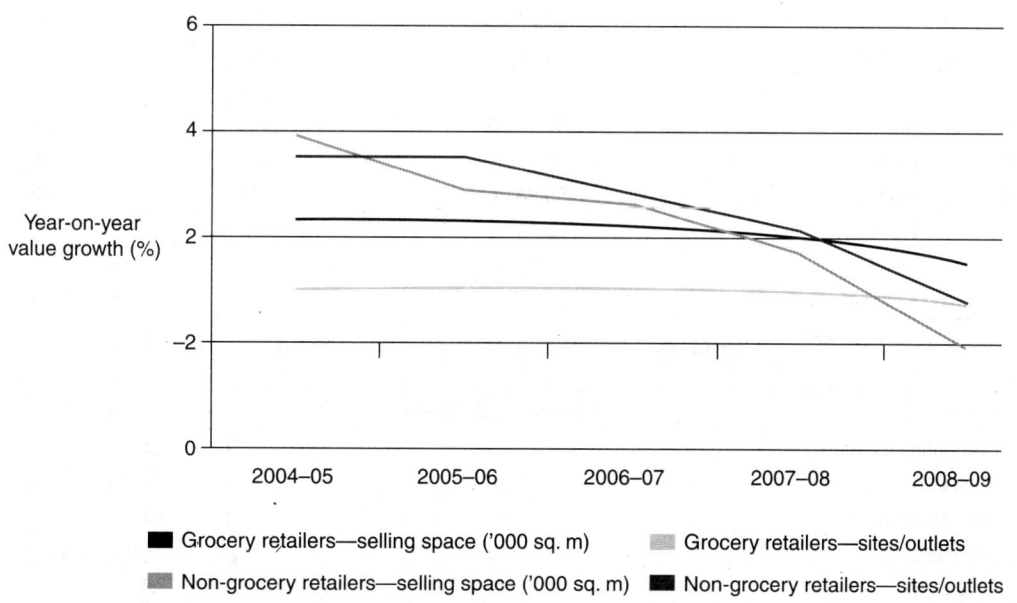

FIG. A3.5   Grocery and Non-grocery Stores

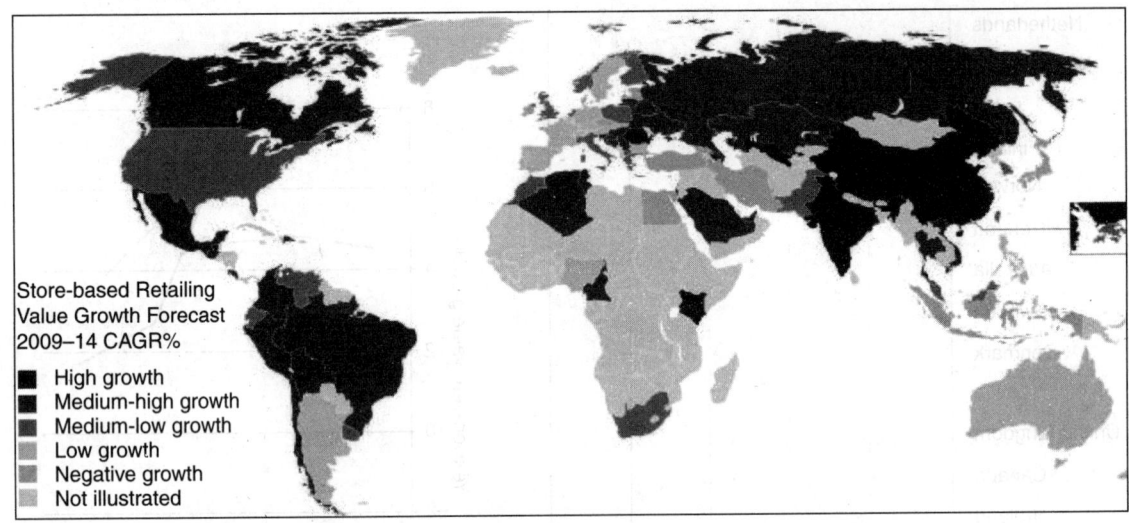

Store-based Retailing
Value Growth Forecast
2009–14 CAGR%

- ■ High growth
- ■ Medium-high growth
- ■ Medium-low growth
- ■ Low growth
- ■ Negative growth
- ■ Not illustrated

FIG. A3.6   Store-based Retailing Value Growth in BRIC Countries

Rank	Name	Sales ($ million 2009)	Sales growth % 2008/09	Two-year trend
1	Wal-Mart	401,258.1	7.5	→
2	Carrefour	121,228.8	1.9	→
3	TeSCO PIC	85,753.3	9.2	↑
4	Seven & I	81,354.7	0.6	↓
5	CVS	74,947.8	10.9	→
6	Target	66,926.7	3.9	→
7	Kroger	66,229.5	3.6	→
8	Schwarz	64,467.2	4.5	↑
9	Walgreen	62,773.2	1.5	↑
10	Aldi	61,953.5	4.0	↑
11	Costco	60,711.7	−4.4	↓
12	Auchan	59,941.0	7.5	→
13	Rewe	52,148.3	3.0	↑
14	AEON	51,756.4	2.4	↑
15	Royal Ahold	50,977.6	−0.9	↓

FIG. A3.7   Leading Retailers of the World

Name	Growth (%) 2008–09	Country
Co-operative Group	98	UK
Edeka Zentrale	19	Germany
Wm Morrison	14	UK
Shinsegae	12	South Korea
CVS Corp	11	US
Metro Inc	8	Canada
Dollar General	7	US
J Sainsbury	5	UK

FIG. A3.8   Fastest Growing Retailers in Various Countries

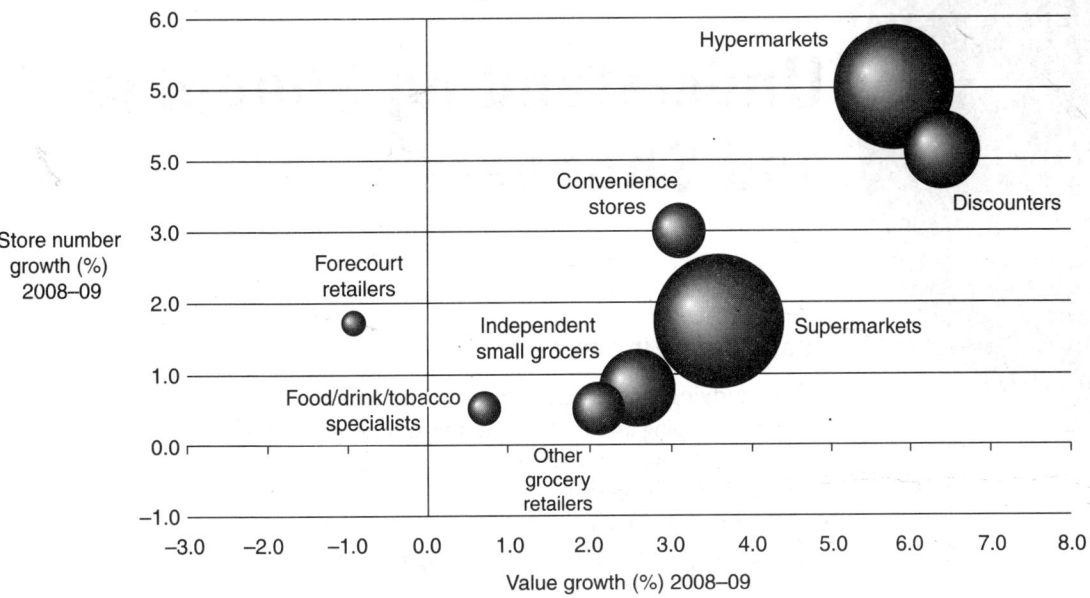

FIG. A3.9 Grocery Channels Value Growth

Note: The size of the bubble represents the amount of additional sales generated in 2009.

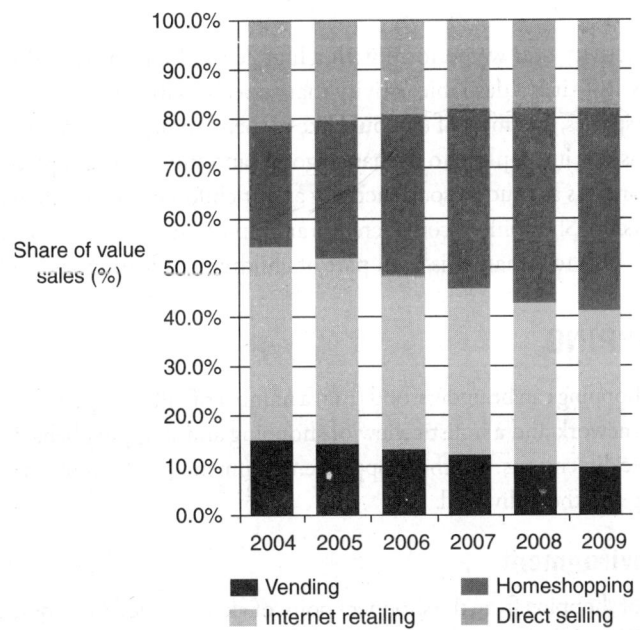

FIG. A3.10 Growth of Internet Retailing

Source: www.euromontior.com, 'Retailing—One Year on from Lehman Brothers' Collapse', January 2010.

4

Understanding Shopping and Shoppers

LEARNING OBJECTIVES

After studying this chapter, you will be able to
- define shopping and understand the shopping process
- describe shopping behaviour
- profile Indian shoppers
- understand the nuances of shopping behaviour
- gain an insight into the existing shopping patterns in India

INTRODUCTION

Shopping is an activity that we perform with a high level of regularity and involvement. It is more than just a necessity—it is a desirable activity that appeals to the inherent nature of humans. We are basically a social species, and most of us would like to spend some part of our leisure time in socializing. Thus, a market is not just a place to exchange goods and money. It is a place to see and be seen at. Going to the market is as much a social activity as our children's cricket match or a visit to a temple or a place of worship. Shopping is considered as an important part of our social life—this is reflected in the fact that a visit to a market is even part of children's education and nursery rhymes.

CONCEPT OF SHOPPING

The concept of shopping can be understood from a number of different perspectives. In order to develop a conceptual framework and a holistic view of shopping and shopping behaviour, shopping could be viewed from three dimensions:[1] (a) the shopping environment, (b) shopping in a socio-cultural context, and (c) shopping and the individual.

Shopping Environment

The importance of shopping from the shopper's point of view emerged towards the end of the nineteenth century in the UK and the US.[2] At the end of the nineteenth and beginning of the twentieth century, economic growth, developments in public transport, and new forms of mass production contributed to the expansion of shops and the phenomenon of shopping. The new formats of the newly opened department stores provided exciting solutions for the growing demands of the affluent, and socially and geographically mobile urban population. For the first time, shoppers were able to enjoy activities that satisfied their functional, social, and aspirational needs.

It has been found that shoppers behave differently depending on the type of shopping situation.[3] They tend to change their process of information search depending on the type of store, even when the same product and, in some cases, even the same brand is being bought. They ask for a particular brand in a *kirana* store and resist change in many cases. However, in a self-service store, they look at more than one brand before reaching a decision. Hence, to some extent, store format can be said to influence behaviour and purchase pattern. In some cases, customers buy only from the shops they patronize, even when it is located at a distance and there are other stores in the vicinity.

Shopping in a Socio-cultural Context

Shopping is an activity that goes beyond the traditional purchasing activities of buying grocery/provisions when required. Modern day shopping is a private pursuit, involving the experience of wandering among a crowd and responding to a wide range of stimuli. It highlights the shop window and the mall environment as a spectacle to be enjoyed and absorbed. Shops are places where the ordinariness of everyday life is transformed into a series of fragmented stimuli.

Shopping can take many shades, as different as being a hedonic recreation or running errands or fulfilling chores. It is a type of ritual that adds cultural meaning and personal relevance to goods, as also an activity that enables information gathering. Essentially, shopping is a means of satisfying many non-purchase-related motives as well as an instrumental means of purchasing.

Although shopping is primarily aimed at collecting information, enabling shoppers to ensure that they make the right decision, it also gives them emotional satisfaction. Shoppers take into consideration the information that they acquire in the store, in addition to the information collected before visiting the store, to decide on purchases.

Shopping facilitates an individual to escape from the realities of the environment and also allows a temporary alteration of the individual's self-concept. Shopping is also a type of compensatory consumption, which includes browsing and window shopping; and, in some cases, the actual purchase becomes a medium to make up for a perceived deficiency. Shopping motives are contextualized within an environment with networks of relationships between the shopper and the store, the merchandise, and other shoppers. Some of the social motives that shoppers seek to fulfil are as follows:[4]

- Social experiences outside one's home
- Communication with others who share similar interests
- Peer group attraction—the patronage of a store sometimes reflects a desire to be with one's peer group or a reference group one aspires to belong to
- Status and authority—many shopping experiences provide the opportunity for an individual to command attention and respect
- Pleasure of bargaining

Traditionally, women have not had the financial resources to indulge in many types of leisure activities, but as the 'business executives of the home' they have had personal control over spending for the family's consumption and housekeeping. Shopping, as an activity, is seen as complementary to female roles.[5] Engagement with, and responsibility for, shopping has had an impact on the traditional role of a woman, which has undergone change due to changes in the shopping environment.

Shopping and the Individual

People's motives for shopping are a function of many variables, some of which are unrelated to the actual buying of products. An understanding of shopping motives requires consideration of satisfactions which shopping activities provide, as well as the utility obtained from the merchandise that may be purchased. The personal motives of shopping could be as follows.[6]

Role-playing   Many activities are learnt behaviours, traditionally expected or accepted as part of a certain position or role in society. A person internalizes these behaviours as required and is motivated to participate in the extended activities. For example, the role a woman plays in the household with regard to shopping is a socially learnt role.

Diversion   Shopping offers an opportunity for diversion from the daily routines and thus represents a form of recreation. For example, shopping may act as a stress buster or an escape from work and monotony.

Self-gratification   Different emotional states or moods may be relevant for explaining why and when someone goes shopping, as in the case of self-gifting.

Learning about New Trends   Products are intimately entwined in one's daily activities and often serve as symbols reflecting attitudes and lifestyles. For example, the purchase of some products may reflect that the buyer keeps abreast with new fashion, products, and stores.

Physical Activity   Shopping provides people with a considerable amount of exercise.

Sensory Stimulation   Retail shops provide many potential sensory benefits to shoppers. Shopping is a see–touch–feel process. For example, our olfactory sense plays an important role in many stores.

While the activity of shopping is performed as a routine, during the last few years, shoppers' orientation towards shopping has changed. Innovations introduced by retailers and marketers in the practice of retailing have provided new paradigms to the way shoppers have been disposed towards the act of shopping.

SHOPPING PROCESS

The shopper decision process can be analysed from two perspectives:[7] (i) the decision process, and (ii) the factors affecting the process. The decision process has six basic steps:

1. Stimulus
2. Problem awareness
3. Information search
4. Evaluation of alternatives
5. Purchase
6. Post-purchase behaviour

The buying process typically begins when a customer recognizes an unsatisfied need. He/she then seeks information about how to satisfy that need, what products/services might be useful, and how they can be bought. This is followed by an evaluation of the various alternative sources of merchandise, such as stores, catalogues, and e-tailing sites, on various parameters, and then the final selection of a particular interface. Eventually, the shopper makes a purchase and consumes the product. Based on his/her experience, the shopper then decides whether the product or service satisfies his/her needs to the desired extent.

The process of decision making can take three forms:[8]

Extended Problem-solving   This is a form of purchase decision in which shoppers devote considerable time and effort to analyse alternatives. This purchase decision involves a high level of risk and uncertainty. Shoppers go beyond their personal knowledge to consult with friends, family members, or experts, and indulge in an extended problem-solving activity. A new product or a product with high cost or technicality would be bought in this fashion.

Limited Problem-solving   This is a purchase decision process involving a moderate amount of effort and time. Shoppers engage in this type of buying process when they have had some prior experience with the product or service and the risk associated with the purchase is moderate. In these situations, customers tend to rely more on personal knowledge than on external information. They usually choose a retailer they have shopped from before and select merchandise they have bought in the past. In such a situation shoppers tend to confirm their decision to buy their usual brands by collecting information about other brands at the store. This behaviour is also exhibited by shoppers in situations where there are small differences among the available brands.

Habitual Decision-making   This is a purchase decision process involving little or no conscious effort. This process is followed mainly in cases of repeat purchase. Brand and store loyalties play a significant role in such purchase situations.

SHOPPING BEHAVIOUR

Shopping is the act of identifying the store and purchasing the product. This behaviour of shoppers differs according to the place where they are shopping and their involvement level with the act of shopping.[9] Shopping is a function of the nature of the product, the degree of perceived risk inherent in the product class, and the level of knowledge or amount of information about alternatives. Observations of shopper behaviour in the store show that every purchase involves part or the whole of a process that follows a consistent pattern of *see–touch–sense–select*.

Shopping behaviour has been classified into the following three categories.[10]

Blinkered Mode   In this mode, shopping is very automatic. It is characterized by shoppers confidently and efficiently zooming in on familiar brands, with no time or interest in logical label reading or studying product attributes. This mode is typically observed in case of low involvement categories and high repeat purchases.

Magpie Mode   In the 'magpie' mode, the shopper allows himself/herself to be distracted and attracted by different brands on display. This mode is associated with situations where the shopper is seeking a change or a treat. This mode can be observed at food or fixture stores.

Browser Mode   The 'browser' mode finds the shopper behaving more rationally, reading the 'back of pack' copy and invariably comparing prices, ingredients, and seeking more information about product attributes, making piece-value comparisons across various brands. This mode is typical of situations where there is a greater perceived 'risk' associated with the brand or purchase.

DEMOGRAPHICS OF INDIAN SHOPPERS

Let us now take a look at the demographics of Indian shoppers in detail.

Population Growth

In 1990, India's population was 850 million. Within a decade it increased to 1 billion, indicating an annual growth rate of 2.05 per cent. The current population of India (in 2011) is around 1.19 billion. By 2030, the population of India will be the largest in the world, estimated to be around 1.53 billion. The estimated birth rate is 20.97 per 1,000 people and the estimated death rate is 7.48 per 1,000 people. The net migration rate is 0.05 migrants per 1,000 people. The current gender composition of males per 100 females is 108. The urban population was 30 per cent of total population in 2010 and the annual rate of urbanization estimated for 2011–15 is 2.4 per cent.[11] The rural population was 633 million in 1990, growing at the rate of 1.73 per cent, and 720 million in 2000, showing a decline in growth rate to 1.15 per cent. It was expected to further decline to 0.53 per cent by 2010 at 772 million.[12]

Life Expectancy

Life expectancy in India, while still low when compared to developed economies, improved during the twentieth century. In 1920, women in India could expect to live to just 20.9 years of age, and men to 19.4 years, with the average figure being 20.2 years. By 1990, these figures had risen to 57.9 years for women and 57.8 for men, while in 2000 it was 62.9 years for women and 62.6 for men. According to the current 2011 estimate, the life expectancy at birth is 65.77 years for males and 67.95 years for females. Improved health care and rising levels of prosperity are helping to increase life expectancy and decrease mortality from many preventable diseases.

Age Segmentation

In 1990, the population between the segment 0–14 years was 36.2 per cent. It showed a further decline at 33.5 per cent in 2000, 31.5 per cent in 2005, and 30.5 per cent according to the 2009 estimate. In 1990, the population above 65 years of age was 4.3 per cent, growing up to 4.9 per cent in 2000, and 5.3 per cent in 2005. It is 5.5 percent according to the 2011 estimate. The current median age is about 26.2 years. According to Euromonitor, it will increase to 31.7 years by 2030.[13] As India's birth rate has traditionally been high, the proportion of the population at the working age (20–44 years) is projected to increase from 35.2 per cent in 1996 to 40.5 per cent in 2016. Those aged 45 and over accounted for just 17.3 per cent in 1996—a proportion that is likely to rise to 23.5 per cent by 2016.

The Middle Class

The middle class is the central theme and the target of the new markets in India. India's middle class, already bigger than the population of the US, is expected to grow to 40–70 million by 2007. Moreover, the age profile of the population is likely to sustain consumer spending as more than 45 per cent of Indians are under the age of 20.[14]

Rural Shoppers

Rural areas, where over 70 per cent of the Indian population still lives, are witnessing widespread changes in the shopper market. In fact, the rural market has outpaced India's urban market in demand for durable and non-durable goods. Estimates suggest that the rural market is growing twice as fast as the urban market. Due to agricultural growth, income redistribution, and the communication revolution, rural India today accounts for a sizeable market share of a wide range of products. However, it has been found that rural shoppers, unlike their urban counterparts, do not distinguish between occupational and personal spending. That is because 70–80 per cent of rural consumers are farmers, who are, in a way, self-employed businessmen. From whatever they earn, they have to spend on the household as well as the farm. As a result, the rural spending basket not only consists of personal and household items, but also occupational expenditure on fertilizers, seeds, pesticides, etc.[15]

Number of Households and Household Size

The number of households rose steadily during the 1990s in India. In 2000, the total stood at 186 million households. It was expected to go up to 231 million in 2010, showing a decline in growth rate to 5.14 per cent. The household number grew between 1995 and 2000 at a rate of 2.28 per cent to 2.36 per cent, but decreased to 2.22 per cent in 2006 and was expected to decline to 2.09 per cent in 2010. It is likely to go down to 1.45 per cent in 2025.[16] The implication of this is that, although more households are being created, the increase is not sufficient to provide more living space, given that the population rose by more than 16 per cent over the same period. The average number of rooms in an Indian household dwelling is three—including kitchen and bathroom. Only a quarter of all Indian families (25%) live in homes with five or more rooms. Nearly half (45%) of all Indian families live in homes with fewer than three rooms, and about one in six families (16%) live in single-room dwellings.

Changing Shopper Profile

India's economic diversity matches its social diversity. Technology ranges from bullock carts with modern wheels to space satellite capability. The demand for shopper goods is also diverse and growing, and includes chewing gum, mineral water, tissue paper, fast food, and denims, besides the necessities. In the area of information and telecom technology, it may range from email, voice mail, fax, and cell phones to PCs, laptops, and Internet access to teleconferencing. Indian shoppers are also buying luxury and entertainment products, such as TVs, home theatres, CD and DVD players, camcorders, and digital cameras.

As households moved to the high and middle-income category, their purchasing power and the basket of goods bought changed. According to a 2008 survey by the National Council of Applied Economic Research (NCAER), the ownership of (select) consumer durable goods among non-poor Indian households was significantly higher than that among poor households. At an all-India level, 33 per cent of non-poor households owned colour television sets, 25 per cent had telephones, 22 per cent had refrigerators, 19 per cent owned cellular phones, nearly 7 per cent had cars, and 2 per cent owned credit cards. In contrast, 8 per cent of poor households owned colour television sets, 4 per cent had telephones, 3 per cent had refrigerators, 3 per cent owned cellular phones, and barely 1 per cent had either cars or credit cards. Armed with this knowledge, marketers came out with innovative products such as sachets of shampoo and detergent powder, and the Tata Nano and the Ginger Hotel chain of the Tata Group for the low-income groups. The spending on these items is bound to increase when the income of the poor households increases. High-income families have been considerably increasing, and by 2025 it is projected to account for 2 per cent of the population but 20 per cent of the consumption, which would mean a significant increase in spending on branded clothing and luxury goods.[17]

The growth in shopper spend and changes in consumption patterns have been facilitated by government policies that increased the availability of a wide range of merchandise, encouraged shopper demand, and helped in developing the market infrastructure.

Socio-cultural Profile

In a study conducted among shoppers, two shopper typologies were developed: the Hindi medium type (HMT) and the English medium type (EMT).[18] These two types of shoppers showed marked differences in their ability to adapt to new concepts and products. While it may be true that HMTs have had their primary education in Indian language medium schools, this was not always the case. Both groups were comfortable in the English language in a work setting, but the HMTs were more comfortable in their mother tongue. They switched to that language at the first opportunity. The HMTs looked up to the EMTs for innovating and were quite happy to follow them. The EMTs did not look up to the HMTs, even for cultural leads, and felt that they were more modern while the HMTs were tradition-bound.

PSYCHOGRAPHIC PROFILE OF INDIAN SHOPPERS

In this section, we shall look at the profile of Indian shoppers, as highlighted in many studies.

Segments of Men

A large urban city study conducted to profile Indian men has shown four broad groups:[19]

1. The *traditional man* is conservative, driven by values, cherishes family, and avoids ostentation. This category spans all age groups, is mostly married, belongs to the second tier in the SEC ladder, and accounts for 36 per cent of the men studied.
2. The *pleasure seeker* is a self-oriented person, driven by status and status symbols. He is a risk-taker and a pleasure-seeker. He is young, unmarried, and lives in a metro city. This category accounts for over 40 per cent of the men.
3. The *social chameleon* is a hypocrite of sorts who wants to project the right image. Tech-savvy and individualistic, he is aged between 30 to 40 years and accounts for 17 per cent of the men.
4. The *intrinsic progressive man* is a futuristic person. He believes in family values and equality of sexes, is non-traditional, tech-savvy, and young, and belongs to the executive class. This category accounts for 7 per cent of the men.

Segments of Women

The above mentioned study categorized Indian women in the following manner:

1. The *contented conservative* is a housewife who is happy with her state of life/society.
2. The *archetypal provider* believes that her role is to provide for and look after the well-being of her family.
3. The *anxious rebel* is a working woman who is not happy with the existing state of affairs.
4. The *troubled homebody* is a housewife who is not sure that she is doing the right thing by sitting at home.
5. The *tight-fisted traditionalist* is a traditional woman who believes in saving for tomorrow.
6. The *affluent sophisticate is* an affluent woman who is comfortable with the finer things in life.
7. The *contemporary housewife* is a housewife who plays an active role in the household and sees herself as equal to her husband.
8. The *gracious hedonist* is a working woman who believes in looking after herself well.

Youth Segments

The youth has been classified into the following five psychographic segments:[20]

Homebodies   They are largely traditional, have low individuality and very few aspirations for self, and keep duty and morality at the core of their values. They are not interested in brands, and are the last to pick up on trends and fashion. They are uneasy with the opposite sex and are focused on their education/job, but not on their 'career'. They are bookworms.

Two-faced youths   They are inwardly traditional and outwardly modern. The body tattoos co-exist with *Kyunki Saas Bhi Kabhi Bahu Thi* (signifying traditionalism). Once married, they know that they will have to abide by prescribed norms, and hence they feel the need to 'enjoy life' to the fullest. They also exhibit openness with the opposite sex and the need to be aggressive to get ahead in life.

Wannabes   This is a large cluster. They are materialistic show-offs. They are extremely competitive. They are desperate to be a part of a crowd, and are trend followers who aggressively seek out lifestyle cues and adapt them to feel more confident and be perceived as 'cool' by others. Although they are uncomfortable with the opposite sex, they tend to show a great desire to attract them.

Rebels   This is the largest cluster. They may be first generation educated professionals, experiencing winds of change in the form of education as the means to a career, wealth, change in lifestyle, and independence. Their parents are very traditional. Their rebellion is not overt. Their responses are guarded as they are either unsure or do not wish to express and commit themselves. They exhibit heavy reliance on friends, and are not understood by their parents.

Cool guys   They are the influencers. Others want to be like them. They fall in the 'work hard, play harder' category. They are confident and have a strong sense of individuality. Their friends are very important to them. They have lots of aspirations. They like to experiment, and are liberal or westernized. They are brand and label conscious. To them the West is a dream for studies.

VALUE AND LIFESTYLE PROFILE OF INDIAN SHOPPERS

The value and lifestyle (VALS) segmentation of shoppers classifies them into different types, based on their unique style of living. American society has been categorized as the pre-World War II shoppers and post-World War II shoppers. Indian shoppers can also be classified into four such typologies:[21]

1. *Pre-independence shoppers* are anti-British, take pride in India, and support local produce, non-violence, and sacrifice.
2. *Post-independence shoppers* are idealistic, independent-minded, non-aligned, sincere, and hardworking.
3. *Pre-Rajiv Gandhi shoppers* are socialistic. For them, corruption is a way of life. They are anti-rich, license-permit drivers and ape and bait the West.
4. *Post-Rajiv Gandhi shoppers* are capitalistic. They have a global orientation, ape the West, and are tech-savvy. They believe in the survival of the fittest.

Lifestyle trends have an impact on how shoppers take purchase decisions and how a marketer needs to address the shopper. This impact is indicated in Table 4.1.[22]

The activities, interests, and opinions (AIO) framework can be used to classify shoppers into various segments. A study using an AIO framework identified five value segments among shoppers. This is described in Table 4.2.

TABLE 4.1   Lifestyle Trends

Lifestyle Trend	Implication for Marketer
Woman becoming assertive	• Depiction of women in advertising
	• Women-oriented durables
Time pressure on women	• Time-saving durables
	• Food products that save time
	• Speciality services that save time
Working couples	• Quick fix meals
	• Holiday packages
	• Crèches/day-care centres
Looks-oriented career males	• Male accessories
	• Ready-made garments
	• Self-help books

TABLE 4.2   Value-based Segments of Shoppers

Cluster Type	Stymied Aspirant	Complete (Wo)man	Struggler	Conservative Housewife	Lone Ranger
Cluster Size	59%	17%	8%	9%	6%
Values	Rather deprived; aspire for upward mobility; see money as a measure of success; religious	Mature; progressive; tolerant; frugal; allow 'space' to others; family supportive; religion important	Very deprived– poor; young– old; looking for money; job for family support; need to work	Wealthy; conservative; traditional; intolerant; lazy; want to have a good time	Liberal; self-aware; bohemian; well-off; locus within; prefer friends to family; not very religious
Demographics					
SEC	SEC B and C	SEC A and B	SEC D/E and C	SEC A	SEC A
Gender	Both males and females	Both males and females	More males	More females	Both males and females
Age	All age groups	Below 40 years	Below 30 or above 50	Below 30 or above 50	Below 40 years
Education	Higher secondary or below	Graduate professional	Higher secondary or below	Graduate professional	Graduate professional
Occupation	Housewife, shop owner, trader, clerk	Housewife, supervisor, executive	Housewife, student, petty trader, skilled	Housewife, businessman	Housewife, senior executive, self-employed professional
Marital status	Married with 2 children	Married with 2 children	More than 2 children	Married with 2 children	Unmarried or 1 child
Religion	Hindus	Hindus/Jains/ Christians	Hindus/ Muslims	Hindus/Jains	Hindus/Jains

(Contd)

(Table 4.2 Contd)

Cluster Type	Stymied Aspirant	Complete (Wo)man	Struggler	Conservative Housewife	Lone Ranger
Activity	Watch TV; visit and entertain family; household chores; *puja/* praying; socially active; go to movies sometimes	Entertain family; read paper; watch TV; high involvement with kids and friends; listen to music—Indian classical; go to temple; go to movies; high use of gadgets; visit museum, library, concert, cultural events; vacation—visit family, religious places; social work-club; dance festival/occasion	Watch TV; visit relatives; go to temple; listen to radio; drink alcohol; play cards	Read; watch TV; go shopping—clothes; household chores; use common gadgets; socially apathetic; enjoy cooking, baking, stitching, knitting; go to kitty parties club; play cards—gamble; vacation abroad	Read; watch TV; listen to pop/western music; shop—toys, gifts, books; not many religious or kids-related activities; repair—house, appliances; drawing—painting; camping—swimming, public speaking; drink alcohol; use new hi-tech gadgets; vacation—tourist places

MEDIAGRAPHICS OF INDIAN SHOPPERS

FCB Ulka's specialist media division, Lodestar Labcentre, has identified segments using media habits in conjunction with lifestyle parameters. Mediagraphics is a method in which demographic characteristics, product ownership, and media data are used to build segments that can be addressed differently by varying product offerings and media plans. The study involved men and women from the top six metros belonging to SEC A and B, who were categorized into several stereotypes.[23]

Men were categorized as follows:

- *Media-mad fast trackers* (8%), who are younger, upwardly mobile, tech-savvy, and have high media consumption.
- *Settled corpos* (10%), who are older and 'mobile', and have high durable ownership and English media and news interests.
- *Couch potatoes* (10%), who are graduates, live in Mumbai/Delhi, are moving up the durable hierarchy, and follow Hindi TV and a bit of English press.
- *Sarkari babus* (8%), which is a Delhi-dominant category. They are non-innovators. They prefer risk-free investments, watch TV, and are usually Doordarshan viewers.
- *Aiyappan sars* (17%), who are clerical staff in south India, have two-wheeler ownership and satellite TV, and exhibit high cinema viewership.
- The *common man* (22%), who has a lower education and smaller business, is Kolkata-/Delhi-based; and has low cable and satellite (C&S) access.
- *Retail Patels* (17%), who are shop owners in Delhi or Mumbai, and show increased ownership of durables and high C&S viewership.
- *Traditionalists* (8%), who are older clerks/shopkeepers, are close to retirement, own durables of the lower-rung of hierarchy, and are heavy TV viewers.

Women in the same study have been categorized as follows:

- *Media-intense modern Ms*, who are younger, more modern, and career-oriented, and show high media consumption across TV, press (English and local), cinema, or radio.
- *Media medley south skews*, who are better educated. There are significant numbers in this category who are working and have a preference for south Indian TV channels.
- *Cine Meenas*, who are not too well-educated, not Western in outlook, and show high TV viewership but a distinct preference for all film-based programmes.
- The *kahani Kkusum ki* category, which is composed of younger housewives who are better than the Cine Meenas, and are heavy watchers of TV, especially soaps and serials.
- The *Mrs traditionalist* category, which is composed of women who are not well-educated, show lower decision-making, and are more of Doordarshan and regional Doordarshan channel watchers.
- *Simple Sudhas*, who have lower education and income levels, not much spare time, and lower consumption of TV.
- The *amma brigade*, which is composed of older middle-class women, mainly from south India. They indulge in very little reading, but are heavy watchers of regional TV channels. They are afternoon TV addicts.

BEHAVIOUR-BASED SEGMENTATION

It has been found that shoppers change their information search process according to stores, even when the same product and, in some cases, the same brand is being bought. Shoppers ask for a brand in a *kirana* store and resist a change in many cases. In contrast, in a self-service store, they look at more than one brand before deciding. In some cases, they buy only from the shops they patronize regularly, even when they are located at a distance and there are other stores that are closer. This behaviour is very evident among cigarette buyers who have a fixed store, either because of long association or because it is on their way to or from work.

In a study where shoppers were observed at stores dealing in groceries, apparel, household appliances, books and music, shoes, lifestyle products such as cards and gift items, cosmetics, and medicine, a store was classified as belonging to the *new format* when the onus of information search is on the shoppers. In such stores, they have access to the merchandise and can touch and feel the products without the help of the shopkeeper/salesperson, even though they can choose to take the help of the salesperson if they wish to do so. Other stores were categorized as *old format* stores. The shopper segments identified are discussed in this section.[24]

Choice Optimizers   These types of shoppers try to derive the maximum out of their shopping. They optimize their value based on the variety of merchandise, information needed in the shopping process, and quality of merchandise. They are completely involved in the shopping process. They make several queries on product quality and price. They browse through many varieties and take time to choose. Sometimes they even return the product when they are not completely satisfied. A few of them force the salesperson to offer more variety and price discounts. This shopper group is quality conscious and driven by the brand. They also show their individualistic nature by taking purchase decisions on their own even when accompanied by other people.

Premeditated Shoppers The shoppers constituting this group go straight to specific racks or a particular section in a store. They seem to have a limited product choice set. They ask for a particular product/service without looking around and do not seem interested in the surroundings. At times they leave the shop immediately when the desired product is not found. Shoppers in this category buy in large quantities. Some of them buy for the whole family. These shoppers come with a list and buy only from the list. In most cases, they do not try any other product. They are generally oblivious to the displays on racks. Such shoppers rarely ask for options or alternatives.

Economizing Shoppers These shoppers are usually price conscious. They seem to be constrained by their budgets. They may change products and brands if these do not fit within their budgets. They rarely buy anything that exceeds their budget.

Many of them hint at buying elsewhere. While selecting or browsing, they check or ask the price first and put the merchandise back if the price does not suit them. They look around for schemes and tend to head straight towards the discount section as soon as they enter a shop. Some of them carry coupons to be redeemed. Most of them want adjustments in prices in lieu of bulk purchase and try to negotiate prices. They repeatedly ask for bargains and cajole the salesperson to reduce the price.

Support Seekers This group consists of shoppers who tend to show low confidence while making purchase decisions. They need help, either from the accompanying person or from the store personnel, to arrive at purchase decisions. Before making the final purchase, they spend a lot of time consulting others. Usually found to be uncomfortable and nervous inside the store, they do not actively seek a store with a good ambience. However, they seem to be affected by the atmospherics of the store. They pick up the merchandise hesitantly and, on several occasions, leave without buying. Some of them make a purchase even when the desired size or design is not available. They are always found to be over-conscious and defensive about their behaviour within the shop.

Frequent Shoppers vs Infrequent Shoppers The study grouped the shoppers according to the frequency of their visits. *Frequent shoppers* enter the store very confidently and move around comfortably. They do not ask for directions. They go straight to specific racks or a particular section of the store. They seem to know the salesperson. Some of them share jokes and shake hands with the salespeople while leaving the store. *Infrequent shoppers* enter the store more hesitantly and with unsure steps. Most of the infrequent shoppers look around, ask for directions, and rush towards the shopping area or section as soon as the salesperson provides them with directions.

Recreational Shoppers These shoppers seem to enjoy their stay at the shop. They try to derive recreational value out of the shopping process. They derive enjoyment from the shop atmosphere and spend time looking at various displays and windows. Their visits to the shop last longer. They see, read, and listen to almost everything on display. By gesture and activity they express their willingness to spend more time in the shop. Shoppers of this kind can be seen browsing with a very relaxed approach. Most of them do not look to be in a buying mode. They are impulsive and buy products on the spur of the moment. In many cases, they buy at the request of accompanying people, without giving too much thought.

Figure 4.1 shows a mapping of the behaviour segments discussed in this section and the associated product categories.

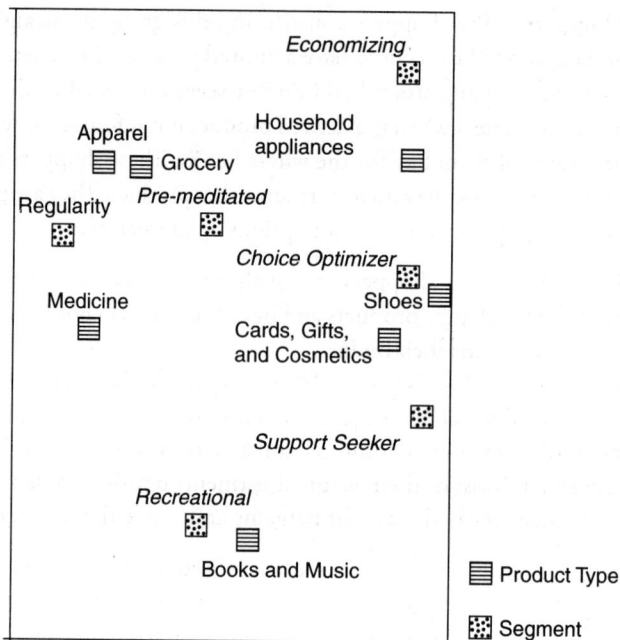

FIG. 4.1   Mapping of the Behaviour Segments
and the Product Category

ATTITUDE-/ORIENTATION-BASED SEGMENTATION

Shopping orientation has been used widely to profile shoppers. This helps in understanding their shopping behaviour. Retailers use such information in formulating their strategies. Orientation-based classification helps retailers to differentiate and target their offerings. Different behaviour by shoppers possessing differing orientations impacts the retailer's decisions with regard to format, location, and promotion. Shopping orientation indicates the way shoppers perform their task of shopping. The evolving retail environment seems to be affecting the orientation. These changes are found to be caused by the decisions taken by the retailer, especially in the areas of store format (such as department store/ online store), socio-economic variables (such as suburban shoppers, middle-class shoppers), and gender. Most studies have found that shoppers seem to have similar demographic profiles in each of these classifications. The typologies, therefore, have been developed on the basis of their attitude and orientation. A summary of typologies recognized in developed countries is given in Table 4.3.

Orientation of Indian Shoppers

A study conducted in India identified orientations that showed similarities in some aspects but also indicated some unique characteristics.

Post-purchase Experience Sharing   The first shopping orientation of Indian shoppers is their inclination towards sharing the shopping experience with friends, colleagues, and neighbours. The subject of these discussions seems to be the merchandise that they found at the store. The respondents want to go shopping as they get an opportunity to look at a variety of merchandise. Shoppers do not seem to attach much importance to the price and touch-and-feel of the merchandise as compared to variety. They show a strong tendency to talk more about the bad experiences of shopping.

TABLE 4.3 Summary of Principal Shopper Typologies[25]

Source/Date	Population	Gender	Sample Size	Research Format	Shopper Types (%)
Stone 1954	Department store shoppers	Female—100%	124	Questionnaire, cluster analysis	Economic (33), personalizing (28), ethical (18), apathetic (17), indeterminate (4)
The Chicago Tribune 1955	Department store shoppers	Female—100%	50	In-depth interviews	Dependent (N/A), compulsive (N/A), individualistic (N/A)
Stephen and Willet 1969	Adult buyers of apparel, shoes, and toys	No reference to gender make-up	315	No. of stores shopped at and patronized	Store loyal (N/A), compulsive/recreational (N/A), convenience (N/A), price/bargain (N/A)
Darden and Reynolds 1971	Head of household	Female	167	AIO statements	Economic (N/A), personalizing (N/A), moralistic (N/A), apathetic (N/A)
Darden and Ashton 1975	Middle-class suburban housewives	Female—100%	116	Self-administered questionnaire, MANOVA	Apathetic (22), demanding (9), quality (19), fastidious (15), stamp preferer (12), convenience (15), stamp hater (8)
Moschis 1976	Cosmetic buyers	Female—100%	206	Questionnaire, factor analysis	Specials (N/A), brand loyal (N/A), store loyal (N/A), problem-solving (N/A), psycho-socializing (N/A), name-conscious (N/A)
Williams, Painter, and Nicholas 1978	Grocery shoppers	Assume 100% female	298	Questionnaire, cluster analysis	Apathetic (20), convenience (27), price (27), involved (11), unclassifiable (15)
Bellenger and Korgaonkar 1980	Adult shoppers	Female—69% Male—31%	324	Self-administered questionnaire, discriminant analysis	Economic (69), recreational (31)

(Contd)

(Table 4.3 Contd)

Source/Date	Population	Gender	Sample Size	Research Format	Shopper Types (%)
Westbrook and Black 1985	Adult shoppers	Female—100%	203	Structured questionnaire, factor analysis	Shopping process involved (12), choice optimizing (18), shopping process apathetic (20), apathetic (10), economic (31), nondescript (9)
Lesser and Hughes 1986	Head of household	Female—55% Male—45%	6,808	Telephone interview, Q-factor analysis	Inactive (15), active (13), service (19), traditional (14), dedicated fringe (9), price (10), transitional (7), convenience (5), coupon saver (5), innovator (4), unclassified (8)
AGB 1987	Housewives	Female—100%	Panel members	Questionnaires, cluster analysis	Caring and conscientious (20), indifferent (21), old fashioned (15), healthy brigade (20), hedonist (23)
Cullen 1990	Principal household shopper	Female—75% Male—25%	2.484	Postal questionnaire, factor analysis	Shopping affect (N/A), economic (N/A), apathetic (N/A), shopping snob (N/A)
Kirk-Smith and Mak 1992	Financial services users	Mixed-unspecified	2,630	Questionnaire, factor analysis	Uninvolved (9), pleasurists (23), conserving carers (22), belongers (24), confident modernists (22)
Jerratt 1996	Adult shoppers	Mixed-unspecified	931	Questionnaire, cluster analysis	Have to (N/A), moderate (N/A), service (N/A), experiential (N/A), practical (N/A), product oriented (N/A)

Managing Stress   Shoppers wish to utilize shopping to manage their stress. They seem to treat shopping as a pastime. They go shopping whenever they are under stress. They feel that salespeople add enjoyment to the shopping experience. There is also a tendency to feel depressed after shopping. This feeling seems to arise out of situations when the time spent on shopping is not seen as utilized well and is considered a waste of time.

Active Information Seeking   Shoppers ask for information actively while shopping. They tend to seek the help of others before making the final decision. In the case of a new product, they may also ask other shoppers at the store for information.

Exploring   Shopping, to the respondents, is found to be similar to exploration. They tend to seek excitement and are curious to know about new things. Shoppers visit new stores to check the merchandise or anything that is novel. They show a tendency to try different things and would not mind visiting several stores.

Feeling Relaxed after Shopping   Shoppers also feel relaxed after shopping. They seem to get a feeling of accomplishment and derive good value from it.

Loyal Shoppers   These shoppers seem to be loyal towards a store. They tend to patronize and buy from a particular store. They are also inclined towards buying branded items. These shoppers feel that shopping takes a lot of effort and hence loyalty to a brand or a store is exhibited. Shoppers with such an orientation feel relaxed before shopping.

Bargain Seeking   These shoppers show an inclination towards seeking bargains. They feel that bargaining is necessary and a shopper could save a lot by bargaining. Such an orientation is found even when shoppers are buying a packaged product where the retail price is fixed or from shops that do not entertain bargaining.

'Go and Grab' Shopping   Some shoppers have the tendency to finish the task of shopping as soon as possible. These shoppers prefer to shop alone. They come to the store, pick or ask for the merchandise, and leave the store immediately after purchasing. They neither spend much time on making decisions at the store nor are they open to any advice.

List Sticking   The shoppers in the study also showed a tendency to make planned purchases. They shop with a list and stick to it in most situations.

Visiting Unplanned   It is found that shoppers do have the tendency to visit the store without planning.

Price-driven Shopping   Shoppers show an inclination towards low price offers. They look for offers that announce lower prices.

Crowd Avoiding   Shoppers also show the tendency to avoid crowds and shop when the store has fewer shoppers.

Shopping from the Nearest Store   Shoppers tend to have a preference for buying from the nearest store. The proximity may not necessarily be from home. It could be from their workplace or from places that they frequent.

Work/Fun Typology

Based on their orientation, shoppers could also be divided into two types: (a) those who enjoy shopping (39%), and (b) those who do not and would, as far as possible, like to avoid it (61%).

Fun Shoppers   These shoppers go to the market with the objective of deriving the maximum value out of their shopping in terms of bargains, information, and enjoyment. For them shopping is another form of entertainment. They make unplanned visits to the store and collect a lot of information before as well as during shopping. They also take the help of salespeople, who they feel add to the enjoyment of shopping. Bargains and low prices attract these shoppers. Bargaining for them is found to be necessary. They feel that a person could save a lot through bargaining. These shoppers also talk about their shopping experiences to others. They seek variety, even when purchasing branded items. Such shoppers consider shopping to be a kind of therapy. They go to the market when they are under stress. They are emotionally charged while shopping and feel relaxed or tense after shopping. Interestingly, this group consists of shoppers who would like to finish shopping as soon as possible and would also like to shop from the nearest store.

Work Shoppers   This group treats shopping as work or an activity that needs to be performed. They consider shopping a waste of time. They would prefer to shop from home. They also tend to avoid crowds. When they do go shopping, it is a pastime. Such shoppers visit stores only when they feel that they have spare time and nothing important to do.

Although there is a lot of similarity in the demographic profile of the shoppers in the two clusters, some differences are noticeable. Fun shoppers consist of more SEC A1, A2, and B1 shoppers as compared to work shoppers. This cluster buys fewer items during its visits to the store. Where the 'work' cluster buys more low-value products, the first cluster buys products of high, medium, as well as low value, compared to the first cluster. There are more men in the second cluster. Also, this cluster consists of shoppers who have been buying from the chosen store for at least three months. However, there is not much difference in the number of shoppers with more than 3 months' association with the store. New format stores attract more fun shoppers than work shoppers. The clusters do not differ in terms of other variables such as the motive of purchase, incidence of purchase on that visit, distance travelled to the store, or the vehicle used for shopping.

SHOPPING PATTERNS IN INDIA

Indian customers are becoming increasingly sensitive in their expectations of products and services, and are seeking a higher standard of quality of delivery. They know what they want. The demands on their time at work and home have made them extremely selective about how they spend their leisure hours. Shopping is also vying with leisure activities. It means that retailers must be better at knowing their customers, predicting their needs and wants, and delivering products and shopping experiences that consistently exceed their expectations so that the shoppers keep coming back to them. Some of the major trends in Indian shopping behaviour are shown in Figs 4.2–4.6 and Table 4.4.

Looking at the spending patterns projected for 2025 in Fig. 4.4, we find that there will be considerable decrease in spending on food, beverages, and tobacco. The share of total consumption would rise for health care and communication.

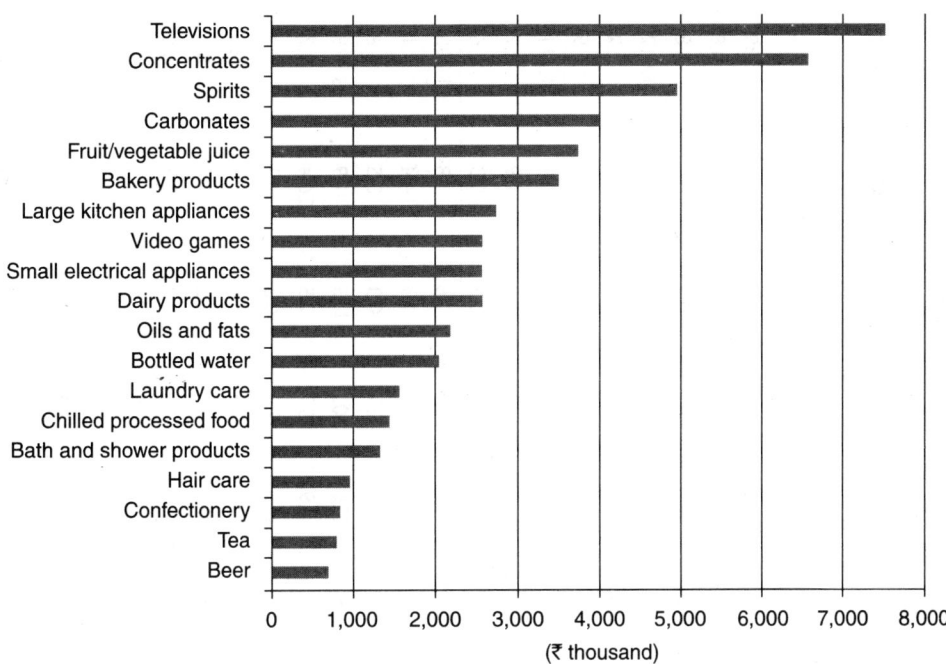

FIG. 4.2   Largest Consumer Market Sectors in India (2010)

Source: Euromonitor International

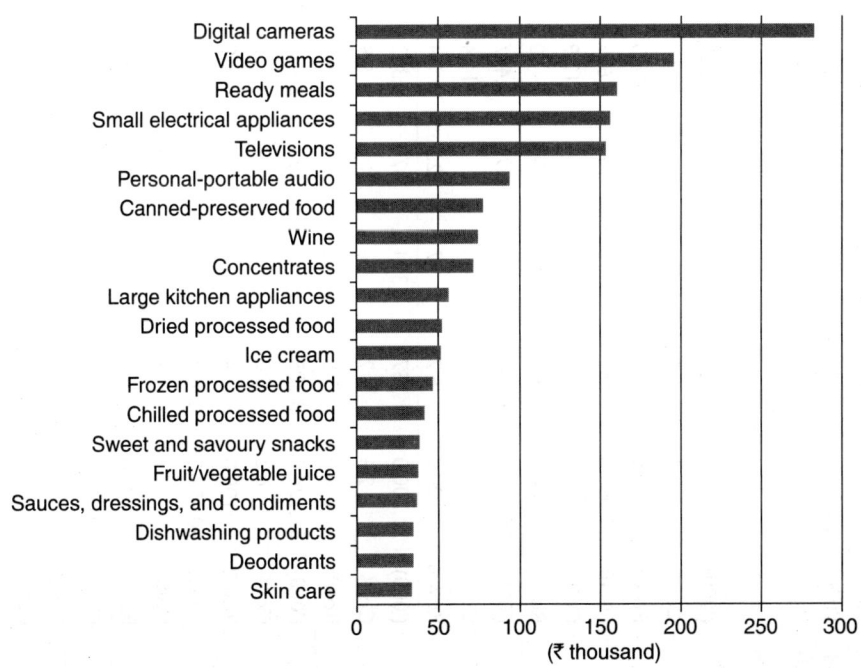

FIG. 4.3   Fastest Growing Consumer Market Sectors (2005–10)

Source: Euromonitor International

TABLE 4.4 Socio-economic Classes—All India

		All	Andra Pradesh	Assam	Bihar	Delhi	Delhi and Urban Environs	Goa	Gujarat	Haryana	Himachal Pradesh	Jammu and Kashmir	Karnataka
Sample	No.	249,990	18,498	4,328	12,353	7,205	10,413	782	14,958	6,072	1,489	785	15,611
Estimated individuals ('000)	('000)	824,288	63,537	21,066	62,839	13,152	15,974	1,203	43,098	18,058	5,220	679	45,013
SECs													
A1	('000)	8852.0	360	91	241	1,623	1,827	14	420	198	18	30	339
	Col%	1.1	0.6	0.4	0.4	12.3	11.4	1.2	1	1.1	0.3	4.4	0.8
	Row%	100.0	4.1		2.7	18.3	20.6	0.2	4.7	2.2	0.2	0.3	3.8
A2	('000)	17,009.0	1,162	216	531	1,695	2,024	31	1,054	413	55	59	1,012
	Col%	2.1	1.8	1	0.8	12.9	12.7	2.6	2.4	2.3	1.1	8.7	2.2
	Row%	100.0	6.8	1.3	3.1	10	11.9	0.2	6.2	2.4	0.3	0.3	5.9
B1	('000)	20,296.0	1,262	342	598	1,497	1,769	58	1,305	358	61	54	1,211
	Col%	2.5	2	1.6	1	11.4	11.1	4.8	3	2	1.2	7.9	2.7
	Row%	100.0	6.2	1.7	2.9	7.4	8.7	0.3	6.4	1.8	0.3	0.3	6
B2	('000)	21,200.0	1,257	334	679	1,302	1,601	61	1,617	574	66	98	1,398
	Col%	2.6	2	1.6	1.1	9.9	10	5.1	3.8	3.2	1.3	14.4	3.1
	Row%	100.0	5.9	1.6	3.2	6.1	7.6	0.3	7.6	2.7	0.3	0.5	6.6
C	('000)	51,524.0	3,305	693	1,283	2,495	3,084	149	3,820	1,202	133	179	3,939
	Col%	6.2	5.2	3.3	2	19	19.3	12.4	8.9	6.7	2.5	26.4	8.7
	Row%	100.0	6.4	1.4	2.5	4.9	6	0.3	7.5	2.3	0.3	0.3	7.7
D	('000)	60,453.0	4,464	782	1,524	2,205	2,747	142	4,371	1,264	106	136	3,963
	Col%	7.3	7	3.7	2.4	16.8	17.2	11.8	10.1	7	2	20	8.8
	Row%	100.0	7.4	1.3	2.5	3.6	4.5	0.2	7.2	2.1	0.2	0.2	6.6
E1	('000)	30,006.0	2,184	346	679	778	1,031	83	2,189	678	59	42	1,727
	Col%	3.6	3.4	1.6	1.1	5.9	6.5	6.9	5.1	3.8	1.1	6.2	3.8
	Row%	100.0	7.3	1.2	2.3	2.6	3.4	0.3	7.3	2.3	0.2	0.1	5.8
E2	('000)	47,479.0	4,622	386	1,886	1,557	1,891	73	3,006	1,179	78	82	2,831
	Col%	5.8	7.3	1.8	3	11.8	11.8	6.1	7	6.5	1.5	12	6.3
	Row%	100.0	9.7	0.8	4	3.3	4	0.2	6.3	2.5	0.2	0.2	6

(Contd)

(Table 4.4 Contd)

		Kerala	Madhya Pradesh	Maharashtra	Orissa	Punjab	Rajasthan	Tamil Nadu	Uttar Pradesh	West Bengal
Sample	No	7,825	11,996	31,895	5,899	6,854	12,760	18,395	39,905	16,782
Estimated individuals ('000)	('000)	27,367	47,862	84,102	30,272	21,033	44,478	56,163	127,250	66,903
SECs										
A1	('000)	180	263	1,590	182	275	282	694	999	746
	Col%	0.7	0.5	1.9	0.6	1.3	0.6	1.2	0.8	1.1
	Row%	2	3	18	2.1	3.1	3.2	7.8	11.3	8.4
A2	('000)	285	939	2,305	436	561	708	1,061	2,033	1,656
	Col%	1	2	2.7	1.4	2.7	1.6	1.9	1.6	2.5
	Row%	1.7	5.5	13.5	2.6	3.3	4.2	6.2	12	9.7
B1	('000)	482	922	3,197	438	744	1,055	1,601	2,272	1,842
	Col%	1.8	1.9	3.8	1.4	3.5	2.4	2.9	1	2.8
	Row%	2.4	4.5	15.8	2.2	3.7	5.2	7.9	11.2	9.1
B2	('000)	489	985	2,968	430	1,000	1,100	1,804	2,530	1,566
	Col%	1.8	2.1	3.5	1.4	4.8	2.5	3.2	2	2.3
	Row%	2.3	4.6	14	2	4.7	5.2	8.5	11.9	7.4
C	('000)	1,494	2,168	8,855	942	1,809	2,130	5,935	5,100	3,312
	Col%	5.5	4.5	10.5	3.1	8.6	4.8	10.6	4	5
	Row%	2.9	4.2	17.3	1.8	3.5	4.2	11.6	10	6.5
D	('000)	2,283	3,334	9,254	1193	1,507	2,485	7,239	6,641	4,939
	Col%	8.3	7	11	3.9	7.2	5.6	13	5.2	7.4
	Row%	3.8	5.5	15.3	2	2.5	4.1	12.1	11	8.2
E1	('000)	1,523	1,856	4,479	574	682	1,381	3,986	2,856	2,459
	Col%	5.6	3.9	5.3	1.9	3.2	3.1	7.1	2.2	3.7
	Row%	5.1	6.2	14.9	1.9	2.3	4.6	13.3	9.5	8.2
E2	('000)	454	3,435	5,695	913	1,147	2,348	39.3	7,492	3,951
	Col%	1.7	7.2	6.8	3	5.5	5.3	6.9	5.9	5.9
	Row%	1	7.2	12	1.9	2.4	4.9	8.2	15.8	8.3

Source: Marketing Whitebook 2009–2010

Share of total consumption, %

Consumption category	United States	Germany	Brazil	South Korea	China	India (2005)	India (2025)
In line with benchmarks							
• Food, beverages, and tobacco	15	21	19	23	35	42	25
• Apparel	4	5	6	4	11	6	5
• Personal products and services	14	10	8	13	4	8	11
Less than benchmarks							
• Housing and utilities	19	27	22	18	9	12	10
• Household products	5	7	9	4	6	3	3
• Education and recreation	12	8	13	16	15	5	9
More than benchmarks							
• Transportation	11	17	13	12	6	17	20
• Communication	1	1	4	2	7	2	6
• Health care	19	4	6	8	7	7	13

Note: Figures are rounded to the nearest integer and may not add up to 100%.

FIG. 4.4 India's Unique Spending Pattern (Share of Total Consumption)

Source: Euromonitor International

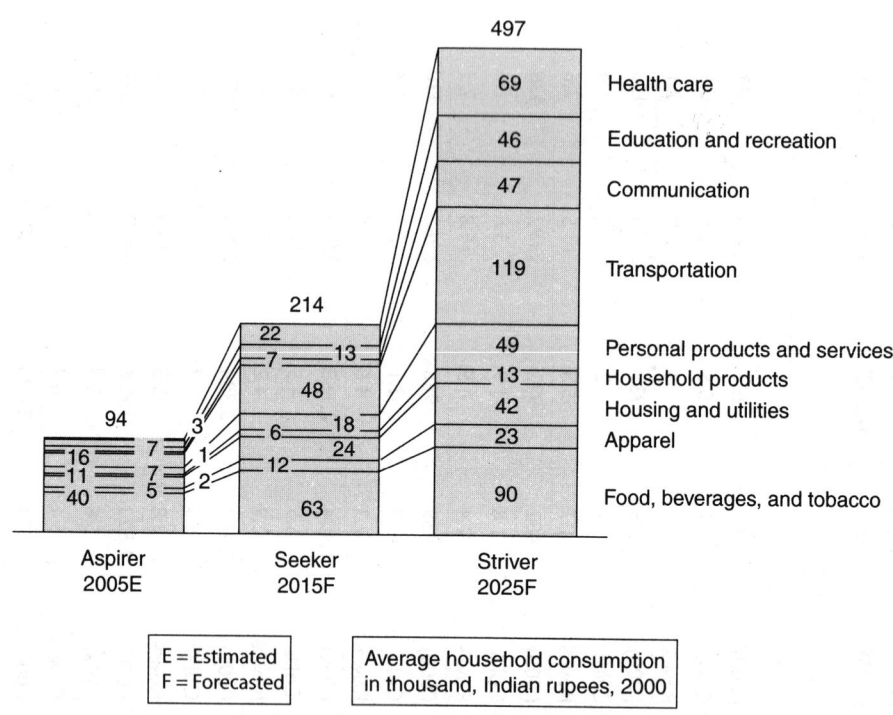

FIG. 4.5 Evolution of Spending for a Typical Household—From Aspirer to Striver

Source: MGI India Consumer Demand Model, v1.0

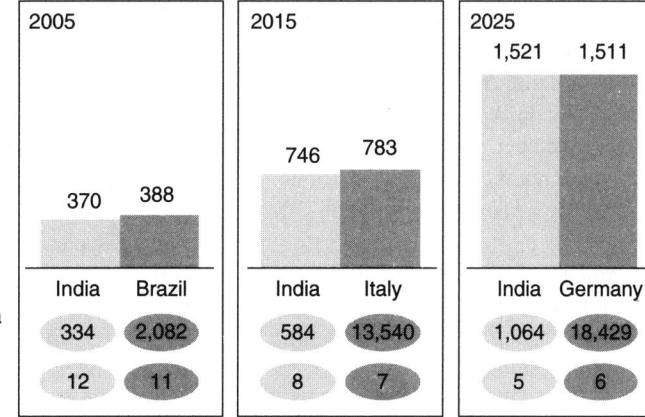

Aggregate private consumption, 2005–25
billion, $, 2000

Note: Figures expressed in billion $, as estimated in the year 2000.

FIG. 4.6 Indian Consumer Market—Poised to Become Fifth Largest in 2025

Source: Global Insight UN Population Division, MGI India Consumer Demand Model, v1.0

SUMMARY

Shopping is an activity that is performed by almost everybody. It involves collecting information for making the best choice. In doing so, customers depict a behaviour which is different from consumption. The values sought by them from shopping tend to be different from the values derived out of consumption. Hence, it is advised that shoppers are treated as a separate class of individuals as compared to consumers. While the economic and demographic profile of both the classes is the same as they may be the same individual or belong to the same household, the gratifications derived out of shopping are different. The costs involved with shopping are of a different nature. Hence, a retailer, unlike a manufacturer, needs to understand customers in a more detailed fashion while profiling them.

To get a holistic understanding of shoppers, it is required that they are profiled from several aspects. A retailer needs to find out the purchase pattern of its shoppers and relate it with the different profiling schemas. It is possible that different segments of shoppers would behave differently. Their behaviour needs to be explained using the most appropriate profiling dimension. In addition to understanding behaviour, it is also important to draw out an attitude-based segmentation of shoppers and determine the association between attitude and behaviour. Several methods are available in the qualitative as well as quantitative research domain for the purpose of drawing attitude-based segmentations of shoppers.

NOTES

1. Woodruffe, Burton H., S. Eccles, and R. Elliott 2002, 'Towards a Theory of Shopping: A Holistic Framework', *Journal of Consumer Behaviour*, February, Vol. 1, No. 3, pp. 256–66.

2. Nava, M. 1996, 'Modernity's Disavowed Women and the Department Store', in Nava, M. and A. O' Shea, (eds), *Modern Times: Reflections on a Century of English Modernity*, Routledge, London.

3. Sinha, P.K. and D.P. Uniyal 2003, 'Using Observational Research for Behavioural Segmentation of Shoppers', presented in the 10th International Conference on Recent Advances in Retailing and Services Sciences, Portland, August 2003.

4. Tauber, E. 1972, 'Why do People Shop', *Journal of Marketing*, Vol. 36, October, pp. 56–59.

5. Kelly, J.R. 1991, 'Commodification and Consciousness: An Initial Study', *Leisure Studies*, Vol. 10, pp. 7–18.

6. Woodruffe, Burton H., S. Eccles, and R. Elliott 2002, 'Towards a Theory of Shopping: A Holistic Framework', *Journal of Consumer Behaviour*, February, Vol. 1, No. 3, pp. 256–66.

7. Berman, Barry and Joel Evans 2003, *Retail Management: A Strategic Approach*, 9th edn, Prentice Hall, Pearson Education, One Lake Street, Upper Saddle River, New Jersey, USA, p. 219.

8. Levy, Michael and Barton A. Weitz 2004, *Retailing Management*, 5th edn, McGraw-Hill Higher Education, Columbus.

9. Berman, Barry and Joel Evans 2003, *Retail Management: A Strategic Approach*, 9th edn, Prentice Hall, Pearson Education, One Lake Street, Upper Saddle River, New Jersey, p. 219.

10. Connolly, A. and D. Firth 1999, 'Visual Planning—the Power of Thinking Visually', *Journal of Brand Management*, Vol. 6, No. 5, pp. 161–73.

11. http://www.indexmundi.com/india/demographics_profile.html, accessed on 22 March 2011.

12. http://www.unhabitat.org/habrdd/conditions/socentasia/india.htm, accessed on 24 April 2004.

13. www.euromonitor.com, accessed on 22 May 2011.

14. AT Kearney, http://www.rediff.com/money/2002/aug/21retail.htm, accessed on 24 April 2004.

15. 'Consumers and Markets: The Rural Consumer', *The Marketing Whitebook 2003–04*; *The Essential Marketer's Handbook, Business World*, p. 96.

16. http://www.unhabitat.org/habrdd/conditions/socentasia/india.htm, accessed on 24 April 2004.

17. www.euromonitor.com, accessed on 22 May 2011.

18. Parameswaran, M.G. 2003, 'Understanding Shoppers: Building Powerful Brands Using Shopper Research', Tata McGraw-Hill.

19. Dobhal, Shailesh 2001, 'Selling to the Indian Male', *Business Today*, September 2.

20. MTV's 2001 survey of India's young adults (15–24 years), *The Marketing White book* 2003–04, *The Essential Marketer's Handbook, Business World*, pp. 108–13.

21. Parameswaran, M.G. 2003, 'Understanding Shoppers: Building Powerful Brands Using Shopper Research', Tata McGraw-Hill.

22. MICA 1998, 'VALS among Residents of Ahmedabad', unpublished study.

23. Parameswaran, M.G. 2003, 'Understanding Shoppers: Building Powerful Brands Using Shopper Research', Tata McGraw-Hill.

24. Sinha, Piyush Kumar and Dwarika Prasad Uniyal 2005, 'Using Observational Research for Behavioral Segmentation of Shoppers', *Journal of Retailing and Consumer Services*, Vol. 12, No. 1, pp. 35–48.

25. Brown, S. and R. Reid 1997, 'Shoppers on the Verge of a Nervous Breakdown', in Brown, Stephen and Turley, Darach (eds), *Consumer Research Post Cards from the Edge*, Routledge, London and New York, pp. 79–149; Westbrook, R.A. and W.C. Black 1985, 'A Motivation-based Shopper Typology', *Journal of Retailing*, Vol. 61, No. 1, Spring, pp. 78–103.

CONCEPT REVIEW QUESTIONS

1. Define shopping and the shopping process. How is shopping different from buying?

2. Describe the shopping behaviour of customers. How is it related to consumption?

3. Based on their behaviour, what are the different ways in which shoppers can be segmented? What are the strategic implications for this segmentation?

4. How do shoppers differ in terms of their orientation towards shopping? How would you use this information in a retail business?

CRITICAL THINKING QUESTION

Discuss the consumer buying process. Identify the position of the shopping process in the complete buying process. Describe the relationship between shopping and other parts of the process. Draw implications for a retailer.

PROJECTS

1. Visit a store. Observe the way customers shop in different types of stores. Draw inferences.
2. Stand in one of the aisles of a self-service store. Observe ten shoppers. Draw the decision-making process and its implications.
3. Meet ten customers before they enter the store. Find out details about the list that they were carrying (physical or mental). Check the list after purchase. Find out whether the actual purchase was different from the list. Assess the reasons thereof.

CASE STUDY

Muebles: The Home Building Store[1]

It was July 2002 and Mr S.N. Patel was flipping through the customer complaint report as a part of his routine weekly activity. A smile of satisfaction appeared in the bearded gentle face of the Managing Director as he went through a report—Many customers had visited the shop 100 times! Muebles had become the talk of the town. Staring through the seventh floor window overlooking the Ahmedabad concrete skyline, he knew his market lay there. However, the composition of his customers had changed from what he had envisaged. When the store had started, it had aimed to reach all those who were building their houses and to sell them the required material. After a year, however, he noticed that the building materials, what he called the invisibles, did not sell as much. They were still being bought from the traditional markets. What was bringing in customers were products that were used to 'fill the shelf', called the visibles. Mr Patel was wondering if he would have to find a new positioning for his store.

Muebles Limited, a home building and improvement store, was a pioneer in its field. Its aim was to provide better-designed home improvement solutions under one roof. It was established in January 2001 as a part of the Casa Moblaje Group's foray into the Indian retailing business. Exhibit CS4.1 lists the goals and objectives of the organization.

Indian Retail Industry

The Indian retail landscape was undergoing a process of evolution, and was poised to undergo a dramatic transformation. The Indian retail industry was not only one of the most fragmented in the world but also the

---

EXHIBIT CS4.1   Mission/Goals of Muebles

Mission   To reduce the trauma of home building

Vision   To accomplish the mission through establishing chain of retail store of home building and improvement.

Goals
- To provide all the merchandise under one roof
- To provide merchandise with improved design content, aesthetics, and functionality
- To provide goods of assured quality at reliable price
- To provide information and customer service for facilitating decision-making
- To assure a pleasant shopping experience unique in this product category

Source: Company documents

---

1. Case written by Prof. Piyush Kumar Sinha, Rowena Rumnong, and Shantanu Varma (PGP 2003–05), Indian Institute of Management Ahmedabad (IIMA).

most challenging due to its unorganized nature. In its nature, the Indian retail market's situation was in sharp contrast to the global situation. The retail sales in India amounted to $180 billion and accounted for 10–11 per cent of the GDP. The Indian retail market had around 12 million outlets and had the largest retail outlet density in the world. However, most of these outlets were basic mom-and-pop stores with very basic offerings, fixed prices, and no ambience. But these were highly competitive stores due to cheap land prices and labour. Also, these stores evaded tax most of the time due to their unorganized format.

There were several challenges that Indian retailing had to face. Prominent amongst them were real estate issues, capital availability, legal framework, human resources, supply chain development and management, and logistics. Retailing as a major sector of the economy had yet to receive any overt political or bureaucratic support, and its success and growth largely depended on the initiatives of the government. Varying sales tax and octroi[2] rates in different states remained the biggest hindrance to the growth of the sector. The high costs of real estate owing to constrained supply were also one of the major factors that were inhibiting the growth. The relevant rules needed to be amended to allow retail stores to operate every day with longer hours, and to enable utilization of part-time employees without incurring any extra cost. The bottlenecks in the supply chain resulted in limited assortments and increased costs of sourcing.

However, Indian retail had strong potential, which was propelled by the dramatic lifestyle changes taking place in the Indian household. In the decade before 2002, India's middle and high-income population had grown at a rapid pace of over 10 per cent per annum, even as the large low-income base had shrunk. The changing Indian woman and family structure drove the demand for convenience. They became more demanding vis-à-vis store ambience and looked for solution providers and external guarantors of quality and usability. Thus, the Indian customer was becoming more demanding and was increasingly focusing on value, convenience, variety, and a better shopping experience. The increase in variety, quality, and availability of products as well as an increase in spending power had resulted in consumers increasingly using supermarkets for their personal shopping. Malls which fused shopping value with entertainment were springing up in many parts of the country.

There was a significant number of new competitors in the retail market, and the established players were expanding. With the government all set to open FDI approvals in retail chains, the entry of multinational retail chains was expected to change the entire retail scenario of the country.

Indian Retail Consumer

The consumer base was growing, that is, the per capita income growth had outstripped the growth in wholesale price index. Consumers were becoming more affluent and, as a result, disposable income had increased. India witnessed around 36 per cent population in the age group of 15–34 years, which was more than that of any other country. This segment, due to the shift in demographics and changes in lifestyle, was seeking parity with global living standards. The demographic shift had occurred due to the phenomena of urbanization, nuclearization of the family, and increase in the number of working women.

All these factors had contributed towards change in attitude of the Indian consumer towards shopping and lifestyle. The consumer had started combining shopping with leisure or socializing, but still, late night shopping was of nascent interest. The Indian consumer did get dissuaded by the brand clutter, was reluctant to pay a premium for the 'brand', and was satisfied with department store shopping.

Home Building Industry

The home building market in India was highly fragmented, undercapitalized, and lacked the 'one stop shop' format, which resulted in inconvenience to the consumer. The organized sector had a small share in the industry, which made shopping for home and building products a time consuming activity. The organized sector consisted mainly of speciality stores with a limited range of merchandise. The unorganized sector had little or no differentiation and price undercutting was a common phenomenon. As a result, the quality of the product varied and low-to-high quality products without any fixed prices characterized the market.

According to a study by the National Council of Applied Economic Research (NCAER), the number of households in the very rich and the consuming class—the target segment for this category of goods—was predicted to increase from 166 million households in 1994 to 200 million households in 2005 (Table CS4.1).

---

2. A tax on various goods brought into a town/city, extensively used in India.

TABLE CS4.1   Customer Segmentation

Segmentation	No. of Households (in Millions)	
	1994	2005
Very rich (₹390,000 p.a.)	1	6
Consuming class (₹81,000–₹390,000 p.a.)	30	75
Climbers (₹40,000–₹80,000 p.a.)	50	75
Aspirants (₹29,000–₹40,000 p.a.)	50	24
Destitute < ₹29,000 p.a.	35	20
Total	**166**	**200**

Source: National Council of Applied Economic Research

The ambience of the market was unfriendly to women/family shoppers and there was limited choice of assortments. In fact, the whole shopping experience was very intimidating to the average consumer who had either no or minimal knowledge and information about the products. The servicing aspect was very crucial because the 'trauma', as some consumer termed the shopping experience, severely discouraged shoppers to repeat their purchases. The small and independent retailer most of the time did not possess adequate knowledge about the product category and after-sales support was inadequate, which further compounded this 'trauma'.

The distribution and retailing of building products was a weak link in the construction industry. Also, material procurement and retail practices were a major cause of dissatisfaction among home builders and renovators.

The home and building store was broadly divided into two major segments.

Building Materials Segment   India witnessed construction worth ₹2,000 billion every year, of which 67 per cent was accounted for materials. The value of the usage of cement had increased from 400 million tonnes in 1996 to 700 million tonnes in 2001. The value of the construction sector had gone up to ₹3,721,450 million in 2001 from ₹970,250 million in 1996.

Soft Furnishing Segment   The market for home improvement products was roughly at ₹16,000 million.[3] The home improvement market was divided into four categories—bedroom (₹7,250 million), bathroom (₹4,000 million), kitchen (₹1,600 million), and hardwood

products consisting of tableware, home décor, storage, and lighting (₹3,250 million). By 2005, this market was expected to grow to roughly ₹18,000–19,000 million, with bedroom accounting for ₹8,500 million, bathroom at ₹4,750 million, kitchen at ₹1,900 million, and hardwood at ₹3,800 million.

Studies had estimated that there were opportunities for at least three organized stores per city, each with a ₹500 million business potential every year. It was also estimated that there was room for at least 3–4 national players retailing such products, in addition to 5–6 regional players.

Competition

Any new retail format in the home and building sector was expected to face stiff challenge from the existing small, independent, and powerful local retailers. The new format was expected to attract major national retail players to invest in this sector. Some of the major retailers in this sector were The Home Store, KSS Homepro, Arcus, and Muebles. International retail giants like Home Depot, IKEA, and Lowe were also eyeing the new Indian home and building market, which was largely untapped by organized retailers. These players, with their experience, best practices, size, and power, posed a major threat to any national retailer in this sector. Speciality stores like Gautier were also going to compete in this segment.

The home and building retail market in India had home improvement stores in line with the global majors such as Home Depot and B&Q, which offered almost all the product categories and services that were required to build a new home or for home improvement or renovation under one roof. Muebles, belonging to the Casa Moblaje Group, was a pioneer in this segment. Homepro, a 350,000 square feet building material supermarket, was India's first building mall consisting of shops, offices, a food court, and entertainment areas. It offered a wide range of building materials, home improvement products, and furnishings. On the services side, this supermarket provided information about land availability and selection, and housed the offices of architects, designers, and financiers. It was also a meeting point for contractors and labour. On the other hand, there were other speciality formats coming up in one or more individual categories. The Home Store and Zeba were in the home furnishing segment; Gautier dealt in furniture; and Johnson Tiles was in the sanitary ware sector.

3. KSA-Technopak, India

Muebles

The background, market size and share, communication strategy, and consumer profile of Muebles are discussed here.

Background

Muebles Limited was set up in November 2000 at Ahmedabad by the Casa Moblaje Group with an objective of creating a national chain of retail stores engaged in retailing home and building products. Since its inception, the store had been a destination store for the whole of Ahmedabad and other cities and towns in and around Ahmedabad even as far off as Jaipur and Baroda. Though the company had initially planned to open 10 stores in 3 years, as the organization moved up the learning curve, it decided to accelerate its activities cautiously. It planned to capture the Ahmedabad market and the surrounding market first. Keeping economies of scale in mind, the company wanted to exploit the goodwill in the present market and align its supply chain properly.

The store had a strategic location. The national highway ran by the side of Muebles. Visibility and traffic, to a great extent, was due to the heavy traffic on this road. The format of the new store was such that visitors could gaze into the store from a distance.

Muebles provided a unique shopping experience to the consumers. On a tangible basis, consumers were provided a wide range and assured quality, competitive prices, and world-class service. This was further accentuated by unique value-added services, such as

- comprehensive design assistance by a panel of professionals and design consultants,
- apartment packages,
- installation and service support,
- infomediation through website,
- home loan consultancy and loans,
- certification programmes for electricians, masons, plumbers, and carpenters,
- educational programme on do-it-yourself techniques and procedures,
- customer loyalty programmes, and
- other services such as cafe, ATM, kids play zone, etc.

Market Size, Share, and Growth

The organization had captured a large market of the home building and construction business in the growing town of Ahmedabad as well as the home improvement

business of the surrounding cities and towns. While Ahmedabad contributed to approximately 60 per cent of the total store traffic, Gandhinagar contributed 35 per cent. The average footfall was around 15,000 per month. The figure was skewed towards weekends (around 800 per day) as compared to weekdays (400–500 per day). The rate of conversion was 35 per cent with an average bill value of ₹14,500.

The company faced seasonality in different times and experienced either slumps or peaks in footfall and sales. For example, before and during any festive season there was tremendous increase in demand, while it witnessed a slump during the rainy season and few visitors came to the store. The company aligned all its departments to the seasonality. For example, during Diwali and other festive seasons, it concentrated its efforts in stocking paints, furnishings, and kitchen appliances.

The store was slowly becoming a destination store for the market it covered and was performing better than expected. Figure CS4.1 shows a break-up of actual versus budgeted sales.

The Store

'Muebles does not have any policy other than satisfying the customer', Mr Patel claimed proudly. In fact, the whole organization and its activities were customer centric. As a matter of policy, managers were supposed to visit the shop floor 3 hours a day to understand shopper's behaviour and needs better.

Each category had 4 floor personnel. The total floor level employees were around 20. The floor employees tracked the customer right from the moment they entered the store and observed them carefully from a distance. The motive was to help the customer in the selection process without interfering. The staff was instructed to respect the privacy of the customers.

The store was laid out in a grid format. It was functional in nature and was based on a 'do-it-yourself' model. Thirty per cent of shop space was given to 12 partners (vendors) who had complete freedom of operation. Design centres were set up using CAD/CAM to assist the consumer choose home décor and furnishings.

The store atmosphere was attractive. The background music and lighting conveyed the seriousness of the store, at the same time, it was sophisticated. The store format aided the consumer in finding the 'right' product. Some products, like toilet fittings, kitchen fittings, or tiles were merchandised in simulated conditions to give the

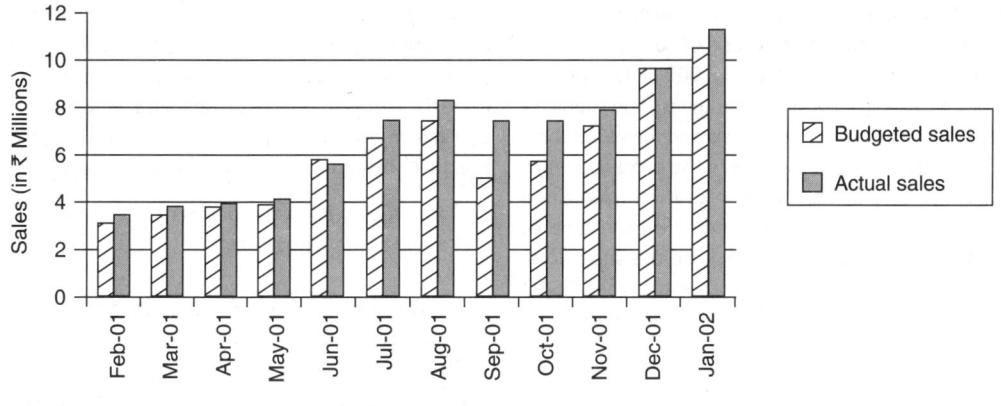

FIG. CS4.1 Budgeted vs Actual Sales

Source: Company documents

customer a feel of the complete range of the store's offering.

The store provides products that were not easily available in traditional hardware stores. Though the merchandise included almost all material of home building and improvement, it offered a narrow and deep selection through a judicious mix of 'one off' and recurring purchase items, hard and soft goods, and imported and domestic goods so that they appealed to both the professional and the consumer.

The store stocked products under five major categories:

- *Kitchen accessories*: appliances, crockery, glassware, ovens, etc.

- *Furniture and furnishing*: sofa set, bed, linen, etc.
- *Bathroom*: tiles, sanitary ware, fittings, taps, and accessories
- *Hardware*: visible (door, window), safety equipment, gardening tools, washing machines
- *Electrical equipment*: lights, luminaries, chandeliers, switches, fans, generators, etc.

The store mainly stocked branded products. The store brand was developed where reputed brands were not available. In the selection of brands, the store policy was to use only the number one brand or the aggressive second. In cases where this was not possible, the company entered into agreements with smaller players who provided them with in-store brands. Over

Muebles: Ambience

the year these suppliers had grown with the store. Suppliers were evaluated on the basis of cost of ordering. The store stocked approximately 12,000 SKUs and had 120 suppliers (30% large branded partners). The suppliers were engaged on a consignment basis and delivered their goods to a central warehouse where the products were bar coded. Normally, 60 days of inventory was maintained at the warehouse. However, depending on the type of product, there would be more stock on the shop floor (e.g. light fixings) than in the warehouse. Table CS4.2 provides information on the space utilization within the store.

TABLE CS4.2   Space Utilization at the Store

Categories	Display Space (expressed in percentage)
Bathroom fittings	20
Furniture	15
Kitchen and kitchen appliances	15
Lighting	12
Hardware	15
Electrical appliances	12
White goods	4
Other (paints, furnishings, etc.)	7

Source: Company documents

The store allowed the partners to employ their own personnel and merchandise the space without interference. In return, it charged a fixed rent and a certain percentage over a fixed sales volume. Interestingly, since Muebles has a policy of not favouring any particular brand, the store personnel were differentiated from partners' personnel by their dress code to enable the customer to differentiate between the two.

As the store moved upward in the retail evaluation wheel and gained experience of the local needs and demands, it took the invisible and less involved products off the shelf. Though the store did not stock products such as cement, sand, iron hardware, and bricks, customers could place an order for these products. The visible and high involvement products replaced the invisible. The store was also increasing its share of storing impulse goods in the relevant home decoration and furnishing category.

The pricing policy of the store varied across the product categories. Pricing was competitive and benchmarked against the traditional hardware and home building material stores in product categories which were usually available in traditional hardware stores. In the destination product[4] category, the store charged premium price.

Table CS4.3 gives the performance measures of the store and some categories.

TABLE CS4.3   Performance Measures

Gross margin	10–30%
Net sales last year	₹77 million
Revenue per sq. ft	₹2600
Service (design and home building consultancy) contributes to the whole revenue	10%

Category	Net sales	Margin
Furnishing and furniture	25%	> 25%
Hardware and electrical	30%	15%
Homebuilding project	8%	8%

Communication Strategy

As a response to its analysis of its potential customer base, Muebles decided to pursue a multi-pronged approach to increase the levels of awareness. They broadened the base with which they were communicating by using a mix of media for brand and tactical advertising and used the Gujarati and English media to reach out to their target segment. They developed two separate communication packages, one for the lay consumers with low comprehension of Muebles's value proposition, and another for the professionals (home builders) who had a relatively higher awareness of the concept.

For invisible products, some of the issues that they had to resolve included the fact that home builders usually contracted the shell and the woodwork of the house and got involved in the finishing stage. Moreover, the purchases were likely to be infrequent, and the builder difficult to communicate with and likely to be 'overawed' with Muebles. Thus, Muebles had to decide how to persuade the contractors to buy cement, steel, and wood from Muebles.

In order to increase sales in this sector, Muebles decided to educate the home builder. The homebuilder

---

4. A destination product is defined as a product not available in traditional stores.

package consisted of developing a critical mass of professionals by rewarding their purchase and then working towards giving them Muebles accreditation through a professional course so that they would buy all their material from Muebles. It would enable them to learn as well as socialize with other consumers and build a loyal customer base for Muebles. Muebles estimated the cost of acquisition of these customers to be ₹300–400 per customer and anticipated business of about ₹1 million from them.

The apartment package consisted of using direct mails and tie-ups with companies such as Electrolux, Pergo, and ICI to give special deals to the five different types of apartment owners. Apartments were classified into four categories according to value (Table CS4.4). They targeted the HR departments in companies and offered special deals. The biggest hurdle to this strategy was the acquisition of a database of apartment owners as apartments change hands frequently and there was no way of knowing the final owner.

TABLE CS4.4   Categories of Apartments (by value)

Flat Type	Value (in millions)	Finishing (in millions)
Luxury	Over 5	0.3–0.5
High income	Over 2.5	0.25–0.3
Middle income	Over 1.5	0.15–0.2
Low income	Over 0.7	0.1–0.15

Changing Customer Profile

The changing customer profile of Muebles is described in this section.

Mr Muebles of Yesteryears   When Muebles started out in November 2000, it categorized the ideal 'Mr Muebles' as a homebuilder, a renovator, and an apartment owner.

Home builders   This includes that segment of customers who wanted to build a new home from scratch, demolished existing houses to construct new ones, or added new floors to the existing house.

Renovators   These were customers who were constructing additional rooms, changing fittings, floorings, and electric finishings, or constructing additional rooms.

Apartment owners   This group includes all those who were looking to get additional facilities or improve

existing facilities, such as good flooring, quality electric wiring, furnishing, bathrooms or to construct additional rooms.

Among the last two segments, basic furniture (wardrobes, closets, and cabinets) and renovation of kitchen/bathrooms claim priority over other types of constructions/improvements. The store quickly realized, however, that although the potential 'Mr Muebles' was aware of the store, he could not comprehend the concept that Muebles proposed. He perceived the store as 'expensive' and exclusive.

Apart from the three categories mentioned here (which they termed as the 'lay consumer'), Mr Muebles could also be a professional such as an architect, an interior decorator, a contractor, or a sub-contractor.

Process of Construction/Improvement   The target customers usually had a rough estimate of their budget based on the money available and their own or their acquaintances' experiences.

The process followed by the individual differed depending on the type of construction/improvement. The process of construction followed by the three segments is shown in Figs CS4.2 and CS4.3.

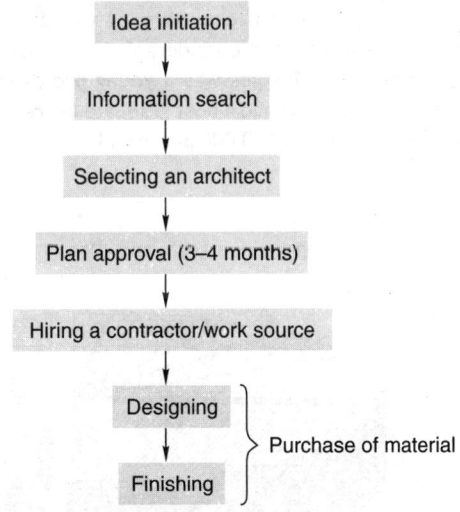

FIG. CS4.2   New Home Builders: Process of Construction

In addition, this market was also subdivided into two product categories, namely structure or invisibles (e.g., cement, sand, Badarpur bricks, metal rods, stone charcoal), and finishing or visibles (wood, marble/granite,

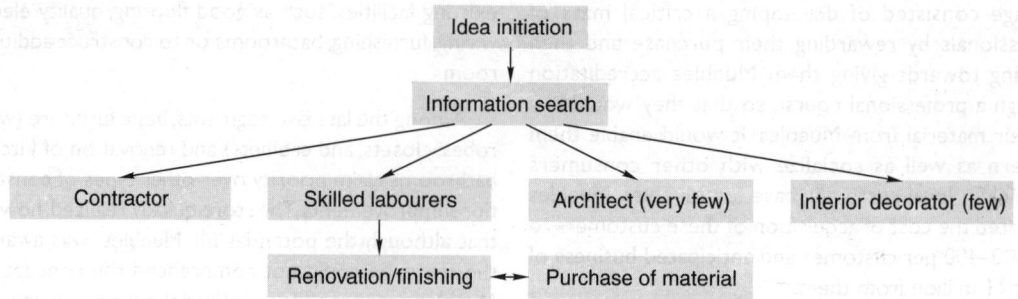

FIG. CS4.3   Renovators/New Apartment Owners—Process of Construction

hardware/sanitary ware, fittings, glassware, electrical fittings, paints).

Muebles needed to provide its potential Mr Muebles with a compelling reason to visit it because, once the customer was there, the store would sell itself. Muebles was confident that the customer would be a satisfied customer because of the range of products and the prices at which they would be offered. However, they needed to provide the consumer with an incentive to visit the store.

The Changed Mr Muebles   Recent studies had shown, however, that the profile of the average 'Mr Muebles' had changed considerably in the last few years. The new Mr Muebles was a young professional who was well educated, had a post graduate degree, and earned well (more than ₹30,000 per month). He drove a

car, usually a big one, had credit cards, and owned all the consumer durables proudly, would soon be replacing his TV/fridge, and was likely to buy the latest laptop. To put it succinctly, Mr Muebles had 'arrived' (Fig. CS4.4).

Mr Muebles was building his own house or was renovating his old one (Fig. CS4.5). He had taken the advice of his spouse or his friends while buying accessories for his kitchen or his bathroom or electrical fittings that reflected his lifestyle (Fig. CS4.6). He liked to shop at Muebles because it was convenient, and because he was sure of the quality and confident of finding what he needed (Fig. CS4.7). He was no longer the Mr Muebles of yesteryear who had not been aware of Muebles and, in fact, had high expectations of Muebles on all his visits. Mr Muebles was likely to visit the store frequently. About 84% of Muebles customers were repeat customers, with

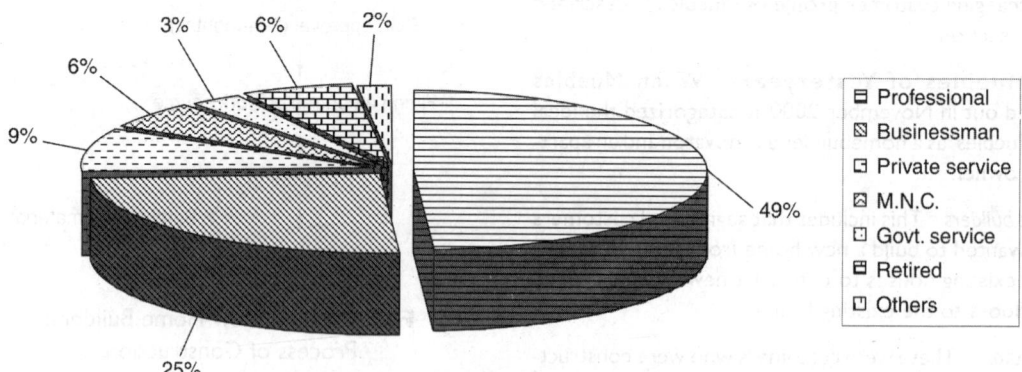

FIG. CS4.4   Demographics of Mr Muebles

Source: Company documents

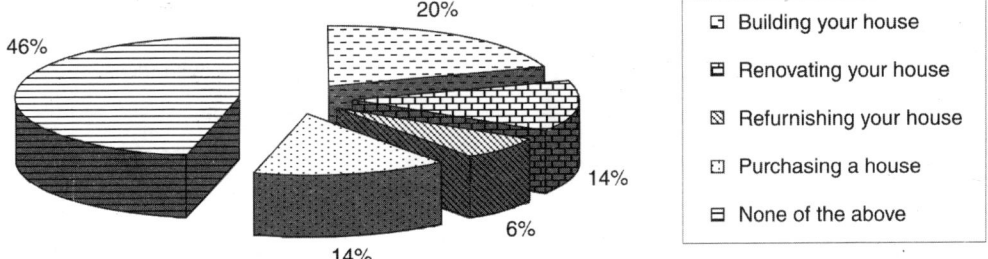

FIG. CS4.5 Potential Customers of Muebles

Source: Company documents

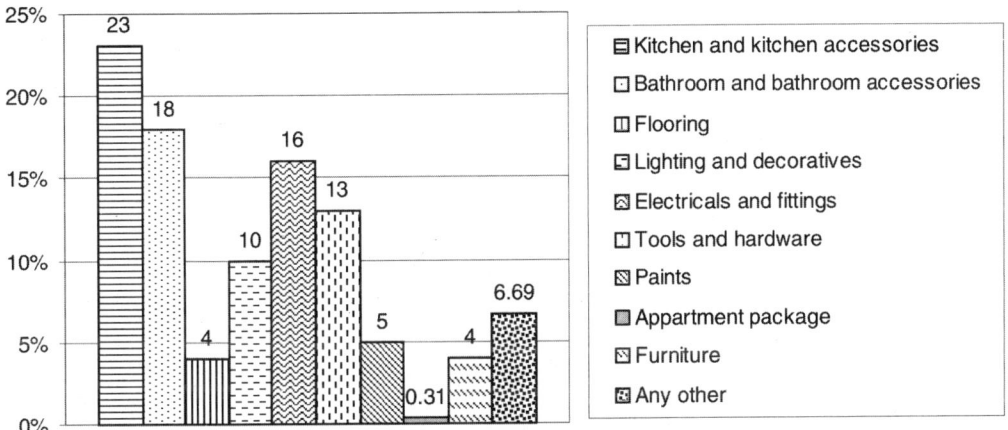

FIG. CS4.6 Purchase by Category

Source: Company documents

over 65% having visited the store more than 5 times. Figures CS4.8—CS4.10 provide more information on Mr Muebles.

The Road Ahead

Mr Patel faced a challenge in the changed environment. The store was planning to open new outlets in the year 2002. The top management team had put forward a strategy that aimed to reposition the store from being a home and building product retailer to being a solution provider in the area of home renovation and furnishing. They wanted the store to become a partner in the process of home improvement. 'While this seems possible, I am concerned about the changes we would have to bring to merchandise and the delivery mechanism for rendering the service. Although in the past two years we have doubled our sales, I am worried that in case of a shift from the home and building position we might invite competition also from stores like IKEA who are planning to enter India soon,' cautioned Mr Patel. Some of the questions with which he was grappling with included:

How should Muebles change its positioning to address this new consumer? In fact, should Muebles change its positioning? Should it change the way it viewed its target customer? Should it redefine its market, its scope, and its reach? What was the way forward for Muebles?

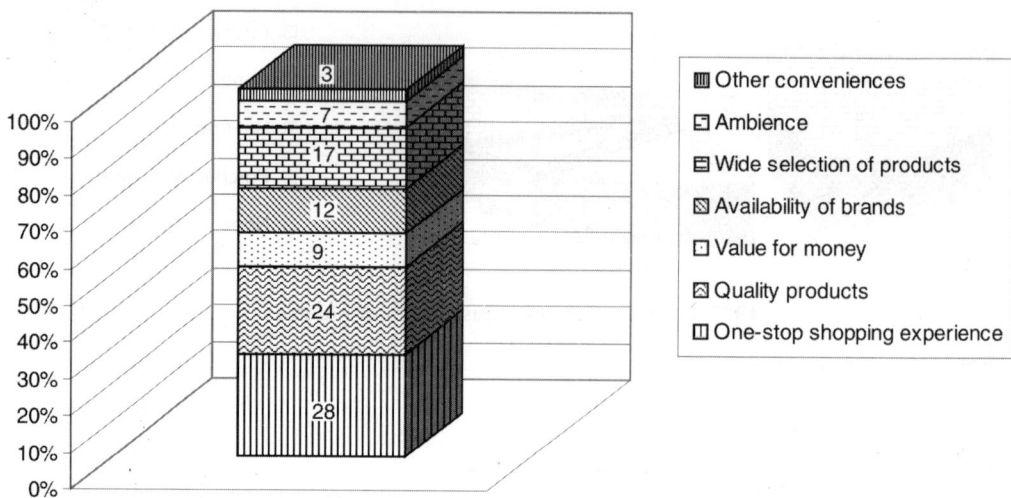

FIG. CS4.7   Perceptions about Muebles

Source: Company documents

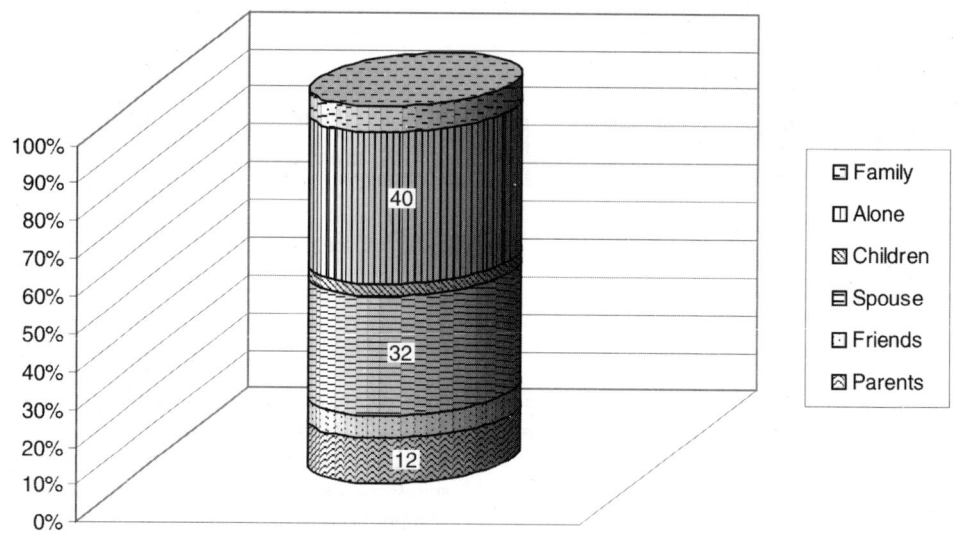

FIG. CS4.8   Purchase Influencers

Source: Company documents

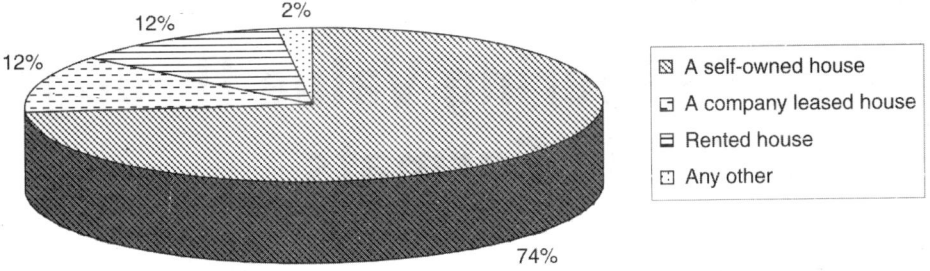

FIG. CS4.9 House Ownership

Source: Company documents

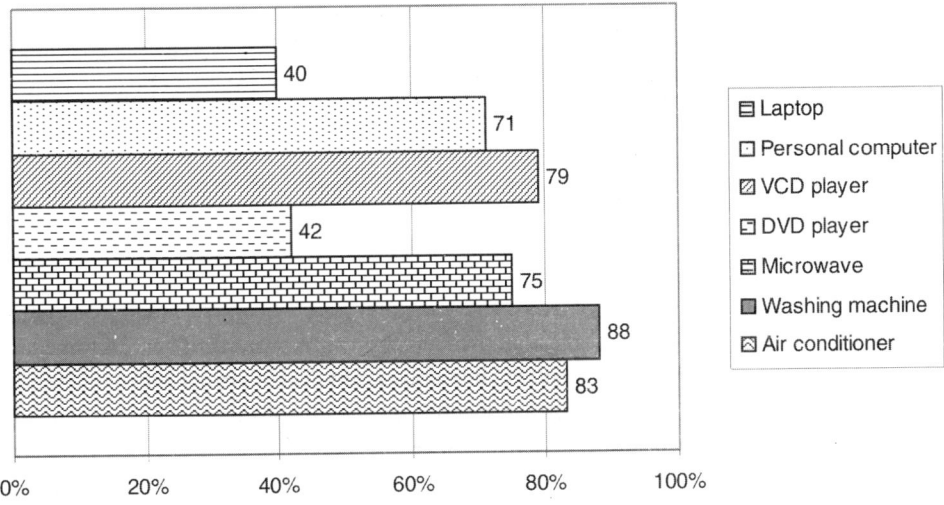

FIG. CS4.10 Durable Ownership of Mr Muebles

Source: Company documents

Questions

1. Enumerate the differences in the profiles of the old and the new customers of Muebles. What changes does it bring with regard to consumer's behaviour?

2. Discuss the changes the store may have to bring about in light of the changing scenario.

3. Should Muebles think of changing its positioning? What would the new positioning be? What would be some of the major changes it may have to bring in order to establish its new positioning?

5 Delivering Value through Retail Formats

LEARNING OBJECTIVES

After studying this chapter, you will be able to
- understand the formats used by retailers
- develop an appreciation of the challenges in e-tailing
- differentiate formats on the basis of values derived by the customers
- chalk out a process for deciding the format for delivering the required value

INTRODUCTION

The retail format is the store 'package' that the retailer presents to the shopper. A format is defined as a type of retail mix used by a set of retailers.[1] It is a place, physical or virtual, where the vendor interacts with his/her customer.[2] The store format depends on the mix of variables such as assortment, price, transactional convenience, and experience that retailers use to develop their business strategies.[3]

Each retailer needs to evaluate the enablers and deterrents for succeeding in the marketplace. This primarily involves identifying the key drivers of growth, the shoppers' profile, and shopper expectations. It also requires the retailer to evaluate the nature of competition and challenge in the marketplace. The retailer then decides the elements of the retail mix to satisfy the target market's needs more effectively than its competitors. The choice of retail mix elements enable it to decide the type of format or structure of business.

CLASSIFICATION OF FORMATS

The term 'retail institution' refers to the basic format or structure of a business. The classification of retail institutions is necessary to enable firms to better understand and enact their own strategies: selecting an organizational mission, choosing an ownership alternative, defining the goods and service category, and setting objectives. Figure 5.1 shows a breakdown of the three categories of retail institutions.[4] The classification is not mutually exclusive; that is, an institution may be correctly placed in more than one category. For example, a department store unit may be part of a chain, have a store-based strategy, accept mail order sales, and have a website.

The format choices have been studied for retail format evolution, price format sensitivity of shoppers and its impact on shopping basket size, stability of format choices through comparison of inter- and intra-format switching behaviour and role of market conditions, perceived shopping

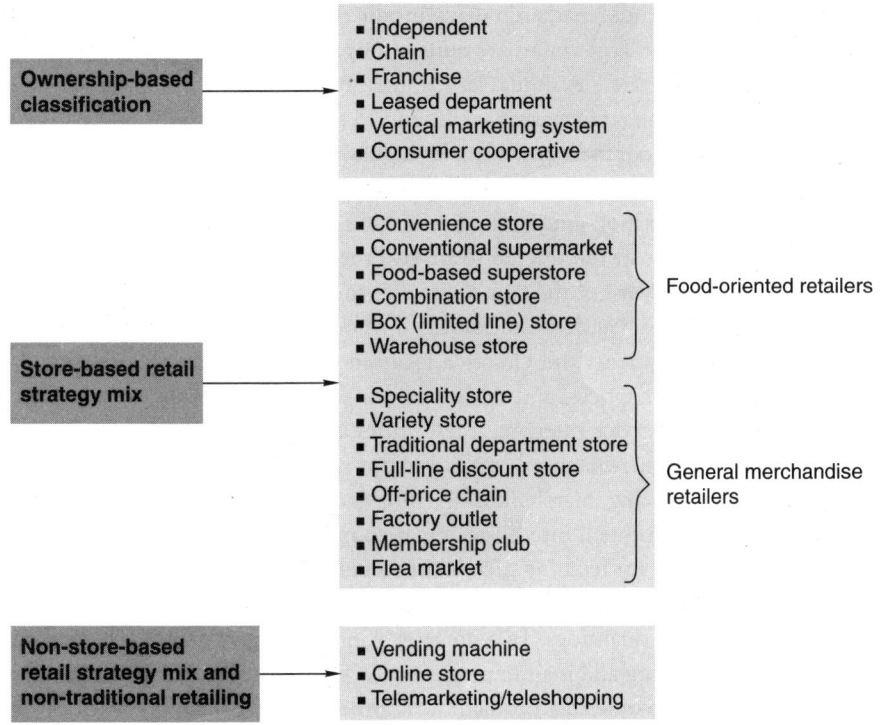

FIG. 5.1 Classification of Retail Institutions

Source: Berman and Evans 2001.

utility of different price formats, effects of exogenous variables and pricing formats on store choice, retail format competition, and providing entertainment. Format choice is also expected to be more stable than store choice with customer switching among stores but remaining within the format.[5]

Ownership-based Classification

Retailing is one of the few sectors where entrepreneurial activity is extensive. More than 80 per cent of all stores across the world operate with one outlet and over one-half of all firms have less than two paid employees.

Retail firms may be independently owned, chain owned, franchisee operated, leased departments, owned by manufacturers or wholesalers, or consumer owned.[6] From a positioning and operating perspective, each ownership format delivers unique value. In order to be successful, retailers need to keep in mind the strengths and weaknesses inherent in each of these formats.

Independents

An independent retailer owns a single retail unit. Independents account for more than 80 per cent of the total retail establishments. However, their share varies based on the development of the economies. While in the US these firms account for just 3 per cent of the total US store sales, in developing countries such as India, their share is almost 97 per cent. A majority of them are run entirely by the owners and their families and have no paid workers. The high number of independent retailers is associated with the ease of entry into the marketplace, owing to low capital requirement and simple licensing procedures.

This creates a very fragmented market in many product categories. For example, in the grocery store category in the US, where large chains are quite strong, the five largest grocery retailers account for only about 22 per cent of sales.[7] A similar large format in India contributes less than 3 per cent of the total retail sales. The Indian retail market has around 15 million outlets and has the largest retail outlet density in the world. Most of these outlets have very basic offerings and offer over-the-counter service. These are highly competitive stores due to cheap land prices and labour.

There is fierce competition among firms, resulting in a high rate of failure. It is estimated that one-third of new retailers in the US fail to survive their first year, and two-thirds fail to continue beyond their third year. Most of the failures involve independents.

Independents enjoy a great deal of flexibility in choosing retail formats and locations. They look for smaller consumer segments and choose a location so that they can serve the customers with a targeted merchandise mix, prices, and other services. A large number of them tend to specialize in a particular product or service category. These stores are labour intensive with a very low level of technology. These are owner-managed establishments with the owner taking all the decisions. Most of the work related to buying, merchandising, and fund management are carried out by the owner. Independents tend to allocate limited time and resources to long-term planning. Other people in the store are used mainly for fetching merchandise and managing the racks.

While they have several advantages, independents have limited bargaining power with suppliers as they often buy in small quantities. They are largely influenced by the other channel members. Due to low economies in buying and maintaining inventory, the transportation, ordering, and handling costs are higher. To overcome this problem, a number of independents form buying groups. To offset the disadvantage of economies, these retailers offer complementary merchandise and services. Compared to other formats, independents tend to use less of advertising and more of personal and point of purchase (PoP) communication. The most common advertising media in India are the free standing inserts in newspapers. Since most independents offer home delivery, the delivery person becomes another source of information. The personal attention paid to the customers by the owner is the most potent tool for customer retention.

Chains

A chain retailer operates multiple outlets (store units) under a common ownership and name. Retail chains can range from comprising two stores to over 1,000 stores. Some retail chains are divisions of larger corporations or holding companies. In developed economies, they account for nearly a quarter of retail outlets and over 50 per cent of retail sales.

Chain retailers have several advantages. They enjoy strong bargaining power with suppliers due to the volume of purchases. They generally bypass wholesalers—many of them buy directly from the manufacturers. Suppliers service the orders from chains promptly and extend a higher level of service and selling support. New brands reach these stores faster. Most of these chains sell private label brands. Wider geographic coverage of markets allows chains to utilize all forms of media. Most chains invest considerable time and resources in long-term planning, and in monitoring opportunities and threats.

Chain retailers suffer from limited flexibility as they need to be consistent throughout in terms of prices, promotions, and product assortments. They have high investments in fixed assets and rent, product assortments, and employees. Due to their spread, these retailers have reduced control, poor communication, and time delays. Thus, such retailers focus on managing a specific retail format for a better strategic advantage and increased profitability. They use innovative strategies to manage costs. In India, chains like Subhiksha implement just-noticeable changes with respect to *kiranas* and manage to differentiate themselves at a low cost.

Franchising

Franchising is one of the most common modes of expansion in retailing. More than one-third of all retail sales are made by franchisees. It signifies a contractual agreement that allows the franchisee to operate a retail outlet using the name and format of the franchiser. The franchisee pays a fee and royalty on all proprietary for operating a store on behalf of the franchiser. The franchiser provides assistance in locating and building the store, developing the products and services sold, management training, and advertising.[8] In return, the franchisee operates the outlet based on the norms and practices laid down by the franchiser.

There are two types of franchising: *product or trademark franchising* and *business format franchising*. In product or trademark franchising, the franchiser allows the use of the identity but does not control the operations. The franchisee may draw up certain operating rules in consultation with the franchiser. In a business format franchising arrangement, the two parties enter into a symbiotic relationship. The franchiser draws out the strategic plans and lays the procedures for operations. The aim is to deliver similar service across all outlets. The franchisees are responsible for the operations and profitability of the stores under the given guidelines. For instance, in the convenience stores located at the BP petrol stations, the merchandise mix, markups, and planograms of the stores are decided by the company. The franchisee can change the merchandise mix to the extent of 20 per cent only to suit the local requirements.

Due to its several advantages to franchisees as well as franchisers, franchising is one of the most popular formats. Franchisers gain a wide presence quickly and with less investment. It improves cash flow as money is obtained from fees, royalties, and merchandise sales. Individual franchisees can become part of a chain and take advantage of the economies as well as knowledge of the franchiser with relatively small capital investment. Since franchisees are owners and not employees, they tend to bring their entrepreneurial skills in growing the business. Franchisees may also have to face certain disadvantages. The agreement does not allow any territorial exclusivity and hence franchisers can open new stores in the same trading area, leading, many times, to over-saturation. On the other hand, bad franchisees can harm a retailer's overall reputation. Ineffective franchisees impact the profitability and may lead to a network with a long tail.

Leased Departments

A leased department is a department in a retail store rented by a manufacturer. The manufacturer is responsible for running the department. It pays the store a rent for using the premises. Leased departments are run on similar lines as an exclusive company store, except that they are located in another store. The leased departments are generally given to non-core product lines. Some common examples of leased departments are food courts, studios, and banks. They require a different set of skills that the main store personnel may not posses and hence complement each other despite being independent. Leased departments help the stores in generating greater traffic and providing one-stop shopping. This arrangement reduces expenses as many of them are shared. However, there may be inflexibility due to the restrictions imposed by the operations of the main store. Also, the main store may seek to replace the existing lessee with newer companies and hence always demand a rise in rent even when lessees are successful.

Consumer Cooperatives

A consumer cooperative is a retail firm where consumers invest in the enterprise. The profits are distributed among the members as dividends. Consequently, even when these stores sell at the same prices, consumers tend to gain. The stores are managed by elected officials. They are started mainly to guard against the malpractices that many retailers indulge in terms of higher prices or inconsistent quality. Consumer cooperatives are limited in number because consumers are usually not experts in buying, handling, and selling goods and services, and the cost savings and low selling prices have not been as expected in many cases. Many of them also become a hotbed of politics. Apna Bazaar in Mumbai is an example of a consumer cooperative.

Store-based Classification

Retail institutions may be classified on the basis of store-based strategy mix and divided into food-oriented and general merchandise retailers. Selected aspects of the strategy of store-based retail institutions are shown in Table 5.1.[9]

Food-oriented Retailers

The major strategic formats used by food-oriented retailers are convenience stores, conventional supermarkets, food-based superstores, combination stores, box (limited-line) stores, and warehouse stores. These formats are discussed in this section.

Convenience Stores　A convenience store is a neighbourhood store. These stores are also known as *kirana* stores in India. Ease of shopping and personalized services are the major reasons for the patronage of these stores, even when they charge average to above-average prices and carry a moderate number of items. They stay open for long hours and provide an average atmosphere. The service levels are moderate within the store, although in India, they provide home delivery and credit as well. Convenience stores are often referred to as 'mom-and-pop' stores. They are visited for fill-in merchandise, and emergency purchases. Most customers shop at least two to three times a week at these stores. These stores carry up to 1,000 SKUs. In India, they are generally over-the-counter (OTC) serviced outlets. Convenience stores face most competition from supermarkets that have started providing longer hours and better stocks of non-food items.

Conventional Supermarkets　A conventional supermarket is a self-service food store offering wet and dry groceries and with a limited range of non-food items, such as health and beauty aids and general merchandise. They carry 5,000 to 10,000 SKUs. They are chosen due to variety, self-service, and promotions. Self service allows supermarkets to cut costs as well as increase volume. The conventional supermarket was once the most common format.[10] However, competition from other formats due to different value drivers, such as better prices from hypermarkets and better service from *kirana* stores, has led to a reduction in the number of such stores in developing markets. India, however, is witnessing growth of this format.

Hypermarkets　Hypermarkets are combination stores that unite supermarket and general merchandise sales in one store, with the latter typically accounting for 25–40 per cent of total sales. Consumers choose them for one-stop shopping and do not mind travelling to visit these stores. Hypermarkets achieve operational efficiencies and cost savings through their large-scale operations. Impulse sales are high in such stores, even when the visit is planned.

TABLE 5.1 Store-based Retailers

Type	Retail Mix Elements			
	Location	*Assortment*	*Services*	*Prices and Promotions*
Traditional department store	Business district, shopping centre, or isolated store	Extensive width and depth of assortment, average to good quality	Good to excellent	Average to high prices, heavy advertising and catalogue use, direct mail, personal selling
Full-line discount store	Business district, shopping centre, isolated store, or strip centre	Extensive width and depth of assortment, average to good quality	Slightly below average to average	Low prices, heavy use of newspaper advertising, price-oriented, moderate sales force
Speciality store	Business district, shopping centre, or regional mall	Very narrow width of assortment, extensive depth of assortment, average to good quality	Average to high/excellent	High prices, heavy use of displays, extensive sales force
Hypermarket	Stand-alone	Average	Low	Low
Variety store	Business district, shopping centre, or isolated store	Good width and depth of assortment, below average to average quality	Below average	Heavy use of newspaper advertising, self-service
Off-price chain	Business district, suburban shopping strip, or isolated store	Moderate width but poor depth of assortment, average to good quality, low continuity	Below average	Use of newspaper advertising, brands not advertised, limited sales force
Factory outlet	Out-of-the-way site or discount mall	Moderate width but poor depth of assortment, some irregular merchandise, low continuity	Very low	Little, self-service
Membership club	Isolated store or secondary site	Moderate width but poor depth of assortment, low continuity	Very low	Little, some direct mail, limited sales force
Flea market	Isolated site, race track or arena	Extensive width but poor depth of assortment, variable quality, low continuity	Very low	Limited, self-service
Drugstore	Stand-alone, strip centre	Very deep	Average	Average to high
Home improvement centre	Stand-alone, power strip centre	Very deep	Low to high	Low

Box (limited-line) Stores The box (limited-line) store is a food-based discounter that focuses on a small selection of items and few additional services. The merchandise consists of few or no refrigerated items and few SKUs and brands per item. Items are displayed in cut cases. Customers carry the merchandise in their own bags. Box stores depend on low-priced private label brands. They aim to price merchandise 20–30 per cent below that of supermarkets. They are very similar to convenience stores, except in terms of merchandise, price, and service.

Warehouse Stores A warehouse store or club is a retailer that offers food and general merchandise with limited services and at low prices, mainly to other retailers, although the final consumers can also buy directly from these stores. These stores appeal to price-conscious consumers who do not mind buying in large quantities and stocking them at home. Warehouse stores are membership-based retail outlets. Such stores are large in size and are generally located in low-rent areas. The store layout is simple and race-track type. As in a warehouse, the aisles and racks are large, suitable for large trolleys to move around. The proportion of private brands in such stores is higher. The assortment is planned on the basis of prices and availability of merchandise. Customers may not get the same brand or SKU of merchandise in every visit.

General Merchandise Retailers

The major formats used by general merchandise retailers are department stores, full-line discount stores, speciality stores, off-price stores, variety stores, and flea markets. These are discussed in this section.

Department Stores   A department store is known for its large assortment and service. The goods and services are organized into separate departments, with each department looking after its own operations. These stores cater to customers who are not price-conscious and are ready to pay for the service. Ambience plays a very important role in such stores. These stores offer a full range of products and services. They offer branded products as well as store brands that are known for quality. They have well-planned merchandise return policies and run loyalty programmes. These stores are the anchors in a shopping centre or mall. They help in attracting very high traffic. Conversion rates are low in such stores. A department store with 30 per cent conversion rate is considered very successful. These stores have to face competition from all formats as they deal in several products and services.

Full-line Discount Stores   A full-line discount store is known for offering an assortment at a price that is discounted up to 50 per cent of the prices charged by department stores. It targets the mass market that looks forward to the best bargain. It is likely to carry the range of merchandise similar to a department store. It reduces its costs through a very low level of service, private brands, and spartan fixtures and ambience. Competition is forcing these stores to improve the experience and service to the customers without compromising on the price.

Speciality Stores   A speciality store deals in a specific product or service. Speciality stores also provide a high level of service to their customers. These stores carry medicine, books, photography, toys, jewellery, hardware, and home improvement products. Category killers and do-it-yourself (DIY) stores belong to this category.

A *category killer* is a specialist discount store. It attracts customers by offering a particular product at the lowest price and the largest assortment. Category killers are known to kill brands by making price the most important buying consideration. In the process, they commoditize the category. According to a report in the *European Retail Digest*, the category killer format will be burnt out due to increasing competitive intensity. These retailers concentrate on reducing costs by increasing operational efficiency and expanding into less competitive international markets. Although they are generally large in size, some category killers are choosing to downsize their format to make it fit small towns, though to a mixed result.[11]

Do-it-yourself stores are a popular format, but are yet to find success in many parts of the world. These stores are category specialists who offer equipment and material mainly to contractors to make home improvements. They look like warehouse stores. Salespeople are available to assist customers in selecting merchandise through demonstrations and workshops. Individual customers also buy from such stores. One such store that has made DIY the core benefit and leveraged it to become one of the largest retailers is IKEA. Unlike warehouse stores, it is a place where customers can be creative and choose what they visualize with the help of design consultants.

Off-price Stores   Off-price retailers sell branded merchandise and designer labels at a low price. They generally offer a range of out-of-season designs, seconds, and order rejects. The buying is totally opportunistic, though many of them have evolved buying strategies that establish long-term relationships with suppliers. Three special types of off-price retailers are *factory outlets*, *closeouts*, and *single-price retail stores*. Off-price retailers are affected most by discount stores and better planning by the manufacturers. However, the unpredictable nature of fashion products results in excess stock and rejects. Factory outlets have become popular formats mainly due to the trend of out-of-town shopping coinciding with the rise of discount formats, creating a climate suitable for the growth of value retailing, and the relaxation of planning guidelines for the development of new out-of-town retail formats.[12]

Variety Stores   A variety store handles a wide assortment of inexpensive and popularly priced goods and services, such as stationery, gift items, women's accessories, health and beauty products, toys, imitation jewellery, and greeting cards. They do not carry full product lines. Transactions are often on a cash basis. They face competition mainly from speciality stores, discount stores, hypermarkets, and closeout off-price retailers.

Flea Markets   A flea market is a form of traditional street selling. It is a place with many retail vendors offering a range of products at lower prices. Shoppers pick and sample the products. Bargaining for prices is common. These markets are located mainly in places where there is high traffic or people come together for a function or an event. At a flea market, individual retailers rent space based on the duration of occupation, which could be on a daily, weekly, or seasonal basis. However, there are many flea markets that are permanent in nature and have become landmarks of the town. They have found a place on the Web too, with offers from eBay and Amazon.com's zShop.

Non-store-based Classification

Non-store retailing is a form of retailing in which sales are made to consumers without using physical stores.[13] Non-store retailers are known by the medium they use to communicate with their customers, for example, direct marketing, catalogue stores, vending machines, and e-tailing. Non-store retailing formats are patronized by time conscious consumers, consumers who cannot easily go to stores, and compulsive buyers.[14] Most non-store retailers offer consumers the convenience of making purchases anytime throughout the year and delivery at a location and time of their choice.

Non-store sales are now growing at a higher rate than sales in retail stores. The high growth rate is primarily due to the growth of e-tailing. The growth of sales in catalogue stores and other non-store retailing formats such as TV home shopping, direct selling, and vending machines is slower.[15]

Vending Machines

A vending machine is a retailing format involving the coin- or card-operated dispensing of goods (such as beverages) and services (such as life insurance sales at airports).[16] It eliminates the need for sales personnel and allows for round-the-clock sales. Machines can be placed wherever they are most convenient for the consumers—inside or outside a store, in a hotel corridor, at a station, airport, or a street corner.

Although many attempts have been made to 'vend' other products, beverages and food items remain the largest category. Hotels, restaurants, and train stations are highly visible spots for vending, but vending accounts for a small proportion of sales. High priced items have not sold well through vending machines because too many coins are required for each transaction and many vending machines are not equipped with currency note changers. Many consumers are reluctant to purchase more expensive items from vending machines as they cannot see them displayed or have them explained, and there is the difficulty of returning unsatisfactory merchandise. In evolved markets, vending machine sales have experienced little growth in the period 2000–2005, largely due to the changes in the workplace.

To improve productivity and customer relations, vending machine retailers use microprocessors to track consumer preferences, trace malfunctions, and record receipts. The devices transmit data back to the host computer. This data is analysed and communications are sent to route drivers, informing them of stock-outs and malfunctions. Some machines even have voice synthesizers. Video kiosks enable consumers to assess the merchandise and also use their credit cards to make a purchase. In India, vending machines are at a very nascent stage. Almost all of them are operated by an attendant. Even coffee machines are operated with assistance. Companies such as Cadbury and Malayala Manorama (a newspaper publishing house) have installed them at places that attract a lot of traffic, such as at the airport. However, sales from these are limited.

Electronic Retailing (E-tailing)

Electronic retailing, also called e-tailing, online retailing, or Internet retailing, is a retail format in which the retailer and customer communicate with each other through the Internet. After an electronic dialogue between the retailer and the customer, the customer can order the merchandise. The merchandise is then delivered at an address of the customer's choice.

Started on venture capitalist (VC) or initial public offering (IPO) money, e-tailing had attracted a lot of hype by 1999. Consumers were thought to be ready to make a deliberate choice of buying from e-tailers rather than retailers. E-tailing seemed to fulfil the consumer dream of no queues, no geographic barriers, low prices, and unlimited selection—what retailing had failed to deliver.[17] However, e-tailing ended up disappointing consumers, who found that traditional shopping was easier. The Ernst & Young statistics for the 1999 Christmas season revealed that US online buyers spent only 26 per cent of their holiday spending (averaging $1,080 per capita) online, while they devoted 67 per cent of their total holiday expenditure to in-store purchases, and the remaining 7 per cent on catalogue products. More than 90 per cent of e-tailers closed down in the period from the end of the 2000 holiday season to January 2001.[18] E-commerce witnessed the collapse of several online grocers, drugstores, auto dealerships, pet supply stores, and other budding e-commerce ventures, and hundreds of dotcom investors abandoned their dreams of getting rich quick with e-commerce.[19]

However, retail e-commerce sales grew to $7.5 billion, up to 24.7 per cent in the second quarter of 2001, compared with just under $6 billion in the second quarter of 2000.[20] It was expected that online retail sales would exceed $30 billion by 2007.[21] European customers were likely to spend more money on the Internet than American customers. More than 5 per cent of grocery shopping would be carried out on the Internet. In the UK, this figure was likely to be 7 per cent, whereas the Nordic countries were expected to buy 6 per cent of their grocery through the Internet. France and Germany were supposed to account for more than 3 per cent of the sales on the Internet in 2007.[22] However, the global online retail sector grew by 14.5 per cent in 2009 and reached a value of $348.6 billion. In 2014, it is projected to have a value of $778.6 billion, an increase of 123.3 per cent since 2009. The largest segment of this sector is electronics, accounting for 22.6 per cent of the sector's total value. The Americans account for 45.7 per cent of the global sector value.[23] The present players in the market are trying to learn the lessons from the failures and success of extinct and surviving e-commerce pioneers.

Forrester Research put out a new five-year forecast predicting that e-commerce sales in the US will keep growing at 10 per cent compound annual growth rate (CAGR) through 2014. It forecasts that online retail sales in the US will be nearly $250 billion, up from $155 billion in 2009.[24]

The Internet can serve one or more of the following roles for a retailer:[25]

1. Project a retail presence.
2. Generate sales as the major source of revenue for an online retailer or as a complementary source of revenue for a store-based retailer.
3. Enhance the retailer's image.
4. Reach geographically dispersed consumers, including foreign ones.
5. Provide information to consumers about the products carried, store locations, usage information, answers to common questions, customer loyalty programmes, and so on.
6. Promote new products and fully explain and demonstrate their features.
7. Furnish customer service in the form of email, 'hot links', and other communication.
8. Be more personal with consumers by letting them point and click on topics they choose.
9. Conduct a retail business in a cost efficient manner.
10. Obtain customer feedback.
11. Give special offers and send coupons to web customers.
12. Describe employment opportunities.
13. Present information to potential investors, potential franchisees, and the media.

The role assigned to the Web by a given retailer depends on whether it is predominantly a traditional retailer that just wants to have a web presence or a newer firm that wants to derive most or all its revenues from web transactions.

The strong growth of Internet retailing is evident from Figs 5.2 and 5.3. It can be clearly seen that the economic downturns have had least impact on the growth of online retail sales and Internet users worldwide.

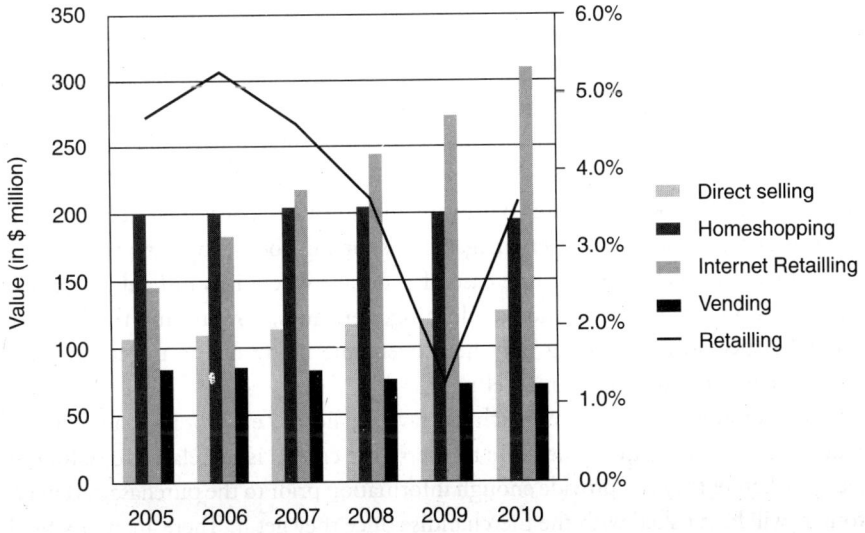

FIG. 5.2   Growth of Online Retail Sales

Source: Euromonitor International

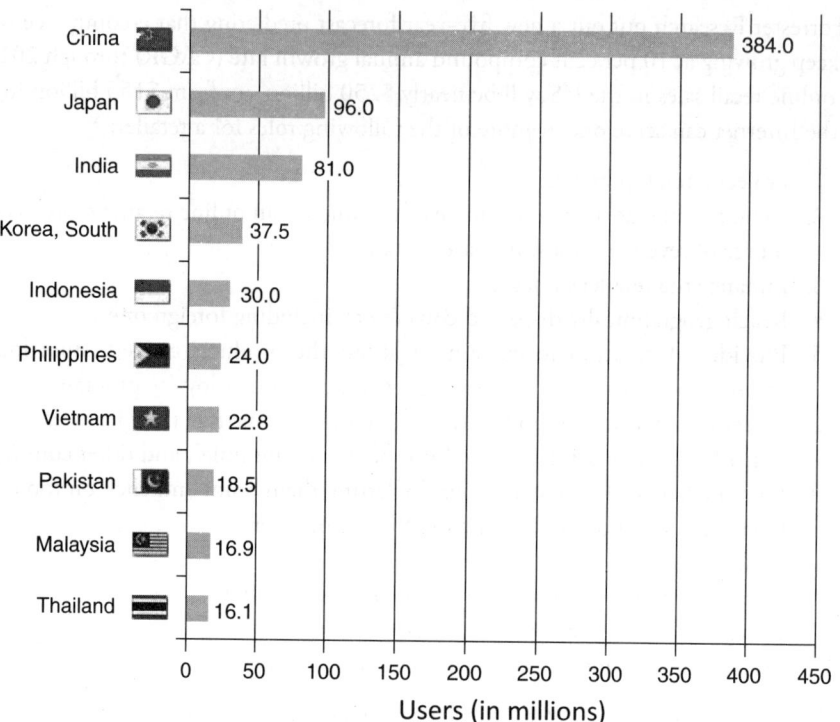

FIG. 5.3   Growth of Internet Users in Asia

Source: www.internetworldstats.com/stats3.htm

Forrester Research forecasted that, in 2007, 13 per cent of US retailing would be conducted via the Internet.[26] Non-US markets accounted for about 30 per cent of the e-commerce industry.[27] In India, non-store retailing represented by direct selling and e-tailing was estimated at ₹1,100 crore. Although only 19 per cent of all retailers had an e-tailing initiative, the number of retailers with plans to venture into e-tailing within one year and those with no plans were almost equal. Significantly, 10 per cent of retailers had discontinued their e-retail initiatives by then. The main reason for retailers to stay away from e-tailing is predominantly non-viability of business and resource constraints.[28] It was estimated that 5 per cent or more of retail sales of goods and services such as apparel, banking, books, computer hardware and software, consumer electronics, gifts, greeting cards, insurance, music, newspapers/magazines, sporting goods, toys, travel, and videos would be made online.[29] It is believed that, the case of products where it is difficult to provide 'touch and feel' information electronically, such as clothing, perfumes, flowers, and food, electronic retailers may not be successful. Branding may help overcome many of the uncertainties in purchasing merchandise without touching and feeling it.

In some products and services, such as travel or hotels, electronic retailers have been able to provide superior information than store retailers. The critical issue related to selling successfully for e-tailers is whether they can provide enough information prior to the purchase and make sure that the customers will be satisfied with the merchandise once they get it. There are many buying situations in which electronic retailers can provide sufficient information, even though the merchandise has important 'touch and feel' attributes, as in case of books and music.

According to the Ernst & Young Global Online Retailing report, the main reasons that non-buyers avoid buying online are discomfort in sending credit card information, preference for seeing the product before purchasing, no existence of credit card, insufficient information about products to make decisions, lack of confidence in online merchants, and non-availability of the opportunity to talk to salespeople. In addition, the main concerns of online buyers are overly high shipping costs; need to try for fit in the case of apparel; high prices; inappropriateness of the format for large, perishable, and luxury items; need to feel and see; and concern of privacy.[30] The report also indicated that consumers restrict their online shopping due to price, security, and ease of navigation.

E-tailers have high fulfilment costs. It could be as high as US$16 per order. Lack of scale makes the business unprofitable. Poor inventory management also causes major losses. E-tailing also involves higher marketing costs. According to Thomas Weitzel Partners, while a superstore spends an average of US$2.50 promoting a product, e-tailers spend US$17.29 per product. Also, experienced offline brands spend about 18 per cent less than start-ups on establishing retail websites. Most consumers still need to be persuaded to go online and, at the same time, almost all e-tailers lose money on every customer. Their customers generate too few orders and too little profit per order to cover the costs of winning them, which can be as high as 65 per cent per order. According to a study conducted by McKinsey in July 2000, e-tailers would need efficient order fulfilment processes, average orders of at least US$100, and gross margins of at least 25 per cent to achieve a comfortable contribution on each transaction.

E-tailing Myths   The common myths earlier were that online selling required low investment and low cost and hence had no entry barriers and it was easy to succeed. There are some other myths that can mislead e-tailers while managing e-commerce operations.[31]

Stickiness is good   Many sites aspire to keep customers on the site as long as possible by adding features and design navigation. On the contrary, it has been observed that customers would rather complete their purpose than waste a lot of time on a site when looking for a particular product. Their behaviour has been found to be very goal oriented.

More is better   Some sites try to attract customers with flashy graphics, animation, and sound effects. A survey from Jupiter Media Metrix found that visitors were twice more likely to return to a site with faster loading pages than to sites that provided rich media. It was also found that 59 per cent of those surveyed would be more likely to return to a site that offered more product information.[32]

Personalization drives profitability   Personalization was supposed to be the key to business-to-consumer (B2C) e-commerce. However, personalization per se does not help to complete sales. Customers buy a complete offer from the retailers. Also, in many cases, customers' purchases may not reflect their interests. Instead of investing in expensive personalization technology sites, e-tailers would be better off devoting their energies to proper merchandising by answering questions and arranging items logically.[33]

E-commerce cannot make money[34]   E-commerce is a high investment business requiring substantial investment to set up the website, the software for data capture, records, and interactive systems for customer dialogue. These are sometimes underestimated and often cause downfalls. However, these are investments like in any bricks and mortar business; only the heads under which they are made are different. E-commerce can be made profitable by generating volumes to make money, giving it time to mature, and by developing strategies to change customer behaviour. However, e-commerce cannot be a gold mine.[35]

Factors Affecting the Growth of E-tailing[36]   The critical factors affecting the adoption of shopping electronically are the experience that customers would get while trying it for the first time, risks they perceive, and the benefit that the e-tailers deliver.

Trying out electronic shopping   In September 2002, about 605.60 million people around the world had access to the Internet. Majority of these Net surfers were living in Europe, followed by Asia-Pacific, Canada and USA, Latin America, Africa, and the Middle East. According to the United Nations Conference on Trade and Development report, Internet usage is seeing an annual rise of about 30 per cent, which is equivalent to about 2.5 per cent of the global population.

A growing share of new Internet users is in developing countries, which accounts for nearly a third of all new Internet users worldwide. In 2010, Asia was the world's hottest area of Internet growth. Asia's emerging markets such as China, India, and Malaysia are expected to show explosive digital growth. The region's two largest economies—China and India—already boast of approximately 500 million Internet users, and McKinsey forecasts that nearly 700 million more will be added by 2015.[37]

With more than 80 million people under 18 years of age expected to be online globally, teenagers and children constitute one of the fastest growing Internet populations. Surfing the Net is a highly regarded activity by this age group. However, adults over 50 years are one of the fastest growing markets online. A large number of people in this age group have home access to the Internet. Studies have revealed that older people are receptive to new technology and have time, money, and enthusiasm to surf the Web regularly. Apart from staying in touch with far-flung family and friends, older people tend to purchase merchandise and services online because shopping in stores can be difficult for them.[38]

Perceived risks in electronic shopping   Technological developments are reducing the risk of electronic shopping by enabling secure transactions and increasing the amount and quality of information available to electronic shoppers. However, the security of credit card transactions remains one of the major concerns, especially in developing economies.

The time lag between order and delivery is one of the important reasons for low usage of e-tailing, especially when the goods are perishable or are bought for an occasion. In the case of store-based retail formats, the delivery time of merchandise is immediate, but in the case of non-store retail formats, consumers usually have to wait for several days to get the merchandise.

Benefits delivered by e-tailers   The biggest benefit of electronic retailing compared to other retail formats is the vast number of alternatives that become available to consumers. The success of Amazon.com is attributed to the fact that no physical bookstore can offer millions of titles at one place. Accessibility is another benefit. For example, a person living in India can shop electronically at Harrods in London in less time than it takes to visit the local supermarket. Since electronic retailers do not have to spend money building and operating stores at convenient locations, they have much lower costs—as much as 25 per cent lower than in-store retailers. Another potential benefit of electronic retailing is the ability to select a small set for the customer to look at in detail. Suggestive selling is very easy on the Net.

E-tailing, however, does have its limitations. Shoppers may not visit all the sites selling the product. This may be a time-consuming exercise unless the consumer is focused and finds a few items to study in detail. In spite of the above-mentioned advantages, electronic retailers (or the customers) will have to incur higher costs to get the merchandise to homes, deal with the high level of returns, and attract customers to their website. Customers bear these costs when they buy from a physical

TABLE 5.2   E-tailing and Other Formats—Comparison of Benefits

	Model Comparison for Grocery				
	Hypermarket	Supermarket	Kirana	Online	Call-in
Benefits to the Retailer					
Break-even volumes	High	Medium	Low	Medium	Medium
Scalability	High	High	Low	High	Medium
Up-front investment	High	Medium	Low	Medium	Medium
GM based on volumes	High	High	Low	Medium	Medium
End customer experience	Medium	High	Low	Medium	Medium
Benefits to Customers					
Pricing	Low	High	High	High	High
Services	Low	High	Low	High	High
Atmosphere	Medium	High	Low	Medium	Medium
Convenience	Low	Medium	High	High	High
Range	High	Medium	Low	High	Low
End customer experience	Medium	High	Low	Medium	Medium

TABLE 5.3   E-tailing and Other Formats—Comparison of Cost of Operation

Sales/Sq. ft	₹500	₹750	₹1000	₹1250
Hypermarket (%)	13.33	10.23	8.68	7.75
Supermarket (%)	19.96	14.52	11.81	10.18
Kirana (%)	7.60	5.57	4.55	3.94
Superkirana (%)	16.85	11.68	9.10	7.55
Sales/Location	₹14 lakh	₹18 lakh	₹26 lakh	₹38 lakh
Online* (%)	13.29	9.62	8.03	7.16

* *Notes:*
1. Online cost does not include marketing and technology costs.
2. Location is treated as mainly a large city when the store's service centre is located.
3. Lakh = 100,000.

store. A comparison of various formats in terms of their economies and the cost of operation for a format in food stores are given in Tables 5.2 and 5.3.[39] The comparison reveals that online retailing scores over all newer formats in terms of benefits to retailers. It scores over even hypermarkets with respect to benefits to the customers. It is also observed that its operation costs are similar to that of other formats. Therefore, in order to succeed, an e-tailer should try to achieve large volumes as soon as possible.

OTHER RETAILING FORMATS

The practice of retailing is continuously evolving. New formats are born and old ones fade. Incessant pressure to improve efficiency and effectiveness and a continual effort to serve the customer better force the retailers to find new ways of doing business. Some of the new formats that have developed recently are discussed in this section.

Supercentres   Supercentres, one-stop combinations of supermarkets and discount department stores that carry at least 80,000 items and often more than 100,000 products ranging from televisions to peanut butter to fax machines, are the new format for the mass merchants. These stores offer the customer the convenience of one-stop shopping with service and variety. They draw customers from very far. They are similar to hypermarkets in their operations, but are much larger in size.

Malls   Malls are formats that house a cluster of stores that are owned and managed by independent retailers. Malls are generally designed to offer products and services that would complete the basket. They also contain cinemas and eateries. Most customers come to malls to spend almost the whole day. These malls are very large. They are either spread over a very large area located away from the city or have many floors when located within the city. While most malls offer a wide variety of merchandise, there are malls that specialize in a particular category, such as the New Gold Souk in Dubai. Malls are designed to accommodate department stores, hypermarkets, speciality stores, exclusive branded outlets, variety stores, and several other formats. In Asian markets, these are the most preferred formats at present.

A Mall in India

Source: http://www.pbs.org/wnet/wideangle/shows/india2/images/
pic_india6.jpg, accessed on 20 October 2006.

Recycled Merchandise Retailers   Recycled merchandise retailers sell cast-off clothes, furniture, sporting goods, and computers. They include pawnshops, thrift shops, consignment shops, and even flea markets. A fast growth of this format has been observed over the past five years. Even as a large number of retailers were closing down in the mid-1990s, recycled merchandise retailers were growing. While in the US, Europe, and Latin America they grew at 10 per cent, in Japan they grew at 20 per cent per annum. One of the most popular stores in Japan, Per Gram Market, sells items at eight cents a gram. Thus, a second-hand T-shirt would cost around US$ 8.50 in such a store, but a silk scarf would sell for US$2.80.[40]

Liquidators   Liquidators are retail formats that come in and liquidate leftover merchandise when an established retailer shuts down or downsizes. They are often called retailing's undertakers or vultures. They earn by buying the merchandise at a price that is 30 per cent less than the wholesale price for the closeout retailers. Retailers utilize the services of liquidators because running closeouts requires some special retailing skills. Liquidators also have to develop special incentive plans to make it more profitable for store personnel to stay and work rather than quit or walk off with merchandise.[41]

Video Kiosks   The video kiosk is a freestanding, interactive, electronic computer terminal that displays products and related information on a video screen. It often uses a touch screen for consumers to make selections. Video kiosks can be situated in high traffic zones such as store aisles or hotel lobbies. They enable consumers to place orders, complete transactions, pay mostly with a credit/debit card, and arrange for products to be shipped. Kiosks can be linked to retailers' computer networks or tied in to the Web.

At the beginning of 1999, there were about 250,000 video kiosks in use throughout the US. At present there are about 2 million kiosks in the US. Video kiosk sales seem to have grown four times from its figure of $830 million in 1999. Worldwide, nearly 80 per cent of kiosks are involved with retail-related transactions. North America accounts for 59 per cent of kiosk sales, the Pacific Rim for 20 per cent, Europe for 16 per cent, and the rest of the world for 5 per cent.[42]

Car Boot Sales   Car boot sales are becoming increasingly popular, where often a vehicle is modified for the sale of a variety of merchandise, such as books, magazines, clothes, music cassettes, export surplus and/or rejects, and fast food items. The boot sale boom has given vendors such as software pirates 'an ideal outlet and quick getaway'. It also provides opportunities for small traders who may lack the capital for permanent premises. They are often situated near university campuses and commercial areas. Their target audience is lower middle class and middle class customers looking for 'value for money products'.

Mobile Vans   Mobile vans are modified vehicles that usually sell books, newspapers, poultry, and meat products. They move from location to location, for fixed periods of time, thus providing convenience by coming closer to customers.

Catalogue Stores   A catalogue store, unlike regular stores, does not house and display all products. Customers can view the products available in the store from a printed or online catalogue. Catalogue stores also give the customers the advantage of browsing through the products on the catalogue from home at any time without taking the pain to visit the physical store, thereby creating a virtual store. The catalogue can be purchased from the store counter at a nominal fee. After deciding the catalogue purchase, the order form is filled and submitted at the store counter where a representative either gets the product from the warehouse or delivers it to a prescribed destination of choice of the customer, after the payment is received.

Here, the retailer not only saves the cost of high rentals in big malls, but also cuts down the store management costs. In US and UK, catalogue stores are a lot more visible. In fact, 78 per cent of the population in UK enjoy catalogue shopping. The momentum of catalogue stores has not been substantial in India when compared with other countries, as this format still needs more time for acceptance from the customers, for them to realize its real potential. Hypercity Retail (India) Ltd and Shoppers Stop Ltd discontinued their catalogue retail operations under the Hypercity–Argos brand as they could not get their target investments back in the planned period. Big players such as Hypercity and Croma have remained unsuccessful in catalogue retailing, but there are also exceptions such as Elvy Lifestyle, where all products are delivered on orders, and payments for the same are made on delivery only if the customer accepts the order after getting a feel of the product.[43]

Shopping Strips   A shopping strip is an open area where the shops are arranged in a row with a pavement (sidewalk), along with a parking space in the front. In the US and Canada, shopping strips are found in every city or town. They are like a hub to the neighbourhood communities. Today in India, although malls have been on a phenomenal rise, shopping strips are still increasingly gaining attention. The preferences of the people are changing towards convenience and locally obtained services.

When compared to the other formats, shopping strips provide more control over purchases in the present shopping environment. The success of this format depends upon the acceptance level of the customers because in many places such as Australia, such formats are facing stiff competition from the evolution of larger formats.

Rural Marts   The main idea behind the format of a rural mart is to facilitate the marketing process for those who are not able to procure the right price, sizeable production, and effective display. Rural marts at the district and sub-district levels are significant to large corporates who want to tap the immense opportunities in the rural markets. In India, the National Bank for Agriculture and Rural Development (NABARD) launched rural marts with effect from 19 September 2005 in nine states and extended them to all the states during 2006–07. The main objectives are to facilitate marketing linkages for the artisans, for their handicrafts and agro-based products, through the setting up of a retail outlet and cover the risk involved in the initial stages of this process.[44]

In India this format is multiplying with the basic objective to help the rural consumer to procure higher returns and also avail additional crop advisory services, water services, and training. The transition phase of Indian farmers graduating towards mechanized farming would be the major reason behind the success of this format.

Flower Markets   This format is currently picking up in India because of government support although the industry as a whole suffers from logistical bottlenecks. Connaught Place in Delhi hosts what is arguably the largest flower market in Asia. The development of this format is hindered by multiple factors, such as lack of subsidies and transportation problems. Moreover, inadequate cold storage and display facilities also happen to be the major obstacles for the development of this format in India. Delhi has the maximum flower traffic in Asia and flowers being 100 per cent perishable, traders of this format have to deal with the extreme climatic conditions of India with extra care.

India's annual flower production stands at around 1,000 tonnes and the country's floriculture industry has a miniscule 0.01 per cent share in the international market.[45] According to a report of the International Labour Organisation (ILO), in India, inadequate purchasing power hinders sizeable imports and similarly inadequate quality hinders sizeable exports. The success of this format in India depends upon many factors, such as optimum temperature, moisture conditions during storage, transportation, and emphasizing on the quality of flowers reaching the end customers.

Cattle Fairs This format has its origins in India from ancient times. The biggest cattle fair of Asia, the Sonepur Cattle Fair, is held on the full-moon day and lasts between fifteen days and one month. Numerous stalls are erected, selling a wide variety of animals, garments, furniture, toys, utensils, jewellery, and handicrafts. Pushkar Fair, the largest camel fair of the world, is held in Rajasthan (Ajmer). Dadri Cattle Fair is also one of the largest fairs in India taking place in Ballia town in Uttar Pradesh. People from all over India gather here to buy and sell cattle. The Nagaur Fair of Rajasthan is the second largest fair in India. Here animals are garlanded with accessories, to give them a vibrant look.

Besides providing the platform for cattle trade, this format also provides a great opportunity to enjoy various leisure activities such as tug of war, cockfights, and bullock fights. People from around the world have been attracted to this format because it offers them a lifetime experience alongside campfire, and enjoying folk music.

Westside—A Chain Store

Neighbourhood *Kirana* Store

FoodWorld—A Conventional Supermarket Store

Shopping Strip

Different Types of Retailing Formats (contd)

A Hypermarket

A Department Store

Warehouse Club

Toys "R"Us—A Speciality Store

TJMax—An Off-price Retailer

Egg Vending Machine in Japan

Different Types of Retailing Formats

VALUE-BASED MODEL OF STORE FORMAT CHOICE

It is evident that each of the formats discussed in this chapter offers some unique benefits that help in attracting shoppers. What is also interesting is that, even with the proliferation of formats, each one of them is surviving. Shoppers have split their purchases across formats. In some cases, different merchandise is bought through specific channels. So, while books and music are being bought in large volumes through the Internet, grocery and high value purchases are being bought through store-based formats. Some shoppers are also buying similar merchandise through separate formats. Due to the choices available to shoppers, there is an effort to optimize the value derived and hence split purchases between formats. However, it is also noticed that shoppers tend to make one of the formats their primary choice and make most of their purchases from that format. It is, therefore, imperative that a retailer should select the value and then choose the format that delivers the value to the fullest. A *format* can be conceptualized as a *system for delivering the value promised to the shoppers so as to create a sustainable competitive advantage.*

Deciding the Format

The process of deciding a format involves several steps, as shown in Fig. 5.4. At the core of the process is the value proposition that the retailer chooses to offer to its customers, based on which it develops a positioning for the store.

FIG. 5.4   Process of Format Selection

Define Value Proposition

The first step in deciding the format is to identify and select the value proposition that the store would like to offer to shoppers. Shoppers have several reasons for choosing a store.[46] A study conducted in India indicated that proximity and merchandise were the primary reasons. More than 70 per cent of the respondents indicated these as their strongest reason for choice. The third reason was ambience (8%) and patronized store (8%). Only 40 per cent could provide as many as three reasons. Seventy per cent had at least two reasons. This indicates that shoppers generally have just one good reason, and, at the most, two reasons for visiting a particular store. A store would thus build a value proposition based on its target customers, competition, and company objectives. Each retailer would need to vary its offering by different combinations of the elements of value mix, referred to as the retail value proposition.[47]

Identify Enablers and Deterrents

Each of the formats would yield optimum results only when certain conditions are fulfilled. A store needs to identify these conditions and the variables causing them. These variables then need to be classified as enablers or deterrents. Enablers are factors that could be utilized to manage the format successfully. Deterrents consist of variables that would impede the successful working and growth of the format. The retailer needs to conduct a thorough analysis of the macro and microenvironment that affect its business. Toys "R" Us (TRS) found that, in entering Japan, its biggest challenge was finding space for large stores. The largest stores in Japan were about one-third of the existing stores. Toys "R" Us is a category killer. It drives the value from focusing on one category and offering price and depth. It would require large space to deliver value to its customers.

Find Out What It Takes to Deliver the Values

Based on the value identified and the environmental factors, retailers develop a mix by using the following five elements:

Variety and Assortment of Merchandise   *Variety* is the number of different merchandise categories a retailer offers. *Assortment* is the number of different items in a merchandise category. Each different kind of merchandise is called a stock-keeping unit (SKU). For example, department stores, discount stores, and toy stores all sell toys. However, department stores sell many other categories of merchandise in addition to toys. Thus, they have greater variety. The toy stores stock more types of toys (more SKUs). For each type of toy, such as dolls, the speciality toy retailer will offer more assortments (more models, sizes, brands, and deeper assortments) than general merchants such as department or discount stores. Elements such as product quality, uniqueness, and reliability can also be clubbed with this factor of the retail mix.[48]

Customer Service and Facility   Services provided by retailers to facilitate the shopping process for customers are called customer services. Customer service could include easy access to product and price information, employing in-store salespeople, parking, accepting modes of payment suitable to customers, express checkouts, home delivery, gift wrapping, rest and refreshment facility, and childcare facility.

Store Design, Display, and Ambience   Ambience can be described as non-visual, background conditions in the store environment, including elements such as temperature, lighting, music, noise levels, air quality, and scent.[49] Display and design factors are the environmental elements that are more visible in nature than ambient factors. These include factors such as layout, width of aisles, equipment, furnishing, and cleanliness. Kotler[50] has proposed *atmospherics* as being an important part of retail marketing strategy. Shoppers also determine the value of the merchandise based on monetary as well as non-monetary costs.[51] The shopping experience, as created by the store environment, plays an important role in building store patronage. Along with the merchandise, it triggers affective reaction among shoppers[52] and contributes to creating store patronage intentions[53].

Pricing   It is one of the strategic decisions that plays a vital role in store selection. Pricing decisions such as premium pricing, everyday low pricing (EDLP), high-low (HILO) pricing, and discount pricing are some of the pricing considerations offered to the customer. The shopper may also evaluate each of these situations in the light of the cost incurred and the utilities derived from shopping. These costs can be classified as fixed and variable costs of shopping.[54] The variable cost is related to the basket size or the list and hence is likely to change with every trip. The fixed costs, such as the location of the store or the price format, would remain unchanged over list size. It is suggested that these costs can be converted into utilities for each of the shoppers by the store. In a study of two price formats, EDLP and HILO, it was found that the store could influence the choice of shoppers by enhancing the perceived utilities.[55] It is also argued that the shopper may evaluate a shopping situation in the light of costs incurred and utilities derived out of shopping.[56]

Accessibility   It is the convenience component of the retail mix. Store location, travelling time, parking facility, and service hours are considered as important elements. The first decision is the problem of store location choice. The second is the problem of shopping trip incidence relating to the timing of shopping trips. The two decision processes are correlated. It is found that, overall, shoppers give prominence to proximity of the store, merchandise, and service provided by the store.[57]

Decide on Brick or Click or Brick and Click

Offline retailers have realized that the online model can help in an unmatched expansion in customer base at a very low cost. The click model also enables retailers to offer many value added services to their customers, which perhaps will be the only differentiating factor in the emerging global marketplace.[58] For the pure play online retailers, such alliances offer a chance to leverage the extensive distribution infrastructure, credibility, and stability of the established offline players. It also helps in customer acquisition as shoppers tend to be more comfortable in making online purchases when the familiar offline retailers have an online presence.

Offline retailers can include their web addresses in their communication. Moreover, they can also tie their store loyalty cards and mailing lists to increase awareness and usage of the online channel. They can find out new shoppers on their site and their conversion. However, integrating offline and online store operations is a complex process. Initially, pure plays were concerned about erosion in their valuations. On the other hand, offline retailers were concerned about the potential cannibalization of the sales. The advantages, however, have outweighed the disadvantages. Table 5.4 highlights some points that a retailer needs to keep in mind while deciding on this issue. The primary

TABLE 5.4   Pure Play, Click and Brick, and Brick and Mortar

Factors	Pure Play	Click and Brick	Brick and Mortar
Ease of distribution	Low	High	High
Scalability	High	Moderate	Low
Market valuation	High	Moderate	Low
Inventory costs	Low	High	High
Infrastructure cost	Low	High	High
Security of payment	Low	Mixed	High
Variable costs	High	Low	Low
Consumer tracking	Easy	Easy	Difficult
Channel conflict	Low	High	Low
Brand equity	Low	High	High
Customer acquisition cost	High	Moderate	Low

Source: Adapted from Meyer 2000.

concern in integration is the cultural fit. The two types of retailers represent different business and retailing environments. The shoppers behave differently, the technology is different, and so are the processes.

ATTITUDE-BASED MODEL OF STORE FORMAT CHOICE[59]

There is merit in building a favourable consumer attitude towards the format, as attitude is a strong antecedent of consumer behaviour and the relationship is well mediated through intention. The affective and cognitive components of attitude have differential impacts on the choice of store formats. Usually, the affective component is a stronger predictor of intention than the cognitive component, indicating that the consumers primarily do a global assessment of the format proposition rather than a detailed evaluative assessment. It may be indicative of the stage of format evolution and familiarity with it, as the recent formats such as hypermarket show the highest cognitive evaluation while the oldest format, namely the *kirana*, has shown the highest affective component (Table 5.5). It may therefore be possible to conjecture that the basis of consumers' format evaluation undergoes a transition from cognitive to affective with the increased familiarity and evolution of the format. As a result, it becomes important for the store formats to know the attitude profiles of their target group from time to time as it may form the basis of the retail format's communication decisions and business proposition changes. A largely affective target group may be approached primarily with affective cues while cognitive cues may be communicated sporadically. On the other hand, a cognitive profile heavy target group, as in the case of hypermarkets, may be targeted primarily with evaluative or utilitarian cues such as value for money positioning or discounts/savings made in a shopping trip or a loyalty promotion. An illustrative example is presented in Fig. 5.5 to highlight the role of different attitude components and their possible transition over time.

The role of the affective components seems to be very critical in determining intention and hence the marketers would need to study the formation and reinforcement process among grocery customers to be able to impact their store format choice process. The marketing stimuli that are able to influence both the components are likely to be the most rewarding from the marketing point of view.

The consumer involvement in the grocery and bulk shopping categories has come out as a significant factor in determining intention and it is a new finding for the former, which has traditionally been described as having had low involvement. This may be because of the association of greater risk with bulk grocery than grocery in general. As an implication, it may be possible to identify different involvement groups within the grocery consumers and target them with suitable communication plans to impact behaviour.

TABLE 5.5 Cross-sectional View of the Target Group Composition across Store Formats (An Illustrative Example)

Store Formats Studied (in ascending order of emergence in Indian retail)	Target Group Composition		
	Affective	Cognitive	Composite
Hypermarket (Most recent)	++	++++	++
Internet	+++	++	++++
Discounters	++++	++	+++
Supermarket	++++	+	++
Kirana (Oldest)	+++++	−	−

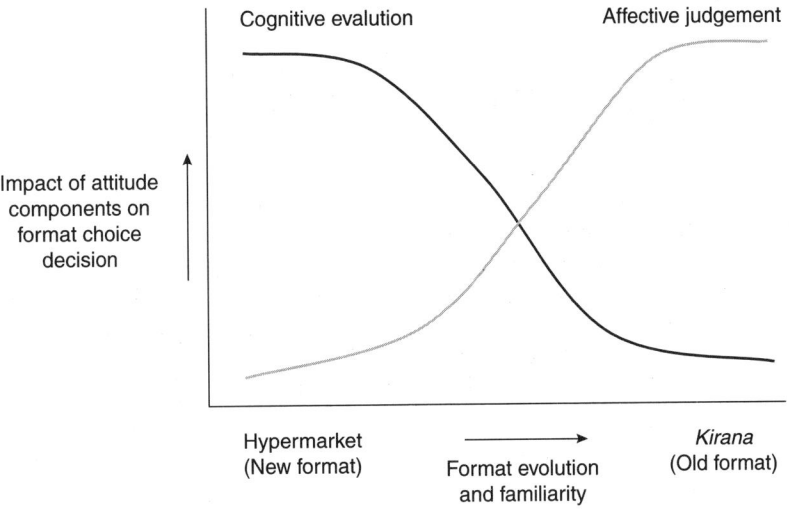

FIG. 5.5 Temporal Effect of Affect and Cognition on Store Format Choice

Apart from attitude and involvement, factors such as subjective norm and perceived behavioural control also significantly impact intention. Newer or niche formats such as the Internet are likely to have low generalized social acceptability; hence increasing awareness and trials can mould customers' subjective norms and behavioural intentions significantly. Perceived operational capability to use a format impacts the actual behaviour, indicating that higher the complexity of task or barriers in accessing and using a format, lower would be the actual usage of that format. The past positive experience has shown to have little role in affecting behaviour. The impact of involvement, cognition, and affect has been depicted in Fig. 5.6.

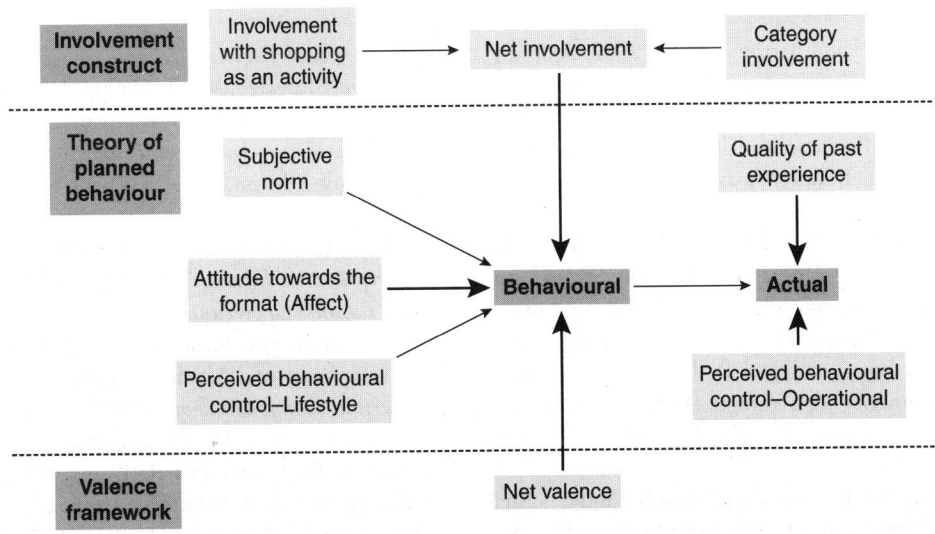

FIG. 5.6 Attitude-based Model for Store Format Choice

SUMMARY

Formats are systems through which retailers deliver their values to the chosen segments of customers. Based on the value chosen for delivery and the success parameters of each of the formats, a retailer tries to differentiate itself from competitors and create a customer franchise. In many cases, the retailer chooses a combination of values as it aims to cater to different segments and their expectations. There is a wide variety of formats from which the retailers can choose. These are classified broadly into store-based and non-store based formats.

Store-based retailers operate in a given physical area defined by their value and merchandise. This form of retailing has been in existence since a long time and has evolved with changes in consumer preferences and compulsions of the retailers. They cover both food and non-food retailing. There are several choices that a retailer has in a physical store, based on the merchandise and ownership. Each of them has unique characteristics and requires a particular skill to operate and compete efficiently. Chain stores are one of the most common ownership formats as they provide the reach as well as volume for buying better and providing the customer a similar experience all over. Retailers use franchising as the route to expand fast without much capital investment from the franchisers. The biggest challenge in the chain stores is to create ownership among the store managers to achieve a high level of value delivery. The competition in the retail business has brought hypermarkets and other large formats which serve as one-stop shops for the customers, giving them competitive prices and convenience.

Non-store-based retailing is mainly in the non-food area. Their area of operation is determined by the feasibility and cost of delivery to the customers at the desired location. Non-store retailing has its own challenges. It requires the retailers to serve the customers without the presence of either the shopper or the retailer in a physical setting. Shoppers have been using this format since a long time through catalogue and teleshopping networks. The advent of the Internet as a new retailing format brought new environments for customers to shop. It started with a lot of insecurity but has been able to establish itself as a good alternative format. Customers have found it entertaining but have restricted major purchases to information-heavy purchases such as books and music. This has forced many retailers to think of having a hybrid format where customers can choose to buy from a physical as well as a virtual format of the same store.

NOTES

1. Levy, Michael and Barton A. Weitz 2002, *Retailing Management*, Tata McGraw-Hill, 4th edn, p. 172.
2. Enders, Albrecht and Tawfik Jelassi 2000, 'The Converging Business Models of Internet and Bricks-and-Mortar Retailers', *European Management Journal*, October, pp. 542–50.
3. Messinger, Paul R. and Narasimhan Chakravarthi 1997, 'A Model of Retail Formats Based on Consumers' Economising on Shopping Time', *Marketing Science*, Vol. 16, No. 1, pp. 1–23.
4. Berman, Barry and Joel R. Evans 2001, 'Retail Management—A Strategic Approach', Eastern Economy Edition, 8th edn, Prentice-Hall India, p. 115.
5. Anand, Kamaljit Singh and Piyush Kumar Sinha 2009, 'Store Format Choice in an Evolving Market: Role of Affect, Cognition, and Involvement', *The International Review of Retail, Distribution, and Consumer Research*, Vol. 19(5), pp. 505–34.
6. Berman, Barry and Joel R. Evans 2001, 'Retail Management—A Strategic Approach', Eastern Economy Edition, 8th edn, Prentice-Hall India, p. 115.
7. Caffey, Andrew A. 1997, 'Opportunity Knocks', *Entrepreneur Magazine's Buyer Guide to Franchisee and Business Opportunities*, p. 3.
8. Fernie, John and Suzanne I. Fernie 1997, 'The Development of a US Retail Format in Europe', *International Journal of Retail and Distribution Management*, Vol. 25, No. 11, pp. 342–50.
9. Berman, Barry and Joel R. Evans, 2001, 'Retail Management—A Strategic Approach', Eastern Economy Edition, 8th edn, Prentice-Hall India, p. 115.

10. Doris, Newton J. 1993, 'Non-traditional Retailers Challenge the Supermarket Industry', *Food Review*, Washington, January–April.
11. 'Category Killers in Europe—A Retail Format for the Future', *European Retail Digest*, Spring 1996, p. 42.
12. Fernie, John and Suzanne I. Fernie 1997, 'The Development of a US Retail Format in Europe', *International Journal of Retail and Distribution Management*, Vol. 25, No. 11, pp. 342–50.
13. Levy, Michael and Barton A. Weitz 2002, *Retailing Management*, Tata McGraw-Hill, 4th edn, p. 172.
14. Crossen Cynthia and Ellen Graham 1996, 'Pressed for Time or Pressed for Money?', *The Wall Street Journal*, March 8, p. 4; George Milne and Mary Ellen Gordon 1994, 'A Segmentation Study of Consumer's Attitudes toward Direct Mail,' *Journal of Direct Marketing*, Vol. 8, Spring, pp. 45–52.
15. Berman, Barry and Joel R. Evans, 2001, 'Retail Management—A Strategic Approach', Eastern Economy Edition, 8th edn, Prentice-Hall India, p. 115.
16. Berman, Barry and Joel R. Evans, 2001, 'Retail Management—A Strategic Approach', Eastern Economy Edition, 8th edn, Prentice-Hall India, p. 115.
17. Lindstorm Martin, Don Peppers, and Martha Rogers 2001, 'Clicks, Bricks and Brands: The Marriage of Online and Offline Business', Kogan Page, London, p. 11.
18. 'Electronic Retailing and eMarketing', 2000, *Newsletter Hermes*, Issue 5, September–October.
19. Mello, Adrian 2001, 'Four Myths of Online Retailing', November 7.
20. 'Electronic Retailing and eMarketing', 2000, *Newsletter Hermes*, Issue 5, September–October.
21. 'Electronic Retailing and eMarketing', 2000, *Newsletter Hermes*, Issue 5, September–October.
22. 'Electronic Retailing and eMarketing', 2000, *Newsletter Hermes*, Issue 5, September–October.
23. http://business.ezinemark.com/vision-shopsters-online-retail-global-industry-guide-1671b2d078a.html, accessed on 9 October 2010.
24. http://techcrunch.com/2010/03/08/forrester-forecast-online-retail-sales-will-grow-to-250-billion-by-2014/, accessed on 9 October 2010.
25. Berman, Barry and Joel R. Evans 2001, 'Retail Management—A Strategic Approach', Eastern Economy Edition, 8th edn, Prentice-Hall India, p. 115.
26. Nongkran, Lertpittayapoom and Suresh Tadisina 'The Antecedents of Customer Satisfaction in Electronic Retailing', Working paper, Department of Management, Southern Illinois University Carbondale.
27. Byliner: Amazon.Com's VP on Global Electronic Retailing, 18 May 2000.
28. 'Changing Gears: Retailing in India', ET Knowledge Series, p. 134.
29. *Business Week* e.biz, 7 February 2000.
30. *Business Week* e.biz, 7 February 2000.
31. 'Electronic Retailing and eMarketing', 2000, *Newsletter Hermes*, Issue 5, September–October.
32. Nongkran, Lertpittayapoom and Suresh Tadisina 'The Antecedents of Customer Satisfaction in Electronic Retailing', Working paper, Department of Management, Southern Illinois University Carbondale.
33. Nongkran, Lertpittayapoom and Suresh Tadisina 'The Antecedents of Customer Satisfaction in Electronic Retailing', Working paper, Department of Management, Southern Illinois University Carbondale.
34. Sudhakar, V.S. 2004, 'E-tailing—The Opportunities and the Challenges', Presentation at Indian Institute of Management Ahmedabad.
35. 'Electronic Retailing and eMarketing', *Newsletter Hermes*, Issue 5, September–October 2000, pp. 98–100.
36. Levy, Michael and Barton A. Weitz 2002 *Retailing Management*, Tata McGraw-Hill, 4th edn, p. 81.
37. http://www.mckinseyquarterly.com/Riding_Asias_digital_tiger_2667, accessed on 14 October 2010.
38. Cleaver, Joanne 1999, 'Surfing for Seniors', Marketing News, July 19, pp. 1–7; and Gapper Justina 1998, 'The Rise of the New Media Greys,' *New Media Age*, January 29, pp. 10–12.
39. Nongkran, Lertpittayapoom and Suresh Tadisina 'The Antecedents of Customer Satisfaction in Electronic Retailing', Working paper, Department of Management, Southern Illinois University Carbondale.
40. 'Used Products are Hot as Japanese Discover the Joy of Buying Second-hand', *Wall Street Journal*, 22 June 2000.
41. 'Everything Must Go—To The Liquidators', *Business Week*, 15 January 1996, p. 52.
42. Frost and Sullivan 1999, 'Interactive Kiosk Markets', San Francisco.

43. http://retail.franchiseindia.com/articles/Retail-Business-Practice/Retail-Renovation/Catalogue-Retailing-in-Infancy-300/, accessed on 18 October 2010.

44. http://www.nabard.org/nonfarm_sector/pp_mt_ruralmart.asp, accessed on 19 October 2010.

45. http://www.indiatogether.org/2004/nov/eco-flower.htm, accessed on 19 October 2010.

46. Sinha, Piyush Kumar, Arindam Banerjee, and Dwarika Prasad Uniyal 2002, 'Deciding Where to Buy: Store Choice Behaviour of Indian Shoppers', *Vikalpa*, Vol. 27, No. 2, pp. 13–28.

47. Stevenson, Lawrence N., Joseph C. Schlesinger, and Michael R. Pearce 1999, *Power Retail*, McGraw-Hill, Canada, pp. 58–84.

48. Levy, Michael and Barton A. Weitz 2002, *Retailing Management*, Tata McGraw-Hill, 4th edn, p. 172.

49. Spenberg, E.R., A.E. Crowley, and P.W. Henderson, 1996, 'Improving the Store Environment: Do Olfactory Cues Affect Evaluation and Behaviours', *Journal of Marketing*, Vol. 60, No. 2, pp. 67–80.

50. Kotler, Philip 1973, 'Atmospherics as a Marketing Tool', *Journal of Retailing*, Vol. 49, Winter, pp. 48–64.

51. Zeithaml, V. 1988, 'Consumer Perception of Price, Quality and Value: A Means-End Model and Synthesis of Evidence', *Journal of Marketing*, Vol. 52, July, pp. 2–22.

52. Baker J., D. Grewal and Levy 1992, 'An Experimental Approach to Making Retail Store Environmental Decisions', *Journal of Retailing*, Vol. 68, Winter, pp. 445–60.

53. Baker, J., D. Grewal, A. Parasuraman, and B. Glenn 2002, 'The Influence of Multi-store Environmental Clues on Perceived Merchandise Value and Patronage Intentions', *Journal of Marketing*, Vol. 66, April, pp. 120–41.

54. Bell, David R., Teck-Hua Ho, and Christopher S. Tang 1998, 'Determining Where to Shop: Fixed and Variable Costs of Shopping,' *Journal of Marketing Research*, Vol. 35, August, pp 352–69.

55. Tang, Christopher S., David R. Bell, and Teck-Hua Ho 2001, 'Store Choice and Shopping Behaviour: How Price Format Works,' *California Management Review*, Vol. 43, No. 2, Winter, pp. 56–74.

56. Messinger, Paul R. and Narasimhan Chakravarthi 1997, 'A Model of Retail Formats Based on Consumers' Economising on Shopping Time', *Marketing Science*, Vol. 16, No. 1, pp. 1–23; Sinha, Piyush Kumar; Arindam Banerjee, and Dwarika Prasad Uniyal 2002, 'Deciding Where to Buy: Store Choice Behaviour of Indian Shoppers', *Vikalpa*, Vol. 27, No. 2, pp. 13–28; Leszczyc, Peter T.L. Popkowski, Ashish Sinha, and Harry J.P. Timmermans 2000, 'Consumer Store Choice Dynamics: An Analysis of Competitive Market Structure for Grocery Stores,' *Journal Of Retailing*, Vol. 59, No. 2, Summer, pp. 75–105; Van Kenhove, Patrick, Kristof De Wulf, and Walter Van Waterschoot 1999, The Impact of Task Definition on Store Attribute Salience and Store Choice, *Journal of Retailing*, Spring, Vol. 75, pp. 125–35.

57. Fernie, John and Suzanne I. Fernie 1997, 'The Development of a US Retail Format in Europe', *International Journal of Retail and Distribution Management*, Vol. 25, No. 11, pp. 342–50.

58. Harvey, Meyer 2000, 'Building a Click and Mortar World', *Journal of Business Strategy*, March/April, Vol. 21 (2), pp. 20–25.

59. Anand, Kamaljit Singh and Piyush Kumar Sinha 2009, 'Store Format Choice in an Evolving Market: Role of Affect, Cognition, and Involvement', *The International Review of Retail, Distribution, and Consumer Research*, Vol. 19(5), pp. 505–34.

CONCEPT REVIEW QUESTIONS

1. Define formats. Describe store-based formats and differentiate them.
2. What myths plague e-tailing? How does an e-tailer guard against such myths?
3. Describe the value-based model of deciding formats. Illustrate it with an example.
4. What are the bases of deciding on using a brick and/or click combination?

CRITICAL THINKING QUESTION

In the context of developing economies, where the retail canvas is full of mom-and-pop stores, which format has the maximum chance of success? What parameters would you use to evaluate your options of formats?

PROJECTS

1. Talk to the owner of your neighbourhood *kirana* store. Find out the challenges faced in the new competitive scenario.
2. Visit a hypermarket and find out why customers patronize this format. Indicate what present and future challenges it faces. Suggest a course of action in view of these.
3. Pick a store that sells ready-made garments, gift items, cards, and music. Compare and contrast the customer flows, revenue per customer, and stock turns of the store. Determine the profitability drivers on these bases. Suggest ways to improve each of the three dimensions.

CASE STUDY

Planet Health[1]

In early 2001, Rohit Patel, Managing Director, Sagar Group of Industries (SGI), was reviewing the plans for entering the retail business of pharmacy and health care products. On the basis of a report submitted by SGI's consultants, Rohit Patel had to decide whether to enter the business and, in case he did the entry strategy and plan.

Company Background

Sagar Group of Industries, situated in Ahmedabad, Gujarat—a state in western India—was started in 1956 as Shanker Chemical Works by J.S. Patel, father of Rohit Patel. The group had grown from a turnover of ₹4 million in the late 1970s to ₹750 million in 2000. While the annual turnover had witnessed fluctuating growth trends, the group had registered a whopping increase of 660 per cent in the net worth during the decade starting from 1990–91 (Fig. CS5.1). The group had grown primarily through vertical integration. In 2001, SGI had ten companies that were involved in manufacturing and/or marketing bulk pharmaceuticals, drug intermediates, drug formulations, fine chemicals, dyes, dye intermediates, and food preservatives (Table CS5.1). Its two manufacturing facilities were located at Ahmedabad.

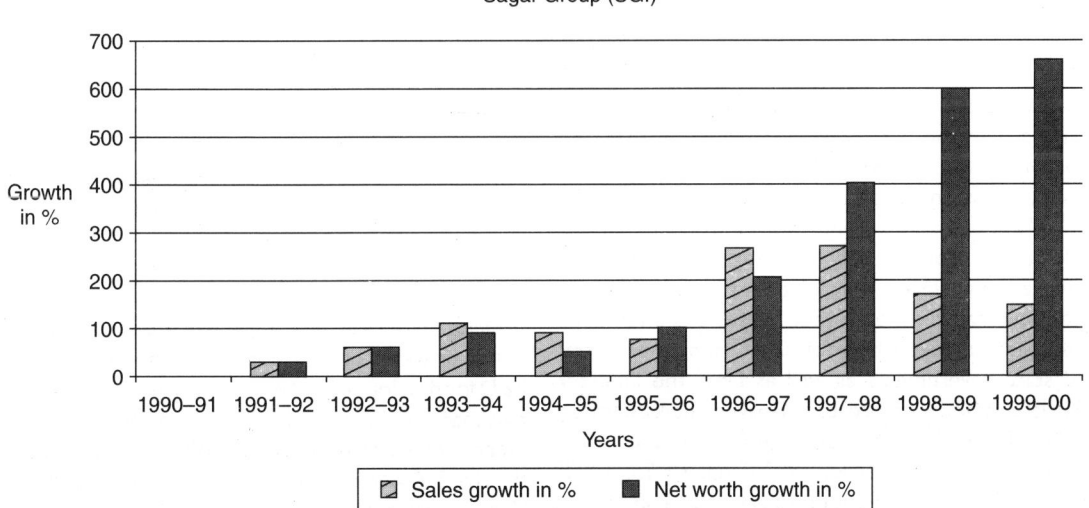

Sagar Group (SGI)

FIG. CS5.1 Sales and Net Worth Growth

---

1. Prepared by Professor Abhinandan K Jain, Professor Piyush Kumar Sinha, and Mr Preshth Bhardwaj, Indian Institute of Management Ahmedabad. Teaching material prepared as a basis for class discussion. Cases are not designed to present illustrations of either correct or incorrect handling of administrative problems. © Indian Institute of Management Ahmedabad, 2003.

TABLE CS5.1   Range of Products of Sagar Group

Dye and Dye Intermediates	Bulk Pharmaceuticals
• Vinyl Sulphone Ester (Acetanalide Base)	• Sulphamethoxazole I.P., B.P.
• Vinyl Sulphone Ester(Ortho Anisidine Base)	• Ciprofloxacin Hydrochloride U.S.P.
• Vinyl Sulphone Ester (Para Cresidine Base)	• Ciprofloxacin Lactate
• Vinyl Sulphone Ester (2:5 Dimethoxy Aniline Base)	• Analgin I.P.
• Acetanalide	• Sodium Methoxide Solution in Methanol
• 4, 4' Diamino Stilbene 2, 2' Disulphonic Acid	• Trimethoprim I.P., B.P.
• 4, 4' Dinitro Stilbene 2, 2' Disulphonic Acid	• 2-Mercapto-5-Methoxy Benzimidazole
• 4' Nitro 4' Amino Stilbene 2, 2' Disulphonic Acid	• Astemizole
• Para Amino Azo Benzene 4' Sulphonic Acid	• Enalapril Maleate U.S.P
• Para Amino Azo Benzene 3, 4' Disulphonic Acid	• Omeprazole
• 1, 3 Phenelene Diamine 4 Sulphonic Acid	• Acetamide
• 3 Amino Acetanilide 4 Sulphonic Acid	*Fine Chemicals*
• 1, 3 Diaminobenzene 4, 6 Disulphonic Acid	• Sodium Bi Sulphite
• 4 Nitro 2 Amino Phenol	• Sodium Sulphite
• 1, 4' Phenelene Diamine 2 Sulphonic Acid	• Stannous Chloride
• Nigrosine (Spirit Solution)	• Aniline Salt
• Nigrosine (Water Solution)	• Ammonia Bi Sulphite
• Nigrosine (Oil Solution)	*Fatty Acids and Derivatives*
	• Stearic Acid
	• Rice Bran Fatty Acid

Source: Company records

The major customers of SGI comprised quality conscious companies in the pharmaceutical, textile, leather, and food processing industries. Its products were mostly exported to countries in Europe, South East Asia, and the US. SGI's business philosophy revolved around delivering high quality products and following ethical business practices. This helped it in building trust among its buyers. The group had received several prestigious awards for its outstanding export performance from the central and state governments as well as from the industry associations by the Ahmedabad Management Association (AMA). Rohit Patel was adjudged the Outstanding Entrepreneur of the Year for 1997 (Exhibit CS5.1). SGI was also involved in various social and professional activities including sponsoring a computer training centre at the AMA that would be run by IBM.

Thinking about Diversification

By the year 2000, while the group was performing well in its current business, Rohit Patel realized that, as China was emerging as a major player in chemical exports, the pharmaceutical business was likely to undergo a major change. The implementation of the product patent regime under the WTO agreement by 2005[2] would lead to a significant change in the competitive situation. Since most Indian pharmaceutical companies had not focused on R&D for development of new molecules, it was expected that many of them would either manufacture for large brand owners or produce only off-patent drugs. While the share of generic medicines in the Indian market was likely to increase, the number of branded generics was likely to decrease. In such a scenario, the market might become very competitive for manufacturers of bulk

---

2. The WTO agreement required a change from the current regime of 'process patent' to 'product patent'. This was expected to have a major impact on all industrial sectors, including the pharmaceutical industry.

EXHIBIT CS5.1   Awards and Contributions

Awards

From Gujarat Dyestuff Manufacturers' Association

(a)	Award for outstanding export performance	1988–89 and 1992–93
(b)	Second award for export performance	1989–90 and 1990–91
(c)	Export trophy for the year	1995–96
(d)	First award for direct export of self-manufactured dye intermediates	1996–97, 1997–98

From the Government of Gujarat

(a)	Export award small trophy	1989–90
(b)	Silver trophy for export performance	1990–91 to 1997–98

From Chemexcil (Basic Chemicals, Pharmaceuticals and Cosmetic Export Promotion Council)

(a)	Top award in small scale sector for best export performance for dyestuff and dye intermediates	1989–90
(b)	Second award in small scale sector for best export performance (overall second amongst all chemexcil categories in various trades)	1993–94

From the Ahmedabad Management Association

(a)	AMA Atlas Dyechem outstanding entrepreneur of the year award	1997

Contributions

Sagar Group is the promoter of Sagar Drugs—AMA Computer Center at Ahmedabad Management Center, where IBM has taken the training responsibility.

drugs, suppliers of formulations to larger companies, and the formulation manufacturers themselves. This change would exert considerable pressure on the margins.

Under these conditions, Rohit Patel felt a strong need to look for diversification opportunities. The natural choice that came to his mind was to do something related to pharmaceuticals due to the group's long association with the sector. Two other sectors, software and retailing, were also identified on the basis of their growth opportunities. Software was dropped from further consideration due to rapid technological change, high attrition rate of skilled manpower, high investment, and severe competition in the industry. It was also felt that even though the group had the financial resources and knowledge of international markets to enter the business, the investments might not be recoverable in the event that the business did not perform as expected.

The retailing sector in India, as a whole, was showing strong signs of 'modernization'. The size of the retail market in 2000 was about ₹90,000 crores, of which the organized[3] sector contributed about ₹20 crore. Of the various important segments of retailing, Rohit Patel zeroed in on pharmaceutical retailing. This was because of the in-house knowledge of the pharmaceutical industry and the relative lack of know-how and resources in other segments. In pharmaceutical retailing, prescription (ethical) drugs accounted for around ₹14 crore, while non-prescription (over-the-counter) drugs accounted for about ₹2 crore.

Initial Assessment of Pharma Retailing

Rohit Patel had known that the pharmaceutical drugs business was characterized by high trade margins of up to 40 per cent. The margins remained primarily with the retailers. In Rohit Patel's assessment, this scenario

---

3. Organized retailing is a phrase used in the industry to differentiate the new retailers, with institutionalized systems and procedures, from the traditional retailers where the operations are person/owner dependent and there is a problem of scalability.

of the pharmaceutical industry was unlikely to change in the near future even after the implementation of the WTO agreements.

Almost the entire retail pharma business was with the traditional retailers. Organized pharma retailing had seen some developments in the recent past. A large business house, the RPG Group, had started a chain, Health and Glow, for retailing drugs, health, and beauty products. Some of the newly built multi-speciality hospitals, such as the Apollo Hospitals Group, were entering the pharmacy business. Rohit Patel noticed encouraging changes in consumer profiles. Among the consumers, the average age, education level, income, and awareness about health care was going up. Nuclear families and shifts to urban centres were on the rise. There were also indications of an increasing behavioural and attitudinal shift from curative to preventive medicines. These, together with early onset of lifestyle diseases such as diabetes, hypertension, asthma, and arthritis, were contributing significantly to the growth in expenditure on health and personal care, especially for children and elders. The availability of health products in all categories, such as cold and cough remedies; pain relievers; remedies for stomach disorders; medicated derma, hair, and oral care products; personal hygiene products, especially for women; and health foods and beverages (neutraceuticals) had increased significantly. There were clear evidences of a desire for better quality products. Consumers were also showing a preference for alternative systems of medicine, such as Ayurvedic and herbal products. To Rohit Patel, the most interesting aspect of the business was that the recession and other macro-economic factors had insignificant effect on the medicine business.

Prevalent Retail Practices

The initial assessment mentioned above helped Rohit Patel to think about venturing into pharmacy retailing. Since SGI did not have experience in retailing, it planned to buy 50 ongoing stores. However, he requested a team from SGI to come up with an in-depth analysis of the pharma retailing opportunity. The team found that almost all of the pharma retail stores were family-run and small in size. They measured between 150 and 250 sq. ft. Many of them did not have the necessary equipment to preserve the medicines properly. In many outlets, the mandatory refrigerator was either switched off during non-working hours for saving electricity or was not working, being under repair. In many areas, there

were regular power cuts, but there were no standby arrangements for power supply. This situation could lead to reduction in the efficiency of drugs that needed to be kept under refrigeration. Also, a significant number of medicines were supposed to be stored at temperatures ranging from 8°C to 24°C. This required air conditioning. However, very few stores were air conditioned.

The drugstores/chemists[4] could be classified into three categories: those attached to hospitals, those around areas with a high concentration of chambers of consulting doctors, and those in residential or market areas. The 'hospital' stores were generally attached to hospitals or nursing homes. They catered mainly to the requirements of patients admitted in the hospital and hence planned their merchandise accordingly. They were housed either in the hospital building or its compound and dispensed a limited number of medicines. Most of them measured about 120 sq. ft on an average. The stores located around consulting doctors' chambers, though part of the main marketplace, dealt in medicines prescribed by the consulting doctors. Selection of merchandise was guided by the specialities of the doctors and their brand preferences. Some of the doctors also had interest either in formulation manufacturing or in a nearby medicine store. The third category of stores, near the residential areas, provided the benefits of proximity and personalized service to consumers. Some of these stores offered home delivery and credit to regular customers. Almost all of these stores dealt in other consumer goods, especially products of personal consumption. However, in a large number of stores, the shoppers had to stand outside the store, be it summer or monsoon. Rohit Patel reflected, 'The most important person in the business is the most neglected in this business.'

The SGI team found that the pharma retail business was fraught with irregularities in adhering to laws and had other malpractices. The sale of medicines was regulated by the Foods and Drugs Act. However, the Act was followed more in letter than in spirit. For example, every store was required to have a pharmacist for dispensing medicines in the store. However, a pharmacist was either only on the payroll or was generally absent during important working hours. The team also reported that a part of the business was done on cash basis to save on government taxes. In such a system, a pharmacy employee could replace the prescribed drug by a

---

4. Drugstore: A retail shop where medicine and other articles are sold.
   Chemist: A health professional trained in the art of preparing and dispensing drugs (http://www.hyperdictionary.com).

more profitable one. He could also get the drug from a neighbouring store and pocket the customary trade margin without the owner ever coming to know.

The country had about 300,000 pharmacy outlets, of which about 12,000 were in Gujarat. They dealt in all forms of medicine, including the alternative systems of medicine. Allopathic drugs were dispensed more in urban markets. India had about 27,000 manufacturers that produced over 60,000 brands/SKUs of drugs. Any pharmacy, depending on its size and location, would have to keep about 500–10,000 SKUs. In comparison, a small grocery store would keep 200–500 SKUs. The problem of counterfeit drugs was also rampant. Retail outlets had little control over their inventories. Most of them were carrying about 6 months' inventories and many times failed to even return expired medicines to respective manufacturers within the prescribed time.

The report was not very encouraging for the SGI, which valued ethical working. Rohit Patel was quite doubtful about being able to manage the existing outlets because of the prevailing business practices and style of working of staff in the sector. He kept the plan of entering pharma retailing on hold.

Rethinking on Entering Pharma Retailing

In the year 2000, Rohit Patel had sought the advice of an independent consulting firm for SGI's generic formulations business and to explore avenues for business diversification. Mr K.K. Sureka, an independent consultant who had the experience of managing the pharmaceutical business of one of the leading business houses in the country, participated on behalf of this firm. He observed that, in the previous decade, while all disciplines of the health care business—drug manufacturing, hospitals, diagnostics, investigations, surgical equipment and procedures, and medical specialities—had witnessed tremendous modernization on par with global standards, pharma retailing was one area that had made no progress. This was because the business was still in the hands of small-time private traders. The business was highly fragmented and no new investments were coming in. The retailers were highly united and resisted change. They could also carry on like this due to a lack of effective regulatory set up. Sureka felt that the time was ripe to take an initiative as customers would welcome a change for the better. He suggested that, as in the case of large-scale retailing of other products such as grocery and apparel, it was

possible to corporatize pharma retailing. He advised that the scope of drug retailing itself could be enlarged to cover a whole range of health care and wellness products. He suggested that it would be possible to achieve large volumes of business through a franchisee model, which, in turn, would help in spreading risks and improving procurement costs and efficiencies. This discussion led to a decision to explore the retail pharmacy business once again. Discussions revealed that it would be possible to take care of Patel's earlier concern about management through proper implementation of systems and use of information technology. It was felt that investment in real estate could be considered quite safe in the context of increasing real estate prices. The investment in inventory could be recovered through discount sales in case the venture did not succeed. Having thought through the risk attached to the business, Rohit Patel requested the consultants to proceed with the detailed feasibility study of the proposal and to recommend a suitable strategy.

Developing the Concept of Planet Health

The consultants proposed to study the pharmacy market in India and abroad—mainly the US and Europe—in order to develop a model that would suit the company's objectives and values. Field visits of leading pharmacy retailers of the country and desk research were carried out.

Pharmacy Practices in the US and Europe

The pharmacies in the US were well-organized and dealt in many products, including photography and personal products, but focused mainly on personal consumption products. Medicines accounted for 50–70 per cent of their sales. The number of medicines stocked was less than 1,000 and about 100 of them contributed a large part of the revenue. There was no price control in the US market, but due to Intellectual Property Rights (IPR) protection, drug prices were 15 to 20 times higher than those prevailing in India. Also, the prices of products remained relatively stable over their life cycle. The likelihood of new product introduction was limited to new FDA approvals. The power of the doctors to switch the medicine was limited as only a few brands of an active ingredient and its analogues[5] were available. The customers had limited influence on selection of medicines, though they were far more knowledgeable about the drugs because of higher education and higher exposure to medicinal literature and media. Pharmacists played an important role as a link between the doctor

---

5. Analogues: A structural derivative of a parent compound that often differs from it by a single element (http://www.hyperdictionary.com).

and the patient. Some of the pharmacies were licensed to make drug compounds as well.

The role of pharmacists in the developed world, including Europe, was very important in hospitals as well as pharmacies. The pharmacists were supposed to be a repository of knowledge regarding drugs available in the market. They knew about their properties, mechanism of action (MOA), adverse effects, interaction with other drugs and food items, and their administration and compliance. They also kept themselves abreast of newly reported side effects and off-label uses of existing drugs as well as the introduction of new drugs. In major hospitals, there were pharmacists who accompanied the doctors on their rounds. In such cases, doctors diagnosed the disease and prescribed a class of drugs, while the pharmacists decided on the specific brands and their doses. They advised the pharmacy on the stocking of drugs. They also guided and advised patients in proper administration of drugs. In Europe, pharmacies, referred to as apothecaries,[6] were not merely drug dispensing outlets. The attached pharmacists played the role of advisors in the consumption of medicines. They were authorized to compound drugs as well.

Study of Pharmacy Retail Chains in India

The consultants made field visits to understand the working of key retail chains in Chennai, Delhi, and Mumbai. These were the major towns in India where organized retailing of medicines was beginning to appear. Chennai, the capital of Tamil Nadu, a state in the south of India, could truly take credit for successfully pioneering the culture of drugstore chains in the country. Apollo, a large chain started by the Apollo hospitals group a family owned chain called Muthu Pharma; two multi-product chains, Health & Glow and Subhiksha; and another chain, Tru Value, were studied in Chennai. During their field visits to Delhi, the Model Pharmacy Project at Hamdard University, the pharmacy outlet at Indraprastha Apollo Hospital, and Lifespring were among the major chains studied. In Mumbai and Vadodara, Medicine Shoppe, a franchisee-based retail drugstore chain promoted by Cardinal Healthcare Inc., USA, was studied. The US chain operated 1,400 stores in 10 countries (the US, Canada, Mexico, Taiwan, Philippines, Indonesia, Thailand, Malaysia, and Australia).

From the published report it was found that the private final consumption expenditure (PFCE) of Indian consumers has gone up from ₹14698 crore in 1990–91

to ₹98168 crore in 2000–01. One of the reasons for the increasing investments in medicines is that there has been an increase in the number of people of advanced age. Table CS5.2 provides the key indicators of health for the periods 1990–91 and 2000–01.

Visit reports (Exhibit CS5.2) were studied to understand the strategies and operations of different formats followed by pharmacies such as the Apollo group's pharmacies, Medicine shoppe, etc. Each of the stores differed in their business models. Most of them sold cosmetics and toiletries, while Subhiksha mostly sold groceries from the store. Most of the stores were operated through franchisees. Some, especially Apollo, practised central purchasing, while Medicine Shoppe had authorized its franchisees to source locally. Lifespring in Delhi, promoted by an Indian from Australia, was also planning to attach a gymnasium and a spa to the store. Other stores sold products similar to the current pharmacies.

Evolving the Concept

Sureka was influenced the most by the Model Pharmacy Project, Delhi. In this pharmacy, a qualified pharmacist advised the shoppers. The concept was similar to the pharmacies in Europe where the pharmacists played the role of advisors in the purchase and consumption of medicines. This was unlike in India where a pharmacy was merely a drug-dispensing unit for shoppers. From his experience, Sureka knew that drug consumption in India was based more on cure than on prevention and, in a large number of cases, the patients did not complete the course as they 'felt' that they had been cured. The doctors did advise the patients about dosages, but most of them had no time to explain the rationale for a particular drug or its dosages. Moreover, the explanation provided by the doctor might not be fully comprehended by the patient or the accompanying person. Some patients sought such advice from other staff in the doctor's clinics. Many others tried to gather information at the chemist shops. The person at the counter, not necessarily a pharmacist, was usually not able to provide the information sought. This, reportedly, led to higher deaths due to negligence in the administration of drugs. Sureka felt that this void at the retail outlets needed to be filled. It would add a lot of value to the consumers. He decided to recommend that SGI should follow the business model of a retail chain of community pharmacies.

---

6. The word 'apotheca' originated in the 14th century from the Greek word 'apotheke' to describe one who prepares and sells drugs or compounds for medicinal purposes.

TABLE CS5.2   Health Indicators (1990–91 and 2000–01)

Health Indicators		1990–91	2000–01
Population	National	846,387,888	1,027,015,247
	Urban	253,916,366	285,354,954
Income Classes		**1995–96** **(in crore)**	**2000–01** **(in crore)**
The very rich (above ₹2,15,000 p.a.)	National	0.7	1.5
	Urban	0.5	1.1
Consuming class (₹45,000–2,15,000 p.a.)	National	18.6	26.5
	Urban	9.3	15
Climber (₹22,000–45,000 p.a.)	National	31.2	42.9
	Urban	9.4	9.8
Aspirant (₹16,000–22,000 p.a.)	National	25.4	19.2
	Urban	4	2.2
Destitute (less than 16,000 p.a.)	National	19.1	14
	Urban	3	1.6
Life expectancy	National	58 yrs	61 yrs
	Urban	NA	NA
Literate population	National	359284417	566703280
	Urban	133140330	200031868
Avg. size of family	National	5.8	5.7
	Urban	6.1	5.5

Source: The Marketing Whitebook 2003–04; *Business World*; and www.censusindia.net

EXHIBIT CS5.2   Other Pharmacy Retailers in India

1. *Apollo Hospital Pharmacy Chain*

Apollo Hospital, Chennai, has a chain of 60 pharmacies under the following categories:

Hospital Pharmacies: These are pharmacy stores attached to an Apollo Hospital. They are presently operating in Chennai, Hyderabad, and Delhi. The Chennai Hospital Pharmacy (measuring 250/300 sq. ft) records daily sales of ₹3 lakh (₹11 crore/annum). The pharmacy stocks around 6000 Rx brands/presentations. Almost all the business comes from Rx products. The consumption of Rx and other hospital products is not included in this turnover. The hospital pharmacies in Hyderabad and Delhi have achieved daily sales of ₹1 lakh and ₹1.5 lakh, respectively. For the current year, additional hospital pharmacies have been planned at Apollo's upcoming hospital projects in Coimbatore, Madurai, and Chennai.

Clinic Pharmacies: These are pharmacy stores attached to an Apollo clinic. The clinic pharmacies are attached to Apollo clinics in Chennai, Hyderabad, and Vishakhapattanam. The pharmacy attached to Apollo Clinic, T. Nagar, Chennai, has daily sales of ₹60,000. Depending on the location and flow of visitors to the attached clinics, other clinic pharmacies have registered daily sales of ₹15,000 to ₹40,000. The interiors of each pharmacy differ from place to place, depending on the availability of space. One common feature, however, is that the furniture in these pharmacies is made of white

(Contd)

(Exhibit CS5.2 Contd)

cedarwood. All clinic pharmacies are open round the clock, seven days a week.

IOC Pharmacies: Apollo has entered into an agreement with Indian Oil Corporation (IOC), the country's largest petroleum retail company, to set up around 100 pharmacy stores at their petrol pumps. About 20 such stores have been set up in Chennai, Delhi, Hyderabad, Ahmedabad, and Gandhinagar. Based on the location of the petrol pump, Apollo Hospital is required to pay a lump sum amount of annual lease rent and 4 per cent royalty on sale of its products to IOC.

Stand-alone Day-and-night Pharmacies: Apollo operates around 45 stand-alone day-and-night pharmacy stores. The size of these stand-alone stores, depending on the location and their residential/commercial potential, varies from 150 to 350 sq. ft. Most of the stores in this category, however, are close to 150 sq. ft in size. The stand-alone locations include high-traffic areas such as airports. All these stores operate on a 24 × 7 format. Apollo has plans to soon start stand-alone pharmacies in all district headquarters of Tamil Nadu, and a couple of stores in New Delhi. The total sales of the stand-alone day-and-night pharmacy stores in Chennai are estimated to be between ₹4 to 4.5 lakh per day (average daily sale: ₹20,000 per store). These pharmacies record higher sales (55 to 60 per cent) in the night shift. The Rx products sales (appx. 6,000 brands/presentations) account for 80 per cent of the total sales by value. The non-Rx products account for the remaining 20 per cent of total sales by value.

Purchasing: Apollo has centralized all its procurement operations of pharma products by obtaining stockistship of 160 pharma companies in respective states through its group company Keimed, headquartered in Hyderabad. Over the counter (OTC) products and fast moving consumer goods (FMCG) are procured through the local stockists of respective companies. Apollo places much emphasis on direct procurement of Rx products as they offer the highest contribution—around 34 per cent, comprising 20 per cent retailer's margin, 10 per cent stockist's margin, and 4 per cent discount against cash payments. Against this, while the contribution on OTC products varies from 10 to 20 per cent, that of FMCG varies between 8 to 12 per cent. For this reason, Apollo is not too keen on promoting the sale of non-Rx products.

Storage and Distribution: Apollo's central storage and distribution units are located at Chennai, Hyderabad,

and Bangalore, which service the requirements of stores located in respective territories. The distribution of Rx and non-Rx products to pharmacies in Chennai (except for hospital pharmacies) is centralized. These products are distributed through the Central Distribution Cell. The salient features of the Chennai Central Unit are as under:

Area:	1,200 sq. ft
No. of Employees:	33
Transportation Vehicles:	LCV – 1, Van – 1
Operating Days:	365
Frequency of Delivery:	Alternate Day
Stock:	6,000 Rx brands and 4,000 non-Rx brands. Few Ayurvedic products are stocked. Imported products are not stocked.

2. Health & Glow

Health & Glow is a pharmacy retail chain promoted by RPG Guardian Ltd—an RPG Group company—in a 50:50 joint venture with Dairy Farm International (DFI). It is modelled on the famous 'Guardian' chain stores in Singapore. Dairy Farm International is a large international retailer based in Hong Kong, with over 2,500 outlets spread over Singapore, Hong Kong, Malaysia, Australia, and New Zealand. It has a turnover of US$12.8 billion.

Health & Glow launched it first store in February 1997 in Anna Nagar, Chennai. In a year's time, more stores were started in Harrington Road, Puraswalkam, TTK Road, Kasturiba Nagar, and Thiruvanmiyur. The stores stock over 4,500 products consisting of a wide range of medicines, cosmetics, skin care products, hair care products, medical care products, health food/drinks, special diet products, fitness products, music cassettes and CDs, and many more items of personal use. The stores are aesthetically designed and offer a pleasing environment although the material used for constructing the display shelves is of average quality. The Rx section stands out because of its style. The inputs for décor have been provided by the franchiser company's Hong Kong outfit. Currently, the chain operates about 10 pharmacy outlets in Chennai and 3 retail outlets in Bangalore. The retail outlets range from 400 to 800 sq. ft in size and register daily sales of ₹20,000 to ₹40,000. All the outlets are operated

(Contd)

(Exhibit CS5.2 Contd)

on company ownership basis with premises on lease rent. The company employs around 100 employees to manage the 10 retail outlets in Chennai. Health & Glow believes in encouraging bulk purchases. It offers 10 per cent discount on single Rx purchase of over ₹1,000.

3. Muthu Pharmacy

Muthu Pharmacy operates a chain of 14 pharmacy stores in Chennai. The main pharmacy located at Pursawalkam has a daily turnover of ₹65,000 (70 per cent Rx products and 30 per cent non-Rx products). This outlet is considered to be the largest pharmacy outlet in southern India. The company stocks approximately 8,000 pharmaceutical (Rx plus OTC) products. The pharmacy offers counselling and door delivery facilities to its customers. It proposes to start a quick delivery service with two independent telephone lines to book orders from its customers. Muthu Pharmacy does not believe in offering discounts to its customers. It feels that the customers are mostly interested in the availability of genuine products and quick delivery of required items at their doorstep.

4. Tru Value

Tru Value was a pharmacy chain promoted by Tamil Nadu Dadha Products Ltd (TDPL), a company taken over by Sun Pharma Ltd, Mumbai. The chain operated around 15 pharmacy outlets in Chennai. The outlets used to offer Rx products at an across-the-board discount of 10 per cent and hence ran into trouble with the local traders (distributors as well as retailers). The trade association stopped supplies through its members and the chain was forced to close down.

5. Subhiksha

Subhiksha, meaning 'prosperity' in Sanskrit, is a chain of pharmacy and grocery stores in Chennai. The chain operates about 80 stores in Chennai and 20 stores in the rest of Tamil Nadu. It has an average daily sale of ₹40,000 per outlet. Subhiksha's main emphasis is on items of grocery and provisions, which account for 90 per cent of its total sales. Rx products account for the remaining 10 per cent of total sales. Most of the private medical stores look neater, cleaner, and more well-presented than Subhiksha.

6. Model Pharmacy Project, New Delhi

M/S Apothecaries Ltd, New Delhi, has set up a 'Model Pharmacy' at Hamdard University. The pharmacy was commissioned in April 2000 and operates on a 24 × 7 basis. Daily sales have grown from ₹15,000 on the first day to ₹26,000 in May 2001. The store occupies an area of 600 sq. ft with an additional area of 100 sq. ft for counselling. The average inventory level is ₹10 to 12 lakh (equivalent to 40/45 days' sales). The stores employ a total of 14 pharmacists (10 regular employees and 4 trainees). The medicine sales (Rx plus OTC products) account for almost 85 per cent of the total sales. Cosmetics and other FMCG products contribute the balance 15 per cent of total sales. The sale of Rx products is around 60 per cent of medicine sales. The OTC products contribute 35 per cent of total sales. The peak sale hours are from 8 a.m. to 2 p.m. as 60 per cent of daily sales occur during this period. The night shift (8 p.m. to 8 a.m.) accounts for only 10 per cent of the daily sales. The location of outlets within the hospital premises (especially during OPD timings) governs the peak sale period. The pharmacy caters to the needs of the Hamdard University campus population (1,000 families) and residential population of surrounding areas like Alaknanda.

The pharmacy does not dispense the medicine without prescription and dispensed prescriptions are marked as 'dispensed'. However, at times, medicines are dispensed without prescription to (i) known patient suffering from chronic ailments and known to be consuming the medicine on a regular basis, or (ii) patients who genuinely appear to be in need of a particular medicine. The dispensed medicines are marked with useful instructions and are packed in a paper envelope/box or plastic bag displaying the Model Pharmacy catch line 'Rx PharmAssist' in bold. The supply of medicines is invoiced using custom software and every dispensing is invoiced. The small value supplies (where the customer does not care to have an invoice) are invoiced through an 'open bill' for the shift/day. The pharmacy does not 'substitute' medicines without consulting the doctor and substituted supplies are marked as 'Please refer to your doctor'. The pharmacy does cut strips and stocks the balance quantity in packets. The inventory is maintained using an alphabetical classification system and all brands containing the same AI are kept in a common box. The procurement/purchase of medicines is done through the local distributors and hence the store has to work on a 'retailer's margin' basis. The average margins are: 9 to 10 per cent for well-advertised FMCG goods/cosmetics, 12 to 13 per cent for other FMCG products, 18 to 20 per cent for Rx products, above

(Contd)

(Exhibit CS5.2 Contd)

20 per cent for generic Rx products, 100 per cent for surgical products, and 15 to 45 per cent for OTC and proprietary products. The pharmacy store has obtained licenses for wholesale as well as retailing of all categories of medicines. The pharmacy occasionally runs promotion programmes (screening sessions, disease workshops, counselling sessions, etc.) in the community area. Sometimes, during these programmes, a discount coupon (worth ₹10) is provided to attract customers. The pharmacy does not seem to make any other promotional efforts in a serious manner. The pharmacy has so far not been able to expand to multiple locations (except for a very small outlet in Delhi with daily sales of ₹6,000) in spite of its willingness to offer franchising free of cost. The lack of strong marketing and commercial capabilities appears to be the key reason for the absence of growth.

7. All India Chemist and National Medical Store

All India Chemist and National Medical Store have two stores located in the subway connecting All India Institute of Medical Sciences (AIIMS) and Safdarjung Hospital. Both the stores operate from very small premises (barely 150 sq. ft each) and occupy a part of the subway width to conduct business. The daily combined sales of both the stores are estimated at ₹4 to 4.5 lakh.

8. Medicine Shoppe

Medicine Shoppe is a franchising-based retail drug chain promoted by Cardinal Healthcare Inc., USA. The drugstore chain operates 1,400 stores in 10 countries (USA, Canada, Mexico, Taiwan, Philippines, Indonesia, Thailand, Malaysia, and Australia). In India, it operates through a mater franchisee—Melrose Trading Company Ltd, Mumbai, a company promoted by Dolphin Laboratories and the CI Gandhi family of Calcutta. It started its operations in 1998. The company has set up 11 'Medicine Shoppe' drugstores. The company had planned to set up 65 franchisee outlets in western India during the period 2001–02. It had an ambitious plan to set up a chain of 500 'Medicine Shoppe' stores by 2005. The company lays great emphasis on the opening day sale of its new outlets. Melrose had set up the first 'Medicine Shoppe' drugstore at Lokhandwala complex, Andheri, Mumbai, in February 1999. The company initially operated this store for 9 months to gain retailing experience and to develop franchising plans for the Indian market.

The average opening day sale is reported at ₹16,000. Marketing efforts are focused towards increasing retail outlet memberships. Generally, a membership of 500 is achieved on or before the opening day. The Merchandising Department negotiates special discounts with non-pharma suppliers for the supply of such goods to franchisee outlets. These discounts are then passed on to the outlet members. Generally, 4 to 5 products are offered under special discount schemes every month. Medicine Shoppe outlets have a set of marketing programmes. Some of these are as follows:

- The loyal customer programme (5% discount to members whose purchases exceed ₹600 within a period of 2 consecutive months)
- Referral programmes (₹10 to 20 discount offered to members for referring a new member)
- Display shelves hire scheme
- Promotion schemes
- Free checkup/screening on specified dates at the outlet
- Free counselling sessions on specified dates at the outlet

The franchisee outlets obtain their prescription drugs directly from the approved local distributors. Melrose assists in negotiating the terms of supply with these distributors. It permits the franchisee outlets to sell drugs (26 categories), customer products (13 categories), and surgical products (not specified). Melrose proposes to undertake centralized purchase of the prescription drugs in the long run.

During the initial period, the franchisee is advised to maintain the stocks/inventory equivalent to 2 months' sales. It is required to target reduction in stocks/inventory to 1 month's sales level after a period of one year. Melrose provides a 'start-up list' and initial order quantities of medicines. The Medicine Shoppe outlet at Calcutta has entered into a corporate tie-up with ITC to supply medicines at a special rate to its employees at the nearby Calcutta office. Melrose provides 5 days' training to the owner and pharmacist of the Medicine Shoppe franchisee outlet prior to opening of the outlet. The outlet employs two pharmacists, two assistants, and one helper supervised by an outlet manager who is also responsible for accounts and inventory management. The stores are run for 14 hours from 8 a.m. to 10 p.m. and employees work in two shifts.

EXHIBIT CS5.3   I am a Pharmacist

1. I have information about most of the drugs.
2. I provide medicines and pharmaceuticals.
3. I sincerely attempt to keep myself abreast of current developments in my profession.
4. I help patients to understand the proper use of medicines.
5. I assist patients in their choice of OTC (over-the-counter) drugs and on prescription.
6. I encourage and promote sound personal health practices.
7. My professional services are available to all at all times.
8. I promote the laws governing the practices of pharmacy and help in their proper implementation.

This is my calling. This is my pride.

In this model, the pharmacists would counsel and educate the shoppers about the drugs and their consumption (administration). They would serve as a link between, doctors and patients whenever required. The core value of this concept resided in the duties and responsibilities of a pharmacist that were developed on the basis of a document of the International Pharmaceutical Federation, the Netherlands, that described the Standards for Quality of Pharmacy Services, referred to as the 'Good Pharmacy Practices' (GPP). It indicated that good pharmacy practice requires that

(i)   a pharmacist's first concern in all settings is the welfare of patients;
(ii) the core of the pharmacy activity is the supply of medication and other health care products of assured quality, appropriate information and advice for the patient, and monitoring of the effects of use;
(iii) an integral part of the pharmacist's contribution is the promotion of rational and economic prescribing and of appropriate use of medicines; and
(iv) the objective of each element of pharmacy service is relevant to the patient, is clearly defined, and is effectively communicated to all those involved.

The role of a pharmacist for the proposed pharmacy was adapted keeping the Indian conditions in mind while retaining the basic values. The modified description, as given in Exhibit CS5.3, was utilized to draw up the guidelines for developing the business concept. The consultants also proposed that this distinct concept could be operationalized through a chain of franchised stores to successfully tap the pharma retailing opportunity in India.

Operationalizing the Concept

The concept of community pharmacists required a total shift from the current practice of pharmaceutical retailing. The focus was to shift from diseases or medicines to wellness. The key decisions in operationalizing the concept were to be in line with the corporate philosophy of ethical practices and business excellence. The broad decisions were regarding the brand name, operating philosophy, merchandise to be offered, retail formats to be adopted, and the level of customer service and relationship management to be practised.

Corporate Philosophy   The cornerstone of corporate philosophy of SGI was that the law of the land, even though it meant much higher investment in human resource and materials, must be followed in letter and spirit. This would imply that, among other things, SGI would have to hire qualified pharmacists, provide air conditioning and refrigeration facilities, arrange standby storage and power supply equipment, and sell all merchandise on bills for its new venture. This would definitely increase the costs of running the stores compared to the existing drugstore format.

Selecting Brand Name   An observation of the names of current stores revealed that their names were based on the names of owners' family members, gods/goddesses, or something that did not mean anything. There was a lot of debate on whether the name should be in Hindi, Sanskrit, or a local language (Gujarati). As Rohit Patel wanted the chain to be pan-Indian, Hindi and local languages were discarded in favour of English and Sanskrit. It was decided that the name of the store had to connote health or medicine and should have a national appeal. It was then felt that a foreign-sounding

EXHIBIT CS5.4   List of Brand Names

Pink Health	Health Street	Medimall	Rapheal	Dawa Ghar
Green Health	Health Square	Medipoint	Your Health	Dawasthan
Precious Health	Health Point	Medisquare	My Health	Dawa Sagar
Glowing Health	Healthway	Medimart	Wellness Home	Charak
Golden Health	Health Star	Medimind		Meri Dawa
Healthy Happy	Health Mart	Mediwall		Chikitsa
Healthy Wealthy	Health Sagar	Medihome		ILAJ
Health Wealthy	Planet Health	Mediplus		Suraksha
Happy Healthy	Health Planet	Medirelief		
Mega Health	Health Home	Medishop		
Good Health	Health Plus	Medihatt		
Pure Health	Health Shop	Medihut		
True Health	Health Shoppee	Mediindia		
	Health India	Medicross		
		Medigreen		

name might help in making a positive impression on the prospective shoppers. The consultants generated a large number of names for the chain (Exhibit CS5.4). After evaluation by the internal team, the name Planet Health was chosen. This reflected a range that encompassed health activity. Health products and medicines formed a core part of the business. At a later date, it could also encompass other disciplines of the health care business. This name would also serve well when Planet Health would decide to expand its operations outside India.

Operating Philosophy   The operating philosophy of the business would be to provide the best service and world-class ambience and shopping experience of pharma products to the customer. This translated into

(i)   genuine and properly stored products;
(ii)   health-related merchandise, including monitoring devices;
(iii) multiple products and brands, including Ayurvedic products;
(iv)   counselling for shopping;
(v)   counselling for proper administration of products, especially medicines;
(vi)   home delivery;
(vii) 24 × 7 service;
(viii) tie-up with doctors and paramedical services; and
(ix)   loyalty programme for a long-term relationship.

It was realized that such a business model would involve high investment in real estate and equipment

and increased costs of energy and manpower. It would also involve the problem of shrinkage, common in large-scale retailing, while earning the same margin as other retailers. Sureka believed that, as a pioneer in providing world-class drug retailing suitable for Indian conditions, these costs would have to be incurred. These could be recovered by attaining high volumes in the quickest possible time by providing superior service and products (especially, better preserved products) as compared to what the customers had so far experienced in India. In the beginning, it was envisaged that, as in the current pharmacy retail format, medicines would contribute 70–80 per cent of the sales while occupying 20–25 per cent space. The higher ratio of medicines would be reduced slowly with increase in the sale of other items without compromising the growth in medicines.

In the beginning phase, it was proposed that SGI should run some stores on its own. It was felt that, after gaining sufficient experience in managing the stores, it would be possible to design a good franchisee model and also guide the franchisees better.

Merchandising   The guiding principle of the merchandising policy of Planet Health was that all products should have a bearing on health care. In the area of drugs, as far as possible, the store was to adjust the mix in such a way as to satisfy the largest numbers of customers in their first visit. The relevant product categories besides prescription and over-the-counter medicines were to be alternative medicines, nutraceuticals, health food and health supplements, personal care, baby care and mother care products, pet care products, surgical and rehabilitation products, and health monitors and devices. There were doubts, however, about the food and snacks category. For recommending the mix of medicines, an analysis of the stocking patterns of the retailers obtained from the study of retail business was used.

It was found that although they carried a wide variety of drugs (2,000–10,000 SKUs), about 20 per cent of them contributed to more than 75 per cent of their sales. The merchandise mix varied with the location, and, more significantly, with the association to hospitals or nursing homes. The prescription drugs accounted for more than 80 per cent of the medicine sales in most of the stores. For providing a high level of service, it was proposed to include a number of sub-categories that had several products and brands. The total number of SKUs was planned to be about 20,000 and the number of brands around 600. The proposed merchandise mix and its classification are given in Table CS5.3.

The merchandise was to be procured locally, especially in the beginning, as the order size was not going to be large enough for approaching manufacturers directly. This would also avoid double taxation and other formalities related to it[7]. However, there was a threat of the likely resistance from traders' associations due to the organized nature of the proposed business. This threat had to be managed well for the business to succeed. It was also decided not to carry any of the suppliers' products if their business practices conflicted with the ethical values of the group, even though this might result in non-stocking of some highly profitable items.

It was planned to carry stock with a targeted fill rate of 95 per cent. A 1–2 day order cycle was planned. To tackle the problem of shrinkage, a system of bar codes was proposed. The proposed code consisted of several digits, of which some would not be accessible to the operating personnel. Only Rohit Patel could decide these 'non-accessible' codes. Nevertheless, shrinkage of 1 per cent was expected. The estimated investment in hardware and software for this purpose would be ₹20 lakh. The information system was proposed to be specially developed, as the available retail software did not suit the requirements of Planet Health.

Store Format and Location Experience of drug buying by consumers indicated that a visit to a pharmacy was a

forced visit. Shoppers were always in a hurry to collect the medicines and leave the store. To provide a good shopping experience it was planned to provide a relaxed but efficient shopping environment to the customer. Keeping this in mind, it was decided to locate the stores in residential areas. The presence of doctors or hospitals in the area would be an added advantage.

The target customers of the store were to be the educated middle and upper class households. Residential localities having many high-rise buildings in the trading area were to be preferred. The trading area was expected to be about a kilometre's radius from the location of the store. The sites were to be selected so that the store had prominent visibility and there was enough parking space. The location, if possible, should also attract shoppers who would walk in at leisure.

In order to deliver the shopping experience, it was proposed to open a set of 'mother and daughter' combinations in each town. The mother store, measuring about 2,000 sq. ft, was to be the largest store and was expected to set the benchmark for the shopping experience and created an identity of Planet Health, distinct from other pharmacies. It would also deal in all health-related merchandise. The daughter stores, smaller in size but having a similar identity, were to be designed to suit the requirements of the trading areas they served. Daughter stores were classified as base, suburban, and central pharmacy. The smaller cities might have only daughter stores. A description of the stores is given in Table CS5.4.

Store Design and Layout All stores were to have a similar identity. The design was to be based on building trust among the shoppers through purity, transparency, and openness. It would provide a full view of the store to passers-by, a complete view of the layout to the customer at entry, and separate entries and exits so that a customer could walk through the shop. To facilitate the walkthrough, the merchandise on display, prescription medicines, and billing counters were to be as distant from the entry as possible. The store had to look rich and elegant without being opulent like a lifestyle store.

Unlike in the developed countries, where the prescription needed to be fed into the system and the shoppers would wait for long for billing and deliveries, Indian shoppers were always found to be in a hurry. Therefore, the store was to be designed in such a way

---

7. The country's sales tax policy required that companies paid central as well as state taxes if the purchase and sale happened in two different states.

TABLE CS5.3 Categories Planned

First Level Categories	Second Level Categories	Third Level Categories
Health care products	Pain relief	11
	Cough and cold	8
	Stomach remedies	10
	Diabetes management	8
	First aid	17
	Anti-allergens	4
	Anti-smoking	2
	Bandages and supports	6
Vitamins and nutritional care products	Diet and nutrition	10
	Vitamins	12
	Minerals and nutrients	9
	Other supplements	12
Baby care products	Accessories	6
	Diapers and bath needs	5
	Food and formula	2
	Health remedies	8
Personal care products	Deodorants and antiperspirants	6
	Eye and eye care	10
	Family planning and contraceptives	6
	Feminine care	8
	Foot care	10
	Hair and scalp care	7
	Health appliances	11
	Incontinence	6
	Mouth care	12
	Shaving needs	6
Beauty care products	Bath and spa	8
	Cosmetics	16
	Fragrance	3
	Skin care	14
	Manicure/pedicure	8
	Hairstyling and colours	9
Food and snacks products	Candy and gum	4
	General grocery	8
Alternative medicines and other products	Nutritional products	2
	Hosiery	8
	Personal gymnasium equipment	3
	Ayurvedic preparations	NA
	Homoeopathic preparations	NA
	Herbal products	2

TABLE CS5.4 Comparison of Different Formats

Base Pharmacy	Suburban Area	Central Pharmacy	Mother Pharmacy
Near hospital/near consultants	Residential area	Mid town/shopping	Central
250+ sq. ft	500 sq. ft	1,000 sq. ft.	2,000+ sq. ft
Prescription (Rx) drugs	Prescription (Rx) drugs	Prescription (Rx) drugs	Prescription (Rx) drugs
Proprietary drugs	Proprietary drugs	Proprietary drugs	Proprietary drugs
Non-prescription (OTC) drugs	Non-prescription (OTC) drugs	Non-prescription (OTC) drugs	Non-prescription (OTC) drugs
Infusions and surgical products	Infusions and surgical products	Infusions and surgical products	Infusions and surgical products
Health care products	Health care products	Health care products	Health care products
Vitamins and nutritional products	Vitamins and nutritional products	Vitamins and nutritional products	Vitamins and nutritional products
	Baby care products	Baby care products	Baby care products
	Personal care products	Personal care products	Personal care products
	Herbal preparations	Beauty care products	Beauty care products
	Ayurvedic preparations	Herbal preparations	Food and snacks
		Ayurvedic preparations	Pet products
		Homeopathic preparations	Herbal preparations
			Ayurvedic preparations
			Homoeopathic preparations

that the shopper spent more time buying or browsing before reaching the billing counter. It was thought that this would not only give the opportunity to expose the store to the shoppers but also increase the bill size and value. The prescription drug section was to be separated from the other products by the billing counter. There was also to be a provision to dispense medicines from a side window during late-night hours. The window could be open to a drive-through. Separate entry and exit points were planned. An information kiosk and a counter that provided information on the loyalty programme was to be placed near the exit point. It also had to provide for night working with adequate safeguards. Guidelines were to be developed and given to the interior designer.

Promotion The launch of Planet Health was to be planned in one town. Ahmedabad was the obvious choice as it was the home of SGI. Six stores (5 daughters and 1 mother) were planned in Ahmedabad to create the visibility to capture the differences in shopping behaviour across the city. It was found that, initially, for one or two stores, the mass media would not be cost effective for creating awareness. TV would be wasteful and print very

expensive. Local language newspapers would be far more costly than English newspapers. It was planned to open the campaign with teaser advertisements that would be carried in the city supplement of the largest English daily. It would be supported by bilingual (Gujarati and English) freestanding inserts in both English and local language newspapers in order to reach about 100,000 households.

It was felt that customer loyalty would play a crucial role in building the business quickly as well as in increasing the stakes for competition. The loyalty programme would entitle the members to several value-added services related to their health needs. It was planned to approach about 5,000 households personally by a team of canvassers. The shoppers would be told about the importance of properly preserved and professionally dispensed genuine medicines in a professionally run medicine store through a presentation. The canvassers would also approach doctors and hospitals to build a network and to provide health services to its customers. The total cost of promotion, including advertising, was estimated at ₹10 lakh during the first year.

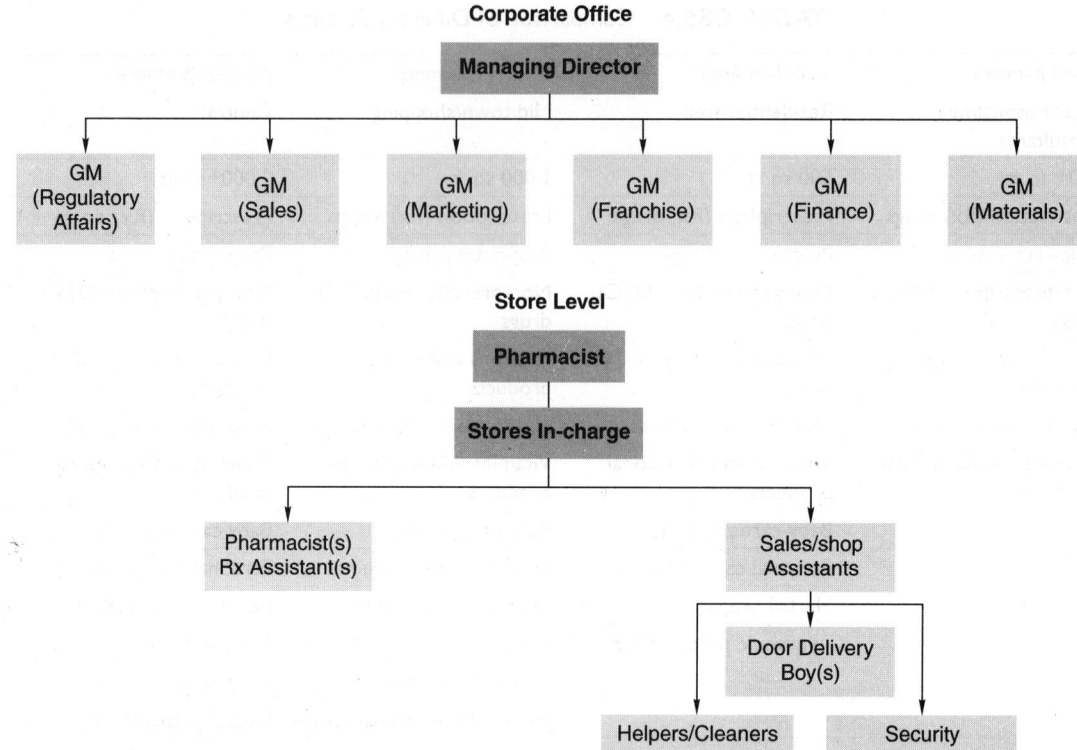

FIG. CS5.2   Organization Chart

Organization of Planet Health

It was proposed to have a team of six general managers at the corporate office: one each for procurement, finance, sales, marketing, franchise, and regulatory affairs (Fig. CS5.2). It was felt that till the business grew to a certain size, Planet Health could draw upon SGI's resources for managing procurement and finance functions and have one person look after sales and marketing. A franchise manager would be appointed after finalizing franchise policy.

A key decision which would help in the process design and management was to organize the stocking of drugs by alphabetical order so that a person knowing basic English could locate and fill the orders. The current practice was to stock the drugs according to the manufacturer's name. This was followed as the supplier's salespeople could visit the store and book requirements for replenishing the stock without disturbing the store personnel. However, this resulted in difficulties in providing quick service to customers as only persons having knowledge of individual manufacturer's brands could fill the customer prescriptions.

Recruitment of suitable pharmacists and recruitment and training of front room and back room staff was thought to be crucial for success. The staff was to have a proper uniform matching the image of the store.

The Decision

The consultants met Rohit Patel regarding the feasibility of the proposed retail business concept and guidelines for implementation. Detailed financial projections for different store formats were presented (see Tables CS5.5a and CS5.5b) by Sureka. At the end of the presentation, Sureka added, 'If we are able to generate a revenue of about ₹1,000 per sq. ft per month, we can venture into this business.' While the concept was appealing, Rohit Patel reflected about the higher investment and operating cost as compared to competing retail formats. He was concerned whether the revenue projections would come right. He looked at the statements and said to the presenting team, 'The whole thing sounds interesting, but let me sleep over it.' and he left the room.

TABLE CS5.5(a)   Profitability Analysis

Summary Profit and Loss Estimates (in ₹ '000)

Particulars	250 sq. ft Store					500 sq. ft Store				
	1	2	3	4	5	1	2	3	4	5
Gross sales/ daily	17.00	22.10	28.73	35.91	44.89	24.00	31.20	40.56	50.70	63.38
Gross sales/ annual	6,205	8,067	10,486	13,108	16,385	8,760	11,388	14,804	18,506	23,132
% contribution from sales	18.40	18.94	19.21	19.48	19.75	18.15	18.69	19.23	19.77	19.77
Contribution from sales	1,142	1,528	2,014	2,553	3,236	1,590	2,128	2,847	3,659	4,573
Gross income	1,212	1,638	2,168	2,756	3,498	1,703	2,310	3,097	3,986	4,992
Interest on FV of premises	112	112	112	112	112	224	224	224	224	224
Gross expenses	1,259	1,499	1,835	2,255	2,642	1,882	2,215	2,684	3,271	3,808
Net profit	−47	139	333	501	856	−179	95	413	715	1,184
Cash profit	250	426	612	781	1,140	314	575	883	1,187	1,661
Cumulative cash flow	250	676	1,288	2,070	3,210	314	888	1,771	2,958	4,619
Startup cost (Capex)			2,081					3,684		

Particulars	1,000 sq. ft Store					2,000 sq. ft Store				
	1	2	3	4	5	1	2	3	4	5
Gross sales/daily	29.00	37.70	49.01	61.26	76.58	38.00	49.40	64.22	80.27	100.34
Gross sales/annual	10,585	13,761	17,889	22,361	27,951	13,870	18,031	23,440	29,300	36,625
% contribution from sales	19.25	19.79	20.06	20.33	20.60	20.45	20.72	20.99	21.26	21.80
Contribution from sales	2,038	2,723	3,588	4,546	5,758	2,836	3,736	4,920	6,229	7,984
Gross income	2,160	2,916	3,854	4,892	6,201	2,975	3,950	5,213	6,610	8,471
Interest on FV of premises	449	449	449	449	449	897	897	897	897	897
Gross expenses	2,428	2,808	3,344	4,018	4,625	3,428	3,899	4,568	5,406	6,150
Net profit	−268	108	510	874	1,576	−453	51	645	1,204	2,321
Cash profit	608	970	1,361	1,728	2,437	1,064	1,551	2,135	2,694	3,820
Cumulative cash flow	608	1,578	2,939	4,667	7,103	1,064	2,615	4,750	7,444	11,264
Startup cost (Capex)			6,897					12,550		

TABLE CS5.5(b)   Profitability Estimates (500 sq. ft)

	Capex	Year 1	Year 2	Year 3	Year 4	Year 5
Gross sales/daily		24	31	41	51	63
Gross sales/daily (non-FMCG)		18	24	32	41	51
Gross sales/daily (FMCG)		6	7	9	10	12
Gross sales/annual		8,760	11,388	14,804	18,506	23,132
Contribution from sales		1,590	2,128	2,847	3,659	4,573
Annual display space rental income		48	86	115	144	173
Annual income—value-added services		21	38	60	91	131
Miscellaneous income		44	57	74	93	116
Other income		113	181	250	327	419
Gross income		1,703	2,310	3,097	3,986	4,992
Expenses						
Salaries and wages		468	538	619	712	819
Energy		309	340	374	411	452
Others		161	172	184	197	211
Operating expenses		938	1,050	1,177	1,320	1,482
Membership programme		20	10	12	13	16
Discounts		169	219	285	356	445
Advertising and promotion expenses		175	228	296	370	463
Marketing expenses		364	457	593	739	924
Marketing expenses (%)		4.20	4.00	4.00	4.00	4.00
Royalty fees		88	228	444	740	925
Direct expenses		1,389	1,735	2,214	2,799	3,331
Interest on inventory		55	42	32	35	40
Interest on fair value of premises	2,243	224	224	224	224	224
Amortization	354	53	53	53	53	53
Depreciation	1,088	142	142	142	142	142
Deferred revenue expenditure		18	18	18	18	18
Int., amortiz., dep., and def. rev. exp.		493	480	470	472	477
Gross expenses		**1,882**	**2,215**	**2,684**	**3,271**	**3,808**
Net profit/(loss)		**−179**	**95**	**413**	**715**	**1,184**
Cash profit/(loss)		**314**	**575**	**883**	**1,187**	**1,661**
Cumulative cash flow	**3,684**	**314**	**888**	**1,771**	**2,958**	**4,619**

Questions

1. Find out the profitability of each of the formats discussed in the chapter and suggest which one Planet Health should adopt.
2. What values does Planet Health want to deliver? How does each format stand with regard to delivering these values?
3. How does each format relate to the location of stores?
4. What changes are required for each of the formats with regard to categories, layout, and branding decisions?

6 Deciding Location

LEARNING OBJECTIVES

After studying this chapter, you will be able to
- understand the critical role of store location in retail business
- discuss the process of deciding location
- understand the process of trading area analysis and site identification
- decide locations for retail outlet networks

INTRODUCTION

A store is a place, real or virtual, where the shopper comes to buy goods and services. The sales transaction occurs at this junction. Location becomes a critical decision for a retailer for several reasons. First, location is generally one of the most important factors customers consider while choosing a store. Second, a bad location may cause a retailer to fail even if its strategic mix is excellent. On the other hand, a good location may help a retailer succeed even if its strategic mix is mediocre. Third, store location is the least flexible element of a retailer's strategy mix due to its fixed nature, the amount of investment, and the length of lease agreements. Even when a lease provides easier exit options, a frequent change in location is a high-risk decision. Shoppers get irritated, and frequent shifts can also give the impression that the store is not performing well. Fourth, a store 'inherits' a lot of its character from its location. A store on a high street portrays a different identity compared with a similar store in a residential area.

PROCESS OF DECIDING LOCATION

In deciding a store location, decisions need to be taken on two broad issues: (i) the current and the future potential of the catchment area of the store and (ii) the exact site of the store. The process could consist of the following steps:

1. Evaluate alternate geographical (trading) areas in terms of the potential characteristics of residents, offices, commercial settlements, and existing retailers.
2. Determine what type of sites are desirable from the three basic locational formats: isolated, unplanned district, or planned centre.
3. Select the general locations for the store.
4. Evaluate specific alternative store sites.

A flowchart of the location decision-making process is shown in Fig. 6.1.

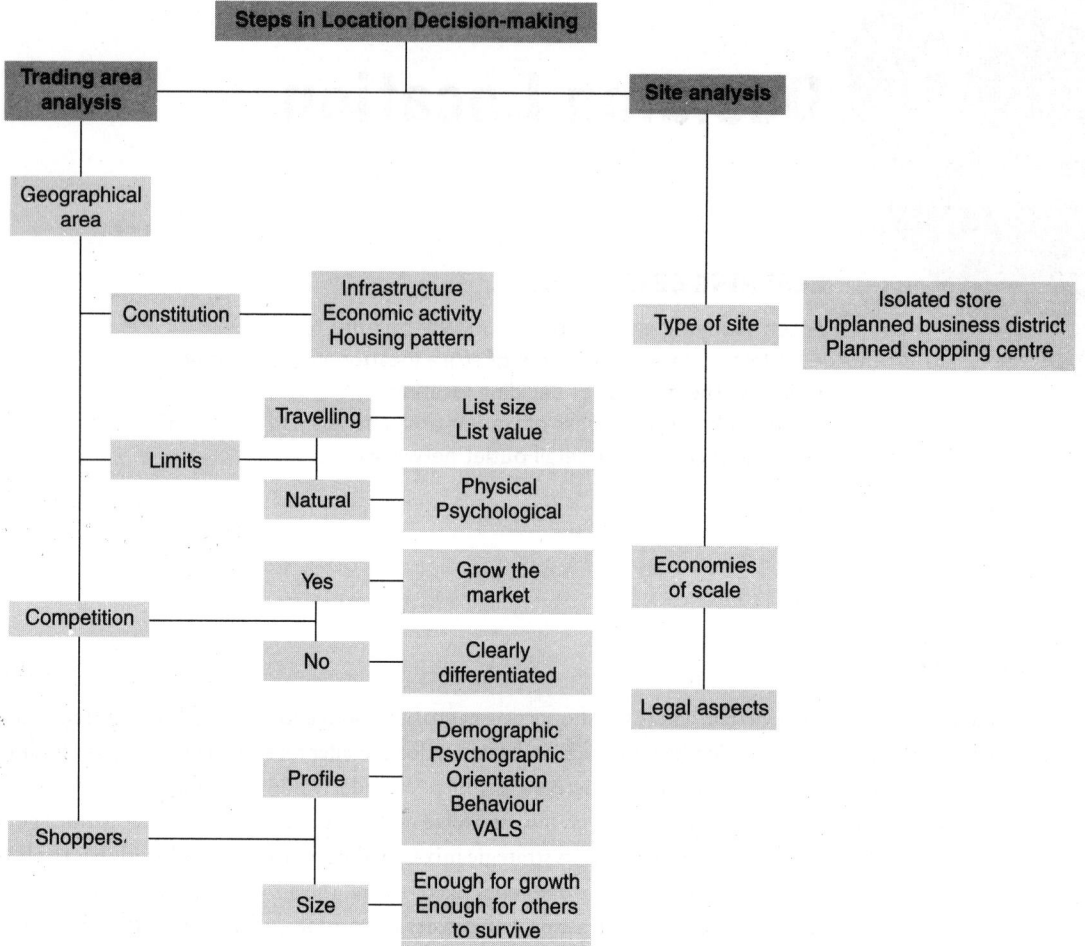

FIG. 6.1   Steps in Deciding Store Location

Trading Area Analysis

A retailer investigates alternative trading areas as the first step in choosing a store location. A trading area is a geographical area containing the customers of a particular store or group of stores for specified goods or services. The trade areas can be divided into three zones—primary zone, secondary zone, and tertiary zone. The *primary zone* is the geographical area from which the store or shopping centre derives 50 to 80 per cent of its customers. It is the area closest to the store and possesses the highest density customer population and the highest per capita sales. There is little overlap with other trading areas (both intra-store and inter-retailer). The *secondary zone* is the geographical area of secondary importance in terms of customer sales, generating about 20 per cent of a store's sales. It is located outside the primary area and the customers are more widely dispersed. The *tertiary zone* (the outermost ring) includes customers who occasionally shop at the store or shopping centre. It typically includes some out shoppers who are willing to travel greater distances to patronize certain stores.

Figure 6.2 defines the trade areas for Indian consumers for different products in the years 2000 and 2001.[1]

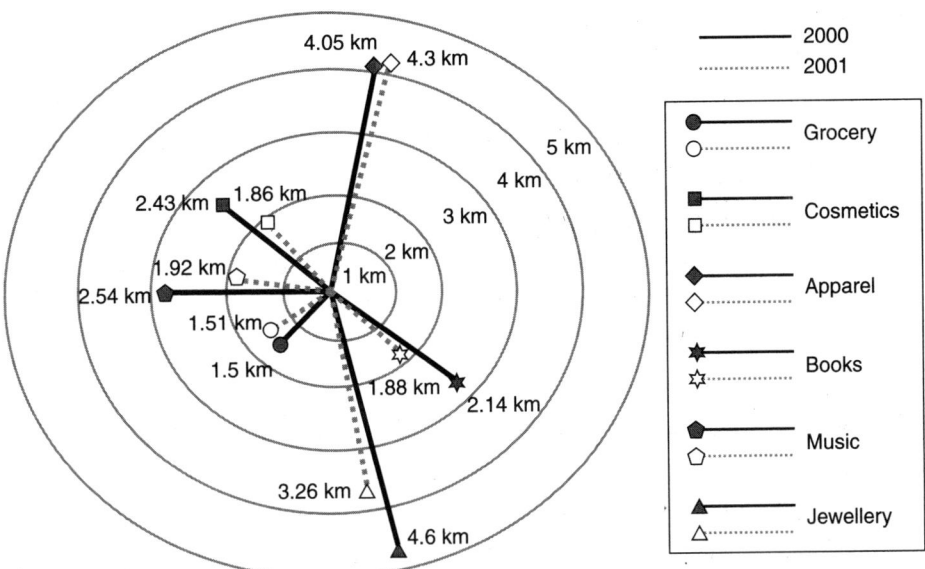

FIG. 6.2 Trade Areas for Various Products (2000 and 2001)

Source: KSA Technopak—Consumer Outlook 2002

In the figure, a shift is noticed in the constitution of the trading area over a period of one year. In some product categories, such as grocery, the distance is reducing as new stores spring up and the shoppers do not perceive any difference among stores. The distance increases in high involvement categories or in categories where shoppers exhibit a variety-seeking behaviour.

A store considers several factors while determining its trade area. The impact of geographical area, competition, and shopper profile is discussed here.

Geographical Area

For deciding on the store location, a retailer needs to assess the geographical terrain of its trading areas. It also needs to consider the infrastructure, economic activities, and housing pattern in that area.

A retailer should keep in mind the infrastructure development trends in a given area. Transportation networks, banking facilities, and other support services play an important role in the development of retail in a given area. Travel or driving time has an influence on the size of a trading area. Physical barriers, such as toll bridges, poor roads, high traffic, railway crossings, and one-way streets, would reduce the size and determine the shape of the trading areas. Economic barriers such as difference in sales tax between towns also affect the size and shape of trading areas. If a state has lower taxes, the size of its trading area increases as it is able to entice customers to travel long distances in order to save money. In addition to physical barriers, customers may also build up psychological barriers. For instance, stores located 'on the route' may be patronized more than those away from it. Sometimes, locations may be avoided because of racial, religious, or historical considerations and biases. Travel time has also been found to be influenced by the size of purchases in terms of either number or value of items.

The economic prosperity of an area can be gauged by the commercial and industrial establishments in the region. Bengaluru, for instance, has become a major retailing hub, since it has a large software industry that represents a younger and richer population as compared to Chennai, which has more traditional industrial settlements. It is also useful to know the sources of income of the people residing in the concerned area. An area with more residents in the salaried class has a different spending pattern as compared to one with a dominant business community. Similarly, the spending pattern of those working for large multinational companies is different from those working for small and medium-sized firms. Market employment is an indication of the changes in the purchasing power of the shoppers in the given area. An area with a diversified employment base is better as the impact of cyclical trends will be less significant.

The density of population has a direct impact on the type, size, and number of stores in a given area. In areas where most of the population lives in multi-unit housing facilities, the trading areas tend to be small, leading to several shopping clusters.

Competition

Competition can affect the success of a store in a particular location in two ways. The presence of competition reduces the effort required by a store to build traffic in the store. While the absence of competition does promise higher potential, presence of competition is an indication that the customer expectation has been proved and is relatively easy to manage. When examining competition in an area, a retailer analyses factors such as the number, size, and distribution of existing stores, the rate of new store openings, the strengths and weaknesses of competing stores, trends, cycles, and the level of saturation. These factors need to be evaluated in the light of an area's population size and growth.

Depending on the level of competition, an area can be defined as saturated, understored, or overstored.[2] A *saturated trade area* offers customers a good selection of goods and services. Customers come to these areas because of a wider selection and the assurance that they will be able to purchase the desired merchandise and their trip will not go waste. In such areas, retailers have to ensure that they have the required merchandise, competitive prices, and good service. The grouping of stores increases the trading area for each store and more consumers are attracted to such locations. Some retailers choose such areas since competing with strong retailers enables them to develop robust methods and systems. In some areas, when it is found that many retailers are at the brink of closure, a new store may come with a redefined value proposition and rejuvenate that area.

Most retailers want to be located in an *understored trade area* that has very few stores selling a specific good or service to satisfy the needs of the population. It provides a large trading area for each of the retailers. In many cases, the target markets do not overlap much. Each of the stores can grow without being in direct competition.

Overstored areas develop due to the entry of retailers during events that indicate high potential. These are also witnessed in newly developed areas where retailers expect the city to grow. However, due to changes in the city development plans, such areas later become unattractive to customers. Sometimes, overstored areas also develop when the retailers fail to consider or assess the entry of competition.

Saturation can be measured with the help of certain ratios based on the throughput of the stores in a given area. These could include average sales per retail store, average sales per retail store category, average sales per square foot of selling area, average sales per employee, and average store sales per capita. These ratios need to be calibrated for different areas and their saturation levels. For instance, a petrol pump in a city would sell different amounts of petrol and diesel compared to one located on a highway. Similarly, an area with a high concentration of two-wheelers would generate more bills but the sales revenue might be less than a station in an area with a large four-wheeler population. In calculating the saturation level in an area based on sales per square foot of selling space, the retailer should take even new proposed stores into account. Sales per square foot of selling area decline when new outlets are added slowly. Furthermore, retailers also have to consider whether a new store will expand the total consumer market for a specified good or service category in a trading area or just increase the firm's market share in that area without expanding the total market. Similarly, it needs to consider whether a competing store would expand the market or eat into the incumbent stores' shares. A retailer may open another store to stop competing retailers from entering the market or to defend its market share.

Competitive information can be accessed through secondary sources such as the directories published by trade associations, chambers of commerce, Yellow Pages, specialized trade magazines, real estate brokers, and local newspaper advertising departments. Websites of most large retail chains list not only all the current locations but also future sites.

Shopper Profile

Growth of population and income are the most important considerations in selecting a trading area. The size and composition of households in an area can also be important determinants of success. For example, a lifestyle store is generally located in areas with high-income households, whereas a toy store retailer would look for locations that have a higher number of families as compared to young singles or retired couples. In fact, the composition of the population can be a crucial factor that influences the decision. For example, in Ahmedabad, new large self-service retail outlets are opening in areas that have a high density of cosmopolitan population and mostly nuclear families. These households tend to buy smaller units on a monthly basis in contrast to the typical Gujarati households that purchase cereals, pulses, oil, and spices on a yearly basis. It has been observed that nuclear families tend to purchase smaller units on a monthly basis compared to joint family households.

Some retailers often venture into new areas in the anticipation that the surrounding area will develop to create demand. In such cases, the household size is not a very critical issue as most retailers try to attract customers from other areas by offering value to the customers. Usually, retailers prefer areas that are cosmopolitan in nature. However, some choose to be part of an area that has a high concentration of a particular community and focus on their specific requirements. It is very common in India to find that stores dealing in a particular commodity such as textiles, meat and poultry, and jewellery tend to be located in a particular area as most of the retailers belong to a specific community.

Knowledge about an area's population characteristics can be gained from survey reports of organizations such as the Central Statistical Organisation (CSO), National Council for Applied Economic Research (NCAER), ACNielsen, and the Indian Market Research Bureau (IMRB). These agencies provide data regarding population size, number of households, income distribution, education level, age distribution, consumption pattern, and similar details. Besides, retailers also collect information that helps in profiling the shoppers psychographically, behaviourally, or on any other basis that can help in developing targeted strategies.

The size, shape, and characteristics of the trading areas of an existing store, shopping district, or shopping centre can be delineated quite accurately with the help of records (secondary data) or specific studies (primary data) and the buying power index (BPI). In the US, retailers use PRIZM—a computerized system for identifying communities by lifestyle clusters for procuring in-depth demographic and lifestyle data—and geographic information system (GIS) to map customers' location and density. The buying power index is a measure of a given market's ability to buy. The basic BPI is measured by assigning weights to three significant factors that exist in every market: (i) total income, (ii) total retail sales, and (iii) total population. This measure is used to determine the extent of each market's ability to buy. Thus, all other factors being constant, a region with a high BPI is preferable to a low BPI area. No matter how a trading area is delineated, a retailer should take into account the impact of weekends, special events, and sales promotions that attract people from greater distances for only time-specific periods. After the event is over, the trading area may drop.

Analysing the Site

Having identified the area in which the retailer would trade, it is equally important to identify a site that suits the positioning, costs, merchandise, and customers. This is decided mainly on the basis of the type and size of the store, the economies of scale, and the legal aspects of the site and its surroundings.

Store Type and Size

The type and size of stores also influence their trading area. Stores situated in the same shopping district or shopping centre can have different sized trading areas. The trading area of a destination store would be much larger than that of a competitor with a less unique appeal. Such stores may offer an extensive assortment in their product category or an unmatched shopping experience, use promotions more extensively, and create a stronger image. Therefore, although situated in the same shopping centre, an apparel chain with a distinctive image may attract shoppers who are willing to travel up to 30 km as compared to a non-distinct shoe store which may get shoppers from only a few kilometres.

Another type of outlet, called a parasite store, does not create its own traffic and has no trading area of its own. The store depends on customers who are drawn to the location for other reasons. For example, a magazine stand in a hotel lobby and a snack bar in a shopping centre are parasite stores that depend on the customer base of the hotel/shopping centre. In India, some of the most common places where there is a high concentration of such stores are temples, bus stations, and railway stations. Airport retailing is a significant store type in this category.

Isolated Store   An isolated store is a freestanding retail outlet located on either a highway or a street. There are no adjacent retailers with which this type of store shares traffic. There are various advantages in choosing such a retail location. There is no competition, rental costs are relatively low, and there is flexibility in terms of space and location choice. The store has better parking facilities and traffic visibility. The facilities can be designed to individual specifications. There are also various disadvantages in this type of retail location. As a rule, unplanned business districts and shopping centres are more popular than isolated stores with consumers who generate the bulk of retail sales. Therefore, it may be difficult to attract initial customers. Most people, especially the variety seeking ones, will not travel very far to get to one store on a continuous basis. Operating costs such as outside lighting, security, and maintenance costs cannot be shared. Advertising costs may also be high. Isolated stores may be appropriate for stores involved in one-stop or convenience shopping, or for destination stores.

Unplanned Business District   An unplanned business district is a type of retail location where two or more stores are situated together (or in close proximity) in such a way that the total arrangement or mix of stores is not due to prior long-range planning. Stores are located on the basis of what is best for them, and not for the district. Thus, four ice-cream stores may exist in an area with no pharmacy store. There are four types of unplanned business districts: (i) central business district, (ii) secondary business district, (iii) neighbourhood business district, and (iv) string.

A *central business district* (CBD) is the hub of retailing in a city and is synonymous with the term 'downtown'. The CBD exists in that part of the town or city which has the greatest density of office buildings and stores. It has high vehicular and pedestrian traffic. It draws shoppers from the whole urban area and includes all classes of people. The CBD has at least one major department store and a broad grouping of speciality and convenience stores. The arrangement of these stores follows no pre-set format as it depends on history (first come, first located) and retail trends.

Central business districts have several strengths that attract a large number of shoppers—potential as well as actual. A typical CBD has good access to public transportation, excellent goods and service assortments, wider range of prices, a variety of store types and customer services, a high level of pedestrian traffic, and proximity to commercial and social facilities. However, CBDs suffer from problems such as inadequate parking, traffic and delivery congestion, high rents and taxes, and older retail facilities. They can be unattractive to people living in suburbs. Some of the best examples of CBDs are around the Fountain area in Mumbai and *Teen Darwaza* in Ahmedabad. Although most cities have a single CBD, a metro may have several.

A *secondary business district* (SBD) is an unplanned shopping area that is located on service roads or at the intersection of two major streets in a city. The kinds of goods and services sold in SBDs are similar to those in CBDs, but SBDs have smaller stores, less width and depth of assortment, and a smaller trading area, so that the consumers do not have to travel far. SBDs sell a higher proportion of convenience-oriented items.

The major strengths of SBDs include good product assortment, access to thoroughfares and public transportation, and more personal service. The major weaknesses of secondary business districts are discontinuity of offerings, parking difficulties, and fewer outlets than in CBDs.

A *neighbourhood business district* (NBD) is an unplanned shopping area that appeals to the convenience shopping and service needs of a single residential area. An NBD contains several small stores, such as a dry cleaner, a stationary shop, a beauty salon, a liquor store, and a restaurant. The leading retailer is typically a supermarket, a large drugstore, or a variety store. Neighbourhood business districts are situated on the major street(s) of residential areas. The major advantages offered by NBDs are convenient location, longer hours, good parking, and a relaxed atmosphere. On the other hand, they offer a limited selection of goods and services and higher prices.

A *string* is an unplanned shopping area comprising a group of retail stores, often with similar or compatible product lines, located along a street or highway. There is little extension of shopping onto perpendicular streets. Restaurants, gift shops, and shops selling music cassettes are examples of retailers often situated in a string. A string location has many of the advantages of an isolated store site, such as lower rent, more flexibility, better road visibility and parking facilities, and lower operating costs. However, it suffers from less control over prices, lower store loyalty, and limited product variety.

Planned Business District   These are locations developed as independent shopping areas in most parts of the city. These include malls, government developed markets, and such developments that become parts of the urban development. These form part of the development plans of the cities or housing areas. A good example of this is seen in Chandigarh, the capital of Punjab and Haryana, where some of the sectors have been identified as shopping areas. The city is laid out in such a manner that this area becomes accessible easily. This area caters to almost all the requirements of the residents of the whole city. Stores in other areas are generally filler stores. The area has entertainment, eating places, and even hotels. Unlike malls, this area has stores that are independent.

Central Business District in a Large City
Source: www.bbc.co.uk

Central Business District in a Rural Area
Source: www.greatmirror.com/images

Medium Town Bazaar
Source: http://www.sos-arsenic.net

Unplanned Market
Source: http://alljames.com

Unplanned Business Areas in Rural and Urban Locations

Economies of Scale

Retailers do not usually decide the store location on the basis of what would be the one best location. Instead, they prefer locations that might not be the best, but would be beneficial for the company to open more stores in the long run. This enables them to achieve economies of scale in promotion and distribution. The choice regarding the number of stores would depend upon the ownership and objective of the owners. For example, in the case of company-owned stores, the objective is to maximize profits for the entire chain. In this case, the retailer would continue to open stores as long as the marginal revenues achieved by opening a new store are greater than the marginal costs. This strategy worked successfully for Home Depot in the US, but met with limited success for FoodWorld, which opened multiple stores in Chennai. The success lies in avoiding cannibalization of each other's market. The same scenario is being observed in Ahmedabad in the context of multiplexes (festival malls) which are getting concentrated in the same area.

Legal Issues

Issues that need to be specifically addressed in India are inflexible zoning, rent, strong pro-tenancy laws, and taxation. Zoning laws, rent controls, and protected tenancies 'freeze' land in city centres that would otherwise be available for new retail outlets and residential buildings. Protected tenants cannot be evicted, and do not voluntarily surrender their cheap tenancies, so the ancient buildings are not being renovated. These laws also restrict competition. For example, subsidized rents allow traditional inner-city counter stores to overlook their operational inefficiencies. In contrast, in Chennai, where rent control and zoning laws are less stringent, modern supermarkets already account for almost 20 per cent of the total food retailing compared to less than 1 per cent in cities with higher average incomes such as Mumbai and Delhi.[3]

METHODS OF ESTIMATING DEMAND

There are several analytical methods of estimating demand for a new store. These take into account environmental parameters such as opportunity, size, and competition while estimating demand and shopper behaviour.

Space–Sales Ratio Method

This method is based on the assumption that a store's sales are dependent on its size in comparison to that of its competitors'.[4] Thus, the market share of a store in a specific category would be proportional to the share of total space occupied by retailers in that category. In order to arrive at the demand estimates, the store first estimates the trading area and also classifies it as core, secondary, or primary. Then, the per capita sales of the category in the trade area is determined. Similarly, the total retail space for the category is established. The sales for a new store would be equal to its share of the total retail space for all the categories that it would deal in.

This is a very commonly used method due to its simplicity. It is more accurate in cases where the trade area matches with city limits as, in such cases, the trading area can be defined more accurately. This method does not consider the impact of the strategies and capabilities of stores or their competition. It is likely to induce more error in case of stores that already enjoy a good ratio of space and sales.

Proximal Area Method

This method attaches great importance to the proximity of the store location to the customers. Propounded by Christaler in 1935 and re-emphasized by Losch in 1954, it assumes that convenience is the primary driver of store choice. It follows the classical *central place theory* which states that shoppers, when faced with the problem of choice among similar stores, would select the one nearest to them. It modifies the definition of trading area and relates it to 'spatial advantage' rather than physical distance. In such a case, a store estimates demand by analysing the profile and buying habits of the population residing in this 'proximal area'.

The proximal area is determined by constructing Thiessen or Dirichlet polygons.[5] It is drawn by first designating the store (say, *A*) on the map of the area and joining it with each of the neighbouring stores *B*, *C*, and *D*. Then, the perpendicular bisector of each of the lines is drawn at *L*, *M*, *N*, and *O*. Also, the diagonals *AD* and *BC* are drawn (see Fig. 6.3a). The perpendicular bisectors are extended in such a way that the lines drawn at *L* and *O* meet at a point (say, *P*), and the lines drawn at *M* and *N* meet at a point (say, *Q*). Now, *P* and *Q* are joined and the lines *LP*, *MQ*, *NQ*, and *OP* are

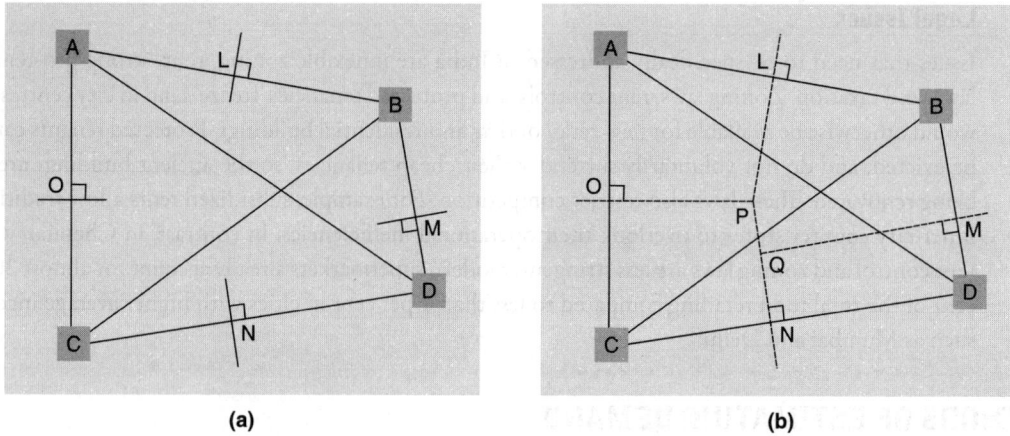

FIG. 6.3 Steps in Determining Proximal Areas

extended to meet the periphery of the map (see Fig. 6.3b). The area covered by intersecting lines *LP*, and *OP*, *LQ* and *QM*, *OP* and *PN*, and *QM* and *QN* represent the territories of stores *A*, *B*, *C*, and *D*, respectively.

Analogue Model

In this model, in order to estimate the size and sales potential of a new location, the retailer would like to match the customer demographics, competition, and the sales of currently operating stores with similar parameters at a prospective location.[6] This model helps in market expansion without bringing about major changes in the retailer's strategy due to the similarity of the target market.

The analogue approach is divided into three steps. First, the current trade area is determined. Second, based on the density of the customers of the store, the primary, secondary, and tertiary trade area zones are defined. Finally, the characteristics of the current store location are matched with a potential new store location to determine the best site. A sample set of data of the top 8 metros of India is given in Tables 6.1 and 6.2. Comparison shows that Ahmedabad and Kolkata are similar in terms of SEC profiles. Hence, a store based in Ahmedabad might consider Kolkata more than any other city if it determines its location on the basis of SEC.

Reilly's Law

The purpose of Reilly's law of retail gravitation is to establish a point of difference between two cities or communities, so that the trading area of each can be determined.[7] The point of difference is the geographical breaking point between two locations at which consumers would be indifferent to shopping at either of the two. According to Reilly's law, more consumers are attracted to the larger location or community because a greater number of store facilities exist there, making the increased travel time worthwhile. The law may be expressed algebraically as

$$D_{ab} = \frac{d}{1 + \sqrt{(P_b/P_a)}}$$

where D_{ab} = limit of location *A*'s trading area, measured along the road to location *B*; d = distance along a major roadway between locations *A* and *B*; P_a = population of location *A*; P_b = population of location *B*.

TABLE 6.1 Household Demographic Data (Top 8 Metros)

	All India	Ahmedabad	Bengaluru	Chennai	Kolkata	Delhi	Mumbai	Hyderabad	Pune
Estimated households ('000)	179,898	833	1,173	1,369	2,625	2,666	3,522	1,021	802
SEC (Urban)									
A1	1.0	4.1	6.5	7.3	4.4	8.4	4.4	5.1	6.1
A2	1.7	8.5	7.0	6.0	4.7	8.6	5.4	10.2	6.0
B1	2.5	10.8	7.2	8.7	10.0	12.0	9.1	8.8	9.0
B2	2.4	9.8	7.9	7.7	7.6	8.8	7.5	7.0	5.8
C	6.3	20.9	26.0	24.7	17.7	21.9	28.3	20.7	25.3
D	7.0	24.8	22.5	22.9	26.2	19.5	24.5	18.6	23.5
E1	3.4	8.9	8.8	13.2	13.4	7.9	10.8	8.2	9.8
E2	5.5	12.2	14.2	9.6	16.0	12.8	9.9	21.3	14.5
Monthly Household Income									
Up to ₹3,000	77.7	47.4	50.9	53.7	54.5	33.2	38.6	46.4	46.8
₹3,001–6,000	16.2	30.3	33.3	26.4	29.7	35.0	41.7	29.0	32.6
₹6,001–10,000	4.0	12.4	9.9	11.6	9.9	19.4	13.2	12.8	10.1
₹10,001–15,000	1.4	7.7	5.2	5.2	3.6	8.8	4.2	7.3	6.8
₹15,001–20,000	0.4	1.7	0.3	2.0	1.4	2.1	1.5	2.8	2.5
Greater than ₹20,000	0.1	0.6	0.3	1.3	0.9	1.5	0.8	1.7	1.2
Urban CWE Occupation									
Unskilled worker	7.5	13.4	17.6	24.7	23.1	18.8	20.3	24.2	23.7
Skilled worker	6.9	27.2	34.3	28.5	24.7	22.7	24.9	24.8	29.0
Petty trader	4.0	16.9	8.5	3.9	14.8	7.2	13.4	6.5	10.4
Shop owner	3.5	10.8	11.0	7.4	10.1	10.7	8.5	8.4	5.0
Businessman/industrialist	1.1	8.4	2.4	4.9	2.3	8.2	3.6	4.3	5.8
Self-employed professional	0.3	0.9	0.3	0.7	1.3	0.8	1.0	0.9	1.1
Clerk/salesman	3.4	12.5	9.4	14.4	11.4	15.4	14.3	13.2	9.8
Supervisory level	1.6	4.7	4.6	4.9	6.2	5.2	5.7	5.4	5.3
Officer/exec-junior	1.0	2.8	4.6	4.2	2.1	5.4	4.9	7.8	3.7
Officer/exec-mid/senior	0.7	2.6	7.2	6.4	3.9	5.7	3.4	4.4	6.1
CWE Education									
Illiterate	34.1	10.8	12.9	6.9	12.5	13.1	8.6	19.8	10.4
Literate-non-matriculate	39.4	37.5	32.2	36.3	44.5	26.2	34.7	26.8	35.3
Matriculate-non-graduate	19.1	31.7	37.6	37.9	23.0	33.3	40.0	31.5	37.9
Graduate +	7.4	20.0	17.3	18.9	19.9	27.4	16.7	22.1	16.6

(Contd)

(*Table 6.1 Contd*)

	All India	Ahmedabad	Bengaluru	Chennai	Kolkata	Delhi	Mumbai	Hyderabad	Pune
Urban Housewife Occupation									
Unskilled worker	2.6	5.7	11.8	6.1	7.7	3.7	5.3	12.1	13.5
Skilled worker	1.0	4.6	5.0	2.6	4.2	2.0	2.4	5.4	4.2
Petty trader	0.9	5.0	2.7	1.5	2.2	0.7	4.0	2.0	3.5
Shop owner	0.5	1.0	2.2	1.2	1.8	1.4	1.7	2.6	0.7
Businessman/industrialist	0.1	0.5	0.3	0.6	0.4	0.5	0.2	0.9	0.6
Self-employed professional	0.1	0.3	0.0	0.1	0.7	0.1	0.2	0.3	0.4
Clerk/salesman	0.6	1.7	2.1	2.5	1.0	2.9	2.5	3.3	3.0
Supervisory level	0.4	1.2	1.8	1.4	1.2	0.7	1.4	2.2	1.4
Officer/exec-junior	0.1	0.2	0.5	0.7	0.3	0.3	0.6	1.8	0.3
Officer/exec-middle/senior	0.1	0.1	0.3	0.6	0.1	0.5	0.3	0.6	0.5
Not working/housewife	64.1	77.6	72.0	80.0	77.4	84.8	78.8	61.3	68.3
Student	1.1	0.6	0.6	1.0	0.9	1.9	0.7	5.1	1.6
Retired	0.6	1.5	0.6	1.7	2.2	0.5	1.8	2.4	2.0
Housewife Education									
Illiterate	54.9	24.4	20.5	15.6	22.1	30.5	20.4	27.8	20.8
Literate-non-matriculate	30.2	38.7	38.5	41.8	48.2	26.7	42.0	28.0	38.0
Matriculate-non-graduate	11.3	25.3	29.1	30.7	17.4	25.3	26.9	29.5	29.2
Graduate +	3.7	11.7	12.0	11.8	12.3	17.7	10.7	14.6	12.0

Source: The Marketing WhiteBook 2003–04; The Essential Marketer's Handbook; Business World

Thus, if the distance between location *A* and location *B* is 20 km; location *A* has a population of 90,000, and location *B* has a population of 10,000, according to Reilly's law, location *A* will draw more customers as it has a larger population. Further, the point of indifference will be 15 km away from location *A*, and 5 km away from location *B* (Fig. 6.4):

$$D_{ab} = \frac{20}{1 + \sqrt{(10,000/90,000)}} = 15 \text{ km}$$

Reilly's law rests on the following assumptions: (i) two competing areas will be equally accessible from the major road, and (ii) retailers in the two areas would be equally effective. Other factors such as the dispersion of the population are held constant or ignored. Reilly's law is useful because of its ease of calculation. It is also useful in situations when other data is not available or when the cost of compiling data is too great. The retailer could use this technique along with other techniques to determine the trading area. Despite its usefulness, Reilly's law has at least three key limitations. First, distance is measured by major thoroughfares and does not involve cross streets, even though some people will travel shorter distances along cross streets. Second, travel time does not necessarily reflect just the distance travelled. Today, time can be a more important driver for a consumer than distance. Third, actual distance may not correspond with people's perception of distance. For example,

TABLE 6.2 Individual Demographic Data (Top 8 Metros)

	All India	Ahmedabad	Bengaluru	Chennai	Kolkata	Delhi	Mumbai	Hyderabad	Pune
Estimated individuals ('000)	707,237	3,132	4,371	5,053	10,869	9,534	12,739	4,022	2,850
Age Group									
12–14	9.8	9.4	8.7	7.8	7.7	9.4	8.2	10.5	8.8
15–19	13.6	13.5	13.8	13.3	12.4	13.5	12.5	14.9	12.9
20–24	12.9	13.8	14.9	14.5	12.6	14.5	14.4	14.2	14.4
25–34	22.2	24.2	24.7	23.7	23.3	25.6	25.7	23.7	24.5
35–44	16.4	16.9	16.5	16.6	17.9	16.3	17.5	16.1	16.9
45–54	11.6	10.9	10.2	11.3	12.4	10.3	11.1	10.0	10.7
55+	13.6	11.2	11.2	12.8	13.7	10.4	10.6	10.6	11.7
Sex									
Male	51.9	56.9	52.7	51.2	53.6	54.9	54.9	51.6	52.7
Female	48.1	43.1	47.3	48.8	46.4	45.1	45.1	48.4	47.3
Male Education									
Illiterate	13.5	4.0	3.7	1.8	6.0	5.6	3.4	8.0	3.4
Literate-non-matriculate	24.5	25.2	20.2	20.4	25.2	19.1	23.1	17.5	20.9
Matriculate-non-graduate	10.7	18.4	21.4	19.2	13.3	19.3	20.8	17.2	21.5
Graduate +	3.2	9.2	7.4	9.9	9.1	11.0	7.6	9.0	6.9
Female Education									
Illiterate	25.0	8.5	9.0	7.5	9.5	11.0	7.5	13.8	9.3
Literate-non-matriculate	16.4	18.4	20.7	20.8	23.9	15.1	20.2	17.6	18.6
Matriculate-non-graduate	5.4	11.3	12.8	15.2	8.1	12.4	13.0	12.1	14.0
Graduate +	1.4	4.8	4.7	5.3	4.9	6.6	4.4	4.9	5.4

Source: The Marketing WhiteBook: 2003–04; The Essential Marketer's Handbook; Business World, p. 96

a store with few services and crowded aisles is likely to be perceived to be at a greater distance than a similarly located store with a more pleasant atmosphere.

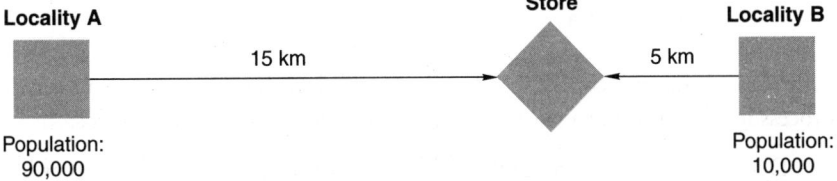

FIG. 6.4 Point of Indifference

Huff's Gravity Model

Huff's gravity model is used by retailers to define their trade areas and forecast sales.[8] This model is based on the premise that the probability that a given customer will shop in a particular store or shopping centre increases with the size of the store or centre and reduces with the distance or travel time. The objective of Huff's model is to determine the probability that a customer residing in a particular area will shop at a particular store or shopping centre. To forecast sales, the probability of the customer shopping at a particular place is multiplied by an estimate of the customer's expenditure. Then, all the estimated expenditures in an area are aggregated to estimate the sales from the area. Huff's model can be expressed as follows:

$$P_{ij} = \frac{S_j \div T_{ij}^b}{\sum S_j \div T_{ij}^b}$$

where P_{ij} = probability of a customer at a given point of origin i travelling to a particular shopping centre j; S_j = size of shopping centre j; T_{ij} = travel time or distance from the customer's starting point to the shopping centre; and b = an exponent to T_{ij} that reflects the effect of travel time on different kinds of shopping trips.

The model indicates that the larger the size (S_j) of the shopping centre compared to its competing stores, the greater the probability that the customer will shop at the centre. A larger size is generally a reflection of more assortment and variety. Travel time or distance (T_{ij}) has a negative effect on the probability that a customer will shop at a given store. The greater the travel time or distance from the customer compared to competing shopping centres, the smaller the probability that the customer will shop at the centre. Customers tend to shop at promixal stores.

The exponent b reflects the effect of travel time on different kinds of shopping trips. The larger the value of b, the larger the effect of travel time or distance (T_{ij}). A larger value of b is assigned when a store deals in convenience goods rather than shopping goods; and b is usually determined through surveys of shopping patterns or from previous experience.

Huff's gravity model can be illustrated with a simple example. Let us assume that a bookstore is planning to open a new store at University Plaza. Two major stores—Bookshelf and Kitab Kendra—also sell books in that locality. Table 6.3 provides data regarding the size of these stores and distance from the university.

TABLE 6.3   Data for University Plaza, Bookshelf, and Kitab Kendra

Shopping Centre	Size (sq. ft)	Distance from the University (km)
University Plaza	5,000	3
Bookshelf	1,000	5
Kitab Kendra	500	1

It is expected that the University Plaza store will draw heavily from the nearby university area. The process for determining a sales forecast would involve the following steps:

1. Determine the probability that a student in this university will shop at University Plaza. Using the formula for Huff's model and data for the centres,

$$P_{ij} = \frac{5,000 \div 3^2}{(5,000 \div 3^2) + (1,000 \div 5^2) + (500 \div 1^2)} = 0.51$$

2. Forecast the number of students who will buy their books at University Plaza. For this, the probability is multiplied by the number of students. Therefore, the number of students who are likely to buy their books is

$0.51 \times 12,000$ students $= 6,120$ customers

3. Determine the sales forecast. Assuming that each customer will spend an average of ₹150 on books, the forecasted sales will be

$6,120$ customers $\times$ ₹150 $=$ ₹918,000

Similarly, the forecasted sales for Bookshelf is ₹65,720 and that for Kitab Kendra is ₹821,500. Therefore, the total forecasted book sales for the entire trade area is ₹1,817,220.

Multiple Regression Model

The multiple regression model is a common method of defining retail trade area potential for retail chains with more than 20 stores.[9] The multiple regression model uses logic similar to the analogue approach, but uses statistics rather than judgement to predict sales for the new store. This approach is divided into three steps. First, an appropriate measure of performance, such as per capita sales or market share, is identified. Second, a set of variables useful in predicting performance is created. Finally, a regression equation is used to project performance for future sites.

The following example illustrates how the model works. The data for ten stores that deal in apparels in a given market is given in Table 6.4. Normally, such an analysis is carried out with several independent variables, but here, only one predictor variable—the population within a 4 km radius of the store—has been used.

TABLE 6.4 Monthly Sales and Population of Apparel Stores

Store No.	Monthly Sales (₹ '000)	Population
1	600	75,000
2	700	60,000
3	800	60,000
4	300	20,000
5	400	25,000
6	325	25,000
7	1,000	80,000
8	1,200	70,000
9	400	25,000
10	600	75,000

Assume that a proposed site had a population of 40,000 potential customers within 3 km. The regression line is derived from the equation

$$Sales = a + b_1 x_1$$

where a = a constant; b_1 = a coefficeint that defines the relationship between sales and the predictor variable(s); and x_1 = the predictor variable (0–3 km population).

Therefore, the projected performance for the proposed site is

$$Sales = 103 + (0.01 \times 40,000) = ₹503$$

In this case, as the population in that area is 40,000, and a is derived as ₹103,000, the sales is forecasted as ₹503 per month.

This simplified illustration uses only one predictor variable. In case the retailer finds that the average family income also has a strong and statistically significant relationship to sales, the new regression equation would be

$$\text{Sales} = a + b_1x_1 + b_2x_2$$

Using the multiple regression method, then, a retailer can predict the sales of a new store using variables that have been successfully used to predict sales in other stores. However, the regression method has its limitations. To be reliable, a sizeable database is required. Since regression is an averaging technique and finds the best fit, it seldom identifies extremely good or extremely poor potential locations. Finally, it assumes that the past is automatically a good reflection of the future.

Figure 6.5 shows the scatter plot of regression analysis based on the data given in Table 6.4.

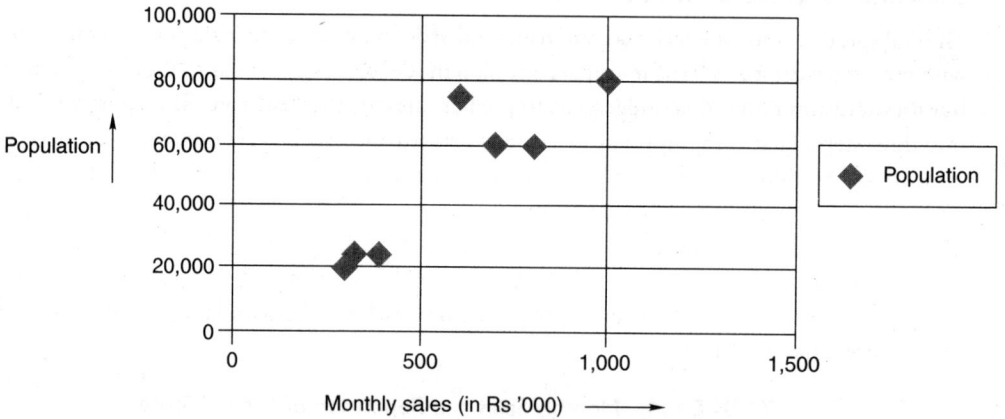

FIG. 6.5   Scatter Plot of Regression Analysis

Converse's Breaking-point Model[10]

Converse's Breaking-point Model, based on *Reilly's Law of Retail Gravitation*, generates mixed results in terms of visually confirmable trade area calculations.

The revision of the Converse's Breaking-point Model has been proposed on the basis of changed retail patterns from the original derivation of Reilly's Law and therefore it is reviewed in addition to the Converse Breaking-point Model, with revised formulae logic and applications.

In this model, Reilly's Law is extended by defining the breaking-point of trade between two cities. A customer staying at this trade breaking-point would be indifferent to the trade area. He would have an equal probability of shopping at each of the two cities in question for non-speciality goods. In particular, this ability to attract trade between the two cities or trade areas is in direct proportion to the square root of the populations of the two cities and in inverse proportion to the distance between these two cities. This relationship is expressed as follows:

$$D_{a \to b} = \frac{d}{1 + \sqrt{P_b/P_a}}$$

where $D_{a \to b}$ is the breaking-point from city a measured in miles to city b; d is the distance between city a and city b (travel time may be substituted for distance); P_b is the population of city b; and P_a is the population of city a.

Converse's Breaking-point Model and formula specifies the 50 per cent shopping probability or breaking-point in trade between two cities in either miles or travel time. The original breaking-point formula derived from Reilly's Law was criticized for being based on factors such as relative cost of travel, relative travel time, and travel convenience. It was argued that breaking-point is more easily determined in rural areas, but as the population density increases the accuracy gets affected.

DETERMINING LOCATIONS FOR NETWORKS

Developing retail outlet networks is one of the most important avenues of growth for retail firms. Locating new outlets expands the geographical area served by the firm, enabling it to increase sales, profit potential, economies of scale in advertising, distribution, and labour costs, and minimizing the uncertainties of market environment. Developing such a network requires evaluation of the impact of each store on the entire network of outlets. Therefore, traditional methods of site selection may not be ideally suited for this purpose as they focus on analysis for single store locations. Some of the methods for network locations are outlined in Exhibit 6.1.[11]

Determining Location for Online Retailers

Distance is an important criterion while determining the location for online retailers. Distance means not only space between objects but also psychological distance. Online retailers need to manage psychological distance while deciding the location, to develop the trust factor in consumers.[12] Trust remains one of the most significant factors to be dealt with during online purchase decisions. Traditional methods of site selection are of less value to today's retailers, who are concentrating on the emergence of semiotic neighbourhoods (semiotics is the study of signs, their forms of expression, and content), which have gained reputation, thereby attracting people to these neighbourhoods to browse through goods and services.[13] The retailers have to consider semiotic qualities, which have considerable influence on the retail value of the goods.

An online retailer has to make a location decision relatively along the lines of targeting potential consumers. Store-based retailers can reach out to potential customers easily with various advertising and promotional strategies. Online retailers have a different problem. Since the number of online customers is practically unlimited, it is hard to find and target them because of the wide geographical dispersion and limited resources.

In general, retailers tend to prefer markets with lower retail wages, markets where a majority of families have children and vehicles, and markets closer to the base or headquarters.[14] For online retailers it is a different scenario altogether, as they have to primarily deal with reduction of ambiguity, uncertainty, and trustworthiness of consumers, before moving on to other factors.

Understanding local geography while deciding the location has become very crucial for 'borderless' retailing. A local retail outlet delivers a sense of credibility online. The geographical proximity of the local physical outlet of an online store gives a perception of similarity to the consumers, which influences the online purchase decisions. A study by the Internet Crime Complaints Center (IC3 2003) reveals that 71 per cent of the online shoppers look at the physical address of the seller before making a purchase from an unknown retailer online.[15]

As online shopping becomes more common and as customers' expectations for customized services grow, online retailers have to take greater care in determining the ideal location to deliver relevant products and services, and enhance customer relationships.

EXHIBIT 6.1   Location Allocation Models

1. **Proximal-area-based Models**
   Competition ignoring model (CIM)
   Objective function: Minimize total travel distance
   Allocation rule: Travel to nearest centre
   Comments: Assumes negative linear relationship between distance and utilization. Ignores competitive locations
   Market share model (MSM)
   Objective function: Maximize demand within the proximal areas of outlets belonging to the firm
   Allocation rule: Travel to nearest outlet
   Comments: Consider the location of competitive outlets. Locates in interstitial sites between proximal areas of existing outlets
2. **Spatial-interaction-based Models**
   Objective function: Maximize expected market share or profit
   Allocation rule: Based on the spatial interaction model
   Comments: Considers trade-off between distance and non-distance factors. Allocates fixed demand among outlets based on the spatial interaction model
3. **Covering Models**
   Set covering model
   Objective function: Locates minimum number of outlets to serve all demand within specified accessibility criterion
   Allocation rule: Consumers patronize nearest outlet
   Comments: Optimal location pattern assures universal accessibility
   Maximal covering model
   Objective function: Minimize proportion of demand within accessibility criterion
   Allocation rule: Consumers patronize nearest outlet
   Comments: Determine trade-off between service level and investment in outlets
   Weighted covering model
   Objective function: Maximize utilization
   Allocation rule: Travel to nearest outlet
   Comments: Assumes step-wise relationship between accessibility and utilization

CHOOSING THE BEST ESTIMATION METHOD[16]

The analogue and Huff approaches are best when the number of stores with obtainable data are small, usually fewer than 30. These approaches can also be used by small retailers. The regression approach is best when multiple variables are expected to explain sales. Huff's model explicitly considers the attractiveness of competition and customer's distance or travel time to the store or shopping centre in question. Since Huff's model uses demographic variables, it is particularly important to use it in conjunction with the analogue or regression methods. Therefore, when a combination of techniques is applied and a similar conclusion is reached, the retailer has more confidence in the decision.

The methods discussed can also be applied to online stores. Although accessibility to online stores is unlimited and shoppers from across the world can buy from these stores, the trading area is determined by the cost of fulfilment. Online stores, of course, have a distinct advantage as they generally do not share the site. However, they do suffer when not listed at the top of the first or second page of the results from any search engine.

SUMMARY

Location is a critical decision for a retailer. It is the most important 'fixed' expense of retail companies. Retailers need to be careful in making locational decisions. Location determines one of the most tangible costs for customers and determines proximity. Two analyses are undertaken in this regard: trading area analysis and site analysis. The former determines the current and the future potential of the 'catchment' area of the stores. This helps the store in delineating the primary, secondary, and tertiary markets. This also determines the nature of competition in the given area for the category. The second analysis helps in determining the character of the store on the basis of its neighbourhood, and tells the retailer whether the responsibility of building the traffic lies with the store.

The extent of a store's trading area is also affected by the size of the store. As a store or centre gets larger, its trading area usually increases. This relationship exists because size generally reflects the assortment of goods and services. The trading area, however, does not increase proportionately with store or centre size. As a rule, trading areas for supermarkets are greater than those for convenience stores. Because of their size, supermarkets have a better selection of products, while convenience stores appeal to consumers' needs for fill-in merchandise. In a shopping centre, department stores typically have the largest trading areas, followed by apparel stores and gift stores. In cases where a store can manage to serve a larger trading area, the location could be decided more on the basis of other stores in the vicinity.

Several methods are available for both the analyses. A retailer should use multiple methods to arrive at a judicious decision regarding trading area and the location of the store.

NOTES

1. KSA Technopak—Consumer Outlook, May 2002.
2. Berman, Barry and Joel R. Evans 2002, 'Trading Area Analysis', *Retail Management: A Strategic Approach*, 8th edn, Prentice Hall India, p. 299; Levy, M. and B.A. Weitz 2002, 'Site Selection', *Retailing Management*, 4th edn, Tata McGraw-Hill, p. 267.
3. Lewis, William 2001, 'Unlocking Potential: Remove Barriers to India's Growth', *The Wall Street Journal*, 11 September.
4. Ghosh, Avijit and Sara L. McLafferty 1987, 'Sales Forecasting and Store Assessment Methods', *Location Strategies for Retail and Service Firms*, Lexington Books, p. 64.
5. Thiessen, A.H. and J.C. Alter 1911, 'Precipitation Averages for Large Areas', *Monthly Weather Review*, Vol. 39, pp. 1082–4; Dirichlet, G.L. 1850, 'Uber die Reduktion der Positiven Quadratischen Formen mit Drei Unbestimmten Ganzen Zahlen', *Journal fur die Reine und Angewandte Mathematik* 40: 216, in Ghosh, Avijit and Sara L. McLafferty 1987, *Location Strategies for Retail and Service Firms*, Lexington Books.
6. Applebaum, W. 1968, 'The Analogue Method for Estimating Potential Store Sales', *Journal of Retailing*, Summer, Vol. 44, Issue 2, pp. 73–7.
7. Reilly, W.J. 1931, *The Law of Retail Gravitation*, Knickerbocker, New York.
8. Huff, D.L. 1964, 'Defining and Estimating a Trade Area', *Journal of Marketing* 28, pp. 34–38.
9. Levy, M. and B.A. Weitz 2002, 'Multiple Regression Model', 'Site Selection', *Retailing Management*, 4th edn, Tata McGraw-Hill, p. 267.
10. Anderson, Steven J., Volker, John X., Phillips, Michael D. 2010, 'Converse's Breaking-point Model Revised', *Journal of Management & Marketing Research*, Vol. 3.
11. Ghosh, Avijit and Sara L. McLafferty 2002, 'Developing Retail-outlet Networks', *Location Strategies for Retail and Service Firms*, Lexington Books, p. 175.
12. Edwards, Steven M., Jin Kyun Lee, La Ferle Carrie 2009, 'Does Place Matter When Shopping Online? Perceptions of Similarity and Familiarity as Indicators of Psychological Distance', *Journal of Interactive Advertising*, Vol. 10, Issue 1, pp. 35–50.
13. Koskinen, Ilpo 2009, 'Design Districts', *Design Issues*, Vol. 25, Issue 4, pp. 3–12.
14. Zhu, Ting and Vishal Singh 2009, 'Spatial Competition with Endogenous Location Choices: An Application to Discount Retailing', *Quantitative Marketing & Economics*, Vol. 7, Issue 1, pp. 1–35.

15. Edwards, Steven M., Jin Kyun Lee, and Carrie La Ferle 2009, op. cit.

16. Levy, M. and B.A. Weitz, 'Site Selection', *Retailing Management*, 4th edn, Tata McGraw-Hill, pp. 283–4.

CONCEPT REVIEW QUESTIONS

1. Why is location so important to retailers? What are the implications of a bad location decision?
2. Enumerate the process of trading area analysis. Describe the importance of traffic pattern and competition in detail.
3. What factors should a retailer keep in mind while identifying a site for a store? How is it different from selecting a site for a retail outlet network?
4. Describe Huff's model. Why is it the most used law?
5. Using a regression analysis, find out the expected sale of a new location. The sales of other locations are given in the table:

Area	Population	Sales (₹ Million/Month)
A	35,000	2.5
B	35,000	1.9
C	65,000	6.5
D	45,000	2.5
E	33,000	1.5
F	63,000	4.9
G	70,000	6.3
H	43,000	3.7
I	23,000	1.5
J	18,000	1.2

CRITICAL THINKING QUESTION

How would a store forecast its sales when

(a) it is located on the main road in a central business district,

(b) it is a destination store, and

(c) it is located on a highway?

PROJECT

Visit a petrol station on a highway. Discuss with the owner the decision to locate the station at that particular site. Find out how the trading area is decided, especially when there is a tie-up with a fleet operator.

CASE STUDY

Aakash Book Store[1]

'Aakash Book Store is a reflection of ourselves,' said Aakash Shetty, the owner of Aakash Book Store in Calicut. Aakash belonged to a family that cherishes reading. He was also an avid reader. After a three-year stint as an engineer in a manufacturing firm, Aakash decided to convert his passion into his profession. Within three years, Aakash Book Store had become a chain with four outlets in Kerala. Besides books, the stores sold magazines, music, stationery, and gifts. The stores were about 2,000 sq. ft in size.

Recently, he visited Ahmedabad, a city in western India, on a *Bharat Darshan* tour organized by one of his friends. During his city trip he noticed that there were not many bookstores in the city. He was able to spot just about six. On enquiring, he found out that the residents here did not indulge in a high level of reading. They would rather spend time on other leisure activities. During the conversation, however, it was mentioned that some activity had lately been seen in book retailing. Crossword, a major national book retailer, had established itself in

---

1. Case written by Prof. Piyush Kumar Sinha, IIMA, based on a course project report by M. Siddharth, Anjana Sasidharan, Vishnu Saraf, Shreya Deb, Suneil Chawla, and Shameek Chakravarty (PGP 2005–07). Cases are written to illustrate a decision situation and do not indicate the effectiveness of the decision.

the city with two large format and three small format stores. Recently, OM Book Shop had opened a small format store. Crossword had been in Ahmedabad for more than five years and had become a household name in book retailing.

Aakash felt that the city had space for many more stores. He had read that the Indian book retailing market was big (₹30 billion)[2] and had the potential to reach 60 billion in the next two years. In such a case, the growth had to come from large cities. Ahmedabad had recently been granted the status of a mega-city.[3] One of Aakash's cousins was doing his MBA from Indian Institute of Management Ahmedabad (IIMA). He met him to discuss his thoughts of entering into book retailing in Ahmedabad. His cousin assured him that he would study the book retailing market. Three months later, Aakash received a report from his cousin, which stated that his gut feel was right. There was potential in the city. Aakash immediately wrote to his cousin to identify the locations where he could open his stores.

Book Retailing in India

Indian book retailing was changing at a rapid rate. The current market size of the industry was estimated to be around ₹30–60 billion. It was expected that the industry would grow by about 15 per cent per annum for the next five years. Indian retailing was changing and so was book retailing. Consumers visited stores that provided experiences in line with international stores. Traditionally, it was observed that shopping for books was restricted to book lovers. Thus, browsing through these bookstores was seen as a book lover's hobby. Now, however, bookstores were offering their consumers the experience of comfortable seating and cheerful interiors that encouraged them to stay and browse for as long as they wanted. Most of them had cafés within the store. Positioned as lifestyle bookstores, they tried to provide their consumers a complete experience. R. Sriram, CEO, Crossword Bookstore, felt that books add tremendous value to people's lives and there exists a large potential. 'We believe in the WW concept, which is "wallet and watch". We give our customers an absolute warm and friendly experience. All our stores are designed keeping the customer benefits in mind'.[4] Kolkata-based Oxford Book Store had launched a forum for aspiring actors and young writers, wherein aspiring authors were invited to present their works before an audience, who were invitees at the store and consisted primarily of customers of the store.

Distribution of books in India was largely through more than 500,000 independent retailers.[5] Their business was dependent mainly on textbooks, some activity books, and stationery. They did not provide a good shopping ambience. They accounted for less than 15 per cent of the market for English books. The new format stores had about 10 per cent of the market share. These stores were essentially non-textbook retailers. They sold books, music, magazines, stationery, and greeting cards.

A report in *The Hindu* (Thursday, 7 September 2006) stated that, in Tamil Nadu, more than three-fourths of the people between the age of 15 and 40 bought books for education. About half of them preferred to read English books. While English was associated with better employment opportunities, the upwardly mobile young adult group still seemed almost evenly split between reading English and local language books. More than a fourth of them said that books for leisure reading were important, while around a fifth of all respondents preferred reading personality development books. More than 40 per cent bought books from book fairs, though about the same proportion frequented bookshops. Online book shopping seemed to be picking up slowly with around 2 per cent choosing that mode of shopping. Most readers preferred to read at home in the evenings or night. Around half the number had personal book collections at home. The principal factors affecting the choice of books were reviews in magazines, the reputation a particular book gained by word of mouth, and the author's popularity.[6] Consumers spent about 8 per cent of their retail spending on books and music. More than 70 per cent of the customers bought from at least three stores. Some of them (5–7 per cent) also had the experience of buying books abroad at stores like Borders and Barnes and Nobles. The findings of this study were also valid for Ahmedabad.

---

2. 10 million = 1 crore
3. A megacity status put Ahmedabad in between metro and class—A cities. This had resulted in a heightened retailing activity.
4. www.etretailbiz.com/sept04/booksmart.htm
5. http://www.imagesfashion.com/back/retail/retailfeb.html
6. http://prayatna.typepad.com/satya/2006/09/book_reading_ha.html

The City of Ahmedabad

Ahmedabad, the biggest city in Gujarat, lies on 23° 1′ North latitude and 72° 37′ East longitude on the banks of the river Sabarmati. With an area of about 200 sq. km and a population of 3.2 million, it is the seventh largest city in the country. Details of the composition of its population and households are given in Tables 6.1 and 6.2 (refer to the section on 'analogue model' in the chapter).

The city is divided into East and West by the Sabarmati River. Old Ahmedabad was within the walled city. The city had grown much beyond it by now. A partial map of the city is given in Fig. CS6.1. The city had many book stores that sold textbooks. It had two main players in the non-textbook category—OM Book Shop and Crossword.

OM Book Shop

OM Book Shop belonged to a book distributor from Delhi. It had five stores in and around Delhi. The Ahmedabad store was the first store outside Delhi.

The store was located on Vastrapur road near IIMA and Ahmedabad Management Association (AMA). There were about five restaurants within half a kilometre of the store. It was visible to the traffic on the road that connected the main city to the residential area of Vastrapur, about 2 km away. Many students and executives came from all parts of the city to AMA, which conducted courses in management. Most customers had come to know of the store because of its location. An open space measuring around 10′ × 15′ led into the store entrance. Four coffee tables and chairs were placed in this area for people to sit and read. It had a tie-up with a neighbouring restaurant to serve coffee and snacks to its customers. The store, with a carpet area of 1500 sq. ft, carried books, magazines, gift articles, and children's games. The store layout is shown in Fig. CS6.2. The store looked spacious and was well lit. The interiors had a brick finish, giving the store an aesthetic appeal.

Figure CS6.3 shows the customer profile of OM Book Shop. Over half of the customers of OM Book Shop were in the age group of 15–25 years. About

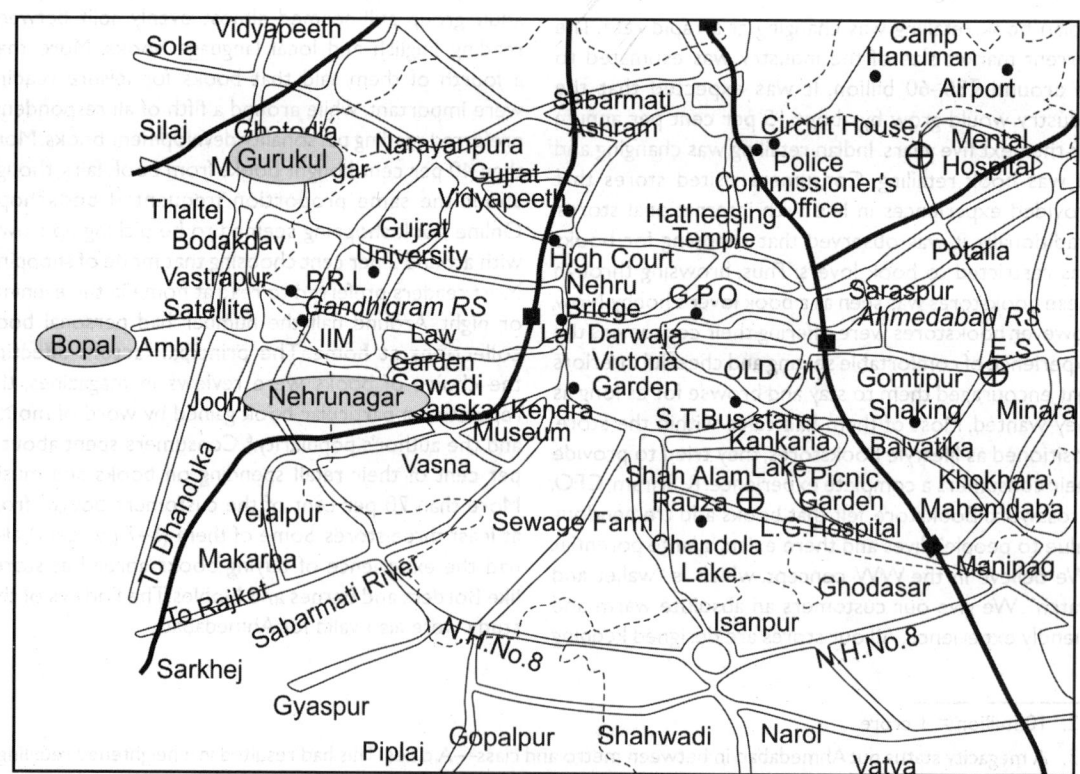

FIG. CS6.1   Partial Map of Ahmedabad[7]

7. www.mapsofindia.com

Entrance

Sitting Area

Book Shelves

Display Near the Entrance

Aisle

OM Book Shop, Ahmedabad

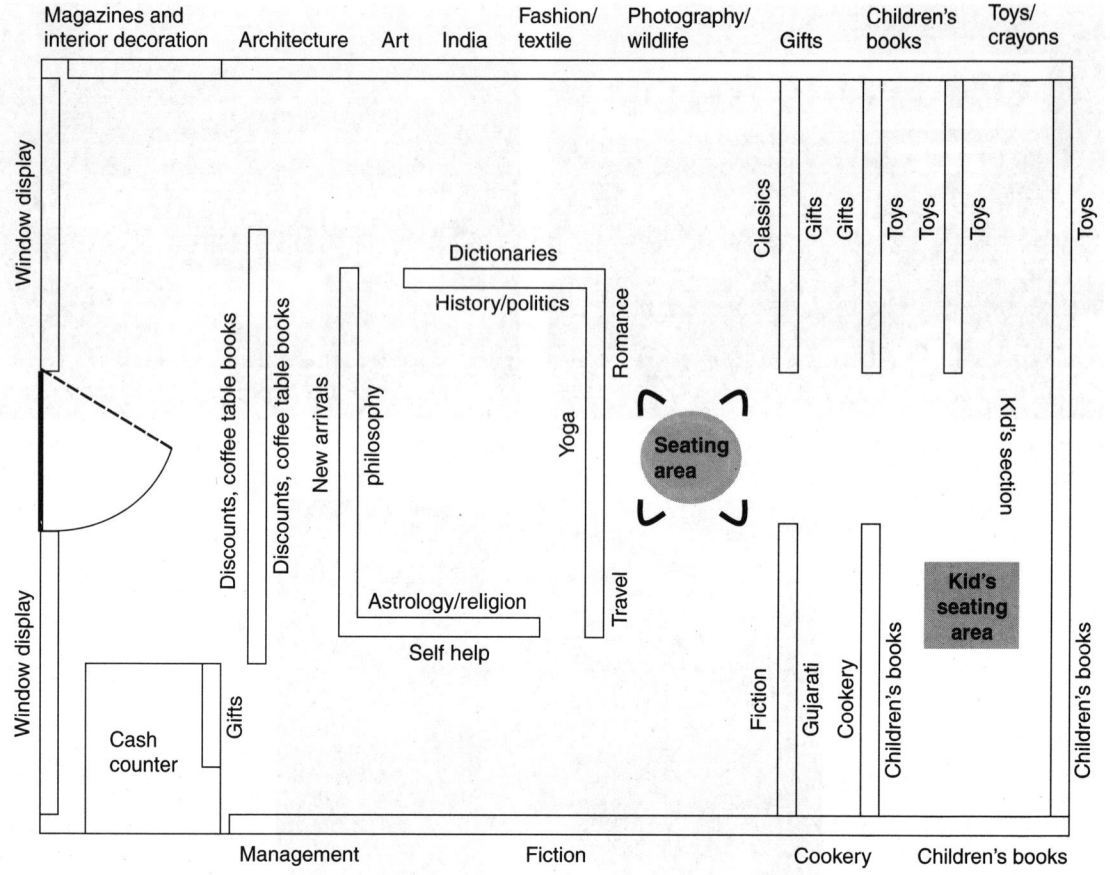

FIG. CS6.2 Store Layout of OM Book Shop

two-thirds of them were unmarried. More than 75 per cent did not have children. Most of the customers came through referrals. Passing by the store and invitations were the main reasons for customers to visit the store. Advertisements did not bring many customers. The store had made a good impression in the minds of its customers, with around 63 per cent of the customers stating that they preferred OM Book Shop to other similar stores. The location of the store was the most important reason, followed by the merchandise selection and ambience. Customers spent less than one hour in the store. Most customers were infrequent visitors. This could be because the store was only four months old. The store attracted about 50–100 visitors per day.

The sales personnel at OM Book Shop were friendly and non-intrusive, but they were not very knowledgeable about books in general. If a customer was interested in a particular genre of books, the sales personnel were not able to recommend any books to the customer. However, the owners of the store often talked to the customers to build more personal relations. When a book was not available in their store, they arranged for the book within two weeks and informed the customer over the phone about the arrival or non-availability of the book. More than 80 per cent of the customers expressed satisfaction with the service provided. The store ran a loyalty programme called the Privilege Club. A customer who bought books worth over ₹500 was offered this service.[8] So far, not many members had enrolled.

Crossword

Crossword operated two types of formats. Large stores (8,000–10,000 sq. ft) were called 'Crossword' and the small stores (500–2,000 sq. ft) were called 'Crossword Corners'. The city of Ahmedabad had two

---

8. http://www.om-books.com/aboutus/pri.asp

23% 63%

14%

☐ Prefer OM   ☐ Don't Prefer OM   ☐ Can't Say

(a) Preference for OM Book Store

9%   0%   9%   82%

☐ < 500   ☐ 500–1000   ☐ 1000–2000   ☐ > 2000

(b) Amount Spent per Visit to OM Book Store

☐ Convenient location   ☐ Ambience
☐ Selection of merchandise   ☐ Discount policy
☐ Helpful sales personnel   ☐ Others

(c) Reason for Preference for OM Book Store

Ranking for different attributes of OM Book Store

☐ Rank 5   ☐ Rank 4   ☐ Rank 3
☐ Rank 2   ☐ Rank 1

(d) Ranking for Different Attributes of OM Book Store

5%   45%

50%

☐ Less than 30 minutes
☐ Between 30 to 60 minutes
☐ More than 60 minutes

(e) Time Spent by a Visitor at OM Book Store

41%   0%   9%   23%

9%

18%

☐ More than once a week   ☐ Once a week
☐ Once a fortnight   ☐ Once a month
☐ Less than once a month   ☐ First time

(f) Frequency of Visit to OM Book Store

FIG. CS6.3   Customer Profile of OM Book Shop (Contd)

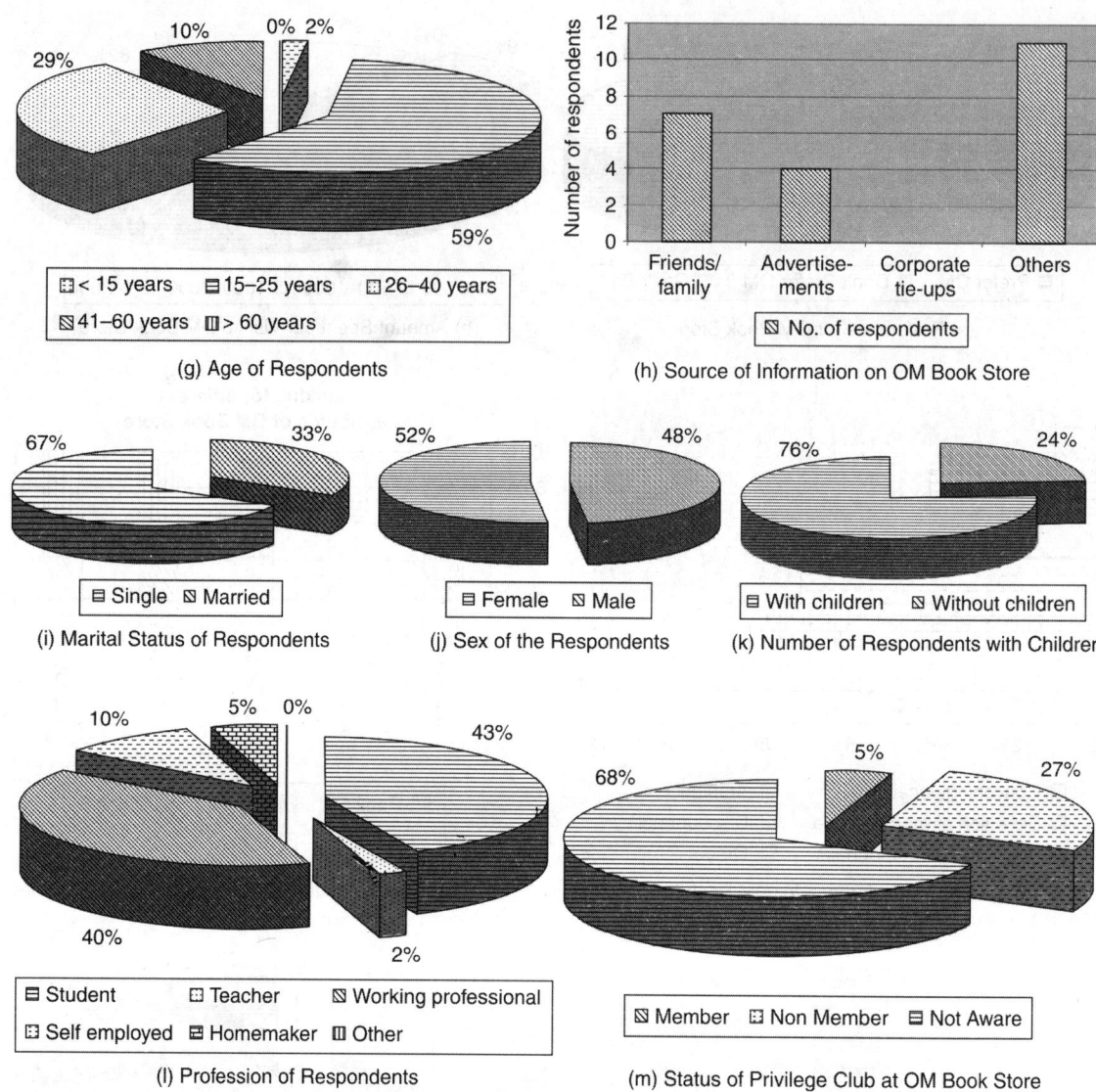

FIG. CS6.3 (Contd) Customer Profile of OM Book Shop

large Crosswords and four Crossword Corners. The two large stores were located near Law Garden and the Satellite–Ambli crossing. The former store was located in a basement and the latter was on the floor of a mall. These stores attracted 150 visitors on a weekday and about 500 on weekends. Customers tended to spend about 2 hours on average. Very few of them came alone.

Approximately 60 per cent of the space was occupied by books. The remaining area contained music, toys, gifts, magazines, and stationery. The aisle spaces were wide and the shelves were low in height, giving an impression of the store being large since a customer could see over the shelf and right across the store. There were chairs located at regular intervals for people to sit and read. A coffee outlet was located within the store, but it was a separate entity. Impulse merchandise such as candies, pens, notepads, and stickers were placed near the billing counter. There were helpdesks located at regular intervals and customers would ask store employees to search for a particular book in the computerized database. The billing counter often had long queues. Here also, the sales personnel were helpful but not very knowledgeable about books. Crossword operated a

Law Garden   Satellite–Ambli Crossing

Crossword Stores

Book Rewards Programme (BRP) in which any customer could become a member by paying a registration fee of ₹150. This programme contributed 32 per cent of its total sales.

Tables CS6.1 and CS6.2 and Figs CS6.4–CS6.7 profile the BRP programme members.[9] More than 50 per cent of its members were married. The average purchase of a BRP customer was ₹2,500 per annum. This was 2.6 times more than that of the walk-in customers. Crossword had classified its customers into five segments. 'Crossword tribes' constituted 10 per cent of its members and accounted for 48 per cent of BRP sales. They generally spent about ₹450 in one visit or ₹1,000 in two visits in a year. 'Crossword core customers' (12 per cent) were very frequent visitors and spent ₹200–400 per visit, contributing 17 per cent of the sales. About 15 per cent of the sales came from 'Crossword climbers' (45 per cent), who spent less than ₹500 per annum at the shop, and purchased less than 5 items. Those who purchased less than 10 items with a cumulative bill value of ₹500–1,000 per year were classified as 'Crossword eager beavers' (14 per cent). The other category consisted of 'Crossword wannabes' (19 per cent), who contributed less than 4 per cent of the BRP sales with an average bill value of ₹100–200 per year. More than 80 per cent of the BRP customers had shown a high commitment and 40 per cent intended to increase their purchase from the store.

Locations for Aakash Book Store

Aakash became more confident after reading the report and visited Ahmedabad. He noted that a large number of customers at Crossword came from the western part of the city, which was far more cosmopolitan in nature than the other parts. He identified three locations at Satellite, Gurukul, and Bopal. Aakash and his cousin went around and evaluated the trading area and the sites (Table CS6.3). Each of these sites was about 5 km apart.

Satellite

The area consisted of old as well new settlements, although it was a newly developed area. The road got its name from the office of the Indian Space Research Organisation (ISRO) on this road near the highway. More than 70 per cent of the settlement had mushroomed in the last ten years. It was primarily a residential area with a lot of retailing activity in the last three years. Crossword's new store was located at the end of this road, about 4 km away, on the Satellite–Ambli crossing. This place had developed as the hub of new retailing with two festival malls (multiplexes), two hypermarkets, and two malls. The third mall being built nearby was supposed to be the largest in Ahmedabad. This road connected Bopal to the main city. It was also the road used by people travelling to Gandhinagar and the western parts of Gujarat. The area's population had a skew towards higher-class people and consisted more of SEC A, B, and C population in comparison to the rest of the city. These residents were more educated and had higher income levels. It was estimated that about 10 per cent of the city's population lived within a 2 km radius of the road. There were few restaurants and no hotels on this road. However, the road connecting the Satellite–Ambli

9. Crossword: Customer Relationship Management, IIMA Case

TABLE CS6.1   Average Purchase (₹ per annum) for Three Groups of Crossword Customers

Store	Avg.	Avg. A*	Avg. B*	Avg. C*
Mahalaxmi	3,830	8,962	2,835	1,071
Ahmedabad	3,317	7,862	2,804	1,087
Chennai	1,808	7,116	2,707	954
Chembur	2,011	6,889	2,791	1,069
Hyderabad	2,163	7,202	2,728	1,089
New Delhi	2,407	6,582	2,777	1,231
Pune	1,821	6,122	2,733	1,030
Vadodara	2,464	7,616	2,763	1,086
Average	2,478	7,294	2,767	1,077

Note: Customers were divided into three groups, A, B, and C, on the basis of their purchasing habits.

TABLE CS6.2   Contribution of Cohorts of Crossword Customers

% of BRP Sales	Top 10 (%)	Top 50 (%)	Top 100 (%)	Top 250 (%)	Top 500 (%)	Top 1000 (%)
Mahalaxmi	5	11	17	29	43	60
Chembur	4	12	20	35	52	72
Chennai	7	18	27	44	63	85
Hyderabad	5	15	23	39	56	77
Ahmedabad	7	21	32	76	76	97
New Delhi	7	22	34	59	81	NA
Pune	3	9	14	25	39	59
Vadodara	8	23	35	57	76	98
Average	6	16	25	46	61	69

crossing and Thaltej crossing had emerged as a major retailing centre, mainly for furniture and restaurants.

Aakash had identified a site near the Nehrunagar crossroads. There was no large retail property within 2 km of the site. This site was a newly built retail property. The owner of the property informed him that a hypermarket, two fast food joints, two restaurants, and several small retailers had confirmed their bookings here. So far, no branded store had booked a site, though two of them had shown interest. Half a kilometre away was a small book store. OM Book Shop was at a distance of about 1.5 km on a road parallel to Satellite Road. The available shop measured 10,000 sq. ft and was located on the ground floor, with a road-facing frontage.

Gurukul

The location was on the road that connected Thaltej and Sheelaj to the city. The former was a settlement of

customers in the middle-income group, while the latter had emerged as a residential area for high-income people with large houses who wanted to live in the serene countryside. Drive-in Theatre and Doordarshan were located on this road. There were two major hospitals and three schools in this area. It covered about 13 per cent of the city's population within a radius of 2 km. The households had a skew towards SEC B and SEC C, with a good number belonging to SEC D also. The road was used by people travelling to North Gujarat and Gandhinagar. The area had a high level of retailing activity, but it mostly had small stores. Only recently, a hypermarket and a fast food joint had opened. There were several offices, restaurants, and commercial organizations. There was no bookstore within 3 km of the site. OM Book Shop would be the closest book store.

Aakash had identified a shop in a mall that had a hypermarket and a fast food joint. The shop measured

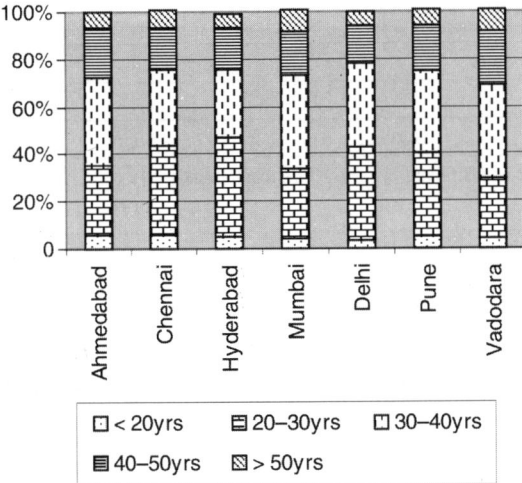

FIG. CS6.4 Age Distribution of Crossword Customers in Different Cities

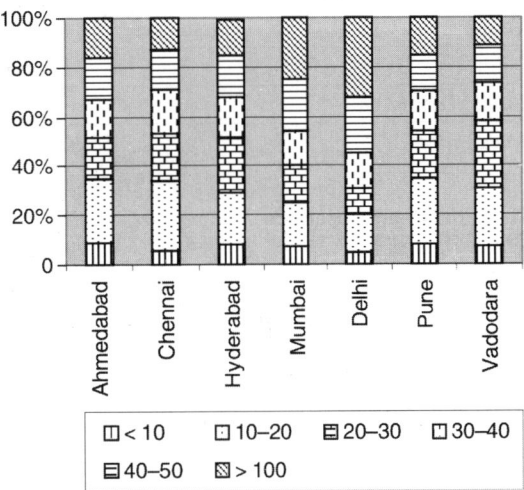

FIG. CS6.5 Income Distribution of Crossword Customers (₹ '000 per annum) in each City

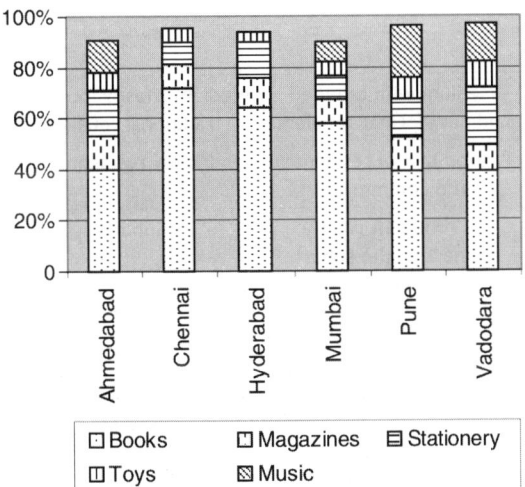

FIG. CS6.6 Type of Merchandise Purchased in each City

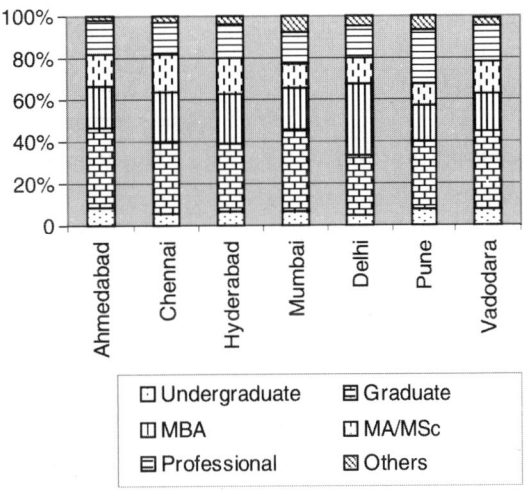

FIG. CS6.7 Educational Profile of Customers in each City

8,000 sq. ft and was located on the ground floor. The shop opened into a courtyard. Once inside the mall, customers could see the store. It had a good frontage.

Bopal

Bopal was a suburb of Ahmedabad. It used to be a sleepy town till about two years ago when a ring road was constructed, which diverted the highway traffic away from the city into Bopal. There was a spurt in construction activity, mainly residential in nature. It

was estimated that Bopal had about 7,000 households, mostly belonging to SEC C, though a large number of SEC A and B households had moved into the outskirts. The population composition would be similar to that of Ahmedabad city. It had a large public school besides another small school. Most of the population worked in and around Ahmedabad. A large number of them would go to work or travel through Satellite Road/Gurukul Road to go to the city. There was very little commercial activity. There was a Crossword Corner located at the

TABLE CS6.3   Evaluation Report[10]

Location Parameters			
Building Description			
Trading Area	*Satellite*	*Gurukul*	*Bopal*
Score out of 10 points, where 10 denotes ideal			
Target catchment population	8	7	7
Branded retailers	5	7	10
Other book retailers	5	8	8
Target residential population	8	9	10
Target corporate population	7	7	3
Target schools/colleges	5	9	8
Target restaurants/hotels	6	8	3
Target tourist population	8	6	3
Proximity to railway station/ airport	2	2	1
Quality and amount of pedestrian traffic	6	9	7
Quality and amount of vehicle traffic	10	8	5
Retail activity	High with branded and new-format retailers	Medium with branded and new-format retailers	Medium, mostly local and traditional retailers
Construction activity	Mostly residential	A good mix of residential and commercial	Mostly residential
Road characteristics	Prominent road connecting the suburb and city centre	Prominent road connecting the suburb and city centre	Suburb
Site Features			
Size (sq. ft)	10,000	7,000	2,000
Site	Part of a mall	Part of a mall	Part of a shopping centre with residences starting from 3rd floor
Existing occupants	Hypermarket fast food joint	Hypermarket fast food joint	Small shops
Proposed space description	Left side of the main entrance	Right of the main entrance	Front
Quality of the road/street	10	10	8
Proximity to important roads/ streets	10	10	8
Shopfront visibility	8	6	9
Signboard visibility	8	6	9

(Contd)

10. Format based on the author's personal experience and discussions with retail executives and store managers.

(Table CS6.3 Contd)

Location Parameters			
Building Description			
Trading Area	Satellite	Gurukul	Bopal
	Score out of 10 points, where 10 denotes ideal		
Width of the shopfront (Ideal 40 ft)	8	6	7
Layout of the space	7	7	7
Single floor/two floors	Single	Two	Single
Ceiling height	8	8	8
Number of columns/width of columns	Low	Low	Low
Access from the main road/high street	10	10	10
Ground level/basement/1st floor (Ideal: Ground)	10	10	10
Width of entrance/lobby	8	6	8
Parking within the complex	6	5	4
Parking outside the complex	7	5	7
Rent (₹ per sq. ft)	30	25	12
Escalation	20% p.a.	10% p.a.	5% p.a.
Advance payment (% of three year rent)	30%	20%	None
Refurbishment cost	New construction	New Construction	Two year old construction
Maintenance	Low	Low	Low
Lease tenure	5 years	7 years	12 years

centre of the area. The shop identified by Aakash was located on the outskirts of the city, where the ring road passed. It was about 3 km from the Satellite–Ambli crossing. New upper class houses were coming up in this area. The shop was situated in a shopping complex. It was on the first floor. It had a good frontage and could be seen from the ring road as well as from roads coming from Ahmedabad. With two shops together, Aakash could get a space of about 2,000 sq. ft.

Journey to Calicut

In addition to data regarding the trading area in different locations of Ahmedabad, Aakash and his cousin also took into consideration the available data on the profitability of large book retailers (Table CS6.4). Aakash was informed that about 500 customers visited such book retailers every day. About half of them purchased books during their visit. Large book retailers dealt in many categories that had differing returns, as shown in Table CS6.5.

Armed with the data regarding book retailing in India, and, specifically, in Ahmedabad, Aakash boarded the flight from Ahmedabad to Calicut. During the flight, he thought about his business plans and decided to come back to Ahmedabad soon. He wanted to start operations within three months. His father had indicated that 25 March 2007 would be a good day to start. However, before that, he had to convince his bankers to extend a loan, and also his family to come with him for at least six months to Ahmedabad. It all depended on choosing the right location and format for his entry into Ahmedabad.

Questions

1. Analyse the data provided in the case study to decide on an appropriate store location for Aakash Book Store. Which method would you use and why?
2. Which of the three locations would be profitable for the store?

TABLE CS6.4 Profitability of a Typical 10,000 sq. ft Store (₹ '000)[11]

	Year 1	Year 2	Year 3	Year 4	Year 5
Income					
Sales	36,000	43,200	51,840	59,616	68,558
Other income	1,000	1,000	1,000	1,000	1,000
Total income	37,000	44,200	52,840	60,616	69,558
Expenses					
Cost of goods	25,200	30,240	36,288	41,731	47,991
Rent	3,600	4,320	5,184	6,221	7,465
Electricity expenses	1,440	1,584	1,742	1,917	2,108
Manpower costs	2,093	2,344	2,625	2,940	3,293
Franchise royalty	720	864	1,037	1,192	1,371
Other operating expenses	550	594	642	693	748
Shrinkage and pilferage	270	324	389	447	514
Commission—credit cards	288	346	415	477	548
Direct marketing expenses	230	276	332	382	439
Computer expenses	200	216	233	252	272
Administration expenses	550	594	642	693	748
Printing and stationery	180	194	210	227	245
Communication	180	194	210	227	245
Maintenance	150	162	175	189	204
Marketing and advertising expenses	120	132	145	160	176
Packing material	162	194	233	268	309
Discount on sales	108	130	156	179	206
Purchase-related expenses	61	73	88	101	117
Sales-related expenses	58	69	83	95	110
Net operating expenses	10,960	12,611	14,540	16,659	19,118
Total expenses	36,160	42,851	50,828	58,390	67,108
PBIDT	840	1,349	2,012	2,226	2,450
Interest and depreciation	1,175	588	441	294	147
PBDT	(335.41)	761	1,571	1,932	2,303

TABLE CS6.5 Merchandise Mix of Large Book Retailers[12]

Merchandise	Sales mix (%)	Margins (%)	Net margin (%)	Merchandise	Sales mix (%)	Margins (%)	Net margin (%)
Books	60	30	18	CDROMs	6	31	2
Music	10	24	2	Toys	8	28	2
Magazines	3	25	1	Stationery	8	32	3
Cards	2	30	1	Café	3	30	1

11. Based on the author's personal experience and discussions with retail executives and store managers

12. Personal Discussion with R. Sriram, ex-CEO, Crossword, and Co-Founder, Next Retail Practice

7 Category Management

LEARNING OBJECTIVES

After studying this chapter, you will be able to
- understand category management and its need
- appreciate the strategic role of category management
- develop an understanding of the process of category management
- discuss specific category management strategies and tactics used by retailers
- describe how the performance of a chosen category can be evaluated

INTRODUCTION

Category management is a practice used for managing retail operations by classifying the assortment of a retailer into categories on the basis of consumer needs, and not just on the basis of individual brands. This method is used to group products and plan their pricing, promotions, and display in such a way that consumer needs can be met more efficiently and the sales and profits of a category can be maximized. Category management has emerged as a strategy to aid retailers in successfully competing in each retail category to enhance shoppers' loyalty and profitability.[1] As a cornerstone of efficient consumer response (ECR) initiatives, category management is designed to help retailers provide the right mix of products, at the right price, with the right promotions, at the right time, and at the right place.[2] Category management is important as it estimates the demand for each item and feeds this information into the supply chain so that correct assortment of products moves efficiently. It helps retailers to maximize sales in the category through an optimal mix of brands and SKUs, based on the consumers' perspective and historical sales data.[3] Category management makes the retailer's categories, rather than the manufacturer's brands, the focus of retailers' resources. It is a retailer's concept where the manufacturer plays a supportive role. Together, the retailer and the manufacturer identify and harness profit opportunities by optimizing market potential by category and retail outlet.

The philosophy behind category management is the close relationship between the retailer and the manufacturer directed at optimizing category profits.[4] From the perspective of relational exchange, the retailer and the supplier establish a bilateral relationship in which the two parties jointly seek to achieve category goals.[5] Retailers and manufacturers set objectives for meeting consumer needs that are specific to the product category and the location of the particular retail outlet. Category management forces retailers to think about what they want to be, who their competitors are, and what they want out of a particular category.[6]

FACTORS AFFECTING THE GROWTH OF CATEGORY MANAGEMENT

The growth of category management is the result of three major factors. These can be classified as (i) changes in consumers, (ii) intensified competition, and (iii) technological advancements.

Changes in Consumers

Consumers' needs, population growth rates, consumer spending, and their lifestyles have been changing rapidly. Consumers have now become more informed and discerning. A large number of consumer buying decisions regarding the product category are being made within the store. In the Netherlands, for example, 20 to 80 per cent of the consumers' buying decisions regarding the product category are made in the store. Shoppers start from home with a choice set, and not just a single brand, in mind. They look for choice and service, quality and freshness, and a reasonable price. But what they get is complexity through non-essential variety, aggressive and widespread promotions, and, finally, a cluttered market. This may have repercussions in terms of less stable consumption patterns in customers and may discourage loyal customers from maintaining their usual shopping pattern. The illusion of choices often creates a gap between what the customers want and what they actually get. Retailers know that failure to recognize and reward consumer loyalty can be costly. Research has shown that while the loyal consumer may only account for 20–30 per cent of consumer traffic, this shopper base can account for 60 per cent or more of a retailer's turnover and profit.[7]

Shoppers define their needs in terms of benefits such as hair care, breakfast food, and fresh breath, whereas retailers have departments based on merchandise. Therefore, the use of category descriptors that do not relate in direct ways to how consumers define their needs can cause a lack of connection between how consumers 'come to market' and how retailers and suppliers 'go to market' in an attempt to meet consumer needs. Retailers and suppliers need to make efforts to understand consumer needs better and to meet those needs more effectively. Category management draws attention to these kinds of unproductive departmental separations by emphasizing that categories should be defined first and foremost by consumer need, and not by departmental separations. It helps in fine-tuning the merchandise offer so that it suits such buying patterns.

At the core of the category management concept is the focus on a better understanding of consumer needs as the basis for retailers' and suppliers' strategies, goals, and work processes. This focus causes a re-evaluation of many current business practices where categories are described and managed in a fragmented manner across departments. Category management helps identify this lack of connection by emphasizing consumer-defined needs and provides solutions for decisions on how products and categories would be marketed. It is a solution towards orienting a store's merchandise to consumer demand. Retailers can then influence consumer purchases through merchandising, pricing, and promotion more effectively by developing strategies for different categories, assigning each category an appropriate role in the product portfolio, and each sub-category the appropriate tactics.

Pantaloons—a leading apparel retailer in India—has employed the concept of category definition, especially in the apparel segment, in its day-to-day function. It is based on the assumption that customers are more product driven than brand driven. They found that, out of every 100 customers that enter a retail store to buy a specific product, 98 are not very particular about the brand. This is primarily because there are various factors, such as price, quality, texture, and colour, that influence a customer's choice of merchandise. The customer's preference for a particular brand gets overshadowed by these other aspects, which lead to the ultimate decision. Thus, managing merchandise by category is more effective than managing individual brands. The idea of category management as implemented by Pantaloons is to create products across the length and breadth of a category at different price points on the basis of fabrics, designs, types, seasons, colours, and sizes, without giving special importance to a particular brand. Figure 7.1 depicts Pantaloons' use of the concept of category management. The aim is to create products that are traffic builders and margin managers within the store, rather than brands that compete with each other. Pantaloons stresses on promoting a product category, thus making brand management a secondary function. For example, John Miller is a range of formal and semi-formal shirts; Bare is a range of denim and casual wear; and Annabelle is a range of western wear for women over 25. Clearly, the significance of brands is limited, and even at the stage of brand management, the company deals with product category.[8]

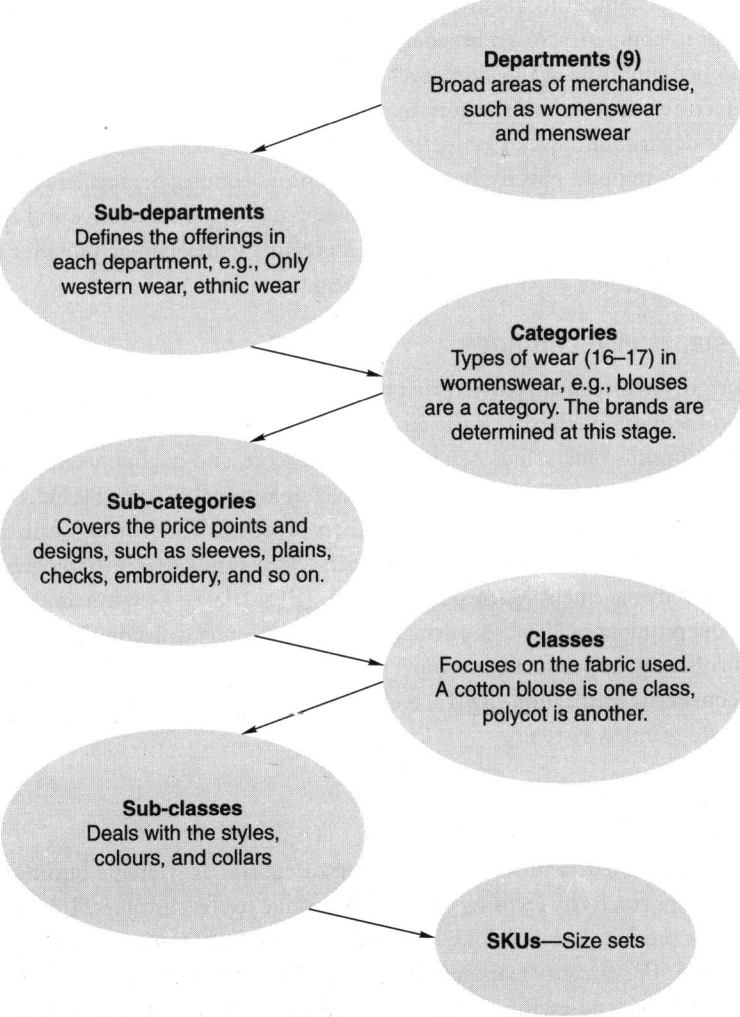

FIG. 7.1 Category Definition at Pantaloons

Intensified Competition

Retailers have emerged as a potent force by delivering convenience and variety to the customers that is unmatched by any manufacturer. This has led to a reduction in the power of a large number of brands. The battle is now being fought at the stores. Each company is vying for a better position of merchandise in the stores. Consequently, retailers are focusing more on the turnover of a category of products than that of a particular brand. Simultaneously, competition is on the rise among retailers too. Each tries to offer a better value to its customers. This has created immense pressure on the earnings of retailers. They cannot afford inefficiency and slack. Thus, every stock-keeping unit (SKU) counts, leading to a focus on category.

Some retailers have used category as their speciality and are delivering high value to customers by providing an unmatched range at very competitive prices. These retailers, called category killers, have successfully entered several categories such as toys, coffee, pet food and supplies, cigarettes and tobacco, non-alcoholic beverages, bath and personal care products, baby care products, and prepared meals. This type of competitor focuses on a category, and does not operate at a total store level. There is no attempt to compete across a broader base of categories. The implication is that other retailers have to compete not only at the store level but also at the category level. This is directing retailers and manufacturers to focus on category management and derive competitive differentiation at the store level or department level. Competitive pressures have also forced retailers to look at the cost of operations. To respond effectively to these economic conditions, retailers and suppliers need to operate more efficiently. They are taking initiatives that develop innovative and efficient approaches in replenishment and demand management. Category management provides the processes and designs to achieve greater efficiencies in these areas.

Advancements in Technology

Effective category management requires that retailers and suppliers are capable of gathering, organizing, analysing, and acting upon the data gathered from the customers and other members of the supply chain. All data regarding customers, merchandise, processes, cost, and quality need to be used to achieve a competitive advantage. Advances in information technology make it possible for retailers and suppliers to share information and change collective business practices. The growing availability of syndicated studies, consumer panel data, and the move to open systems and other technologies are facilitating the adoption of new management systems. Point of sales (POS) data is used by retailers and manufacturers to decide about promotions, displays, pricing, and other aspects of delivering better value to customers. It also helps in offering the product in a manner suitable to customers at different locations. The adoption of radio frequency identification (RFID) technology by large retailers is a major step in the direction of developing a seamless system.

CATEGORY MANAGEMENT PROCESS

Category management is a process of managing categories as strategic business units, producing enhanced business results by focusing on delivering value to the customer. This could be achieved by optimizing new product introductions, enhancing repeat purchases, and increasing the turnaround of the merchandise. The category management process ensures that shoppers find every visit to the store rewarding, enriching, and exciting. This process involves certain strategic and operational decisions. The main components of the process are depicted in Fig. 7.2.

Defining Categories

Category definition is the first step in the category management process. At this point, the category is defined and the product assortment is determined from the consumer perspective. The roles of sub-categories and/or individual SKUs are considered within the category. The category definition leads

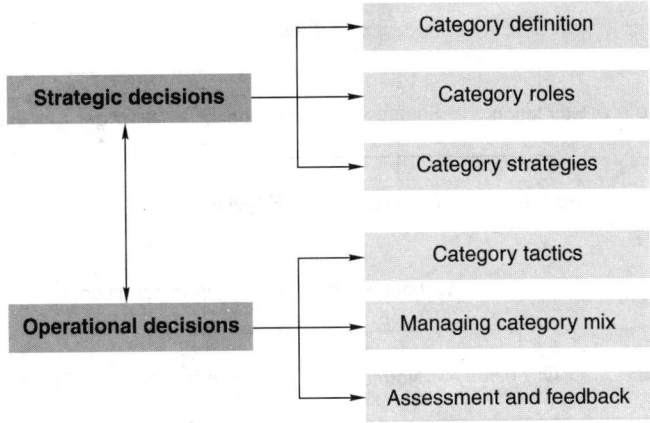

FIG. 7.2 Category Management Process

to the formation of departments and sections in the store. The concept has been illustrated in Fig. 7.3 with the help of an example. It illustrates how retailers can use their understanding of the consumer's definition of the category and its structure to build a product assortment. For this, retailers need to understand the way consumers organize product forms, price options, sizes, and brands when they buy and use the category. This yields a specific name for the category in light of the benefit or solution sought by consumers. It provides the clustering of products and their SKUs that belong to the category. Retailers can draw the decision tree of the consumers based on their choice patterns. Retailers take into consideration the customers' perspectives and store operations, such as customer flow, display, and stock filling, in taking this decision. For instance, most of the pharmacy retailers in India define the category by the name of the manufacturers. This has reduced the stocking and supply burden on the retailers as the manufacturers' salespeople replenish the stock during their visits to the store. Although this mode of working is easier for suppliers, retailers need to have trained employees who are well-informed about the drugs and their manufacturers.

Planet Health, a pharmacy retailer, chose to categorize medicines alphabetically. This step eliminated the need to know about the manufacturers and also enhanced the ease of servicing the customers' prescriptions. The level to which the retailer needs to define its categories depends on the extent of control it wishes to exercise and the level after which the differences in behaviour of customers become insignificant. The former would depend on the depth of data available. With the help of current technology, most retailers can collect information on each SKU. A retailer would stop at a level beyond which the definition becomes meaningless in taking merchandise decisions.

Assigning Roles to Categories

Each category, as defined in the first step, needs to be assigned specific and strategic roles. The roles are derived after comparing the categories in the light of customers, competition, and retailer's objectives. These roles would help each category to allocate different portfolios so as to develop distinct and focused strategies. Such an assignment helps in targeting the merchandise at specific customers and their needs. By focusing on the roles, retailers develop strategies that would utilize resources efficiently. Category roles are developed with the consumer in mind and reflect typical consumer shopping behaviour. It enables retailers to understand why competitors are doing better or worse than they (or the market) are, enabling the retailer to reallocate its resources across categories to improve its overall market position. It

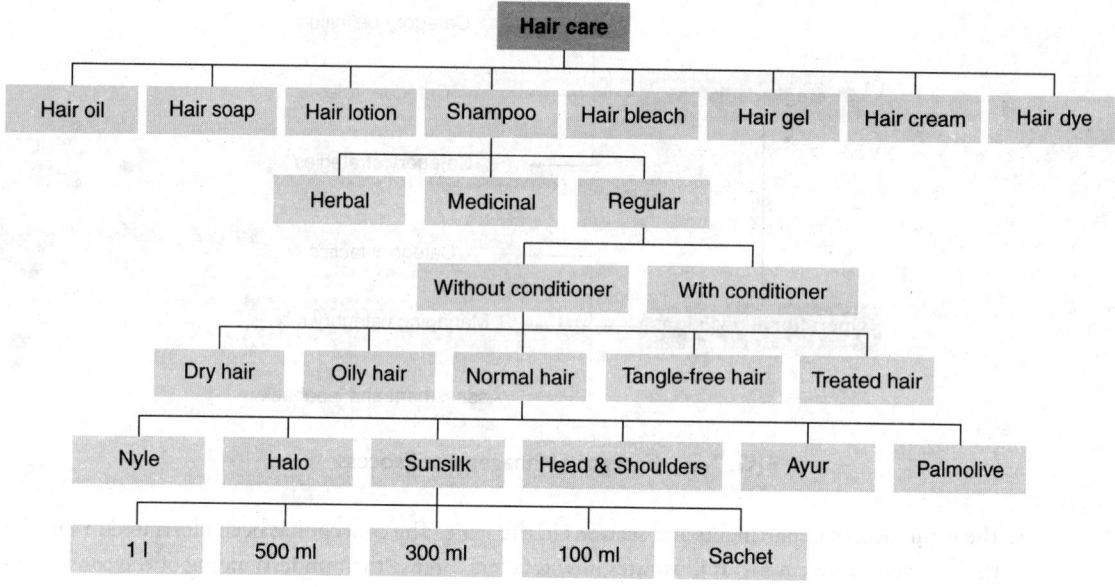

FIG. 7.3 Category Definition—Shampoo

helps manufacturers allocate their scarce marketing resources better across retailers and categories. For example, manufacturers can help both better performing and underachieving retailers by reallocating more money to the marketing actions that have the biggest impact on a category's performance (e.g., displays versus feature advertisements versus depth or breadth of assortment).[9]

A store can have up to 500 categories. In a typical supermarket, there are normally 150–200 categories. In a hypermarket format, there can be almost 500 categories. Each category has to play a significant role in achieving the retailer's mission, goals, and strategies. Categories are assigned roles based on the purchase behaviour of the customers. Two variables that may be taken into consideration for assigning roles are (i) the penetration of the category and (ii) the frequency of purchase. This yields a classification that can be used for developing strategies.[10] As seen in Fig. 7.4, this method can be used to classify product roles as staples, niches, variety enhancers, and fill-ins, and adequate strategies can be developed accordingly. Table 7.1 provides a description of roles for different categories as assigned by FoodWorld.[11] Similarly, Planet Health, a pharmacy retailer, categorizes its products as primary (first-level), secondary (second-level), and tertiary (third-level), as shown in Table 7.2.[12]

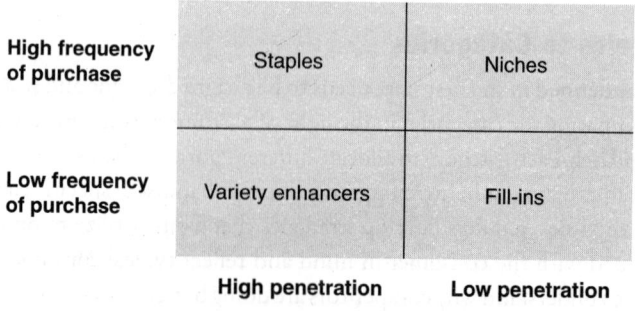

FIG. 7.4 Scheme of Categorization

TABLE 7.1 Categories at FoodWorld

Main Group	Total No. of Categories	Total No. of Sub-categories	Total No. of SKUs	% Revenue (Oct. '98)	Weighted Average Margin
Staples	5	35	523	28.39	14.79
Typical Categories: Cereals, pulses, flours, spices, edible oils					
Processed Foods	16	70	954	16.22	18.20
Typical Categories: Biscuits, canned non-veg., canned fruit, canned veg., desserts, tinned milk, breakfast foods					
Beverages	4	26	319	13.39	16.78
Typical Categories: Drinks, tea/coffee, health drinks, liquor					
Non-food	6	28	449	8.69	17.94
Typical Categories: Detergents, house cleaning, paper goods, cigarettes, pet food					
Health and Beauty	9	53	1,069	12.10	14.97
Typical Categories: Skin care, hair care, oral care, OTC, baby needs, cosmetics, herbal					
Perishables	4	19	310	15.79	20.18
Typical Categories: Dairy products, frozen foods, bakery, vegetables					
H/ware and Home App.	3	33	1,693	5.60	23.24
Typical Categories: Batteries, misc. hardware					
Total	47	264	5,317	100.00	126.09

The most commonly described roles of categories are discussed here.

Destination   This category consists of products and services for which the retailer is the primary provider. Through products in this category, the retailer delivers unmatched value to the consumer. This role is significant as it helps the store in building a distinct position. Generally, the store is known for the products and services in this category either across the chain or in selected markets. Categories with a *destination role* have the responsibility of creating a clear competitive advantage for the store. Typically, 5 to 7 per cent of the categories are assigned this role.* In many cases, these categories are available only at this store. This also sets the requirements of personnel, technologies, systems, processes, and other marketing efforts. It is found that manufacturers' coupons are used to promote this category, and these are less promoted products. The objectives of categories with this role are to enhance consumer satisfaction, service level, and market share.

Preferred   Categories with this role are used to induce the customers to prefer the store to its competitors. These categories at the store provide competitive value to the target consumer. They help in building volume for the store. Typically, 55–60 per cent of a retailer's categories perform this role. Maximum activity happens with regard to these categories. They serve almost all the customers of the retailer. Stores use feature advertisements, displays, and other promotional schemes for these products to score over competitors. The primary objectives of these categories are to deliver profit, cash flow, and return on assets (ROA).

Convenience   Categories assigned this role add the value of convenience in shopping. They help enhance the image of the retailer as a one-stop shopping place. They play a supportive role to the

---

* This is the proportion of categories and not SKUs. SKUs in the 'convenience' role may be much larger in number when compared to categories with a 'preferred' role.

TABLE 7.2 Categories at Planet Health

First-level Categories	Second-level Categories	Third-level Categories
Health Care Products	Pain relief	11
	Cough and cold	8
	Stomach remedies	10
	Diabetes management	8
	First aid	17
	Anti-allergens	4
	Anti-smoking	2
	Bandages and supports	6
Vitamins and Nutritional Care Products	Diet and nutrition	10
	Vitamins	12
	Minerals and nutrients	9
	Other supplements	12
Baby Care Products	Accessories	6
	Diapers and bath needs	5
	Food and formula	2
	Health remedies	8
Personal Care Products	Deodorants and anti-perspirants	6
	Eye and eye care	10
	Family planning and contraceptives	6
	Feminine care	8
	Foot care	10
	Hair and scalp care	7
	Health appliances	11
	Incontinence	6
	Mouth care	12
	Shaving needs	6
Beauty Care Products	Bath and spa	8
	Cosmetics	16
	Fragrance	3
	Skincare	14
	Manicure/pedicure	8
	Hairstyling and colour	9
Foods and Snacks Products	Candy and gum	4
	General grocery	8
Alternative Medicines and Other Products	Nutritional products	2
	Hosiery	8
	Personal gymnasium equipment	3
	Ayurvedic preparations	NA
	Homoeopathic preparations	NA
	Herbal products	2

preferred categories in completing the shopping basket of the customers. Typically, 15–20 per cent of categories are assigned this role. These categories help the store in holding the customers from going to other stores. Since these are not major purchases, customers tend to optimize their shopping trips. They do not mind trading off the extra effort of going to other stores with slightly higher prices. These categories play an important role in profit generation through higher margins. The performance of this role is measured on per unit earnings.

Occasional/seasonal These categories are offered by the retailer to cater to the seasonal and occasional needs of its customers. These include products that are specific to a season, such as umbrellas and raincoats during monsoons or woollen products during winter. Festivals and events are major drivers of purchase of several products. For instance, sales of gifts, sweetmeats, and chocolates witness an increase during these times. Similarly, festivals such as Diwali and Christmas are celebrated with major purchases. During these times, customers look for merchandise that is appropriate for the festival/occasion. Stores that provide a good range of products and value to customers witness high sales. Besides enhancing the image, largely through the excitement created in the store, these categories provide a very good supportive role in increasing profit, cash flow, and ROA. For most retailers, 15–20 per cent of categories are managed with this role.

The roles assigned to product categories provide a logical framework for the allocation of the retailer's resources. They work as guidelines for the allocation of inventory, shelf space, and promotional spending. As a result, the retailers and the suppliers come together to manage their categories efficiently and improve their return on assets. Interestingly, even though category management is a retail strategy, it is the manufacturers who have developed the expertise in this area. They help the retailers in deciding the assortment, pricing, promotions, and placement of the various brands and sizes of each SKU for the category. Manufacturers know a great deal about the consumers of the category in which they are involved. They are well-informed about the kind of products their customers buy, their brand preferences, frequency of products purchased and consumed, and the distribution channels used by them.[13] Retailers usually select a category captain from the manufacturers and provide store-level data for the category consisting of all brands, including store brands. Based on this, the manufacturer in the role of the category captain helps in developing a category plan most suited to the retailers and the manufacturer.

Category Strategies

At this stage, the retailer develops appropriate strategies for each of the categories on the basis of their roles and performance objectives. These strategies also need to be cascaded to sub-categories and other levels to which the retailer wants to extend control. The strategies should entail retailer plans to purchase, merchandise, service, and sell the category. The strategies are developed on the basis of how these categories are performing, how they relate in delivering values to the customers, and how they derive competitive advantage. This process yields a set of strategies and specific action plans. One of the tools that retailers can use for this purpose is the growth–share matrix shown in Fig. 7.5.[14] Each category needs to be plotted on the basis of its sales growth and share in the total business. The process may be conducted within each category so that the category managers are aware of their status. The characteristics of the categories plotted in Fig. 7.5 are discussed here.

Winners Winner categories and items are the cash generators. They are highly profitable and attract a large number of customers. These categories enjoy a high share and grow faster. Such categories include products that have a higher penetration and are bought frequently. They are also price sensitive and are

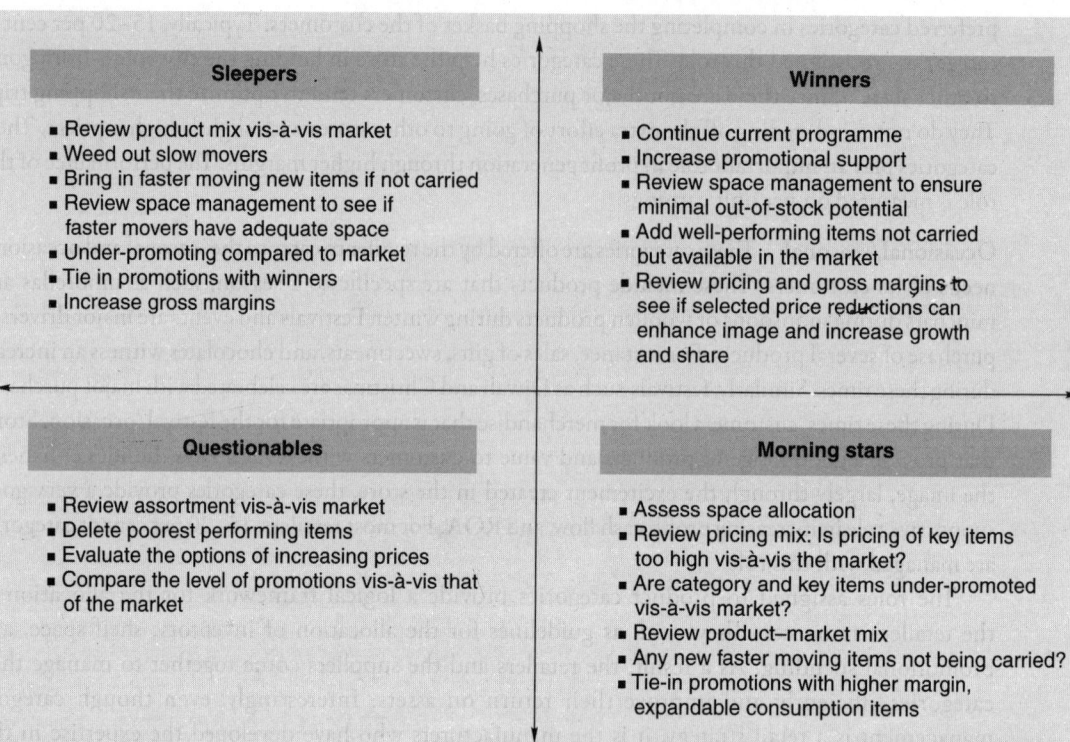

Sleepers

- Review product mix vis-à-vis market
- Weed out slow movers
- Bring in faster moving new items if not carried
- Review space management to see if faster movers have adequate space
- Under-promoting compared to market
- Tie in promotions with winners
- Increase gross margins

Winners

- Continue current programme
- Increase promotional support
- Review space management to ensure minimal out-of-stock potential
- Add well-performing items not carried but available in the market
- Review pricing and gross margins to see if selected price reductions can enhance image and increase growth and share

Questionables

- Review assortment vis-à-vis market
- Delete poorest performing items
- Evaluate the options of increasing prices
- Compare the level of promotions vis-à-vis that of the market

Morning stars

- Assess space allocation
- Review pricing mix: Is pricing of key items too high vis-à-vis the market?
- Are category and key items under-promoted vis-à-vis market?
- Review product–market mix
- Any new faster moving items not being carried?
- Tie-in promotions with higher margin, expandable consumption items

FIG. 7.5 Growth–Share Matrix

promoted frequently by the competitors. Most of the categories with preferred roles and a few with destination roles would constitute this set. The basic strategy for the retailer is to maintain and defend its position on the strengths of these categories. The retailer has to invest in these categories for building the share. It should ensure that the merchandise is available all the time in the required number and variations. These products also need to be displayed properly so that the customers can shop with ease. These are the core sets that strengthen the loyalty of the customer. These also help in enhancing the image of the store. The retailer should focus on maximizing the cash generation and defending against competitors. This category should be allocated a higher share of the resources.

Morning Stars These are categories that contribute significantly to the retailer's business. They account for a high share of the retailer's sales. However, the rate of growth has either stabilized or is witnessing a decline. This category includes products that were introduced recently. Some of the destination categories may also fall in this group. These categories have either lived their purpose due to changes in consumer preferences or have lost their value as competing stores have also added this category and have started delivering equally good value. For such products, a retailer needs to assess whether there has been a fall in the overall demand or the competitors are weaning away the customers. The primary strategy followed for such categories includes profit maximization and creation of excitement around the merchandise. A store has to keep a constant watch on these categories as they have significant implications for profits and image building. These categories may also be evaluated and, based on their performance, shifted to the winner group. Some retailers may decide to let this category decline if a new category comes up that outshines this category. In such as situation, a retailer may like to maximize the profits before phasing out the category. However, in many cases, it should be possible to turn this category into a winner rejuvenating it.

Sleepers This category consists of products that do not move fast. It includes products that either have low purchase frequencies or are not preferred by customers. These categories need to be pushed. Attention needs to be paid to their shelf placement, promotion, and other tactical measures. These categories consume a lot of space and a retailer may have to consider reducing the number of items in each of these categories. Studies have shown that there is a threshold for the number of items, beyond which customers do not mind having less of one item/category and more of their preferred categories and items. These categories would not be a big draw for the customers and hence promoting them alone may not yield the desired results. Most categories with convenience would face this situation. These may require placement near the destination or preferred categories or tie-in promotions with them. In these categories, competitors would be involved in heavy promotions, trying to gain an edge. This group of categories ride on other categories and play the role of value enhancers or fill-ins.

Questionables These are categories that no longer fit with the store strategies and plans. These may include categories that have been included in anticipation of some trend, occasion, or season. Essentially, these include categories that have either lived their lives or were procured to meet expressed demands that did not materialize. They are generally the result of poor forecasting and buying. Retailers with these categories follow the strategy of category rationalization. They need to assess the merchandise–customer fit to identify opportunities for carrying on with these categories and products. In most cases, when no such fit exists, they may have to be deleted and phased out. In case of those that may fit, retailers would either assess the possibility of promoting them to reach some segments of customers that may still want them, or clear the stocks. There is distinct danger in promoting questionables with winners or morning stars as they might reduce the value of the bundling. The effort should be to earn as much cash from this category as possible. It may be used as a traffic builder.

Each of the strategies discussed in this section set directions for developing plans for other decisions related to sourcing, buying, inventory management, store layout, shelf placements, and other marketing and supply chain activities. They take into consideration the category roles, their performance measures, product characteristics, and purchase behaviour of the target customers.

Category Tactics

The strategies developed for each of the categories are the bases for planning the tactical moves for the categories. *Category tactics* are a set of store variables that the retailer uses to keep the store and its offer relevant to its target customers. These variables are grouped into assortment, pricing, display, and promotion tactics. The guiding principles for these tactics are derived from their strategies, targets, and role for the chosen categories. A set of such tactics for a retailer is called a *tactogram*. These inter-linkages and principles are evaluated periodically for synergy and results, based on which required changes are brought into the tactics. Because of changing markets, a retailer needs to look at its tactogram at very frequent intervals. While major changes may happen at longer intervals, a category manager would need to look at it almost daily as it ensures continued performance for every category and the products within it. These tactics need to be formulated primarily in light of the roles of the categories, as shown in Table 7.3.[15]

TABLE 7.3   Category Tactics and Linkage to Category Roles

Category Role	Category Tactics			
	Assortment	*Pricing*	*Shelf Presentation*	*Promotion*

Destination	• Complete variety
	  – variety in market
	  – sub-categories
	  – segments
	  – brands
	  – SKUs
		• Leadership best value
		  – per unit of use
		  – entire category
			• Prime score location
			  – high traffic
			  – high exposure time
			• High cube allocation
				• High level of activity
				• High frequency
				• Multiple vehichles
				  – customized

Preferred	• Broad variety
	• Competitive in market
	  – sub-categories
	  – major brands
	  – major SKUs
		• Competitive-consistent
		  – equal to competition (per unit of use)
		  – major components of category
			• Average store location
			  – high frequency
			• High cube allocation
				• Average level of activity
				  – average frequency
				  – average duration
				  – multiple vehicles

Seasonal/ Occasional	• Time variety
	  – sub-categories
	  – segments (per unit of use)
		• Competitive-seasonality
		  – clean to competition
		  – some components of category
			• Good store location
			  – high traffic
			• Average cube allocation
				• Seasonal/timely activity
				  – multiple vehicles

Convenience	• Select variety
	  – major brands/ SKUs
		• Acceptable
		  – within 15% of competition (per unit of use)
			• Available store
			• Low cube allocation
				• Low level of activity
				  – selected vehicles

Assortment Tactics

Assortment is one of the most tangible variables that can be used by retailers to create differentiation. Customers generally use assortment as a criterion to classify retailers on the basis of the products and services offered by them. They also differentiate retailers on the basis of the breadth and depth they offer. Therefore, the purpose of this tactic is to offer an assortment that balances the needs of consumers with the business objectives of the retailer and suppliers. At this stage, a retailer takes a decision on the variety and range to be offered to consumers. It also lays down the rules and criteria for taking decisions with regard to carrying and deleting items in a category.

The variety and range offered by a retailer help in catering to a larger and heterogeneous segment of customers. A wide variety and range not only bring in a large number of customers but also make them buy. Each brand in a category offering the best possible breadth and depth would result in a better performance of the category. It is very likely that when category sales are distributed evenly over brands, customers will perceive that there are more brands on offer and this creates an image of the retailer as more effective in meeting customer needs.[16]

A retailer manages its assortment by finding the right mix of breadth and depth. In markets and product categories that witness a high level of penetration and proliferation, it is likely that investment in breadth and depth may provide smaller returns as both tend to reach saturation.[17] In many categories, reduction in assortments does not affect consumer intentions to purchase at a store when the pruned brand is not a favourite and the amount of space provided is not altered much. Consumers' use of such simple cues enables a 25 per cent reduction in the items without any significant negative impact on assortment perception. The threshold for perceiving a reduction lies between 25 and 50 per cent.[18] Additionally, item reduction may have a positive impact on store image as customers find it easier to locate their choices. This is witnessed in categories with long tails.

One of the many important decisions that a retailer takes with regard to assortment planning is the share of private brands. Many retailers use private brands as the primary differentiating factor and utilize them for building store traffic. These are targeted mainly at the value-conscious segments. In many cases, they help the customers complete the purchase as retailers offer specific SKUs that the brand manufacturers do not provide, as their interests are wider than that of the retailers. Private labels are found more in categories that are bought for utilitarian purposes.

A store generally follows a practice of uniform categorization across the chain. However, some changes may be required to cater to customers at different locations. These changes are more at the sub-category or item level than at the broad category level. A store also changes its tactics depending on the strategy being followed. For instance, in case of profit maximization, categories with a higher margin would have a higher share of the space as well as facings. In this case, it is possible that the store would push the private labels more than other brands. In order to build traffic, stores use a mix that has a higher proportion of categories from the winner segment. To build excitement, destination and newly introduced categories and products are given a higher share of the category or the space.

Pricing Tactics

Price is a strong differentiator for retailers. The emergence of price formats, such as discounters and category killers, is an evidence of the power of price. Since shopping is an effort and a cost for the customer, price becomes a benchmark for assessing the value delivered by retailers. Lower prices even affect the trading area of retailers. Customers do not mind travelling longer for a better bargain. Walmart, Sam's Club, Big Bazaar, and Vishal Mega Mart are examples where such behaviour is often seen.

The set of pricing tactics helps the retailer in managing its price on the basis of the requirement of the category. The prices of categories are set primarily on the basis of their roles. Categories with destination and convenience roles can be sold at a higher price. Preferred categories generally need to have a very competitive price. Customers are price sensitive to categories that are purchased with high frequency and have heavy usage. A retailer uses price to create an image, build traffic, and to keep the value delivered to customers competitive.

Very frequent price changes may be detrimental to the image of the retailer. Therefore, unless warranted, retailers usually resort to temporary reductions that are communicated within the store and hence do not impact store traffic. Temporary price reductions are most effective in categories which many customers are likely to notice and possibly make an opportunistic purchase on that shopping trip. Such reductions have lower impact on other categories and frequent reductions may lead to the retailer giving away margins without gaining much in return.[19] Customers show high price sensitivity to some categories.[20] In case of these categories, retailers try to ensure that their prices match those of the competitors almost on a daily basis. This may result in a 'floor-effect', that is, minimal prices, and, hence, a reduction in the variability of prices. It is also possible that a promotional programme that is very desirable from the brand manager's perspective may, in fact, lead to reduction in the total sales of the category if much of the merchandise moves at a promotional price.[21]

Assortment Plans of an Appliance Brand

Assortment Tactics by a General Retailer

Assortment Tactics

The roles assigned to a category come into play while determining the prices. For the destination category, the retailer has the liberty of charging prices that may be higher. It has an opportunity of being the price leader for that category and applying to the total category. In other categories, it may have to use different prices for the sub-categories and items, depending on the competitive pressures. A category manager, therefore, would make pricing decisions based on his/her judgement, information on the value provided to target customers, and the current price image of the category and the retailer. It should always be kept in mind that price is a delicate variable and price tactics may have far-reaching consequences.

Promotional Tactics

Promotional tactics are the source of creative selling ideas. They enable both the retailer and the manufacturer to meet objectives when brand substitution occurs both within and across the store. The retailers gain higher margins due to a better trade deal and the manufacturers sell out higher volumes of their brands. Tactics in this area determine the promotions to be offered to the consumer in the category. These include tools such as feature advertising, displays, sampling, contests, and coupons. Retailers define each of these promotional tactics and prepare a calendar of these promotional events in line with the strategy and role of the categories. Market characteristics such as brand market share, couponing activity, display activity, and feature activity explain a considerable amount of the variation in promotional price elasticities.[22] Such display, featuring, and price promotion strategies used by stores can result in increased sales for the brand within the store. Part of the increase is due to brand substitution within the store, primarily as a result of the price promotion. Some of the increase can also be attributed to customers' substitution of stores in order to buy the product being promoted.[23]

In some categories, of the total sales increase due to promotions, more than 80 per cent is accounted for by brand switching, about 15 per cent by purchase time acceleration, and the remaining 5 per cent by stockpiling.[24] Promotions induce consumers to buy more and consume faster. They increase consumption rates within the category.[25] This effect varies across categories due to differences in primary demand effects of promotion. Products such as bacon, salted snacks, soft drinks, ice cream, and yoghurt exhibit primary demand expansions as a result of promotions, while bathroom tissue, coffee, detergent, and paper towels exhibit stockpiling only.[26]

It is to be kept in mind that promotion does not always have positive effects, especially on the long-term profitability of the retailers. The sales displacement caused by stockpiling often reduces the non-promotional sales of the promoted products in subsequent periods.[27] It may also lead to reduction in the demand of the competing products.

A retailer uses several tools to promote its merchandise. Each has a different impact. This impact varies with the purchase behaviour of the customers. As indicated in Table 7.4, merchandise that are purchased frequently and have high penetration respond more to features, while those with high penetration but low frequency respond to coupons as well.[28] The strategies followed by retailers impinge upon the promotional tactics. Feature advertising is utilized more for traffic building, whereas in-store promotions are used to increase the size of transactions. Retailers choose themes to create excitement around the products being promoted. Seasons and festivals influence the timing of promotions and categories to be promoted. Stores also use off-season promotions to clear old stocks.

Promotions are very common in retailing. However, a retailer must make an appropriate choice of the tactics to be used, based on the strategy and role of the category, type of products, time and duration, and expected consumer response. The choice of promotion tactics must be validated to

TABLE 7.4   Sales Impact of Promotion Mix

Buying Characteristics	Feature, No Display	Display and Feature	Coupons	Low Promotion
High penetration—high purchase frequency	High	Medium	Low	Low
High penetration—low purchase frequency	High	Medium	Medium	High
Low penetration—high purchase frequency	Low	Low	Low	High
Low penetration—low purchase frequency	Low	Low	Medium	High

TABLE 7.5   Promotional Tactics at a Supermarket

Sub-class	Merchandise Category	Category Role	Funding Promotion	Frequency of Promotion
Additives	Baking needs	Convenience	Vendor-backed	At least once in 2 months
	Coconut milk	Convenience	Vendor-backed	At least once in 2 months
	Salad dressing and spreads	Convenience	Vendor-backed	At least once in 2 months
	Essence	Convenience	Vendor-backed	At least once in 2 months
	Sauces	Desirable	Preferably vendor-backed	Every month
	Sweetners	Convenience	Vendor-backed	At least once in 2 months
	Vinegar	Convenience	Vendor-backed	At least once in 2 months
Preservatives	Jams	Desirable	Preferably vendor-backed	Every month
	Loose pickles	Convenience	Vendor-backed	At least once in 2 months
	Pickles	Desirable	Preferably vendor-backed	Every month
	Preserves	Convenience	Vendor-backed	At least once in 2 months
Instant mixes	South Indian mixes	Convenience	Vendor-backed	At least once in 2 months
	North Indian mixes	Convenience	Vendor-backed	At least once in 2 months
	Other mixes	Convenience	Vendor-backed	At least once in 2 months
Italian delicacies	Vermicelli	Convenience	Vendor-backed	At least once in 2 months
	Other pastas	Speciality	Vendor-backed	At least once in 2 months
	Macaroni	Speciality	Vendor-backed	At least once in 2 months
	Spaghetti	Speciality	Vendor-backed	At least once in 2 months

Source: Kar, Sanjay Kumar, Piyush Kumar Sinha, and B.B. Mishra, 'Category Management Practices in India', unpublished Ph D thesis.

determine whether the actions will be able to generate sufficient sales and profit improvements. A judicious mix of these tactics brings a product or category into the consideration sets of the customers.[29] Table 7.5 illustrates the promotional tactics followed by a supermarket.

Shelf Presentation Tactics

Shelf presentation or position sensitive tactics have a significant impact on sales. The position of the shelf, number of facings, and pack size affect the sales. Shelves above the mid-point (about four to five feet above the floor) and the bottom shelf contribute most to sales. While top shelves are influential due to the tendency to focus on products at the eye level, the bottom shelf is important due to the large size of the containers that appeal to the value or heavy user customers.[30] The type of product also affects this arrangement. For instance, in case of wines, large size is associated mostly with table wines and not dessert or sparkling wines. Seasonality also affects placements, which are designed to achieve higher sales during the shortest possible time. Placements have a direct impact on the equity of a brand as the arrangement of brands and customers' perceptions about them are related. Display conditions that do not fit with the customer expectations lead to a re-evaluation of the brand. High-equity brand valuations by customers are influenced by an unfamiliar context brand when (a) a mixed display structure leads customers to believe

Shelf Presentation Tactics of a Men's Apparel Section

Display Tactics of a Paint Brand

Shelf Presentation Tactics

that the context brand serves as a benchmark or a diagnostic tool for judging the high-equity brand; (b) the precedence given to one brand over others in display makes expectations about brand differences or similarity accessible; and (c) the unfamiliar context brand disconfirms these expectations.[31]

While manufacturers like to display their brands along with other brands that have a similar positioning, retailers may like to mix the brands to increase the sale of the lesser known categories. Shelves need to be arranged in the way customers shop. They generally move in the direction of reading. Thus, for products that are labelled in English or in other scripts that are read from left to right, it is advisable to position the brand immediately to the right of the most dominant brand, and, within the same brand, featured products are to be positioned immediately to the right of the most popular products.[32]

Tactics in this area determine how the category will be presented to the consumers at the point of sale. Some of the key decisions made at this stage are vis-à-vis the criteria used for managing shelf space (in the category, sub-categories, segments, and SKUs), category location in the store and in aisles, category layout, on-shelf service levels (e.g., minimum days of supply, packing units, etc.), and specific sub-category/segment and SKU space allocation. Table 7.6 provides some general guidelines for selecting shelf presentation tactics that support the various category strategies.[33] Figure 7.6 depicts one such planogram. Table 7.7 illustrates the importance of shelf presentations.

Managing Category Mix[34]

A retailer manages the category mix taking into consideration several variables, such as customer choice, fashion, inventory, productivity, retail space, and retail margins. For example, the category mix at Shoppers Stop, a department store, is decided on the basis of consumer buying pattern and not merely on product type (Fig. 7.7). The merchandise is divided into sections on the basis of many factors, such as the average turnover of the product, customer buying patterns, and planning efficiency. Men's denims and formal shirts are found to be usually purchased according to brand preferences, and these products are segregated according to brand names for planning purposes. Shoppers Stop has about 90

TABLE 7.6 Shelf Presentation Tactic Guidelines—An Example

Strategy	General Tactical Approach
Transaction building	• Shelf sets should direct consumer attention to higher priced SKUs
	– Consider blending higher priced SKUs throughout set to increase consumer response and purchase
Traffic building	• High profile location and competitive category space allocation
	• Overall shelf should be attractive and invite consumers to return to the store
	• Highlight loyalty SKU segments
Turf protecting	• Planograms should direct consumer attention to higher margin SKUs
	– Capitalize on impulse items
	– Locate higher margin categories in high-traffic aisles
	• Consider blending higher margin SKUs throughout set to increase consumer exposure and trade-up
	• Maximize visibility of private label and high profit SKU segments
Cash generating	• Planogram highlights new/high profile SKUs/segments
	• Adequate space to get consumer attention

TABLE 7.7   Importance of Shelf Presentation

Category	Aspects of Shelf Presentation				
	Shelf Level	Visible Stock Quantity	Attractive PoP posters with Gondola	Bright Colour Pack	Gondola with Beauty Advisors
Soaps	■				
Hair care		■	■		
Skin care—upper range					■
Skin care—lower range	■				
Processed foods		■		■	

Source: Tambawala, Ammar and Chinmay S. Thattey, Project on 'A Study of the Linkage between Shopping Behaviour at the Point of Purchase and In-store Execution for FMCG Products', PGP (2008–10), IIMA.

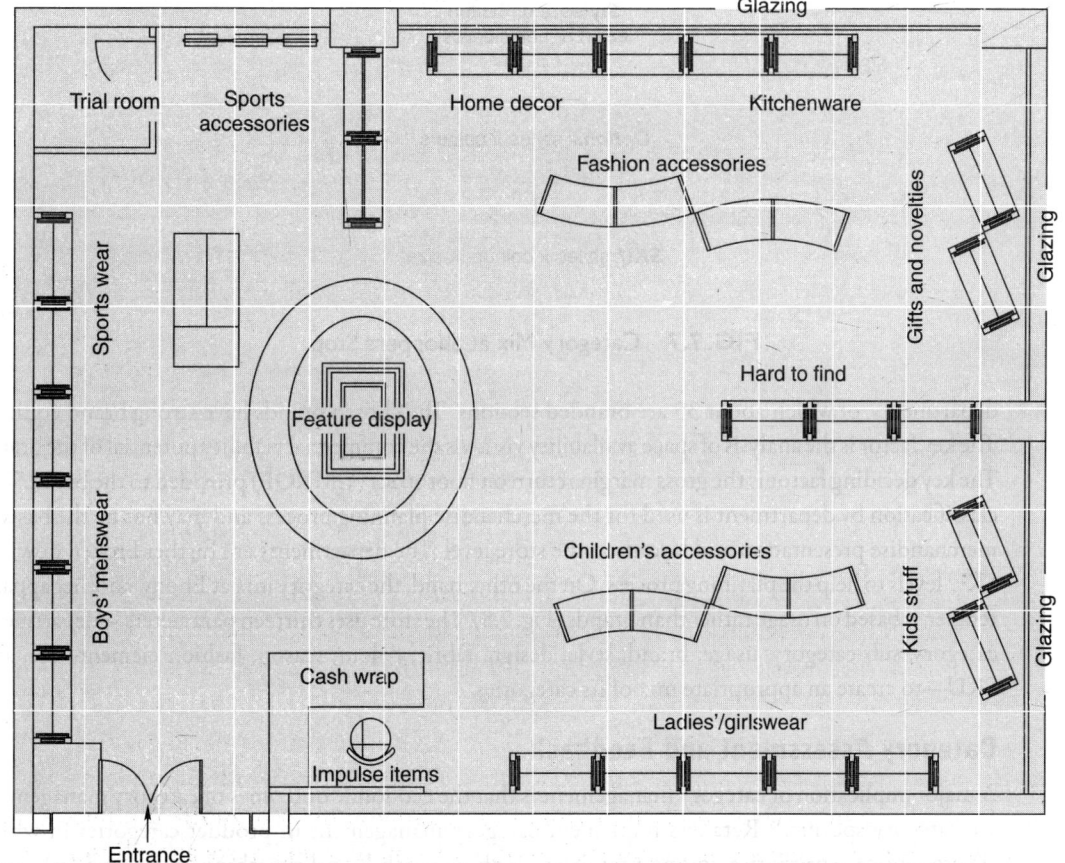

FIG. 7.6   Planogram Showing Shelf Presentation Tactics of a Store

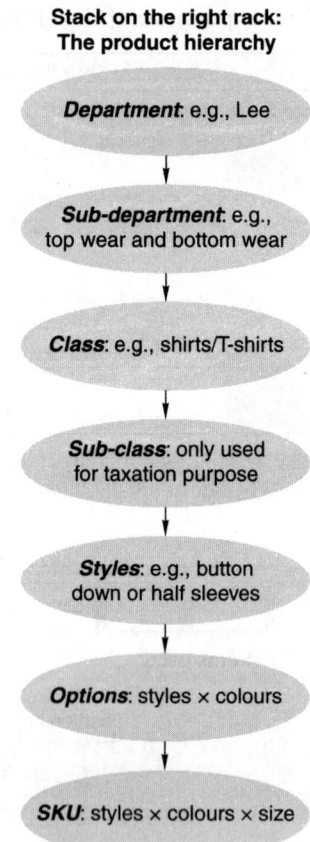

FIG. 7.7   Category Mix at Shoppers Stop

departments, of which about 35 are branded sections. The chosen brands have strong brand equities. The key factor is the analysis of space availability vis-à-vis the commercial viability potential of the brand. The key deciding factor is the gross margin return on floor space (GMROF) provided to the brand. This classification by department is used for the merchandise planning process and may not be the basis of merchandise presentation and layouts at the store level. The departments are further broken down to SKU levels to help the planning process. On the other hand, the category mix at Ebony, another apparel retailer, is based on usage rather than brands (Fig. 7.8). The store uses thirteen parameters—department, category, sub-category, usage, brand, style, design, fabric, colour, season, fashion element, size, and SKU—to create an appropriate mix of its categories.

Category Assessment and Feedback

A major implication of category management is that the economic outcomes of category management are category specific.[35] Retailers implement category management in product categories in which (i) cross-price sensitivities among brands are high or much brand switching exists, and (ii) cross-store price sensitivities are low or little price-based cross-store shopping takes place for brands in the category. A study that tested the effect of one of the common outcomes of category management—SKU reduction—found that, to a certain extent, item reduction leads to increases in consumer satisfaction.[36] Another study suggested the need for assortment differences across regions.[37]

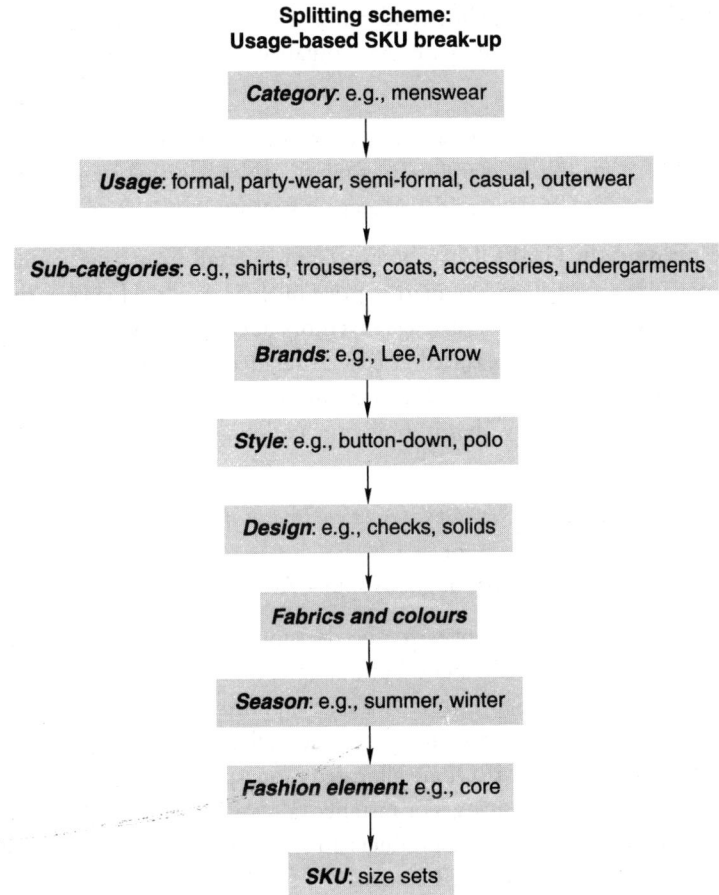

FIG. 7.8 Category Mix at Ebony

Retailers need to assess the performance of their categories on a continuous basis. They need to develop a system that would obtain, organize, and analyse the current performance of the category. They should also identify the areas of greatest opportunity for improved results in turnover, profits, and return on assets in the category. The performance of categories could be assessed from two broad perspectives—economic and perceptual. The measurement of the economic performance of a category includes the profit generation by the categories based on sales, inventory, space, and people. This analysis also encompasses the assessment of the performance of suppliers and the processes employed by the retailers for managing the categories. The evaluation of the perceptual performance of a category includes the assessment of the perception of customers in terms of their roles in creating a store image and patronage.

Assessing Economic Performance

The following measures can be used to assess the economic performance of a retailer.

Gross Margin Return on Inventory (GMROI)   GMROI measures the gross earnings of the retailer for the investment in merchandise. The gross margin and inventory turnover are used to calculate a category-specific return on investment measure called GMROI. It can be used to evaluate departments, merchandise classifications, vendor lines, and items. Since GMROI combines the effects of profits and turnover, it enables the store to compare and evaluate departments with different margin/turnover profiles.

$$\text{GMROI} = \text{Gross margin percentage} \times \text{Sales-to-stock ratio}$$
$$\text{or (Gross margin} \div \text{Net sales}) \times (\text{Net sales} \div \text{Average inventory})$$
$$\text{or Gross margin} \div \text{Average inventory}$$

Average inventory in GMROI can be expressed at retail or at cost. Some retailers use retail inventory since it closely reflects the market price of their goods. However, the preferred method of calculating GMROI is to express average inventory at cost because inventory is the denominator and a return in investment is measured at cost. A retailer's investment in inventory is the cost of the inventory, and not its retail value. This measure is called the sales-to-stock ratio. It is a measure of the productivity of inventory, that is, how much sales can be generated from the investment in inventory.

$$\text{Sales-to-stock ratio} = \text{Net sales} \div \text{Average inventory at retail}$$
$$\text{or}$$
$$\text{Sales-to-stock ratio} = \text{Cost of goods sold} \div \text{Average inventory at cost}$$

The inventory turnover ratio supports the decision of many retailers to remove certain slow moving categories from their assortment. For example, food and apparel have been found to have a higher turnover as compared to furniture. This data supports the decision of many discount stores to remove furniture from their assortments. The retailers allocate space on the basis of the GMROI of the items. Items with higher GMROI are allocated more space. The retailer should find a judicious mix in order to maximize its returns. For instance, a retailer dealing in consumer electronics (low GMROI items) may also stock other products anticipating that, while customers are at the store, they would also purchase higher GMROI items.

Gross Margin Return on Floor Space (GMROF)   GMROF is a measure of the productivity of space. It determines the sales generated from the investment in space. This measure guides the retailer in the space allocation of items. Items with higher GMROF would get more space allocation. For example, a 200 gm pack of a commonly bought cereal has a higher GMROF than a 500 gm item. GMROF is calculated as follows:

$$\text{GMROF} = \text{Gross margin} \div \text{Space provided}$$

Gross Margin Return on Persons Employed (GMROP)   GMROP is a measure of the productivity of salespeople employed in a particular product category. The higher this ratio for a particular department, the higher would be the productivity of the people in that department. GMROP is calculated as follows:

$$\text{GMROP} = \text{Gross margin} \div \text{Persons employed}$$

Table 7.8 shows the indices for category performance for better understanding.

Direct Product Profitability (DPP)   This method has been developed to address the issue of allocating costs to different categories/SKUs. The gross margin methods are easy to compute but do not portray the profitability at the SKU level in its true sense. Direct product profitability identifies each of the costs

TABLE 7.8 Indices for Category Performance

Metric	Description
GM—Category	Sales – COGS
GM—Sub-category	Sales – COGS
Share of GM of category	GM category/GM store or department
Share of GM of sub-category	GM sub-category/GM category
Inventory	
GMROI—Category	GM/Average stock
GMROI—Sub-category	GM/Average stock
Average stock	Safety stock or average of MBQ and safety stock
MBQ	Minimum base quantity for ordering
Inventory Turns	Sales/Average stock
Space	
Space—Category	Linear/Square feet
Space—Sub-category	Linear/Square feet
GMROF—Category	GM/Space utilized
GMROF—Sub-category	GM/Space utilized
Inventory space efficiency	GMROI × GMROF
Promotions	
Markup	(Sales price – COGS)/COGS
Markdown	(Sales price – COGS)/Sales price
Discounts	Original sales price – Actual sales price
Premiums	Any non-price offer
Bundling	Any other product tied
Direct Product Cost (DPC)	
Inventory cost at store	COGS
Inventory cost at warehouse	COGS
Promotions	Markdowns/Discounts/Premium/Bundling
Direct product profit	GM – DPC

related to a given category/SKU. Then it classifies these into costs allocable to the unit and 'overheads'.[38] This profitability in case of DPP would always be lower than GMROI since costs are being allocated to units as per the efforts and are not spread equitably.[39] A sample calculation of DPP is given in Table 7.9. The proponents of activity-based costing support DPP as it allocates costs even to the SKU level and the retailer is able to get the real profitability of the merchandise.[40] It is considered as a tool that helps the retailer to view the profitability and its antecedent across the value chain.[41] It helps in dealing with the suppliers and arriving at a good bargain. DPP, however, suffers from the limitation of being static and may not reflect the dynamic changes brought into shelf space allocation or cross selling.

TABLE 7.9 Estimation of Direct Product Profitability (DPP)

Sl. No.	Particulars	Amount per Unit (₹)
1.	Retail price	100
2.	Cost of goods	70
	Gross margin	**30**
Discounts and Allowances		
3.	Cash discount	2
4.	Merchandise allowances	2
5.	Others	1
	Total	5
	Adjusted gross margin	**25**
Direct Distribution Costs		
6.	Warehouse space	0.5
7.	Warehouse handling	1.0
8.	Warehouse inventory costs	2.0
9.	Transportation to store	1.0
10.	Store space costs	3.2
11.	Store inventory costs	4.0
12.	Store handling costs	6.0
	Total direct product cost	**17.7**
13.	**DPP**	**7.3**

Marketing Profit of a Category

The profit impact of a retailer's decision to merchandise a product category, or the *marketing profit* of a category, is the total profit a store makes from the consumers for whom the category is the lead category. It is a profit measure which takes into account the cross effects of merchandising one category on the profits of the other categories in the store.[42] It focuses on consumers and their store choice behaviour and is particularly pertinent to the calculus of marketing decision-making. The marketing profit of category i can be expressed as

$$\text{MP}_i(s) = \Pi(s) - \Pi(s_{-1}) - h_i\, s_i \tag{1}$$

where MP_i denotes the total marketing profits from category i, $\Pi(s_{-1})$ denotes the total store profits when all consumers with category i as the lead category on their shopping lists decide to shop elsewhere, and $h_i\, s_i$ denotes the costs incurred in maintaining the shelf space h_i at store s_i. In this model, $\Pi(s_{-1})$ is derived from $\Pi(s_1)$ by letting p_i approach 0 in Eqn (1). Here, it is assumed that the alternative to an actively merchandised category, which draws consumers with the category as their lead category into the store, is to have the category perish on the shelf in the sense that only consumers with some other category as their lead category may purchase from the category. A measure with such a strict condition would highlight the importance and immediacy of proper category management. Since the shelf space allocated to a category is only relevant to the shopping decisions of the consumers for whom the category is the lead category, the costs incurred in maintaining the shelf space ($h_i s_i$) should be entirely attributed to these consumers. The above equation establishes the linkage between the marketing profits of a category and the allocation of shelf space. The measure of marketing profits assumes that the retailer has incorporated the aspect of shelf space allocation. This means that the shelf space in Eqn (1) is chosen by a retailer so that

$$s^* = \arg \max_{(s_1, s_2, \ldots s_n)} \Pi(s) \tag{2}$$

such that $$\sum_{i=1}^{n} s_i \leq \overline{S} \tag{3}$$

that is, shelf space occupied by each category is a result of the retailer's efforts to optimize allocation of the total amount of shelf space available to the retailer $\overline{S}$. In Eqn (2), s_1, s_2, and s_n denote the spaces allocated to different categories.

The optimal allocation of shelf space requires that s^* satisfy the first order conditions

$$\frac{\partial \pi_i}{\partial s_i} + \sum_{k \neq i} \frac{\partial \pi_k}{\partial s_i} = \lambda \quad \text{for} \quad i = 1, 2, \ldots, n \tag{4}$$

Here, λ is the shadow price of the shelf space—the profit that the retailer can gain by increasing the total shelf space available by a unit—and it is also the opportunity cost of shelf space for the retailer. Equation (4) implies that marginal profit contributions from each category carried by a store must be the same if the shelf space is occupied optimally. Equation (4) and shelf space constraints (3) implicitly define the optimal allocation of shelf space s^* for the retailer.

The concept of marketing profits and its measurement is important as it focuses on customer profitability rather than the DPP. It provides a more accurate measure of the performance of various categories, allowing the retailers to develop better plans for different department and category managers. It also provides retailers with information on the value of the shelf space. This can be useful in slotting allowance negotiations. A retailer may also use this information to allocate promotional resources more effectively. Since the yardstick used to measure category management differs between organizations, a universal definition of category management would take into consideration the category performance as the overall retail sales volume and the profitability of the category relative to the same category at relevant comparative prices.

Recent developments have provided a number of tools that may be used to make the relevant decisions and judge the benefits of local adjustment.[43] There is a widespread application of scanning techniques and related software. It provides retailers with the opportunity of deducting the influence of prices and promotions, enabling them to assess the influence of local environment on category performance. There are several tools available to map consumer behaviour, buying behaviour, and media exposure. The consumer database can be a valuable and useful source of information for suppliers. Retailers as well as manufacturers have started receiving information through toll free telephone lines and a variety of promotions. Many retailers are implementing customer cards and loyalty programmes for building databases with information of usage, brand choice, and brand loyalty. Modelling techniques are also available to gauge the relations between different variables (e.g., environment, customers, sales, etc.). These techniques, such as market basket analysis, can provide insights into the potential for a category in an individual outlet or a cluster of outlets based on the presence of certain types of consumers and the competition in the catchment area(s) of the store(s).

Assessing Perceptions

Retailers need to find out the impact of their category management efforts in light of the impact it has on the perceptions of the customers. Merchandise and its presentation have been found to have a positive influence on store loyalty and patronage. Within a given trade area, the 'uniqueness of assortment' as a way of influencing store loyalty and patronage has been emphasized. In terms of consumer priorities, assortment and variety come after convenience and price.[44] Given that consumers are favourably inclined to revisit a store where they have had positive shopping experiences and found something they could not find anywhere else, these studies suggest that competing stores need to differentiate themselves on the basis of the type and quality of assortment they offer. The emphasis here is on tailoring the cues using retail mix elements to foster loyalty.

SUMMARY

The benefits of category management are higher levels of consumer satisfaction and returns from a more consumer-focused procurement, marketing, and merchandising programme. It leads to increased revenues and profit. Through efficient business processes, it also reduces system and marketing costs. Category management results in more customer-oriented product assortments, better new product introductions, more efficient promotion programmes, and effective shelf placements. It brings greater cooperation and compatability among the retailers and their suppliers through an integrated approach to managing the merchandise and the stores.

A store needs to lay out a detailed category management process. It starts by defining the category and assigning roles to each of them in the light of the store's positioning, objectives, and market requirements. For each of the categories, it then draws out strategies for enhancing the returns as per the objectives. These strategies lead to the tactics and the mix that the retailer would like to offer its customers within each of the categories. The retailer then draws out a plan for assessing the performance of its category in terms of economic parameters and consumer perception in order to enhance store loyalty and patronage. It may also use tools such as the growth–share matrix for assessing the performance and opportunities for each of the categories.

Implementation of category management may require several hurdles to be crossed. The cost of achieving efficiencies using ECR may outweigh the benefits. The full implementation of category management requires retailer restructuring. It may not be easy to create partnerships with suppliers. Full and complete information may not flow across the system. Sometimes, it may lead to over-concentration and, hence, lack of variety in product offerings to customers. To curb this, several countries (such as France) place small suppliers at an advantage, often decreeing by law that up to 10 per cent shelf space be reserved for them. Otherwise, category management may help the category champions to derive undue advantage due to their position.

NOTES

1. Blattberg, Robert C. 1995, *Category Management Guides*, Vol. 1–5, Food Marketing Institute, Washington DC.
2. Gruen, Thomas W. and Reshma H. Shah, 'Determinants and Outcomes of Plan Objectivity and Implementation in Category Management Relationships', *Journal of Retailing*, Vol. 76(4), pp. 483–510.
3. Gruen, Thomas W. and Reshma H. Shah, 'Determinants and Outcomes of Plan Objectivity and Implementation in Category Management Relationships', *Journal of Retailing*, Vol. 76(4), pp. 483–510.
4. 'European Retail Marketing', *European Retail Digest*, Winter 1994/95, pp. 4–11.

5. Macneil, Ian R. 1980, 'The New Social Contract: An Inquiry into Modern Contractual Relations', Yale University Press, New Haven.

6. Johnson, Maureen 1999, 'From Understanding Consumer Behaviour to Testing Category Strategies', *Journal of Marketing Research Society*, Vol. 41 (3), 259–88.

7. Singh, Jerry 2004, 'Category Management', www.categorymanagement.com, accessed on 12 April 2004.

8. 'Stores that Score, Apparel Industry Case Studies', 'Changing Gears: Retailing in India', *The ET Knowledge Series*, pp. 58–59.

9. Dhar, Sanjay K., Stephen J. Hoch, and Nanda Kumar 2001, 'Effective Category Management Depends on the Role of the Category', *Journal of Retailing*, Vol. 77, pp. 165–84.

10. Fader, P.S. and L.M. Lodish 1990, 'A Cross-category Analysis of Category Structure and Promotional Activity for Grocery Products', *Journal of Marketing*, Vol. 54(3), pp. 52–65.

11. Koshy, Abraham, G. Raghuram, and Bibek Banerjee 1998, 'FoodWorld A', Indian Institute of Management, March, p. 325.

12. Jain, Abhinandan K., Piyush Kumar Sinha, and Presth Bhardwaj 2004, 'Planet Health', Indian Institute of Management, Mar–353.

13. 'European Retail Marketing', *European Retail Digest*, Winter 1994/95, pp. 4–11.

14. Johnson, Maureen 1999, 'From Understanding Consumer Behaviour to Testing Category Strategies', *Journal of Marketing Research Society*, Vol. 41 (3), pp. 259–88.

15. Johnson, Maureen 1999, 'From Understanding Consumer Behaviour to Testing Category Strategies', *Journal of Marketing Research Society*, Vol. 41 (3), 259–88.

16. Hoch, S.T., E.T. Barlow, and B. Wansink 1999, 'The Variety of an Assortment', *Marketing Science*, Vol. 18 (4), pp. 527–746.

17. Dreze, X., S.J. Hoch, and M.E. Purk 1994, 'Shelf Management and Space Elasticity', *Journal of Retailing*, Vol. 70 (4), pp. 301–26.

18. Bromarczyk, S.M., W.D. Hoyer, and L. McAlister 1998, 'Consumers' Perception of the Assortment Offered in a Grocery Category: The Impact of Item Reduction', *Journal of Marketing Research*, Vol. 35 (2), pp. 166–76.

19. Walter, R.G. and S.B. MacKenzie 1988, 'A Structural Equation Analysis of the Impact of Price Promotions on Store Performance', *Journal of Marketing Research*, Vol. 25 (1), pp. 51–63.

20. Hoch, S.J., B. Kim, A.L. Montgomery, and P.E. Rossi 1995, 'Determinants of Store Level Price Elasticity', *Journal of Marketing Research*, Vol. 32 (1), pp. 17–29.

21. Raju, J.S. 1992, 'The Effect of Price Promotion on Variability in Product Category Sales', *Marketing Science*, Vol. 11(2), pp. 207–20.

22. Bolton, R. 1989, 'The Relationship between Market Characteristics and Promotional Price Elasticity', *Marketing Science*, Vol. 8(2), pp. 153–69.

23. Kumar, V. and R.P. Leone 1988, 'Measuring the Effect of Retail Store Promotions on Brand and Store Substitution', *Journal of Marketing Research*, Vol. 25 (2), pp. 178–85.

24. Gupta, S. 1988, 'Impact of Promotion on When, What and How Much to Buy', *Journal of Marketing Research*, Vol. 25, Nov, pp. 342–55.

25. Ailawadi, K.L. and S.A. Neslin 1998, 'The Effect of Promotion on Consumption: Buying More and Consuming it Faster', *Journal of Marketing Research*, Vol. 35, pp. 390–98.

26. Bell, D.R., J. Chiang, and V. Padmanabhan 1999, 'The Decomposition of Promotional Response: An Empirical Generalisation', *Marketing Science*, Vol. 18, pp. 504–26.

27. Frank, R.E. and W.F. Massy 1967, 'Effects of Short-term Promotional Strategy on Selected Segments', in P.M. Robinson (ed.) *Promotional Decision Using Mathematical Models*, Allyn and Bacon, Boston, pp. 147–225.

28. Fader, P.S. and L.M. Lodish 1990, 'A Cross-category Analysis of Category Structure and Promotional Activity for Grocery Products', *Journal of Marketing*, Vol. 54(3), pp. 52–65.

29. Allenby, G.M. and J.L. Ginter 1995, 'The Effects of In-store Displays and Feature Advertising on Consideration Sets', *International Journal of Research in Marketing*, Vol. 12, pp. 67–80.

30. Folwell, R.J. and A.D. Moberg 1993, 'Factors in Retail Shelf Management Impacting Wine Sales', *Agribusiness*, Vol. 9 (6), pp. 595–603.

31. Buchanan, L., C.J. Simmons, and B.A. Bickart 1999, 'Brand Equity Dilution: Retailer Display

and Context Brand Effects', *Journal of Marketing Research*, Vol. 36 (3), pp. 345–55.

32. Young, Scott 2003, 'Winning at Retail: Research Insight to Improve the Packaging of Children's Products', *Advertising and Marketing to Children*, October–December, pp. 17–22.

33. Johnson, Maureen 1999, 'From Understanding Consumer Behaviour to Testing Category Strategies', *Journal of Marketing Research Society*, Vol. 41 (3), pp. 259–88.

34. 'Stores that Score, Apparel Industry Case Studies', 'Changing Gears: Retailing in India', *The ET Knowledge Series*, pp. 58–59.

35. Basuroy, S., M.K. Matrala, and R.G. Walters 2001, 'Impact of Category Management on Retailer Prices and Performance: Theory and Evidence', *Journal of Marketing*, October.

36. Bromarczyk, S.M., W.D. Hoyer, and L. McAlister 1998, 'Consumers' Perception of the Assortment Offered in a Grocery Category: The Impact of Item Reduction', *Journal of Marketing Research*, Vol. 35 (2), pp. 166–76.

37. Grewal, D., M. Levy, A. Mehrotra, and A. Sharma 1999, 'Planning Merchandise Decisions to Account for Regional and Product Assortment Differences', *Journal of Retailing*, Vol. 75 (3), pp. 405–24.

38. Borin, Norm and Paul Farms 1990, 'An Empirical Comparison of Direct Product Profit and Existing Measures of SKU Productivity', *Journal of Retailing*, Vol. 66, Issue 3, pp. 297–314.

39. Bookbinder, James H. and Feyrouz H. Zarour 2001, 'Direct Product Profitability and Retail Shelf-space Allocation Models', *Journal of Business Logistics*, Vol. 22, Issue 2, pp. 183–208.

40. Cooper, Robin and Robert S. Kaplan 1991, 'Profit Priorities from Activity Based Costing', *Harvard Business Review*, Vol. 69, No. 3, pp. 130–42.

41. Pinnock, A.K. 1990, 'Direct Product Profitability: A Supply Chain Philosophy', in Fernie J. (ed.) *Retail Distribution Management*, Kogan and Page, London.

42. Chen, Y., J.D. Hess, R.T. Wilcox, and Z.J. Zhang 1999, 'Accounting Profits versus Marketing Profits: A Relevant Metric for Category Management', *Marketing Science*, Vol. 18 (3), pp. 208–29.

43. 'European Retail Marketing', *European Retail Digest*, Winter 1994/95, pp. 4–11.

44. Kunkel, J.H. and L.L. Berry 1968, 'A Behavioural Conception of Retail Image', *Journal of Marketing*, Vol. 32 (October), pp. 21–7; Korgaonkar, P.K., D. Lund, and B. Price 1985, 'A Structural Equations Approach toward Examination of Store Attitude and Store Patronage Behaviour', *Journal of Retailing*, Vol. 61 (Summer), pp. 39–60; Reynolds, F.D., W.R. Darden, and W.S. Martin 1974, 'Developing an Image of the Store Loyal Customer', *Journal of Retailing*, Vol. 50, pp. 73–84.

CONCEPT REVIEW QUESTIONS

1. Describe category management and its role in enhancing store performance.
2. Describe the process of category management. Why are some elements strategic and others tactical?
3. What different roles can a category play? How are they linked to the definition of the categories?
4. What are the different shelf presentation tactics that are used by retailers to enhance sales? How are they decided?
5. Assortment planning is critical to category management. What steps are taken by retailers in developing this plan?
6. How are categories evaluated? What are the differences in GMROI and DPP? Which is a better method and why?
7. Promotions are common in category management. What are the different types of promotional tactics used by retailers? How do retailers decide about these?

CRITICAL THINKING QUESTIONS

1. Should mineral water be categorized with soft drinks? What factors would you consider while taking a decision regarding the issue?
2. Air curtains are used by cold products storage devices. What could be the major reasons for it?
3. Why is it that stores dealing in similar merchandise categorize them differently?

PROJECTS

1. Talk to the owner of a *kirana* store about the merchandising practice for bread and milk.
2. Visit a supermarket and a hypermarket to find out the locations of different categories as defined in the text. Compare and contrast them.
3. Meet a category manager and discuss the challenges faced in managing the categories and their profitability.
4. Visit three stores and gather information about innovations undertaken in managing the categories and the results achieved from these innovations.

CASE STUDY

Girish Food Store[1]

Girish had been watching the changes that were occurring in the Indian retail scenario in Ahmedabad. He was a third generation entrepreneur. His grandfather had started the store. In 2005, the store would celebrate its golden jubilee. The store had withstood the changes in the marketplace by providing a high level of personalized service to its customers, but the scenario had never been as competitive as it was now. He was facing stiff competition from modern retail formats such as hypermarkets, supermarkets, and discounters. Upgraded *kirana* stores also posed a challenge to his store. Within a span of one year, Big Bazaar and Star India had opened hypermarkets that were located on the same road as Girish Store. Adani had started a chain of supermarkets and three of them were opened within two kilometres of Girish Food Store. Several *kirana* stores had upgraded their operations by improving their merchandise display and layout. Some of them had installed computers. Some had also installed air conditioners in their stores.

Girish needed to develop a plan for the year 2005–06. In the 50th year of operation, he wanted to announce his plan to open more stores. Although the store had been performing well, the new challenges required a new way of managing the business. 'Our competition is no more at the same store level. It has become multi-faceted. We have to start competing by delivering value

that is not just different but also sustainable. So, we are concentrating on understanding consumer shopping behaviour in the store. Over the last few years, we have collected information of the shoppers' basket[2] along with their response to different promotional stimuli in some product categories. I am sure that we will gain some insight into consumer behaviour and will also be able to install category management practices in our store, especially when we have plans to expand from five to twelve more stores in the next one year.'

Indian Grocery Industry

Retailing was one of the largest industries in India and provided employment to 5 per cent of India's total workforce. Retailers contributed roughly ₹30 billion in sales in 2005, which was 10 per cent of India's GDP at current prices in 2005.[3] Food and grocery retailing was the leading contributor to total retail sales in India. The food distribution system had seen a consistent growth in sales due to increase in population and strong economic growth. Sales through mass grocery retailers were estimated to reach US$2.95 billion in 2006—an increase of 163 per cent from 2005.[4] The market was being driven by youth population and the consumer group aged 20–45 years was emerging as the fastest growing consumer segment.

---

1. This case is prepared by Piyush Kumar Sinha, Professor of Marketing, Indian Institute of Management Ahmedabad and Sanjay Kumar Kar, Academic Associate, IIMA, based on a project as a part of a course.

   Teaching material of Indian Institute of Management Ahmedabad is prepared as a basis for class discussion. Cases are not designed to present illustrations of either correct or incorrect handling of administrative problems.

2. *Shoppers' basket* is a term used to refer to the products bought by a customer on a regular basis.
3. http://www.gmid.euromonitor.com/Reports.aspx
4. http://www.foodanddrinkinsight.com/file/34144/india—mass-grocery-retail-forecasts.html

Modern retailers contributed around 3 per cent of the total retail sales in India; the rest was contributed by *kirana* stores. There were supermarkets in India but their number was significantly low in comparison to traditional corner shops, which account for 95 rupees (£1.10) of every 100 rupees spent in India.[5] The new retail formats were coming up mainly in metros and bigger cities, though smaller cities and towns were also witnessing some developments. The most popular new formats were supermarkets and hypermarkets. Supermarkets registered 28 per cent growth in 2005[6] over the previous year. These new formats were also creating excitement in the market by offering wider product assortments, promotional schemes, and product offerings at affordable prices. In many cases, they offered prices lower than those offered by *kirana* stores.

According to NCAER, the number of households that fell under the consuming class was estimated to be 91 million by 2007, as compared to 55 million in the year 2000. It was observed that this class was spending more across grocery, non-grocery, and non-store channels. Credit mechanisms, including credit cards and personal loans, also further bolstered higher retail spending. The average Indian spent more on food, which accounted for around 38 per cent of consumer spending in the year 2003–04. Consumers in India spent about 43 per cent on food and non-alcoholic beverages, which was much higher than the consumers' spend of about 7 per cent in the US. A household in Ahmedabad spent ₹2869 in a month on products such as soap, shampoo, nail polish, washing powder, footwear, tea, coffee, cigarettes, and electric bulbs.

Different Formats in Grocery Retailing

Grocery in India was sold through several formats. These were *kiranas*, upgraded *kiranas*, supermarkets, hypermarkets, wholesalers, telephone (only in a small part of Mumbai), and online (present only in Bangalore). A description of each of the physical stores is given here.[7]

Kirana

This traditional format was the most prevalent in India. *Kiranas* accounted for more than 98 per cent of the grocery sales. These stores were small in size, measuring not more than 500 sq. ft. Most of them would measure less than 250 sq. ft. They sold goods to neighbouring households. They had customers who bought from them regularly due to convenience, credit, home delivery, and a merchandise mix that suited their requirements. They sold goods at the MRP.[8]

Discounts were given only when there were promotions run by the companies. They remained profitable largely due to their low cost of operations.

Upgraded Kirana

They offered values similar to *kirana* stores, but were well lit and had a better display of merchandise. They allowed customers to browse and pick the products on their own, though most of the customers still ordered at the counter and waited for the order to be fulfilled. They were able to offer prices that were 7–10 per cent lower than *kirana* stores', mainly due to bulk buying from the distributors or manufacturers in some cases. The average size of these stores was less than 1000 sq. ft. Most of these stores were independents. The larger chain stores generated an annual revenue of about 20 million. Margin Free Market and Subhiksha were leading chain stores in the country in this category. Only Subhiksha was present in Ahmedabad. Girish Store belonged to this format. This was the fastest growing segment.

Supermarkets

The most widely used definition of a supermarket is that of a store with a selling area of between 400—2,500 sq. ft, selling at least 70 per cent foodstuff and everyday commodities. The contribution of supermarkets to food sales was currently small as compared to independent grocers that sold through all kinds of stores, including stalls and carts. Supermarkets offered a wider product assortment as compared to independent grocers or *kirana* stores. Supermarkets were expanding from a considerably larger base as compared to hypermarkets. They were expected to witness a high increase at a CAGR of 26 per cent over 2005–10 and more than triple to exceed 5,000 in 2010.[9]

---

5. http://news.independent.co.uk/world/asia/article1959040.ece

6. http://www.gmid.euromonitor.com/ReportSearch.aspx

7. Sinha, Piyush Kumar, Mathew, E. and Kansal, A. (2005), 'Format Choice of Food and Grocery Retailers', W.P No 2005–07–04, Indian Institute of Management. Ahmedabad.

8. Maximum Retail Price that is printed on the packet. Retailers would not sell beyond this price.

9. http://www.gmid.euromonitor.com/Reports.aspx

Hypermarkets

These are stores with a sales area of over 10,000 to 40,000 sq. ft, with at least 35 per cent of selling space devoted to non-food items. They are much larger compared to an average department store. Hypermarkets entered the Indian retail scene in 2001. The first hypermarket to be established was Giant, set up in Hyderabad by RPG Enterprises in June 2001. This was followed in October 2001 by Pantaloon Retail, which set up its Big Bazaar hypermarkets in Kolkata and Hyderabad. Trent India Limited started Star India Bazaar in Ahmedabad in November 2004. Hypermarkets had a wide range of product categories (about 20,000 SKUs), essentially in groceries, food, home needs, fresh food, garments, and consumer durables. These items were sold at low prices made possible due to the economies of large-scale buying and operations. They offered discounts that varied from 6 per cent to 60 per cent. Hypermarkets were designed to generate higher revenues and delivery gains in terms of branding, merchandising, display, variety, and choice for partners, consumers, retailers, and the government. Owing to the huge volume of sales generated at hypermarkets, overheads were low and they were able to function like discount stores. Groceries gave the highest per sq. ft. sales and were the major determinants of profitability. Hypermarkets were likely to lead the growth of grocery retailing in India. It was estimated to grow in value terms at a CAGR of 52 per cent over the next three years. The number of outlets was expected to reach about 300 by 2010.

Wholesalers

Ahmedabad presented this format as one of the major players in grocery retailing. A large number of Gujarati families would buy grains, cereals, pulses, edible oil, and spices for the whole year when the new crop would arrive in the market. At this time of the year, the prices would also be lower than other times. Customers would stock these items for the whole year. This practice was so prevalent that every retailer offered bulk buying, though the prices would differ across formats. Wholesalers offered prices that were 20–30 per cent cheaper than those offered by retailers, and still made about 10 per cent gross profit. They could offer such low prices as they bought the products directly from the farms. Although these wholesalers were present all over the city, most of the purchases were usually made from the wholesale market situated in the city centre. These stores were small in size and kept samples or small-size packs. The supply would be made from a warehouse. In most cases, they offered home delivery and cleaning and adding of oil for preservation. One of the leading outlets was PZ, which had many namesakes in the city.

Shopper Analysis

Girish Food Store attracted more than 600 shoppers per day and generated more than 575 bills. The shoppers used two payment modes. Cash payments dominated with a share of about 90 per cent. Girish realized that, in the highly competitive environment, understanding shopper behaviour was as important as any other marketing mix element. The previous year, the store had conducted a study of its shoppers. Three segments of shoppers emerged from the study: (i) fill-in or convenience shoppers, who purchased 1–8 items, (ii) routine shoppers, who bought 9–30 items, and (iii) stock-up shoppers, who purchased 31 or more items. These three shopper segments are profiled in Table CS7.1.

The fill-in category of shoppers came to the store because of convenience. They had time constraints and spent only half the time spent by the routine shoppers. These shoppers bought fewer items and spent about 12 minutes to finish their shopping activities. Shoppers from this category had low usage of shopping lists and coupons. They did not interact with store personnel much and, in most cases, picked the items themselves. Male shoppers constituted close to 35 per cent of this group. The fill-in shopper segment was the largest one. The average bill size per customer was ₹80.

The routine shopper segment spent about 24 minutes on an average. More than 55 per cent of them used store coupons. The average sale per customer in this category was about ₹245 per trip. In this category, close to 80 per cent were female shoppers. About 40 per cent of them used a shopping list.

The last segment, that is, stock-up shoppers, spent about 40 minutes in the store. More than 65 per cent of them preferred to carry a shopping list. Sixty five per cent of shoppers used store coupons for redemption. This segment consisted mainly of women (90 per cent). In Ahmedabad, the dry weather allowed households to stock food grains and grocery items for a longer time. The stock-up shoppers were always considered to be major contributors to the supermarkets' business. Their bill size was much higher than that of the other two segments, and they were believed to be the most loyal shoppers. These heavy buyers accounted for 25 per cent of the store's customers. They normally purchased food products frequently and staple products less frequently.

TABLE CS7.1 Shopper Profile at Girish Food Store

| | Types of Shoppers | | | |
	Fill-in	Routine	Stock-up	Total for the Store
Number of items	1–8 items	9–30 items	31+ items	
Percentage of shoppers	40	35	25	100
Average sales per customer per visit (₹)	80	245	700	400
Average shopping time (minutes)	12	25	43	27
Average no. of items	4	19	37	19
Customers using store coupons (%)	12.50	56.40	67.20	32.50
No. of coupons per using customer	1.5	2.9	3.7	2.6
Average no. of coupons used	0.25	1.5	2.22	0.9
Customers using manufacturer's coupons (%)	12.30	34.39	55.65	28.30
No. of coupons per using customer	1.6	3.56	5.8	3.85
Average no. of coupons used	0.24	1.3	3.25	1.1
Customers shopping before noon (%)	25.50	23.50	28.00	26.60
Customers shopping after noon (%)	35.50	33.00	37.40	34.40
Customers shopping in the evening (%)	40.00	43.50	34.60	39.00
Male shoppers (%)	35.60	22.25	12.40	24
Female shoppers (%)	65.40	77.75	87.60	74
Customers using shopping list (%)	10	37	67	26

The study also collected data on sales, cost, and space utilization by different categories and sub-categories (Table CS7.2). Girish found that each of the sub-categories posed different issues. They not only sold differently but would also use space differently and had different turnover rates. Girish also conducted a consumer basket analysis, which showed that his shoppers bought sugar, oil, and rice together in most occasions. Also, shoppers purchased related items together, for example, baby cream and baby lotion. This data was derived on the basis of a data mining exercise. A comprehensive list of pairs is provided in Table CS7.3. Girish has been very aggressive compared to other upgraded *kiranas*. The store planned several promotions and also used the local media, such as the press and local cable network, to announce the schemes. In the previous year, it had run several promotional schemes that fell in four categories, as shown in Table CS7.4. He found that these promotional measures did not behave in a similar fashion for every category.

'I need to crack this puzzle like any other "organized" retailer and am sure that I will become more competitive in terms of costs as well as value delivered to my customers. I believe that the investment that we have made in data management and analysis will give me a sustained advantage over all other competitors, including those from other formats,' Girish said to his father.

Questions

1. Analyse the data provided in the case study and suggest category tactics based on the profitability of each of the sub-categories, GMROF, and category share.
2. Suggest an assortment-based competitive strategy for Girish to meet the challenges posed by *kirana* stores and hypermarkets.
3. Analyse the performance of the promotional efforts of the store. Draw implications and suggest measures to improve category and sub-category promotional performance.
4. Draw out a classification plan for the different categories and identify their roles based on the sales data and strengths of other formats.

TABLE CS7.2   Category Sales and Other Details

	Weekly Unit Sales	Weekly Sales Amount (₹)	Weekly Cost of Goods Sold (₹)	Weekly Direct Product Cost (₹)	Minimum Base Quantity	Safety Stock	Linear Feet on Shelf Space
Grocery Products							
Baby food/formula	543	18,467	17,780	2,589	543	233	26.23
Baking mixes/pancake mixes	253	13,844	11,424	1,286	253	108	19.39
Baking needs	261	1,6417	12,260	1,420	261	112	19.87
Sugar	1,344	90,035	87,236	5,445	1,344	576	65.22
Bottled water	128	6,782	4,696	1,258	128	55	17.95
Candy	682	28,434	19,148	5,188	682	292	40.17
Cereal/other breakfast food	728	86,723	71,352	4,388	728	312	31.99
Tea	220	31,669	26,573	1,502	220	94	16.90
Bread	1,647	88,593	65,828	6,819	1,647	706	57.27
Sauces	499	28,582	22,087	2,538	499	214	41.28
Cookies	553	42,815	31,468	3,458	553	237	51.42
Desserts	260	8,974	6,943	984	260	112	13.04
Flour/meal	67	2,903	2,760	464	67	29	7.64
Canned fruit	402	17,349	13,405	1,663	402	172	20.56
Dried fruit	18	1,312	913	93	18	8	3.09
Fruit drink mixes	258	8,422	6,522	697	258	111	10.54
Jams/jellies/spreads	194	18,218	15,168	976	194	83	18.95
Juices/drinks	548	38,198	29,798	2,713	548	235	40.82
Milk	69	2,872	2,481	286	69	30	3.72
Milk modifiers	30	2,816	2,281	229	30	13	3.67
Oils/shortening	97	10,235	8,138	673	97	42	13.09
Pasta products	215	9,697	6,486	946	215	92	21.91
Pickles	150	10,886	7,062	781	150	64	17.41
Prepared foods	730	38,050	29,526	3,845	730	313	46.64
Salad dressings	290	19,463	16,973	1,280	290	124	17.86
Salt/spices	170	13,586	8,400	720	170	73	17.91
Snacks	1,128	92,605	66,314	6,901	1,128	483	76.07
Soup	778	24,817	20,205	2,873	778	334	29.03
Beverages	181	12,710	10,781	1,024	181	77	6.09
Syrup	54	5,458	4,359	352	54	23	5.91
Coffee	71	7,160	5,911	566	71	30	12.92
Dried vegetables	153	8,978	6,631	818	153	65	17.09
Total	**12,721**	**807,071**	**640,911**	**64,776**	**12,721**	**5,452**	**791.65**

(Contd)

(Table CS7.2 Contd)

	Weekly Unit Sales	Weekly Sales Amount (₹)	Weekly Cost of Goods Sold (₹)	Weekly Direct Product Cost (₹)	Minimum Base Quantity	Safety Stock	Linear Feet on Shelf Space
Personal Products							
Conditioners	274	18,949	16,250	1,585	274	117	16.41
Hair colours	196	16,077	11,718	1,194	196	84	13.92
Hair creams	89	8,779	7,350	560	89	38	7.60
Hair gels	122	6,649	5,857	456	122	52	5.76
Hair oils	990	58,476	48,706	4,320	990	424	50.63
Hair powders	24	700	511	67	24	10	0.61
Shampoos	1,465	145,117	115,631	9,510	1,465	628	125.63
Oral care accessories	15	209	181	20	15	6	0.18
Toothbrush	910	21,306	14,254	2,025	910	390	18.45
Toothpaste	1,950	80,975	70,105	7,087	1,950	836	70.10
Toothpowder	22	567	485	45	22	9	0.49
Sanitary pads	670	34,756	30,050	2,656	670	287	30.09
After shave	83	8,513	7,165	450	83	36	7.37
Cartridges	118	10,698	9,062	586	118	51	9.26
Razors	858	39,332	29,042	2,876	858	368	34.05
Shaving brushes	39	1,772	1,327	167	39	17	1.53
Shaving creams	324	11,494	9,475	887	324	139	9.95
Shaving foams	60	5,601	4,839	440	60	26	4.85
Shaving gels	58	4,904	4,251	369	58	25	4.25
FB deodorants	620	67,084	48,073	6,605	620	266	58.08
Body lotions	1,452	112,503	89,268	7,105	1,452	622	97.40
Body oils	24	2,435	2,014	132	24	10	2.11
Cosmetic bleaches	76	2,937	2,259	151	76	33	2.54
Face cleansers	176	9,413	7,587	876	176	75	8.15
Face wash	416	15,198	11,149	1,054	416	178	13.16
Hair removers	79	3,285	2,832	316	79	34	2.84
Hand wash	267	14,350	10,958	989	267	114	12.42
Shower gels	25	1,662	1,417	157	25	11	1.44
Skin care accessories	46	4,799	3,817	426	46	20	4.15
Skin creams	1,227	70,400	53,769	4,754	1,227	526	60.95
Sunscreens	94	5,633	4,543	487	94	40	4.88
Body wash	84	5,047	4,345	476	84	36	4.37
Soaps	4,596	152,224	111,782	9,554	4,596	1,970	131.78
Talcs	645	32,624	23,142	2,623	645	276	28.24
Total	**18,094**	**974,468**	**832,561**	**71,005**	**18,094**	**7,755**	**843.62**

TABLE CS7.3   List of Two-pair Baskets

No.	Product Line I	Product Line 2	Basket Logic
1.	Baby cream	Baby lotion	Baby products
2.	Toilet roll	Paper napkins	Home hygiene products
3.	Cosmetic cream	Moisturizer	Personal care products
4.	Baking powder	China grass	Dessert ingredients
5.	Packed meals	Ice cream	Customers having packed food as well as dessert
6.	Sunscreen	Moisturizer	Personal care products
7.	China grass	Jelly	Dessert ingredients
8.	Antiseptic cream	Baby soap	Baby products
9.	Toilet roll	Broom	Home hygiene products
10.	Baking powder	Corn flour	Baking ingredients used together
11.	Pasta	Macaroni	Italian food ingredients
12.	Baby cream	Baby powder	Baby products
13.	Baby lotion	Baby powder	Baby products
14.	Baby body oil	Baby food	Baby products
15.	Floor duster	Paper napkins	Home hygiene products
16.	Ice cream	China grass	Dessert ingredients
17.	China grass	Custard powder	Dessert ingredients
18.	Body wash	Body lotion	Personal care products
19.	Sweet corn	Corn flour	Sweet corn soup ingredients
20.	Shaving foam	Toothbrush	Personal care products
21.	Bajra	Jowar	Basic grains; often eaten together
22.	Baby lotion	Baby shampoo	Baby products
23.	Baby food	Nappies	Baby products
24.	Baby body oil	Baby powder	Baby products
25.	Jelly	Custard powder	Dessert ingredients
26.	Rubs	Cold cream	Personal care products
27.	Potato	Onion	Basic vegetables
28.	Body lotion	Cold cream	Baby products
29.	Baby lotion	Baby soap	Baby products
30.	Ice cream	Jelly	Dessert ingredients
31.	Naphthalene	Room freshener	Home hygiene products
32.	Baby powder	Baby soap	Baby products
33.	Packed meals	Soups	Ready to cook/eat products bought by consumers who do not have time to cook
34.	Baby shampoo	Baby powder	Baby products
35.	Macaroni	Corn flour	Italian food ingredients
36.	Shaving brush	Shaving cream	Shaving products bought together
37.	Anti-marks cream	Fairness cream	Cosmetics

(Contd)

(Table CS7.3 Contd)

No.	Product Line 1	Product Line 2	Basket Logic
38.	Ice cream	Custard powder	Dessert ingredients
39.	Paper napkins	Naphthalene	Home hygiene products
40.	Baby body oil	Baby soap	Baby products
41.	Citric acid	Jaggery	Indian sweets ingredients
42.	Baby food	Baby shampoo	Baby products
43.	Baby food	Baby powder	Baby products
44.	Baby shampoo	Baby soap	Baby products
45.	Sunscreen	Deodorant	Personal care products
46.	Sunscreen	Toothbrush	Personal care products
47.	Baby shampoo	Face wash	Products bought by young mothers
48.	Macaroni	Soyabeans	Italian food ingredients
49.	Black peas	Green peas	Peas are ordered together
50.	Rangoli	Incense sticks	Festival products
51.	Body lotion	Face wash	Products bought by young mothers
52.	Rubs	Talcum powder	Personal care products
53.	Potato chips	Snacks	Packed food
54.	Baby food	Baby soap	Baby products
55.	Floor duster	Broom	Home hygiene products
56.	Paper napkins	Scrub pad	Home hygiene products
57.	China grass	Soft drink concentrate	Dessert ingredients
58.	Semiya	Til	Indian sweets ingredients
59.	Corn flour	Custard powder	Dessert ingredients
60.	Dish wash tub	Scrub pad	Sink cleaning products
61.	China grass	Milk	Dessert (Pudding) ingredients
62.	Baby lotion	Shaving cream	Personal care products
63.	Soya milk	Corn flakes	Health food
64.	Green peas	White peas	Peas are ordered together
65.	Chyawanprash	Honey	Indian health food
66.	Paper napkins	Aluminium wrap	Packaging material
67.	Potato chips	Deodorant	Possible basket of urban male youth
68.	Hair dye	Fairness cream	Cosmetics
69.	Dish wash tub	Glass cleaner	Home hygiene products
70.	Toilet roll	Disinfectant	Home hygiene products
71.	Cold cream	Face wash	Personal care products
72.	Black peas	White peas	Peas are ordered together
73.	Hair removal cream	Sanitary napkins	Women's personal care products
74.	Nappies	Baby shampoo	Baby products
75.	Cold cream	Talc	Personal care products

TABLE CS7.4 Promotion Analysis at Girish Food Store

	Weekly Unit Sold on Promotion	Weekly Incremental Volume due to Promotion		Average % Increase in Unit Sales over the Base Level			
		Unit	₹	Temporary Price Reduction +10%	Price Reduction Plus Feature Ad	Price Reduction Plus Display	Price Reduction Plus Feature Ad and Display
Grocery Products							
Baby food/formula	125	34	1,157	6	18	25	NA
Baking mixes/pancake mixes	268	145	7,938	32	65	90	164
Baking needs	326	123	7,745	24	45	86	150
Beverages/carbonated	465	249	16,675	35	56	75	300
Bottled water	40	12	635	21	56	48	170
Candy	390	230	9,586	15	89	88	145
Cereal/other breakfast food	376	178	21,212	28	67	98	155
Tea	208	127	18,316	24	59	154	187
Bread	500	254	13,661	15	37	132	145
Sauces	160	68	3,894	19	36	111	143
Cookies	180	75	5,809	34	54	132	154
Desserts	230	124	4,274	29	50	112	156
Flour/meal	148	43	1,850	23	45	125	178
Canned fruit	100	32	1,382	26	48	132	157
Dried fruit	90	54	3,933	45	67	122	150
Fruit drink mixes	170	87	2,839	32	62	121	157
Jams/jellies/spreads	189	98	9,218	45	80	132	200
Juices/drinks	280	154	10,734	36	76	145	233
Milk	50	24	1,000	25	68	87	189
Milk modifiers	48	13	1,211	30	70	110	147
Oils/shortening	85	37	3,899	21	83	130	230
Pasta products	175	78	3,525	35	87	122	189
Pickles	86	34	2,473	32	78	111	200
Prepared foods	56	27	1,407	41	87	143	230
Salad dressings	216	89	5,970	46	69	150	240
Salt/spices	96	46	3,669	23	98	160	300
Snacks	400	205	16,835	29	121	156	345
Soup	76	38	1,211	15	85	97	253
Sugar	300	165	11,615	19	90	132	270
Syrup	43	21	2,123	25	78	154	320
Coffee	65	32	3,241	33	89	121	253
Dried vegetables	49	14	823	39	92	160	290
Total	**5,990**	**2,910**	**184,629**	**28**	**69**	**118**	**206**

(Contd)

(Table CS7.4 Contd)

Merchandise Categories	Weekly Unit Sold on Promotion	Weekly Incremental Volume due to Promotion		Average % Increase in Unit Sales over the Base Level			
		Unit	₹	Temporary Price Reduction +10%	Price Reduction Plus Feature Ad	Price Reduction Plus Display	Price Reduction Plus Feature Ad and Display
Conditioners	132	34	2,351	12	30	45	120
Hair colours	89	25	2,051	14	43	53	89
Hair creams	34	14	1,381	16	34	60	86
Hair gels	48	16	872	20	38	70	125
Hair oils	354	140	8,269	32	58	80	140
Hair powders	18	6	175	15	30	60	NA
Shampoos	650	240	23,773	25	54	75	240
Oral care accessories	6	2	28	24	65	90	NA
Toothbrush	530	260	6,087	25	34	65	245
Toothpaste	850	375	15,572	23	65	86	250
Toothpowder	10	4	103	24	45	75	210
Sanitary pads	390	215	11,153	15	32	74	180
After shave	34	13	1,333	23	45	68	85
Cartridges	45	18	1,632	26	34	65	120
Razors	432	132	6,051	14	43	68	156
Shaving brushes	23	11	500	15	45	58	65
Shaving creams	145	67	2,377	23	46	54	95
Shaving foams	25	9	840	28	34	65	80
Shaving gels	34	12	1,015	16	45	85	90
FB deodorants	456	254	27,483	15	37	65	120
Body lotions	567	312	24,174	13	50	85	140
Body oils	8	3	304	16	45	87	160
Cosmetic bleaches	25	9	348	15	46	57	169
Face cleansers	67	27	1,444	17	32	68	98
Face wash	215	115	4,201	13	32	63	89
Hair removers	34	12	499	22	45	67	87
Hand wash	136	65	3,494	21	43	85	110
Shower gels	9	3	199	17	25	45	88
Skin care accessories	21	12	1,252	26	54	68	96
Skin creams	475	247	14,172	24	67	87	120
Sunscreens	43	22	1,318	14	35	87	133
Body wash	29	16	961	15	45	87	143
Soaps	2,754	789	26,133	17	43	57	200
Talcs	295	134	6,778	26	47	87	98
Total	**8,983**	**3,613**	**198,324**	**19**	**43**	**70**	**132**

8 Supply Chain Management

LEARNING OBJECTIVES

After studying this chapter, you will be able to
- elucidate the importance of supply chain management
- discuss the fundamental requirements for an efficient supply chain
- explain the key drivers of supply chain management
- gain an insight into the key focus areas for efficient supply chain management
- understand the framework for supply chain management in terms of three interrelated aspects—network structure, business processes, and management processes
- familiarize yourself with the process of supply chain management

INTRODUCTION

Supply chain management (SCM) is a term that has grown significantly in use and popularity since the late 1980s. It addresses issues of order cycle, item assortments, and promotions. It is particularly important in mature or declining markets and during periods of economic slowdown when market growth cannot conceal inefficient practices. It is also critical in new product and market developments where the organization needs to take decisions related to distribution and facilitate faster delivery of products in the markets.[1]

The term *supply chain management* was coined by Keith Oliver of the strategy consulting firm Booz Allen Hamilton in 1982. It refers to the process of planning, implementing, and controlling the operations of the supply chain with the purpose of satisfying customer requirements as efficiently as possible.[2] It is the integration of key business processes from the end user through to the original supplier that provides products, services, and information that add value for customers and stock holders.[3] Supply chain management can also be defined as the design and operation of the physical, managerial, informational, and financial systems needed to transfer goods and services from the vendor to the customer (point of production to point of consumption) in an effective and efficient manner.[4] Information about customer choices and demands, assortments, and sales returns travel in the reverse direction.

Supply chain management is a process where bottlenecks, value adding factors, and liability factors in the value chain are identified and addressed, enabling the retailer to have an efficient supply chain. Efficient SCM in retail operations ensures that the right product is in the right place, at the right time, and at the right cost.

Supply chain management is a much broader concept than logistics. Although they have several common aspects, the difference lies in how companies perceive them.

Supply chain management is the integration of key business processes from the end user to the original suppliers who provide products, services, and information that add value for customers and other stakeholders.[5]

The Council of Supply Chain Management, earlier known as the Council of Logistics Management, states, 'Logistics is that part of the supply chain process that plans, implements, and controls the efficient and effective flow and storage of goods, services, and related information from the point of origin to the point of consumption, in order to meet customer requirements.'[6]

Supply chain management involves increasing efficiency across the members of a supply chain who are directly or indirectly interacting from its origin to the destination. Their involvement in the supply chain could be either at the primary level or the subsidiary level. The primary level would consist of those who perform the important functions in the business; the subsidiary level would comprise those who help primary members do their tasks.

Customer service management has always been the vital component of any supply chain. If the suppliers are not satisfied, it would be difficult to keep up with the volatile customer demand, and this would adversely affect their performance. Customer service management becomes a critical part of SCM because it helps to determine whether the existing customers will continue as customers in the long term. Customer service audit is used for attaining these goals in SCM.

FACTORS FOR SUCCESSFUL SCM

The fundamental requirements for efficient SCM are (i) single entity, (ii) inventory perspective, (iii) strategic decision-making, (iv) a systems approach, and (v) doing what one can do best.[7]

The responsibility of planning and control functions across the supply chain generally rests with a single entity. This reduces administrative delays and improves efficiency across the supply chain. In developed markets, retailers control a significant portion of this process. In emerging markets such as India, as retailers have not yet achieved critical size, this process is managed largely by the manufacturers. In certain mofussil markets, the intermediaries hold control of the process.

A supply chain consists of processes and systems that enable a 'leaner and cleaner' system of inventory management. Efforts are made to improve flexibility, reduce lead times and uncertainties, and improve quality. This not only reduces inventory but also helps retailers to keep their assortment contemporary.

Decisions in the supply chain have strategic implications rather than just operational ones. It needs the attention of top management and cannot be left only to the buyers or merchandisers. Most retailers create teams of senior managers to plan inventories as it has a direct impact on the profitability of the company. This necessitates an integrated concept of supply chain that enables interfacing between the vendor and the customer with many subsystems interacting with each other. Some of the principles followed in this regard are given in Exhibit 8.1. The role of information technology cannot be undermined in such cases. Supply chain management also focuses on allocating activities so as to add maximum value to the retailer and its customers. The complexity and uncertainty of supply has implications on outsourcing, in-sourcing, and effective partnership building. In the case of supplies that have extensive logistics requirements and which have higher uncertainty in supply, a retailer would like to in-source the activity. In other cases, the activity could be outsourced.

Supply chain management is an interactive process that requires leadership, commitment, and empowerment for successful implementation. It focuses on the need to look at value delivery to the

EXHIBIT 8.1   Seven Principles of SCM

The most requested article in the 10-year history of *Supply Chain Management Review* was one that appeared in our very first issue in the spring of 1997. Written by experts from the respected Logistics practice of Andersen Consulting (now Accenture), 'The Seven Principles of Supply Chain Management' laid out a clear and compelling case for excellence in SCM. The insights provided here remain remarkably fresh ten years later.

Principle 1: Segment customers based on the service needs of distinct groups and adapt the supply chain to serve these segments profitably.

Principle 2: Customize the logistics network to the service requirements and profitability of customer segments.

Principle 3: Listen to market signals and align demand planning accordingly across the supply chain, ensuring consistent forecasts and optimal resource allocation.

Principle 4: Differentiate product closer to the customer and speed conversion across the supply chain.

Principle 5: Manage sources of supply strategically to reduce the total cost of owning materials and services.

Principle 6: Develop a supply chain-wide technology strategy that supports multiple levels of decision-making and gives a clear view of the flow of products, services, and information.

Principle 7: Adopt channel-spanning performance measures to gauge collective success in reaching the end user effectively and efficiently.

Source: Anderson, David L., Frank F. Britt, and Danavon J. Favre 2007, 'The 7 Principles of Supply Chain Management', *Supply Chain Management Review*, 1 April 2007, accessed on 16 May 2007.

customer comprehensively. Such values are delivered by the retailer through defined business activities in the form of flow of goods and services, information, and cash.[8] The value flow manifests itself as goods and services flow largely from the vendor to the customer through the retailer. Occasionally, there could be reverse flows of material due to returns, rework, or recycling. The information flow consists of flows both from vendor to customer and from customer to vendor. This is the main driver of the concept of supply chain. In the forward direction (the direction of the major value flow), information that helps in managing estimates, stock availability, dispatch services, stock transfer notes, quality assurance reports, and warranties is passed from one entity in the chain to the other. The major components of the backward flow (against the direction of the major value flow) are inputs for such activities as sales forecasts, marketing plans, dispatch plans, procurement quantities and timing plans, quality feedback, and invoked warranties. The cash flow consists mainly of money paid for goods and services received, and credit periods/advances to customers and vendors. The cash usually flows with the information, such as order specifications, invoicing, purchase orders, and receipts. An efficient SCM would match the value flow with an appropriate cash flow structure.[9]

DRIVERS OF SCM

Increased customer expectations, technological developments, and changing management attitudes are the key drivers of supply chain management.

Customers expect increased value addition from retailers. They are becoming more and more sensitive to response time, reliability, cost consciousness, and information accessibility and provisions.

As a result, retailers are moving towards reduced lead times and costs in their operations. The value that firms seek to provide to their customers is increasing. Recent developments in information technology and flexible manufacturing technology allow newer initiatives in this direction. This has led to a change in the attitude of managers, who now welcome integration and partnership with complementary entities (rather than the traditional principal-agent approach) and recognize the need for continuous process improvement. Retailers are realizing the ill effects of high inventories and inefficient flow of goods. Attempts are being made to manage the system with reduced inventories so as to not only bring down working capital costs but also reduce stock costs through shorter lead times.

SCM AND COMPETITIVE ADVANTAGE

Retailers have now realized the importance of the supply chain and SCM is quickly becoming a new source of competitive advantage. This is being achieved by focusing on the key areas of SCM, leading to specific decisions, as will be discussed here.[10]

Minimizing Uncertainty   A retailer faces three distinct uncertainties with regard to SCM: (i) supply uncertainty, caused due to unreliability of vendors, (ii) process uncertainty stemming from internal processes, and (ii) demand uncertainty. Supply uncertainties are addressed through initiatives such as vendor development and certification, sharing of stock planning information, and joint attention to transport arrangements. Process uncertainty caused by machine breakdowns, uncertain yields, absenteeism, and lack of attention to detail can be addressed through good maintenance practices, better technology, and development of robust systems and processes. Demand uncertainty can be reduced to a large extent by using robust forecasting techniques and through better communication with customers.

Reducing Lead Times   Time is a critical factor in SCM. The processes, when not designed and managed well, increase lead time at different stages of procurement, conversion, and distribution. Retailers using bar codes and UPC scanners tend to spend a lot of time in re-coding merchandise as there is a lack of a uniform coding system. All such activities need to be mapped. Critical activities among them can be identified and managed to increase efficiency. Reducing set-up or changeover times in various processes and the use of flexible assembly techniques improves the flexibility of response. For efficient SCM, retailers may often require different supply chains for different customer segments based on response requirements. The tendency to club supply chains in the interest of efficiency can be counterproductive to effectiveness. Lead time can also be cut down by faster modes of transport and better planning practices.

Minimizing the Number of Stages   The number of stages that goods and services pass through adds to the complexity of SCM. Unification of tasks and reducing the number of stages makes coordination of decision-making easier. This can be achieved through business process re-engineering. Retailers benefit a great deal by sourcing from as high up the supply chain as possible. This not only reduces costs but also improves the quality of merchandise.

Improving Process   Quality SCM builds long-term competitive advantage through the service aspects of value delivery to the customer. Product quality and features can only be short-term advantages. Competing on service requires close attention to processes. Doing things right the first time is a prerequisite to effective SCM. This can be achieved through statistical process control, root cause analysis of poor quality, and improvement of process capability. Efficient process technologies help in reducing inventories and wastage. Improved supply chain practices will require integrated process orientation rather than functional organization. Job rotation and having flatter and leaner organizations also help.

Managing Demand Uncertainty and anticipated variations in demand are an integral part of SCM. To reduce uncertainty, a retailer would have to develop not only a good forecasting system but also strategies that smoothen demand. This can be achieved through appropriate promotion and branding. This will enable better control of the supply chain right from demand generation. This can also be managed by postponing the value addition as close to the customer as possible, so that precise customer needs can be met without holding committed stocks in the entire chain. This is very important, especially for retailers that deal in fashion or seasonal goods. For example, United Colors of Benetton, an apparel retailer, has shifted the colouring process closer to the market. It manufactures and stocks only grey fabric. Depending on the demand of the season, it can colour its fabrics and bring them to the market faster than any other retailer.

Initiatives at an Industry Level Efficient SCM requires a developed network of transportation and communication infrastructure, besides the competence of retailers. Industry-level, rather than firm-level, initiatives in specific product categories can focus on transport and/or warehousing inadequacies and help develop appropriate service providers.

FRAMEWORK FOR SCM

The SCM framework has three key nodes—(i) the supply chain network structure, (ii) supply chain business processes, and (iii) supply chain management components (Fig. 8.1). These nodes are interrelated. The *supply chain structure* is a network of channel members and the links between the members of the supply chain. *Business processes* are the activities that produce a specific output of value to the customer. The *management components* are the managerial variables by which the business processes are integrated and managed across the supply chain. The implementation of supply chain management involves identifying the supply chain members, the processes that need to be linked with each of these key SCM, and the type or level of integration that applies to each process link. Efficient SCM involves various activities related to sourcing, storing, and transporting. The objective of SCM is to maximize competitiveness and profitability for the company, as also for the whole network, including the end customer.[11]

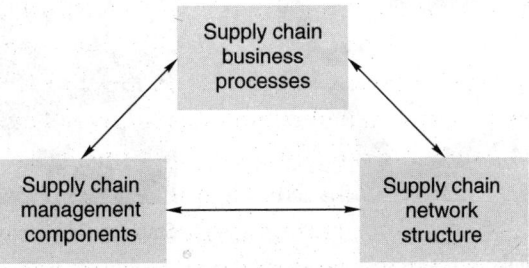

FIG. 8.1 Framework for SCM

Storing in a Warehouse
Source: www.schenker.co.uk

Picking
Source: www.tnt.com

Shipping
Source: www.tnt.com

Sending
Source: www.tnt.com

Tracking
Source: www.no-ordinary-city.co.uk

Stacking (Hypercity, Mumbai)

Supply Chain Activities

Supply Chain Network Structure

The supply chain structure is a network of channel members and the links among these members. It is a network of agencies that come together to ensure that the desired value is delivered to the members. The members and the structure of the chain change with the requirements of the value delivery process that the chain wishes to follow. Retailers are integral to the supply chain. They connect the customer to the rest of the supply chain. Retailers are in a unique position to collect purchase information of every customer and every transaction, gauge customer wants and needs, and share the information with suppliers to plan production, promotion, deliveries, assortments, and inventory levels. Customers benefit from fewer stock-outs and a better assortment of merchandise. These benefits translate into higher sales and lower markdowns and, hence, higher profitability for the retailer.

Channel Structure

Bucklin developed a theory of channel structure, which is based on the assumption that the purpose of the channel is to provide consumers with a desired combination of outputs (lot size, delivery time, and market decentralization) at minimal cost.[12] Consumers influence the channel structure by seeking the desired combination of service outputs. A channel where no group or institution generates more profit or consumer satisfaction per unit of product cost is considered ideal. Otherwise, the activities/ functions of channel members that generate less profit get shifted to other channel members in order to achieve the most efficient and effective channel structure. This shifting of specific functions may lead to the addition or deletion of channel members.

The decision regarding when and where to use channel intermediaries leads to the 'make-versus-buy' or outsourcing decision. Outsourcing represents an opportunity that should be considered in supply chain design and evaluation of existing supply chains. For example, DHL—a courier delivery company—has, in addition to the handling of shipments, also ventured into storage and management of inventory. After successfully establishing a network of distribution centres and fleets to ensure prompt delivery, DHL leveraged its assets by offering logistics services to its customers.

Costs in the channel can be reduced by postponing changes in the form and identity of a product to the last possible point in the marketing process, and by postponing inventory location to the last possible point in time, since risk and uncertainty costs increase as the product becomes more differentiated.[13] Postponement results in savings and reduces risk and uncertainty costs. Speculation, which is the opposite of postponement, means that a channel institution assumes risk rather than shifting it. It can reduce marketing and transportation costs through economies of large-scale production, reduction of stock-outs and their associated costs, and reduction of uncertainty. To reduce the need for speculative inventories, many retailers use time-based promotions for improving inventory turns, leading to enhanced productivity, competitive position, and customer satisfaction. Time-based management systems use technology such as bar coding and EDI, and rely on information sharing among suppliers, manufacturers, and retailers regarding lead times and forecasts of sales, production, purchase needs, shipping, new product plans, and payment.

Channel structure is affected by technological, cultural, physical (e.g., geography, size of the market, location of production centres, and concentration of population), social, and behavioural variables and local, state, and federal laws. Figure 8.2 depicts the different supply chain structures. The three primary decisions that influence the network structure of a company will be now discussed:

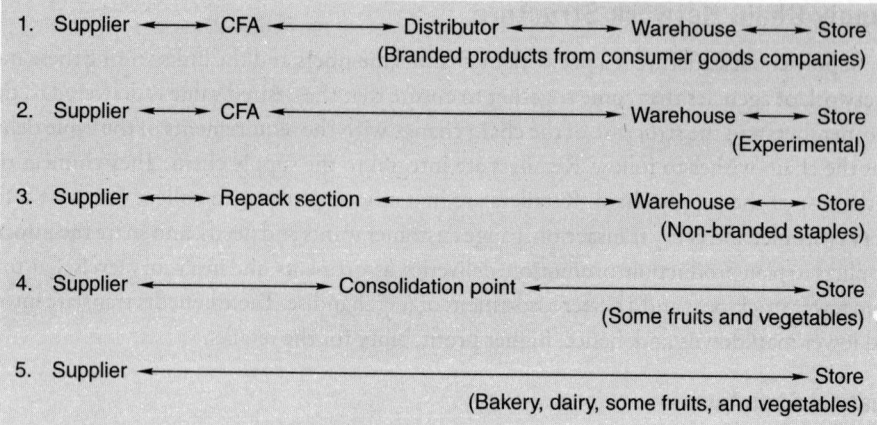

FIG. 8.2   Different Supply Chain Structures

Identifying the Members of the Supply Chain   A supply chain consists of primary and secondary members. The *primary members* of a supply chain are the units who perform operational and/or managerial activities in the business process designed to produce a specific output for a particular customer or market. The *secondary* or *supporting members* of a supply chain are companies that provide resources, knowledge, utilities, or assets for the primary members of the supply chain.[14] Supporting members include banks that lend money to the retailer; building owners that provide warehouse space; and companies that supply equipment, print marketing brochures, or provide transportation. The distinction between primary and supporting members of a supply chain are not obvious in all cases. The same member can perform primary activities related to one process and supporting activities related to another process. Coordination with all the members of the supply chain can be complex and unmanageable. Retailers tend to identify the critical members on the basis of the contributions made to various flows of product, title, payment, information, and promotion and allocate managerial attention and resources accordingly.

Determining the Structural Dimensions of the Network   The supply chain network can take three structural dimensions: (i) a vertical structure, (ii) a horizontal structure, or (iii) the retailer's position from the source of supply. The term *vertical structure* refers to the number of tiers in the supply chain. The supply chain may be long, with numerous tiers, or short, with few tiers. The term *horizontal structure* refers to the number of suppliers/customers represented within each tier. A retailer can have a narrow vertical structure, with few companies at each tier level, or a wide vertical structure with many suppliers or customers at each tier level. A retailer can position itself at or near the initial source of the supply. For instance, Walmart has set up procurement centres in India for its global sourcing of textiles and other products. Different combinations of these structural variables are possible. Outsourcing logistics, marketing, or product development activities would change the supply chain structure. Members of the chain depend on each other for successful integration and management of business processes, even across the domain of the businesses of members of the supply chain.

Managing the Process Links   A supply chain consists of many processes and sub-processes. Four fundamentally different types of business process links can be identified between members of a supply chain.[15] *Managed process links* are links that retailers find important to integrate and manage. This might be carried out in collaboration with other member companies of the supply chain. *Monitored* *process links* are not as critical to the retailer, but it is important that the process links are integrated and managed appropriately between the concerned members of the chain. Successful retailers monitor the management and integration of each process link periodically. *Not-managed process links* are links in which the retailers are not actively involved, nor are they critical enough to use resources for monitoring. In such cases, retailers trust the other members to manage the process links appropriately. Sometimes, in case of limited resources, retailers leave them to manage on their own. *Non-member process links* are links between members and non-members of the supply chain. Though these links are not integral to the supply chain, they may affect the performance of the retailer and its supply chain.

Supply Chain Business Processes

A supply chain consists of processes that can be viewed as a network of activities designed with a focus on customers and with a purpose of dynamic management of flows of products, information, cash, knowledge, and ideas in the chain. Efficient supply chain management requires integrating activities into key supply chain processes as opposed to managing individual functions. It aims at achieving trade-offs within and among members regarding inventory and activity allocation. An integrated supply chain requires continuous sharing of information so as to create the most optimum product flows. A process approach yields significant benefits in terms of cost reductions and service improvements. The key business processes for efficient SCM include efficient consumer response (ECR), buying and merchandising, and product development, including the development of private labels.

Efficient Consumer Response

Efficient consumer response (ECR) is a process for providing consumers with the best possible value, service, and variety. As a step towards an integrated SCM, it identifies key customers or customer groups that are critical to the retailer. Customer-focused teams in the retail organization develop strategies to provide mutually beneficial products and services. New customer interfaces are designed, which lead to improved communications and better predictions of customer demand, which, in turn, lead to improved services for customers. Performance of these changes are evaluated in light of customer profitability and the levels of service provided to customers. Efficient consumer response consists of activities that focus on replenishment, category management, customer service management, demand management, and customer order fulfilment. Through ECR, retailers implement systems for quick response, inventory planning, electronic data interchange, and logistics planning, resulting in increased efficiency and reduced distribution costs.

Efficient product replenishment is the smooth, continual flow of product, matched to consumption and supported by a timely, accurate, and, preferably, paperless information flow. Efficient replenishment techniques aim to ensure that all members of the supply chain benefit from the process. A retailer needs to be careful while choosing a technique so that the benefits generated for one supply chain player do not have adverse consequences for others. Otherwise, it may disturb the balance of costs between manufacturers and retailers.[16] In the US, it is estimated that by applying efficient replenishment techniques, the total grocery supply chain inventory could be reduced from more than 100 days of sales to around 60 days. *Category management* practices aim to optimize the range of products stocked in store, the efficiency of promotions, and new product introductions. Similarly, a continuous replenishment programme involves several techniques. The most commonly described technique is vendor managed inventory (VMI), especially in a fixed order quantity (FOQ) environment. This involves daily reviews of the retail sales and stock position using EDI communication from the retailer to the supplier, which help in forecasting future sales on the basis of which new orders are estimated. Vendor managed inventory system is also suitable for use where EDI is not sufficiently advanced. The key elements in the replenishment are the order review cycle, the replenishment lead time, and the target safety stock level.

Customer service management provides a single source of information. It is the point of contact that efficiently handles inquiries with regard to shipping dates, product and pricing information, product availability, and after-sales service. Another critical process for effective ECR is *customer order fulfilment*. This requires integration of the distribution and transportation plans.

The objective of implementing ECR is to develop a seamless process from the supplier to the retailer and then to various customer segments to meet their requirements and reduce the total delivery cost to the customer. Most of the time, there is variability in inventory due to variance in process, supply, and demand. Customer demand, characterized by irregular order patterns, is by far the largest source of variability. Given this variability in customer ordering, *demand management* is crucial to the success of SCM. The demand management process gathers, compiles, and updates customer demand continuously to match requirements with supply. Advanced SCM systems synchronize customer demand and supply rates to manage inventories globally.

Buying and Merchandising

Buying involves development of plans with suppliers to support the product flow management process as also development of new products. Suppliers are generally categorized according to their contribution and importance to the retailer. Long-term partnerships are developed with a small core group of suppliers that allows for quick response and continuous improvement. The key suppliers are involved right from the planning stage, leading to reduction in product sourcing cycle times. Early supply input reduces cycle time through better coordination among other functions. Better margins are achieved through appropriate sourcing and negotiations and by achieving efficiencies in the distribution system.

The merchandising function involves determining the specific products/brands to offer and their sourcing. The merchandising strategy begins with studying customer preferences in terms of product range, variety for choice in a given product, freshness, availability, and other factors that are important to the customer. Based on customers' shopping lists and budgets, the merchandise offer could be categorized into destination, strategic, convenience, and speciality. The various categories, depending on their attributes, would entail different strategies regarding the width (brand choice), depth (number of variants), price, and tactical usage for drawing customers to the store.

Product Development and Private Labels

As part of a strategy for ECR, many retailers get directly involved in developing products suitable for their customer segment. This becomes imperative for retailers who deal in products that are heavily dependent on the variations in customers' tastes and preferences with season, time, and store location. Retailers are required to integrate their customers and suppliers into the product development process so that they can minimize the new product development process and successfully launch new products/categories in the minimum possible time and remain competitive. In many cases, the limitation of current suppliers leads to product development by retailers. A private label brand (also called 'own label' or store brand) is defined as a product line that is owned, controlled, merchandised, and sold by a specific retailer, in its own stores.[17] Typically, the retailer or its category managers develop product specifications for the merchandise and find a supplier/manufacturer. It is the retailer and not the manufacturer who is responsible for promoting the brand.

Private labels have evolved mainly due to the need of retailers to differentiate themselves from similar format retailers and to cope with the neighbourhood *kirana* store. A retailer differentiates itself through a portfolio of private label products that is seen as relevant by consumers in terms of economics (price premiums and market share), attitude (consumer perceptions), and behaviour (customer loyalty). Private labels also help improve gross margins and retain footfalls. Store brands are perceived to deliver a better value proposition for customers as they cost less and are of comparable quality. Stores such as Westside have more than 90 per cent of merchandise under private labels. Ebony has been successful in launching private labels in categories not filled by other brands, as in the case of size 46˝ shirts and men's *kurtas*. This has helped the store establish a distinctive identity. Pantaloons' launch of a range of merchandise for customers who wear larger sizes has also been received well.

Studies show that about two-thirds of consumers believe that retailer brands are as good as or even better than manufacturers' brands. A global survey of private labels by ACNielsen in 36 countries and 80 different categories has shown a steady growth in their value. In the period between March 2002 and 2003, private label sales in terms of value rose by 4 per cent to $85 billion. It constituted 15 per cent of the total sales. Among five regions that the survey covered, Europe had the highest value share of private labels at 22 per cent and a growth rate of 6 per cent. In North America, their value share was 16 per cent. The emerging markets (comprising Hungary, South Africa, Czech Republic, and Poland) showed the fastest growth of 48 per cent, although the value share was only 4 per cent. Growth in Latin America and Asia Pacific continues to rise as multinational retailers expand into these markets.

Private labels have a large share in paper products, plastic bags and wraps (29%), and food categories—refrigerated food (28%) and frozen food (28%). Personal care products (4%), cosmetics (2%), and baby food (1%) have fewer private labels. In urban India, private labels are present in almost half of all stores classified as modern format stores. All the Indian hypermarkets stock private label packaged consumer goods. About 60 per cent of the over 1,400 supermarkets possess store brands. Department and health and pharmacy stores register the lowest penetration of private labels at 14 per cent and 9 per cent, respectively. There is a greater presence of store brands in supermarkets in southern cities, such as Coimbatore (100%), Hyderabad (82%), Bengaluru (82%), Madurai (75%), and Vizag (81%). Private labels are also found in the northern cities, such as Lucknow (100%), Kanpur (80%), and Ludhiana (100%).[18]

There are several reasons for retailers' growing interest in their own brand sales. These are as follows:

1. Private labels are priced 20 to 30 per cent lower than manufacturer brands. They offer quality, style, and consistency. On a global basis, private label products are found to offer consumers an average discount of 31 per cent when compared to manufacturers' products. The price differential is the widest in Poland (50%), and the lowest in Hong Kong (10%). In India, in some cases, the profits have been found to be double those of the branded products.[19] For instance, Big Bazaar has its own brand of tea, which is 40 per cent cheaper than the competitors' brands and accounts for half of its tea sales.

2. The exclusivity of strong private labels boosts store loyalty. Private labels create a relationship based on the experience of the product, and not just the shopping experience.

3. Retailers have more control over distribution, display, promotion, and quality of merchandise in case of private labels.

4. It is easier for the retailer to manage the inventory in terms of volume and segmentation.

Private labels also offer several advantages to the producers. They provide them an opportunity to build strategic partnerships with selected retailers. Smaller suppliers who do not have promotional capabilities can enter bigger stores at a lower cost. They can get more shelf space in the store.

Despite these advantages, the retailer must be cautious of placing too much emphasis on its own brands. This is because of the following reasons:

(a) The retailer needs to make significant investments to design merchandise, create customer awareness, and develop a favourable image for its private label brands.

(b) The sales staff may need additional training to help them sell private label brands.

(c) Customers who are loyal to manufacturers' brands would shop at other stores when the preferred brands are not stocked or when the full variety is unavailable.

(d) Private labels, especially in the current Indian retailing environment, may fail to pose a 'threat' to manufacturer brands as these offer a wider choice of merchandise. In addition, manufacturers often provide retailers greater visibility through advertising and promotional incentives. The dominant small format stores also restrict the use of private labels due to their size of operation and inability to offer a wider choice than manufactures.

Supply Chain Management Components

The management components constitute the third element of the SCM framework that determines the integration and efficiency of the supply chain. Each component has several sub-components whose importance varies depending on the process being managed. The primary components of SCM are planning and control methods, workflow/activity structure, organization structure, communication and information flow facility structure, product flow facility structure, management methods, power and leadership structure, risk and reward structure, and culture and attitude. These components can be divided into two groups: (i) physical and technical and (ii) managerial and behavioural components. The first group includes the most visible, tangible, measurable, and easy-to-manage components. The second group is comprised of the managerial and behavioural components that are less tangible and visible and are often difficult to assess and alter. They define the organizational behaviour and influence how the physical and technical management components can be implemented. There is interdependence among the two groups and successful SCM is established by understanding each of these management components and their interdependence. Each component is briefly described in Table 8.1. To establish a supply chain, retailers would consider various factors such as market coverage objectives, product characteristics, customer service objectives, and profitability.[20]

RETAIL INVENTORY MANAGEMENT

Retail inventory management is about efficiently handling merchandise assortment while keeping the ordering, shipping, and other related costs under control. One of the biggest challenges in the retail industry is managing the store inventory. Retailers have limited space in the store to keep products that are large in number and wide in variety. The challenge for a retailer is to strike the right balance between too much inventory and too little inventory. In case of too much stock, the profitability of the retailer would be affected and in case of too little inventory, he/she would lose potential customers to competitors.

TABLE 8.1   Management Components of SCM

Component	Description
Planning and control methods	The control aspects can be operationalized as the best performance metrics for measuring supply chains.
Workflow/activity structure	The workflow/activity structure indicates how the firm performs its tasks and activities.
Organization structure	Organization structure can refer to the individual firm and the supply chain. The use of cross-functional teams suggests a process approach and a more integrated supply chain.
Communication and information flow facility structure	It refers to the information network that has been developed for management of the supply chain. EDI would be integral to this. The Internet has been proving very useful in this regard.
Product flow facility structure	It refers to the network structure for sourcing, manufacturing, and distribution across the supply chain. It also determines the extent of coordination of new product development and product portfolio planning processes across the supply chain.
Management methods	They include corporate philosophy and management techniques. The level of management involvement in day-to-day operations can differ across supply chain members.
Power and leadership structure	The power and leadership structure across the supply chain will affect its form and the level of commitment of other supply chain members.
Risk and reward	The anticipation that risks and rewards will be shared across the supply chain affects the long-term commitment of members.
Culture and attitude	The culture of an organization determines how employees are valued and incorporated into the management of the firm, which is very necessary for the supply chain to perform as a coordinated network.

Some activities involved in the management of inventory are replenishment, carrying cost management, inventory forecasting, quality management, handling of defective goods and waste products, inventory price management, inventory storage, and inventory valuation. In retail inventory management, keeping a track of all the stock that is available in the warehouse and shop floor along with those in transit is a challenge for the retailer. For these reasons, an effective retail inventory management system is very important.

Retail inventory management is important to maintain control over activities such as ordering, shipping, tracking inventory, storage, and warehouse distribution. Effective inventory management helps the retailer not only to make steady profits but also to reduce inventory wastage and control theft. All big retail houses such as Walmart, Tesco, and Carrefour attach a lot of significance to good retail inventory management systems, to increase their corporate profitability.

Retail inventory management broadly consists of the following activities:

- Managing the inventory
- Managing store markdowns
- Evaluating the sales of certain products
- Evaluating shopping comparison with competitors
- Analysing stores on individual level
- Implementing an effective review system

A major cost decision that a retailer is always concerned about is the trade-off between carrying cost and stock-out costs. Integrating these with total cost is very significant. Retailers must decide on the order quantity as well as on the reorder level policies. The most frequently used model for determining the inventory level by minimizing carrying costs and ordering costs is known as the *economic order quantity* (EOQ) model.

The EOQ model can be calculated using the following formula:

$$EOQ = \sqrt{2 \times O \times D / (C \times V)}$$

where O is the ordering cost; D is the annual demand; C is the carrying cost; and V is the average cost or value of one unit of inventory.

Economic batch quantity (EBQ) is also an associated concept. According to this concept, the profitability would be adversely affected if the inventory level is too low or too high, and hence an optimum level should be maintained, which leads to profitability. The EBQ model has got its own limitations but it is widely used in the industry for managerial decision-making.

The inventory management technique used when there is uncertainty in the environment is the *fixed order quantity model*. Here, the order is placed when the inventory reaches a minimum level, the reorder point. There is also another model known as *fixed order interval model* in which orders are placed at fixed intervals—weekly or monthly. It requires large quantities of safety stock to cover the risk of a stock-out.

Another common tool used is ABC analysis. The basic postulate of the ABC model is that 20 per cent of the firm's products contribute to 80 per cent of the sales, which guides a retailer to manage the products in important categories for better output. We focus here on key items and divide the products into different product categories. The high volume stock items would be placed at retail locations, moderate items at warehouse locations, and slow-moving items at a centralized distribution area. The product categories help in setting the inventory level accordingly.

Another model named VED (vital, essential, and desirable) is also used in inventory management. In this model, the inventory level is decided based on the criticality of use of the product.

Forecasting is also an important technique used with respect to inventory management. If data about buyers' intentions to buy the products are gathered, it would help the retailer in developing a sales forecast, which would finally guide them to the desired inventory level management.

Most large businesses today utilize computerized systems for inventory management. Retail software packages can reduce costs by reducing the time spent in manually counting the inventory and creating purchase orders. Retailers are required to handle thousands of SKUs, which makes it impossible to manage inventory manually. There are many systems that help in inventory management, such as bar code readers, point-of-sale terminals, and electronic product catalogues (such as those used successfully by Argos).

A retailer can have several issues if the inventory management system does not fall in place. These issues include lack of sufficient storage space, increase in cost of maintaining order level, customer turnover, cancelled orders, increase in obsolete items, and adverse relations with intermediaries. It also becomes essential for a retailer to conduct physical inspections of the stock, as computerized systems always need accuracy checks. In retail, the inventory management system works broadly on the lines of delegation; it becomes very crucial for the retailer to maintain strategic control to reduce the loss of inventory through theft and wastage.

The maintenance of inventory level has a considerable impact on customer service for a retailer. Every retailer will always try to follow the minimum safety stock policy to ensure a good service level.

Retailers use enterprise resource planning (ERP) systems to improve inventory management. The ERP systems help in improving the order processing system, and thus help in reducing inventory requirements and increasing the speed of invoicing, thereby improving the performance levels.

RETAIL LOGISTICS MANAGEMENT

Logistics management could be described as an extension of transportation and associated areas, to attain an efficient and effective distribution system.[21] Over the years, we have witnessed a gradual transformation from physical distribution and material management to logistics management. An excellent logistics system not only reduces costs and enhances service quality, but also provides the retailer a competitive edge in the long run. The widespread use of information technology and systems has helped retailers to provide better service to consumers, by offering them quality products and meeting their volatile demands. The importance of retail logistics can be represented in terms of the generic value chain by Michael Porter, as shown in the Fig. 8.3. Accordingly, every firm has a collection of primary activities and support activities. Primary activities of a firm have two important components:

Inbound Logistics   This is related to the movement of merchandise into the store or distribution centre/warehouse of the retailer.

Outbound Logistics   This is related to the deliveries made to the customers, especially prominent in online retailing and durable retailing.

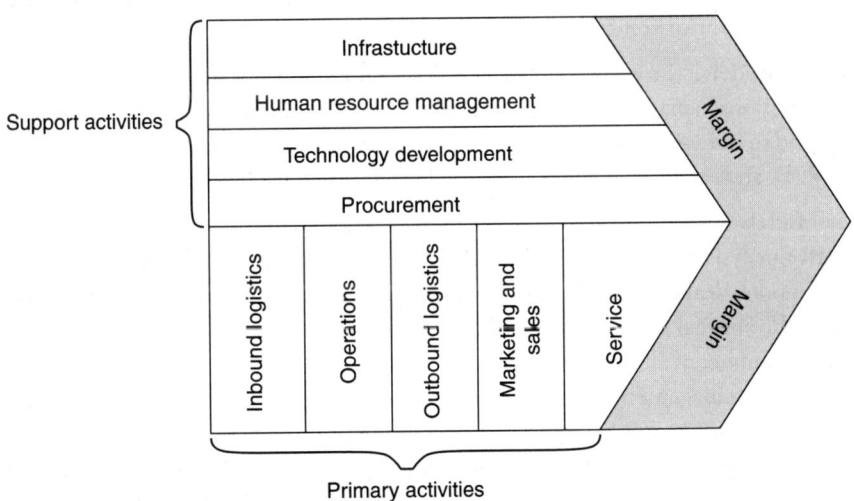

FIG. 8.3   Michael Porter's Generic Value Chain

Source: Porter, M.E. 1985, *Competitive Advantage*, The Free Press, New York.

Logistics management in retail has to be carefully undertaken because in case of discrepancies, the mistakes prove to be expensive. Therefore, managers give their best efforts to allocate the resources judiciously along the supply chain. The retailers need to quickly react to the changes in the demand and supply, and this reaction depends highly on efficient logistic operations all along the chain. Some of the critical decisions in retail logistics lie in deciding the warehouse location to meet the ever-changing consumer demand, scheduling transportation, managing inventory, materials handling, packaging, and managing information effectively.

There are also external factors attached to retail logistics, such as government intervention in terms of various legislations (i.e., excise duties, octroi tax, Motor Vehicle Act, modified value added tax, packing material regulations, etc.). Retailers have moved a step ahead and are by and large also concentrating on reverse logistics, whereby recycling and reduction in the materials used portray them as being more environmentally conscious. The coverage of retail logistics has also highly broadened, since present-day retailers have gone global and the product/information flow in logistics have turned out to be international.

Owing to these challenges, it becomes very important for a retailer to conduct quantitative analysis for critical decision-making in relation to logistics management.[22] Some of the basic models used in this context are as follows:

Forecasting Models Here, we take past data into consideration and attempt to predict the demand based on that data. There are several forecasting models; regression models and time series models being the most frequently used ones. Regression models are used to find the nature of relationship between the dependent and the independent variables. Time series models are used to predict the trend, seasonality, and cyclicity. Forecasting models do have their own limitations in terms of the degree of error, but the acceptable degree of error would depend on the retailer's risk-taking appetite.

Mathematical Programming Models Linear programming, integer programming, and non-linear programming are some methods used with the objective of either cost minimization or revenue maximization. These models help in various aspects such as better planning of location, optimal resource allocation, and efficiency of the distribution network. Non-linear programming models are more difficult to compute in comparison with the other models.

Inventory Models Inventory models are based on lines of inventory control similar to those used in the operations management. They are used to solve the fundamental problems related to inventory control and to trade-off different costs associated with inventory. Several models, such as EOQ, EBQ, ABC, VED, and safety stock models, are used for deciding the inventory control levels.

Other Models There are several other models, such as routing models, scheduling models, and alternative analysis models, which allow a retailer to examine various decisions in logistics management. Routing models deal with finding the best routes for delivery. Scheduling or resource allocation models deal with the optimal allocation of resources. Alternative analysis models deal with the decision made with fewer number of alternatives chosen.

Logistics management has been influenced to a great extent by the developments in the information technology (IT) sector. The developments in IT have helped many retailers restructure the entire distribution network and control the supply chain costs, to gain competitive advantage. The World Wide Web, electronic commerce, electronic data interchange, bar code scanners, etc. have all changed the way businesses are managed. Data management through the use of IT has aided decision-makers in manipulating data to achieve high performance levels. A variety of integrated system frameworks such as EDI (electronic data interchange), MRP (material requirement planning), and DRP (distribution resource planning) are used at different levels of logistics management, thereby facilitating long-term efficiency.

Logistics cost is a very important issue for a retailer because it has considerable influence on profitability.[23] In retail, inaccurate logistics costs lead to decisions that adversely affect the profitability of the firm. The reduction of retail logistics costs does not mean individually decreasing the transportation, warehouse, or inventory cost, but minimizing the cost in totality to achieve greater proficiency. One of the methods adopted to deal with the problem of insufficient cost data is activity-based costing. Cooper and Kaplan have recommended activity-based systems to examine the demands that are made by particular products or consumers on indirect resources.[24]

To arrive at the accurate logistics cost, it is important to consider the total cost and measure the value based on profit contribution. Firms in the first stage of the value creation process find out innovative ways to add value to customers. In the second stage, they make the customer realize the benefits received by them. In the final stage, firms connect the value created for the customers to the value for the shareholder value.[25]

Once the retailer gathers accurate information about the logistics cost, the next task is to control and monitor logistics performance. Logistics performance is monitored through standard cost, budgetary practices, productivity ratios, and statistical methods, to raise the product and service quality. With the help of IT, logistics performance measurement has become more simplified, as a retailer can track an order and its related costs right from its origin to its destination.

After the onset of e-commerce, businesses have started working more or less in a paperless environment, which has not only helped them save resources but also contributed towards gaining a competitive edge by using advanced technology. Technology has helped retailers improve the quality of decision-making five fold. It has also helped them deal with the logistics challenges more efficiently and generate more cost savings. Information is a vital component for planning and controlling the retail logistics system.

The logistics plan must be embedded in the marketing plan so that the overall corporate plan can be executed smoothly. A strategic logistics plan would probably include areas such as marketing, manufacturing, purchasing, accounting inputs, and logistics inputs. Logistics inputs mainly comprise the broad objectives and logistics operational plans. It further includes logistics forecasts, financial statements, and most importantly the description of the logistics strategy, which specify the impact on corporate profits and other business functions. The most important criterion in a strategic logistics plan would be to balance the cost and service effectiveness. Logistics audit is done by retailers because they want to satisfy customers at the lowest cost. To achieve this, regular checks on logistics operations are conducted to bring out any loopholes in the system.

EDI IN SUPPLY CHAIN MANAGEMENT

The usage of EDI in the area of SCM has helped not only to maintain efficient inventory levels, but also to effectively deal with stocks-outs and last minute delays. The National Institute of Standards and Technology, in a 1996 publication,[26] defines electronic data interchange (EDI) as 'the computer-to-computer interchange of strictly formatted messages that represent documents other than monetary instruments. Electronic data interchange implies a sequence of messages between two parties, either of whom may serve as originator or recipient. The formatted data representing the documents may be transmitted from the originator to the recipient via telecommunications or physically transported on electronic storage media.'

Electronic data interchange can be defined as a process where one computer communicates with another, or a process where companies use a computer to exchange business information. Electronic data interchange, in other words, replaces the verbal and written interaction carried out through emails and messages. It has become very popular, and this has lead to business houses adopting it very quickly because of the cost benefits and time savings attached.

Certain EDI standards must be followed for data interchange. These include common communication standards, common interpretations, and common formats as also computer compatibility. Retail industry associations tend to develop their own EDI standards for ease of functioning. Value added networks (VANs) are most widely used in EDI.[27] Here, all the EDI details are routed to a third party vendor, which again routes it to the suppliers. There are four major sets of EDI standards.[28]

1. The UN-recommended UN/EDIFACT is the only international standard and is predominant outside of North America.
2. The US standard ANSI ASC X12 (X12) is predominant in North America.
3. The TRADACOMS standard developed by the ANA (Article Numbering Association) is predominant in the UK retail industry.
4. The ODETTE standard is used within the European automotive industry.

Electronic data interchange saves money for the retailer by reducing continuous human interaction and promoting paperless transactions. It also helps in storing and manipulating data, thereby reducing another set of expenses. The speed with which the trading partners complete the transactions increases manifold. It also helps in reducing inventory due to planned accuracy and information availability. Electronic data interchange, combined with artificial intelligence, enhances the overall supply chain management.

For good performance of EDI, retailers need to ensure stability and uniformity of the EDI systems used by their trading partners. On both the ends, the implementation of EDI needs to be uniform. Security in the information age is a very crucial area that needs to be dealt with cautiously. There are various ways to increase the security level while using EDI, starting with the use of passwords for user identification. Connection to the Internet should also be secured with reliable systems for data integration and safety.

Implementing an EDI system requires good planning and controlled execution. It may involve the following steps:[29]

Developing the Organizational Structure   To implement an EDI system, the first step would be to develop an organizational structure where there is a dedicated person or team handling the process and the interaction with outsiders.

Deciding Where to Implement EDI First   Once a person or team is appointed, the next step would be to strategically review the business operations and then to find out which area would benefit most from implementing the EDI.

Developing an EDI Solution   Based on the area for implementation, retailers would identify an EDI network and software provider, either internally or hire an expert in these areas for a solution fit for their use.

Integration with Other Systems   The integration of EDI with other back-end systems would help cost savings and efficiency in the overall operation of the business.

Analysis of Internal Business Processes   Mapping of all the business documents and systems would ensure smooth flow of information across the EDI network.

Trial with the EDI System   Once the EDI system has been implemented, it is important to run a trial process to remove any deficiencies.

Finalization of EDI System   Once the trial has been declared successful and all deficiencies have been removed, the last stage would be to integrate the trading partners with the new EDI system.

Retailers communicate with the supply chain as part of their daily routine activity. The overall development of SCM would include the members of the supply chain to effectively coordinate the production and logistics activities. It requires integration of the company's internal activities, with suppliers' production, transportation, and inventory activities. Information technology can provide supply chain coordination efficiency on both the ends. The usage of EDI helps supply chain members maximize their efforts towards the accomplishment of common goals.

SUMMARY

Supply chain management is the process of ensuring that the store has the desired merchandise whenever its customers want it. It consists of sub systems that deal with ECR, buying, and management of the supply chain. It is a critical part of the retail operations. Many retailers have been able to build their competitive advantage by managing their supply chain efficiently. Supply chain management is especially applicable to retailers who want to offer their merchandise at unmatched prices. Walmart has made this a hallmark of its own. Similarly, fashion retailers also need to pay much attention to their supply chain as their products have a short life and the demand needs to be known much before the season. They cannot afford to miss either the season or the fashion trends. For products that are perishable, such as fruits, flowers, and vegetables, the supply chain needs to be very efficient to prevent the loss of quality.

The SCM framework includes the network structure, business processes, and their management. A retailer would have to decide about each of these aspects based on the requirements of its customers. This would help in achieving the highest level of customer response. Supply chain management is not just internal to the company, nor is it outside the retailer's area of influence. The core of SCM is the assessment of the demand of the customers not just in terms of volumes but also in terms of the type of merchandise and stock-keeping units (SKUs). It ensures profitability to the retailer by managing higher stock turn and ensuring freshness of merchandise. The process is aimed at ensuring that markdowns are reduced and the pipeline functions smoothly with no bottlenecks and piling. At the core of this is the extent of sharing of information across the value chain. This has led to the integration of the supply chain through the use of information technology and other tools such as bar coding and radio frequency indicator devices (RFID).

A good supply chain management, therefore, would ensure that the merchandise is fresh, is of good quality, and is available in the right quantity. Today, when retailers source their merchandise from all over the world, this activity becomes very critical to their success.

NOTES

1. Lambert, Doughlas M., Martha C. Cooper, and Janus D. Pagh 1998, 'Supply Chain Management: Implementation Issues and Research Opportunities', *The International Journal of Logistics Management*, No. 2, p. 1.

2. http://en.wikipedia.org/wiki/supply_chain, accessed on 30 May 2011.

3. Lambert, Doughlas M. and James R. Stock, *Strategic Logistics Management*, 4th edn, McGraw-Hill International Edn, Marketing/Advertising Series, p. 54.

4. Logistics 1999—2nd International Exhibition and Conference on Logistics Management, Confederation of Indian Industry.

5. Lambert, Doughlas M., Martha C. Cooper, James D. Pagh 1998, 'Supply Chain Management: Implementation Issues and Research Opportunities', *The International Journal of Logistics Management* 9, No. 2.

6. http://cscmp.org/aboutcscmp/definitions.asp, accessed on 10 December 2010.

7. Logistics 1999—2nd International Exhibition and Conference on Logistics Management, Confederation of Indian Industry.

8. Logistics 1999—2nd International Exhibition and Conference on Logistics Management, Confederation of Indian Industry.

9. Logistics 1999—2ⁿᵈ International Exhibition and Conference on Logistics Management, Confederation of Indian Industry.

10. Logistics 1999—2ⁿᵈ International Exhibition and Conference on Logistics Management, Confederation of Indian Industry.

11. Lambert, Doughlas M. and James R. Stock, *Strategic Logistics Management*, 4ᵗʰ edn, McGraw-Hill International Edn, Marketing/Advertising Series, p. 59.

12. Bucklin, L.P. 1966, *A Theory of Distribution Channel Structure*, IBER Special Publications, Berkeley, California; and Bucklin, L.P. 1972, *Competition and Evolution in the Distributive Trades*, Prentice-Hall, Englewood Cliffs, New Jersey.

13. Bucklin, Louis P. 1965, 'Postponement, Speculation and the Structure of Distribution Channels', *Journal of Marketing Research*, Vol. 2, No. 1, 16 February, pp. 26–31.

14. Lambert, Doughlas M. and James R. Stock 2001, *Strategic Logistics Management*, 4ᵗʰ edn, McGraw-Hill International Edn, Marketing/Advertising Series, p. 63.

15. Lambert, D.M., M.C. Cooper, and J.D. Pagh 1998, 'Supply Chain Management: Implementation Issues and Research Opportunities', pp. 7–9.

16. Fernie John and Sparks Leigh, *Logistics and Retail Management: Insights into Current Practice and Trends from Leading Experts*, CRC Press, Kogan Page, Washington D.C.

17. Gupta, Shivani (IB) MBA 2002–04, 'Growth of Private Labels: The Indian Scenario'.

18. 'Retail: The Power of Private Label', an ACNielsen Survey, *Business Today*, 26 October 2003, pp. 105–10.

19. 'Retail: The Power of Private Label', an ACNielsen Survey, *Business Today*, 26 October 2003, pp. 105–10.

20. Cooper, M. Bixby, Doughlas M. Lambert, Donald A. Taylor, and Donald J. Bowersox 1979, *Management in Marketing Channels*, McGraw-Hill, pp. 201–9.

21. Raghuram, G. and Rangaraj N. 2000, *Logistics and Supply Chain Management*, Macmillan India Limited.

22. Raghuram, G. and Rangaraj N. 2000, *Logistics and Supply Chain Management*, Macmillan India Limited.

23. Stock, James R. and Douglas M. Lambert 2001, *Strategic Logistics Management*, McGraw-Hill.

24. Cooper and Kaplan 1988, 'Measure Costs Right: Make the Right Decision', *Harvard Business Review*, pp. 96–103.

25. Christopher, Martin and Lynette Ryals 1999, 'Supply Chain Strategy: Its Impact on Shareholder Value', *The International Journal of Logistics Management* 1, No. 1.

26. Kantor, Michael and James H. Burrows 1996, 'Electronic Data Interchange (EDI)', *National Institute of Standards and Technology*.

27. Stock, James R. and Douglas M. Lambert 2001, *Strategic Logistics Management*, McGraw-Hill.

28. http://en.wikipedia.org/wiki/Electronic_Data_Interchange, accessed on 11 December 2010.

29. http://www.edibasics.co.uk/implementing-edi/, accessed on 11 December 2010.

CONCEPT REVIEW QUESTIONS

1. Define supply chain management and describe its role in increasing a retailer's competitiveness.
2. What are the drivers that lead to the adoption of good SCM practices?
3. Describe the three interrelated aspects of SCM. Elaborate on the management component.
4. How does SCM help in achieving efficient customer response?

CRITICAL THINKING QUESTION

What is the difference between a warehouse and a warehouse retailer in terms of SCM?

PROJECTS

1. Analyse the supply chain of a *kirana* store and a hypermarket.
2. Try to understand the priorities of a retailer of fast moving consumer goods (FMCGs), fashion products, and base apparel.

CASE STUDY 8.1

FoodWorld-B[1]: Supply Chain Strategy Introduction

'Given where we are, the key to our success lies in effective supply chain management,' was the sentiment echoed by Mr Shiv Murti, the portly, affable Vice President (Merchandising) of FoodWorld. Having established itself as a long-term, large, and 'here-to-stay' player in the organized food retailing industry, the primary supply chain management concern for FoodWorld was how to negotiate the best terms for the supply of products and source them from as upstream as possible in the supply chain.

FoodWorld operated with over 6,000 stock-keeping units (SKUs), of which 80 per cent were from the organized sector. The remaining, which were from the unorganized sector, consisted of two supply channels. One was the *perishables*, which needed to be sourced fresh, with a focus on quality and direct delivery to stores. The other was the *non-perishables*, which were repacked and sold under the FoodWorld brand. The challenge in the organized sector SKUs (which were essentially branded non-perishables) was to be able to deal with the principal directly and obtain as much of a price advantage as possible. The challenge among the unorganized sector SKUs (which were growing in number and volume as per customer expectations, and also had the potential of high margins) was to identify the right sources and have good quality management processes.

In a functional sense, the key issues to be dealt with were (a) what to stock, (b) whom and where to source from, (c) how to reduce total delivery time from vendor to store, and (d) how to reduce the cost of procurement.

Company Background

FoodWorld was a division of Spencer's, the retailing company under RPG Enterprises (RPG). RPG was among the top five business houses in India, with sales of about ₹65 billion in 1996–97. Its asset base was over ₹75 billion in 1997. RPG's business interests spanned a variety of sectors including power, tyres, agribusiness,

telecommunications, retailing, and financial services. RPG got into retailing with the acquisition of Spencer's & Co. in 1989. It had a large number of partnerships with international companies, including Fortune 500 companies. For FoodWorld, there was a partnership with Dairy Farm International, a large retail house in Hong Kong.

Spencer's & Co. had been founded in Madras (now renamed as Chennai) in 1865 as a retailer offering imported items to the large British expatriate and military population. By 1897, it had grown to be the largest store in India with 65,000 sq. ft of shopping space. At its peak in 1940, it had 50 stores in most of the major cities in India. It had also integrated backward, producing some of the products that it sold, such as soft drinks, cosmetics, etc. After India gained independence from the British in 1947, sales dropped significantly, though Spencer's somehow survived and continued to offer food, clothing, cosmetics, and other high-priced speciality items. The customers were primarily the expatriate community.

Due to its deteriorating sales, Spencer's had been open for acquisition. In the early 70s, ownership changed once. In 1989, RPG purchased Spencer's, and established it as a separate division under the leadership of P.K. Mohapatra, a senior RPG executive. The primary motive for this acquisition was the undervalued real estate.

At that time, Spencer's had nine stores and was the largest retail chain in India. Though one of the options was to simply focus on the development of the real estate offered by Spencer's, the RPG executives looking after Spencer's felt that the retail business potential should not be given up easily. It was decided to experiment with one store to test its potential. If the experiment failed, RPG would close the retail operations. The departmental store in Bangalore was modernized in 1991, retaining its product profile of hardware, food, kitchen appliances,

---

1. Case prepared by Professors G. Raghuram, Bibek Banerjee, and Abraham Koshy, Indian Institute of Management Ahmedabad. Research assistance of Parvathy Raman and Anita Basalingappa is acknowledged.

The authors wish to thank Mr P.K. Mohapatra, Mr Shiv Murti, Mr Ganesh Chella, and other top managers of FoodWorld for their generous cooperation and financial support in preparing this case.

Cases of the Indian Institute of Management Ahmedabad are prepared as a basis for class discussion. Cases are not designed to present illustrations of either correct or incorrect handling of administrative problems.

Copyright ©1999 by the Indian Institute of Management, Ahmedabad.

and clothing. When the store opened, sales increased to four times the previous levels and returned a healthy contribution. Shiv Murti, who had joined Spencer's to head merchandising, had played a significant role in this turnaround. This settled the issue in favour of continuing with the more important Spencer's activities including retailing, the airline general sales agency (GSA) and pharmaceuticals. From ₹250 million at the time of acquisition, the turnover had risen to ₹1 billion by 1994 through a careful process of nurturing the three activities while dropping over 20 others. The airline GSA accounted for over 80 per cent of the turnover.

During 1994–95, the RPG group went through a reassessment of its portfolio of activities with the help of a large international consulting firm. It was recommended that retail business development should be one of the key thrusts (along with telecommunication and financial services), since it offered a lot of growth potential. There was an emerging middle class that had barely had a glimpse of modern retailing. Retailing had traditionally been in the 'non formal' small sector, and had remained unchanged for over a century.

The issue then was whether to build on Spencer's image or to consider a fresh start. Leveraging on Spencer's for retail business development had its risks. While the 'Spencer's' brand name was widely associated with quality, it also had a connotation of high prices. The popularity of this was reflected in the expression, 'paying the Spencer's price', which was commonly used to suggest the payment of high prices. Further, the existing Spencer's employees were both poorly qualified and underpaid. It was decided that a new retailing format, with no link to Spencer's, would be developed.

Based on a study of retail chains world over, it was felt that the retail format should be 'mass-based' rather than 'niche-based,' since it would offer greater growth potential. In order to develop a mass base, it was decided that the retailing format should focus on the daily livelihood of people. Food, clothing, and health care products were considered. Clothing was dropped, since RPG had no background in either the fashion industry or textile manufacturing, considered essential for success in this area. Food was selected as the first area of entry, to be followed by health care products.

FoodWorld

After a study of customer preferences in early 1996, the supermarket format was selected to offer (a) value based on price and quality, (b) choice through self-service from a spread of merchandise, and (c) a better shopping environment. In terms of location, three choices were considered (in decreasing order of property prices): (a) commercial high street, (b) residential high street, and (c) out of town area. Since the supermarket was to be positioned as a one-stop shop for all food-related items during a shopping outing, the commercial high street was not that important. Further, with the mass-based positioning, the middle income group was considered the primary target. This group would not have access to personal transport or would not fancy spending time on transportation for supermarket shopping. Hence, the out of town location concept was dropped and the residential high street was decided on.

Various 'ideal' sizes were considered, keeping in mind likely costs and availability of properties, ranging from 1,200 sq. ft to 6,000 sq. ft. Given the self-service format and the merchandising choice, a minimum size of 3,000 sq. ft was considered essential, while 4,500 sq. ft would be the preferred size. All stores would be air-conditioned, offering extensive assortments of groceries, personal care, cleaning products, kitchenware, and tableware. There would also be a 'fast food' and 'bakery' section. The attempt would be to provide a pleasant ambience and offer outstanding customer service. With this concept in view, a name had to be selected for the supermarket retail chain. After brainstorming for a suitable name, and some market research, the name 'FoodWorld' was selected, along with a logo and the bright red and orange signature colour.

The first FoodWorld store was launched on 9 May 1996 in Chennai. This was followed by a store in Bangalore (20 August 1996), and then by two more in Chennai (1 September 1996). In 1996, the M.G. Road, Bangalore and a part of the Mount Road, Chennai Spencer's stores were converted as FoodWorld stores. New stores were opened at regular intervals, until it reached the current tally of nineteen (6 in Chennai, 8 in Bangalore and 5 in Hyderabad). Table CS8.1 provides a description of these stores. In the FoodWorld chain, an investment of ₹650 million had been made so far. The turnover was ₹210 million during 1996–97, and ₹420 million during 1997–98, with a projection of ₹870 million in 1998–99 (of which ₹520 million had been achieved during April–November, 1998). Table CS8.2 shows the performance trends for 1996–97, 1997–98, April–November, 1998, 1998–99, and 1999–2000 classified and aggregated according to the stores opened during the three periods. The gross margin on this turnover was 16.7 per cent in 1996–97, 18.4 per cent in 1997–98, and projected at 20.5 per cent in 1998–99. (The actuals during April–November 1998

TABLE CS8.1   Store-wise Description

Store Location	Date of Opening	Total Area (Sq. Ft)	Trading Area (Sq. Ft)	Store Type Based on Trading Area	Store Type Based on Sale	Oct. '98 Sale (₹ '000)	Oct. '98 Gross Margin (%)	Operating Expenses (₹ '000)	PBIT (₹ '000)	PBT (₹ '000)
Chennai										
Store 1	Dec. 96	14,065	7,257	A	A	9,156	22.41	694	1,358.09	1,005
Store 2	09.05.96	3,000	2,404	C	B	4,415	19.43	351	506.66	428
Store 3	01.09.96	4,494	3,094	B	B	4,619	20.12	392	537.34	398
Store 4	01.09.96	4,231	3,177	B	B	5,431	20.39	399	708.33	538
Store 5	09.05.98	5,000	3,305	B	B	4,151	19.89	485	340.80	137
Store 6	23.10.98	3,500	2,700	C	B	1,269	19.89	212	40.45	−60
Bangalore										
Store 1	Dec. 96	9,500	6,492	A	A	11,487	19.04	754	1,433.13	1,265
Store 2	20.8.96	5,720	3,976	B	B	4,072	16.61	494	182.36	127
Store 3	5.6.98	2,565	2,472	C	B	4,910	17.18	420	423.54	285
Store 4*	29.12.96	4,362	3,729	B	B	4,242	17.40	480	258.11	61
Store 5	5.4.97	3,650	3,421	B	C	2,180	15.75	324	19.35	−44
Store 6	4.5.97	2,862	2,437	C	B	2,910	16.84	342	148.04	95
Store 7	30.7.98	3,024	2,494	C	B	4,825	16.81	388	423.08	65
Store 8*	25.4.98	3,000	2,656	C	C	2,569	16.40	324	97.32	−4
Hyderabad										
Store 1	26.9.97	4,500	2,971	C	B	3,117	16.78	349	174.033	150
Store 2	13.12.97	4,000	3,278	B	A	4,690	16.20	426	333.78	301
Store 3*	17.4.98	3,000	2,168	C	C	2,520	16.71	264	157.09	137
Store 4	1.10.98	4,084	3,500	B	B	3,445	16.63	426	146.90	120
Store 5*	31.10.98	3,500	3,000	B	B	179	14.22	143	−117.55	−190

* Some of the data are estimated.
Source: Company Records, December 1998.

was 18.4 per cent.) Each one of the stores had broken even within a few months of starting and had made a contribution towards regional and corporate expenses. The store operating expenses as a percentage of sales reduced over time, as seen in Table CS8.2. This figure was higher for later stores during the first year of operations, reflecting higher startup costs. The M.G. Road store in Bangalore had a gross margin and store operating expenses (as a percentage of sales) of 13 per cent and 7.2 per cent respectively in 1996–97, 18.7 per cent and 7.4 per cent respectively in 1997–98, and 18.3 per cent and 6.8 per cent respectively for April–November 1998. Within the store operating expenses, salaries and wages accounted for about 2.5 per cent of sales, rent about 2.2 per cent, shrinkage about 1.6 per cent, and

depreciation about 0.7 per cent. In the future, salaries and wages, rent, and depreciation were expected to increase as newer and more expensive properties were to be acquired. FoodWorld as a business enterprise was still in the red. This was typical of large retail startup businesses where a critical number of outlets were necessary before the bottom-line was positive.

Apart from increasing turnover in each of the stores by leveraging a large store network, it would be imperative to increase margins to ensure sustainability and growth of the enterprise. This would require appropriate sourcing and negotiating with suppliers for better margins, and achieving efficiencies in the regional distribution system that FoodWorld had in place. In

TABLE CS8.2   Performance Trends

Year	1996–97 Budget (₹'000)	% of Sales	1996–97 Actuals (₹'000)	% of Sales	1997–98 Budget (₹'000)	% of Sales	1997–98 Actuals (₹'000)	% of Sales	YTD Apr. '98–Nov. '98 Budget (₹'000)	% of Sales	YTD Actuals (₹'000)	% of Sales	1998–99 Projected (₹'000)	% of Sales	1999–2000 Projected (₹'000)	% of Sales
New Stores (NS)																
NS 96–97	8		7													
NS 97–98					13		4									
NS 98–98									10		8					
Total No. of Stores	8		7		20		11		21		19					
Sales																
NS 96–97	2,577		2,088		3,366		3,654		2,830		3,148					
NS 97–98					1,118		579		764		898					
NS 98–98									1,241		1,106					
Subtotal	2,577		2,088		4,484		4,233		4,835		5,152		8,665	100	12,957	100
Gross Margin																
NS 96–97	382	14.8	349	16.7	633	18.8	671	18.4	530	18.7	587	18.6				
NS 97–98					152	13.6	107	18.5	143	18.7	147	16.4				
NS 98–98									234	18.9	212	19.2				
Subtotal	382	14.8	349	16.7	785	17.5	778	18.4	907	18.8	946	18.4	1,774	20.5	2,786	21.5
Store Operation																
NS 96–97	346	13.4	266	12.7	480	14.3	444	12.2	286	10.1	286	9.1				
NS 97–98					171	15.3	126	21.8	115	15.1	112	12.5				
NS 98–99									284	22.9	165	14.9				
Subtotal	346	13.4	266	12.7	651	14.5	570	13.5	685	14.2	563	10.9	1,408	16.2	2,119	16.4

(Contd)

Table CS 8.2 (Contd)

Year	1996–97				1997–98				YTD Apr. '98–Nov. '98				1998–99		1999–2000	
	Budget (₹ '000)	% of Sales	Actuals (₹ '000)	% of Sales	Budget (₹ '000)	% of Sales	Actuals (₹ '000)	% of Sales	Budget (₹ '000)	% of Sales	Actuals (₹ '000)	% of Sales	Projected (₹ '000)	% of Sales	Projected (₹ '000)	% of Sales
Warehouse/ Regional Office																
NS 96–97	136	5.3	134	6.4	219	6.5	268	7.3	143	5.1	167	5.3				
NS 97–98					73	6.5	42	7.3	39	5.1	48	5.3				
NS 98–98									63	5.1	58	5.2				
Subtotal	136	5.3	134	6.4	292	6.5	310	7.3	245	5.1	273	5.3	437	24.6	494	17.7
Corporate Opex																
NS 96–97	112	4.3	96	4.6	57	1.7	76	2.1	32	1.1	40	1.3				
NS 97–98					19	1.7	12	2.1	9	1.2	11	1.2				
NS 98–98									13	1.0	14	1.3				
Subtotal	112	4.3	96	4.6	76	1.7	88	2.1	54	1.1	65	1.3	95	1.1	104	0.8
EBIT																
NS 96–97	–212	–8.2	–147	–7.0	–123	–3.7	–117	–3.2	69	2.4	94	3.0				
NS 97–98					–111	–9.9	–73	–12.6	–20	–2.6	–24	–2.7				
NS 98–98									–126	–10.2	–25	–2.3				
Subtotal	–212	–8.2	–147	–7.0	–234	–5.2	–190	–4.5	–77	–1.6	45	0.9	–166	–1.9	69	0.5

Notes:
1. Figures exclude notional rent on owned properties.
2. POS Maintenance included under Maintenance.
3. Warehouse & Corporate Opex apportioned to existing and new stores on the basis of sales.
Source: Company Records, December 1998.

this context, the merchandising function (what specific products/brands to offer, who to source from) and the distribution strategy (how to organize the logistics of supply to the stores) gained significance as critical success factors.

Merchandising Function

The merchandising function was carried at both the centralized (in the corporate office of FoodWorld at Chennai) and the regional level. Figure CS8.1 presents the organization structure of FoodWorld, showing the merchandising function along with other key 'line' and support functions, including the regional setup. Figure CS8.2 shows the organization structure of the regional setup. The position of FoodWorld along with other profit centres, and corporate level staff functions under Mr P.K. Mohapatra is given in Fig. CS8.3. Each of the six units (consisting of profit centres and/or corporate level staff functions) was headed either by a president or a general manager.

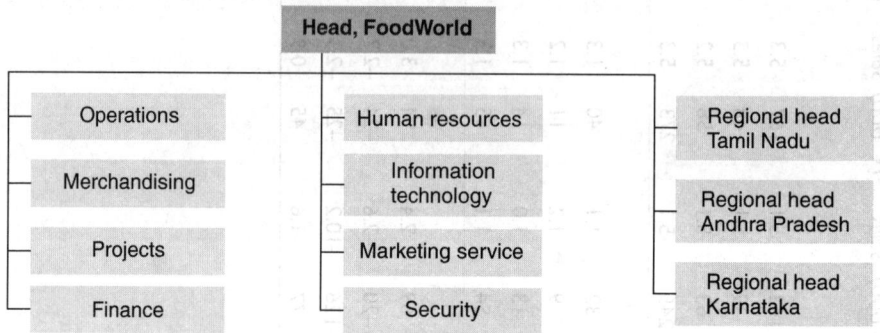

FIG. CS8.1   FoodWorld Organization Structure

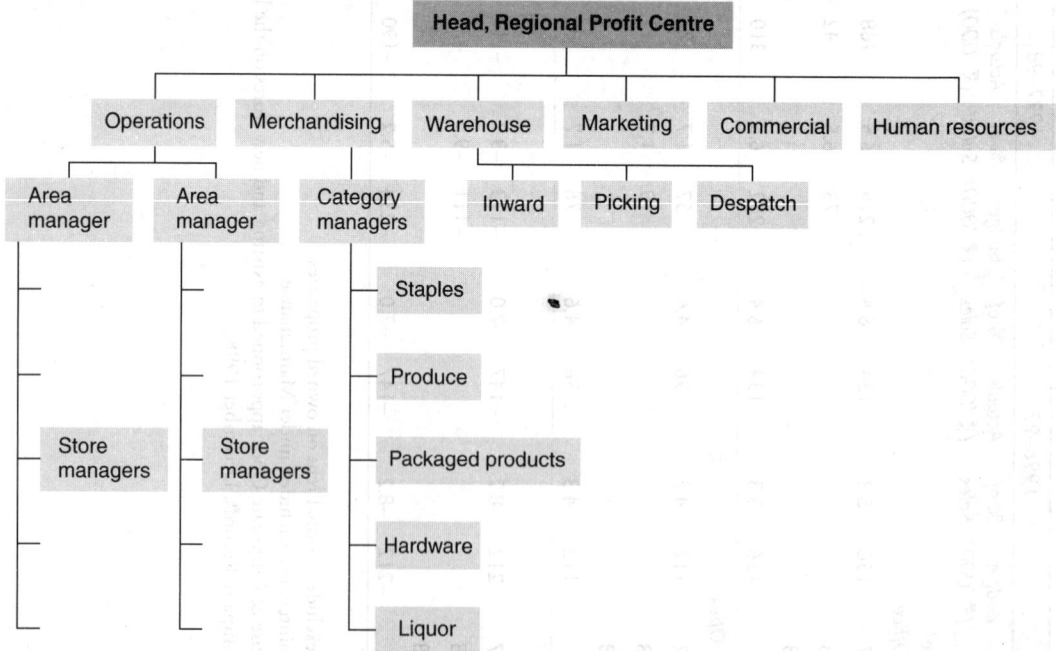

FIG. CS8.2   Regional Organization Structure

Source: Company Records, December 1998

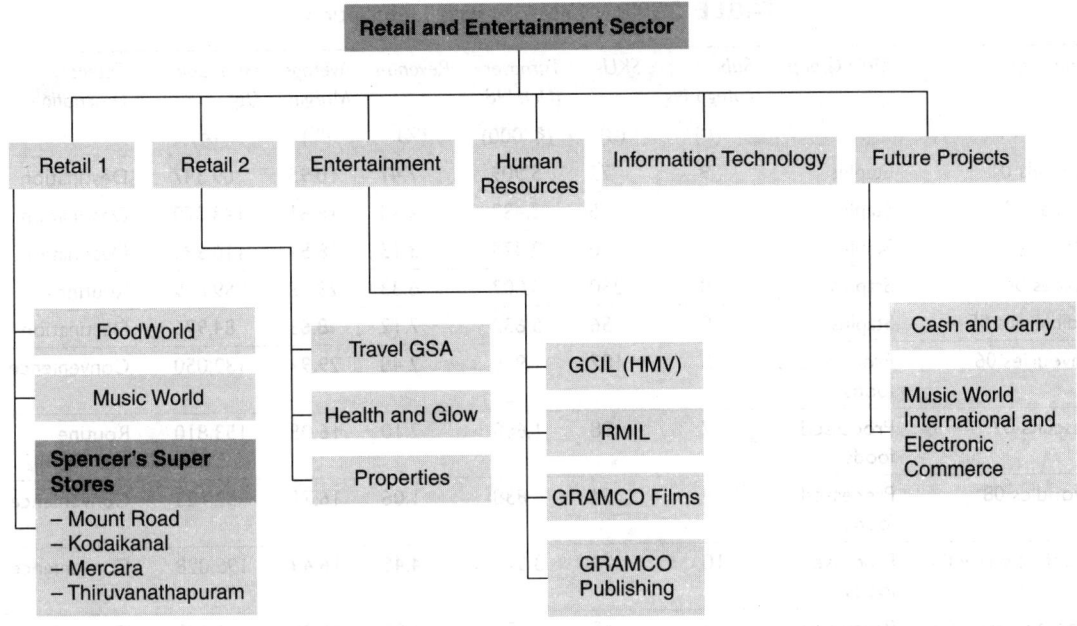

FIG. CS8.3   Retail and Entertainment Organization Structure

Source: Company Records, December 1998

The merchandising strategy began with the customer preference study mentioned earlier. This study highlighted the following customer expectations in terms of considering the store for food purchase:

- Product range
- Variety for choice in a given product
- Freshness
- Availability
- Reasonable price (not more than neighbourhood stores)

In response to this, FoodWorld executives decided that the core range of products would consist of everything that a household shopped for on a daily/weekly/monthly basis. Insights into this were obtained on the basis of customers' shopping lists and budgets. A merchandising offer consisting of seven major groups, namely staples, processed foods, beverages, non-food items, health and beauty items, perishables, and hardware and home appliances, was finalized. These were divided into 49 categories, with a category descriptor as destination, strategic (routine), convenience, and speciality (occasional), depending upon essentiality in the customers' purchase basket and frequency of purchase. Table CS8.3 provides a category-wise description as of December 1998. These categories were further divided into about 270 sub-categories, to enable sourcing, keeping in mind the range of products available from suppliers. The total number of SKUs in the original list was more than 6,000 (4,500 in six categories and 1,700 in hardware and home appliances, also called general merchandise. However, most stores carried about 150 basic items in general merchandise, unless there was an explicit section for this).

The strategies for various categories depending on their attributes, regarding the width (brand choice), depth (number of variants), price, and tactical usage (for drawing customers to the store) are listed in Table CS8.4. In any category/sub-category, a minimum of *two* brands would be on offer.

TABLE CS8.3　Category-wise Description

Category	Main Group	Sub-categories	SKUs	Turnover (Oct. '98)	Revenue	Average Margin	Hash Sale Qty	Category Description
		(#)	(#)	(₹ '000)	(%)	(%)	(#)	
Cereals 01	Staples	9	72	5,909	7.47	10.95	69,347	Destination
Pulses 02	Staples	4	75	3,432	4.34	16.61	143,070	Destination
Flours 03	Staples	5	70	2,475	3.13	18.54	116,394	Destination
Spices 04	Staples	8	250	5,007	6.33	23.18	259,619	Routine
Edible oils 05	Staples	9	56	5,632	7.12	8.63	84,976	Destination
Savouries 06	Processed foods	5	187	1,959	2.48	29.91	132,050	Convenience
Biscuits 07	Processed foods	7	98	1,660	2.10	16.05	153,810	Routine
Noodles 08	Processed foods	4	64	838	1.06	16.71	52,123	Convenience
Confectionary 09	Processed foods	10	74	3,519	4.45	16.49	195,028	Convenience
Can non-veg. 10	Processed foods	2	15	51	0.06	18.25	1,182	Convenience
Can fruit 11	Processed foods	3	15	25	0.03	21.94	475	Convenience
Can veg. 12	Processed foods	3	3	78	0.10	16.72	2,071	Convenience
Desserts 13	Processed foods	6	90	582	0.74	15.75	23,242	Convenience
Jams 14	Processed foods	4	58	580	0.73	15.27	15,938	Routine
Tinned milk 15	Processed foods	2	20	279	0.35	9.12	5,495	Convenience
Sauces 16	Processed foods	7	29	619	0.78	16.34	20,678	Routine
Pickles 17	Processed foods	4	106	538	0.68	17.29	14,696	Routine
Ready to fry 18	Processed foods	3	99	569	0.72	24.50	39,357	Routine
Soups 19	Processed foods	2	26	462	0.58	14.37	20,272	Convenience
Breakfast foods 20	Processed foods	4	37	841	1.06	12.71	18,099	Routine
Baby foods 21	Processed foods	4	33	234	0.30	9.27	2,475	Routine
Drinks 22	Beverages	9	94	2,071	2.62	22.44	83,500	Convenience
Tea/coffee 23	Beverages	4	90	2,443	3.09	9.84	50,649	Routine

(Contd)

Table CS8.3 (Contd)

Category	Main Group	Sub-categories (#)	SKUs (#)	Turnover (Oct. '98) (₹ '000)	Revenue (%)	Average Margin (%)	Hash Sale Qty (#)	Category Description
Health drinks 24	Beverages	5	37	1,432	1.81	10.25	19,568	Routine
Liquor 25	Beverages	8	98	4,482	5.67	20.05	30,899	Routine
Detergents 26	Non-food	4	70	2,425	3.07	10.09	92,479	Routine
House cleaning 27	Non-food	6	114	2,319	2.93	16.80	104,996	Routine
Paper goods 28	Non-food	5	40	463	0.59	40.32	14,995	Occasional
Household needs 29	Non-food	9	170	1,253	1.58	28.75	69,973	Routine
Cigarettes 30	Non-food	3	20	348	0.44	9.34	11,156	Convenience
Pet food 31	Non-food	1	35	62	0.08	30.00	131	Occasional
Skin care 32	Health & beauty	9	250	3,281	4.15	12.81	143,241	Routine
Hair care 33	Health & beauty	6	160	1,551	1.96	14.16	32,011	Routine
Oral care 34	Health & beauty	5	85	1,378	1.74	16.28	58,231	Routine
Sanitary goods 35	Health & beauty	4	30	615	0.78	12.52	14,398	Routine
Shaving needs 36	Health & beauty	4	85	1,299	1.64	15.45	21,386	Routine
O.T.C. 37	Health & beauty	5	70	369	0.47	22.71	14,249	Convenience
Baby needs 38	Health & beauty	3	55	546	0.69	15.84	10,202	Routine
Cosmetics 39	Health & beauty	10	94	197	0.25	19.50	2,695	Convenience
Herbals 40	Health & beauty	7	240	331	0.42	24.77	4,262	Convenience
Dairy products 41	Perishables	7	60	2,008	2.54	12.00	104,150	Destination
Frozen foods 42	Perishables	7	75	1,610	2.04	17.00	41,704	Convenience
Bakery 43 & 44	Perishables	3	65	4,497	5.69	27.78	157,159	Convenience
Vegetables 45 & 46	Perishables	2	110	4,365	5.52	17.28	407,030	Destination
Batteries 47	H/ware and home app	4	48	306	0.39	23.98	11,967	Occasional
Misc. 48	H/ware and home app.	5	210	1,770	2.24	20.21	10,116	Occasional
Hardware 49	H/ware and home app.	24	1,435	2,350	2.97	25.42	51,446	Convenience
Total		264	5,317	79,060	100.00	17.17	2.932,990	

Source: Company Records, December 1998.

TABLE CS8.4 Strategies for Various Categories

	Destination	Strategic	Convenience	Speciality
Width	High	High	High	High/Medium
Depth	High	Low	Low	Low
Price	Aggressive 'Key SKUs' Best in City	Aggressive Value Added Price Range for Margin	MRP/KVI	MRP
Tactical Usage	High	Medium	Medium	Low

Most of the store sales came from branded non-perishables. However, perishables and non-branded repack SKUs were expected to witness the highest growth, with higher than average margins. The revenue share and margin spread of the main items were as given in Table CS8.5.

TABLE CS8.5 Revenue Share and Margin Spread of Main Items

Item	Revenue (%)	Margin Spread (%)
Perishables	15	
• *Branded*		
Frozen		10–20
Dairy		4–10
• *Unbranded*		
Bakery		30
Fruits and Veg.		25
Repack	10	5–20
All others	75	15

Almost all of the 'repack' items belonged to the staples group and carried a store branding. However, the total staples group had branded products of other companies categorized under 'all others'. While the repack items constituted 10 per cent of revenue, the staples group constituted 28 per cent of revenue. The top 1,000 SKUs accounted for 70 per cent of the revenue. Within this, the growth was expected to be in repack and perishable items, which constituted about 100 SKUs.

Interior design and layout of a store was a fairly involved subject, taking into account basic ergonomics, purchase preferences, items on promotion, basic layout of the property, etc. This also involved design of appropriate display hardware such as gondolas (an open rack, typically eight feet in length and five feet in height, with five or six shelves), gondola ends (for special promotional displays), coolers and freezers, special display hardware for increased attention, channels on the gondola shelves for stickers, hardware for promotional material, and signages. It was also important to design a bay (a set of gondolas) keeping in mind factors such as the alignment of shelves. The number of checkout counters (tills), staff assignment, assignment of tills for different types of customers (large/small volume, cash/credit), and security features were also decisions of significance.

In terms of product display, the destination categories (which was an essential component of the purchase basket) would typically be in the far end of the store. This would attract customers right into the store. The strategic and convenience categories were displayed so as to provide good visibility and access, like in the eye-level shelves rather than in the top or bottom shelves. The various procedures followed for display in a store, signages, shelving, and stacking were determined and documented with a lot of 'science' behind them. These procedures were to be followed by the customer service supervisors and representatives. The daily routines of the key store staff, including the customer service supervisors and representatives, cashiers at the checkout counters (tills), goods, and receiving staff, were developed to a great level of detail and constantly reinforced through training and periodic meetings including one before every shift. The typical number of bays and SKUs, based on the type of the store, was as given in Table CS8.6.

Each bay was three feet in width, with a height of five or six feet. The corresponding number of shelves per bay was either six or seven. All the shelves had a depth of 15 inches, except for the bottom one, which was of 18 inches, for increased visibility. A bay with six shelves thus had 18 running feet and could accommodate 45–70 facings of SKUs, depending on the SKU dimensions. An SKU may have one to three facings depending upon the sales volume and desired visibility. A description of SKUs in two bays is given in Table CS8.7. (The 'MBQ' and 'SUF' attributes are described later under the indenting process.)

TABLE CS8.6 Number of Bays and SKUs in Stores

Store Type	Trading Area (Sq. Ft)	No. of Stores	Example Location	Typical No. of Bays	No. of SKUs
A	6,000+	2	MG Road (Bengaluru) Mount Road (Chennai)	120+	6,000
B	3,000+	9	Himayatnagar (Hyderabad) Gandhi Nagar (Chennai)	80–95	4,500
C	2,000+	8	Jaynagar (Bengaluru) Marredpally (Hyderabad)	65–75	3,000

TABLE CS8.7 Description of SKUs in Two Bays

Bay No: 35					Section: Tea (Ht 5 feet, 6 shelves)				
No.	SKU Code	SKU Description	Company Name	Shelf	Depth	MBQ	Facings	SUF	Cost	MRP
1.	191148	Taj Mahal Tea bags 25'S	HLL	1	15"	12	2	6	63.80	69.00
2.	191146	Green Label 100 g	HLL	1		12	2	6	23.44	25.00
3.	191087	Yellow Label 100 g	HLL	1		12	2	6	15.89	17.00
4.	191154	Kotada Tea 100 g	Kotada	1		8	1	3	11.90	14.00
5.	191052	Top Star 100 g	HLL	1		12	2	6	17.46	18.25
6.	191057	Taj Mahal 100 g	HLL	2	15"	18	3	6	17.75	18.50
7.	191027	Red Label 100 g	HLL	2		18	3	6	14.20	15.00
8.	191147	Green Label Tea W.B. 250 g	HLL	2		4	1	3	94.12	110.00
9.	191086	Yellow Label Tea 250 g	HLL	2		12	2	6	64.15	68.00
10.	191059	Taj Mahal Tea 250 g	HLL	3	15"	12	3	6	45.50	76.50
11.	191026	Red Label 250 g	HLL	3		12	2	6	38.25	43.00
12.	191064	Green Label Tea 250 g	HLL	3		8	2	6	64.15	68.00
13.	191053	Top Star 250 g	HLL	3		8	2	3	39.86	76.50
14.	191144	Taj Mahal Tea Bags 100'S	HLL	4	15"	6	2	3	63.80	69.00
15.	191025	Red Label 500 g	HLL	4		8	2	3	70.00	73.00
16.	191085	Yellow Label 500 g	HLL	4		8	2	3	79.44	85.00
17.	191058	Taj Mahal Tea 500 g	HLL	5	15"	8	2	3	78.00	82.00
18.	191000	Red Label 500 Jar	HLL	5		6	2	3	83.58	88.00
19.	191020	Sargam Tea 250 g Jar	Duncan	5		6	1	3	28.98	30.00
20.	191153	Kotada Tea 250 g	Kotada	5		12	1	6	24.23	28.50
21.	191060	Top Star 500 g	HLL	5		6	2	3	73.91	76.50
22.	191145	Taj Mahal Tea bags 200'S	HLL	6	18"	4	1	3	112.73	124.00
23.	191101	Sargam Tea 250 refill	Duncan	6		6	1	3	23.93	25.00
24.	191021	Red Label 250 Jar	HLL	6		12	2	6	41.75	44.00
25.	191065	Lipton Green Label 500 g	HLL	6		12	1	6	128.30	136.00
26.	191152	Kotada Tea 500 g	Kotada	6		6	1	3	56.10	66.00
27.	191035	Sargam Tea Jar 500 g	Duncan	6		12	2	6	76.36	83.00

(Contd)

Table CS8.7 (Contd)

| Bay No: 36 | | | Section: Coffee (Ht 5 feet, 6 shelves) | | | | | | | |
No.	SKU Code	SKU Description	Company Name	Shelf	Depth	MBQ	Facings	SUF	Cost	MRP
1.	190015	Green Label Coffee 50 g	HLL	1	15"	36	3	12	7.28	7.75
2.	190012	Bru 50 g	HLL	1		36	3	12	24.30	28.00
3.	190053	Nescafe 25 g	Nestle	1		18	3	6	26.10	28.00
4.	190088	Sunrise Premium 50 g	Nestle	2	15"	36	4	12	26.90	30.00
5.	190014	Bru Sachet Strongm 50 g	HLL	2		24	2	12	24.30	26.00
6.	190060	Nescafe Select 50 g	Nestle	2		12	2	6	52.92	59.00
7.	190092	Sunrise Extra 50 g	Nestle	3	15"	36	3	12	23.35	25.00
8.	190009	Tata Kapi 50 g	Tata Tea	3		24	2	12	24.23	28.00
9.	190064	Nescafe Select 100 g	Nestle	3		24	2	12	104.30	114.00
10.	190056	Nescafe Select 100 g Jar	Nestle	3		24	2	12	105.00	115.00
11.	190091	Sunrise Premium 100 g	Nestle	4	15"	12	1	6	54.25	58.00
12.	190007	Bru 100 g	HLL	4		12	1	6	50.49	54.00
13.	190029	Coorg Pure Filter 100 g	Tata Tea	4		12	1	6	12.75	15.00
14.	190016	Green Label 100 g	HLL	4		12	1	6	14.09	15.00
15.	190034	Brooke Bond Cafe 100 g	HLL	4		12	1	6	10.33	11.00
16.	190042	Coorg Double Roast 100 g	Tata Tea	4		12	1	6	10.84	12.75
17.	190090	Sunrise Premium 100 g Jar	Nestle	4		8	1	3	51.40	55.00
18.	190084	Sunrise Premium 200 g	Nestle	5	15"	12	1	6	101.87	115.00
19.	190008	Bru 200 g	HLL	5		12	1	6	104.67	112.00
20.	190031	Coorg Pure Filter 200 g	Tata Tea	5		12	1	6	25.16	29.60
21.	190041	Coorg Double Roast 200 g	Tata Tea	5		12	1	6	21.25	25.00
22.	190010	Tata Kapi 200 g	Tata Tea	5		12	1	6	89.25	105.00
23.	190065	Food World Pure Filter Coffee 200 g	Store brand	5		12	1	6	30.00	36.00
24.	190072	Nescafe Select 200 g	Nestle	5		12	1	6	193.95	212.00
25.	190080	Nestle Sunrise Extra 200 g	Nestle	6	18"	12	1	6	84.15	90.00
26.	190020	Green Label Coffee 200 g	HLL	6		12	1	6	28.57	30.00
27.	190024	Green Label Coffee 500 g	HLL	6		9	1	3	70.48	74.00
28.	190027	Coorg Pure Filter Coffee 500 g	Tata Tea	6		9	1	3	62.05	73.00
29.	190040	Coorg Double Roast 500 g	Tata Tea	6		9	1	3	60.00	65.00
30.	190066	Food World Coffee 500 g	Store brand	6		9	1	3	75.00	90.00
31.	190043	Coorg Double Roast 500 g	Tata Tea	6		9	1	3	67.38	73.00
32.	190076	Nescafe Select 500 g	Nestle	6		9	1	3	475.75	520.00

Note: HLL—Hindustan Lever Limited (now HUL)

Source: Company Records, December 1998.

Distribution (Supply Chain) Strategy

The key elements of FoodWorld's distribution strategy, which actually addressed the supply chain management, were as follows:

Minimum Suppliers This would yield benefits due to economies of scale, both in purchasing and supply logistics, reduced overheads and control requirements, and easier vendor development.

Creation of Regional Hubs Three regional offices were set up at Chennai, Bangalore, and Hyderabad to address the state-wise requirements. This facilitated over 90 per cent central distribution. The remaining 10 per cent was supplied directly to the store (mostly perishable items like fruits and vegetables, and bakery).

Replenishment Frequency The desired servicing of stores from the warehouses was daily, while the supply frequency for any specific SKU was twice a week. The desired ordering and servicing frequency from suppliers to the warehouses was weekly. Hardware and general merchandise items were treated as exceptions, to be indented and ordered as required.

Sourcing with Minimum Intermediaries The idea was to source from as 'upstream' as possible in the supply chain. This would help reduce losses and increase margins for FoodWorld.

Indenting Process

This referred to the request for stocks made by the different stores on their servicing warehouse/direct supply. Most SKUs could be indented twice a week on nominated days for which supply would be made from the warehouse after a gap of a day, again on nominated days (Table CS8.8). The nominated days enabled synchronization of indent processing at the warehouse. Direct supply products were indented daily, directly from the suppliers. Hardware items were indented based on need, and by using the information of the ordering schedule from suppliers by the warehouse (Table CS8.9).

Each SKU in a store had two specific attributes that helped indenting, namely minimum base quantity (MBQ)

and supply unit factor (SUF). The MBQ was determined as follows:

$$MBQ = \frac{120\% \text{ of highest sales achieved per month}}{4}$$

The rationale behind this was there should be enough stocks even if there is (a) a surge in demand and (b) short/no supply from the warehouse until the next indent, thus providing for a week. The indent quantity was determined after a physical verification of store stocks on nominated indent days, as follows:

Indent quantity = (MBQ – Physical stock)
in multiples of SUF

The average stock turns per year was 12 in 1997 and expected to be higher in 1998. The quantity was in multiples of SUF to enable convenient repacking of suppliers' stocks at the warehouse. For most SKUs, the shelf space volume was less than the MBQ. This was by choice, to enable frequent replenishment and to provide a sense of fullness in the shelves. The indenting process was being automated, so that the stock levels would be obtained based on point of sale data. As a result, indent quantities would be automatically generated. Key indicators like stock-out percentage would also then get generated.

A random examination of certain records gave a 20 per cent stock-out figure. As explained by a store manager, the true stock out was only 10 per cent. The rest was accounted for by items which had been discontinued, but not yet deleted from the indent records. The indent fill (no. of SKUs) rates from the warehouse were typically 60 per cent, while the case fill (SKU quantity) rates were 85 per cent. For certain SKUs, they were even more than 100 per cent, especially if other sizes of the same brand or brands of the same item were not available. If the case fill rate was less than 75 per cent, it was considered as the indent not having been serviced. Table CS8.10 gives a sample of two successive indents from the same store for the tea/coffee category. The stock in the store, the indented quantity, and the picked quantity for supply from the warehouse are given.

TABLE CS8.8 Schedule of Indents and Despatches for a Region

Store Indent Schedule	Warehouse Despatch Schedule
Sunday	
Dessert mixes, breakfast cereals, biscuits, jams, hot drinks, branded flours, household needs, hair care, liquor, pickles, Amul products, rice flour, and daily indent	Baby food, tin milk, tea/coffee, confectionery, household cleaning, paper goods, detergents, oral care, OTC, spices, and daily indent
Monday	
Soup, drinks, noodles/vermicelli, sauces, oils, branded spices, branded rice, skin care, shaving needs, herbal cosmetics, baby needs, cheese, spices, and daily indent	Canned food, ready to fry, BR savouries, sanitary products, batteries/electrical, dal, and daily indent
Tuesday	
Tea/coffee, confectionery, household cleaning, paper goods, oral care, detergents. *Please do top up indenting today.*	Dessert mixes, breakfast cereals, biscuits, jams, hot drinks, branded flours, household needs, hair care, cigarettes, rice flour, and daily indent
Wednesday	
Jams, hot drinks, biscuits, breakfast cereals, dessert mixes, BR savouries, hair care, sanitary, household needs, pickles, dal, and daily indent	Soups, drinks, noodles/vermicelli, sauces, oils, branded spices, branded rice, skin care, shaving needs, baby needs, pickles, cheese, spices, and daily indent
Thursday	
Drinks, noodles/vermicelli, sauces, oils, branded spices, skin care, shaving needs, baby needs, cheese, rice flour, and daily indent	Tea/coffee, confectionary, household cleaning, paper goods, detergents, oral care, Only despatch of top up items, baby needs, cheese, rice flour, and daily indent
Friday	
Tea/coffee, confectionary, household cleaning, paper goods, oral care, detergents, baby food, tin milk, OTC, spices, and daily indent	Dessert mixes, breakfast cereals, biscuits, hams, hot drinks, branded flours, household needs, hair care, sanitary, branded savouries, herbal cosmetics, dal, and daily indent
Saturday	
Canned food, ready to fry, BR savouries, sanitary, batteries/electrical, cigarettes, dal, and daily indent	Drinks, noodles/vermicelli, sauces, oils, branded spices, skin care, shaving needs, baby needs, pickles, cheese, rice flour, and daily indent

Source: Company Records, December 1998.

TABLE CS8.9 Hardware Indent Schedule for a Region

Monday	Bharat/Klassik
Tuesday	Yera Glassware, Anjali Kitchenware, Walt Disney/Fiskars, Hallmark Mugs
Wednesday	Clearline, La Opala, Philips, SS Cutlery, Decopride, Ramsons Cutlery
Friday	Archana Products, AB Plastic Containers
Saturday	Shripet Plasticware, Prestige Cookers, Butlers/Anupam
Sunday	Rosewood Items, HIP Flask, M/W Proof Containers

Source: Company Records, December 1998.

TABLE CS8.10   Store Indent on a Warehouse

Report No: 0F8

Indent Date: /11/98 (Sunday)

Store No: 863

Store Name: AAA

No.	Item Code	Category: Tea/Coffee	Stock Qty	Indent Qty	Picked Qty
Sub Category: 2301 Ground Coffee					
Indent Number: [630486]					
1.	190046	Brooke Bond Green Label Coffee	278	6	6
2.	190024	Brooke Bond Green Label Coffee	244	12	12
3.	190027	Coorg Filter Coffee 500 g	74	9	9
4.	190040	Coorg Double Roast Coffee 500 g	83	12	12
5.	190043	Coorg D.R. 500 g Jar	0	12	
6.	190065	F.W. Pure Filter Coffee 200 g	0	12	
7.	190066	F.W. Pure Filter Coffee 500 g	0	12	
Sub Category: 2302 Instant Coffee					
Indent Number: [630487]					
1.	190007	Brooke Bond Bru Instant Coffee	0	12	
2.	190014	Bru Super Strong 50 g	0	12	
3.	190053	Nescafe 25 g Jar	0	12	
4.	190056	Nescafe Inst Coffee 100 g Jar	0	12	
5.	190064	Nescafe Select Inst Coffee 100 g	0	12	
6.	190090	Nestle Sunrise Premium 100 g	0	12	
7.	190091	Nestle Sunrise Premium 100 g	0	12	
Sub Category: 2303 Dust Tea					
Indent Number: [630488]					
1.	191037	Sargam Dust Tea 500 g	0	12	
2.	191039	Double Diamond Dust Tea 250 g	0	12	
3.	191147	Lipton Green Label Tea 250 w.b.	0	12	
Sub Category: 2304 CTC Tea					
Indent Number: [630489]					
1.	191000	Brooke Bond Red Label 500 g j	18	6	6
2.	191006	Brooke Bond 3 Roses 250 g ja	0	6	
3.	191021	Brooke Bond Red Label 250 g ja	0	12	
4.	191025	Brooke Bond Red Label Tea 500 g	134	12	12
5.	191026	Brooke Bond Red Label Tea 250 g	310	12	12
6.	191027	Brooke Bond Red Label Tea 100 g	250	12	12
7.	191028	Cheers Darjeeling Leaf Tea 250 g	21	12	12
8.	191043	Devan Tea 100 g Green	208	6	6
9.	191047	Kannan Devan Leaf 250 g	75	12	12
10.	191111	Runglee Rungliot Darjeeling Tea	0	12	
11.	191129	Duncon Double Diamond Leaf Tea	0	6	

(Contd)

Table CS8.10 (Contd)

No.	Item Code	Category: Tea/Coffee	Stock Qty	Indent Qty	Picked Qty
12.	191146	Lipton Green Label Tea 100 g	207	6	6
13.	191148	Lipton Tajmahal Tea Bags 25's	368	24	24
14.	191150	Prime Tea 25 Bags	0	24	
15.	191151	Kotada Tea Bearer 250 g Brand	0	6	
16.	191152	Kotada Tea Bearer Brand 500 g	0	6	
17.	191153	Kotada CTC Spl Dust 250 g	0	6	
18.	191154	Kotada Bearer Brand Tea 100 g	0	6	

Sub Category: 2301 Ground Coffee
Indent Number: [630633]

No.	Item Code	Category	Stock Qty	Indent Qty	Picked Qty
1.	190016	Brooke Bond Green Label Coffee	212	24	24
2.	190020	Brooke Bond Green Label Coffee	205	24	24
3.	190024	Brooke Bond Green Label Coffee	217	18	18
4.	190027	Coorg Filter Coffee 500 g	47	12	12
5.	190029	Coorg Pure Filter Coffee 100 g	66	18	18
6.	190031	Coorg Pure Filter Coffee 200 g	83	24	24
7.	190034	Brooke Bond Cafe 100 g	125	12	12
8.	190040	Coorg Double Roast Coffee 500 g	68	12	12
9.	190041	Coorg Double Roast Coffee 200 g	101	12	12
10.	190042	Coorg Double Roast Coffee 100 g	98	18	18
11.	190043	Coorg Double Roast Coffee 500 g Jar	0	3	
12.	190065	F.W. Pure Filter Coffee 200 g	0	12	
13.	190066	F.W. Pure Filter Coffee 500 g	0	12	

Sub Category: 2302 Instant Coffee
Indent Number: [630634]

No.	Item Code	Category	Stock Qty	Indent Qty	Picked Qty
1.	190007	Brooke Bond Bru Instant Coffee	0	18	
2.	190008	Brooke Bond Bru Instant Coffee 20 g	271	24	24
3.	190010	Tata Kaapi 200 g	58	6	6
4.	190012	Brooke Bond Bru Inst Coffee 50 g	381	12	12
5.	190014	Bru Super Strong 50 g	0	24	
6.	190053	Nescafe 25 g Jar	0	24	
7.	190056	Nescafe Inst Coffee 100 g Jar	0	24	
8	190060	Nescafe Classic 50 g	254	12	12
9.	190064	Nescafe Select Inst Coffee 100g	0	12	
10.	190084	Nescafe Sunrise Premium Inst 2	291	12	12
11.	190088	Nescafe Sunrise Premium Inst Co	323	12	
12.	190090	Nestle Sunrise Premium 100 g	0	12	
13.	190091	Nestle Sunrise Premium 100 g	0	12	
14.	500207	Nescafe 3-in-one 180 g	0	12	

(Contd)

Table CS8.10 (Contd)

No.	Item Code	Category: Tea/Coffee	Stock Qty	Indent Qty	Picked Qty
Sub Category: 2303 Dust Tea					
Indent Number: [630635]					
1.	191020	Brooke Bond Super Dust Jar 500	0	3	
2.	191037	Sargam Dust Tea 500 g	0	3	
3.	191039	Double Diamond Dust Tea 250 g	0	3	
4.	191101	Sargam Tea 250 g Refill	0	3	
5.	191147	Lipton Green Label Tea 250 w.b.	0	3	
Sub Category: 2304 CTC Tea					
Indent Number: [630636]					
1.	191000	Brooke Bond Red Label 500 g j	6	6	
2.	191006	Brooke Bond 3 Roses 250 g j	0	6	
3.	191009	Brooke Bond 3 Rose Tea 500 g	69	6	6
4.	191021	Brooke Bond Red Label 250 g ja	0	6	
5.	191025	Brooke Bond Red Label Tea 500	110	6	6
6.	191026	Brooke Bond Red Label 250	262	6	6
7.	191027	Brooke Bond Red Label 100	190	12	12
8.	191029	Chakaragold 100 g	55	12	12
9.	191030	Chakaragold 250 g	59	6	6
10.	191035	Duncans Sargam Tea Jar Garden	0	6	
11.	191043	Kannan Devan Tea 100 g Green	190	6	6
12.	191047	Kannan Devan Leaf 250 g	51	12	9
13.	191052	Lipton Topstar Tea 100 g	186	12	12
14.	191053	Lipton Topstar Tea 250 g	168	6	6
15.	191057	Lipton Tajmahal Tea 100 g	112	12	12
16.	191058	Lipton Tajmahal Tea 500 g	71	12	12
17.	191059	Lipton Tajmahal Tea 250 g	195	12	12
18.	191064	Lipton Green Label Tea 250 g	42	12	12
19.	191065	Lipton Green Label Tea 500 g	1	6	
20.	191085	Lipton Yellow Label Tea 500 g	86	6	6
21.	191087	Lipton Yellow Label Tea 100 g	190	12	12
22.	191111	Runglee Rungliot Darjeeling Tea	0	3	
23.	191129	Duncon Double Diamond Leaf Tea	0	3	
24.	191146	Lipton Green Label Tea 100 g	171	12	12
25.	191148	Lipton Tajmahal Tea Bags 25's	242	12	12
26.	191150	Prime Tea 25 Bags	0	12	
27.	191151	Kotada Tea Bearer 250 g Brand	0	6	
28.	191152	Kotada Tea Bearer Brand 500 g	0	3	
29.	191153	Kotada CTC Spl Dust 250 g	0	6	

(Contd)

Table CS8.10 (Contd)

No.	Item Code	Category: Tea/Coffee	Stock Qty	Indent Qty	Picked Qty
30.	191154	Kotada Bearer Brand Tea 100 g	0	3	
31.	500218	A V T Assam Tea 250 g Jar	6	6	
32.	500219	A V T Premium Tea 500 g	92	6	6
33.	500220	A V T Premium Tea 250 g	92	6	6

Source: Company Records, December 1998.

Ordering Process

The category managers in the warehouse monitored the stock position of the SKUs under their control and placed orders from the suppliers. Table CS8.11 gives an example of three SKUs for which the base quantity stocks have been defined. For example, Cadbury's 5 Star (38 gms) had a base quantity (MBQ of 240, 96, and 48 for A, B, and C category stores, respectively) totalling 420 units in the warehouse (D). The actual stocks being 1,046, no order was yet due. However, an order would be due for Surf Excel since actual stocks were less than the warehouse base quantity. Tables CS8.12 and CS8.13 show sample purchase orders placed on vendors and the goods receipt note from the vendors, respectively. In all the three cases, supplies were received within the third day.

TABLE CS8.11   Ordering Process

FoodWorld Warehouse	Product Master (Master Maintenance Menu)		
Product Name	Cadbury's 5 Star 38 gms	Cadbury's Crackle 35 gms	Surf Excel Refill 500 gms
Product Code	263607	263573	901039
UOM	gms	gms	Gms
Packout	36	24	6
Description	Confectionery count lines	Confectionery block chocolate	Detergent powder
Dept/Group Code	906	905	2602
Tax Code	88	88	88
Stock Movement Flag	NA	NA	NA
Indent Flag	0	0	0
Prod-Company Code	50 Cadbury's	50 Cadbury's	125 Hindustan Lever
Vendor Code	CRA024 Ashwini Distributors	CRA024 Ashwini Distributors	CRU034 Upmarkets
ABC Code	A	A	A
Power Item	N	Y	N
Base Quantity	A:240 B:96 C:48 D:420	A:60 B:36 C:24 D:120	A:48 B:24 C:18 D:420
Buyer Code	003	033	007
Cost Price	₹8.83 from 24.9.98 WIP: 8.83	₹12.37 from 24.9.98 WIP: 12.37	₹59.28 from 3.12.98 WIP: 59.28
MRP	10.00 from 11.2.98	14.00 from 3.9.98	65.00 from 9.5.98
Prev Cost Price	8.89 from 15.9.98	12.46 from 15.9.98	59.58 from 21.11.98
Prev MRP	10.00 from 11.2.98	12.00 from 2.3.98	60.00 from 9.2.98
Stock Qty at Warehouse	1046	664	13

Source: Company Records, December 1998.

TABLE CS8.12 Sample Purchase Orders

No.	Product Name	Code	MRP	Qty	Cost	Value
Hex Trading						PO No: 37337
1.	Brooke Bond 3 Roses 500 gms Jar	191007	101.50	24.00	96.97	2,327.28
2.	Brooke Bond Inst Coffee 200 gms	190008	124.00	180.00	115.89	20,860.20
3.	Brooke Bond Bru Inst Coffee 50 gms	190012	26.00	120.00	24.30	2,916.00
4.	Brooke Bond Green Label Coffee 50 gms	190015	8.15	80.00	7.65	612.00
5.	Brooke Bond Green Label Coffee 500 gms	190024	78.00	120.00	74.29	8,914.80
6.	Brooke Bond Red Label 500 gms Jar	191000	86.00	48.00	81.50	3,912.00
7.	Brooke Bond Red Label Tea 250 gms	191026	43.00	96.00	41.25	3,960.00
8.	Brooke Bond Red Label Tea 250 gms Jar	191021	43.00	72.00	41.25	2,970.00
9.	Brooke Bond Green Label Coffee 200 gms	190020	31.60	120.00	30.10	3,612.00
10.	Lipton Green Label Tea 250 gms	191064	88.25	144.00	84.38	12,150.72
11.	Lipton Green Label Tea 100 gms	191146	31.50	120.00	29.98	3,597.60
12.	Lipton Tajmahal Tea Bags 200's	191145	130.00	18.00	118.18	2,127.24
Dhanalakshmy Agencies						PO No: 37554
1.	Nescafe Select Inst Coffee 50 gms	190060	61.00	224.00	55.80	12,499.20
2.	Nescafe Sunrise Extra 200 gms	190080	100.00	72.00	93.50	6,732.00
3.	Nescafe Sunrise Inst Extra 50 gms	190092	27.00	256.00	25.25	6,464.00
M S Vel & Company						PO No: 37810
1.	Coorg Double Roast Coffee 500 gms	190040	74.00	96.00	74.00	7,104.00
2.	Coorg Double Roast Coffee 200 gms	190041	30.00	120.00	30.00	3,600.00
3.	Coorg Filter Coffee 500 gms	190027	83.00	72.00	83.00	5,976.00
4.	Coorg Pure Filter Coffee 100 gms	190029	17.00	180.00	17.00	3,060.00

Source: Company Records, December 1998.

For almost all of the SKUs, the supplies were made from the nearest vendor, who was the dealer appointed by the supplying company. Dealer margins were anywhere up to 10 per cent. Most dealers were willing to operate with a weekly frequency of supplies to the warehouse, by consolidating all SKUs to be supplied by them. The average number of SKUs per vendor (supplying company) was about 20. Table CS8.14 gives the list of the top vendors from whom the cumulative purchase value in a month was 75 per cent of the total purchase, in which 63 vendors accounted for 4,106 SKUs. (The top five companies accounted for about 1,400 SKUs.) The order fill rate was typically in the range of 60 per cent to 75 per cent. More than one category manager could be dealing with the top few vendors for raising orders. For example, five category managers dealt with Hex Trading.

TABLE CS8.13 Sample Goods Receipt Notes

No.	Product Name	Code	MRP	Qty Accepted	Cost	Value
Hex Trading						DC No: 8201
1.	Brooke Bond Bru Inst Coffee 200 gms	190008	124.00	180.00	115.89	20,860.20
2.	Brooke Bond Bru Inst Coffee 50 gms	190012	26.00	120.00	24.30	2,916.00

(Contd)

Table CS8.13 (Contd)

No.	Product Name	Code	MRP	Qty Accepted	Cost	Value
3.	Brooke Bond Green Label Coffee 50 gms	190015	8.15	80.00	7.65	612.00
4.	Brooke Bond Green Label Coffee 500 gms	190024	78.00	120.00	74.29	8,914.80
5.	Brooke Bond Red Label 500 gms Jar	191000	86.00	48.00	81.50	3,912.00
6.	Brooke Bond Red Label Tea 250 gms	191026	43.00	96.00	41.25	3,960.00
7.	Brooke Bond Red Label Tea 250 gms Jar	191021	43.00	72.00	41.25	2,970.00
8.	Brooke Bond Green Label Coffee 200 gms	190020	31.60	120.00	30.10	3,612.00
9.	Lipton Green Label Tea 250 gms	191064	88.25	144.00	84.38	12,150.72
10.	Lipton Green Label Tea 100 gms	191146	31.50	120.00	29.98	3,597.60
11.	Lipton Tajmahal Tea Bags 200's	191145	130.00	18.00	118.18	2,127.24
Dhanalakshmi Agencies						**DC No: 8205**
1.	Nescafe Select Inst Coffee 50 gms	190060	61.00	224.00	55.80	12,499.20
2.	Nescafe Sunrise Extra 200 gms	190080	100.00	72.00	93.50	6,732.00
3.	Nescafe Sunrise Inst Extra 50 gms	190092	27.00	256.00	25.25	6,464.00
M S Vel & Company						**DC No: 8207**
1.	Coorg Double Roast Coffee 500 gms	190040	74.00	96.00	74.00	7,104.00
2.	Coorg Double Roast Coffee 200 gms	190041	30.00	120.00	30.00	3,600.00
3.	Coorg Filter Coffee 500 gms	190027	83.00	72.00	83.00	5,976.00
4.	Coorg Pure Filter Coffee 100 gms	190029	17.00	180.00	17.00	3,060.00

Source: Company Records, December 1998.

TABLE CS8.14 List of Top Vendors for a Sample Month

No.	Vendor Name	No. of SKUs	Total Hash Qty	Purchase Value from Vendor	Company Name	Purchase Value %	Cumulative %
1.	Hex Trading	1,076	94,381	2,235,908.67	HLL	10.43	10.43
2.	Tamil Nadu State Marketing Corpn Ltd	112	17,220	1,564,409.00	Tasmac	7.30	17.72
3.	Venkateswara Agencies	61	49,461	716,526.40	Cadburys	3.34	21.07
4.	Dhanalakshmi Agencies	96	14,541	524,534.02	Nestle Culnery	2.45	23.51
5.	Arihant Agencies	128	52,775	518,428.91	Britannia	2.42	25.93
6.	Gajalakshmi Agencies	34	33,737	479,216.90	Nestle Confectionery	2.24	28.17
7.	Sathya Fruits	18	18	474,801.80	Fruits	2.21	30.38
8.	Fresh 'N' Green	37	37	398,832.05	Vegetable	1.86	32.24
9.	Mahanth Enterprises	22	5,395	396,753.23	ITC	1.85	34.09
10.	Dew Consumer Products and Services Ltd	54	54	377,733.51	Bakery	1.76	35.85
11.	Sri Ganesh Agencies	26	13,190	377,540.90	Aavin	1.76	37.61
12.	Bhawar Sales Corporation	59	6,470	353,170.10	P&G	1.65	39.26
13.	J J Udyog	4	12,100	326,025.00	Dal, Jalgaon	1.52	40.78

(Contd)

Table CS8.14 (Contd)

No.	Vendor Name	No. of SKUs	Total Hash Qty	Purchase Value from Vendor	Company Name	Purchase Value %	Cumulative %
14.	V R Muthu & Brothers	11	5,092	301,768.00	V V S Idayam	1.41	42.19
15.	Bhikshu Marketing	87	11,513	299,039.89	R C I	1.39	43.58
16.	E I D Parry (India) Ltd	4	20,000	276,000.00	Parry—sugar	1.29	44.87
17.	Sakthi Soft Drinks Ltd	17	4,425	248,985.05	Coca Cola India	1.16	46.03
18.	Akash Marketing Centre	41	14,132	242,436.90	Gujarat Co-op. Milk—Amul	1.13	47.16
19.	Mac Marketing Company	44	4,797	237,024.90	Nestle—Imported	1.11	48.27
20.	Sri Jeet Traders	65	19,503	229,731.90	Dry Fruits, Masalas, Wholesale	1.07	49.34
21.	Suresh Enterprises	31	8,993	218,623.37	Kellogg's	1.02	50.36
22.	Sandhya Agencies	54	4,037	218,378.52	ISPL	1.02	51.38
23.	Sri Sai Enterprises	118	7,351	218,004.92	Johnson & Johnson	1.02	52.39
24.	Godrej Pillsbury Ltd	25	8,540	216,546.90	Godrej Pillsbury	1.01	53.40
25.	K Ahamed Hussain & Sons	40	9,282	214,779.84	SKB	1.00	54.41
26.	Associated Agencies	320	5,935	202,409.19	Hardware	0.94	55.35
27.	Shree Manish & Co.	79	10,368	195,430.74	Colgate Palmolive	0.91	56.26
28.	Chang Foods Pvt. Ltd	40	40	188,287.55	Old Chang Kee	0.88	57.14
29.	Srijeet Enterprises	47	14,488	180,802.85	Dals, Dry Fruits	0.84	57.98
30.	K Narayanasami	12	12	165,758.40	Vegetable	0.77	58.76
31.	Pankaj Traders	31	10071	157,127.50	Dals	0.73	59.49
32.	Agri Flora	24	24	151,176.30	Exotic F&V	0.71	60.19
33.	M S Vel & Company	47	4,363	147,066.10	Tata Tea	0.69	60.88
34.	Amudhan Agencies & Services Pvt. Ltd	150	1,834	146,564.95	Modi Revlon	0.68	61.56
35.	Fathima Agencies Pvt. Ltd	84	7,933	135,679.05	Pondicherry Mineral Water	0.63	62.20
36.	Service Unlimited	41	12,186	133,302.15	Chilly, Daniya	0.62	62.82
39.	Amalgam Foods Limited	113	1,523	126,132.75	Sumeru' Amalgam Foods Ltd	0.59	64.60
40.	Salecha Industries	1	4,900	124,950.00	Dals,	0.58	65.18
41.	Raja's Marketing Co.	38	6,098	121,382.00	Henkel Spic	0.57	65.74
42.	Sree Subha Milk Products	75	7,949	118,424.00	Dairy Products	0.55	66.30
43.	Venkat	1	3,000	112,050.00	Fruits and Vegetable	0.52	66.82

(Contd)

Table CS8.14 (Contd)

No.	Vendor Name	No. of SKUs	Total Hash Qty	Purchase Value from Vendor	Company Name	Purchase Value %	Cumulative %
44.	The Nilgiri Dairy Farm Ltd	15	15	111,299.60	Dairy Products, Nilgiri's	0.52	67.34
45.	Sri Singhi Spices Pvt. Ltd	12	2,084	110,940.00	Satnam Overseas, Kohinoor Bas	0.52	67.86
46.	Bullwork Traders	29	9,942	105,224.40	Jaggery, Tamarind,	0.49	68.35
47.	Naveen India	50	6,129	99,579.34	Best Food International, CPC	0.46	68.81
48.	Five Star Agencies	41	13,859	98,799.65	Nutrine	0.46	69.27
49.	Balajee Associates	23	23	98,188.60	Bakery	0.46	69.73
50.	Coral Enterprises	19	8,190	91,231.00	Chilly, Dania, Pepper, Dals	0.43	70.16
51.	Bawar Sales Corporation	15	2,154	91,190.95	P&G	0.43	70.58
52.	Sil Agencies	67	2,607	90,081.39	Kaytis, Costas, Prutina—Tin Veg. & Non-veg., Suzaane	0.42	71.00
53.	Kamal Stores	103	8,100	89,891.00	Savories, Unbranded	0.42	71.42
54.	Pazha Mudir Cholai	6	6	88,077.20	F&V	0.41	71.83
55.	Tobacco Centre	43	3,170	83,941.63	ITC	0.39	72.22
56.	Raaj Trade Linghs	89	2,911	82,943.15	Park Avenue, J K Helen Curtis	0.39	72.61
57.	Ashok M. Lulla	33	33	81,501.15	New Gangodhri, Chat Items	0.38	72.99
58.	New Bharath Enterprises	29	1,964	80,697.57	Dabur India	0.38	73.37
59.	Jain Marketing	70	3,673	78,293.68	Haldiram Nagpur	0.37	73.73
60.	Saroj Enterprises	24	6,134	76,111.66	MTR Foods	0.35	74.09
61.	Sri Saravan Enterprises	11	1,586	75,693.20	Goodnight, Godrej Hi Care	0.35	74.44
62.	N. Suresh Babu	2	7,500	74,962.50	IDLI Rice	0.35	74.79
63.	S K Swamy Enterprises	27	5,029	74,962.39	Karnataka Soaps, Mysore Soaps	0.35	75.14
	Total of top 63	**4,106**	**596,847**	**16,110,360.74**			
	Others	**3,697**	**283,168**	**5,330,701.33**			
	Grand total	**7,803***	**880,015**	**21,441,062.07**			

* The total number of SKUs include many which have been discontinued, but have not yet been taken off from the database.

Source: Company Records, December 1998.

Generally, the products were received through LCV trucks (one to three tonners). On receipt at the warehouse, a quantity and quality check was undertaken before accepting the goods. The next step was to paste bar coded stickers as per FoodWorld's code, to enable easy processing at the point of sale. However, there were certain items such as some of the vegetable oils and tetrapack drinks for which sticker sheets were only enclosed with the cartons and left as a task for the stores to complete before display. This was due to the fact that such SKUs were sensitive to additional handling.

Indents received from stores during a given working day, say, day 1, were processed on day 2 and then despatched to the stores on day 3. Non-branded staples were repacked using the FoodWorld brand, in a separate 'repack' section in the warehouse, equipped with weighing and packet sealing machines. Most of the processing in the warehouse and in the store was computerized. However, integration had not yet been achieved. The store representatives and the warehouse staff consisted of both permanent and temporary personnel. The ratio was roughly even.

Vendor Development

The key elements of the vendor development process were as follows.

- Identification of the supplying company's one-point contact.
- Driving towards standardized trading terms across all three regions on the following dimensions:
  - Credit
  - Promotion
  - Single point sources of supply across SKUs/categories, preferably direct from the company's depot/carrying and forwarding agent (CFA)
  - Margins (over and above product retail margins) for turnover, distributors' allowance, new store opening, bar coding (for data), and trade schemes

This strategy would also be driven by when a supplying company was willing to take notice of FoodWorld. This would depend on the volume of sales and perceived value of the level of services offered by FoodWorld. For FoodWorld, with an annual turnover of ₹1 billion, dealing with a company like Hindustan Lever Ltd (now Hindustan Unilever Limited) with an annual turnover of ₹78 billion (Table CS8.15) would be a challenge. In terms of branded food processing, the top five companies (led by Hindustan Lever Ltd, at ₹20 billion) accounted for an annual turnover

TABLE CS8.15 Hindustan Lever Limited: Sales Profile 1997

(A)

Sl No.	Items	Amount (₹ Billion)
1.	Soaps and Detergents	33.60
2.	Beverages	15.44
3.	Personal Products	8.84
4.	Others	6.13
5.	Processed Triglycerides Oils and Vanaspathi	5.42
6.	Animal Feeding Stuffs	2.72
7.	Speciality Chemicals	1.55
8.	Ice Cream and Frozen Desserts	1.53
9.	Branded Staple Foods	1.12
10.	Canned and Processed Fruits and Vegetables	0.97
11.	Diary Products	0.87
	Total	**78.20**

Source: The Economic Times, 30 December 1999.

Branded Food Processing (1996)

(B)

Company	Amount (₹ Billion)
Hindustan Lever Limited	20
NDDB	12
Nestle	10
Sicl	8.5
Britannia	6.5
Total (top five)	60
Cadbury	2.5
Total (top 20)	**100**

Source: Compiled from FAIDA Report, CII & McKinsey and Co., 1997.

of ₹60 billion. The top 20 companies accounted for ₹100 billion. Certain consumer goods companies had been willing to provide better terms and services to FoodWorld, including direct supply from depots or at least by having a specially selected dealer service from the warehouse. The possibility of better information processing through electronic data interchange was also being considered. One of the arguments that suppliers had against direct supply was the implied reduced earning potential for their distributors.

FoodWorld saw a potential of increasing their margins by 4 per cent to 10 per cent, by negotiating and sourcing directly from producing locations for branded products. The scope was even more in non-branded staples and perishables (such as fruits and vegetables), where there could be many intermediaries even between producing locations and the visible suppliers. As seen in Table CS8.16, in comparison to a developed country like the US, intermediaries in India, accounted for a larger share of the margins, while at the same time contributing less in terms of value addition.

As an example, the cost of rice procurement for the Madras region and its variation since January 1997 is given in Table CS8.17. The selling price of the rice and its impact on sales, percentage, and absolute margins are also provided. In the early months, rice of the appropriate quality used to be procured from the wholesale market in Madras. Later on, procurement was organized from the markets near the millers in Andhra Pradesh. The next step was to attempt direct procurement from mills, and then possibly from paddy markets, after which milling would be done on a contract basis. While the scope for increasing margins would increase, FoodWorld might have to get into activities not necessarily within its realm of expertise.

Issue at Hand

FoodWorld felt that the number of SKUs they were dealing with was too large. A rationalization effort focused on reducing the high-end sub-categories/SKUs and low volume SKUs and the depth (number of variants) was considered essential to reduce the maximum SKU count to 3,000. Table CS8.18 gives the expected profile of 'value added' food consumption in India by 2005. Exhibit CS8.1 gives the economics of a typical store, for which the break-even would be ₹2.08 million/month at a 17 per cent store margin.

The Vice President (Merchandising) was aware that, over the next five years, an additional investment of ₹3 billion was planned to increase the number of outlets from the present 19 to 26 by mid-1999, 50 by mid-2000, 120 by 2002, and 300 by 2004. The challenges for supply chain management in this context were going to be significant and needed a proper strategic response. As Mr P.K. Mohapatra said, 'Organized retailing pre-supposes retailer's ability to be able to influence, or, more importantly, manage a set of supply chains to be able to deliver value to the consumer in a commercially viable and sustainable way.'

TABLE CS8.16   Role of Intermediaries—Comparison between India and the US

	India	US
Intermediaries between farmer and consumer (fruits and vegetables)	6 (consolidator, commission agent, trader, commission agent, wholesaler, retailer)	2 (wholesaler, retailer)
Intermediaries between farmer and mill (wheat)	2 (commission agent, grain trader)	1 (grain trader)
Markup	33–50%	9%
Farm-gate prices as share of consumer prices		
• Apples	30%	40%
• Tomatoes	25%	41%
• Milk	90%	NA
Share of intermediary margin contributing to value addition costs	50%	80%

Milk cooperatives in India have demonstrated that by reducing the number of intermediaries, the farmers' share of revenues can be increased from 50% to over 90% of the processor price.
Source: Compiled from FAIDA Report, CII & McKinsey and Co., 1997.

TABLE CS8.17 Ponni Rice Sales and Purchase for Madras Region

Month	Sales	Sales Value	Selling Price	Purchase	Purchase Value	Net Cost	Margin	Absolute Margin
	(kg)	(₹)	(₹/kg)	(kg)	(₹)	(₹/kg)	(%)	(₹)
Jan '97	5,572	109,783	19.70	5,100	74,573	15.72	20.20	22,191.16
Feb '97	4,689	92,703	19.77	4,900	71,894	15.78	20.20	18,710.58
Mar '97	6,147	118,685	19.31	6,000	88,022	15.77	18.30	21,746.81
Apr '97	5,925	114,353	19.30	5,800	85,313	15.82	18.05	20,619.00
May '97	6,974	129,166	18.52	7,100	100,159	15.17	18.10	23,370.42
June '97	10,884	195,011	17.92	11,000	150,300	14.69	18.00	35,125.04
July '97	14,082	265,823	18.88	14,000	201,290	15.46	18.10	48,115.28
Aug '97	13,368	253,456	18.96	13,500	195,194	15.55	18.00	45,583.60
Sept '97	10,192	192,817	18.92	9,900	141,959	15.42	18.50	35,656.36
Nov '97	12,022	201,200	16.74	12,000	153,154	13.72	18.00	36,258.16
Jan '98	11,444	204,414	17.86	11,500	154,357	14.43	19.20	39,277.08
Feb '98	9,848	176,193	17.89	9,000	121,297	14.49	19.00	33,495.48
Mar '98	9,850	174,899	17.76	10,500	142,180	14.56	18.00	31,483.00
Apr '98	9,314	165,888	17.81	9,600	131,138	14.69	17.53	29,065.34
May '98	13,225	242,520	18.34	13,500	185,085	14.74	19.61	47,583.50
June '98	22,959	388,368	16.92	24,000	319,037	14.29	15.50	60,283.89
July '98	69,840	1,098,688	15.73	82500	1,043,625	13.73	12.72	139,784.80
Aug '98	95,760	1,437,846	15.02	150,000	1,891,500	13.43	10.54	151,789.20
Sept '98	106,330	1,603,653	15.08	290,000	3,787,400	13.55	10.15	162,881.50
Oct '98	120,000	2,035,054	16.96	320,000	4,848,000	14.86	12.40	251,854.00

Source: Company Records, December 1998.

TABLE CS8.18 Expected Profile of 'Value Added' Food Consumption in India by 2005

SI No.	Item	Amount (₹ Billion)
1.	Oil	500
2.	Packaged Milk	360
3.	Fresh Poultry	270
4.	Sugar	240
5.	Packaged Atta	150
6.	Soft Drinks	105
7.	Bakery	100
8.	Cereals	100
9.	Processed Meat and Poultry	90
10.	Tea and Coffee	74
11.	Indian Dairy Products	73
12.	Confectionery	65

(Contd)

Table CS8.18 (Contd)

Sl No.	Item	Amount (₹ Billion)
13.	Value Added Western Diary Products	47
14.	Fruit Drinks	20
15.	Fresh Vegetables	12
16.	Spices	12
17.	Puree, Jams, and Sauces	10
18.	Frozen Vegetables	3.5
	Total 'value added' food consumption in 2005 (approximately)	**2,250**
	Total 'value added' food consumption in 1996 (approximately)	**770**
	Total food consumption in 1996	**2,500**

Source: Compiled from FAIDA Report, CII & McKinsey and Co., 1997.

EXHIBIT CS8.1   Economics of a Typical Store

Size	:	3,500 sq. ft
Investment	:	₹4 million/fitout
		₹1 million/rent deposit
Total	:	**₹5 million**

Costs	₹
Rent	90,000
Salaries	80,000
Power/Fuel	50,000
Selling Exp.	15,000
Bank Charges	10,000
Security/Others	10,000
Repair/Maintenance	20,000
Adv./Promotion	15,000
Total	300,000
Depreciation	50,000
Interest on W/Cap	5,000
Total Operating Expenses	**355,000**

Source: Company Records, December 1998.

Questions

1. Evaluate the supply chain management at Food-World.
2. Critically analyse the structure of the supply chain and its suitability for the business. Suggest ways to improve its performance.
3. Suggest ways to reduce the number of SKUs as required in the case. Discuss the implications for supply chain management and suggest ways to manage them.

CASE STUDY 8.2

Woolworths Limited, Australia[1]

It was December 2001. The supply chain executive team (SCET) of Woolworths Limited was called for an important meeting. This meeting was headed by the General Manager, Supply Chain, Michael Luscombe. The main focus was on Project Refresh, which had commenced in August 1999 and was being driven by this team. This project was a plan to 'renew and reinvigorate' the company, leveraging initiatives in the supply chain. Since the commencement of Project Refresh, sales had improved by $2 billion and stripped $0.5 billion from Woolworth's costs. Luscombe and his team members were pleased with these numbers. Most of the benefits were expected to come from the supermarkets division, which accounted for about 85% of the revenues.

The SCET reported to the Supermarkets Executive team and also the Corporate Support Group. It also had to coordinate with the Supermarket Buying and Marketing team. Table CS8.19 gives the composition of these groups and teams. It also provides an insight into the different roles held by the senior management team (related to supermarkets) over the past five years.

A brief description of Project Refresh is given in Exhibit CS8.2, with excerpts from the company's annual reports of 1999, 2000, and 2001. The project was envisaged as a three-level initiative, with increasing sophistication, to yield an expected savings of more than $9 billion over nine years, starting 1999. The initial success of Project Refresh made Luscombe and his team optimistic about advancing to the level 2 initiative. They also decided to rechristen this initiative as Project Mercury, with an increased focus on the end-to-end supply chain and information technology (IT). The team was keen on identifying business process outsourcing (BPO) partners for this initiative. Exhibit CS8.3 gives an overview and significant details of the project, as would be relevant for a BPO partner to work with the company.

One of the most important decisions being considered by SCET was the restructuring of the distribution centre (DC) network. Woolworths was operating 31 DCs to cater to the supply needs of its supermarkets division. The retail outlets were receiving stock from multiple DCs, and did not leverage synergy in supply. The replenishment at the DC level was based on manual processes. Luscombe and his team had to take several decisions. The first was whether to consolidate the 31 DCs to a smaller number, by having multiple product categories (ambient and chilled) supplied from the same DC. If this happened, they would then need to identify the number of DCs and their locations. This would also imply that third-party-managed DCs would now be managed by the company. Initiatives to improve DC operations, including IT, would become critical.

Company Overview

Woolworths was one of the largest retail chains in Australia, retailing food, groceries, liquor, petrol, and general merchandise including consumer electronics. It had also entered into the wholesale business. By the end of 2001, it was operating 1,359 stores in Australia and 33 in New Zealand. It was headquartered near Sydney in Bella Vista, New South Wales (NSW), Australia. Table CS8.20 gives some major events in the growth of Woolworths since the opening of the first store in 1924 in Sydney.

The first store was called Woolworths Stupendous Bargain Basement. Nominal capital was £25,000 and attracted just 34 shareholders. The original concept was to establish a store that sold everyday needs of general merchandise at low prices. Woolworths successfully focused on its low price approach to general merchandise until the late 1950s, when it diversified into food retailing through the supermarkets format. By 1960, Woolworths was the first Australian retailer to operate in all Australian states and territories. The 1960s and 70s

---

1. Prepared by Professor G. Raghuram, Indian Institute of Management, Ahmedabad, and G. Kuberkar.

All data, except those mentioned as 'company data,' has been sourced from the Internet. Support rendered by TCS is gratefully acknowledged.

Cases of the Indian Institute of Management Ahmedabad are prepared as a basis for class discussion. Cases are not designed to present illustrations of either correct or incorrect handling of administrative problems.

Copyright © 2008 by the Indian Institute of Management Ahmedabad.

TABLE CS8.19 Composition of Groups and Teams

I. Corporate Support Group (2001)

Sl No.	Name	Designation
1.	Bradley, Steve	General Manager, Corporate IT
2.	Brookes, Bernie	Chief General Manager, Supermarket Buying and Marketing
3.	**Corbett, Roger**	**Group Managing Director/Chief Executive Officer**
4.	Howard, Judy	General Manager, Human Resources
5.	Jeff, Rohan	General Manager, Corporate Services
6.	**Luscombe, Michael**	**General Manager, Supply Chain**
7.	Mcmorron, Dick	Chief General Manager, General Merchandise
8.	Onikul, Naum	Chief General Manager, Supermarkets Operations
9.	Reid, Gary	General Manager, Business Development
10.	Wavish, Bill	Finance Director

II. Supermarkets Executive Team (2001)

Sl No.	Name	Designation
1.	Flood, Tom	General Manager, Supermarkets Operations
2.	Foran, Greg	General Manager, Merchandising Logistics, General Merchandise and Private Label
3.	McFadzean, Tony	General Manager, Liquor
4.	Pokorny, Peter	General Manager, Fresh Foods
5.	Sidler, Hans	General Manager, Petrol
6.	Winn, Penny	General Manager, Supermarkets Retail Support

III. Supply Chain Executive Team (2001)

Sl No.	Name	Designation
1.	Hill, Paul	National Supply Chain Performance Manager
2.	Hope-Johnstone, Craig	National Supply Chain Operations Manager
3.	Kochanowicz, Daniel	National Supply Chain Strategy Manager
4.	Luscombe, Michael	General Manager, Supply Chain
5.	McLaughlin, Charles	National Transport Manager
6.	Ramsay, Peter	Divisional Programme Office Manager

Source: http://www.woolworthslimited.com.au/resources/files/2001financialreport.pdf

(Contd)

Table CS8.19 (Contd)

IV. Supermarket Buying and Marketing Team (2000)

Sl No.	Name	Designation
1.	Aylen, James	Senior Business Manager, Grocery 2
2.	Brookes, Bernie	Chief General Manager, Supermarket Buying and Marketing
3.	Custance, Gavin	Senior Business Manager, Inventory
4.	Dhnaram, Greg	Senior Business Manager, State Liaison
5.	Dunn, Ian	Senior Business Manager, Trade Development and Relations
6.	Hillen, Bevan	Senior Business Manager, Deli/Bakery
7.	Hunt, David	Senior Business Manager, Merchandising Support
8.	Johnston, Murray	Senior Business Manager, Grocery
9.	MacDonald, Ian	Senior Business Manager, Perishables
10.	McAtamney, Jon	Senior Business Manager, Produce
11.	McEntee, Pat	Senior Business Manager, Meat
12.	Mintzis, Liz	Senior Business Manager, General Merchandise and Cleansing
13.	Nahmani, Avner	Senior Business Manager, Liquor and Tobacco
14.	O'Brien, Grant	Senior Business Manager, Marketing
15.	Pokorny, Peter	General Manager, Fresh Foods

Source: http://www.woolworthslimited.com.au/resources/files/2000financialreport.pdf

V. Career Progression of Woolworths' Senior Management Team (Related to Supermarkets)

Name	1997	1998	1999	2000	2001
Bradley, Steve			Corporate Manager, Information Technology	Corporate Manager, Information Technology	Corporate Manager, Information Technology
Brookes, Bernie	General Manager, QLD Supermarkets	General Manager, QLD Supermarkets	Chief General Manager, Supermarkets Buying and Marketing	Chief General Manager, Supermarkets Buying and Marketing	Chief General Manager, Supermarkets Buying and Marketing
Clark, Grant					Supermarkets Manager, Region 6 (NSW, ACT)
Corbett, Roger	Managing Director, Retail	Chief Operating Officer	Group Managing Director, Chief Executive Officer	Group Managing Director, Chief Executive Officer	Group Managing Director, Chief Executive Officer

(Contd)

Table CS8.19 (Contd)

Name	1997	1998	1999	2000	2001
Cornell, Ian	Chief General Manager, Supermarkets	Chief General Manager, Supermarkets			
Flood, Tom	General Manager, WA Supermarkets	General Manager, WA Supermarkets	General Manager, VIC Supermarkets	General Manager VIC Supermarkets	General Manager, Supermarkets Operation
Luscombe, Michael			General Manager, Supply Chain	General Manager, Supply Chain	General Manager, Supply Chain
Onikul, Naum	General Manager, VIC Supermarkets	General Manager, VIC Supermarkets	General Manager, Supermarkets Operation	Chief General Manager, Supermarkets Operation	Chief General Manager, Supermarkets Operation
Roberts, Trevor	General Manager, Distribution	General Manager, Distribution	General Manager, Distribution		
Wavish, Bill			Chief Financial Officer	Finance Director	Finance Director
Winn, Penny		Store Operations Manager, Big W	National Manager, Ezy Banking	National Manager, Ezy Banking	General Manager, Supermarkets Retail Support

Source: http://www.woolworthslimited.com.au/shareholdercentre/financialinformation/annualreports.asp (1997–2001)

saw further diversification with the acquisition of the Rockmans women's clothing chain and the establishment of the BIG W discount department store chain. In the early 1980s, Woolworths acquired the Dick Smith Electronics chain. Then in 1985, Woolworths bought the Australian Safeway store group from Safeway of the US to become the largest food retailer in Australia.

At the end of the 1980s, Woolworths became the subject of a takeover bid from Industrial Equity Limited (IEL) that was successfully completed in 1989. Woolworths remained a wholly-owned subsidiary of IEL until 1993 when it was re-floated on the Australian stock exchange at $2.45 a share. Woolworths diversified into petrol retailing in 1996, giving discounts to attract customers. The Internet HomeShop service was introduced in 1998 and Ezy Banking followed in 1999. The same year, Woolworths launched Project Refresh with the task of reorganizing many parts of the business.

Chisholm Manufacturing, a processed foods and small goods manufacturer, and Rockmans, the women's clothing chain, were disposed of in 2000, as Woolworths sought to focus on its core businesses of supermarkets and general merchandise. This process continued in 2001 with the sale of Crazy Prices and the acquisition of Tandy Electronics, and 67 Franklins supermarkets.

Woolworths Retail Activities

Woolworths was made up of a number of businesses, all providing the customers with quality, value, and everyday low prices. The company was operating in Australia through several retail banners. Table CS8.21 lists the various retail brands under the Woolworths umbrella. The brands were operated under three divisions: supermarkets, general merchandise, and wholesale. The numbers of brand-wise outlets are given in Table CS8.22. Not all the outlets carried liquor or had a petrol pump.

Supermarkets

• Woolworths: The company's premier supermarkets chain operated in every Australian state and territory except Victoria.

- Safeway: In Victoria, Woolworths was named Safeway.

- Food For Less: Woolworths also operated a number of smaller supermarkets under this brand in some areas.

- Flemings: Group of four supermarkets located in Sydney (the remnants of a chain purchased in the 1960s).

At the end of the financial year 2001, Woolworths had 604 supermarkets distributed around Australia. The distribution of supermarkets was closely aligned with that of the population.

Chisholm Manufacturing was another wholly owned business of Woolworths in the supermarkets division. All the bulk ham, bacon, sausages, and small goods sold in all the supermarkets were packed and supplied through Chisholm Manufacturing.

Plus Petrol

In 1996, Woolworths entered the petrol market, with wholly owned Plus Petrol outlets in Dubbo, NSW. With canopies adjacent to Woolworths supermarkets, it allowed Woolworths to meet more of its customer needs in one location and also helped to increase store sales. The petrol business returned a profit of $4.6 million in fiscal 2001. At the end of fiscal 2001, Woolworths had 166 petrol outlets.

Liquor

The total liquor business was organized under four brands:

- Woolworths Liquor: Liquor stores, either attached or located within Woolworths supermarkets (known as Safeway Liquor in Victoria)

- BWS: Liquor stores located away from the company's supermarkets

- Dan Murphy's: Known as 'liquor supermarkets' and one of the company's best growth performers

- First Estate: Fine wine stores

The total business generated sales of more than $1 billion per annum. Woolworths' share of the national liquor market was around 10% compared with Coles Myer's estimated market share of 13%.

Ezy Banking

Ezy Banking, Woolworths' banking joint venture with the Commonwealth Bank in 1999, was viewed as a separate business from the supermarkets group but was implemented to drive traffic through the stores, and thus generated incremental sales. It was another example of meeting customers' everyday needs in one location and also provided Woolworths an opportunity to learn more about its customers. In just two years, in 2001, 610,000 accounts were opened, exceeding the five-year target of 500,000 accounts.

General Merchandise

The general merchandise division was much smaller than the supermarkets division, accounting for only 13% of sales. The division comprised the following:

BIG W

This discount department store chain sold a wide range of general merchandise. Its direct competitors were Target and Kmart, both members of the Coles Myer Group. Through the implementation of every day low prices (EDLP), improved supply chain management, and other benefits coming out of Project Refresh, Woolworths was able to drive impressive performance improvements from BIG W.

Consumer Electronics

- Dick Smith Electronics: Sold hobby electronic products as well as computer products

- Dick Smith Powerhouse: Innovative and interactive store, which sold consumer entertainment products

- Tandy Electronics: Sold computers, communications, and electronic goods

Woolworth's Metro

These were inner-urban convenience stores located in Sydney and Brisbane, selling a range of pre-prepared meals for the 'time-poor' customer.

Wholesale

The wholesale division covered Australian independent wholesalers (AIW), who traded in Victoria, NSW, and Queensland, and statewide independent wholesalers (SIW), which traded in Tasmania. The latter was only 60% owned by Woolworths. This division, which was the smallest amongst all divisions, contributed only 3% of the total sales of Woolworths.

Australian Retail Industry

The Australian retail environment was dynamic and constantly evolving. There were 70,000 employing retail businesses in Australia. In 2000–01, the industry transacted $197 billion of business, growing at 2–3%

per annum (Table CS8.23). The industry was the largest employer in Australia, employing 920,000 people (about 12% of the workforce). Over the period 1993–2000, employment grew by over 20%. Australia's biggest retailers in terms of sales, market share, and impact on the retail industry were Coles Myer, Woolworths, Foodland, Harvey Norman, Bunnings, and David Jones. Exhibit CS8.4 provides an insight into the supermarket division's competitive environment.

The state-wise population and retail income distribution is given in Table CS8.24. The major supermarket retailers' outlets across the state, as of 1998, is given in Fig. CS8.4.

According to Australian Food Statistics 2001 published by the Department of Agriculture, Fisheries and Forestry, supermarkets and grocery stores accounted for around 66% of total food sales (excluding liquor) of almost $64 billion, in 1999–2000. This result showed a 2.6% increase in sales over the year 1998.

Supermarkets Division

Australia, as a country, was divided into eight administrative states and territories. Figure CS8.5 gives a map of Australia, along with its important cities. The state-wise distribution of the 604 Woolworths supermarkets is given in Table CS8.25. The supermarkets were organized into ten regions, as seen in Fig. CS8.6. Large areas of Australia still did not have an outlet due to a very low density of population.

The main product categories of the supermarkets are given in Exhibit CS8.5. The supermarkets business was viewed as consisting of food, groceries, liquor, and petrol. In terms of supplies, the DCs handled chilled and ambient separately. Produce and liquor, to a significant extent, was handled independently through dedicated DCs. For the financial year ended 24 June 2001, the Supermarkets Division had revenue of $17.5 billion, as seen in Table CS8.26. The earnings before interest and tax (EBIT) were $600 million. Table CS8.27 provides a five-year analysis of the financial results of Woolworths.

Woolworths' sales turnover totaled almost $21 billion and EBIT was just over $700 million. The company recorded a net profit of $428 million. The market capitalization was recorded at $11.6 billion. The market share was in the range of 28% to 40%. Woolworths was the second largest employer in Australia with a staff of over 140,000 people.

Project Refresh

In 1999, Woolworths achieved an operating profit of $312 million, at 4% over the year 1998, and also a 9.6% growth in sales. Though this performance was very good by Australian standards, and placed the company in the top half of Australian listed companies, there was a need to grow shareholder value faster. The management team was determined to have a more dynamic and outward-looking approach, and so, in August 1999, launched 'Project Refresh'. This was an exciting and important programme that identified the developing trends in the retail environment and the need for changes designed to deliver increased customer focus and shareholder wealth.

The major objectives of Project Refresh were as follows:

- Focus on customer needs.
- Control, measure, and track costs.
- Create greater shareholder value through strategic capital management.
- Create a new management structure that will allow decisions to be made faster and by the most appropriate person, whether at store, regional, or national level and will also reduce the costs of unnecessary duplication.
- Focus on supply chain, inventory management, buying and marketing, IT, human resources, organizational redesign, and cost of doing business.
- Provide better supplier relationships.
- Refocus on core businesses of supermarkets and general merchandise retailing.
- Seek buyers for Rockmans and Chisholm manufacturing businesses.

In short, the Project Refresh initiative covered all aspects of business with a view to saving costs, increasing sales, and improving effectiveness.

Project Refresh, since its inception in 1999, concentrated on a number of initiatives, including a significant business restructuring programme as well as numerous cost reduction programmes. These initiatives were collectively known as Refresh Level I initiatives.

While the benefits of Refresh Level I continued to flow, the company shifted its major focus to Refresh Level II. This was called Project Mercury, an integrated, end-to-end supply chain improvement programme spanning over five years in both logistics and enabling technology.

Project Mercury

This project, started in October 2001, was considered the most important initiative driving change in Woolworths' history, and $1 billion would be spent on the upgrade of supply chain and associated IT. This supply chain redesign programme was initiated with a business objective of improving the process of delivering products to the customers. In achieving this, the programme aimed to generate a competitive advantage for its supermarkets. It would impact logistics, buying and marketing, supermarket operations, and IT functions.

The supply chain strategy was developed after evaluating systems and logistics features of leading global retailers following which the company determined an appropriate and optimum solution for Woolworths. This solution would address the following key design considerations:

- Common integrated systems required to support supply chain operations
- Store supply chain costs (from the supermarkets' back dock to the shelf)
- DC location and numbers
- DC function (cross-docking and flow-through)
- Composite supply chain (integrating cold and ambient)
- Transport management (primary and secondary freight)
- Process improvement across the network
- Buying and supply chain systems improvement to help make cost savings in these areas
- Making distribution process easier and more efficient for the stores

Project Mercury would be the umbrella term for all projects across the business that impacted the way in which products were supplied from vendors to customers. It would be the consolidation of many projects already underway within supply chain, buying and marketing, and supermarket operations, with the support of IT and human resources.

One of the important decisions was about consolidating the 31 DC network into a more responsive and cost efficient supply system. Exhibit CS8.6 gives the current DC network. Table CS8.28 gives the specific locations of the DCs and product types being supplied. The proposed DC network and locations are given in Exhibit CS8.7. This network would consist of nine regional DCs (RDCs) and two national DCs (NDCs). Figure CS8.7 gives the before and after structure of flows between DCs and outlets. The rationale for this proposal is given in Exhibit CS8.3.

The NDCs would distribute to over 700 stores nationally. The most significant change and challenge for NDC was to convert its operations from servicing just over 238 NSW stores to servicing nine RDCs and over 700 stores nationally.

For example, the Sydney NDC was one of the two NDCs in Australia. The other was Mulgrave Grocery in Melbourne. Sydney NDC would range ambient products such as slow moving grocery and general merchandise lines. It would service Sydney and Melbourne Metro stores directly from the NDC and service all other stores via their respective RDCs.

Delivery frequencies would change from daily store deliveries to once or twice a week. For example, Yennora DC would move 700,000 cartons in a seven-day operation. Sydney NDC would move 1.3 million cartons, previously a six-day operation.

The RDCs, such as Sydney and Wyong RDCs, would service supermarkets with fast moving lines. They would be a composite facility, providing fast moving grocery, general merchandise, frozen, locally manufactured, and all chilled and fresh products to stores. Two-third of the goods supplied would be from Sydney or Melbourne NDCs. Reducing the 31 DCs into 11 multi-temperature sites would reduce DC operating costs by $14 million in FY08.

Supply Chain

Project Mercury's mission was to implement the world's best practices in supply chain management to provide a better shopping experience for the customers every time. The supply chain strategy would not be just about DCs and transport, but would involve every part of the supermarket's business. This would identify different areas for improvement such as the following:

- The 'flow through' of products from suppliers to stores with less handling and lower cost along the way (Fig. CS8.8)
- Product movement through the supply chain 'ready to fill' directly onto store shelves

- The right amount of stock arrivals at the store when the stores need it
- Inventory management in the supply chain and forecasting stock requirements at DCs and stores
- The efficiency and effectiveness of the transport network (Exhibit CS8.8 and Fig. CS8.9)

The SCET, in partnership with the buying and marketing team, was working with the suppliers to achieve these improvements.

Systems to Support Supply Chain Strategy

The SCET identified possible benefits of implementing IT systems throughout the supply chain. Hence, the team was in the process of considering inclusion of the following systems to support supply chain strategy as a part of Project Mercury:

IT

IT systems would play a major part in implementing the supply chain strategy. The aim was to ensure the maximum service level to the customer with minimum inventory levels and operating costs. All components of the supply chain (including suppliers) would be linked electronically with much greater coordination between their operations. Exhibit CS8.3 provides a description of the IT systems.

IT would deliver maximum benefit to the business from the use of technology for the lowest cost. The systems associated with IT were warehouse management system (WMS), transport management system (TMS), and replenishment system. These were already in use for different operations in DCs and stores. A revamped form of these systems would be executed as a part of Project Mercury. Broadly, the following programmes would be under IT systems:

- Automatic store replenishment with AutoStockR
- DC replenishment with StockSMART
- Computer-based ordering and receiving for direct store deliveries (DSD)
- Tracking stores' stock on hand with Perpetual Inventory
- Better management of the flow of products into and out of DCs with enhanced TMS
- Operations of DCs through WMS

In short, the following programmes in revised form would be executed as part of Project Mercury.

- WMS

- TMS
- Replenishment system

WMS

WMS, a database-driven computer programme, would be an integral part of Project Mercury, which controls the movement of stock, people, forklifts, etc., within the DCs. This was also responsible for running the DCs' operating processes and information flows such as receiving stock from vendors, picking store orders, and dispatching these orders to stores. WMS would provide significant benefits to DCs in terms of speeding up picking times and pick accuracy.

A typical warehouse of Woolworths supermarkets would receive products such as groceries, perishables/frozen food, bakery, deli, fresh produce, meat, and liquor with more than 100,000 lines. The number of cartons received per year would be 680 million and the number of pallets received per year would be 8.5 million.

Woolworths supermarkets were facing the following operational issues, which led to the implementation of WMS under Project Mercury:

Receiving

- Full screen receiving with invoices from the drivers
- No handheld receiving at the docks
- No advanced shipment notice
- No express receiving

Picking

- Picking with labels
- No hands-free picking
- Less accurate and productive, especially non-CLS picking

Replenishment of Pick Slots

- Triggering of replenishments not based on real-time balance on hand

Loading

- Manual paper-based loading
- Consolidation without using the system
- No visibility of loading status

Miscellaneous

- Insufficient pick slots for the products
- Inefficient management of despatch lanes
- No updating of put-away priorities

- No optimization of secondary freight
- No concept of umbrella warehousing
- No proper management of warehouse mark-outs
- Produce warehousing managed by different systems
- Limited cross-docking and flow-through, mostly manual
- Paper-based picking for interstate stores and warehouse transfers
- No capability of rejecting stock before put-away was performed
- No advance shipment notice from vendors; no EDI documents to and from the warehouses

This system would be one of the components of end-to-end supply chain strategy, which supported RDCs and NDCs. The key considerations for redesigning WMS would be safety, accuracy, and cost. The new features of WMS would be the following:

- All product categories in composite multi-temperature DC
- Voice-enabled processes (picking, forklift drivers)
- Cross-dock processes (NDC and vendor)
- Dynamic pick locations (multiple slots, rotating slots)
- RF loading across multiple temperature zones
- Random weight processes

WMS strategy would also be set up for pilot site selection and rollout.

The following would be the business benefits of implementing WMS:

- A single, integrated WMS would be implemented to support the future network of multi-temperature distribution centres (RDCs).
- Quality assurance (QA) management would allow quality assurance of pallets received at the DC and rejection of low quality produce products.
- Products would be maintained with quality suffix and inter-item transfers would be performed.
- Increased picking accuracy
- Increased labour productivity
- Reduced cost of printing and distributing picking documents
- Reduced cost of re-keying order amendments, picking confirmations

- Hands free and eyes free—makes picking easier (helpful for items such as frozen foods, which were handled through gloves)
- Real-time stock updates
- It would enable business to inquire and maintain the cross dock information by transport order, thus enhancing the visibility of the incoming cross dock unit load devices (ULDs) from NDC and the cross dock ULDs that had arrived in RDC but were not yet loaded, thus giving the RDC a better planning capability
- Reduced manual intervention required to manage cross dock ULDs in the warehouse
- Automation of pallet handling (put away, replenishment, empty pallet handling) in ambient component of the facility
- Would satisfy a 2011 design year OM throughput of approximately 225 million cartons per year across all categories

DCs would also consider 'voice picking—hands and eyes free' technology that eliminates need for paper during the order picking process. It would be the best method for improving picking in DCs. It was expected that accuracy of picking would increase substantially. This would be a step towards store friendly principles.

TMS

Primary Transport

Primary transport means movement of product from vendors

- to the NDC/RDC network,
- into an interstate DC for full truck load (FTL) deliveries from vendors,
- DSD.

Shuttle Transport

This was a movement of products between DCs (local, intrastate, and interstate).

Secondary Transport

This was a movement of products from the RDCs or NDCs to the stores and return of ULDs, i.e., roll cages, dollies, crates, etc.

TMS, a web-based software, would help manage primary freight (movement of goods from vendors to DCs). It would keep track of the shipments in the transportation process. This would enable the operators to plan accurately and direct the movement of trucks to get the stock arriving in the DCs at the right time for the lowest cost. This system was used by Walmart, Tesco, and other large retailers overseas.

TMS would be introduced in Project Mercury's supply chain strategy after identifying the following benefits:

- Improved delivery to DCs
- Utilization of Woolworths' volumes to consolidate shipments
- Greater degree of control over flow-through and cross-docking
- Improved visibility of product movement in the supply chain
- Lower inventory

The SCET would manage the transport of stock across the supply chain, from vendors to DCs and stores. The transport operations, serving 700 supermarkets, would be one of the largest in Australia.

CAPs, a vehicle scheduling and routing system, would help plan the transport to stores in case of access restrictions due to curfews or physical restrictions. The system would map out the best possible routes and sequences for trucks to take.

Replenishment System

Various replenishment programmes would be initiated as part of the Project Mercury initiative:

- Automation of the existing replenishment system
- Fresh Food, Produce, and DSD integration into automated replenishment system
- Integration of DC forecasting process and store replenishment process

The following would be the major replenishment systems considered for implementation:

- StockSMART—Improved DC level forecasting including promotions
- AutoStockR—Store forecasting and replenishment
- WOW Link—Improved information to vendors
- DSD conversion project
- Self-ready trays
- Roll cages

A major task would be to build the link between store and DC replenishment to support an integrated solution.

The following would be the future considerations of the replenishment system:

- Store level promotional forecasting/replenishment
- Mix of aggregated store forecasts (fast movers) and DC-level forecasts (slow movers) for DC replenishment
- Introduction of system forecasting and replenishment into fresh food categories
- Closer relationships with key vendors to support flow-through

StockSMART (DC Forecast-based Replenishment)

StockSMART would be an automated forecasting and replenishment system for stock in DCs. It would be implemented in all DCs for grocery and general merchandise items. Service levels would be expected to improve by over 2% while three days' worth of inventory would be removed from the DCs.

AutoStockR (Store Forecast-based Replenishment)

AutoStockR or automated stock replenishment would be a computer-assisted ordering system that would order stocks for departments in supermarkets, including liquor. This system would be a key foundation for Project Mercury. AutoStockR would provide a forecast for each item in every supermarket across the country. This forecast would enable the supply chain to gain greater vision of store requirements, improving DC service levels, and the way in which stock would deliver to supermarkets. AutoStockR would be run in over 100 supermarkets. The potential benefits of this system would be improved productivity, reduction in store out of stocks, unnecessary inventory in stores, and double handling in stores.

WOW Link

WOW Link would be an electronic resource, via the Internet, to monitor Woolworths' information from across the buying and supply chain areas. This would provide Woolworths and its trading partners access to the following:

- Forecast replenishment plans
- DCs inventories
- Details of vendors' purchase orders
- Upcoming promotions
- Service level information
- Allocation details and Woolworths' product records

- Vendors' logistics performance (via scorecards and alert messages)

Developed in collaboration with a pilot team of eight trading partners, WOW Link would be a three-phased system. The initial phase would provide a basic one-way flow of information between Woolworths and its trading partners. The second phase would enable some interaction between the two, in terms of exchanging a range of information. The third phase would provide full interaction and collaboration between Woolworths and its trading partners.

DSD Conversion Project

Woolworths' 15% of volume was supplied directly to stores from the vendors. Another valuable component of Project Mercury would be the DSD Conversion Project. This project was aimed at converting 50% of DSD vendors over to warehouse supply through Woolworths' DCs. Benefits would be experienced not only for Woolworths but also for the vendors. There would be an increase in delivery frequency to the stores, the removal of congestion at stores' back docks, and reduction in the number of invoices to be processed.

Shelf-ready Trays

Shelf-ready trays were packed trays wrapped with film or a cardboard sleeve that could directly be fitted on the shelf for display. These would be identified as efficient shelf replenishment methods, which would improve productivity as well as occupational health and safety at store level and reduce the end-to-end supply chain costs.

Roll Cages

Roll cages were ULDs for transporting products from the DCs to the stores, rather than using a pallet. Roll cages reduced the number of times stock was touched at the store and thus reduced the handling costs. Roll cages would be introduced in Woolworths DCs and stores in Perth and WA. The SCET would proceed with the next stage of the roll cage implementation to other parts of the country.

The rationalization of DCs, combined with new cross-dock and flow-through processes, supported by the new WMS, would utilize the site advantages and further reduce both cost and stock levels, and the cost of transport from DCs to stores. Reducing the volume of DSD and introducing electronic store delivery would reduce costs by utilizing DC infrastructures as well as eliminating administration costs. For stores, the introduction of phased replenishment store restocking capabilities, along with store ready ULDs (for example, shelf ready trays and roll cages) would reduce overall costs.

Looking Forward

Michael Luscombe was looking for a BPO service provider for his company. He expected that the BPO partner should not only see from the IT perspective but should also have a strategic insight for analysing the financials of the company. The BPO service provider should be able to visualize the implications of restructuring the distribution network along with implementation of various IT systems. Most important was the position of the company in the competitive world of other retail companies, in terms of service and cost.

EXHIBIT CS8.2   Project Refresh

In the 1999 Annual Report (published in October 1999), Chairman, John Dahlsen wrote:

In August 1999, we announced Project Refresh, an exciting and important programme which identified the developing trends in the retail environment and the need for changes designed to deliver increased customer focus and shareholder wealth.

Project Refresh will give management the opportunity to build on the organization's market position, by a rigorous focus on customer needs, a more responsive management team, better supplier relationships and best practices in cost control, cost measurement and tracking.

Critically, Project Refresh will see the divestment of non-core assets and the focusing of attention and funds on the core businesses. It will result in important structural changes and the need to continue the process of review and re-invigoration of the organizations' core value proposition—a Customer Centric Business.

The 2000 Annual Report stated the following:

In August last year, we announced the implementation of Project Refresh. It is a significant and far reaching initiative which covers all aspects of our business as we re-examine everything we do.

Whilst the supermarkets' central Shared Service Buying function is the most recognizable change for our suppliers, Project Refresh also covers supply chain, IT, human resources, organizational redesign, and cost of doing business programmes.

The initial benefits will be extended to all areas of our businesses and will become part of our operational and corporate culture. Every effort is being made to achieve our gains without redundancies, by retraining and redeployment. The members of the teams working on Project Refresh are drawn from every state in Australia with around 30 people working on the various initiatives at any one time.

Supermarkets Shared Services

The change to central shared service buying and marketing was the result of a restructure of the business from a state based buying and marketing structure to a single functionally based business. Some of the main building blocks for the new structure—which we have called 'Shared Services'—were developed by examining best practices in supermarkets operations from around Australia and the world.

The new structure replaces a system of six state buying and marketing operations and enables us to buy most products centrally, while still maintaining state buying in some fresh foods categories. It has the capacity to considerably increase efficiency, eliminate duplication, improve supplier relations, and drive supply chain economies.

The new shared services function allows us to buy more effectively, to offer more consistent quality fresh food, and increase value through better buying and reduced pricing. Our decisions will also be better informed because of the establishment of cross-functional teams, made up of people with experience in buying, marketing, stock control, and store management. The new structure will further encourage a strong service culture, enabling business managers to provide quicker service and better support to store managers and their teams.

Supply Chain

As the year progressed, the considerable strategic advantages of our major new warehousing and distribution facilities became more apparent. We saw improved in-stock positions, particularly at the Christmas and Easter peak trading periods. Following a comprehensive review of our supply chain management,

we have formed a single supply chain structure which applies both technology and logistics as one function for the total company. It is expected that this will bring significant advantages to the company, in stock flow, stock turns, and in-stocks. Much more remains to be done in this area and the financial rewards we will generate from a total supply chain management strategy are considerable.

The 2001 Annual Report stated the following:

This far reaching initiative covers all aspects of our business as we examine everything we do with a view to saving costs, increasing sales, and improving effectiveness. In particular, the areas of cost savings cover

- Examination of all line item expenses
- Improvements to the total supply chain and its over-arching IT
- Functional reorganization to a national or shared service basis whilst increasing regional and in-store empowerment

Earlier this year we announced that we expect annual savings as a result of this initiative to reach $185 million, of which $50 million had been realized. In the global environment which influences all aspects of our business and against which we continuously benchmark ourselves, change and cost saving are perpetual. Initially, as a result of Project Refresh and increasingly as a consequence of continuous change, we now expect annual savings over the next five years to increase to approximately 1% of sales. That is further savings exceeding $200 million per annum.

Supermarkets Buying and Marketing

The Project Refresh changes began in August 1999 with a review of how we conduct our supermarkets buying and operations. This resulted in a decision to change our organizational structure from a divisionally based group of businesses in each state to a single, functionally based business. The first concrete realization of this structural change was effected in June 2000, when supermarkets moved to a national shared service environment for buying and marketing.

In line with our objectives of improving the ranging, layout, competitive pricing, and promotional offer to our customers, this was the first major approach to a centralized management environment in supermarkets. It laid the foundation for a streamlined management structure in finance, human resources, operations, and supply chain.

In its first full year of operations, supermarkets buying and marketing put in place new measures to improve communication throughout stores, including the in-house television programme—WOW TV, and Merchant of the Year competitions to encourage competition between store teams to build the best store displays and gain the best incremental sales.

Supplier Relations

The quality of our relationship with our supplier partners is an important ingredient in providing a continually improving offer to our customers.

Our supplier focus groups that have been run each quarter demonstrate an improving supplier relationship and a genuine focus on sales with our suppliers. Suppliers have been pleased with the consistency and uniformity of our interaction. Feedback shows improving supplier relationships with a genuine mutual focus on increasing sales.

Later in the year, we will be hosting a dinner to thank our suppliers and present the Suppliers of the Year Awards. These awards provide us with a great opportunity to recognize the outstanding teamwork between Woolworths and its many suppliers.

Supply Chain

Our supply chain is defined as the 'end to end' linkage of the activities of buying and marketing and store operations. In simple terms, the supply chain strategy focus is on being store friendly. This will ensure that the appropriate products get on the shelf faster and cheaper whilst using less inventory.

A high level strategy for the Woolworths supply chain has been based upon Woolworths' strong existing supply chain network, and on world's best practice, developed during study tours of major retailers in Europe and the USA. Implementation plans for the strategy are being developed, and will be phased in over the next five years.

A significant amount of supply chain work in the financial year revolved around the development of IT systems to support inventory management in the Supermarkets Division. Four major projects underway are IT systems to support:

- Ordering or merchandise into our DCs
- Ordering of merchandise into our stores
- Better visibility of stock holding across the company
- Better management of stock delivered directly to our stores from suppliers

Other projects undertaken in the year under review include

- Development, and implementation of supply chain integration plans for the converted former Franklins stores
- Rationalization of the Victorian distribution facilities, including closure of one site and a major upgrade to the Mulgrave Distribution Centre
- Centralization of the Dick Smith Electronics (DSE) distribution facilities from a multi-site to a one-site operation, based at Chullora in Sydney
- Development of integration plans for the Tandy Electronics supply chain into the DSE business
- Extension of the BIG W Warwick, Queensland distribution facility to handle increased volumes as this business expands
- Brismeat operation–design, tender, and commencement of works to refurbish and extend the Ipswich Meat Facility.

Merchandise Logistics

During the financial year, the Woolworths supply chain merchandise logistics department was formed, with the aim of working with our suppliers to improve the flow of their merchandise through the supply chain. This is an area with potential to remove substantial costs, for both suppliers and for Woolworths.

Woolworths Transport

The Woolworths National Transport Department was formed as part of the new supply chain structure. This group has identified a number of strategic initiatives that will be positive for the Woolworths group and work has commenced on implementation of these initiatives. The National Transport Department has also provided a national approach to transport contract management, with performance based service level agreements, which are providing immediate benefits to the company.

IT

Supply chain system improvement was the main focus of IT. We have a major development programme underway over the next three years, that enables and supports our overall supply chain strategy. The main achievements in the last year were

- The implementation of a new warehouse replenishment system (StockSMART) to better control the inventory levels of our everyday stock
- The pilot of a promotional warehouse replenishment system

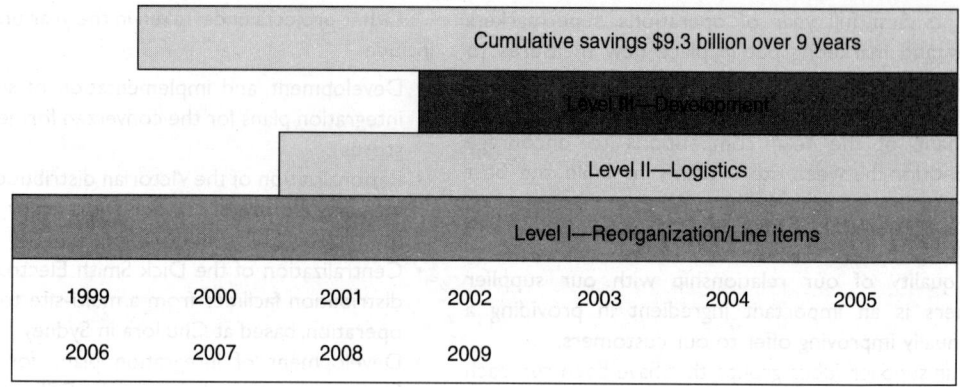

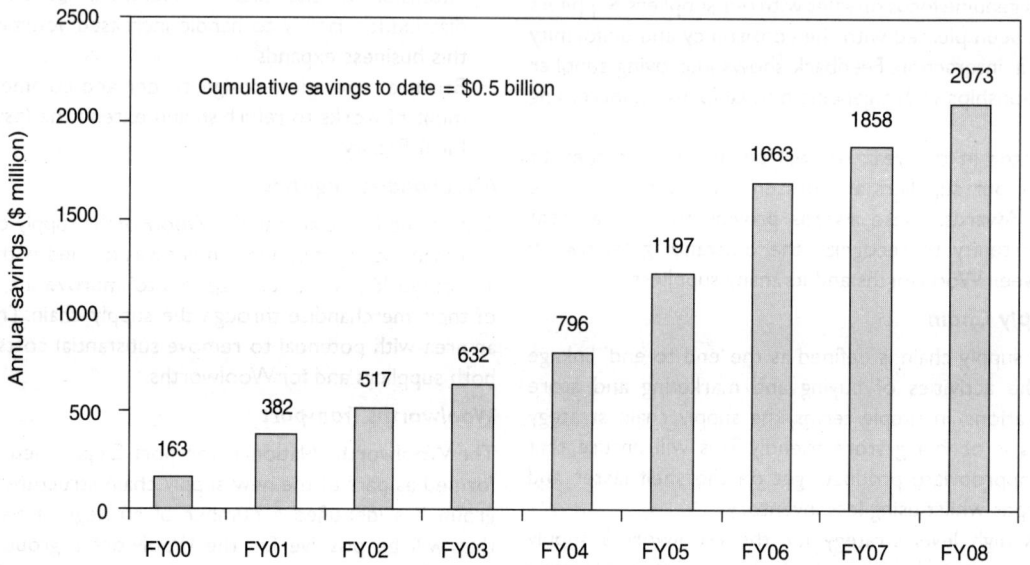

Source: http://www.woolworthslimited.com.au/resources/files/1999financialreport.pdf; http://www.woolworthslimited.com.au/resources/files/2000financialreport.pdf; http://www.woolworthslimited.com.au/resources/files/2001financialreport.pdf

- The pilot of an AutoStockR
- The development of more sophisticated systems to control the ordering and delivery of DSD

We are confident that in the next year, as we roll out the pilot systems, we will gain significant improvements in our in-stock positions, as well as a reduction in our overall stock levels.

We have rolled out new stores back-office infrastructure to over 600 supermarkets. This provides a standard, Microsoft Windows Platform, in every supermarket which will be the basis for many new in-store IT applications in the coming years.

EXHIBIT CS8.3 Project Mercury and Network Model Project

Project Mercury

Project Mercury would be considered as a business transformation for Woolworths supermarkets.

The following were some of the objectives of Project Mercury:

- Changes to business to support the supply chain development programme (SCDP) are wider than the supply chain operations.
- Significant changes required across supply chain, buying and marketing, IT, stores, and vendors.
- Coordinate cross-divisional activities and make it a total business strategy.
- Currently, stores receive stock from multiple DCs.
- A regional distribution centre consolidates these sites into a single point of supply for a group of stores.
- These new DCs process all merchandise categories, requiring multiple temperature environments.
- $14 million result from fractionalizing DC labour cost.
- Together with composite transport, these facilities provide improved service to stores by enabling multiple deliveries for all product categories.
- 100% control of DC network.
- Transport benefits result from reduced number of distribution nodes.

As a part of Project Mercury WMS, TMS, and replenishment systems would be implemented. The respective objectives were as follows:

WMS Project Objectives

Develop the following WMS business requirements, required to support NDCs and RDCs of the future, for all categories:

- New processes: Cross dock, carton flow-through, voice picking, optimized system directed work sequencing, etc.
- User requirements as defined by current WMS business users
- Requirements to support existing processes (interface and integration)

Develop WMS strategy for existing DCs:

- What should be done with existing DCs from a WMS perspective
- Pilot site selection

TMS Project Objectives

- *Execution*: Support the management and execution of all freight within the organization.

- *Visibility*: Provide visibility of freight movement to buyers, vendors, carriers, DCs, stores, and transport operations.
- *Optimization*: Optimize freight movement for both inbound (from vendors) and outbound (to stores).
- *Automation*: Remove much of the administrative overhead currently associated with managing transport.
- *Reporting and Monitoring Decision Support*: Provide comprehensive reporting and monitoring capability for tracking operational performance and cost.
- *Decision Making Regarding Product Flows*: Make decisions regarding product flows to support the new NDC/RDC flow through the network.

Replenishment Project Objectives

Key business requirements to be fulfilled by the future replenishment capability are as follows:

- Support store service level requirements while reducing store inventory and out-of-stocks.
- Support delivery flexibility and one-touch initiatives to minimize store labour.
- Standardize processes/systems for store and DC replenishment across all categories.
- Forecast warehouse demand based on aggregated store demand.
- Be responsive to merchandising strategies such as promotions, events, allocations, and seasonality.

Key input for transport planning:

- Support flow-through (cross dock/reverse pick) processes.
- Provide tools to centrally manage service levels and presentation level policies.
- Support alternate sources of supply to provide disaster contingency.
- Provide medium and long-range forecasts to vendors.
- Provide visibility and measurement of replenishment activities.

Network Model Project

A leading Australian retailer executed a network optimization project and came to a conclusion on the number of DCs to be operated. The following are the details of the network model project:

Project Brief

- Determine the location and number of RDC and NDC facilities.

- Arrive at capital costs for proposed DC infrastructure.
- Determine the optimal range configuration and capacity in each facility.
- Determine the annual throughput level guidelines on range in facilities (taking into account flow-through).
- Be available for iterative use in the event that input data becomes more accurate or identified constraint conditions deem it appropriate.
- The model is required to provide multi-period outputs, to be utilized as an ongoing tool as required.

The project delivered the following:

- The expected number, location, and size of the RDCs and NDCs
- The estimated cost of the network
- Insights into 2008 DC network and flows
- A network data set
- Issues for other project teams
- Next steps in the network modelling process

Key Assumptions

- Five product categories: ambient, chilled, frozen, meat and fish, produce
- Management of peaks and range changeovers incorporated into network flows and DC design projects

- All produce, chilled, and meat and fish ranged in RDCs
- All national frozen lines ranged in NDCs
- All local SKUs (including frozen) ranged in RDCs
- Each market area serviced by only one RDC
- RDCs are allocated the fastest to ambient SKUs, some of which will be ranged and some flow-through

Analysis to Date

- 500, 2,000, 3,500, and 5,000 fastest ambient SKUs allocated to RDCs
- RDCs at Sydney, Melbourne, Adelaide, Perth, Brisbane, Devonport, Townsville, Yass, Newcastle, Tamworth, Seymour, and Albury
- NDCs at Sydney, Melbourne, Brisbane, Albury, and Tamworth
- Other sites (Darwin, Overseas or out of Australia, and Perth NDCs) were considered, but low volumes did not warrant a full analysis.
  Note: Town name only to be taken as approximate location
- Costs included: DC operating (picking, flow-through, and cross dock), transport (primary and secondary), and capital costs
- Costs excluded (for now): Inventory, capital costs of XD, capital cost of FT automation, and DC fixed costs

Suggested Optimal Solution Post 2008

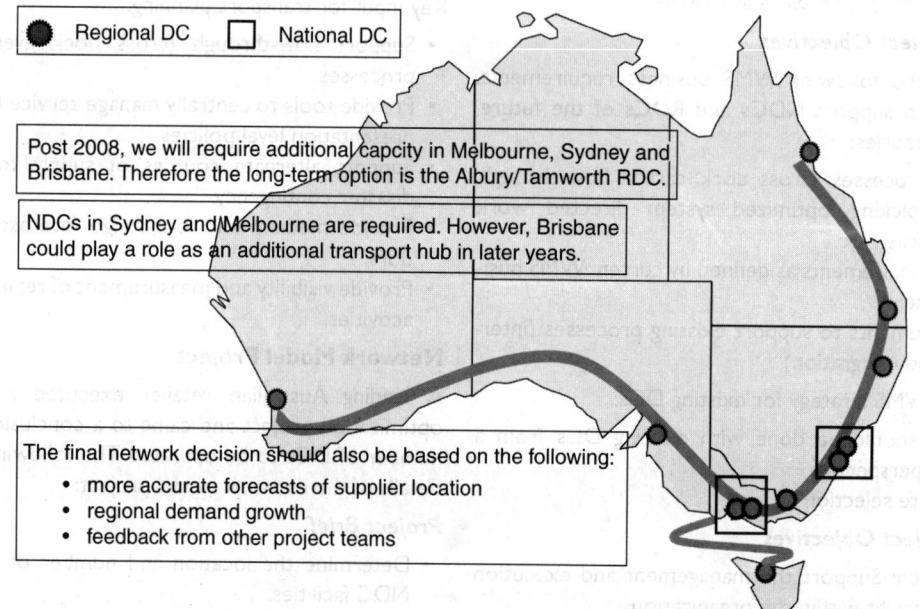

Post 2008, we will require additional capcity in Melbourne, Sydney and Brisbane. Therefore the long-term option is the Albury/Tamworth RDC.

NDCs in Sydney and Melbourne are required. However, Brisbane could play a role as an additional transport hub in later years.

The final network decision should also be based on the following:
- more accurate forecasts of supplier location
- regional demand growth
- feedback from other project teams

2008 and Later Projections

This model offers the flexibility to cater to at least 20% more volume than FY08.

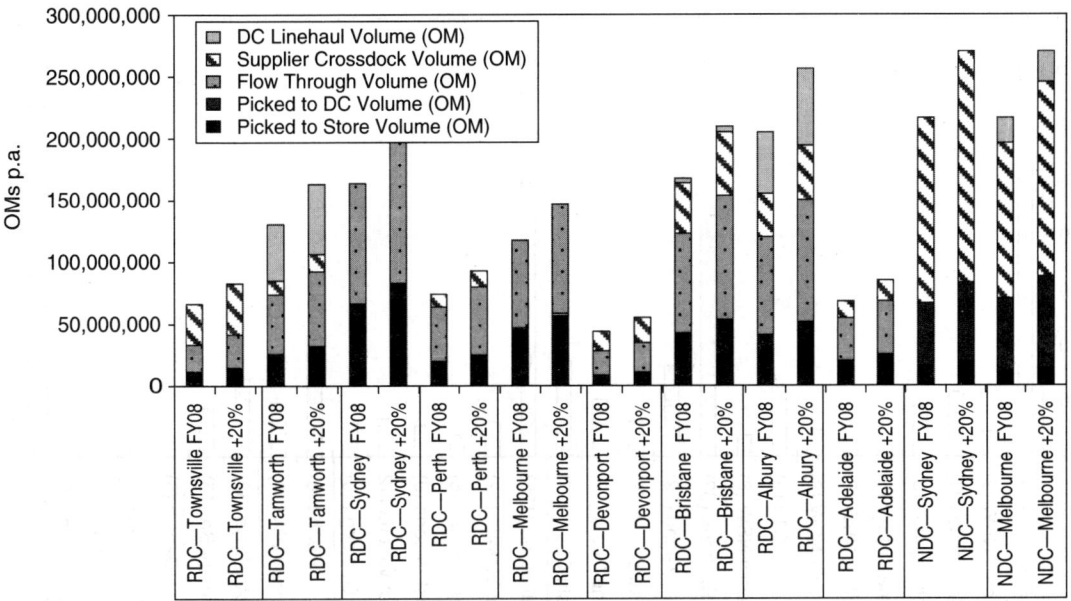

Factors Involved in Developing an Optimal Network

- Where are the suppliers?
- Where is the demand?

Suppliers

Two-thirds of all goods are supplied/made out of Sydney or Melbourne.

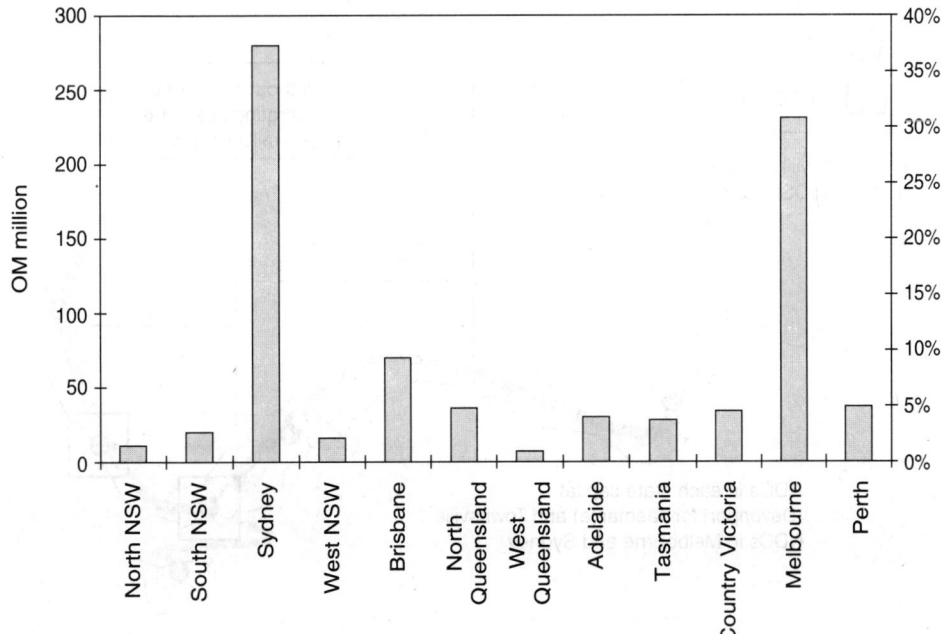

Based on vendor survey of top 50% of each category.

Demand

A third of all demand comes from stores in Sydney and Melbourne.

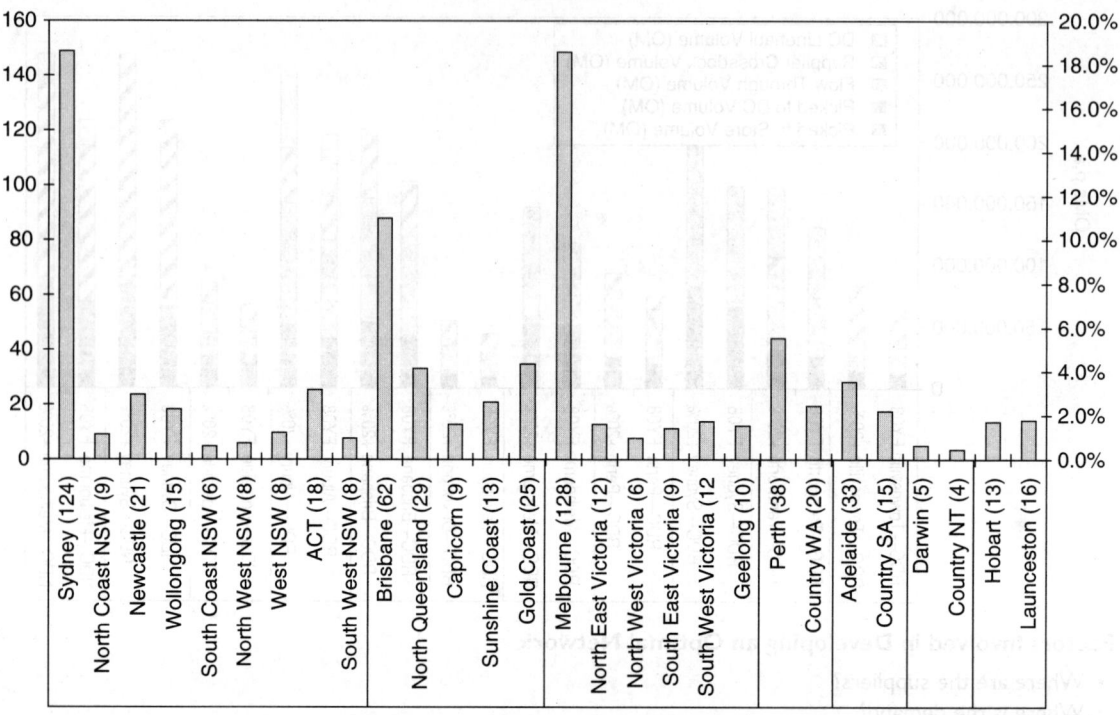

Initial Base Case Network

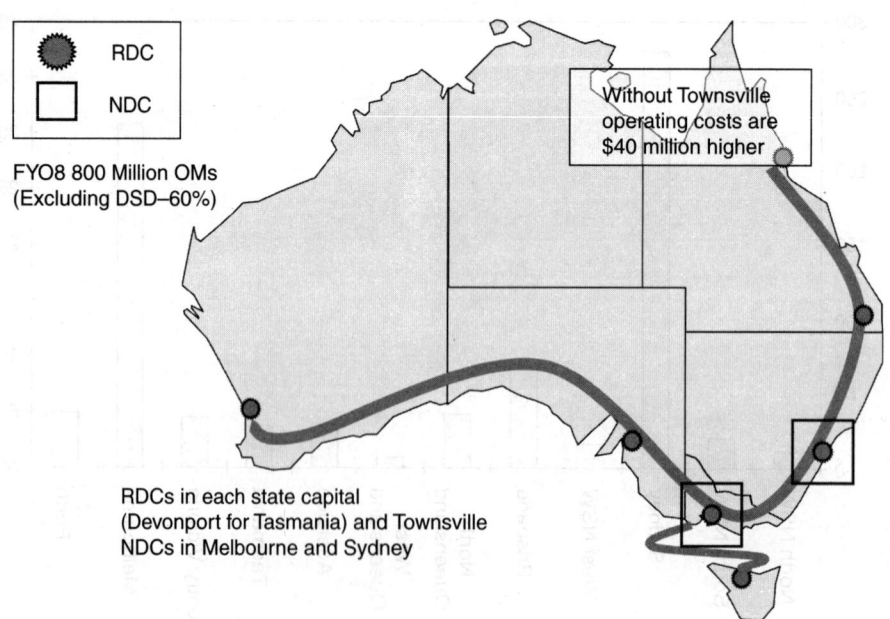

RDC

NDC

FYO8 800 Million OMs
(Excluding DSD–60%)

Without Townsville
operating costs are
$40 million higher

RDCs in each state capital
(Devonport for Tasmania) and Townsville
NDCs in Melbourne and Sydney

Total Costs do not Vary Greatly as RDC Size Varies

Entire supply chain from factory to store

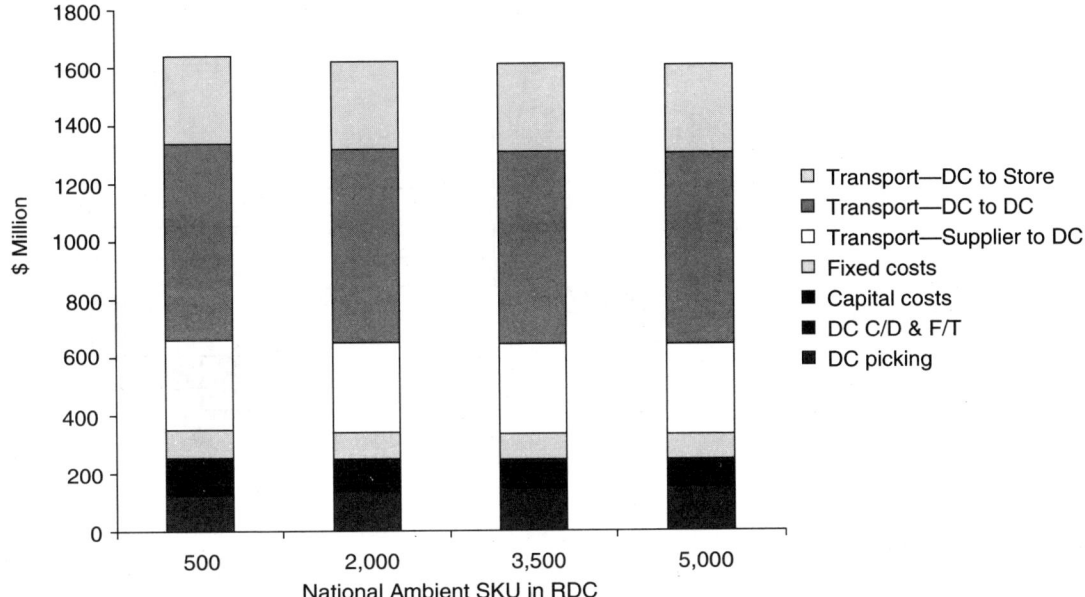

Effect of Changing SKU Allocation on Throughput

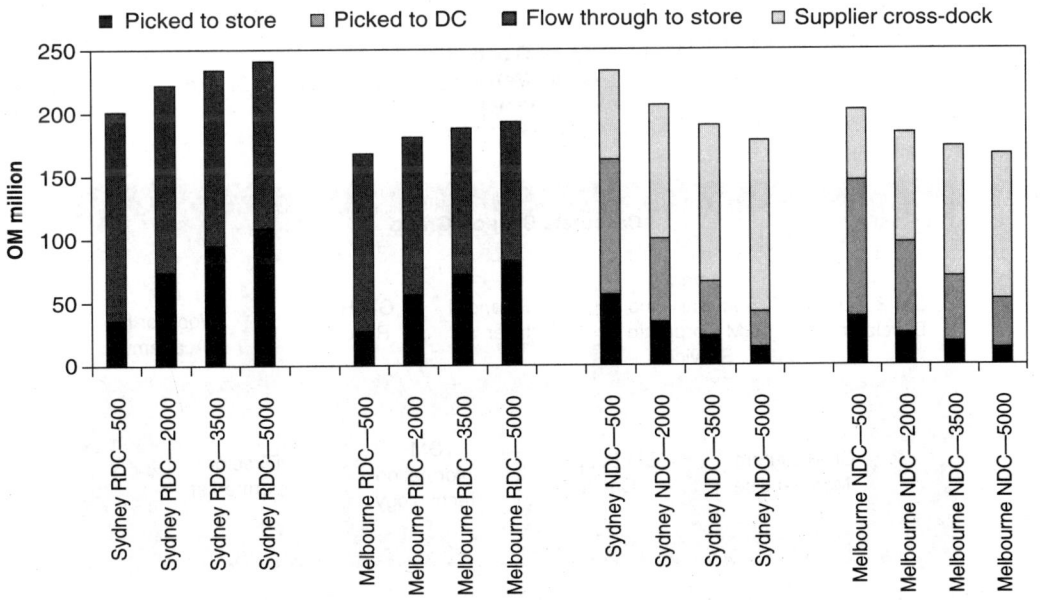

Initial Optimal Network

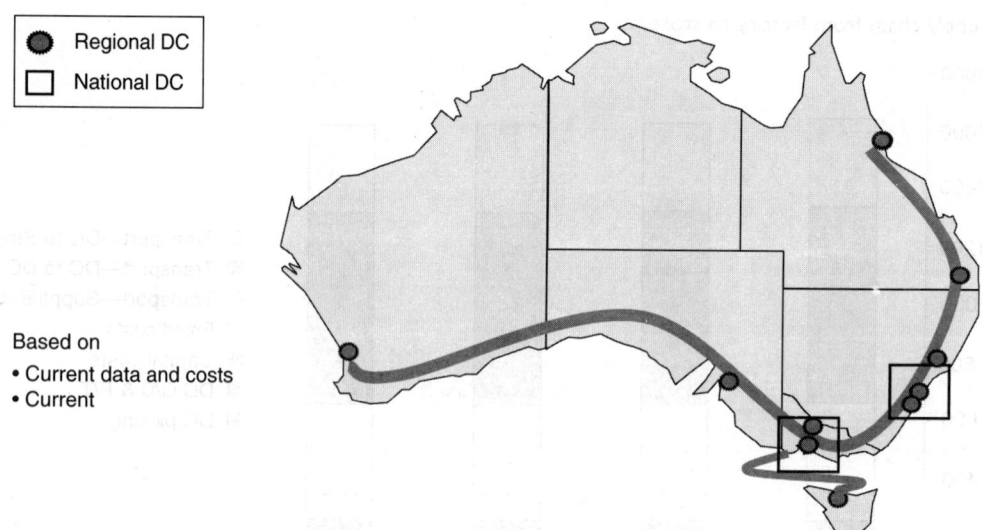

Legend:
- Regional DC
- National DC

Based on
- Current data and costs
- Current

Organizational Structure

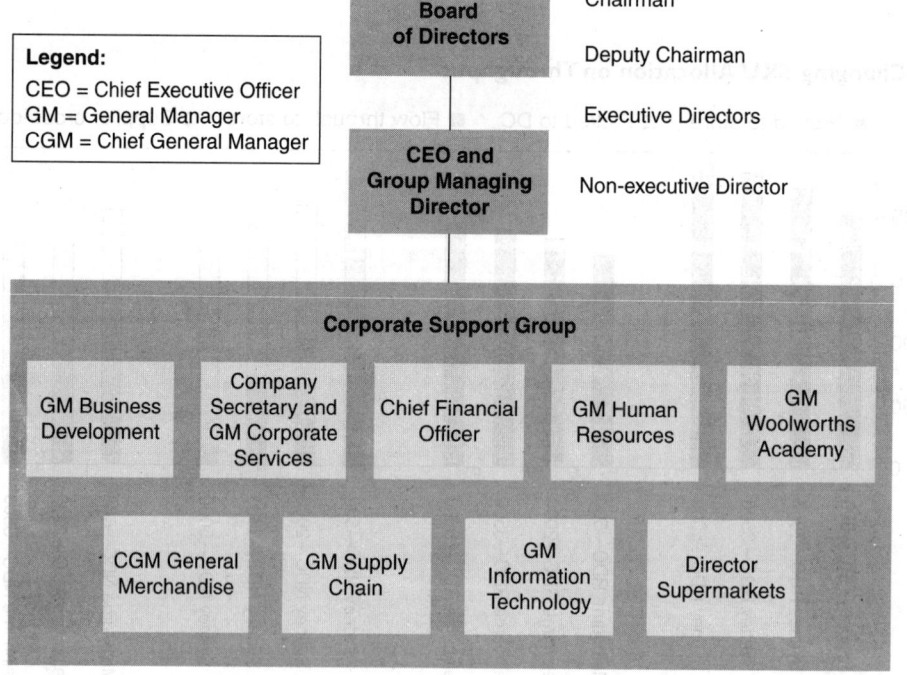

Legend:
CEO = Chief Executive Officer
GM = General Manager
CGM = Chief General Manager

Board of Directors

Chairman

Deputy Chairman

Executive Directors

CEO and Group Managing Director

Non-executive Director

Corporate Support Group

GM Business Development

Company Secretary and GM Corporate Services

Chief Financial Officer

GM Human Resources

GM Woolworths Academy

CGM General Merchandise

GM Supply Chain

GM Information Technology

Director Supermarkets

Larger RDC Organization Structure

Smaller RDC Organization Structure

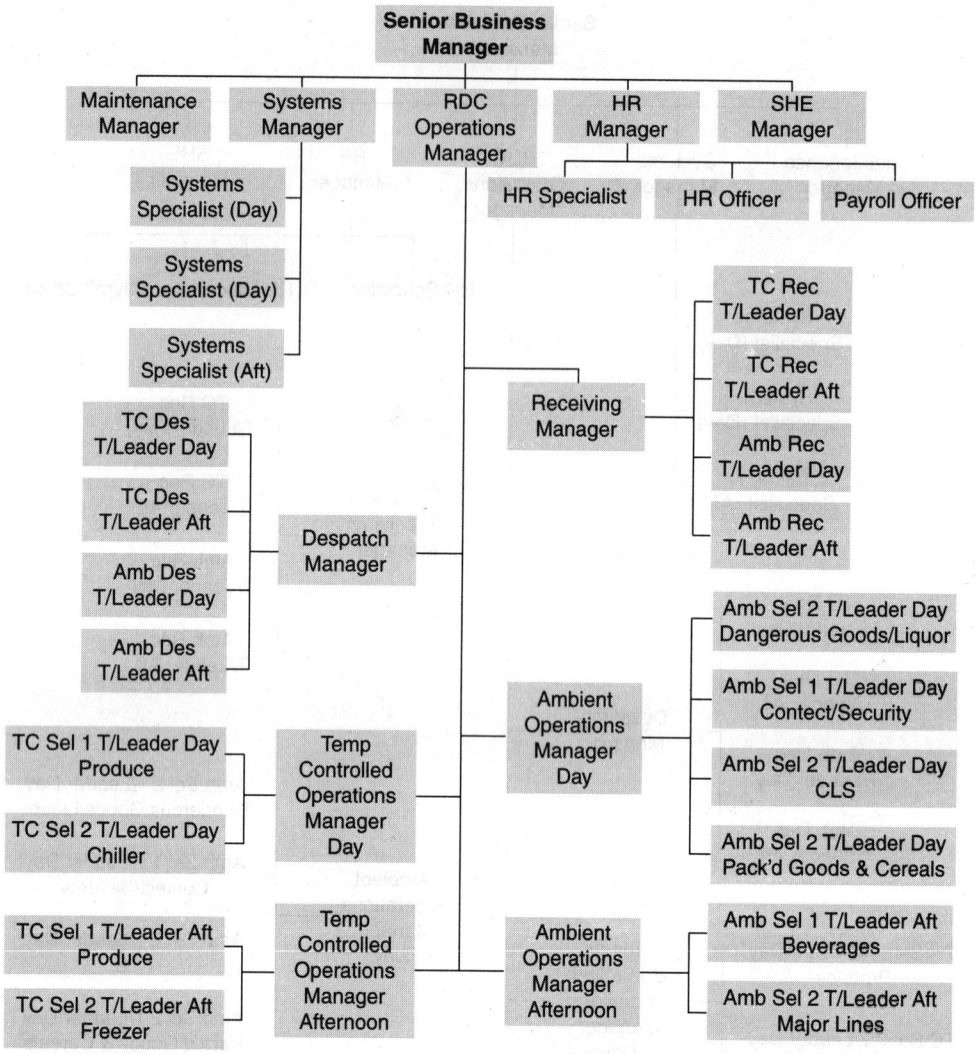

Source: Company data

TABLE CS8.20   Major Events

Year	Events	Location
1924 (5 December)	First store opened: Woolworths Stupendous Bargain Basement	Old Imperial Arcade, Pitt Street, Sydney
1933	Expanded to 23 stores	
1936 (1 April)	Bought eight stores from Edments Ltd	
1955	• 200th store was opened • First supermarket was opened	Civic Center, Canberra Beverly Hills, Sydney
1960	• Acquired Rockmans chain of women's clothing stores • Acquired Flemings supermarket	Sydney

(Contd)

Table CS8.20 (Contd)

Year	Events	Location
1970	First discount department store Big W was opened	
1981	Acquired Dick Smith Electronics consumer electronics chain	
1985	Acquired the Australian stores of the American company, Safeway Inc. (126 stores)	Eastern Australia
1987	Woolworths and Safeway supermarket launched 'The Fresh Food People' campaign	
1989	Acquired by Industrial Equity Limited (IEL)	
1993	Woolworths Limited floated on the Australian Stock Exchange at $2.45 a share	
1996	First Plus Petrol outlet was opened	Dubbo, NSW
1997	First convenience store Metro was opened	Sydney
1998	Internet HomeShop service began	Sydney
1999 (11 August)	First Ezy Banking service to customers was launched	Queensland
1999 (31 August)	Launched Project Refresh to reorganize the business	
2000	Sold Rockmans chain of women's clothing stores	
2000 (11 December)	Acquired Internet grocery retailer GreenGrocer.com.au	
2001 (10 April)	Acquired 224 Tandy Electronics stores from Canada based InterTan Inc	
2001 (4 June)	Purchased 67 of Franklins' 282 supermarket stores from the Hong Kong-based Dairy Farm Group	

Source: http://en.wikipedia.org/wiki/Woolworths_Limited; http://www.answers.com/topic/woolworths-limited?cat=biz-fin; http://www.woolworthslimited.com.au/news/mediareleases/asx_archive.asp

TABLE CS8.21 Retail Brands

Supermarkets			General Merchandise			Wholesale
Food and Groceries	Liquor	Petrol	Discount Stores	Convenience Stores	Consumer Electronics	
Woolworths⁺	Woolworths Liquor⁺	Plus Petrol (in Woolworths, Safeway and Big W)	Big W	Metro	Dick Smith Electronics	Australian Independent Wholesaler (AIW)
Safeway⁺	Safeway Liquor⁺		*Rockmans		Dick Smith Powerhouse	
Food For Less⁺	Dan Murphy's		**Crazy Prices		Tandy Electronics	
Flemings⁺	First Estate		**Woolworths Variety			
Franklins⁺	Mac's Liquor					
	BWS					

⁺ These brands are served by the DCs under examination.
* Sold in 2000. **Sold in 2001.
Source: http://en.wikipedia.org/wiki/Woolworths_Limited; http://www.answers.com/topic/woolworths-limited?cat=biz-fin

TABLE CS8.22   Brand-wise Outlets

Retail Brand	1996 June 23	1997 June 29	1998 June 28	1999 June 27	2000 June 25	2001 June 24
Supermarkets (Food and Groceries)	505	518	542	559	585	604
Woolworths Liquor	–	38	38	42	41	130
Safeway Liquor*						
Dan Murphy's*						
First Estate*						
Mac's Liquor*						
BWS*						
Plus Petrol	–	12	49	98	137	166
Big W	71	78	82	85	87	90
Rockmans	246	252	257	258	–	–
Crazy Prices	74	85	100	116	134	–
Woolworths Variety	1	1	1	1	1	–
Metro*						
Dick Smith Electronics	107	113	115	119	123	138
Dick Smith Powerhouse	–	1	2	4	6	9
Tandy Electronics	–	–	–	–	–	222
Australian Independent Wholesaler*						

* Data not available
Source: http://www.woolworthslimited.com.au/shareholdercentre/financialinformation/annualreports.asp (1997–2001)

TABLE CS8.23   Retail Industry Turnover in Australia

Year	Turnover ($ billion)	Growth (%)
1998	181.0	NA
1999	185.1	2.3
2000	192.9	4.2
2001	196.6	2.0
Forecasts		
2002	202.5	3.0
2003	207.6	2.5
2004	211.9	2.0
2005	217.3	2.5
2006	223.4	2.8
2007	229.8	2.9
2008	235.8	2.6

Source: IBIS Industry Division Report, http://invest.vic.gov.au/NR/rdonlyres/ey7ysvb3esmeunmd2eur7kilsdr74u35dln3hgqve5 cbmq5x4orn3azcf2hplzdbanc6xruwz5qr7b/OverviewofVICRetailind8.pdf

EXHIBIT CS8.4   Woolworths Activities

Supermarkets

At the end of the last financial year, Woolworths had 604 supermarkets distributed around Australia. The distribution of supermarkets is closely aligned with that of the population. This is clearly shown in Chart CS8.1.

Chart CS8.2 shows the growth in store numbers, state by state, over the last five years. New South Wales and Victoria have been the fastest growing states while store numbers in the other states have been relatively static.

Surprisingly, Queensland has not been one of the fastest growing states as might be expected, given the shift in population to that state. However, this may be explained by Woolworths, which had a larger market share in Queensland that any other state apart from Tasmania, had seen almost no increase in store numbers over the period. Refer Chart CS8.3.

During the last fiscal year, an agreement to acquire 67 Franklins supermarkets was entered into.[2] The supermarkets, including refurbishment costs, were to cost $360 million, add an expected $1.5 billion to sales in a full year and be earnings neutral in the current fiscal year. These figures will be a little higher now that the number of supermarkets acquired has increased to 71. All, except six, supermarkets have been delivered and re-opened under Woolworths.

Woolworths also operates a number of smaller supermarkets under the Food for Less banner in New South Wales and Queensland. Some of the smaller Franklins supermarkets are now Food for Less stores. These smaller stores offer mostly non-perishable grocery items and usually include frozen food, dairy, and delicatessen areas. The stores average 1,000 square metres in size and are generally located in secondary or suburban strip shopping centres.

Growth in the retail division will be driven through increasing store numbers and bolt-on acquisitions for both supermarkets and liquor. Under a five year

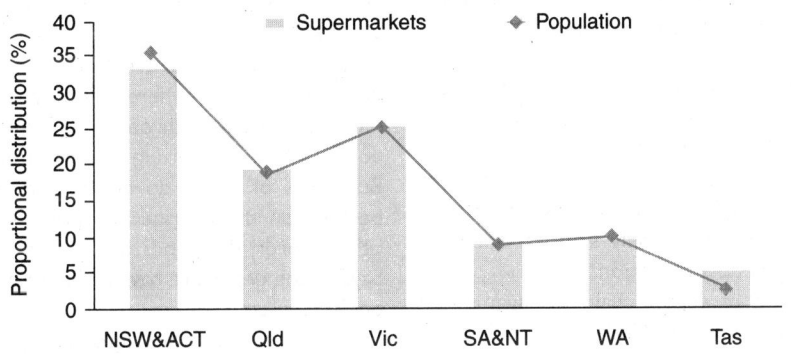

CHART CS8.1   Supermarket and population distribution

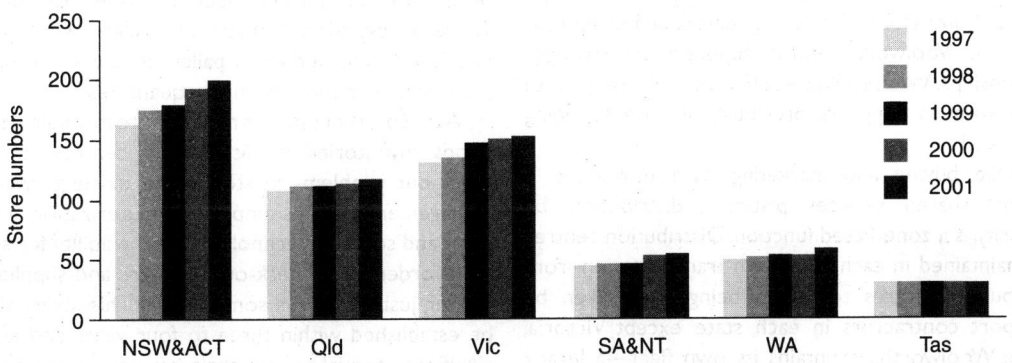

CHART CS8.2   Growth in store numbers by state

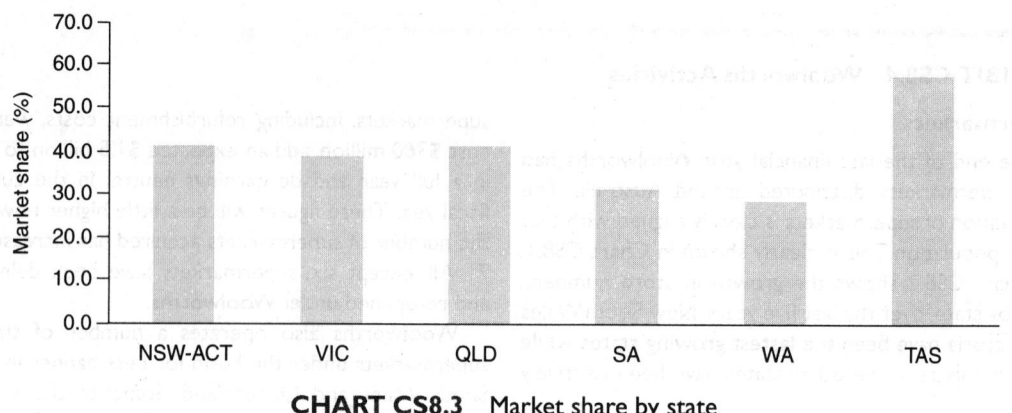

CHART CS8.3   Market share by state

Source: AC Nielson Scan Track, Total Defined Grocery, 28/10/2001

plan supermarket numbers will increase by 15–25 per annum. Some of these will be green field developments while others will come from acquisition of independent operators.

Retail strategy and supply chain management

Woolworths retail strategy can be defined as every day low prices (EDLP). The EDLP strategy is sometimes referred to as the Walmart approach. Walmart is the world's largest and most successful supermarket retailer. EDLP means seeking the best prices from suppliers and maintaining minimum profit margins on every product sold, constantly. It is not 25 per cent off store wide sales, or rotating specials on selected items, and then maintaining higher prices the rest of the time. With EDLP, Woolworths has only specials when the supplier provides the cost reduction.

A critical aspect of supply chain management is relationships with suppliers. Under the old state-based buying function, relationships with suppliers were fragmented and varied. The move to a single, national buying function provided an opportunity for all supplier contracts to be re-negotiated, delivering cost savings to Woolworths and its suppliers, and stronger relationships. Where Woolworths did not always rate highly with its suppliers previously, it rose to being rated No.1.

While buying and marketing have moved to a national shared services platform, distribution, by necessity, is a zone-based function. Distribution centres are maintained in each zone with transportation from distribution centres to stores being undertaken by transport contractors in each state except Victoria, where Woolworths maintains its own fleet—a legacy from Safeway.

Two high velocity distribution centres are operated in NSW and Victoria, these being the Minchinbury and Hume Distribution centres. These centres receive and distribute to Woolworths supermarkets the 4,500 fastest moving grocery items, excluding fresh, chilled, and frozen foods. Minchinbury and Hume service their own stales and some of the needs of Tasmania. This amounts to 180 stores for Hume and more than 200 for Minchinbury.

The distribution centres are hi-tech, fully automated, dedicated facilities where the primary objective is to move the product through the centre as quickly as possible, thus minimizing the investment in inventory. Bulk buys of goods do not go into storage but will be held on the distribution floor as 'cross stock'. In other words, the goods are moved from the arrivals bays to the departure bays within two to three days or preferably less.

Other goods move into a high-rise warehouse, serviced by robotic cranes for storage for periods of three to six weeks, before being moved to the stock picking area prior to distribution to the supermarkets. Cross stock goods remain on pallets while stored goods are removed from pallets in the stock picking area for distribution in smaller quantities.

At the present time it is necessary to maintain sizeable goods inventories in distribution centres to avoid stock-out problems in stores. The existing inventory management systems employ computerization and bar code and scanning technology but the ability for stores to re-order from check-out scanners and suppliers to deliver, just in time, is someway off. This ability should be established within three to four years and lead to significant annual supply chain savings. Lower volume product is processed through separate distribution

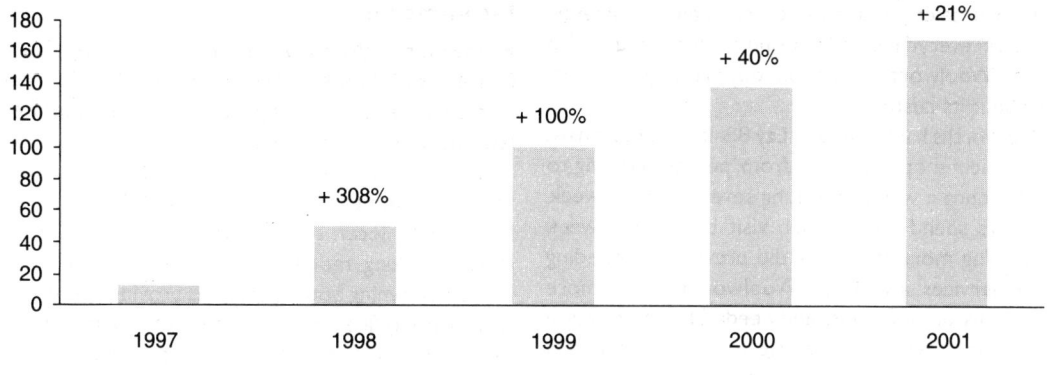

CHART CS8.4   Plus Petrol outlets

centres that are less dependent on technology and more labour intensive. These centres handle 9,000 slower moving items including some general merchandise. There are separate distribution facilities for fruit and vegetable produce, and frozen and chilled foods are handled by P&O Cold Stores.

There is also a national distribution centre at Moorebank in NSW that handles 4,000 lines of general merchandise goods and imported goods for the supermarkets that are not particularly time sensitive.

Plus Petrol

The first Plus Petrol site was opened in Dubbo in 1996. The business has steadily expanded to the point where it generated 4% of the supermarket division's sales but less than 1% of EBIT, last year. Woolworths views the petrol business as an adjunct to its retail offering, creating incremental store sales. Petrol retailing fits with Woolworths' core competency being a high volume, low margin business and, with canopies located adjacent to supermarkets, it allows Woolworths to meet more of its customer' needs in a single location.

The petrol business returned a profit of $4.6 million in fiscal year 2001, before allowing for the cost of the discount given to Woolworths shoppers and the value of incremental sales. While no figures were provided, Woolworths said that incremental sales exceeded the cost of the discount. An independent analysis undertaken by Jebb, Holland, and Dimasi showed that there is a significant incremental sales benefit for stores with adjacent canopies. Moreover, more volume from existing and new outlets will improve the economics of the petrol business.

The number of Plus Petrol outlets rapidly increased, as Chart CS8.4 shows. At the end of fiscal year 2001, Woolworths had 16 petrol outlets and expected to

have 250 by year end. Some of the later growth came from 69 ex-Liberty Oil outlets added to the chain under a lease arrangement. Woolworths has already taken delivery of 35 of the outlets.

Liquor

Woolworths stand-alone liquor business has been much slower to develop. Until fiscal year 2001, the number of stand-alone stores had been constant at around 40 but 90 stores were later added last year to bring the total to 130 by year end. The growth came mostly from a buying spree that saw Woolworths acquire the 13 store Booze Bros chain in South Australia, the 11 store Toohey Bros chain in NSW, and the 45 store Liberty Liquor chain at a cost of $72 million.

The total liquor business has been reorganized under four brands: Dan Murphy, destination outlets; Woolworths Liquor, attached to supermarkets; BWS, neighbourhood stores; and First Estate, fine wine stores. The total business generated sales of more than $1 billion per annum and this increased to as much as $1.5 billion the next year as more stores are added.

One constraint to growing this business was the availability of liquor licences. In Victoria, Woolworths exceeded the cap on the number of licences that can be held. The cap was set at 8% of the licences issued but the legislation was reviewed in 2003.

Woolworths' share of the national liquor market was around 10% compared with Coles Myer's estimated market share of 13%.

Ezy Banking

Ezy Banking, Woolworths banking joint venture with the Commonwealth Bank, is viewed as a separate business from the supermarket group but was implemented to drive traffic through the stores and thus generate incremental sales. It is another example of meeting customers' everyday needs in one location and it also provides Woolworths with an opportunity to learn more about its customers.

Woolworths has found that Ezy Bank customers have changed their shopping habits from, perhaps coming to the store once a week, to visiting several times a week. Customers spend less at each visit but over a week are spending more than they did previously. Providing banking services also helps Woolworths learn more about its customers' habits and needs. This information will become critical in the battle to win and maintain market share in the future

Woolworths runs Ezy Banking under an alliance with the Commonwealth Bank to produce a co-branded product for its customers. Woolworths has no capital risk associated with Ezy Banking. In this respect the model that has been pursued is different from that chosen by other retailers to provide banking services. For example, Tesco in the United Kingdom, is the bank, it holds a banking licence.

At the moment, the Ezy Banking product range extends to a savings and transaction account, a credit card, and rewards scheme. The rewards are vouchers redeemable in the supermarkets and provided by suppliers. The extension of the product range was on the cards, to include insurance and home loans.

In the meantime, in just two years 610,000 accounts have been opened exceeding the five year target of 500,000 accounts.

E-commerce

HomeShop is Woolworths' Internet shopping service. During fiscal 2001 Woolworths acquired a 38% interest in greengocer.com to expand its Internet offering and later moved to 100% ownership.

HomeShop utilizes a store-based model, in other words, customer orders are supplied and delivered from their local store. Greengrocer.com utilizes a central picking model, operating from purpose built facilities. Owning both operations provides Woolworths with back-office synergies and the opportunity to experiment with different operating models.

The capital invested to date is not significant.

Financial performance

The recent financial performance of the whole Supermarket division is presented in a table. Note that EBIT margin is fine as would be expected for this division but return on funds employed is substantial and exceeds that of the other divisions.

The supermarket division enjoyed strong revenue growth in 2000, including the contribution from Plus Petrol (without this, revenue growth would have been only 10%). Sales growth was facilitated by an improved product offering and reduced costs, which also enabled Woolworths to increase market share of ABS measured Food Liquor and Grocery to 25.6% from 24.6%. Project Refresh allowed costs to be reduced by 0.52%, of which 0.38% was passed on to customers and the balance to shareholders.

Recent financial performance—Supermarket division

$ millions	Full Year 27/06/1999	Interim 9/1/2000	Full Year 25/06/2000*#	Interim 7/1/2001	Full Year 24/06/2001
Sales	15,339	8,432	15,724	9,322	17,519
Increase			2.1%	10.6%	11.4%
Contribution on consolidation	84.8%	80.2%	82.8%	80.9%	83.8%
EBIT	515	284	533	317	619
Margin	3.3%	3.4%	3.4%	3.4%	3.5%
Increase		3.6%	11.5%	16.1%	
Contribution on consolidation	95.4%	79.2%	85.7%	79.2%	87.5%
Funds employed	1,443.3	1,322.1	1,295.5	1,080.2	1,312.6
ROFE	35.7%	42.9%	41.1%	58.6%	47.1%
Increase			−10.2%	−18.3%	1.3%
Contribution on consolidation	61.2%	52.1%	67.6%	54.4%	62.2%

* Adjusted for WST # Continuing operations

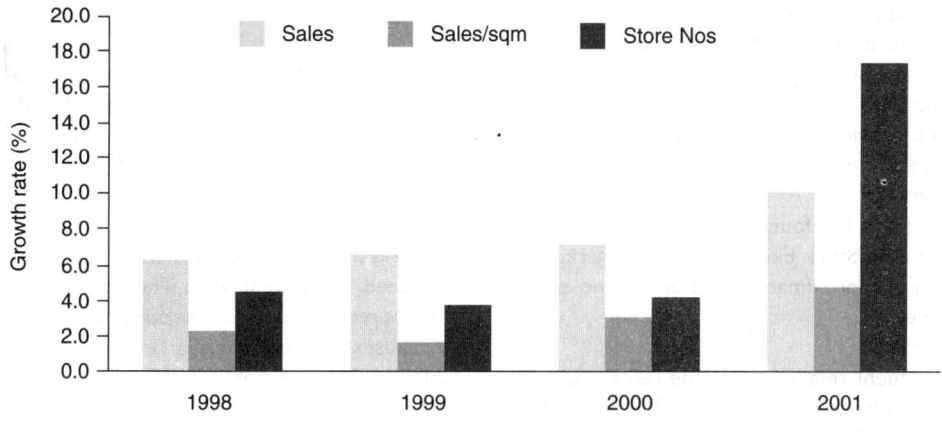

CHART CS8.5 Divisional growth summary

Supermarkets in all states performed strongly with South Australia benefiting from the acquisition of the Booze Bros liquor chain ($12 million), Western Australia from the acquisition of Advantage Supermarkets ($21 million), and Tasmania from the realigning of Roelf Vos and Purity branding with Woolworths.

A five year summary of sales growth for the division (excluding petrol) is presented in Chart CS8.5 along with the key drivers, sales per square metre, and store numbers. Note growth in sales per square metre has been steadily increasing since 1999. This is the result of improving productivity, and in fiscal 2001, the demise of Franklins and vastly increased liquor store numbers, with higher sales per square metre value. These factors all combined to take the growth rate to almost 5% per cent last year.

Major participants and market shares

The industry is dominated by a small number of firms. The two major participants are Woolworths Limited and Coles Myer Limited, then some way behind come Metcash Trading Limited and Foodland Associated Limited, which are wholesalers and distributors to whom independents are aligned under banner groups, and then other independents. The Franklins supermarket group, followed by Kong based Dairy Farm International Holdings Limited, had a similar national presence to Metcash Trading until it exited the industry late in the first half of this year. Its parent Dairy Farm determined that return on investment was insufficient to justify a presence in this industry and its stores were sold off, mainly to Woolworths (71), Coles Myer (20), Foodland (36), and more than 100 to independent grocers aligned with Metcash's IGA distribution group.

Summary details on the other participants are as follows:

- *Coles Myer Limited*

  The Coles and Bi-Lo supermarket chains are subsidiaries of Coles Myer Limited. Coles Myer is Australia's largest private employer with 162,000 employees. Coles Myer has 608 Coles and Bi-Lo supermarkets. The Coles supermarkets are positioned at the 'full service' end of the market and compete directly with Woolworths and Safeway supermarkets, while Bi-Lo is positioned at the 'no-frills' end.

  The supermarket division of Coles Myer also includes liquor retailing through Liquorland and fast food retailing through its Red Rooster stores. Coles Myer is also Australia's largest general merchandiser through its Myer Grace Bros, Kmart, and Target stores.

  Coles Myer has a market capitalization of approximately $9.6 billion.

- *Metcash Trading Limited*

  Metcash is around 75 per cent owned by the South African company, Metro Cash and Carry Limited. Metcash is the successor of the former Davids Limited, and has maintained its position as Australia's largest grocery wholesaler and distributor operating in all states and territories except Western Australia. Metro Cash and Carry acquired its interest in Davids in 1998 following the company's floatation in 1994.

  Metcash's IGA distribution business services more than 1,100 independently owned IGA aligned supermarkets. Employees total 5,220. Market capitalization is approximately $880 million.

• *Foodland Associated Limited*

Foodland is the major distributor and sole independent wholesaler in Western Australia. Apart from the provision of wholesale grocery products, Foodland provides financial incentives and marketing support to FAL franchise and other independent supermarkets.

Foodland is the fourth largest retailer listed on the Australian Stock Exchange. With a market capitalisation of approximately $1.2 billion and employs 15,000 people.

• *Independents*

Independent retailers form the remainder of the sector. The National Association of Retail Grocers of Australia (NARGA) is the main representative body for this group and its figures indicate that there are more than 3,000 independent supermarkets and grocers around Australia.

The independents vary in size from corner stores to full size supermarkets and many operate within the banner groups aligned with the wholesalers, Metcash and Foodland. The number of non-aligned independents is not accurately known but is thought to be around 50 per cent of the total NARGA membership.

The vertically integrated structure of the supermarket operations of Woolworths and Coles Myer provides a number of advantages in purchasing, warehousing, and distribution, and pricing over the independent operators. Centralized buying allows opportunistic purchases of larger volumes than normal before known price increases or as part of joint promotional exercises or pricing campaigns with the producer. This also allows greater scale to coordinate promotional activities and exploit generic advertising advantages.

Centrally coordinated store orders allow larger warehouse pick-up runs enabling efficiencies in distribution to be exploited. Average store orders for independents are much smaller and as a general rule smaller stores are more labour intensive and costly to run. Economies of scale allow larger stores to utilize labour, energy, and floor space more efficiently.

Finally, Woolworths and Coles Myer supermarkets often have the privilege of being anchor tenants in major shopping centres which means they pay substantially less rent per square metre than other tenants and often enjoy more flexible terms and conditions under their lease agreement with the landlord. In addition, prime positions for extended hours trading and high volume customer flows are secured.

With intense competitive pressures such as these, rationalization of the independents will continue. Only larger independents with the capital to refurbish stores and to incorporate the new technologies used by their major competitors are likely to survive. However, unlike metropolitan areas, less competition in rural and regional Australia is likely to protect many smaller independents.

Market share for each of the participants can be measured in different ways. The market share figures are sourced from AC Nielson's ScanTrack service, which uses scanned supermarket sales for Woolworths, Coles Myer, and Franklins, and warehouse withdrawal data for Metcash, Foodland, and other independents.

The product range covered is broad including packaged groceries, dairy, and frozen food but excludes fresh meat and vegetables, delicatessen and bakery goods, milk, and potato chips. The survey also excludes convenience stores, route trade and direct store delivery, about one-third of all grocery categories according to Woolworths.

Source: http://www.ybmarkets.co.uk/downloads/public/11287_0.pdf

References

http://www.answers.com/topic/woolworths-limited?cat=biz-fin

http://www.aph.gov.au/senate/committee/retail_ctte/report/c02.htm

http://www.citypopulation.de/Australia-UC.html

http://en.wikipedia.org/wiki/Woolworths_Limited

http://invest.vic.gov.au/NR/rdonlyres/ey7ysvb3esmeunmd2eur7kilsdr74u35dln3hgqve5cbmq5x4orn3azcf2hplzdbanc6xruwz5qr7b/OverviewofVICRetailind8.pdf

http://www.lonelyplanet.com/mapshells/australasia/australasia/australasia.htm

http://www.myfuture.edu.au/services/default.asp?FunctionID=5104&IndustryGroupID=240

http://www.woolworthslimited.com.au/shareholdercentre/financialinformation/annualreports.asp (1997–2001)

http://www.woolworthslimited.com.au/shareholdercentre/financialinformation/annualreports.asp (1999–2001)

http://www.woolworthslimited.com.au/resources/files/2000financialreport.pdf

http://www.woolworthslimited.com.au/resources/files/2001financialreport.pdf

http://www.woolworthslimited.com/au/resources/full+year+profit+announcement.pdf

http://www.woolworthslimited.com.au/news/media-releases/asx_archive.asp

http://www.woolworths.com.au/Vendors/contact/regions.asp

http://www.ybmarkets.co.uk/downloads/public/11287_0.pdf

http://www.woolworthslimited.com.au/resources/woolies+august+2001.pdf

http://www.woolworthslimited.com.au/resources/files/1999financialreport.pdf

TABLE CS8.24   State-wise Population and Retail Income Distribution

States	Capital	Area (sq. km)	Population ('000)	Population (%)	Retail Income (%)
New South Wales (NSW)	Sydney	801,352	6371.7	33.6	34.2
Victoria (VIC)	Melbourne	227,590	4645.0	24.5	23.8
Queensland (QLD)	Brisbane	1,734,190	3655.1	19.3	19.2
Western Australia (WA)	Perth	2,532,422	1851.3	9.8	9.8
South Australia (SA)	Adelaide	985,324	1467.3	7.7	7.6
Tasmania (TAS)	Hobart	67,914	456.7	2.4	2.2
Australian Capital Territory (ACT)	Canberra	2,349	311.9	1.6	2.2
Northern Territory (NT)	Darwin	1,352,212	210.7	1.1	1.0
Total		**7,703,353**	**18969.6**	**100**	**100**

Source: http://www.citypopulation.de/Australia-UC.html

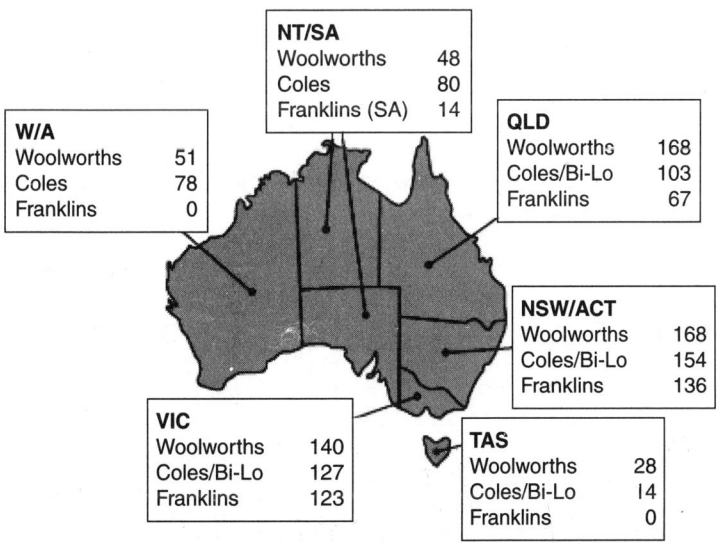

FIG. CS8.4   Major Retailers' Supermarkets in Australia (1998)

Source: Franklins, Submission, pp. 1.2–1.3; http://www.aph.gov.au/senate/committee/retail_ctte/report/c02.htm

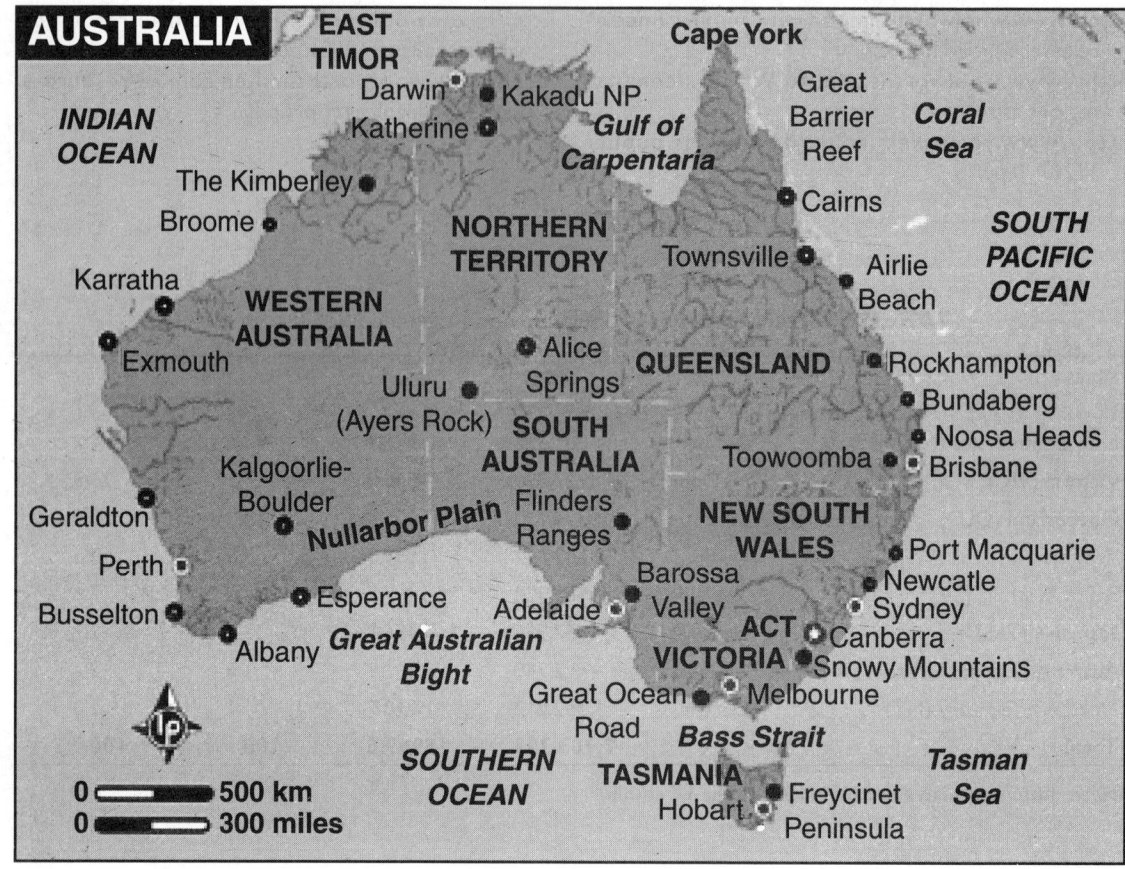

FIG. CS8.5 Map of Australia

Source: http://www.lonelyplanet.com/mapshells/australasia/australasia/australasia.htm

TABLE CS8.25 State-wise Distribution of Supermarkets

States	1997 June 29	1998 June 28	1999 June 27	2000 June 25	2001 June 24
New South Wales (NSW) and Australian Capital Territory (ACT)	162	174	178	192	199
Queensland (QLD)	106	111	111	112	115
Victoria (VIC)	130	133	145	149	151
South Australia (SA) and New Territories (NT)	43	45	45	51	53
Western Australia (WA)	48	50	52	52	57
Tasmania (TAS)	29	29	28	29	29
Total	**518**	**542**	**559**	**585**	**604**

Source: http://www.woolworthslimited.com.au/resouces/files/2001financialreport.pdf

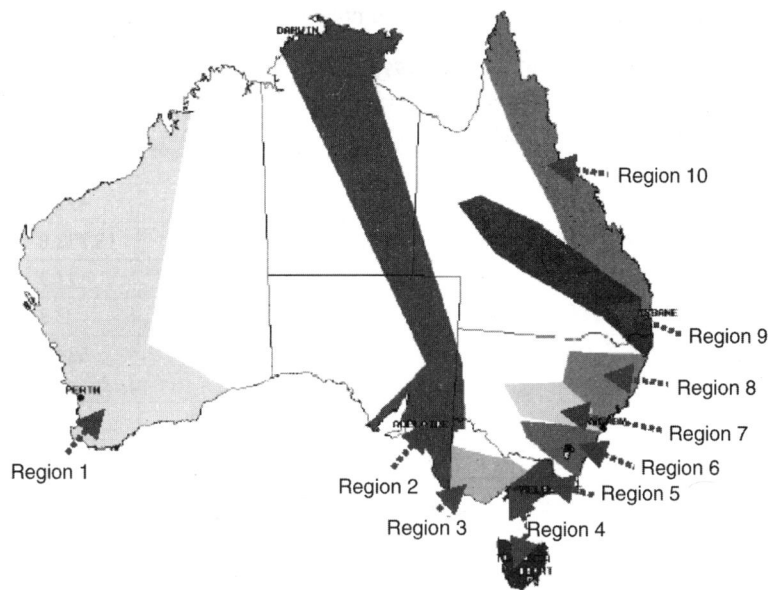

Region 1: WA   Region 2: SA, VIC, NSW, NT, WA   Region 3: VIC   Region 4: VIC, TAS
Region 5: VIC, NSW   Region 6: NSW, ACT   Region 7: NSW   Region 8: NSW
Region 9: QLD, NSW   Region 10: QLD

FIG. CS8.6   Regional Distribution of Supermarkets

Source: http://www.woolworths.com.au/Vendors/contact/regions.asp

EXHIBIT CS8.5   Supermarkets' Product Categories

	Food					Non-food	
Meat	Perishable (Other than meat)	Deli/Bakery	Produce (F&V)	Other Food		Liquor	Petrol
Chilled/Frozen		Ambient					

Source: http://www.woolworthslimited.com.au/shareholdercentre/financialinformation/annualreports.asp

	Purchase within Australia		Share of Australian Produce
	$ million	%	%
Fruits and vegetables (F&V)	1,280	97.5	25.0
Meat	1,140	100.0	14.3
Beef	480		
Lamb	200		
Pork	95		
Chicken	185		
Small goods	177		
Dairy and eggs	627	94.0	9.2

Source: http://www.woolworthslimited.com.au/resources/woolies+august+2001.pdf

TABLE CS8.26   Financial Summary of Supermarkets

		1997 June 29 (53 weeks)	1998 June 28 (52 weeks)	1999 June 27 (52 weeks)	2000 June 25 (52 weeks)	2001 June 24 (52 weeks)
Sales ($ million)	Food, liquor, and groceries	12,583.8	13,374.5	14,247.0	15,251.3	16.772.3
	Petrol	–	–	316.4	472.5	747.1
	Total supermarkets	12,583.8	13,374.5	14,563.4	15,723.8	17,519.4
Cost of doing business (%)		–	–	21.8	21.9	21.4
EBIT to sales (%)		3.1	3.3	3.0	3.3	3.5
EBIT ($ million)	Food, liquor, and groceries	397.6	453.2	451.5	534.0	614.0
	Petrol	–	(3.9)	(2.9)	(1.0)	4.6
	Total supermarkets	397.6	449.3	448.6	533.0	618.0

Source: http://www.woolworthslimited.com.au/resources/files/2001financialreport.pdf

TABLE CS8.27   Five-year Analysis

	2001 52 weeks	2000 52 weeks	1999 52 weeks	1998 52 weeks	1997 53 weeks
Profit and loss					
Sales[1] ($m)					
Food, liquor, and groceries	16,772.3	15,251.3	14,247.0	13,374.5	12,583.8
Petrol	747.1	472.5	316.4	–	–
Total supermarkets	17,519.4	15,723.8	14,563.4	13,374.5	12,583.8
BIG W	2,069.8	1,913.9	1,788.0	1,644.5	1,516.8
Consumer electronics	418.0	338.2	298.6	241.9	223.1
General merchandise	2,487.8	2,252.1	2,086.6	1,886.4	1,739.9
Wholesale	697.8	675.3	520.7	388.8	151.5
Total trading operations	**20,705.0**	**18,651.2**	**17,170.7**	**15,649.7**	**14,475.2**
Discontinued operations[2]	210.1	337.6	356.6	351.4	324.5
Total group	**20,915.1**	**18,988.8**	**17,527.3**	**16,001.1**	**14,799.7**
EDIT[3] ($m)					
Food, liquor, and groceries	614.0	534.0	451.5	453.2	397.6
Petrol	4.6	(1.0)	(2.9)	(3.9)	
Total supermarkets[4]	618.6	533.0	448.6	449.3	397.6
BIG W	83.4	74.3	62.2	56.2	48.0
Consumer electronics	30.8	26.0	20.8	15.7	14.6
General merchandise	114.2	100.3	83.0	71.9	62.6
Wholesale	5.0	2.9	(2.1)	(9.7)	(4.2)
Total trading operations	**737.8**	**636.2**	**529.5**	**511.5**	**456.0**

(Contd)

Table CS8.27 (Contd)

	2001 52 weeks	2000 52 weeks	1999 52 weeks	1998 52 weeks	1997 53 weeks
Net property income	33.1	24.8	33.0	22.3	15.1
Head office overheads	(59.0)	(50.2)	(40.5)	(33.9)	(45.1)
Total unallocated[5]	(25.9)	(25.4)	(7.5)	(11.6)	(30.0)
Continuing operations	711.9	610.8	522.0	499.9	426.0
Discontinued operations	(5.3)	10.8	17.4	16.3	23.0
Total group	**706.6**	**621.6**	**539.4**	**516.2**	**449.0**
EDIT to sales (%)					
Supermarkets	3.53	3.39	3.08	3.36	3.16
General merchandise	4.59	4.45	3.98	3.81	3.60
Wholesale	0.72	0.43	(0.40)	(2.49)	(2.77)
Total	3.38	3.27	3.08	3.23	3.03
Profit and loss ($m)					
Sales	20,915.1	18,988.8	17,527.3	16,001.1	14,799.8
Cost of goods sold	15,561.0	13,983.4	12,790.3	11,710.4	10,856.4
Gross profit	5,354.1	5,005.4	4,737.0	4,290.7	3,943.4
Gross profit margin	25.60%	26.36%	27.03%	26.82%	26.64%
Branch and administration expenses	(3,737.7)	(3,548.3)	(3,400.0)	(3,072.4)	(2,866.4)
(excluding rent, depreciation, and amortisation)	17.87%	18.69%	19.40%	19.20%	19.37%
Ebitdar	1,616.4	1,457.1	1,337.0	1,218.3	1,076.9
Ebitdar margin	7.73%	7.67%	7.63%	7.61%	7.28%
Rent	(600.0)	(546.7)	(527.7)	(479.4)	(442.1)
EBITDA	1,016.4	910.4	809.3	738.9	634.8
Depreciation	(300.7)	(282.8)	(265.0)	(219.9)	(184.1)
Amortization of goodwill	(9.1)	(6.0)	(4.9)	(2.81)	(1.7)
EBIT	706.6	621.6	539.4	516.2	449.0
Interest	(13.1)	(27.8)	(45.5)	(42.8)	(41.2)
WINS distribution	(47.7)	(26.1)	–	–	–
Net profit before tax	645.8	567.7	493.9	473.4	407.8
Taxation	(217.4)	(203.6)	(181.3)	(172.7)	(149.5)
Normal net profit after tax	428.4	364.1	312.6	300.7	258.3
Adjustment for change in company tax rate	–	(8.4)	–	–	–
Abnormal items after tax	–	(60.1)	(55.3)	(21.1)	–
Outside equity interests	(0.4)	(0.1)	(0.3)	(0.2)	(0.3)
Operating net profit attributable to the members of Woolworths Limited after WINS	428.0	295.5	257.0	279.4	258.0

(Contd)

Table CS8.27 (Contd)

	2001 52 weeks	2000 52 weeks	1999 52 weeks	1998 52 weeks	1997 53 weeks
Balance sheet ($m)					
Fund, employed					
Inventory	1,731.8	1,648.3	1,652.6	1,562.4	1,488.3
Accounts payable	(1,666.4)	(1,571.8)	(1,281.1)	(1,202.7)	(1,101.1)
Net investment in inventory	65.4	76.5	371.5	359.7	387.2
Other assets	320.0	443.5	424.7	342.6	301.6
Other creditors	(855.5)	(798.8)	(653.1)	(536.8)	(485.2)
Fix assets	2,587.7	2,194.1	2,216.3	1,890.2	1,589.3
Total funds employed[6]	2,117.6	1,915.3	2,359.4	2,055.7	1,792.9
Net tax balances	(49.0)	(64.4)	(28.3)	(52.6)	(85.0)
Provision for dividend	(155.41	(137.8)	(115.2)	(102.6)	(101.1)
Net assets employed	1,913.2	1,713.1	2,215.9	1,900.5	1,606.8
Net debt[7]	(387.6)	(82.2)	(731.3)	(527.9)	(381.1)
Total equity	**1,525.6**	**1,630.9**	**1,484.6**	**1,372.6**	**1,225.7**
Woolworths income notes	(583.0)	(583.0)	–	–	–
Outside equity interest	(3.7)	(3.3)	(3.2)	(2.9)	(2.5)
Shareholders funds	**938.9**	**1,044.6**	**1,481.4**	**1,369.7**	**1,223.2**
Cash flow ($m)					
EBITDA	1,016.4	910.4	809.3	738.9	634.8
Movement in net investment in inventory	34.6	276.1	4.6	28.3	52.5
Other operating cash flows	8.7	56.7	(11.5)	(22.3)	59.8
Net Interest paid	(25.0)	(33.6)	(53.7)	(42.8)	(41.1)
Tax paid	(225.7)	(142.7)	(174.7)	(193.1)	(46.2)
Operating cash flow	809.0	1,066.9	574.0	509.0	659.8
Gross capital expenditure	(537.4)	(420.8)	(764.9)	(685.0)	(699.4)
Proceeds on disposal	173.1	111.0	145.7	157.7	129.2
Other investing cash flows	(185.0)	16.8	(32.0)	3.2	(19.6)
Free cash flow	259.7	773.9	(77.2)	(15.1)	70.0
Movement in gross debt	211.5	(519.8)	290.9	221.0	53.2
Woolworths' income notes	–	583.0	–	–	–
WINS distribution	(47.7)	(24.7)	–	–	–
Dividends paid	(212.1)	(173.5)	(154.1)	(153.3)	(96.1)
Share buybacks	(349.4)	(548.4)	–	–	–
New shares issued	44.0	26.9	22.7	23.3	12.3
Net cash flow	(94.0)	117.4	82.3	75.9	39.4

(Contd)

Table CS8.27 (Contd)

	2001 52 weeks	2000 52 weeks	1999 52 weeks	1998 52 weeks	1997 53 weeks
Shareholder value					
ROFE[8] (Pre-tax return on funds employed)					
Before abnormals	35.04	29.08	24.43	26.83	26.33
After abnormals	35.04	24.69	20.52	25.11	26.33
DuPont analysis (abnormals excluded)					
EBIT to sales	3.38	3.27	3.08	3.23	3.03
Debt burden[9]	91.40	91.33	91.56	91.71	90.83
Tax burden[10]	66.34	64.14	63.29	63.52	63.34
Asset turn[11]	4.23	3.99	3.99	4.18	4.44
Financial leverage[12]	4.99	3.77	3.08	2.94	2.82
Return on investment[13]	43.19	28.92	21.88	23.15	21.88
Earnings per share					
Ordinary share price closing	10.85	6.18	5.0	5.28	4.31
Market capitalization ($m)	11,235.20	6,550.8	5,764.2	6,019.2	4,842.5
Weighted average shares on issue	1,065.8	1,125.0	1,146.2	1,132.4	1,109.4
Normal basic EPS	40.16	32.36	27.25	26.54	23.26
Total basic EPS[14]	40.16	26.27	22.42	24.67	23.26
EPS pre goodwill amortization	41.01	32.89	27.67	26.78	23.41
Interim dividend	12.0	10.0	8.0	8.0	8.0
Final dividend	15.0	13.0	10.0	9.0	8.0
Total dividend	27.0	23.0	18.0	17.0	16.0
Payout ratio (before abnormals) %	66.37	66.88	66.28	64.34	69.53
Payout ratio (after abnormals) %	66.37	82.40	80.63	69.26	69.53
Price/earnings ratio (times)	27.0	23.5	22.3	21.4	18.5
Price/cash flow ratio (times)	14.28	6.50	10.00	11.70	73.00
Growth rates (% increase)					
Sales	10.14	8.34	9.54	8.12	11.34
Sales per equivalent week	10.14	8.34	9.54	10.20	9.23
Same store sales	6.31	4.74	3.99	4.28	4.39
Sales per square metre	6.22	4.39	1.81	3.61	1.58
EBITDA	11.63	12.49	9.53	16.40	15.38
EBIT	14.04	15.24	4.49	14.97	14.60
NPBT	13.76	14.94	4.33	16.09	13.09
NPAT	44.84	14.98	(8.02)	8.29	10.45
Normal EPS	24.12	18.75	2.68	14.10	6.60

(Contd)

Table CS8.27 (Contd)

	2001 52 weeks	2000 52 weeks	1999 52 weeks	1998 52 weeks	1997 53 weeks
Financial strength					
Interest cover ratio	11.62	11.53	11.85	12.06	10.90
Fixed charges cover	2.40	2.40	2.30	2.30	2.19
Sales to inventory[15]	12.38	11.51	10.90	10.49	10.34
Gross capital expenditure to EBITDA (%)	52.88	46.22	94.52	92.71	110.17
Operating cash flow per share	0.76	0.95	0.50	0.45	0.59
Gearing[16] (%)	20.26	4.80	33.01	27.80	23.72
Current assets to current liabilities (%)	80.71	90.37	109.85	110.81	106.43
Total liabilities to net tangible assets[17]	71.90	64.88	67.86	65.20	64.53
Productivity					
Stores (number)					
Supermarkets					
NSW and ACT	199	192	178	174	162
Queensland	115	112	111	111	106
Victoria	151	149	145	133	130
South Australia and Northern Territory	53	51	45	45	43
Western Australia	57	52	52	50	48
Tasmania	29	29	28	29	29
Total supermarkets	604	585	559	542	518
Freestanding liquor	130	41	42	38	38
Plus Petrol	166	137	98	49	12
General merchandise					
BIG W	90	87	85	82	78
Dick Smith Electronics	138	123	119	115	113
Powerhouse	9	6	4	2	1
Tandy	222	–	–	–	–
Crazy Prices	–	135	117	101	86
Rockmans	–	–	258	257	252
Total	**1,359**	**1,114**	**1,282**	**1,186**	**1,098**

(Contd)

Table CS8.27 (Contd)

Stores (movement)	June 00	Opened/acquired	Closed/sold	June 01
Supermarkets				
New South Wales	192	10	3	199
Queensland	112	3	-	115
Victoria	149	5	3	151
South Australia and Northern Territory	51	3	1	53
Western Australia	52	5	–	57
Tasmania	29	1	1	29
Total supermarkets movements	585	27	8	604
Freestanding liquor	41	90	1	130
Plus Petrol	137	29	–	166
General merchandise				
Big W	87	3	–	90
Crazy Prices/Variety	135	9	144	0
Dick Smith Electronics	123	15	–	138
Dick Smith PowerHouse	6	3	–	9
Tandy	–	223	1	222
Total store movements	1,114	399	154	1,359

	2001 52 weeks	2000 52 weeks	1999 52 weeks	1996 52 weeks	1997 53 weeks
Area (sqm)					
Supermarkets	1,317,840	1,254,744	1,206,202	1,149,431	1,105.518
General merchandise	602,718	614,515	619,333	589,029	552,645
Total	1,920,558	1,869,259	1,825,535	1,738,460	1,658,163
Sales per square metre					
Supermarkets (excluding petrol)	12,727.1	12,154.9	11,811.5	11,635.8	11,382.7
General merchandise	4,127.6	3,664.8	3,369.1	3,202.6	3,148.3
Total	10,028.4	9,363.8	8,947.3	8,778.4	8,638.3

Notes to statistics
1. Sales for prior periods have been restated to exclude WST.
2. Discontinued operations includes Chisholm Manufacturing and Crazy Prices sold in 2001 and Rockman sold in 2000.
3. EBIT for the periods 1998 to 2000 are as previously reported, i.e., excluding individually significant non-recurring items (previously described as abnormal items).
4. Supermarket EBIT for prior periods has been restated to reflect IT costs previously reported as unallocated.

5. Unallocated expense represents corporate costs relating to the Woolworths group as a whole, and profits derived by the group's corporate property division including the disposal of development properties. These amounts are not identifiable against any particular operating segment and accordingly they remain unallocated, as required by Accounting Standard AASB 1005.
6. Funds employed is net assets excluding net tax balances, provision for dividends and net debt.
7. Net debt is gross debt less cash on hand, cash at bank and cash on short term deposit.
8. Return on Funds Employed (ROFE) is EBIT as a percentage of average funds employed for the year.
9. Debt burden is net operating profit before income tax expressed as a percentage of EBIT before abnormal items.
10. Tax burden is normal profit after income tax expressed as a percentage of normal profit before income tax.
11. Asset turn is total sales divided by average total assets for the year.
12. Financial leverage is average total assets divided by average shareholders funds for the year.
13. Return on investment is net profit after income tax, divided by average shareholders funds for the year.
14. Total basic earnings per share is net profit after income tax attributable to Members of the Company after WINS distribution, divided into the weighted average number of ordinary shares on issue during the year. The weighted average number of ordinary shares on issue has been calculated in accordance with Accounting Standard AASB 1027. Fully diluted EPS is not significantly different from basic EPS.
15. Sales to inventory is total sales for the period divided by average inventory.
16. Gearing is net repayable debt divided by net repayable debt plus total equity.
17. Total liabilities exclude deferred income tax liability and provision for dividend and includes outside equity interests.

Source: http://www.woolworthslimited.com.au/resources/files2001financialreport.pdf

EXHIBIT CS8.6   DC Network

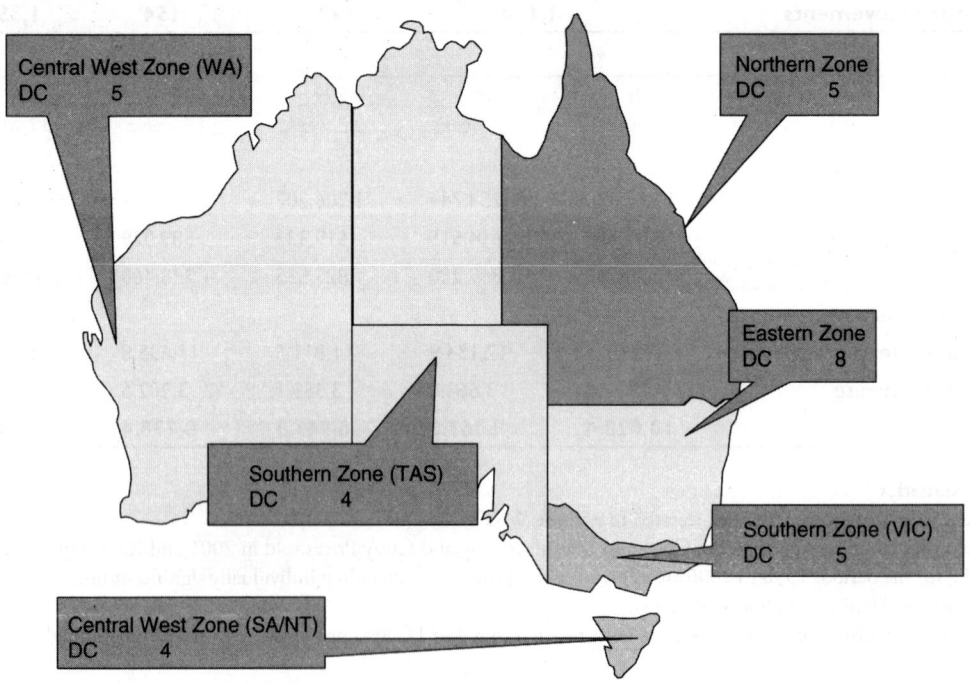

Central West Zone (WA)
DC   5

Northern Zone
DC   5

Eastern Zone
DC   8

Southern Zone (TAS)
DC   4

Southern Zone (VIC)
DC   5

Central West Zone (SA/NT)
DC   4

Source: Company data

(Contd)

Exhibit CS8.6 (Contd)

Location	Zone	Type			Total
		Ambient	Produce	Chilled/Frozen	
Perth (WA)	Central West	3	I	I	5
Adelaide (SA)	Central West	I	I	2	4
Melbourne (VIC)	South	3	I	I	5
Devonport (TAS)	South	2	I	I	4
Sydney (NSW)	East	5	2	I	8
Brisbane (QLD)	North	3	(I)*	I	5
Townsville (QLD)	North		I		I
Total		**17**	**7 (8)**	**7**	**31 (32)**

* Under consideration
Source: Company data

TABLE CS8.28 DC Locations

DC	State	Name	Location	Type
1899	NSW	Moorebank DC	Moorebank	Produce
1904	NSW	Helles Avenue DC	Moorebank	Ambient
1944	NSW	Yennora	Yennora	Ambient
1979	NSW	Sydney RDC—Ambient	Minchinbury	Ambient
1905	NSW	Hume AIW—Liquor	Alexandria	Ambient
1911	NSW	Aiw Warwick Farm	Warwick Farm	Ambient
1947	NSW	Sydney RDC—Fresh	Minchinbury	Produce
1910	NSW	Versacold Arndell Prk Sfd DC	Arndell Park	3rd Party
2899	QLD	Everton Park DC	Everton Park	Ambient
2920	QLD	Acacia Ridge DC	Acacia Ridge	Ambient
2908	QLD	Beenleigh Road DC	Acacia Ridge	Ambient
2953	QLD	Versacold Satellite Warehouse	Murarrie	3rd Party
2919	QLD	Townsville Produce DC	Bohle Townsville	Produce
3902	VIC	Hume DC	Broadmeadows	Ambient
3919	VIC	Mulgrave Produce DC	Mulgrave	Produce
3989	VIC	Clayton DC	Clayton	Ambient
3911	VIC	Melbourne NDC	Noble Park	Ambient
3908	VIC	Versacold Laverton DC	Laverton North	3rd Party
5903	SA	Gepps Cross Produce DC	Epps Cross	Produce
5910	SA	Adelaide RDC—Ambient	Gepps Cross	Ambient
5911	SA	Adelaide RDC—Liquor	Gepps Cross	Ambient
5918	SA	Croydon DC	Ridleyton	Chilled
4899	WA	Miles Road DC	Kewdale	Ambient

(Contd)

Table CS8.28 (Contd)

DC	State	Name	Location	Type
4901	WA	Miles Road DC	Kewdale	Ambient
4905	WA	Perth Produce DC	Perth Airport	Produce
4916	WA	Bunbury DC	Boyanup Road	Ambient
4903	WA	Versacold Spearwood RDC—Freezer	Spearwood	3rd Party
7180	TAS	Derwent Park DC	Derwent Park	Chilled
7380	TAS	Breadalbane DC—SIW	Breadalbane	Ambient
7385	TAS	Prospect DC—SIW	Prospect	Ambient
7191	TAS	Devonport Produce DC	East Devonport	Produce

All 3rd party were for chilled.
Source: Company data

EXHIBIT CS8.7 Proposed DC Network

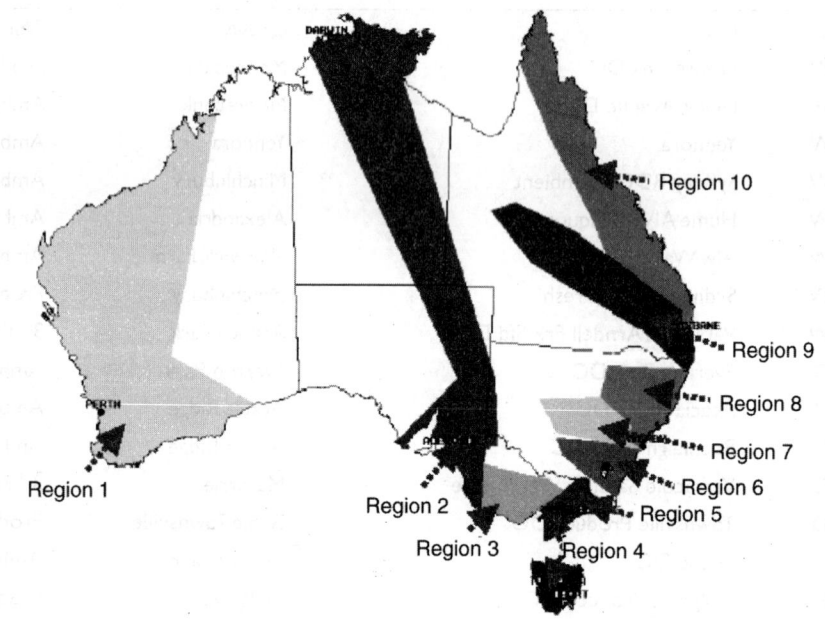

Region 1: WA	Region 2: SA, VIC, NSW, NT, WA	Region 3: VIC	Region 4: VIC, TAS
Region 5: VIC, NSW	Region 6: NSW, ACT	Region 7: NSW	Region 8: NSW
Region 9: QLD, NSW	Region 10: QLD		

Source: Company data

(Contd)

Exhibit CS8.7 (Contd)

Location of Proposed DCs

States	Cities	NDC/RDC
Queensland	Brisbane, Townsville	RDC, RDC
New South Wales	Sydney, Wyong	NDC/RDC, RDC
Victoria	Melbourne, Wodonga	NDC/RDC, RDC
Tasmania	Devonport	RDC
South Australia	Adelaide	RDC
Western Australia	Perth	RDC

Source: Company data

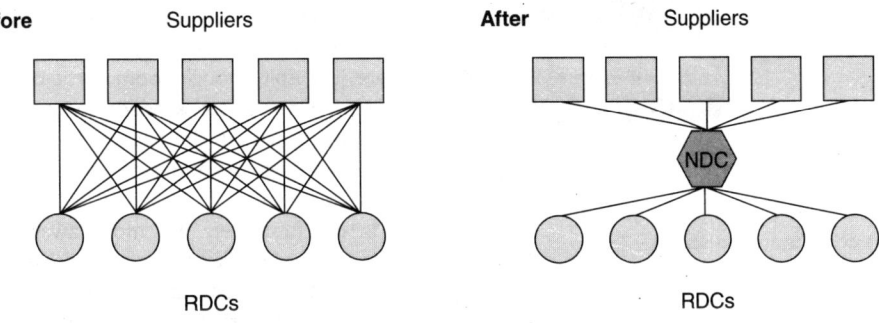

FIG. CS8.7 NDC and RDC Structure

Source: Company data

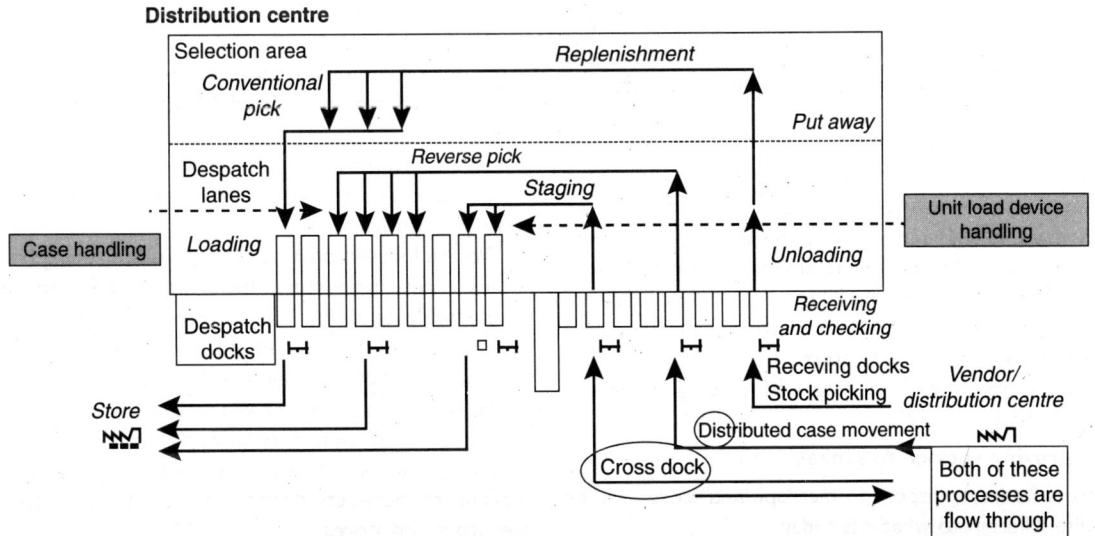

FIG. CS8.8 Flow Through

Source: Company data

EXHIBIT CS8.8 Supply Chain Transport

Making it easier to receive deliveries and clear the backdocks

We've come a long way—a delivery being unloaded in 1956.

In the Supply Chain Division we manage the transport of stock across the supply chain, from vendors to distribution centres and to stores.

Our transport operations are managed in several different ways. For example, in Victoria and Hobart, we own and manage our own transport operations. In other areas, we have commercial arrangements in place with external transport companies to deliver products from our distribution centres to stores.

It all amounts to a massive transport operation. In fact, the combined size of the fleet we use to service our 700 supermarkets is one of the largest in Australia. The size of the transport task provides us with the opportunity to improve efficiencies in many areas.

We are constantly working towards improving our transport operations to ensure that we provide the best possible service to our customers, the stores. One of the ways we are doing this is by taking on this responsibility for the management of our transport, By taking on this responsibility we able to coordinate how our transport operations are run and therefore provide better service to stores.

Here are some of the things we are doing to improve our transport service.

Improving service to stores

In the future, transport to metropolitan stores will be quite different to what it is today.

At present, supermarkets typically receive large loads of product from our distribution centres for each department. For example, on any given day, metropolitan supermarkets may receive deliveries from up to six trucks a day. On average, one of these trucks will carry a load of fresh produce, one will carry chilled and frozen items, three will carry load of dry groceries and one will carry a load of general merchandise.

As many of you well know, disseminating stock into the store is not always easy because sometimes there just isn't enough room for it on the shop floor which means the stock needs to be stored on top of the capping area, in the backdock or in the coolroom. Delivering large quantities of one type of product adds to this problem.

In the future we will move away from delivering large loads of similar product to delivering the various products to the stores as and which they need it. We will do this by using trucks that can carry composite loads. A composite load is a mixture of product categories on the one truck. Smaller quantities of products from different categories will come off the truck on Roll Cages and then be put straight out on display, ready for purchase by the customer. This means there will be less stock in the backdock.

To enable composite loads, future trucks will have trailers which can transport different products on the same loads. Trailers will have separate areas for produce, chilled and frozen items, and dry grocery and general merchandise. We will be trailing composite loads soon in South Australia.

We are focused on assisting stores in keeping back rooms as clear as possible through the timely removal of returnable items like Roll Cages, pallets, and bins. The returnable items are loaded onto empty trucks leaving the store. This not only helps reduce the clutter in back rooms but is a much better way of utilizing our trucks.

We are also working hard towards improving on time delivery to stores through improved communication procedures between distribution centres, transport operators, and stores.

Focusing on safe operations

We only do business with reputable companies who value safety as highly as we do and who have similar safety standards. The transport companies we do business with must have

- drivers who are skilled and take part in regular training
- high quality equipment that is well maintained

- responsible driving programs including fatigue management programs
- environmental policies and standards, such as vehicle disc brakes to cut down noise levels and low emissions form tucks with modern refrigeration units.

Source: http://www.woolworthslimited.com.au/resources/woolies+august+2001.pdf

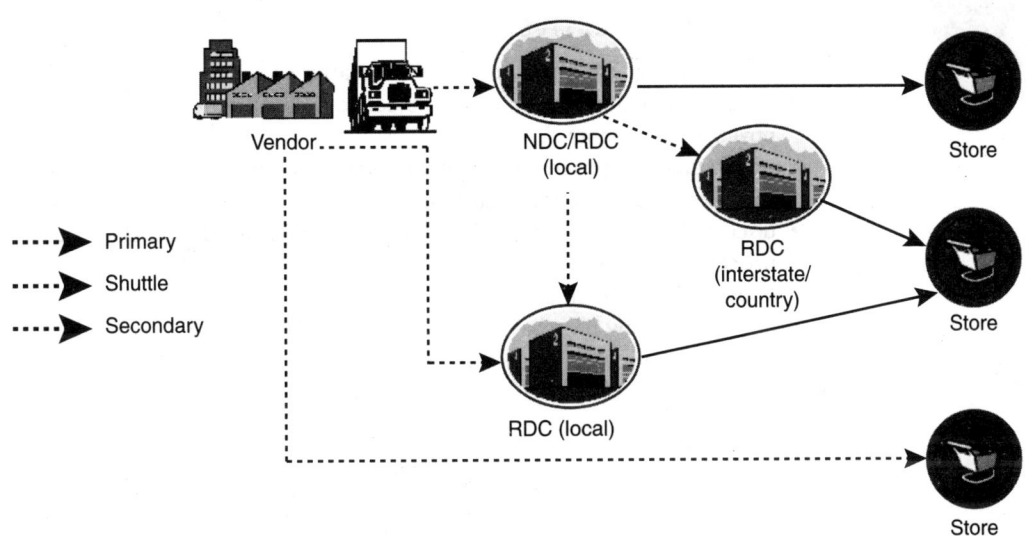

FIG. CS8.9 Transport Network

Source: Company data

Questions

1. Did Project Refresh meet its desired objectives to leverage the supply chain initiatives?
2. Should Michael Luscombe consolidate the DCs to a smaller number and elaborate the areas he needs to concentrate, if he goes with the decision?
3. What are the key areas of improvement in the operations of a DC?
4. How far would the BPO service provider help Luscombe in restructuring the distribution network and consolidating the position of the company?

9 Retail Buying

LEARNING OBJECTIVES

After studying this chapter, you will be able to
- develop an understanding of the objectives and role of retailers' purchase/buying departments
- understand the process of organizational buying and look at retail buying as a special case of organizational buying
- discuss the relevant models of retailer buying behaviour and chalk out the process of buying
- know how to become a good buyer
- understand how merchandise plans and assortment plans are developed
- discuss the advantages of retail buying groups

INTRODUCTION

The main function of the purchase department of a retailer is to obtain the maximum possible value from the money spent by the retailer in procuring merchandise. The purchase department is responsible for supporting the retail operations with a satisfactory flow of materials in congruence with the retailer's positioning based on a given set of operating and market conditions. It is also responsible for combining the various elements of material quality and cost, supplier know-how, cooperation, and service. This has to be carried out in an environment where the market and operating principles change with time. This poses a challenge for purchase and supply management.

OBJECTIVES OF BUYING

The objectives of buying can be viewed from three levels—(i) from a general managerial level, (ii) from a more specific functional or operational level, and (iii) from a detailed level at which the precise strategic buying plans are formulated.[1]

From a top managerial perspective, the objectives of the purchase department include the five 'rights'—acquisition of the right quality, from the right supplier, in the right quantity, at the right time, and at the right price. A sixth factor, which is part of these objectives, is the desired services necessary for optimal supply and utilization of materials. From an operating or functional level, eight basic objectives are identified—(i) to support company operations with an uninterrupted flow of materials and services, (ii) to buy competitively, (iii) to buy wisely, (iv) to keep inventory investment and investment losses at a practical minimum, (v) to develop effective and reliable sources of supply, (vi) to develop good relationships with the supplier community and continuing relationships with active suppliers, (vii) to achieve maximum integration with other departments of the firm, and (viii) to handle the buying function proactively and in a cost-effective manner. The purchase department formulates policies which serve as general guidelines to channel their actions towards the attainment of desired objectives. The purchase and supply policies establish the ground rules for the department's relationship with other departments, and inform the buying personnel about the expected conduct of department activities.

ORGANIZATIONAL BUYING

Webster and Wind (1972) defined *organizational buying* as the decision-making process by which formal organizations establish the need for purchased products and services and identify, evaluate, and choose among alternative brands and suppliers.[2] The *business market* consists of all organizations that acquire goods and services used in the production of other goods or services that are sold, rented, or supplied to others. Compared to consumer markets, business markets generally have fewer and larger buyers, a close customer relationship, and more geographically concentrated buyers. Demand in the business market is derived from the demand in the consumer market and fluctuates with the business cycle.

The decision-making unit of a buying organization is called the buying centre. It comprises all those individuals and groups who participate in the buying decision-making process, who share some common goals and risks arising from the decisions.[3] The buying centre consists of initiators, users, influencers, deciders, approvers, buyers, and gatekeepers. These parties are affected by environmental, organizational, interpersonal, and individual factors in arriving at a buying decision. The environmental factors include the level of demand for the product, the overall economic outlook, the rate of technological change, political and regulatory developments, competitive pressures, and social responsibility. The buyer keeps in mind the organization's objectives, policies, procedures, organization structures and systems, and trends towards buying. At the interpersonal level, the buying centre includes participants with different interests, authority status, empathy, and persuasiveness. The buying department seeks to derive high value from fewer and better suppliers, which may involve global sourcing and partnering.

RETAILER BUYING BEHAVIOUR

Retail chains have become gatekeepers to consumer markets.[4] Without the retailers accepting products, it is difficult for producers to market them. In many markets, retailers have grown large and powerful, leading to the elimination of wholesalers. Wholesalers' functions have been shifted either forward or backward in the channel. Many retailers buy products directly from the producers. Even in markets where the retail industry is still evolving and the structure has not yet changed, the stagnation of markets is forcing manufacturers to focus on the point of sale. Therefore, knowledge about retailer buying behaviour has become important for producers while developing their marketing strategies. Retailers are more like consumers in what they buy and more like producers in how they buy the merchandise. A number of factors justify the treatment of retailer buying as a special case of organizational buying:

1. Retailers buy primarily finished products but sell more than just the products. They add value through activities such as delivering a good shopping experience.[5]

2. The retail buyer is responsible for not only controlling costs but also generating revenue.[6]
3. In industrial buying, the decision is often influenced by users or merchandisers/buyers. In retail buying, the decision is influenced by marketing, logistics, and merchandising.[7]
4. Retailers are members of different retail buying associations, which may limit the number of suppliers to choose from.[8]
5. In retailing, the adoption of one's own labels has resulted in the retail buyer becoming more and more involved in product development, sales forecasting, and market analysis.[9]
6. Developments in information technology have given the retailer decision-making tools that differ from those of industrial buyers.[10]

Models of Buying Behaviour

Several attempts have been made to conceptualize retailer buying behaviour.[11] Sheth (1973) has proposed one of the most commonly used models, as depicted in Fig. 9.1. The merchandise requirements are the buying motives and criteria used by retailers to evaluate different product offerings. These are influenced by inter- and intra-organizational factors. *Inter-organizational factors* include retailer size, type, location, and management mentality. *Intra-organizational factors* encompass the requirements of the retailer, which differ for every product that is bought. These factors are the type of merchandise, product positioning, and regulatory constraints. The merchandise requirements of the retailer influence its choice calculus. The construct of *choice calculus* captures the retailers' decision rules, such as trade-off, dominant, or sequential choice calculus. The choice calculus is also influenced by the accessibility of suppliers. *Supplier accessibility* depends on the competitive structure of the supply industry, the corporate image of the supplier, and its relative marketing effort. The competitive structure of the supply industry could limit the number of suppliers available to retailers, especially when the suppliers follow an exclusive

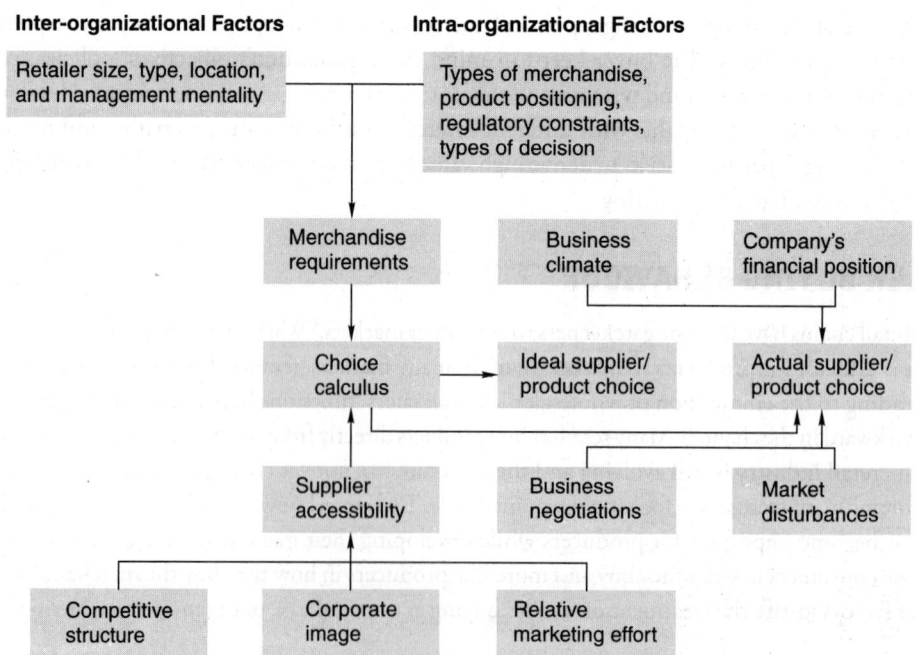

FIG. 9.1   Sheth's Model of Retailer Buyer Behaviour

distribution policy. The image of the supplier influences its accessibility. For example, manufacturers from certain countries may be preferred by retailers because of their positive image.

The concept of the *ideal supplier/product choice* refers to the supplier/product choice that would be the outcome of a rational and formal decision-making process that is influenced by the retailer's merchandise requirements and the accessibility of suppliers. However, these factors together may not always help the retailer to reach a decision as there are several other intervening factors that influence the *actual supplier/product choice*. The negotiations between the manufacturer and the retailers are important for establishing the terms of trade. Market disturbance that includes unexpected events also come in the way of buying decisions. The buying decision is also influenced by the business climate. This construct refers to macroeconomic trends and events concerning the retailer. The retailers' financial position is also a major factor affecting the buying decision.

The process described in Sheth's model is generic and applies to almost all situations. However, with time, there have been changes in the retail scenario, and new factors have been found to be influencing retailers' buying behaviour. As depicted in Fig. 9.2, some of these factors are electronic data interface (EDI), buyer associations, and the changing face of shoppers.[12] These have resulted in differences in the way information is being processed and used for developing buying strategies and plans.

BECOMING A BUYER

Buying has come to occupy a very critical role in retailing as customers seek increased value from retailers in terms of merchandise and price. The emergence of price formats such as discounters, category killers, and supercentres has brought buyers to the forefront of the retail business. Most large retailers have adopted buying structures that involve centralized replenishment and allocation. This has given better bargaining power to the store. It also relieves the store managers from the task of replenishment and allocation, and enables them to focus better on the store. For procurement, they only need to raise an indent and take receipt of the merchandise.

The centralized buying system has also led to the physical separation of functions. Buyers need not be located in the store. On the downside, this implies that buyers no longer rely heavily on one-to-one communication with the customers. With the point of sale data being available to the buyers online, this separation is accentuated. Thus, when the merchandise does not perform well, store managers accuse buyers for not buying well and buyers blame store managers for not selling the merchandise well.

Responsibilities of Buyers

Retail buyers are the essential link between the suppliers and the 'goods inward' functions and the customers and the 'goods outward' functions. Retail buying is one of the most challenging jobs in the retail business. The task has become even more complex as retailers have grown in size and geographical coverage. They have also expanded their product ranges to include a larger proportion of imported merchandise. Most of the tasks of buying are now being handled by specialist persons or agencies, bringing in a supervisory focus to the role of buyers. The various specialist departments that buyers need to interact with, in the order of importance, are merchandising, marketing, product management, physical distribution, retail/store operations, inventory management, packaging/design, technologists, market research/analysis, finance/accounts, advertising, space allocation/planning, and promotions/ publicity, board/top management, corporate planning, and personnel/training.[13] The proportions of

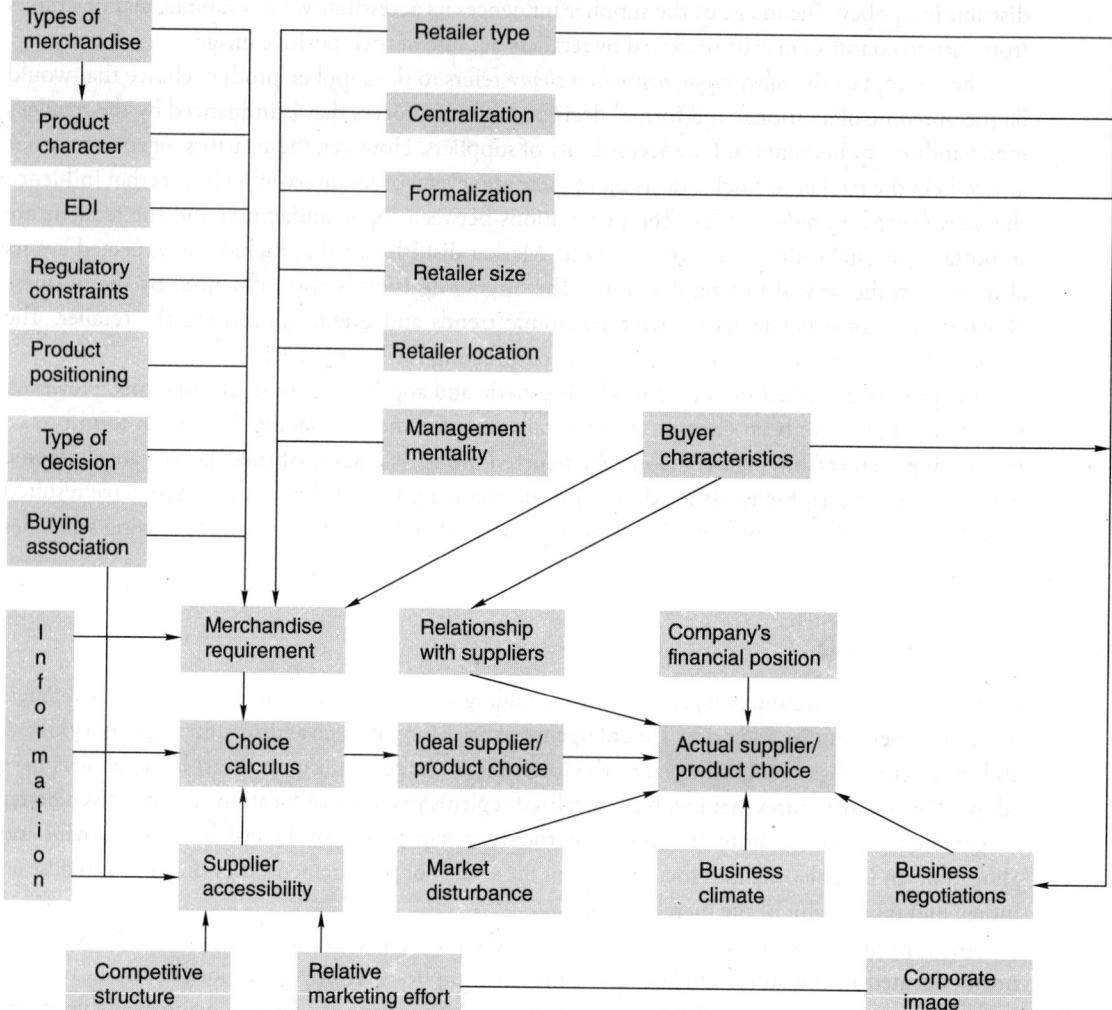

FIG. 9.2 Revised Theory of Merchandise Buying Behaviour

private brands in the store, which vary from 100 per cent in fashion stores to 20 per cent in other stores, provide additional responsibilities. These include negotiating the best deal for off-the-shelf products and managing the fluctuating demand due to markdowns or unsatisfied demands.

Buyers also need to be concerned about ethical and environmental issues in procuring merchandise.[14] This becomes more important as retailers source their merchandise globally. Some retailers, who source from emerging economies, have already implemented a policy of sourcing from only those vendors who provide adequate pay and conditions to their employees. Buyers, therefore, perform several tasks on their own or in association with other departments. These tasks can be broadly classified into three groups: (i) selection, feasibility, and monitoring of merchandise, (ii) selection and appraisal of suppliers and negotiations with them, and (iii) pricing-related decisions of merchandise. Table 9.1 depicts the responsibilities of the retail buying department and the extent to which these responsibilities are shared with other departments, as expressed by the buyers.[15]

TABLE 9.1   Responsibilities of Retail Buyers

Responsibilities (Figures in Percentages)	Buyers' Sole Responsibility	Shared Responsibility	Not Buyers' Responsibility
Proposing which product areas are to be carried	72	19	9
Deciding which product areas are to be carried	44	43	13
Selecting products within a product area	86	14	0
Product design	19	67	14
Specifying product formulations	18	67	16
Assessing the feasibility of products	58	40	2
Specifying product packaging	19	73	8
Quality control	13	62	25
New product launches	41	57	2
Monitoring product performance	60	40	0
Monitoring stock availability	32	55	13
Allocating stock to stores	33	25	42
Physical distribution	7	19	74
Liaising with stores	36	61	3
Space allocation and planning	7	64	29
In-store display	6	60	34
Direct product profitability	55	31	15
Selecting suppliers	86	13	1
Supplier appraisal	71	28	1
Negotiating with suppliers	89	11	0
Progress-chasing with suppliers	58	36	6
Replenishment buying/repeat orders	31	34	35
Market monitoring	34	58	8
Identifying market gaps	48	48	4
Sales forecasting	47	45	8
Initiating sales promotional activity	53	42	5
Implementing sales promotional activity	29	50	21
Initiating advertising activity	19	53	28
Implementing advertising activity	5	36	60
Pricing	82	18	0
Authorizing markdowns	45	34	21
Budgeting for market purchasing	50	36	14
Strategic planning	7	40	53
Training junior buyers	50	44	7

Desirable Characteristics

A buyer needs to be a good negotiator while being sensitive to the demands of both the suppliers and the store managers. Communication skills are very important in this profession. Some desirable personal qualities in an effective buyer are enthusiasm, education, analytical excellence, ability to articulate, product knowledge, objective reasoning, dedication, leadership, appearance, and flexibility.[16] The real power of the buyer comes from the knowledge of customers' purchase patterns and the ability to translate these into finding the most suitable source of merchandise to address these requirements. Buyers are evaluated mainly on the basis of sales turnover, profits, and their ability to meet targets[17] (Table 9.2).

TABLE 9.2   Main Criteria on Which Buyers are Appraised

	Total Sample (%)
Sales turnover	51
Profit—unspecified	44
Meeting set targets/achieving budget	33
% Margin	17
Gross profit	14
Increasing profit	11
Managing/motivating staff	8
Successful new product development	6
Training staff	6
Quality (control)	5
No waste/unnecessary markdowns	5
Stockturn	3
Market share	2
Terms negotiated	2
Creativity/flair	2
Promotional activity	2
Other activity	14

Buying is an acquired skill. Good buyers need to be ruthless, with clear goals in terms of store profitability. An effective buyer would need to have a combination of characteristics in the right mix. Figure 9.3 shows the research data from a study conducted on the importance given to buyer characteristics by the participants of a study conducted among buyers at retail organizations. The study indicated that negotiation skills (42%), market awareness (35%), communication skills (26%), and commercial taste (24%) are the four most important characteristics a successful buyer would possess.

MERCHANDISE AND ASSORTMENT PLANS

Retailers develop two types of plans. The *merchandise plan* is a forecast of specific merchandise purchased and its value, typically for a period of six months or a year.[18] A sample six-month merchandising plan is provided in Table 9.4 (see 'preparation of sales plan'). The buying calendar followed by Benetton is

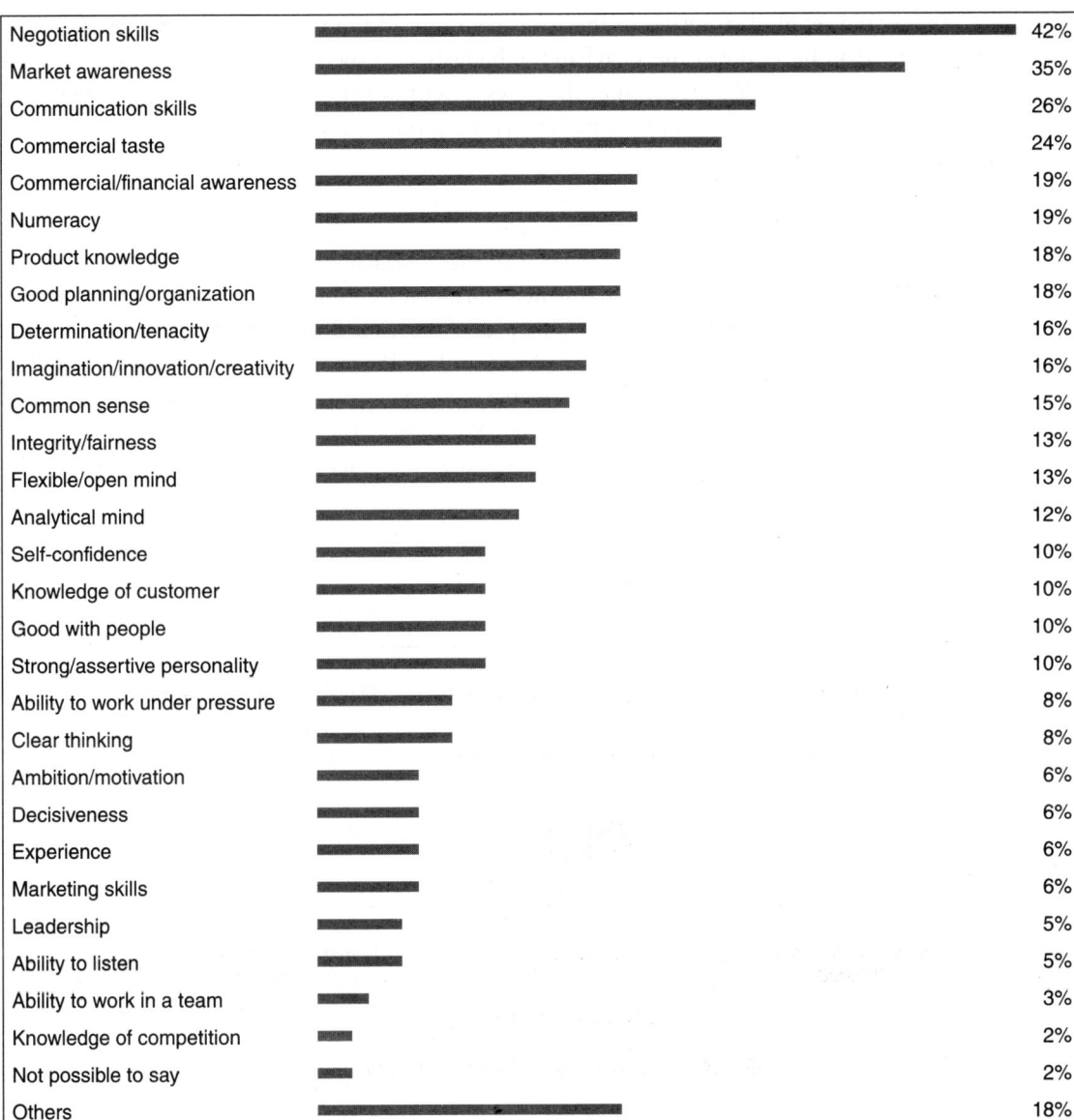

Negotiation skills	42%
Market awareness	35%
Communication skills	26%
Commercial taste	24%
Commercial/financial awareness	19%
Numeracy	19%
Product knowledge	18%
Good planning/organization	18%
Determination/tenacity	16%
Imagination/innovation/creativity	16%
Common sense	15%
Integrity/fairness	13%
Flexible/open mind	13%
Analytical mind	12%
Self-confidence	10%
Knowledge of customer	10%
Good with people	10%
Strong/assertive personality	10%
Ability to work under pressure	8%
Clear thinking	8%
Ambition/motivation	6%
Decisiveness	6%
Experience	6%
Marketing skills	6%
Leadership	5%
Ability to listen	5%
Ability to work in a team	3%
Knowledge of competition	2%
Not possible to say	2%
Others	18%

FIG. 9.3 Important Characteristics of a Retail Buyer

depicted in Annexure 9.1. The key purpose of the merchandise plan is to provide an estimate of the amount of capital required to be invested in inventory for a specified period. This can then be translated into cash flow estimates for the store manager. The plan helps achieve increased turnover, reduced amount of markdowns, improved ability to maintain markups, and minimized inventory investment. It enables the retailer to achieve a balanced assortment of merchandise leading to increased sales and profits by preventing overstocking or understocking of inventory. It regulates inventory levels in accordance with the objectives of the retailer.

The second set of plans relates to the assortment offered to the customers from time to time. *Assortment plans* break down the merchandise budgets into specific units of merchandise to be purchased in terms of SKUs for each of the styles, colours, or sizes. These plans are developed for the entire store, and also for specific departments and product classifications.

Merchandise Plans

Retailers generally follow two methods of developing merchandise plans, as illustrated in Fig. 9.4. In top–down planning (Fig. 9.4a), the top management estimates the total sales for the upcoming period. The expected sales for each department are planned according to its past contribution to the sales of the entire store and its role in the future plan of the store. Bottom–up planning (Fig. 9.4b) is an alternative method used to develop a merchandise plan. The sales for the store are determined by adding together the planned sales figures that are developed by each department manager. Planned sales figures for all departments are then aggregated to arrive at the total planned sales for the store. Most large retailers combine the two approaches to derive the final plan that addresses the interests of all involved.

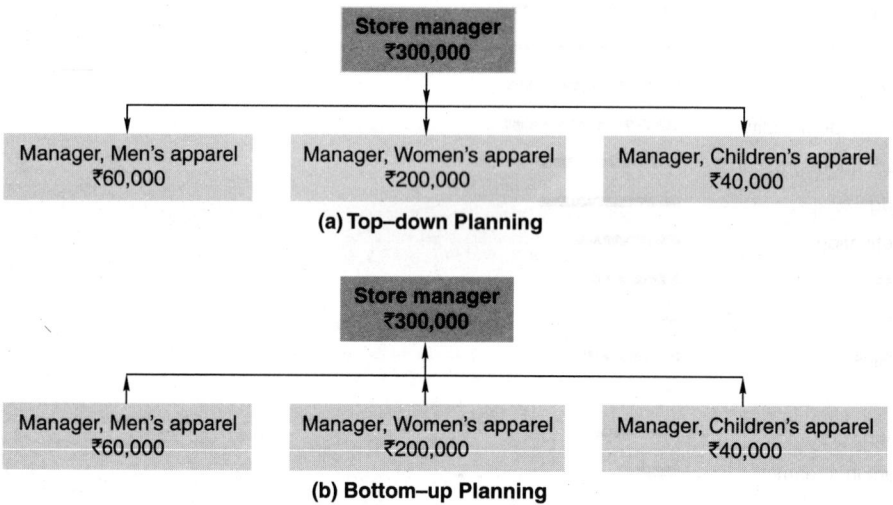

FIG. 9.4 Approaches to Merchandise Planning

Steps in Determining Merchandise Plans

The steps in developing merchandise plans are (i) determining the merchandise requirement, (ii) preparing the sales plan, and (iii) deciding the assortment.

Merchandise Requirements Merchandise is one of the key factors that customers keep in mind while selecting a store. It is the most tangible aspect of the business. The basic decisions with regard to the merchandise are taken on the basis of the value proposition of the store and the categories that would make the customers feel that the store is complete in its merchandise offer. Retailers use several criteria for selecting merchandise. The merchandise assortments are reviewed from time to time, and, based on their performance, changes are made by the retailers. Although sales performance is the primary factor,

TABLE 9.3 Criteria for Estimating Merchandise Requirement

A. Profitability and Sales	F. Supplier Characteristics
• Overall profitability	• Supplier representative
• Rate of turnover	• Reputation and reliability
• Sales potential	• Sales force organization
	• Services and functions
	• Other characteristics
B. Economic Conditions	**G. Competitive Considerations**
• Supplier's price	• Overlap with merchandise
• Gross margin	• Number of stores with similar merchandise
• Allowances and rebates	• Pricing strategy
• Support to cooperate advertising	
• Credit terms	
• Other economic conditions	
C. Assortment Considerations	**H. Distributive Factors**
• Existence of private brands	• Transportation adaptation
• Relations to other products	• Store adaption
D. Consumer Evaluations	**I. Tactical Considerations**
• Overall consumer evaluation	• Upcoming events
• Retail price	• Traffic building
• Product's physical characteristics	• Clearance sales
• Product's psychological characteristics	
• Packaging	
E. Supplier Marketing	**J. Salesperson Presentation**
• Introductory marketing campaign	• Techniques
• Continual marketing	• Utility

retailers use a combination of criteria to arrive at their own metric. A list of these criteria is given in Table 9.3.[19] Retailers set their own targets for all or a chosen set of each of these criteria and arrive at a metric that would determine the choice of merchandise.

Preparation of Sales Plan   A sample merchandise plan for six months is given in Table 9.4. Each month, the actual figures are entered to assist the future planning. They also help in revising the plans. When sales are higher than the planned sales, larger purchases are required to increase the inventory level, as shown in the merchandise plan. On the other hand, when sales are less than the planned sales, the amount of purchases is decreased. The steps involved in planning sales for the upcoming period are discussed in this section.

TABLE 9.4   A Completed Six-month Merchandising Plan

Dept Name _____

Dept No. _____

								Plan (This Year)	Actual (Last Year)
							Workroom cost		
			Six-month				Cash discount %		
			Merchandising Plan				Season stock turnover		
							Shortage %		
							Average stock		
							Markdown %		

Season 2	Month	Jul.	Aug.	Sep.	Oct.	Nov.	Dec.	Season Total
Sales	Last year	₹10,000	₹12,000	₹23,000	₹18,000	₹12,000	₹12,000	₹87,000
	Plan for this year	₹11,005	₹13,207	₹25,265	₹19,810	₹13,206	₹13,206	₹95,700
	Revised							
	Actual							
Retail Stock (BOM)	Last year	₹31,000	₹33,600	₹46,000	₹32,400	₹21,600	₹21,600	₹186,200
	Plan	₹34,116	₹36,980	₹50,530	₹35,658	₹23,770	₹23,770	₹204,830
	Revised							
	Actual							
Retail Stock (EOM)	Last year	₹33,600	₹46,000	₹32,400	₹21,600	₹21,600	₹20,000	₹175,200
	Plan	₹36,980	₹50,530	₹35,658	₹23,773	₹23,773	₹21,000	₹191,714
	Revised							
	Actual							
Reductions	Last year	₹1,001	₹609	₹1,305	₹1,609	₹1,923	₹2,253	₹8,700
	Plan	₹1,100	₹670	₹1,436	₹1,770	₹2,115	₹2,479	₹9,570
	Revised							
	Actual							
Purchases at Retail	Last year	₹13,209	₹25,705	₹11,009	₹9,123	₹14,253	₹19,100	₹92,399
	Plan	₹14,969	₹27,427	₹11,829	₹9,695	₹15,322	₹12,912	₹92,154
	Revised							
	Actual							
Purchases at Cost	Last year	₹7,093	₹13,803	₹5,912	₹4,899	₹7,654	₹10,257	₹49,618
	Plan	₹8,038	₹14,728	₹6,352	₹5,206	₹8,228	₹6,934	₹49,486
	Revised							
	Actual							

Comments _____

Merchandise Manager _____

Buyer _____

Controller _____

Planned sales Forecasting sales is the first and most important part of the plan. All other merchandising decisions are made in relation to forecast sales. The forecast is made on the basis of the sales figures of previous years and the prevailing business environment. For example, from the previous year's merchandise plan, the following sales data are obtained:

Sales	Jul.	Aug.	Sep.	Oct.	Nov.	Dec.	Total
Last year's sales (₹)	10,000	12,000	23,000	18,000	12,000	12,000	87,000

The first step is to calculate last year's monthly sales figures as a percentage of the year's total sales by using the following formula:

Sales of a Month in the Last Year ÷ Total Sales of Last Year

For each month, the percentage of sales would thus be as follows:

	Jul.	Aug.	Sep.	Oct.	Nov.	Dec.
Sales last year (₹)	10,000	12,000	23,000	18,000	12,000	12,000
Total sales last year (₹)			87,000			
Percentage of yearly sales	11.5	13.8	26.4	20.7	13.8	13.8

Let us assume that the percentage of monthly sales for the current year would be similar to that of last year. The retailer can now forecast the sales for the current year each month. Thus, the percentage of monthly sales for the current year would be as follows:

Month	Jul.	Aug.	Sep.	Oct.	Nov.	Dec.
Percentage of yearly sales	11.5	13.8	26.4	20.7	13.8	13.8

The next step is to determine the total planned sales volume for the season. Let us assume a 10 per cent increase in sales is planned for the period. Therefore, the planned sales for the current period would be ₹95,700 (10 per cent over ₹87,000, which is ₹87,000 + ₹8,700 = ₹95,700).

The final step is to plan sales for each month of the current period using the following formula:

Planned Percentage of Monthly Sales × Planned Total Sales

	Jul.	Aug.	Sep.	Oct.	Nov.	Dec.
Planned percentage of monthly sales	11.5	13.8	26.4	20.7	13.8	13.8
Planned total sales (₹)			95,700			
Planned monthly sales (₹)	11,005	13,207	25,265	19,810	13,206	13,206

These figures are entered in the six-month merchandise plan as follows:

	Jul.	Aug.	Sep.	Oct.	Nov.	Dec.	Total
Sales last year (₹)	10,000	12,000	23,000	18,000	12,000	12,000	87,000
Planned monthly sales for current year (₹)	11,005	13,207	25,265	19,810	13,206	13,206	95,700
Revised							
Actual							

Planned beginning of month inventory   The next step in preparing a merchandise plan is to determine the amount of stock required to meet the planned sales. A retailer needs to ensure that there is sufficient opening stock and assortment to meet customer demand. The planned beginning of month (BOM) inventory can be calculated using the following formula:

Planned Monthly BOM Inventory = Planned Monthly Sales × Stock-to-sales Ratio

The stock-to-sales ratios can be obtained from past years' sales and inventory data. The planned BOM inventory for each month can be calculated using the stock-to-sales ratios and planned sales for the current year.

	Jul.	Aug.	Sep.	Oct.	Nov.	Dec.
Stock-to-sales ratio	3.1	2.8	2.0	1.8	1.8	1.8
Planned monthly sales (₹)	11,005	13,207	25,265	19,810	13,206	13,206
Planned monthly BOM inventory (₹)	34,116	36,980	50,530	35,658	23,773	23,773

These figures are then entered in the six-month merchandise plan as follows:

BOM Inventory	Jul.	Aug.	Sep.	Oct.	Nov.	Dec.	Total
Last year (₹)	31,000	33,600	46,000	32,400	21,600	21,600	186,200
Planned (₹)	34,116	36,980	50,530	35,658	23,773	23,770	204,830
Revised							
Actual							

Planned end of month inventory   The end of month (EOM) stock for a particular month is the planned BOM stock for the following month. In our sample six-month merchandise plan, the planned EOM inventory levels would be entered as follows:

EOM Inventory	Jul.	Aug.	Sep.	Oct.	Nov.	Dec.	Total
Last year (₹)	33,600	46,000	32,400	21,600	21,600	20,000	175,200
Planned (₹)	36,980	50,530	35,658	23,773	23,773	21,000	191,714
Revised							
Actual							

Planned reductions   Reductions are an important component in a merchandise plan. They are inevitable due to markdowns, employee discounts, and shrinkages due to employee theft and shoplifting. These reductions are generally estimated on the basis of past experience and are presented as a percentage of the planned sales in the merchandise plan. For the store in consideration, if the planned reductions are 10 per cent (planned markdown percentage = 6.8 per cent, planned shortage percentage = 2.1 per cent, and planned employee discount percentage = 1.1 per cent), the total reductions can be calculated by multiplying the total planned sales for the current year by the reduction percentage. In our example, the total reductions will thus be ₹9,570 (10 per cent of ₹95,700). The planned reductions are calculated for each month and the figures are then entered in the six-month merchandise plan as follows:

Planned Monthly Reductions = Percentage Reductions Planned for the Month
× Planned Monthly Sales

	Jul.	Aug.	Sep.	Oct.	Nov.	Dec.	Total
Last year's monthly reductions (₹)	1,001	609	1,305	1,609	1,923	2,253	8,700
% reductions planned for the month based on last year's data	11.5	7.0	15.0	18.5	22.1	25.9	
Planned monthly reductions (₹)	1,100	670	1,436	1,770	2,115	2,479	9,570
Revised							
Actual							

Planned purchases at retail   On the merchandise plan, purchases must be planned at retail as all other figures are based on retail. The formula used is

$$\text{Planned Purchases} = \text{Planned Sales} + \text{Planned EOM} + \text{Planned Reductions} - \text{Planned BOM}$$

Using this formula and the data entered in the merchandise plan, the planned purchases at retail for the current year can be calculated as follows:

	Jul.	Aug.	Sep.	Oct.	Nov.	Dec.
Planned sales (₹)	11,005	13,207	25,265	19,810	13,200	13,206
Planned EOM (₹)	36,980	50,530	35,658	23,773	23,773	21,000
Planned reductions (₹)	1,100	670	1,436	1,770	2,115	2,479
Planned BOM at retail (₹)	34,116	36,980	50,530	35,658	23,770	23,770
Planned purchases (₹)	14,969	27,427	11,829	9,695	15,322	12,912

These figures are then entered in the six-month merchandise plan.

Planned Purchases at Retail	Jul.	Aug.	Sep.	Oct.	Nov.	Dec.	Total
Last year (₹)	13,209	25,705	11,009	9,123	14,253	19,100	92,399
Planned (₹)	14,969	27,427	11,829	9,695	15,322	12,912	92,154
Revised							
Actual							

Planned purchases at cost   The store wishes to have an initial markup for the period at 46.3 per cent. The planned purchases at cost can be calculated using the following formula:

$$\text{Planned Purchases at Cost} = (100\% - \text{Initial Markup \%}) \times \text{Planned Purchases at Retail}$$

The cost of planned purchases for each month can be calculated and entered in the merchandise plan. The planned purchases at cost are the measure of the amount the retailer would have to spend on merchandise for the season as well as for individual months.

	Jul.	Aug.	Sep.	Oct.	Nov.	Dec.	Total
(100% − initial markup %)	(100 − 46.3)	(100 − 46.3)	(100 − 46.3)	(100 − 46.3)	(100 − 46.3)	(100 − 46.3)	
Planned purchases at retail (₹)	14,969	27,427	11,829	9,695	15,322	12,912	92,154
Planned purchases at cost (₹)	8,038	14,728	6,352	5,206	8,228	6,934	49,486
Last year (₹)	7,093	13,803	5,912	4,899	7,654	10,257	49,618
Planned (₹)	8,038	14,728	6,352	5,206	8,228	6,934	
Revised (₹)							
Actual							

Assortment Plan   After the merchandise plan has been prepared, the retailer develops assortment plans. These plans break down the merchandise budgets into specific units of merchandise to be purchased, such as styles, colours, and sizes. Several factors, such as the type of merchandise carried, store policies, and the variety of merchandise available, are considered while preparing assortment plans. Assortment plans vary with product categories. Assortment plans for fashion merchandise need to be monitored on a much more frequent basis compared to assortments of basic merchandise. The variety of merchandise available will also affect assortment plans. Many manufacturers offer product lines with a wide variety of options whereas others offer only limited choices. For each product category, retail buyers determine the assortment's breadth and depth. Assortments may be offered in either a broad and shallow plan or a narrow and deep one. For fashion merchandise, buyers usually test the market early in the selling season by offering a broad and shallow assortment. As customer demand becomes more clearly defined during the selling season, the assortment is likely to become narrower and deeper. Retailers generally follow a process that involves the following steps:

1. Decide the categories and sub-categories of products the store or department will offer.
2. Determine the brands and price lines the store will offer for each of these sub-classifications. Retailers use their knowledge of characteristics of the target market, their brand preferences, and the role of private labels to arrive at the most appealing price lines.
3. Identify all the general characteristics of an item that customers may consider when buying it. For example, men's shirts have different colours, sizes, sleeve lengths, and collar styles, and are made of different materials. Since it is not possible to plan for every possible customer, only the major characteristics are considered in order to present a balanced assortment. The budget determines the breadth and depth of the assortment. For example, it is possible to stock men's shirts from a size 14 collar to a size 27. However, the bulk of sales could be at around size 15½. The assortment is then adjusted accordingly.
4. Decide on the proportion of one classification to another and determine the proportion in which each selecting factor will be represented in the stock. For example, not all sizes or colours will have the same rate of sale, nor will each colour be equally popular in every size that is manufactured. For some selection factors such as size, these proportions can be calculated using past sales figures. In the case of colour, it is important to find out the readiness of customers to accept new colours as they are introduced.
5. Calculate the specific number of units to purchase.

The following example will help us understand the assortment planning process of a retailer better. Let us assume that a store is selling sweatshirts. The market research indicates that there is no brand loyalty for sweatshirts and the customer is prepared to substitute one brand for another. Past sales records indicate that a particular brand has been very popular with the shoppers. The merchandising buying plan indicates that, for the coming season, a budget of ₹90,000 has been allocated to sweatshirts. If the store decides to stock only that particular brand of sweatshirts costing ₹300 each, the store will be able to purchase 300 sweatshirts. This brand offers sweatshirts in four sizes in 5 different colours. They are also available in 100 per cent cotton and a woollen blend. The brand offers the sweatshirts in hooded and non-hooded designs. Suppose that the past sales records indicate the following size and colour choice distribution:

Size		Colour	
Small	15%	White	20%
Medium	20%	Grey	35%
Large	45%	Black	15%
X-Large	20%	Olive	15%
		Maroon	15%

This data will be taken into account in preparing assortment plans for calculating the number of sweatshirts that need to be purchased for each of the sizes and colours selected:

Size	Number	Colour	Number
Small	45	White	9
		Grey	16
		Black	7
		Olive	7
		Maroon	6
Medium	60	White	12
		Grey	21
		Black	9
		Olive	9
		Maroon	9
Large	135	White	27
		Grey	47
		Black	20
		Olive	20
		Maroon	20
X-Large	60	White	12
		Grey	21
		Black	9
		Olive	9
		Maroon	9

After reviewing these figures, the store may decide to offer only hooded, 100 per cent cotton shirts. If it decides to further break the assortment down by offering both hooded and non-hooded and cotton and cotton/woollen blends, it would not be able to offer an adequate number of sizes and colours. For example, if it decides to offer each colour in a ratio of 80 per cent non-hooded and 20 per cent hooded, and 60 per cent all cotton and 40 per cent blends, the store would be offering only one or two of some types, as the following chart illustrates:

Size	Colour	SKU	Material		Style	
Small	Maroon	7	4 (all cotton)	3 (non-hooded)	1 (hooded)	
			3 (woollen/cotton blend)	2 (non-hooded)	1 (hooded)	

This example shows that the store can buy only one small maroon hooded sweatshirt made of 100 per cent cotton and only one small maroon hooded sweatshirt made of a woollen/cotton blend. Once these sweatshirts are sold, the assortment will be depleted for those sub-categories. In preparing assortment plans, retailers use research and analysis of past records and current trends so that they offer brands for which there is adequate customer demand.

Merchandising Plan for Basic Stocks

The demand for certain categories of merchandise does not change much with season in terms of appearance, composition, or price. Such goods are known as basic merchandise. These may include products of daily use, such as grocery, and those that are bought commonly, such as white shirts and polo-neck T-shirts. Purchases for such merchandise can be planned without using the method outlined in this section. Retailers use a basic stock tool for planning these purchases. The primary decision in this tool is to determine the amount of merchandise a retailer must have on hand or on order so that sufficient merchandise is available throughout the period. The basic stock plan develops a list which provides information such as a description of the items, their retail prices and costs to the store, the maximum and minimum reorder quantity, and the rate of sale.

Maximum Quantity   This is the amount of merchandise that must be on hand or on order at any reordering point. It is the quantity that is sufficient to provide the appropriate amount of merchandise for sale while goods are being delivered. The stock on hand never reaches the maximum as sales occur during the time it takes for the new order to be received. The following formula is used to calculate the maximum level of quantity:

$$\text{Maximum Quantity} = \text{Sales Volume Per Week} \times (\text{Reorder Period} + \text{Delivery Period}) + \text{Reserve}$$

The sales volume per week for each item is obtained by analysing past sales records. The reorder period is the time between two orders for merchandise. Longer periods between reorders require ordering larger quantities of merchandise and keeping larger inventory. The delivery period is the period between the time when the order is placed and the time when the merchandise is available to go on the shelf. The reserve is the quantity of merchandise necessary to meet unanticipated sales. Some retailers use the following formula as a thumb rule to determine the amount of reserve:

$$\text{Reserve} = 2.3 \times (\text{Reorder Period} + \text{Delivery Period}) \times \text{Sales Volume Per Week}$$

Minimum Quantity   This is the point at which the merchandise must be reordered. The formula for determining the minimum quantity is as follows:

$$\text{Minimum Quantity} = \text{Sales Volume Per Week} \times \text{Delivery Period} + \text{Reserve}$$

Open-to-buy Planning

In spite of all the planning, a buyer faces situations that require deviation. These are generally caused due to exogenous variables such as unforeseen changes in weather or sudden opportunities. Under this system, the buyer has the liberty to decide and spend a specific amount for the period. This amount reduces each time a purchase is made. The advantages of open-to-buy planning are that the buyer is assured that a specified relationship between the stock on hand and the planned sales is maintained and the buyer is able to adjust merchandise purchases to reflect changes in sales, reductions, and purchases. It also enables the retailer to determine problem areas, such as the buyer being in an 'overbought' situation due to inaccurate sales forecasts and failure to recognize sales or fashion trends leading to markdowns. Using this system, the buyer can take corrective action through sales promotion and by cancelling outstanding orders. The open-to-buy figures are not listed on the merchandise plan. They are calculated using the planned purchases at cost, as shown in the following example.

Let us assume that a buyer has the following information:

Planned sales (₹)	25,000
Planned BOM (₹)	36,000
Planned reductions (₹)	2,000
Planned EOM (₹)	35,000
Stock on order at cost (₹)	5,000
Initial markup (%)	44.6

The buyer would first find out the planned purchases at retail:

$$\text{Planned Purchases} = \text{Planned Sales} + \text{Planned EOM}$$
$$+ \text{Planned Reductions} - \text{Planned BOM}$$
$$= ₹25,000 + ₹35,000 + ₹2,000 - ₹36,000$$
$$= ₹26,000$$

The planned purchases at retail are then converted to planned purchases at cost by using the following formula:

$$\text{Planned Purchases at Cost} = (100\% - \text{Initial Markup }\%) \times \text{Planned Purchases at Retail}$$
$$= (100\% - 44.6\%) \times ₹26,000$$
$$= ₹14,404$$

The open-to-buy value can be determined as follows:

$$\text{Open-to-buy} = \text{Planned Purchases at Cost} - \text{Stock on Order}$$
$$= ₹14,404 - ₹5,000$$
$$= ₹9,404$$

Therefore, for the given month, the buyer would have ₹9,404 to spend in addition to the planned purchases.

However, over the years, retailers have been able to reduce their dependence on the open-to-buy system by enhancing the capabilities of their merchandise planning. This has been made possible due to the availability of software with improved features, functionality, and technical capabilities and sophisticated planning systems to focus on the customer and improve micromarketing.[20]

RETAIL BUYING GROUPS

Although they are not new phenomena, retail buying groups have evolved and become stronger with time. These are groups of smaller retailers formed with the purpose of buying efficiently. The underlying motive is the pooling of interests to increase buying power.[21] As a group, they wield power that would never be available to smaller retailers. They are a form of alliance between two or more retail companies whereby each partner seeks to add to its competencies by combining some of its resources with those of the partners. Due to the scale of buying, these alliances provide small firms a competitive advantage over large retailers and cooperatives.[22] Retailers derive benefits from their groups in terms of buying, marketing, operations, and replication. Table 9.5 describes these benefits.[23]

TABLE 9.5   Benefits Sought by Retail Buying Groups and Directions of Change

Factor	Incentive to Form a Group	Directions of Change
1. Economies of Scale		
1.1 Buying volumes	• Dependent on the size of discounts which vary by sector and distribution economies among members	• Growth of corporate chains increases pressure for independents to form groups but varies by sector
	• Strong case to maximize size of alliance to achieve full benefits	• Local differentiation provides alternative strategy to compete with multiples
	• Extent of alliances will depend on competition, especially from voluntary chains and non-aligned wholesalers	• Growth in national corporate chains increases territorial coverage necessary for groups but strong voluntary chains in some sectors limit scope for groups, as does falling number of independents
		• Growth of corporate chains increases pressures for independents to form groups but varies by sector
		• Manufacturers concerned about growth of retail concentration may seek to limit discounts to discourage chains and groups, but success will depend on relative power in channel
		• Consumer demand for variety and global product sourcing has increased the need for professional buying skills, the cost of which is more easily sustained through groups
		• Increase in manufacturer concentration results in larger volumes of business with major retailers, which increases the importance of volume-related discounts
1.2 Marketing economies, e.g., retail brands, product testing, advertising, promotion	• Large volume sales allow use of more effective marketing and reduce cost per unit	• Rise in emphasis on retail marketing by corporate chains leads to increased importance of retailer image. Source of potential competitive weakness for non-aligned independents
	• Shared costs of marketing innovation	• Requirement to introduce marketing innovations faster places a premium on marketing information about competitors
	• Greater need to be aware of what other retailers are doing to enable faster diffusion of new concepts being encouraged by larger organizations	• Increased costs of retail brand developments which moves away from 'me too' brands weakens the competitive position of medium-sized retailers
		• Moves to meet the specific demands of local markets encourage local managerial control within alliance-type organizations
1.3 Economies in operations, systems, financial, legal and personnel services	• Bulk purchase can reduce costs but competition is present from alternative providers	• Increased ability of providers to design customer-specific packaging may limit incentive to acquire through the buying group

(Contd)

Table 9.5 Contd

Factor	Incentive to Form a Group	Directions of Change
2. Economies of Replication		
2.1 Recurrent costs, e.g., product ranges, operating systems	• Benefits in competitiveness through improved marketing and lower unit costs by replication across outlets	
2.2 Fixed and capital costs, e.g., equipment provision, format design	• Spreading of costs across members. Retail technology systems costs are responsive to replication economies	• Increased importance of store design and layout and efficient operating have increased the importance of these economies
3. Economies of Scope		
3.1 Combinations of product ranges and services	• Main advantages are the consumer attractions of different assortments, together with the opportunity for lower costs through joint overheads	• Trend towards more specialist retail formats and product ranges in some sectors reduce importance of this factor in those sectors. Where wide range is needed because of convenience elements in shopping, this may strengthen case for alliances
3.2 Promotion	• Economies of scope widely used to underpin promotional activity	• Economies of scope become more important as pressures to raise shelf space and floor space productivity increase

A buying group is a collective activity that has resulted from proactive and innovative strategies. The proactive strategy emanates from the need of independent retailers to counter the power of large chain stores. The benefits of the alliance can be achieved and measured easily. As a result, the purpose of these groups is easy to understand.[24] The working capital required is limited. The initial investment is low. The entry barriers are also low and the commitment is voluntary. It is the result of a crisis-response behaviour.[25] The innovative strategy leads to the formation of buying groups for harnessing a new-found opportunity. In this case, retailers gain competitive advantage due to new products or services. This is widely found in cases where small retailers want to respond to local requirements that the large chains find it difficult to service due to their common offerings. These strategies have an impact on the groups in terms of the emphasis placed on different functions, though many of the structural features of the groups may be similar. Although buying groups suffer from the disadvantage of relying on consensus and cooperative action, the heightened turbulence in the retail industry enhances the occurrence of such alliances. The changing environment impacts the form and the strategies of these groups. Table 9.6 highlights the major factors that influence the formation and growth of buying groups.[26]

TABLE 9.6 Factors Affecting the Formation and Growth of Buying Groups

Factor	Proposition	Direction of Influence
Similarity of product ranges	More similar the trading interests, the greater the incentive to form groups	More emphasis on measurement or returns to sales area leads to greater convergence of product ranges within sector
Size	Similar sizes, whether measured in sales area or in number of retail units within sub-group, are more likely to have similar interests and to form a group	Reduction in number of medium-sized retail chains means that remaining independents are likely to be similar in size

(Contd)

Table 9.6 Contd

Factor	Proposition	Direction of Influence
Non-competing trading areas	Basic prerequisite for success and survival of alliances	Greater consumer mobility increases areas of competition and thus greater geographical coverage is needed to obtain size
Culture	Independent small businesses often value independence	Changing competitive pressures force change in attitudes
Management expertise and attitude	The greater the benefits, the greater the effort and greater the expertise of staff attracted to group	General rise in standards of management leads to greater recognition of benefits
Management ambitions	As the organization develops, it will seek to extend benefits to members by widening its scope since managerial aspirations are most likely to be fulfilled through growth strategies	Older retail groups are likely to have a wider range of functions offered to members than younger groups
Entrepreneurship	Despite cooperative nature, a leader is required to establish the group	Greater need for group increases incentive for entrepreneur to act

NEGOTIATIONS IN RETAIL

Negotiation, in the simplest terms, is a discussion between two or more disputants who try to arrive at a solution to their problem. A retailer would face the issue of negotiation right from the initial stages, which might begin with issues of real estate leases, space utilization, and learning how to get the best prices and terms on products with supplier negotiation. Negotiation basically takes place because the parties who wish to come out with a solution that might work for both of them and end the dispute or argument. The parties involved in a negotiation prefer agreement to argument to get a better deal and mutual benefit. In a negotiation, the mutual benefit is not always mandatory because in a give and take situation, sometimes it can also become a win–lose situation. The disputants would either force a compromise to their benefit or else would go for a mutual agreement.

A successful retailer would tend to understand others in terms of the adjustments and readjustments of their positions during negotiations to influence the outcome. Decision-making skills alone would not suffice for a retailer because negotiation skills would always help him/her get the better out of any deal. The process of give and take has to be followed very judiciously because if one party assumes that there is little compromise from the other side, they may not reach a consensus. It is very important for a retailer to work towards a solution which would optimize the outcome for both the parties.

The tension that exists in a negotiation between cooperation and competition is known as 'The Negotiators Dilemma'.[27] This can be explained thus:

1. If both sides cooperate, they will both have good outcomes.
2. If one cooperates and the other competes, the cooperator will get a terrible outcome and the competitor will get a great outcome.
3. If both compete, both will have mediocre outcomes.
4. In the face of uncertainty about what strategy the other side will adopt, each side's best choice is to compete.

It is also a challenge for a retailer to actually bring the parties to negotiation because often, it is hardly possible for the parties to commit themselves to the negotiation due to their differences. It is also a challenge for a retailer to look into the past of the other side to get more information about their reputation and priorities to have an idea about their future proceedings.[28] It also becomes a prerequisite for the retailer to actually avoid any misunderstanding which would result into arguments on the other side. If the required and interested people do not take part in the negotiation process, then it would be very difficult to reach a solution.

It would be difficult for a retailer to survive the competition if he/she lacks good negotiating skills. In order to remove the roadblocks from various challenging situations, it becomes crucial for a retailer to use various sources of power in negotiation.[29] Power in negotiations means the ability of the retailer to attain his/her objectives by convincing or influencing the other side in favourable terms. Although it is agreed that using threats in the process of a negotiation sometimes has a favourable result, doing so can also prove very costly to the retailer. This has to be a very calculated decision and if it does not fall right, then it could prove dangerous.

There is utmost necessity for planning the negotiation to effectively meet the objectives. The retailer, for reaching a stable argument, has to shape the planning process for the negotiation to be successful. He/she has to set goals and prepare for the negotiations beforehand. If there are strong alternatives with the retailer, then he/she could always exert influence depending upon the circumstances. It is always very important for a retailer to actually influence the other side with a good solution for reaching a common level of understanding; again shaping good solutions majorly depends upon the circumstances.

CONTRACTS IN RETAIL

Contract management is a course of action wherein both the parties involved in the contract come together to meet their obligations, thereby fulfilling the objectives. It aims at building a cordial relationship between the customer and the provider. Contract management includes targeting continuous improvement in performance. Anticipating future needs and taking remedial actions to rectify the deficiencies are steps that are likely to continue throughout the life of a contract.

Contract management activities can be broadly grouped into the following three areas (Fig. 9.5):[30]

1. Service delivery management ensures that the service is being delivered as agreed, to the required level of performance and quality.
2. Relationship management keeps the relationship between the two parties open and constructive, aiming to resolve or ease tensions and identify problems early.
3. Contract administration handles the formal governance of the contract and changes to the contract documentation.

The first stage involves the managing of service delivery, which means to deliver as per the required standards. It involves the assessment and monitoring of the performance of the service provider to achieve the objectives by minimizing the risks.

The second stage mainly deals with relationship building among the involved parties. A good relation is the cornerstone of any contract and is crucial for the survival of the agreement.

The third stage involves contract administration, which binds both the parties to the contract to follow the rules as per contract documentation and clarity in the contract administrative procedures. The combination of all these three areas would actually result in good contract management and the achievement of the desired objectives.

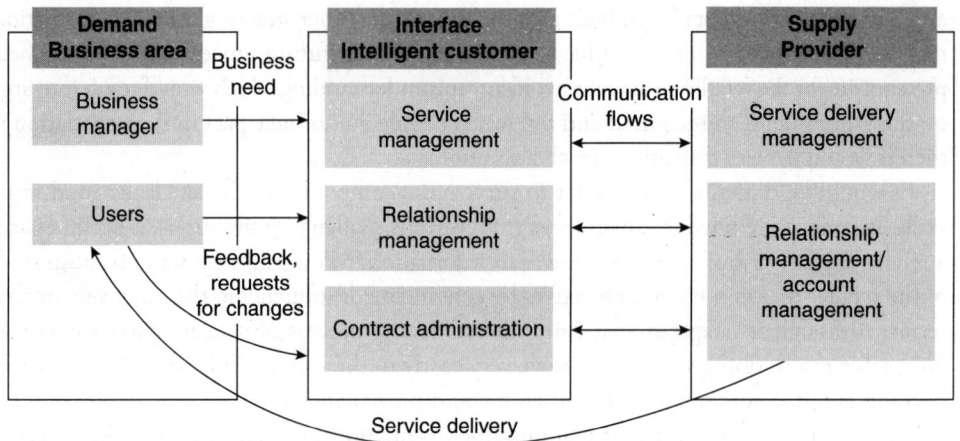

FIG. 9.5 Contract Management Activities

Source: www.ogc.gov.uk, accessed on 25 April 2011.

The requisites of a good contract largely depend on the way a contract is constructed. The terms of the contract should adhere to the requirements of the parties to the contract, ensuring that all types of differences are avoided. It must not only be made on legal foundations, but also exhibit a productive relationship and mutual trust between the parties to the contract.

There would always be a possibility of some tensions or differences between the parties regarding the contract. The basic objective here must be to ease the tensions and also ensure that the agreed terms are properly adhered to. Under any scenario, a retailer can follow these guidelines for the development of a good contract:

1. Clarity in the selection and evaluation of procedures enables the contract to be properly awarded to the concerned party.
2. Clear information about the procedures for dispute resolution eases the process of managing risks in contracts.
3. Parties to the contract must have well-defined objectives, contributions, and mutual understanding about the benefits derived from the contract.
4. Quality management must be followed all through the life of the contract to ensure that customers get value for money.
5. Clarity should be maintained in communicating the terms and conditions of the contract.
6. Roles and responsibilities of the members to the contract must be precisely defined.
7. Benchmarking and performance measurement should be taken care of at regular stages of the contract.
8. Contract manager could be designated to make aware of the contract specifications, if required.
9. Parties to the contract should be willing to deal with any unforeseen problem or issue in a mature way over the life of the contract.
10. Parties to the contract should be able to anticipate and adapt to changing business needs.

Contracts need to be managed by both the parties in an effective and efficient way for them to succeed together as a whole and manage the process smoothly with fewer hassles. An intelligent customer capability has three crucial factors, namely the knowledge of the business, the knowledge of the services provided, and finally the knowledge of the contract itself. Annexure 9.2 shows the snapshots of various contract agreements used by retailers.

SUMMARY

Buying is a function that ensures that the retailer has the right merchandise at the right price. It involves forecasting the requirements of the customers of the store and setting up a plan that incorporates details of the merchandise and the financial implications. A store usually has two sets of plans: one for the category and the other for the assortment within the category. Besides, the plan also indicates the sales at retail price and the estimated markdown.

A buyer has to liaise with several departments to arrive at the plan. The negotiation skills that buyers possess are commendable. Good communication skills, besides knowledge of the right source, add to the efficiency of buying. The activity of buying is a major source of cost advantage for many retailers. As the volume of buying increases with the growth of retailers, smaller retailers come together to form buying groups so as to get the same advantage. A retailer needs to be very careful in managing this function.

Buyers need to master the skill of forecasting the requirements for particular merchandise as well as SKUs. For this, they utilize point of sales data, look at the trends in the marketplace, and identify the correct source of supply. In today's context, a retail buyer needs to be aware of what is happening vis-à-vis the customers of its stores. In addition to this, a buyer should also be aware of the sources across the world that would give them the merchandise at the correct price and in the correct quantity whenever required.

NOTES

1. Doubler, D.W. and David Burt 2001, *Purchasing and Supply Management: Text and Cases*, 6th edn, Tata McGraw-Hill.
2. Webster, Frederick E., Jr and Yoram Wind 1972, *Organisational Buying Behaviour*, Prentice Hall, New Jersey, p. 2.
3. Webster, Frederick E., Jr and Yoram Wind 1972, *Organisational Buying Behaviour*, Prenticc Hall, Ncw Jersey, p. 6.
4. Hirschman, E.C. and R.W. Stampfl 1980, 'Roles of Retailing in the Diffusion of Popular Culture: Micro-perspectives', *Journal of Retailing*, Vol. 56, Spring, pp. 16–30.
5. Davies, G. 1993, *Trade Marketing Strategy*, Paul Chapman, London.
6. Wagner, J., R. Ettenson, and J. Parrish 1989, 'Vendor Selection among Retail Buyers: An Analysis by Merchandise Division', *Journal of Retailing*, Vol. 65, No. 1, pp. 58–79.
7. Swindley, David 1992, 'Retail Buying in United Kingdom', *Service Industries Journal*, Vol. 12, No. 4, pp. 533–44.
8. Robinson, T. and C.M. Clarke Hill 1995, 'International Alliances in European Retailing', *International Review of Retail, Distribution and Consumer Research*, Vol. 5, No. 2, pp. 167–84.
9. Swindley, David 1992, 'Retail Buying in United Kingdom', *Service Industries Journal*, Vol. 12, No. 4, pp. 533–44.
10. McLaughlin, E. and G.F. Hawkes 1995, 'Category Management in the US Grocery Distribution Channcl: A Ncw Mcchanism for Vertical Coordination', 8th International Conference on Research in the Distributive Trades, Centro di Studi sul Commerio Universta (CESCOM), Bocconi University, Milan, pp. 1, 2, September; Swindley 1992, 'Retail Buying in United Kingdom', *Service Industries Journal*, Vol. 12, No. 4, pp. 533–44.
11. Sheth, Jagdish N. 1973, 'A Model of Industrial Buyer Behaviour', *Journal of Marketing*, Vol. 37, Issue 4, October, pp. 50–6.
12. Hansen, T.H. and H. Skytte 1998, 'Retailer Buying Behaviour: A Review', *International Review of Retail, Distribution and Consumer Research*, Vol. 8, No. 3, pp. 276–301.
13. Clodfelter, Richard 2003, 'Preparing Buying Plans', *Retail Buying: From Basics to Fashion*, 2nd edn, Fairchild Publications, p. 224.

14. Nilson, J. and V. Host 1987, *Reseller Assortment Decision Criteria*, JAI Press, Aarhus.
15. Donofrio, Terry J. 'Beyond Basic Product Planning: Where are We Going with Merchandise Planning?', *Retail Systems and Services*, http://www.rs-s.com/Articles/bpp1.htm, accessed on 24 July 2004.
16. McGoldrick, P.J. 1990, *Retail Marketing*, McGraw-Hill, Maidenhead.
17. Swindley, David 1992, 'Retail Buying in United Kingdom', *Service Industries Journal*, Vol. 12, No. 4, pp. 533–44.
18. Swindley, David 1992, 'Retail Buying in United Kingdom', *Service Industries Journal*, Vol. 12, No. 4, pp. 533–44.
19. Diamond, J. and G. Pintel 1985, *Retail Buying*, Prentice Hall, New Jersey.
20. Swindley, David 1992, 'Retail Buying in United Kingdom', *Service Industries Journal*, Vol. 12, No. 4, pp. 533–44.
21. Thompson, J.D. 1967, *Organisation in Action*, McGraw-Hill, New York.
22. Hardy, K.G. and A.J. Magrath 1987, 'Buying Groups: Clout for Small Business', *Harvard Business Review*, Vol. 65, No. 5, pp. 16–22.
23. Shaw, S.A., J.A. Dawson, and N. Harris 1994, 'The Characteristics and Functions of Retail Buying Groups in the United Kingdom: Results of a Survey', *International Review of Retail, Distribution and Consumer Research*, Vol. 4, No. 1, pp. 83–105.
24. Fulop, C. 1962, 'Buying by Voluntary Chains', Allen and Unwin, London.
25. Carney, M.G. 1992, 'The Incentive Structure of Co-operative Retail Buying', *Economic and Industrial Democracy*, Vol. 13, pp. 207–31.
26. Shaw, S.A., J.A. Dawson, and N. Harris 1994, 'The Characteristics and Functions of Retail Buying Groups in the United Kingdom: Results of a Survey', *International Review of Retail, Distribution and Consumer Research*, Vol. 4, No. 1, pp. 83–105.
27. Lax, David A. and James K. Sebenius 1986, *The Manger as Negotiator: Bargaining for Cooperation and Competitive Gain*, The Free Press, New York.
28. http://www.beyondintractabilty.org/essay/negotiation/, accessed on 17 December 2010.
29. Fisher, Roger 2002, 'Network Power in Collaborative Planning', *Journal of Planning Education and Research*, March, pp. 221–36.
30. www.ogc.gov.uk/documents/Contract_Management.pdf, accessed on 28 December 2010.

CONCEPT REVIEW QUESTIONS

1. What are the objectives of the buying function at a retail business?
2. Explain retail buying behaviour. What are the factors that influence a retailer's buying decision?
3. Explain the merchandise planning process with an example.
4. Describe the assortment planning process with an example.
5. What are the differences in open-to-buy and buying of base stock? What parameters would ensure efficiency in each of these cases?
6. What are the responsibilities of a buyer? List the characteristics/attributes that must be present in a good buyer.
7. What are buying centres? What are the factors that have propagated the need for this structure?

CRITICAL THINKING QUESTIONS

1. How would the merchandise plan for a fashion product be different from that of a perishable product?
2. What coordination does a buyer need to build with a merchandise?

PROJECTS

1. Meet the retail buyer of a large store and a small store. Find out the differences in their approaches to buying.
2. Meet a retailer and find out how buyers are selected and evaluated.

ANNEXURE 9.1

Benetton's Buying Calendar

Benetton, an international fashion retailer, is recognized for the best practices it brought into its operations. Benetton's buying process starts at least a year before the season for which the designs and colours are being developed. The buyers visit fashion shows and design studios and meet several designers to gauge the new trends. In order that the new colours and designs are accepted by the customers and a larger proportion of the merchandise is sold at full price, buyers need to forecast the demand and suggest production schedules well in advance.

Spring–Summer Season

	Year 1												Year 2											
	Jan.	Feb.	Mar.	Apr.	May.	Jun.	Jul.	Aug.	Sep.	Oct.	Nov.	Dec.	Jan.	Feb.	Mar.	Apr.	May.	Jun.	Jul.	Aug.	Sep.	Oct.	Nov.	Dec.
Preparation of designs																								
'Pre-presentation' to agents								C																
Reduction of basic line								O																
Presentation to agents								M																
Presentation to store managers								P																
Receipt of orders from stores								A																
								N																
								Y																
Preparation of rough production plans																								
Placement of orders with suppliers, contractors								V																
								A																
Receipts of supplies, work from contractors								C																
Payment of suppliers, contractors								A																
								T																
								I																
In-company production								O																
Delivery of basic collection to stores								N																

(Contd)

Annexure 9.1 Contd

	Year 1												Year 2											
	Jan.	Feb.	Mar.	Apr.	May.	Jun.	Jul.	Aug.	Sep.	Oct.	Nov.	Dec.	Jan.	Feb.	Mar.	Apr.	May.	Jun.	Jul.	Aug.	Sep.	Oct.	Nov.	Dec.
Changes in colours for initial orders								■	■															
'Flash' collection								■																
Presentation to agents								■					▨											
Order collection														▨										
Ordering from contractors															▨									
Receiving from contractors																								
'Reassortment'																								
Retail selling season																								
Receipt of payment from stores																								
Payment of commissions to agents																								
Fall–Winter Season																								
Preparation of designs																								
'Pre-presentation' to agents																								
Reduction of basic line								■	▨															
Presentation to agents						▨	▨	■	▨															
Presentation to store managers								■	▨															
Receipt of orders from stores								■	▨											■				
Preparation of rough production plans											▨									■				
Placement of orders with suppliers, contractors												▨	▨							■				

(Contd)

Annexure 9.1 Contd

	Year 1												Year 2											
	Jan.	Feb.	Mar.	Apr.	May.	Jun.	Jul.	Aug.	Sep.	Oct.	Nov.	Dec.	Jan.	Feb.	Mar.	Apr.	May.	Jun.	Jul.	Aug.	Sep.	Oct.	Nov.	Dec.
Receipts of supplies, work from contractors																								
Payment of suppliers, contractors																				COMPANY VACATION				
In-company production																								
Delivery of basic collection to stores																								
Changes in colours for initial orders																								
'Flash' collection																								
Presentation to agents																								
Order collection																								
Ordering from contractors																								
Receiving from contractors																								
'Reassortment'																								
Retail selling season																								
Receipt of payment from stores																								
Payment of commissions to agents																								

Source: Benetton (A); Harvard Business School.

ANNEXURE 9.2

Snapshots of Contract Agreements Used by Retailers

Illustrative Rebate Agreement

This agreement is made by (the Retailer) .... and (the Supplier) ....

Whereas the purchaser owns and operates the retailing company under the name _____ located in _____ (stores) and is desirous of purchasing products of various descriptions from reputable suppliers for retail sale at the stores, the supplier is in the business of trading in the products which the purchaser is interested in purchasing, and the parties are desirous of setting out the special terms and conditions applicable to the said purchase transactions including the special terms.

Now therefore the parties agree as follows:

Product Range

The special terms enumerated in the schedule attached hitherto shall apply to all products supplied to the purchaser by the supplier pursuant to purchase orders placed during the validity period of the agreement.

Scope

The agreement is not a binding commitment to purchase the products from the supplier but is intended only to record the agreement of the parties with regards to the special terms that would apply should purchases be made.

Shelf Space

The purchaser gives no commitment regarding the duration of the display, shelf space size, and location, except where Gondola fee is paid to the purchaser. These matters shall be at the purchaser's absolute discretion.

Barcoding

All products shall be barcoded. Failure to barcode any products will attract a penalty of _____ per unit.

Merchandising Support

Wherever required by the purchaser, the supplier at its cost shall provide merchandising support at the store.

Out of Stock

Failure to notify _____ product being out of stock for longer than 3 weeks will result in delisting of the product.

Cost Price

The cost price will be binding for the period of the contract, the only exception will be changed in the commodity market.

Validity Period

The agreement shall be valid for the calendar year in which it is executed and shall expire on _____ of such year. Notwithstanding this, these special terms shall apply to deliveries made after the validity period of this agreement, provided the relevant purchase orders were placed during the period of the agreement.

Governing Law

This agreement shall be governed by the laws and regulations of _____. The parties agree to submit any disputes hereunder for the final determination by the courts of _____ in respect of such disputes.

(Contd)

Annexure 9.2 Contd

IN WITNESS WHEREOF THE PARTIES HAVE SIGNED THIS AGREEMENT

DATE: ....

At ....

Title _____ Designation _____   Title _____ Designation _____

(Purchaser)   (Supplier)

Sample Supply Agreement

The agreement hereinafter referred to as the agreement is made on _____ and between _____ hereinafter referred to as the _____ Retail Company and _____ hereinafter referred to as the Supplier. Whereas _____ Retail Company is the owner and the operator of _____ hereinafter referred to as the Products from reputable suppliers for display and sale at the store and the Supplier carries on business of the sale of the products and is duly licensed, competent, able and willing to supply the products to the stores according to the provision hereof, and on the terms and conditions stipulated in the special terms, the local purchase and the Standard Terms all of which are attached hereto.

Now therefore the parties agree as follows:

Expressions used herein shall, unless herein defined, bear the same meaning as respectively assigned to them in the standard terms.

Undertaking to Supply

The supplier undertakes to supply to the stores the full range of the products periodically ordered by the store under local Purchase orders in accordance with the terms thereof and as per the terms and conditions set out in the Standard Terms and the Special Terms. This agreement is not a binding commitment by the _____ Retail Company or its stores to purchase any products but is a record of the terms and conditions that would apply to the purchaser, if and when purchases are made by any of the stores.

Purpose of This Agreement

This agreement is entered into by the Supplier and the _____ Retail Company with the limited purpose of securing uniform terms and conditions that will give the individual purchase transactions initiated, concluded, and paid for by each store at their sole and absolute discretion.

Payment

The respective stores will make payment for the supply of the products in accordance with the Standard Terms and the Special Terms.

Term

The agreement shall be of term of _____ from _____ and shall be valid in respect of the local purchase orders issued to the supplier by the store in this period.

In witness whereof the parties have signed this agreement on the date thereof.

(Contd)

Annexure 9.2 Contd

For and on the behalf of Retailer		For and on the behalf of the Supplier
	Supply Special Terms	
Supplier Origin	Supplier Code	Name
Supplier Origin	Supplier Code	Name
Supplier Origin	Supplier Code	Name
Secions		Product Group Name

Section A—Fixed Rebates

Name of Agreement

Fixed Rebate

Method of Payment

Section B—Progressive Rebates

Desciption

Progressive Rebate

Method of Payment

Section C—Special Agreements

Description	% Amount	Minimum Guaranteed	Starting Date	Ending Date
1. Advertising				
Method of Payment				

Section D—Payment Terms

Days: 15/30th of every month

Section E—Listing Fees

Will be negotiated and agreed for all new products.

Section F—Confirmation of Spend at Store Level

Supplier confirms availability of budgets to support promotional activity at each store.

Section G—Penalty

A penalty of _____ will be paid by the supplier for failure to supply the products which were agreed to be supplied.

Note: This is a common sample used by many retailers.

10 Store Layout and Design

LEARNING OBJECTIVES

After studying this chapter, you will be able to
- understand the importance of an appropriate store layout
- delineate the key elements of layout and discuss the factors that are taken into consideration while designing the layout of a store
- gain an insight into how the store layout and its elements help in enhancing customers' shopping experience

INTRODUCTION

The store, which is the direct point of contact between the retailer and the shoppers, has always occupied a central role in retailing. In a cluttered marketplace, retailers often find that it is very difficult to create a differential advantage on the basis of merchandise, price, promotion, and location. In such a situation, the store itself becomes a point of differentiation. We can very well think of a store as a theatre. The walls and floors are the stage; the lighting, fixtures, and signs represent the sets; and the merchandise and the store personnel represent the show. All components need to work in synchronization to maximize the impact of the merchandise. A customer who is familiar with the store layout is likely to buy more than those unfamiliar with it.[1] The layout helps support the customers' memory of the list of things they plan to buy and where they are likely to find these items in the store. Compared to serviced stores, in many categories, open format stores have led to increased purchase and widening of the consideration set.[2]

OBJECTIVES OF LAYOUT AND DESIGN

Consumer studies indicate that they would like to reduce the time spent on shopping. Many feel that shopping adds stress to their family life.[3] Increased working hours and the rise in the number of working women are exerting pressure on the time that families have and shopping is being seen as a chore to be completed.[4] In addition to time, there are many factors, especially those inside the stores, which create stress. Crowding and 'trolley rage', music, relocation of stock, floor and shelf space, parking, checkout, aisle width, congestion, overheating, badly behaved children, older and slow moving customers, and disabled customers are seen as factors that increase the stress levels of consumers.[5]

The proximate environment that surrounds the shopper is never neutral. The retail store is a bundle of cues, messages, and suggestions that communicate with the shoppers.[6] The retail settings affect the consumer response through the two emotional states of pleasure and arousal. However, these are difficult to measure as (a) they are basically emotional states and thus difficult to verbalize;

(b) they are transient and difficult to recall; and (c) they influence behaviour within the store rather than external behaviour such as store choice.[7] Since most of the attributes that make up the environment and impact shoppers are at or below the conscious level of the customer, their measurement is difficult. This leads to inaccuracies and misinterpretation of findings. Moreover, our common-sense notion of the relationship between architecture and activity is often erroneous.[8] Shoppers react to space, light, acoustics, air quality, temperature, comfort, tidiness, and colour.[9] The point-of-purchase settings affect consumer mood states, which, in turn, may affect in-store beliefs and evaluation.[10] Therefore, in order that the customers enjoy their shopping, stores need to be designed with the following objectives:

1. The store's atmosphere should be consistent with the store's image and strategy.
2. The store design should help influence shopping decisions.
3. It should lead to increased productivity of the retail space.
4. It should enhance the experience of the customer.

ELEMENTS OF STORE LAYOUT

A number of factors need to be kept in mind while deciding on the layout of a store. Type and amount of merchandise, location, floor pattern, and product display are some of the key factors that need to be considered by retailers. This requires an understanding of how customers interact with the retail environment. For instance, in case of malls, where most shoppers come to spend most part of the day, the layout is designed keeping in mind the different shops, their locations, and the fact that the mall should provide good facilities such as restrooms, chairs, eateries, and entertainment. Hypermarkets and most shops that deal in bulky items provide easy access to parking so that shoppers can take their trolleys close to their vehicles.

Every variable within the store—including the layout, furniture, and other customers—sends out some kind of message to the customer. Some basic elements of layout that are primarily responsible for this communication are planning and circulation, storefronts and entrances, merchandising, materials and finishes, lighting and music, and graphics and signage. Let us discuss each of these elements in detail.

PLANNING AND CIRCULATION

Planning and circulation are possibly the most essential aspects of in-store retail communication. However, the amount of effort that goes into planning these aspects is concealed from the shopper since a good plan is seamless and invisible to the shopper. The planning should allow for guiding and helping the shopper through the space naturally. Appropriate planning will help the store to operate effectively, without the design 'getting in the way'. The designer's task in the circulation is largely functional—moving people through and around the retail environment. Good circulation works unobtrusively. No shopper likes the feeling of being herded around the store; they would rather appreciate being helped by logic, convenience, and visual recommendation. A wide range of factors influence store planning and layout. Most designers start with an architectural assessment of the store infrastructure, including the entrances, stock and service area, and staircases. They also consider the relationships between different departments and areas. The plan helps in using space effectively and efficiently.

Circulation Plans[11]

Within the store there is a limited number of ways for shoppers to move—front to back, diagonally across, from side to side, and, in multi-level stores, up and down. Planning the circulation of the store involves determining and facilitating these movements, based on the expected pattern of customer behaviour. Circulation needs to be simple. A complex circulation path distracts and confuses the customer. Narrow aisles create congestion in the store, forcing the shopper to worry about moving through without bumping into people or merchandise. Vertical circulation is treated in the same way as horizontal, clarity and generosity of space being crucial. In a retail store with several levels, the design would encourage shoppers to move up or down from the entrance level, in order to support business in the less popular parts of the store. The means of vertical circulation, such as the stairway, escalator, or elevator, need to be clearly visible.

It can sometimes seem as though only a small number of basic circulation plans exist for retailing. In practice, however, circulation can be endlessly varied. Retailers use a mix of these plans to enhance customer experience. A few basic designs are described here.

Straight Plan   As the name implies, the straight plan provides for the shoppers to cover the store with direct access from front to back. Walls are used for stocks, as are floor-standing units. Projecting walls or the placement of display units to divert circulation helps in breaking the monotony. The simplicity of the straight plan encourages shoppers to move to the back of the store. Retailers use signs of special promotions or features to draw customers to the end of the aisle or remote areas of the store.

Race Track Walkway or Pathway Plan   This type of plan is common in larger stores and consists of a distinct circulation path that helps shoppers move through the store. The pathway may be defined by differing floor materials, changes in the ceiling treatment, or even just a clearing of display units. These pathways work as circulation devices in department stores. Shoppers travel along a well-defined route passing the aisles and shelves until they see something that attracts their attention.

Diagonal Path   This type of plan immediately creates movement by defying the normal rectilinear grid of a store. The focal point where the lines or aisles converge in a diagonal plan is very crucial. For example, a cash-taking service or information desk in a central location or a special display or feature may be a helpful focal point in such a plan.

Curved Plan   Curved plans ensure circulation with the help of curved walls that suggest more movement than straight ones. The aisles are concentric to the wall. As the end of the aisle is not visible, customers tend to feel that they have more to see, and hence keep moving. This may lead to a loss of sense of direction. A store provides exits and signage at strategic points to make shopping convenient. Constructing curved surfaces can, however, be expensive. Retailers need to be careful in this design as it requires structural changes.

Figures 10.1 (a)–(c) show sample layouts of some stores. The circulation plan is related to the extent of 'wandering' allowed by the store. It may also be associated with the type of merchandise, which, in turn, reflects the extent of planning and information search at the store.

Circulation Graphics

Graphics play an important role, especially in larger stores. In large stores, customers need to know exactly where they are and how they can get to each floor. Graphics are used as a directional tool along the circulatory route, at every point of decision. Department or concession signage tell the customers that they have reached the desired place. Even when the store is carefully planned, circulation store directories are necessary. These are placed strategically near entrances, escalators, and other vertical circulation routes. Good planning and circulation within a store or shopping centre is paramount. Signage is the silent salesperson for the business. Studies have shown that as much as 80 per cent of all sales are generated at the point of purchase by signage, displays, and events within the store. In order to differentiate itself from competition and portray the right image, it is necessary to have the right signs. A retailer may keep the following points in mind while choosing signage:

1. Signs should be short and clear. Customers need to see them within 3 seconds.
2. Signages need to have consistency in terms of colour, size, type, style, and layout.
3. Features/benefits or price signs are noticed immediately.
4. Policies need to be stated clearly and positively.

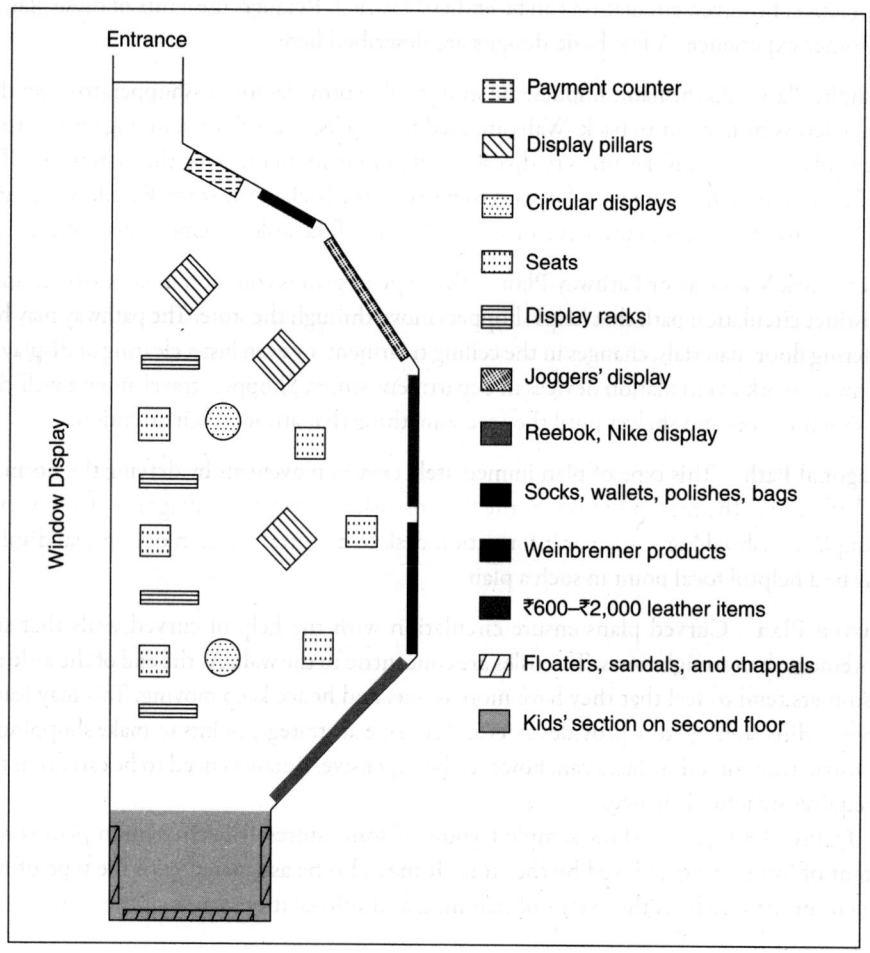

(a) Layout of a Shoe Store

FIG. 10.1 Sample Layout of Some Stores

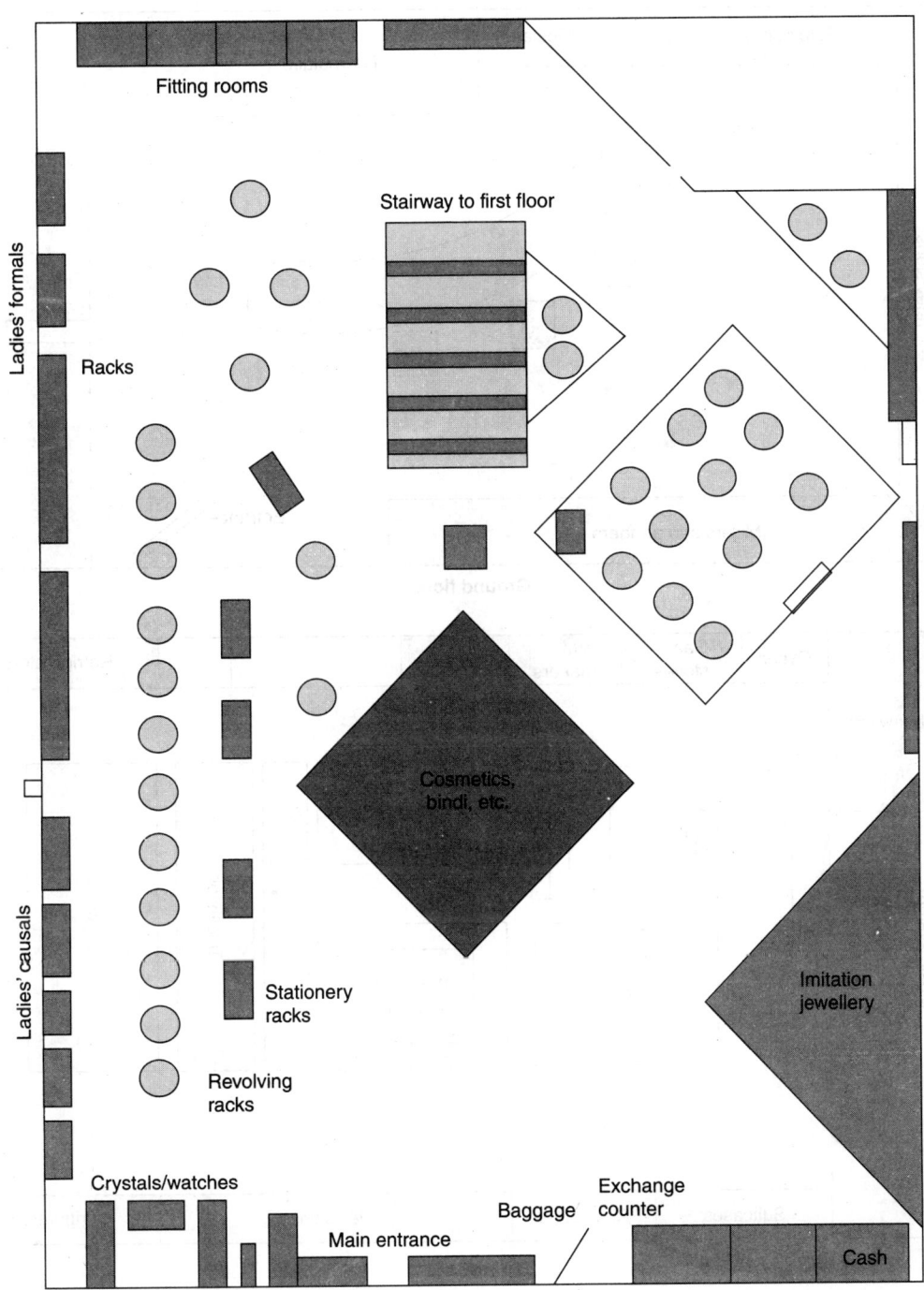

Fitting rooms

Ladies' formals

Racks

Stairway to first floor

Cosmetics, bindi, etc.

Imitation jewellery

Ladies' causals

Stationery racks

Revolving racks

Crystals/watches

Main entrance

Baggage

Exchange counter

Cash

(b) Layout of a Women's Apparel Store

FIG. 10.1 (Contd)

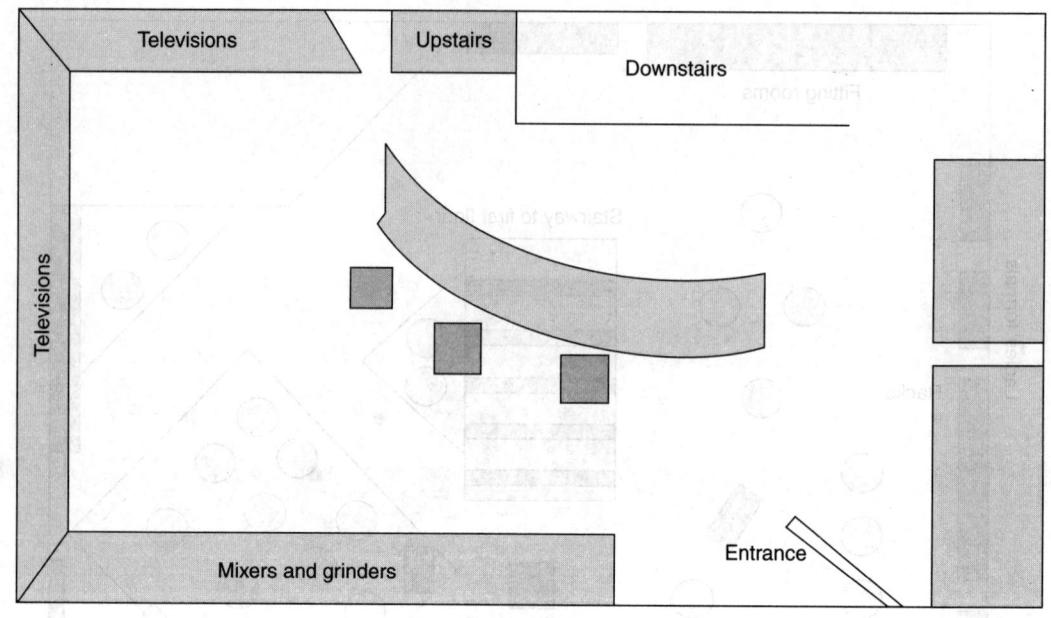

Ground floor

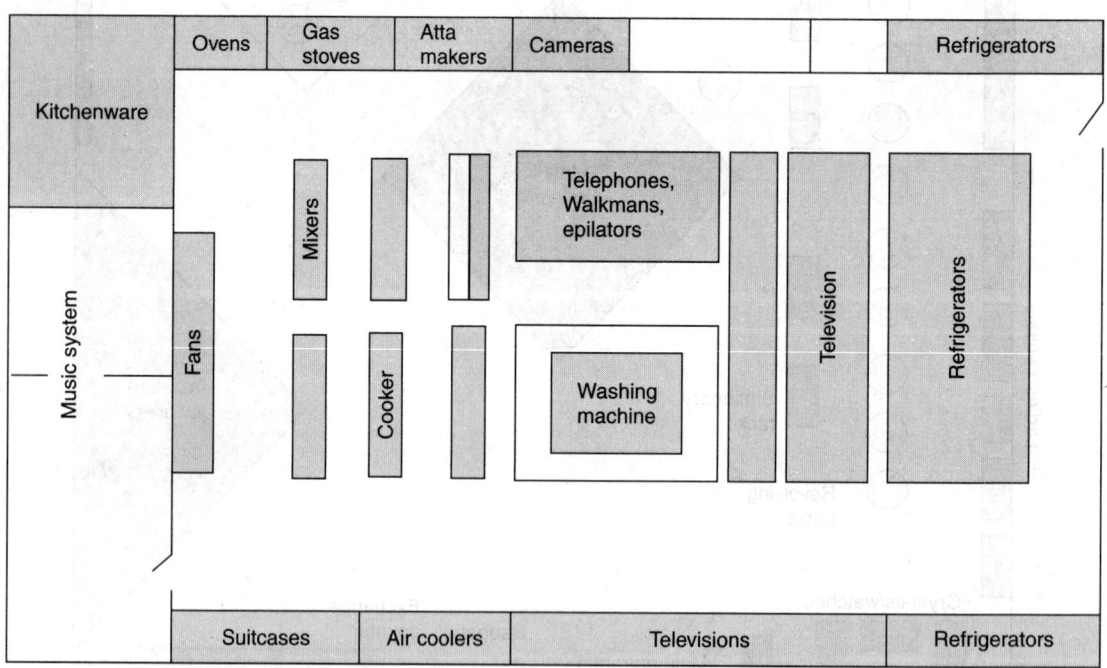

Basement

(c) Layout of a Two-floor Consumer Durable Strore

FIG. 10.1 (Contd)

STOREFRONTS AND ENTRANCES[12]

The first impression created by a store design is critical. The storefront and entrance are a condensed version of everything the design is trying to communicate. The first aim is obviously to attract the target customers to the store. The storefront must be able to communicate whether the store fits the customers' choice. Storefront presentation can be improved with windows or lighting or even with the installation of a better sign. Customers may initially be attracted to a store, but if they discover that the store is not what it seems to be, they are likely to leave, seldom to return. If the storefront is not managed well, it can even turn away shoppers who would otherwise have been attracted to the merchandise inside. Lack of cohesion between the exterior and the interior is likely to create dissonance.

Facades

The exterior communicates its message through many elements: the windows and the character of the window displays, the nature of the entrance, views of the interior, signs, and the material with which the entrance itself is constructed. Each of these elements needs to be consistent and harmonious with the others. The design of the exterior cannot be considered in isolation as such a design is likely to create a disjunction between the interior and the exterior. Creating an exterior that is in sync with the store interior may be difficult. It is even more challenging to create a harmonious design for chain stores. A chain store with sites in varied locations may not have identical storefronts, but it needs to have a common identity across sites.

The choice of a recessed or a projecting storefront is another crucial consideration in designing a storefront. A recessed storefront offers protection from the weather and acts as a funnel drawing shoppers into the store. A projecting storefront intrudes into the street or complex, thus announcing the presence of the store directly to the shoppers. The choice of projecting or recessing depends on the need to differentiate the storefront from its surroundings.

Entrances

All the devices of the facade are preludes to the entrance itself. Except where the openness of the store is a design feature, the entrance provides a sense of transition from the world outside to the world of the retailer inside. There is a direct relationship between the kind of door that is used and the customers' perception of the store. The function of a door is much more than providing security to the store. It can be used to communicate exclusivity.

There are many kinds of doors. Swinging doors are side hinged, usually made of glass, and have a frame of wood or metal. Sliding doors usually open automatically and slide into a side recess. Revolving doors prevent a direct path between the interior and exterior of the store. In a sense, such a door is always closed, so that wind and drafts cannot blow directly into the building. However, revolving doors are extremely expensive. While designing the door, the type and positioning of the door handle or door push should be thoughtfully considered, especially keeping in mind those with armfuls of shopping bags.

Windows

Windows are an ideal way to attract new and existing customers. They are used for selling promotions, image building, seasonal changes, new arrivals, and to showcase high-demand items. Window displays need to be changed frequently so that they do not become stale, and, therefore, easy to ignore. The frequency of changing window displays depends on seasons, type of merchandise, promotional intensity, and festivals and occasions.

Material for Storefronts

The choice of material for the storefront conveys much about the image of the store. In most cases, it provides a clear indication about the culture, values, and interiors of the store. The use of stone, marble, or granite, for example, suggests a solid and enduring quality of the store. In contrast, stainless steel offers an image of a contemporary, mechanistic, and, perhaps, transitory style. The many varieties and adaptability of wood allow it to serve many ends. It is very versatile and can be shaped to suit any design. Metal storefronts require less maintenance and aluminium in particular is extremely cost effective. More expensive metals, such as bronze, brass, or stainless steel, convey an image of excellent quality, but the initial capital investment is very high. The creation of a memorable experience for the customer must be a prime objective of the retail design—a storefront not only serves the retailer's culture appropriately, but also acts as the first point in differentiation.

Window Display of a Computer Hardware Store

MERCHANDISE DISPLAY

Retailers display their merchandise in an appropriate environment in order to encourage the sale of products. They need to organize the merchandise keeping in mind the stock densities and equipment. There are a number of considerations that apply to merchandising in all types of retailing. Since the merchandise is the *raison d'être* of any store, its presentation is of prime importance in determining the character of the store.

Fixtures

Retailers can choose between custom-designed fixtures and off-the-rack or stock fixtures. Most designers opt for custom-designed fixtures. Customized fixtures lend uniqueness to the individual store and are better suited for the merchandise. In some cases, special fixtures can become a part of the store's

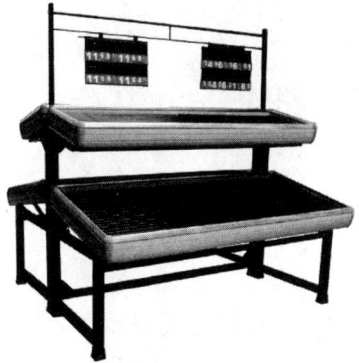

Fruit and Vegetable Display Unit

Display Units for Trousers

Display Units

identity. Special fixtures, however, translate into additional costs and time for the design. The use of stock fixtures, along with some degree of customization in terms of changing finishes or materials and additional features, provides an appropriate and proven solution for many projects. Whether the fixtures are custom designed or stock fixtures, care should be taken to keep the design as simple, as possible. These designs can be altered with changes in the market, sales, and seasons.

Positioning of Merchandise

One of the first considerations in deciding the fixtures for a stores is whether the merchandise should be accessible to the customer. There are situations where the merchandise is not made accessible due to reasons of security, danger, and fragility. Inaccessibility also implies a certain exclusivity and desirability. Placing the fixtures in a position where assistance from the sales staff is essential can also create inaccessibility. The height and position of merchandise in cases where exclusivity is not required needs careful planning. Stores also have to decide whether the fixtures should be wall-mounted/perimeter units or floor-standing units. Most stores use some combination of the two. The ratio is determined on the basis of the size of the store, circulation plans, and stock densities. In some fashion stores, for example, perimeter wall units permit three levels of stock. This high perimeter density can then allow less dense mid-floor presentation. Retailers tend to give the best spaces to high-margin and or destination categories and items. Research shows that shelves at the eye level and just below it are the best shelves to sell from. While allowing for individual creativity, some effective guidelines for displays could be followed:[13]

1. Tell a story or have a theme.
2. Keep displays simple. Avoid putting in too many items.
3. Try displaying products in situations depicting their actual use.
4. Focus on impulse items.
5. Use proper lighting and props.
6. Do power walls (displays of mass amounts to show bestsellers).
7. Show complementary/coordinating items together.
8. Change displays on an ongoing basis.
9. Integrate your advertising into your displays.
10. Use motion, if possible, to attract attention.
11. Focus on bestsellers.

In a study that involved mental mapping of some superstores, shoppers were able to recall the location of some of the merchandise. In most of the cases, however, majority of the answers were incorrect. Of the items recollected, about two-thirds were in peripheral aisles and the rest were in the central area. Almost nine out of ten items that were correctly located were in peripheral aisles.[14] The poor item location recall in the central areas seems to be due to a lack of locational cues or mnemonic aids in what is essentially an undifferentiated area. This has some relation with the kind of products stocked in these aisles. The study found that the items were located twice as accurately in the periphery as in the central area.

MATERIALS AND FINISHES

Materials and finishes for a store are generally determined by three factors: the image they convey, practical considerations, and cost. A wood floor, for example, may stand for either a high-class retailer or a bargain, no-frills environment, depending on the nature of the merchandise. Practical considerations include availability, durability,

A Floor-standing Display Unit

fire resistance, and ease of replacement. While deciding on the material and finishes, retailers consider capital costs and cost of maintenance. Retailers pay particular attention to three basic elements—floors, walls, and ceilings.

Floors

Floor finishes can create different atmospheres, zones, walkways, and even departments. Larger stores use a wide range of floors to differentiate various sections and departments. The flooring in each section

Children's Apparel Store

Luggage Store

Merchandise Display

is chosen in such a way that it matches the look of that particular section and the overall design of the store. Retailers use carpets, wood, and tiles for flooring. Carpets aid the establishment of a store's identity. Wooden floors are seemingly more durable than carpets. Good wooden floors look even better because they take on a colouration and patina and merge with the overall look after some time. The rich patterns and the quality of the wood help in creating traditional, more exclusive environments. Although carpet and wood are likely to be the most common choices for flooring, some 'non-resilient' materials such as marble, terrazzo, mosaic, granite, and ceramic tiles are also used. These floorings are durable and easy to clean but they may be hard and uncomfortable surfaces to walk on and may create much noise in the store. Tiles are more desirable in aisles and other heavy traffic areas. In addition to the various natural forms of flooring, a wide variety of resilient surfaces, such as vinyl and linoleum, are also available. These are available in many versions, including imitation wood, marble, and terracotta.

Interior Walls

There is considerable diversity in finishes and materials for walls. Paint is the least expensive and most flexible of finishes for walls. However, many painted finishes are easily soiled. A well-maintained store requires frequent re-painting. The other common wall finish is plaster. It provides several possibilities. A combination of plaster and paint can give walls a sculptural three-dimensional quality. Plaster can also be mixed with fibreglass, glass, concrete, and different resins to improve structural and weathering qualities. Besides paint and plaster, the store can also choose from brick, marble, concrete, wood, plastic, laminate, mirror, fabric, paper, and other materials, depending entirely on how the wall is to be used. A retailer needs to decide the extent of wall that would be visible. In many stores, where the perimeter is used for display, walls perform a subsidiary role in the design.

Ceilings

The ceiling is one of the most complex parts of a store, usually carrying and concealing many vital services such as lighting, electrical wiring, air conditioning, security equipment, and fire protecting devices. They can become a dominant visual, distracting the shoppers from the merchandise below. The various types of finishes described for walls apply to ceilings as well. Ceilings can be suspended or false.

While the appearance of walls, floors, and ceilings is crucial, retailers should also consider fittings and equipment while deciding on finishes. Fittings and equipment need to not only suit their function but also fit into the overall scheme. Retailers should combine uniqueness and experimentation with practicality, good value, and appropriateness.

LIGHTING

Studies have shown that proper lighting can increase sales by up to 20 per cent. A study showed that consumer reactions vary with the three-way congruence between a store's environmental cues, consumers' cognitive categories representing known store types, and salient situational shopping motivations. For fashion-oriented stores, blue interiors are associated with more favourable evaluations, marginally greater excitement, higher store patronage intentions, and higher purchase intentions than are orange interiors. However, the results change substantially when the effect of lighting in combination with colour is considered. The use of soft lights with an orange interior generally nullifies the ill effects of orange and produces the highest level of perceived price fairness while controlling for price. Additionally, the results suggest that the effects of environmental and price cues are mediated by consumers' cognitive and affective associations.[15] Stores should ensure that there are no burnt out lights. Cheaper bulbs can cause merchandise

Internal Lighting

to look grey and shabby. Spotlights, preferably halogen ones, highlight key selling areas better. The front of the store should glow with light for the store to be noticed. A bright storefront is more attractive and appealing.

Lighting performs the essential function of illuminating the store and its merchandise. It is also one of the most important elements that give the store its atmosphere. Skilful use of lighting can often rescue mediocre designs. Lighting is about the contrast between light and shade. Most stores fit into one of the two broad categories of lighting— ambient lighting and theatrical lighting. *Ambient-lit* stores, such as supermarkets, do-it-yourself stores, or drugstores, require an overall level of illumination while *theatrically-lit* settings are usually preferred for fashion stores or jewellers. Lighting must be considered in the context of the floor plan and the merchandise strategy for the store. Circulation areas can be differentiated using lighting. It is important to understand what part of the merchandise needs to be illuminated. For most items, the front matters more than the top. The problem of glare can be minimized by designing the lighting within the case.

Lighting can sometimes be featured in the plinths of counters, gondolas, and other floor units. This technique can be used to lighten the apparent heaviness of bulky sales counters and can help give counters a floating appearance. In some stores, a dropped bulkhead provides housing for the light fixtures. It also defines the walkway by allowing the side lighting to spill over the rest of the store. To help create a sense of space within a store or to emphasize its spatial qualities, the effect of lighting on walls becomes important. Strong, positive perimeter lighting can help define the total space, particularly in stores with several floors, where it helps the shoppers to get some idea of the store shape and space. Stores utilize natural light in the best possible way as it aids colour rendition and provides spatial interest to the interior of the store. Also, it is free.

MUSIC

Music can be an essential element in a store. It is used to create an environment that influences shopping behaviour positively. Sales have been found to be affected by the kind of music being played in the store. In a study conducted in a grocery store that played muzak, higher sales were recorded compared to stores playing radio music, contemporary music, or no music.[16] Another study found that the sales increased by 38 per cent when a supermarket played a slower music compared to when it played fast music. This was attributed to the pace of the customers. Another study showed that customers in stores that played slower music spent about 20 per cent more time in travelling between two observational points.[17] Not all studies have found a direct impact of music on sales. However, shoppers have been found to spend more time in stores that play soft music as compared to stores that play loud music.[18] In any case, music makes shoppers spend more time in the store and changes their pace, which can be utilized to build

TABLE 10.1 Emotional Expression Ascribed to Various Components of Music

Time-related Expressions

1. Duple rhythm produces a rigid and controlled expression in comparison with triple rhythm, which is more relaxed or abandoned.

2. The faster the tempo, the more is the animation and happiness expressed.

3. Even, rhythmic movement can represent the unimpeded flow of some feeling; dotted, jerky, and uneven rhythms produce more complex expressions.

4. Firm rhythms suggest a serious mood, whereas smooth-flowing rhythms are more playful.

5. Staccato notes give more emphasis to a passage than legato notes.

Pitch-related Expressions

1. 'Up' and 'Down' in pitch not only correspond to up and down in the physical world, but can also imply 'out-and-in' as well as 'away-and-back', respectively.

2. Rising and falling pitch can convey a growing or diminishing intensity in a given emotional context.

3. Songs in higher key are generally considered to be happier than songs in lower keys.

4. Music in the major mode expresses more animated and positive feelings than music in the minor mode.

5. Complex harmonies are more agitated and sad than simple harmonies which are more serene and happy.

Texture-related Expressions

1. Loudness can suggest animation or proximity, whereas low volume implies tranquility or distance.

2. Cresendo (soft to loud) expresses an increase in force, whereas diminuendo (loud to soft) suggests a decrease in power.

3. The timbre of brass instruments conveys a feeling of cold, hard force, whereas reed instruments produce a lonely, melancholy expression.

sales or customer patronage by influencing the mood of the shoppers. The various ways in which music can influence shoppers are given in Table 10.1.

Music can be classified in many ways. In the retail context, it is classified mainly into foreground and background music. Foreground music refers to music with lyrics, played by original artists, whereas background music refers to instrumental music played by studio musicians. Background music tends to be more restricted in terms of tempo, frequencies, and volume. Some claim that foreground music is more suited for retail outlets.[19] Customers, young and old, seem to express a more positive attitude towards foreground music as compared to background music. Shoppers were found to be in a more active mood, especially for planned purchase, when foreground music was played.[20] However, younger shoppers, as compared to older shoppers, spend more time in stores that play background music.

Stores need to be careful and play the kind of music that reflects the products at the store and the type of clientele that the store wants to attract. Stores that deal in music use music to promote the chosen album. It is observed that the sales of such promoted albums increase with 'air displays'. Tuning in to radio stations can sometimes be unsuitable as commercials can kill the mood to purchase, or even advertise a competitor. An appropriately structured music acts on the nervous system and activates the brain with corresponding emotional reactions.[21] Stores need to ensure that appropriate and continuous music is always played. Music has an added effect when combined with scent, as shown in Figs 10.2 (a)–(e).[22] Table 10.2 shows how various elements of music affect our emotional state.

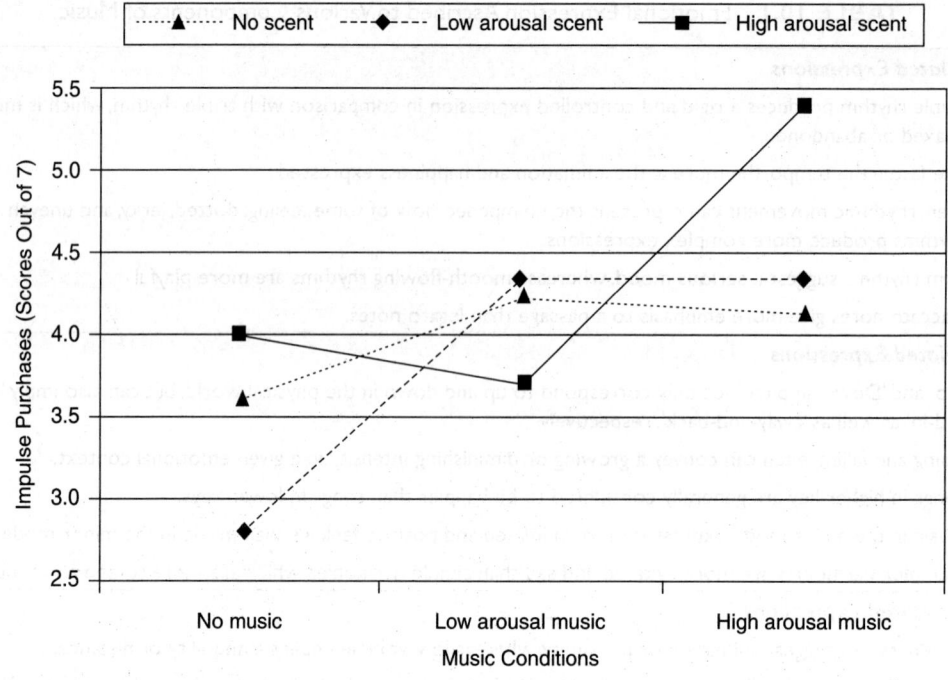

(a) Impact of Scent and Music on Impulse Purchases

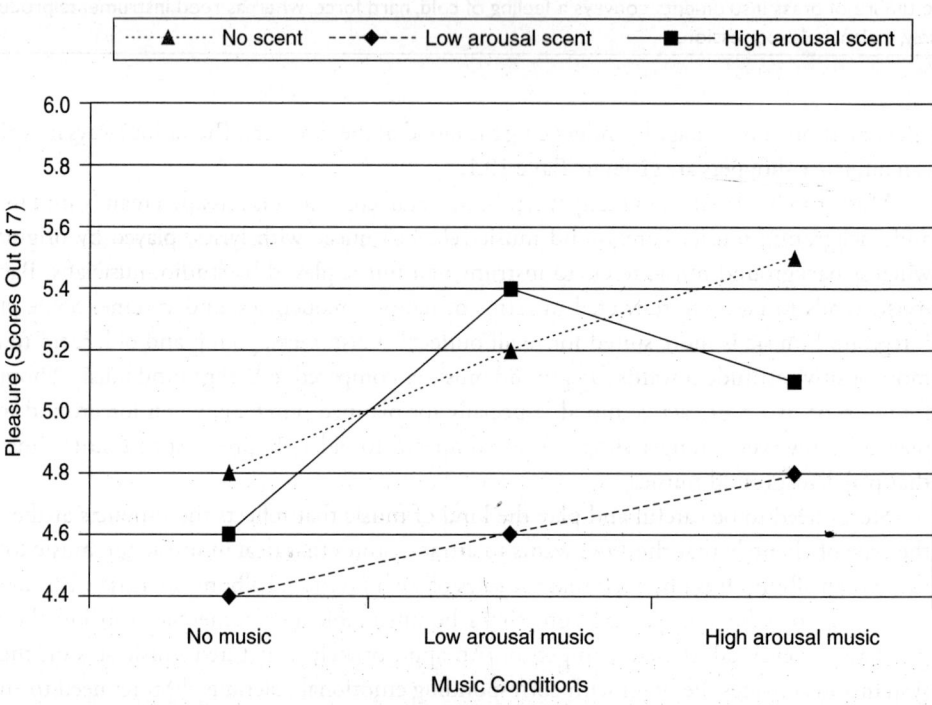

(b) Impact of Scent and Music on Pleasure

FIG. 10.2   Impact of Scent and Music on Shopping

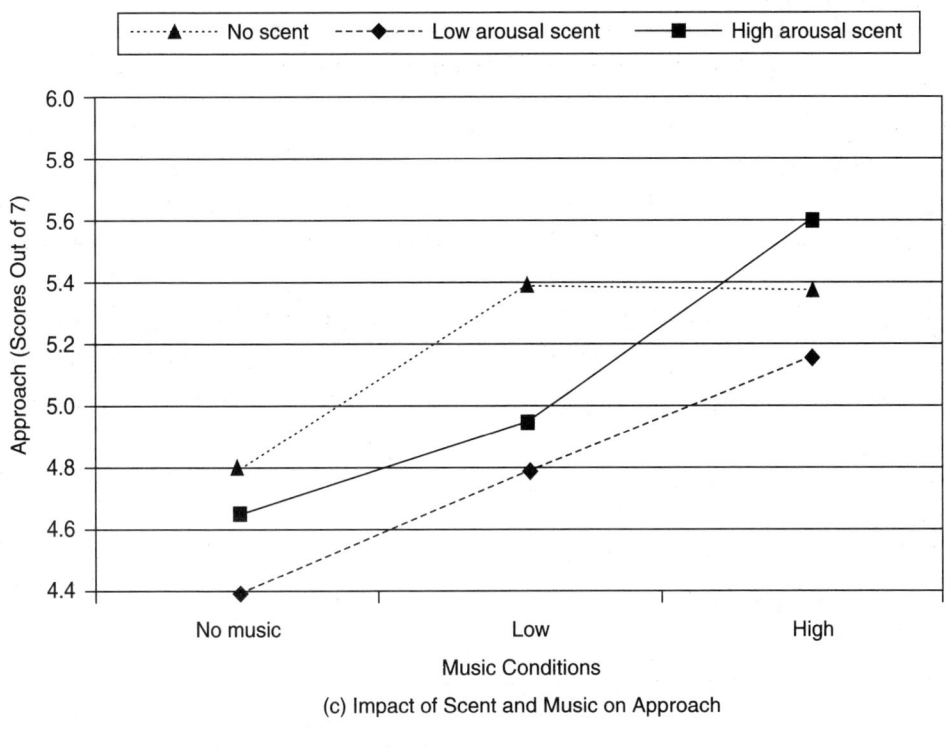

(c) Impact of Scent and Music on Approach

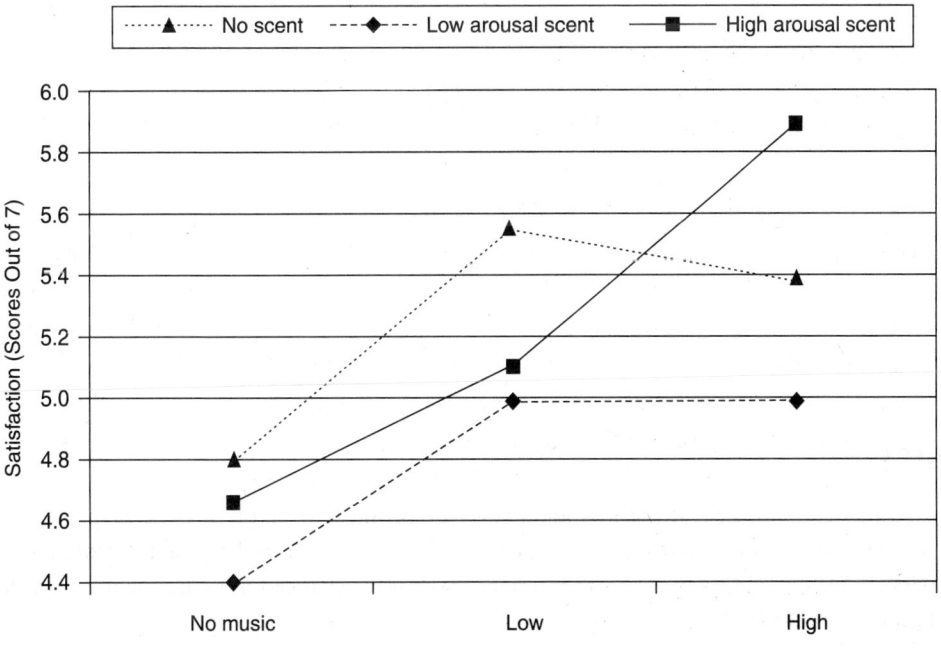

(d) Impact of Scent and Music on Satisfaction

FIG. 10.2 (Contd)

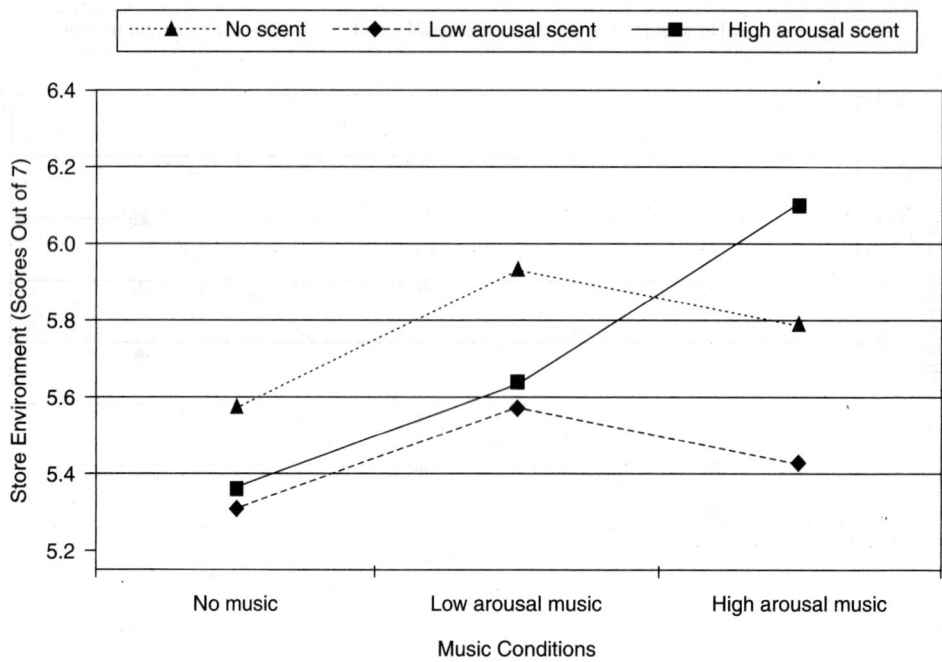

(e) Impact of Scent and Music on Store Environment

FIG. 10.2 (Contd)

TABLE 10.2   Musical Characteristics for Producing Various Emotional Expressions

Musical Element	Emotional Expression								
	Serious	*Sad*	*Sentimental*	*Serene*	*Humorous*	*Happy*	*Existing*	*Majestic*	*Frightening*
Mode	Major	Minor	Minor	Major	Major	Major	Major	Major	Major
Tempo	Slow	Slow	Slow	Slow	Fast	Fast	Fast	Medium	Slow
Pitch	Low	Low	Medium	Medium	High	High	Medium	Medium	Low
Rhythm	Firm	Firm	Flowing	Flowing	Flowing	Flowing	Uneven	Firm	Uneven
Harmony	Consonant	Dissonant	Consonant	Consonant	Consonant	Consonant	Dissonant	Dissonant	Dissonant
Volume	Medium	Soft	Soft	Soft	Medium	Medium	Loud	Loud	Varied

GRAPHICS

Graphics communicate the store's identity to a customer. Underplaying the graphics element can prevent a store from achieving its full potential. They also help in keeping the store contemporary without major changes in the store interior. They can be changed more frequently than most other fixtures in the store.

Exterior Signage

Exterior signage creates the first impression of a store. It works as an advertisement for the store. It communicates the name as well as the character of the store. Retailers strike a balance between unnoticeable discretion and offensive overexuberance. A good signage merges into its surroundings while keeping

Exterior Signage

its distinctiveness. Sometimes, the sign itself can be a major attraction. A store can use typography of its choice. Clarity and store personality should be kept in mind while choosing the typography. Highly reflective surfaces that distort the sign or restrict visibility should be avoided. Most exterior signs are illuminated either from within or by using external lanterns, tubes, or spotlights. The simplest method of an illuminated exterior signage is pasting the signage on the plate glass of the store window. A large number of smaller stores use painted signages that are lit with a bulb or fluorescent tube.

Interior Signage

These graphics have some very specific roles: selling merchandise, giving information, and providing direction inside the store. These separate graphic groups vary with stores but they should project a single image. Different signs often perform different tasks. Signs that provide direction need to be simple and quickly comprehensible. Signs that help the selling process are more complex. They can range from the simple such as the designer label in a fashion store to the highly intricate. Signs that try to convey many things tend to confuse the customer.

LAYOUT FOR E-TAILERS[23]

Customers use three major dimensions—entertainment, organization, and informativeness—to assess a website.

Entertainment

Effective websites integrate information and entertainment. Entertainment has been defined by the look and feel of the website and its aesthetic orientation. It tends to create an impact on users' online shopping experience. The positive sensations caused by heightened levels of entertainment and aesthetics have been directly related to perceptions of service quality within the cyber environment. The positive sensations that one feels as a result of being entertained are a significant predictor of attitude towards a website and overall attitude towards the shopping experience. The entertainment dimension of the website significantly influences customers' purchases and revisit intentions, as well as customer satisfaction. An example of such a website would be www.oyestyle.com.

Organization

Website organization can be defined as the degree to which a website 'presents itself and tour-guides' the user. The way a website is organized impacts its navigation or the ability to explore the interactive environment in alternative ways to seek out information. Navigability or ease of use of website has been identified as a driving factor of e-service quality and repeat patronage. Navigability also influences a

Aisle Sign
Source: www.i5design.com

Shelf Sign
Source: www.i5design.com

Directional Display
Source: http://www.thisbroken.com

Interior Signages Used by Retailers

website's functional convenience by ensuring that customers can successfully complete intended activities. Overall, a website's organization is positively related to purchase intention, customer satisfaction, and site effectiveness, that is, the ability of the site to aid one in meeting his/her needs. Effective site organization and the ease of navigation it creates make it easier for visitors to find exactly what they are seeking and create more pleasurable and rewarding online shopping experiences. Let us take a look at Saffronart's interactive website http://www.saffronart.com/default.aspx for such an experience.

Informativeness

Informativeness refers to the perceived quality of the factual content that a website provides. Content consists of all digital subject matter, including text, video, audio, and graphics, as well as the message specifics pertaining to product/service and informational offerings. Information content has been posited as a driver of the acceptance of new information technologies and a conduit for task-oriented users to achieve their goals and/or solve their problems. Information acquisition, particularly with respect to product availability, price, features, and quality comparisons, is the primary reason individuals are motivated to use online resources. The quantity and credibility of information are critical drivers of online service quality and are predictors of customer preferences for the website, intent to purchase and revisit, and perceptions of the effectiveness and satisfaction with the website. Informativeness, coupled with other design elements, influences a website's attractiveness and longevity. For example, a visit to the website www.indiaplaza.com will help us experience that.

Online environmental cues influence customers' cognitive and affective responses as well as specific shopping behaviours in terms of both approach and avoidance outcomes. Online retailers must attend to the ambient conditions, spatial layout and functionality, and signs, symbols, and objects that combine to create customers' perception of their e-servicescape, thereby capturing the entertainment, organization, and information components of website design, respectively.

SUMMARY

Store layout design is aimed at making shopping an enjoyable experience. Retailers need to design the store layout in such a way that it influences shopping decisions and leads to increased productivity of the retail space. The layout planning exercise can be carried out from the dimensions of planning and circulation, storefronts and entrances, merchandise display, materials and finishes, lighting and music, and graphics and signage. The layout is designed keeping in mind the circulation of the customers so that there are no congestions in the store. The store decides on the path on the basis of the shopping process of the customers. It also keeps in mind the pre-purchase planning that the customer undertakes. When the visit to the store is a planned one, the shopper is not much interested in looking around and prefers a layout that facilitates fast movement. On the other hand, when the shopper wishes to look around while shopping, a straight path is not stimulating.

It has been found that when shoppers spend more time in a store, they not only feel good about it but also tend to purchase more. The image and the business of the store is enhanced due to good layout design. The elements of layout create the right atmospherics by using music, lights, smell, and displays. These elements help the store become a preferred one and it is able to sell products that do not necessarily form part of the shoppers' basket. Well-placed signage helps in finding the merchandise as well as in stimulating unplanned purchases.

NOTES

1. Iyer, Eswar S. and Sucheta S. Ahlawat 1987, 'Deviation from a Shopping Plan: When and Why do Consumers not Buy Items as Planned', *Advances in Consumer Research*, Vol. 14, Issue 1, University of Massachusetts, pp. 246–50.

2. Sinha, Piyush Kumar and Dwarika Prasad Uniyal 2004, 'Using Observation Research for Segmenting Shoppers', *Journal of Retailing and Consumer Research*, Netherlands.

3. Fram, E.H. and J. Axelrod 1990, 'The Distressed Shopper', *American Demographics*, Vol. 12, No. 10, pp. 44–5.

4. Lavin, M. 1993, 'Wive's Employment, Time Pressure, Phone and Mail Order Shopping—An Exploratory Study', *Journal of Direct Marketing*, Vol. 7, No. 1, pp. 42–9; Kelly, D. 1994, 'Doing the Time Crunch—Again', *Prospects*, May 27, Lehman Brothers Global Economics, New York.

5. Yalch, R. and E. Spangenberg 1990, 'Effects of Store Music on Shopping Behaviour', *Journal of Consumer Marketing*, Vol. 7, No. 2, Spring, pp. 55–63.

6. Markin, R.J., C.L. Lillis, and C.L. Narayana 1976, 'Social Psychological Significance of Store Space', *Journal of Retailing*, Vol. 52, No. 1, pp. 43–54.

7. Donovan, R.J. and J.R. Rossiter 1982, 'Store Atmosphere: An Environmental Psychology Approach', *Journal of Retailing*, Vol. 58, No. 1, pp. 34–57.

8. Holahan, C.J. 1978, *Environment and Behaviour*, Plenum Press, New York.

9. Greenland, S.J. and P.J. McGoldrick 1992, 'Researching the Effects of Retail Environment upon Customer Behaviour in the Financial Services Sector', European Marketing Academy Conference, May, Aarhus.

10. Gardner, M.P. 1985, 'Mood States and Consumer Behaviour', *Journal of Consumer Research*, December.

11. Levy, M. and B.A. Weitz 2003, *Retailing Management*, 5th edn, Tata McGraw-Hill, Delhi.

12. Newman, A.J. and P. Cullen 2002, *Retailing: Environment and Operations*, Thomson Learning, 1st edn, pp. 14–15.

13. Sinha, Piyush Kumar and Dwarika Prasad Uniyal 2005, 'Using Observational Research for Behavioural Segmentation of Shoppers', *Journal of Retailing and Consumer Services*, January, Vol. 12, Issue 1, pp. 35–48.

14. Sommers, R. and Susan Aitkens 1982, 'Mental Mapping of Two Superstores', *Journal of Consumer Research*, Vol. 9, pp. 211–15.

15. Babin, Barry J., David M. Hardesty, and Tracy A. Suter 2003, 'Colour and Shopping Intentions: The Intervening Effect of Price Fairness and Perceived Affect', *Journal of Business Research*, Vol. 56, No. 7, pp. 541–51.

16. Ware, Jeff and Gerald L. Patrick 1984, 'Gelson's Supermarkets: Effect of MUZAK Music on Purchasing Behaviour of Supermarket Shoppers', MUZAK Research Report.

17. Milliman, Ronald E. 1982, 'Using Background Music to Affect the Behaviour of Supermarket Shoppers', *Journal of Marketing*, Vol. 46, pp. 86–91.

18. Cain Smith, Patricia and Ross Curnow 1966, 'Arousal Hypotheses and the Effects of Music on Purchasing Behaviour', *Journal of Applied Psychology*, Vol. 50, Issue 3, pp. 255–6.

19. Rath, Lee 1984, 'Store Music Directly Affects Buying Trends: Expert Advises Tailoring it to Suit Clients', *Merchandising*, August.

20. Yalch, Richard and Eric Spangenberg 1990, 'Effects of Store Music on Shopping Behaviour', *Journal of Consumer Marketing*, Vol. 7, No. 2, pp. 55–63.

21. Clynes, M. and N. Nethelim 1982, 'The Living Quality of Music', in M. Clynes (ed.), *Music, Mind and Brain*, Plenum Press, New York, pp. 47–82.

22. Matilla, A.S. and J. Wirtz 2001, 'Congruency of Scent and Music as a Driver of In-store Evaluation and Behaviour', *Journal of Retailing*, Vol. 77, pp. 273–89.

23. Hopkins, Christopher D., Stephen J. Grove, Mary Anne Raymond, and Mary C. Laforge 2009, 'Designing The E-servicescape: Implications For Online Retailers', *Journal of Internet Commerce*, Vol. 8, pp. 23–43.

CONCEPT REVIEW QUESTIONS

1. How would you define a good layout? What are the advantages of a good layout?
2. What are the elements of layout planning? Describe these briefly.
3. What are circulation paths? Which are the different paths available to retailers? What factors are kept in mind while choosing a particular path?
4. Describe the role of music on shoppers, and its interaction with other sensory elements.
5. How does a retailer decide on the signage to be used in the store?

CRITICAL THINKING QUESTIONS

1. Why is it that two retailers selling the same merchandise follow different layouts? What factors impact their decisions?
2. How are the layout decisions of an online retailer different?

PROJECTS

1. Visit a store. Find out which sensory elements are being used to influence shoppers. Check whether these elements change with the time of the day/day of the week/season.

2. Visit an exclusive brand showroom and a multi-brand store dealing in consumer durables. Understand the layout patterns of each store and the reasons behind these.

CASE STUDY

Prerna Stores[1]

Jitendra Chaudhary, the owner–manager of Prerna Stores, had been successful in opening 15 outlets in Chandigarh. He had followed a modular model wherein all stores looked alike and had similar offerings. The layout was primarily similar but could change depending on the site. While, on the whole, the business was doing well, there seemed to exist differences in the sales pattern of stores. Most stores were performing within his expectations. The performance of two stores, however, was very different. Using the Sector 17 store as a benchmark, he asked a team of MBA students to assess the factors causing this phenomenon. Since most of the aspects of the two stores were similar, he requested them to focus on their display and layout of the store. Last week, the group of students submitted the report. Jitendra was wondering on the changes he might have to bring about for the Sector 34 store to perform better.

Snapshot of the Store

Prerna Stores

Prerna Stores was a retail grocery store belonging to the Prerna Supermarket retail chain. It had an image of being a no-nonsense grocery store without much of the frills associated with other supermarkets. The two stores studied were situated in Sectors 17 and Sector 34 of Chandigarh (see Fig. CS10.1). These stores were representative of the layout in other stores as well. These stores had a floor area of approximately 2,500 sq. ft.

Trading Area Profile

Both stores were situated in residential areas, but there was a difference in the location of the stores. The Sector 17 store was situated in the basement of a residential building, whereas the Sector 34 store was situated on the ground floor of a building and had a good frontage. The Sector 34 store was on a service road which connected the suburbs to the city. The store at Sector 17 was situated in an upmarket residential and commercial area of the city. The household income of the residents was high as most of them belonged to business class families that mostly lived in a joint family setup. This store enjoyed the advantage of being centrally located in the city. On the other hand, the store situated in Sector 34 was located at the outskirts of the city comprising young, service class families in a largely nuclear setup. The residents were generally young couples and, in most cases, both partners were working in government services. This sector was developing fast as most of the migrant population from other states and retired people were settling down in this area.

Store Layout

The layout of the two Prerna stores had largely been suggested by the managers in the chain who were

---

1. Case written by Prof. Piyush Kumar Sinha, Indian Institute of Management Ahmedabad, and Vandana Sood based on a study conducted by a group of students of PGP 2002–04.

   Teaching material of Indian Institute of Management Ahmedabad is prepared as a basis for class discussion. Cases are not designed to present illustrations of either correct or incorrect handling of administrative problems.

   © Indian Institute of Management Ahmedabad, 2004

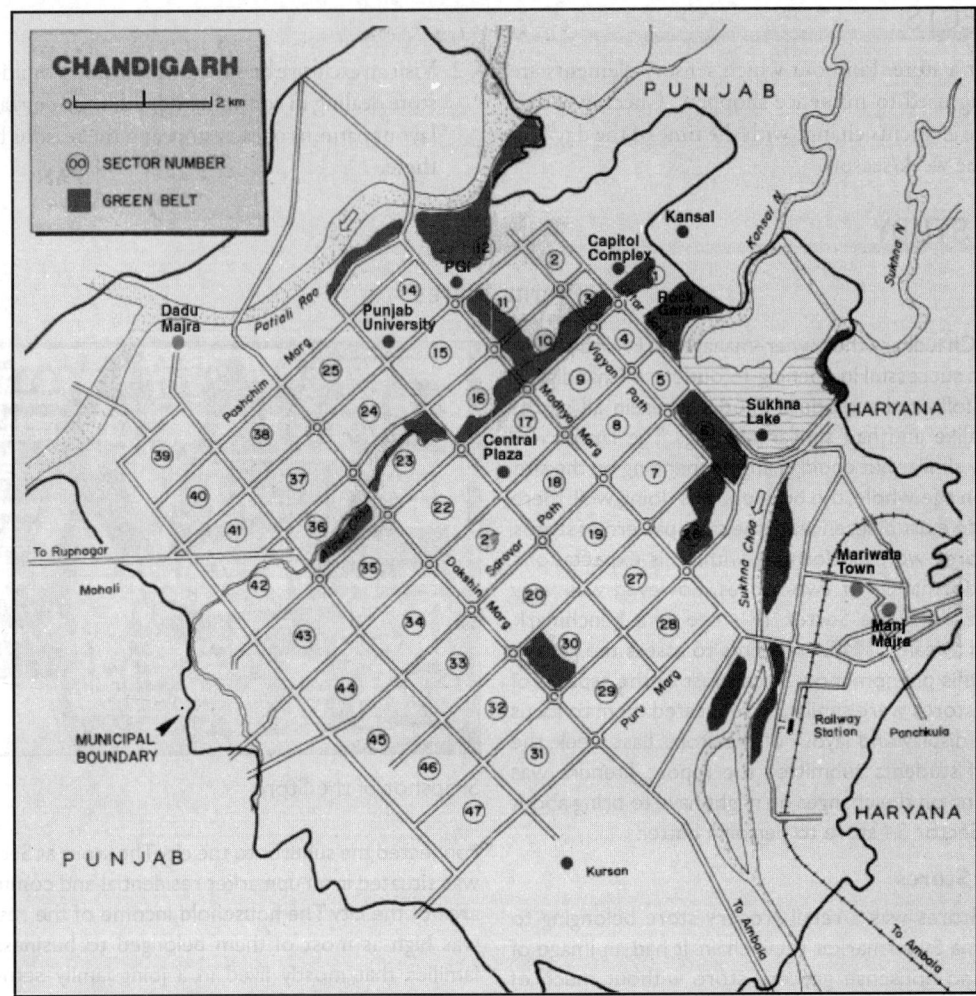

FIG. CS10.1 Map of Chandigarh

involved with retail stores for the past eleven years. The experience and feedback generated by various trial experiments held over the years, rather than any particular scientific study, had influenced the layout of the store. The stores were arranged to facilitate orderly purchases by the consumer. Prerna Stores had adopted the grid layout, which may not have been very aesthetically pleasing, but was convenient for regular customers who could easily make their way through the aisles picking up the merchandise that they needed and move speedily. It also facilitated the movements of the customer in the store by making sure that the customer

did not run into a dead end. The grid layout had a sufficient number of partitions for the consumer to cross aisles if they felt the need for it. The stores took care to use labels like 'Bakery', 'Breakfast', and 'Cosmetics', which hung from the top, indicating the kind of merchandise the customer could expect on the shelves.

Merchandising

The merchandise was categorized[2] under destination, routine, convenience, and occasional. Their positions in the store are shown in Fig. CS10.2 (for the Sector 17 store) and Fig. CS10.3 (for the Sector 34 store). The two stores

2. Destination categories consist of products and service for which the retailer is the primary provider. Routine categories are used to induce the customers to prefer the store over its competitors. Convenience categories add the value of convenience in shopping and help create an image of the retailer as one-stop shopping place. Occasional categories are provided by the retailer to cater to the seasonal or occasional needs of customers.

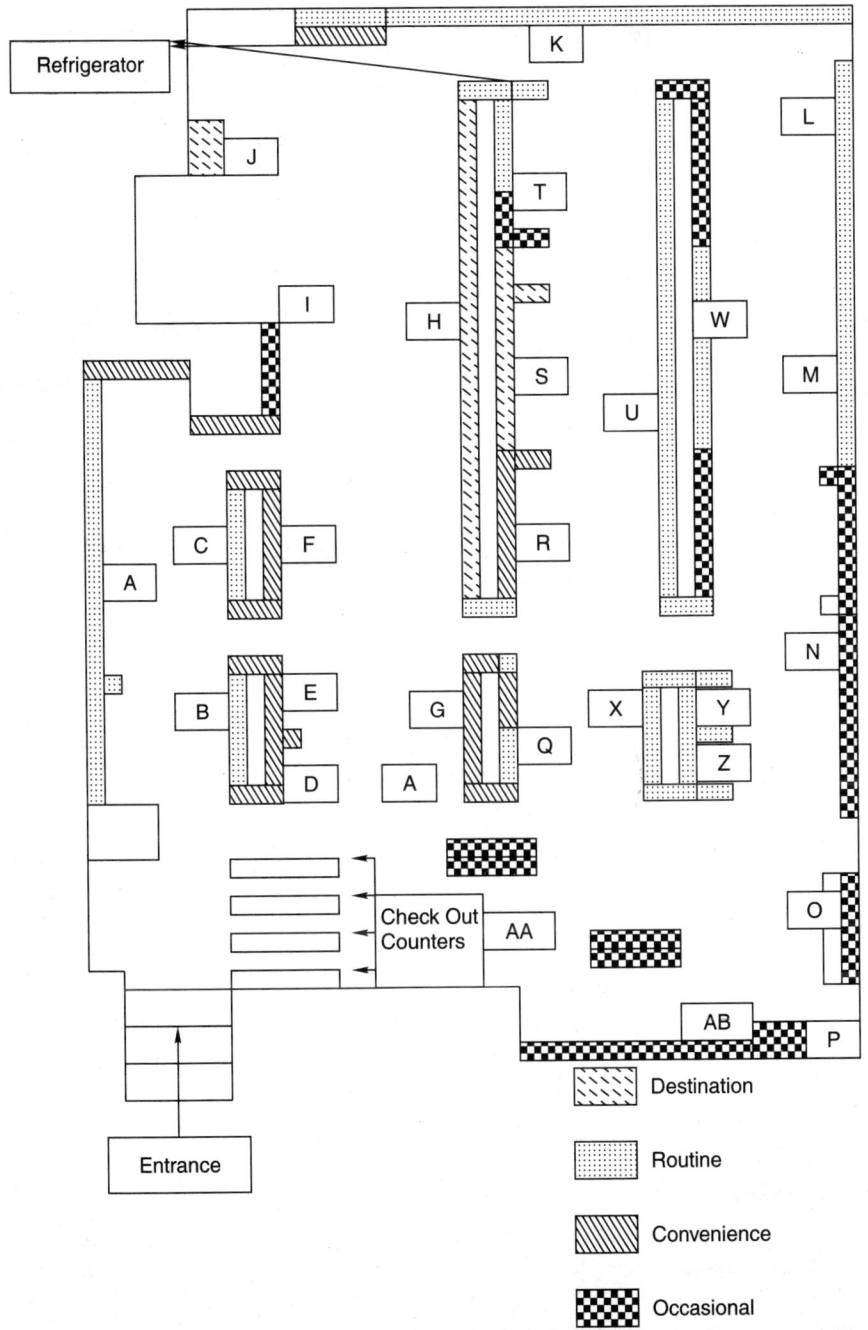

FIG. CS10.2 Category-wise Layout of Merchandise at Prerna Stores, Sector 17

were organized in 27 and 16 product classes respectively, as shown in Table CS10.1 and Table CS10.2. Most of the brands placed at eye level appeared to be either product category leaders (e.g., Wheel, Britannia Cream Treat, and Fair and Lovely), popular imported brands (e.g., Tang, McVities, Kellogg), newly introduced brands (e.g., Nestea and Lipton Iced Tea), or Prerna's own brands (Prerna's Pulses, Prerna's dry fruits, and Prerna oil).

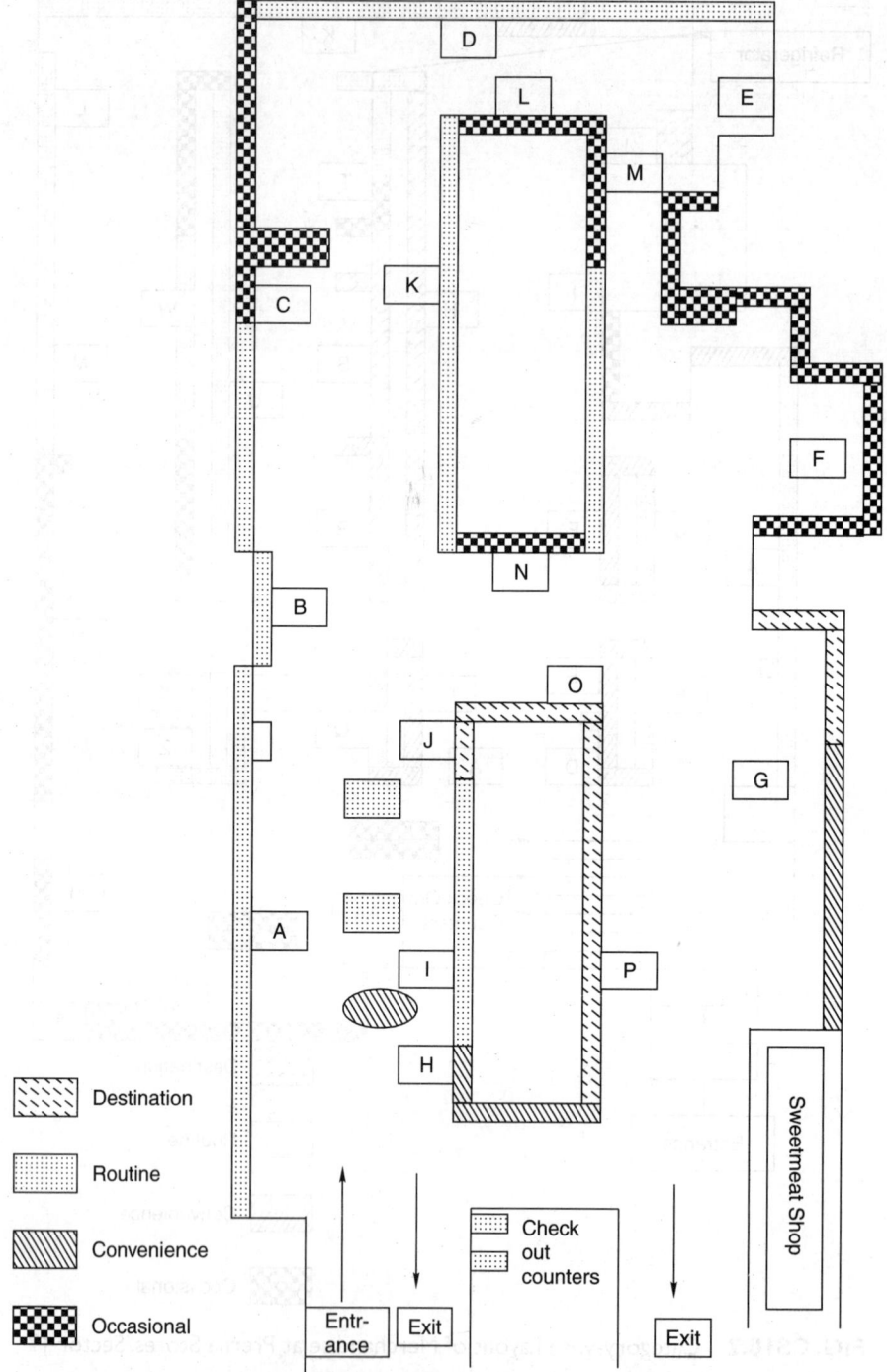

FIG. CS10.3   Category-wise Layout of Merchandise at Prerna Stores, Sector 34

TABLE CS10.1   Category Description of Prerna Stores, Sector 17

Row Code	Product Categories	Row Code	Product Categories
A	Bakery products	L	Detergents
	Wafers		Cleaning agents
	Breakfast cereals/beverages	M	Detergents
	Beverages (tea/coffee)		Cleaning agents
	Groceries (pulses)	N	Plastic ware
	Biscuits		Artificial jewellery
	Kitchens of India (spices)	P	Toys
B	Soft drinks	Q	Pulses
	Namkeen		Dry fruits
C	Soups		Preserved fruits
	Ketchup/Pickles/Jams		Deodorants
	Preserved foods	R	Pasta/Noodles
	Biscuits		Sugar
	Ready-to-fry products	S	Cooking oil
	Papad	T	Electrical goods
D	Ready-to-make/mix foods		Pet foods
E	Ready-to-make/mix foods	U	Shampoos
F	Pickles		Shaving ranges
	Masalas		Oral care ranges
	Miscellaneous grocery	W	Baby care products
G	Chocolates		OTC drugs
	Confectionery		Household products
H	Cereals/Pulses	X	Soaps
	Salt		Deodorants
I	Plastic ware	Y	Sanitary napkins
J	Rice	Z	Skin care products
K	Refrigerated dairy products	AA	Stationery
	Household products	AB	Artificial jewellery

An analysis of the percentage of eye-level SKUs with the basket of goods purchased by each customer revealed that, on an average, 55 per cent of the SKUs purchased at Sector 17 and 35 per cent of the SKUs purchased at Sector 34 were placed at eye level (Table CS10.3). This indicated that sales of eye-level SKUs (taken as a ratio of the number of SKUs sold to shelf space taken) was higher than that of SKUs placed at non-eye-level shelf locations. This also explained the reason for Prerna placing certain brands/SKUs at eye level across all stores. The items were stacked in such a manner that customers usually bought them together. The stores had snacks and breakfast items near the entrance whereas the refrigerators were placed at the back.

Shopper Movement

The store conducted a study to understand the difference in the basket size of the customers of the two stores. Besides the sale of eye-level products, it also tracked customers as they moved in the store. The route maps of the customers of Prerna Stores, Sector 17 and their basket of purchase are given in Figs CS10.4(a)–(i) and Tables CS10.4(a)–(i). Figures CS10.5(a)–(i) and Tables CS10.5(a)–(i) show the route maps and basket

TABLE CS10.2 Category Description of Prerna Stores, Sector 34

Row Code	Product Categories	Row Code	Product Categories
A	Soft drinks	H	Chocolates
	Branded wafers		Confectionery
	Biscuits	I	Namkeen
	Beverages (tea/coffee)		Papad
	Breakfast cereals	J	Spices/Condiments
B	Refrigerated dairy products		Pulses
C	Sanitary napkins	K	Deodorants
	Skin care products		Shampoos
	Baby food		Soaps
	Baby care products	L	Shoe polish
	OTC drugs		Pet food
	Glassware		Locks
	Kitchenware		Safety matches
	Paper tissues	M	Hair oil
D	Detergents		Toothpaste
	Cleaning agents		Toothbrushes
	Pesticides		Body talc
E	Home products		Shaving ranges
F	Toys		Batteries/Torches
	Plastic products		Bulbs
	Stationery	N	Garnier products
G	Pasta/Noodles	O	Rice
	Soups	P	Masalas
	Ready-to-mix/make		Pulses
	Processed foods		Cereals
	Preserved foods		Groceries (Misc.)
	Cooking oil		
	Sugar		

of purchases of each shopper at Prerna Stores, Sector 34. The route maps depict the typical movement of a representative customer through the two stores on the basis of observation. In the Sector 17 store, management of the twilight zone[3] seemed to be done well. Immediately on descending the steps to the floor of the store, there was a booth on the left where the shoppers could entrust anything they might be carrying to the guard for safekeeping. Shop assistants also handed out shopping baskets and most customers generally accepted these unless they chose to take trolleys, which lay ahead. The layout of the store with the cash counters blocking the exit to the right also essentially meant that customers had no alternative but to move ahead into the aisles where soft drinks, bread, biscuits, packed soups, tea, and a variety of other products were kept.

3. Twilight zone is the area that the shopper encounters immediately after entering the store. (Underhill Paco 1999, *Why We Buy—The Science of Shopping*, Simaon and Schuster.)

Most customers who stopped to examine them often ended up making purchases, especially in the biscuits section, where the customers tended to spend more time (around 3–4 minutes). They tended to move to the next aisle to shop for the routine products and thus covered almost the entire store.

In the Sector 34 store, the twilight zone was not as restrictive. Here, most of the customers were lured straight into the aisles where soft drinks, biscuits, and ready-to-eat food products were stored. It was this aisle in the store that was crowded the most at any point in time because any customer who entered the store necessarily visited this area. The typical customer then went on to neglect the aisle at the back of the store as

most of the regular grocery needs were satisfied by the two aisles in front of the store. The customer took a turn at B and went towards the shelves positioned at N, O, and P. They seemed to totally neglect the rear of the store. Among the customers who did venture to the back aisles, viz. K, L, and M, almost none visited the plastic segment and the stationery segments marked as F and E. This probably reflected on the product choice of the store rather than the store layout.

Issues at Hand

Should Prerna rearrange its merchandise or change the layout? Should it look at an alternative site? Should it change the format of the Sector 17 store and make it a service store as opposed to an open format store?

TABLE CS10.3 Brand Sales Analysis

Customer Number	Total SKUs Purchased	Number of SKUs at Eye Level	Proportion of Eye-level SKUs
Sector 17			
1	17	10	58.8
2	18	11	61.1
3	3	1	33.3
4	4	2	50.0
5	9	7	77.8
6	16	7	43.8
7	12	6	50.0
8	10	5	50.0
9	8	6	75.0
Mean			**55.5**
Sector 34			
1	3	2	66.66
2	17	5	29.4
3	6	3	50.0
4	4	1	25.0
5	1	0	0.0
6	1	0	0.0
7	6	3	50.0
8	9	4	44.4
9	19	11	57.9
10	7	2	28.6
Mean			**35.2**

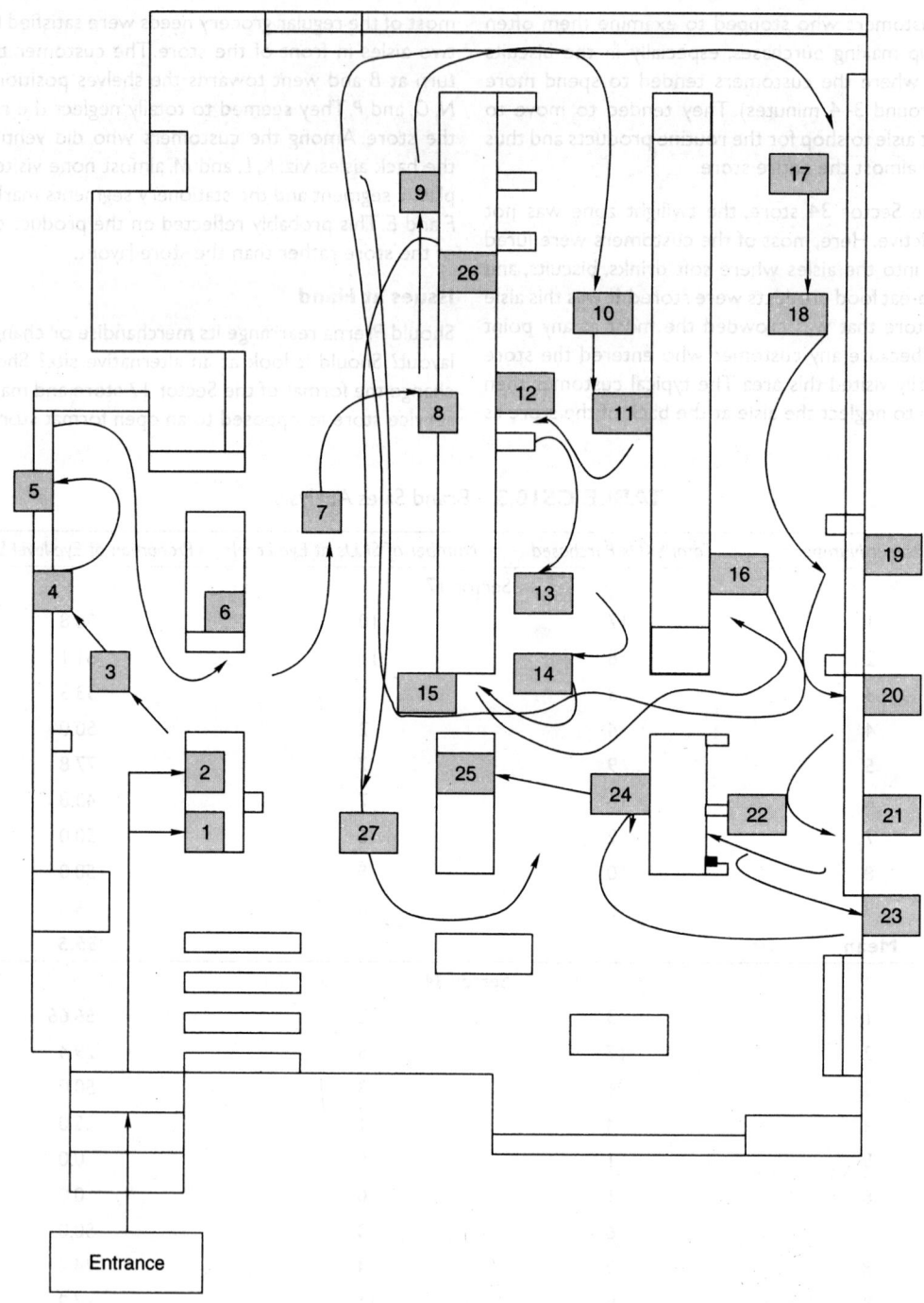

(a) Customer Movement 1

FIG. CS10.4 Customer Movement at Sector 17 Store (contd)

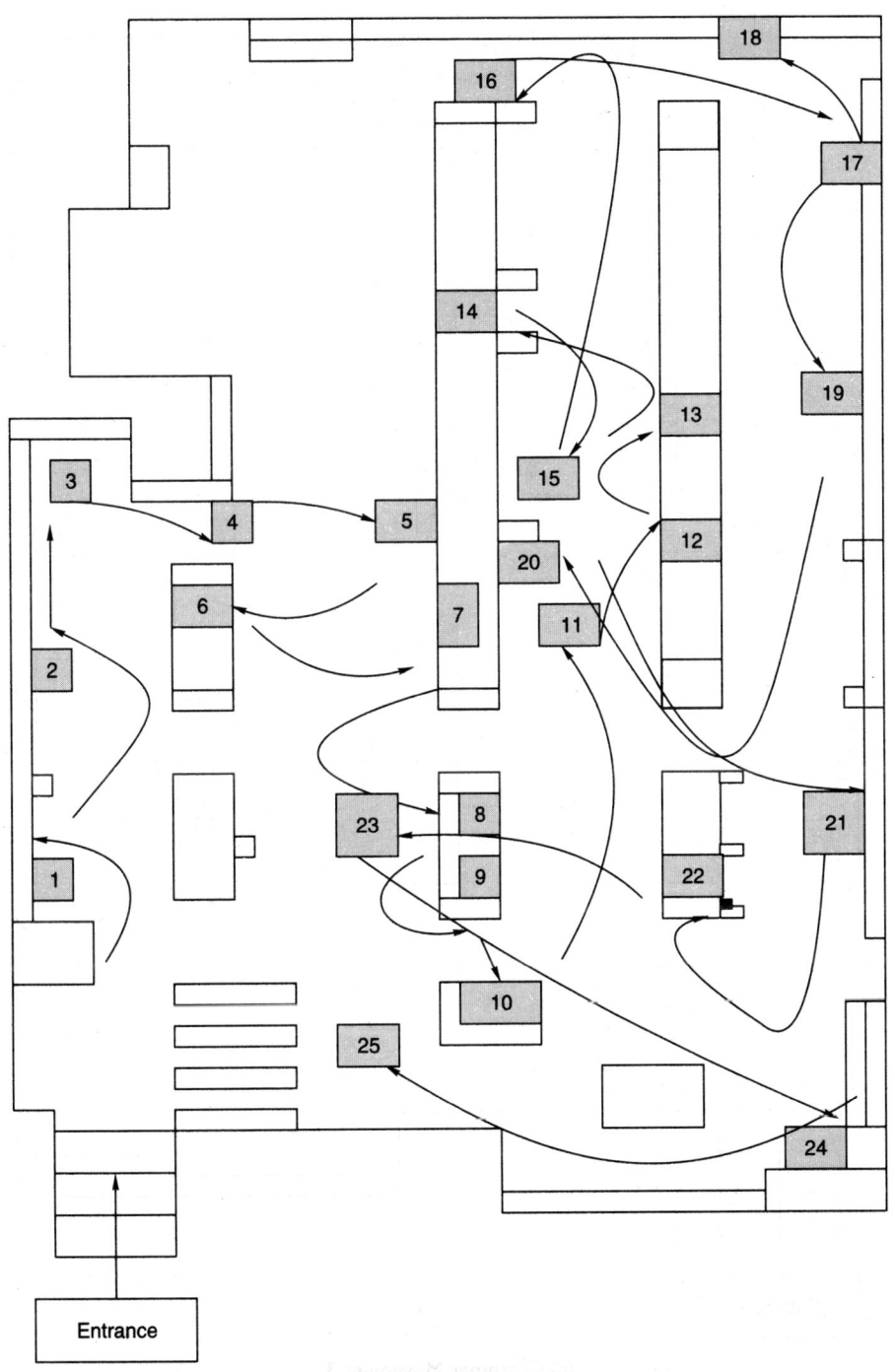

(b) Customer Movement 2

FIG. CS10.4 (Contd)

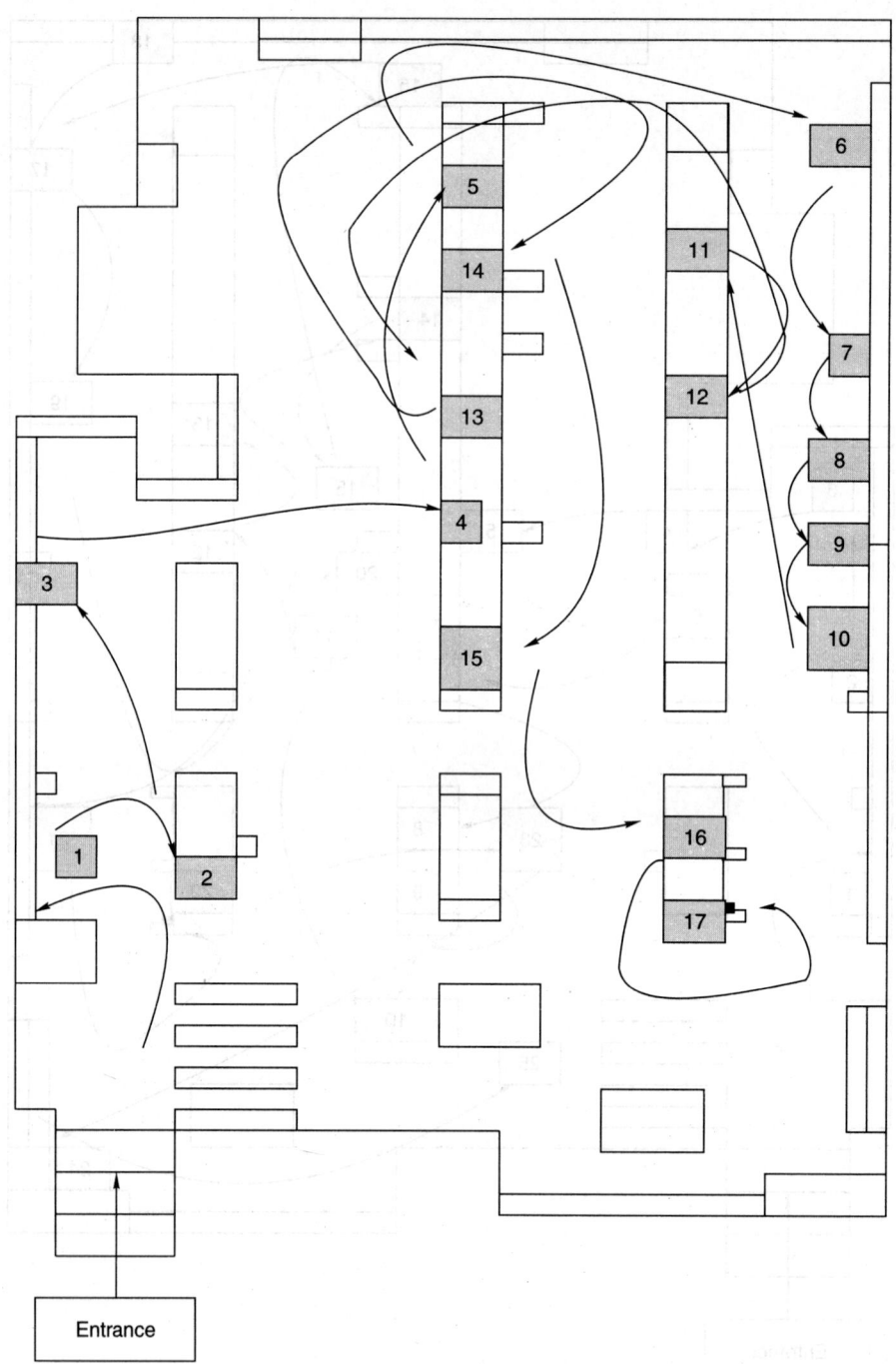

(c) Customer Movement 3

FIG. CS10.4 (Contd)

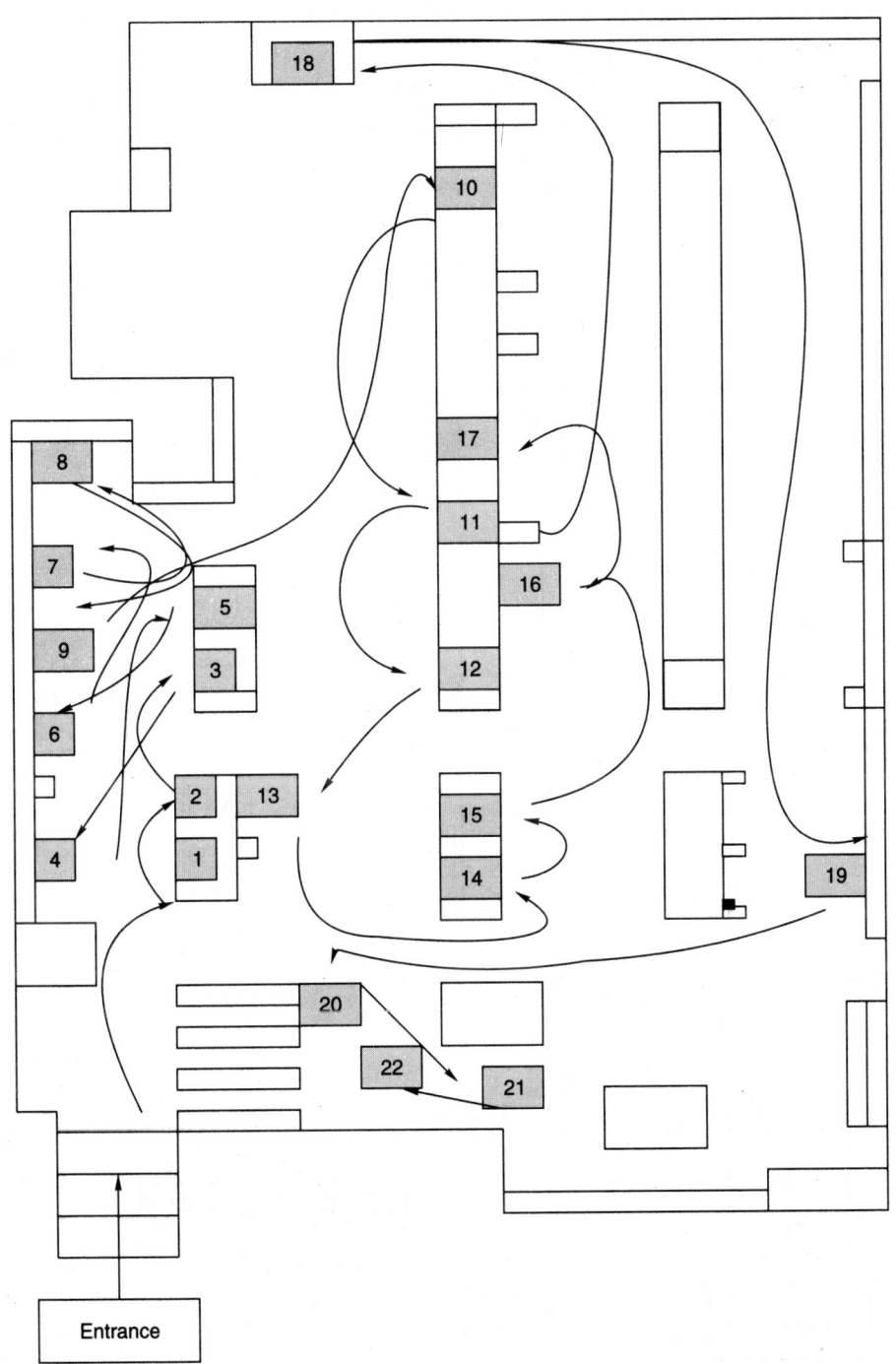

(d) Customer Movement 4

FIG. CS10.4 (Contd)

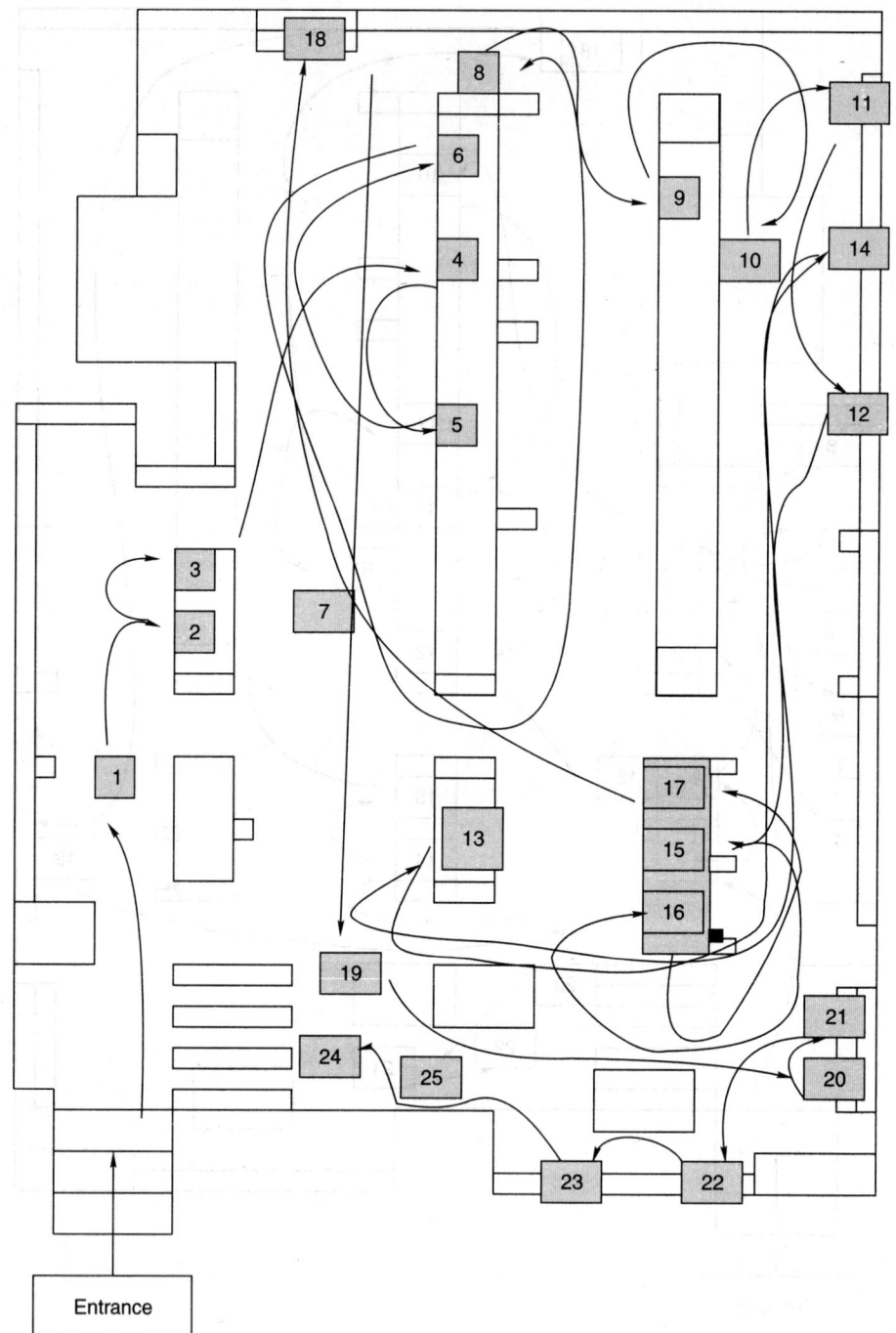

(e) Customer Movement 5

FIG. CS10.4 (Contd)

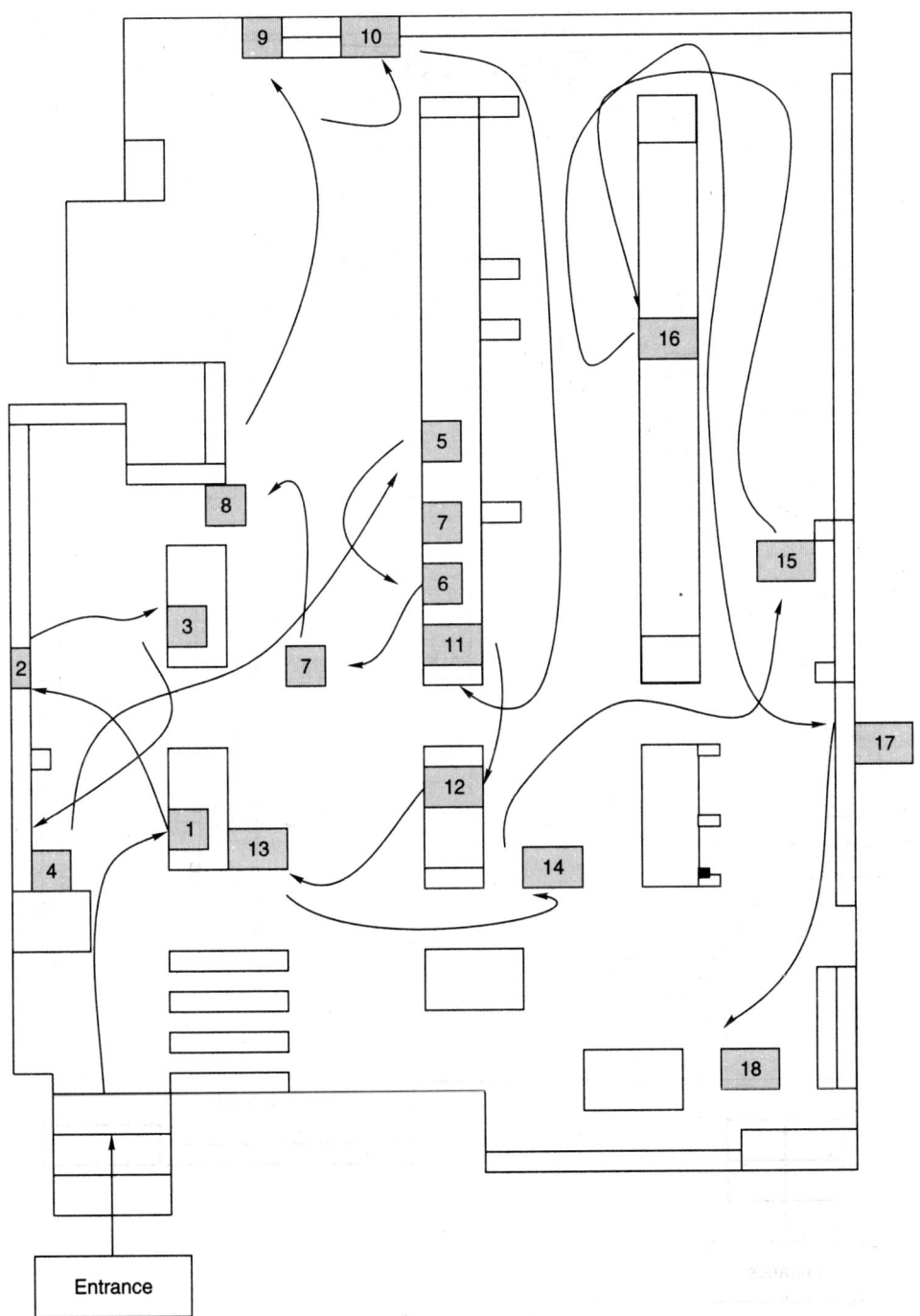

(f) Customer Movement 6

FIG. CS10.4 (Contd)

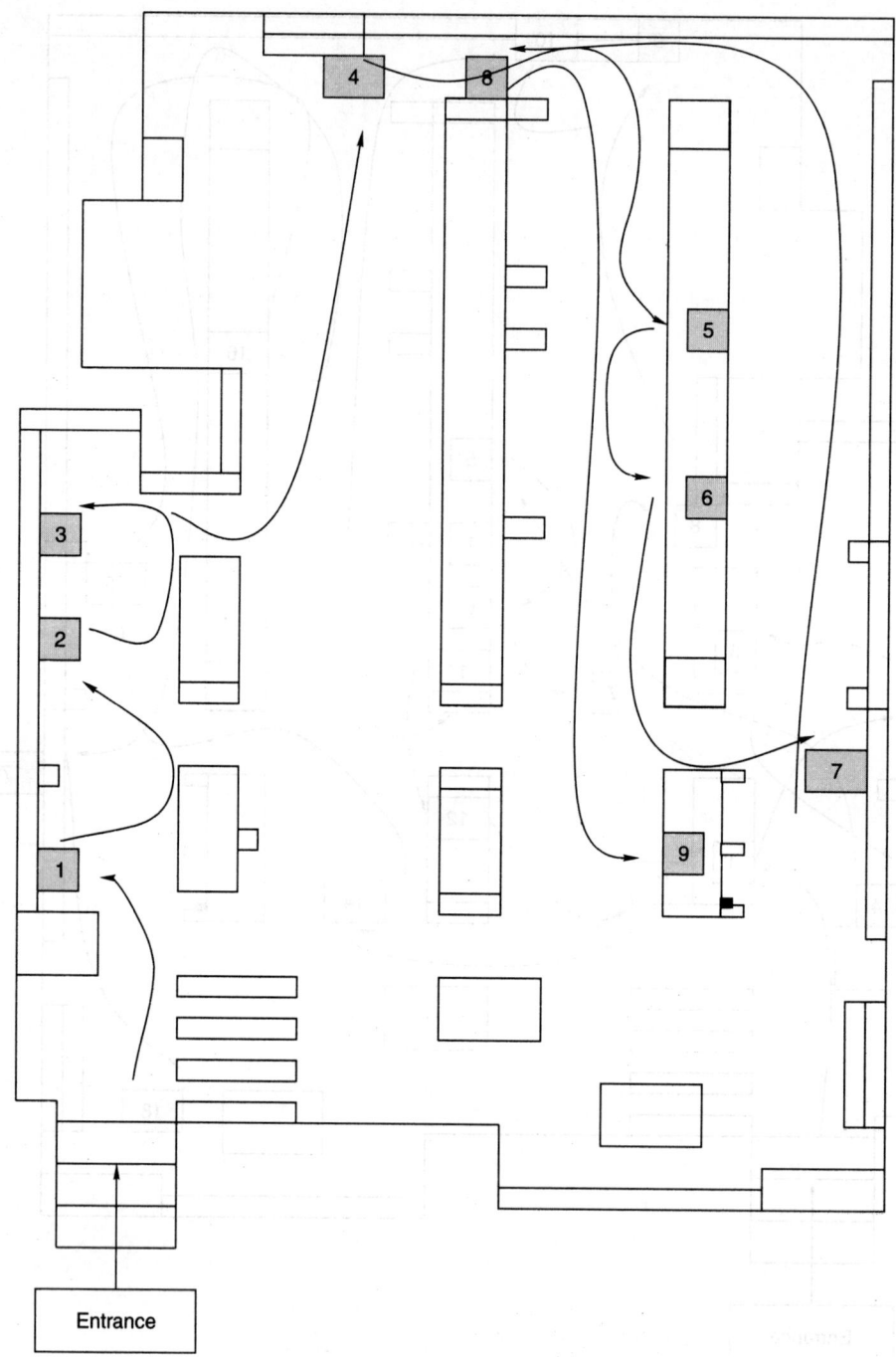

(g) Customer Movement 7

FIG. CS10.4 (Contd)

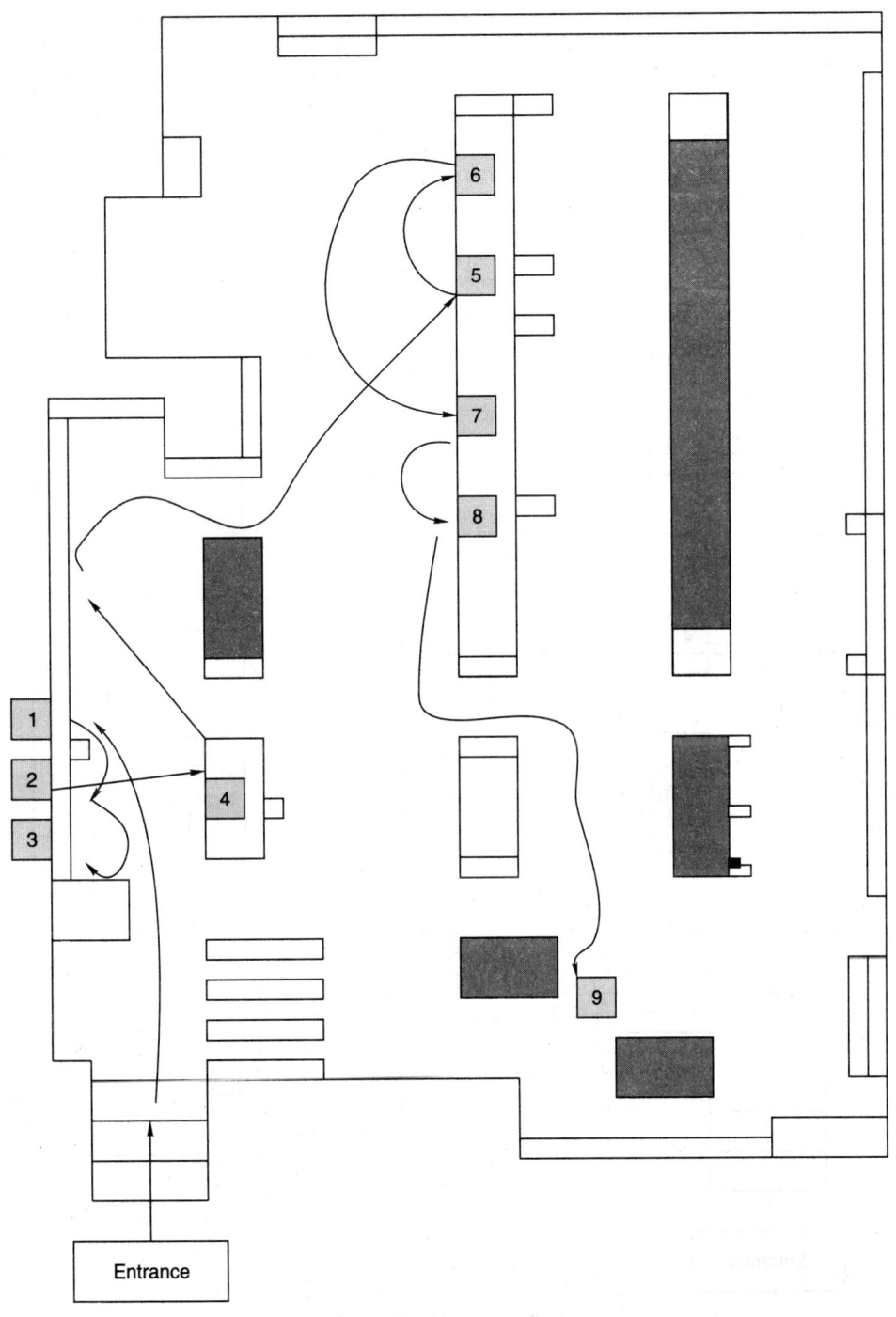

(h) Customer Movement 8

FIG. CS10.4 (Contd)

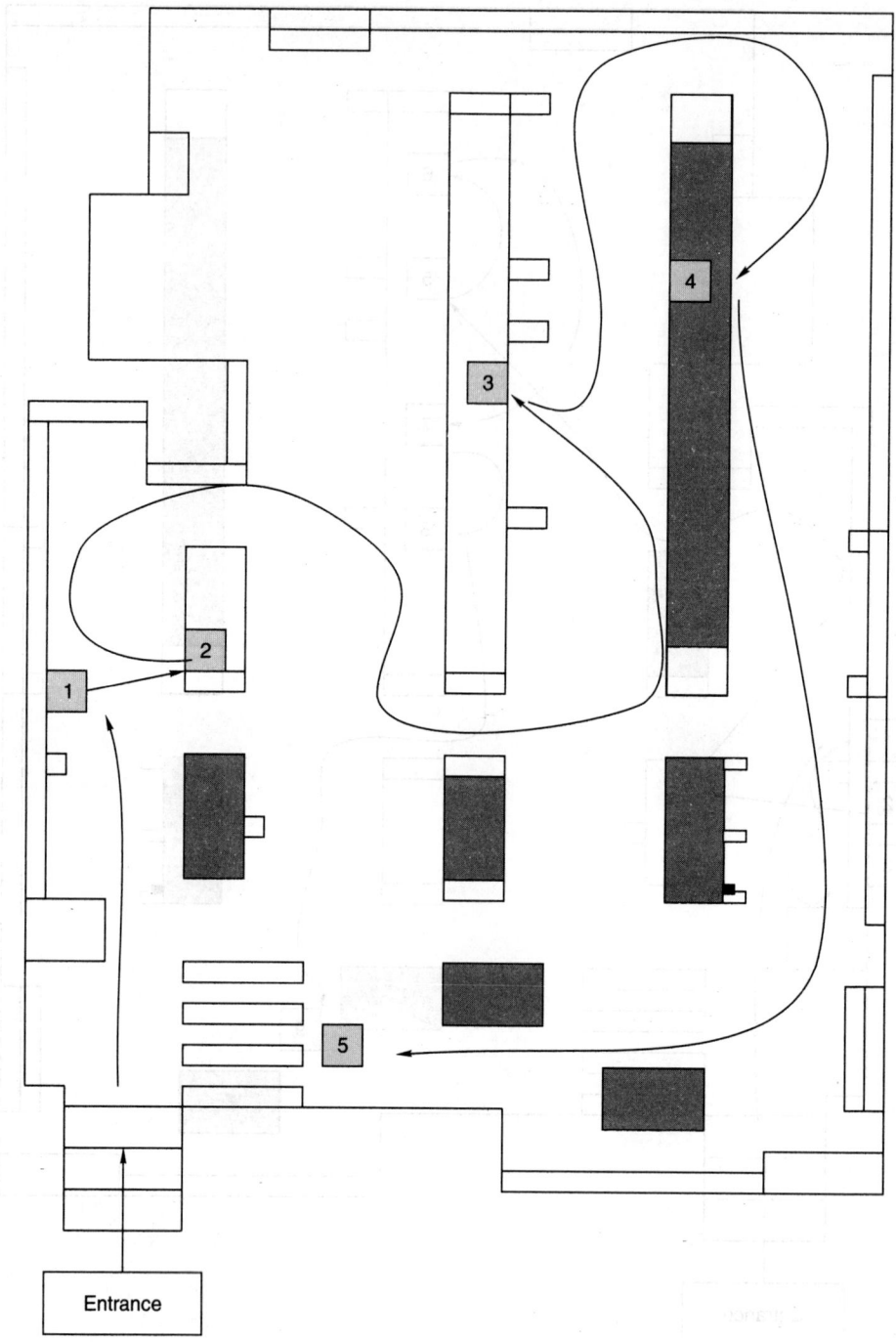

(i) Customer Movement 9

FIG. CS10.4 (Contd)

TABLE CS10.4(a)   Customer Movement 1—Mother and Daughter (Trolley);
Entry: 7:10 p.m. Exit: 8:00 p.m.

1. Picked up Mirinda orange (2 bottles × 1.5 ltr)	14. Checked out Mr Chings' noodles
2. Spent time looking at *namkeen* (picked up quite a few SKUs of different types)	15. Picked up Top Ramen noodles
3. Conversed between themselves	16. Picked up Johnson's baby soap
4. Picked up a small bottle of Horlicks, compared it to Nutramul, discussed and finally picked up Horlicks	17. Picked up Nirma washing powder
	18. Checked out plastic materials; checked out plastic plates
5. Checked out Néscafé refill packs	19. Checked out plastic Tupperware
6. Checked out MTR Pavbhaji Masala, talked to salesgirl, looked for *rasam* powder, spent 10 minutes in doing so	20. Picked up big plastic storage boxes
	21. Browsed the plastic section again, picked up another plastic container
7. Browsed along	22. Mother checked out sanitary napkins, picked up a small Whisper pack
8. Checked out *besan*, picked up the same	
9. Browsed along the *dal*/pulse section	23. Spent a substantial time at the skin care aisle and picked up Nivea lotion
10. Picked up	
11. Mother took out a shopping list	24. Picked up Medimix soap
12. Talked to salesgirl, picked up Saffola (2 packs), daughter looked disinterested	25. Mother checked out dry fruits
	26. Daughter picked up *bajra*, *dal* packets
13. Checked out the sugar-branded with Prerna, spent time discussing with salesgirl	27. Daughter picked up Perk discount pack

TABLE CS10.4(b)   Customer Movement 2—Lady in Green Salwar 50 yrs (Trolley);
Entry: 6:36 p.m., Exit: 7:05 p.m.

1. Observed cheeselings, did not pick it up	14. Checked out hair oil, wanted something specific, called salesgirl, picked up Navratna oil, put it back and then picked up Parachute oil
2. Went to the tea section, conversed with another shopper (no purchase)	
3. Picked up Britannia Time Pass, Bourbon Treat, browsed along	15. Picked up cooking oil—Mastan brand
	16. Picked up cheese slices, Britannia on discount, checked with the salesgirl
4. Picked up Lijjat papad	
5. Observed a promotional offer on soap (fluorescent sticker)	17. Picked up Wheel Active (2 packs)
	18. Spent long time observing Pril packs and picked up Minita scrubber
6. On consulting a salesgirl, picked up some 'Gujju' brand of products	
	19. Checked out Nirma (5 for 3 offer) and picked it up
7. Picked up two 10 kg packs of an edible oil	20. Talked to salesgirl, picked up pasta (macaroni) and hakka noodles (Ching's Secret)
8. Talked to salesgirl and haggled for the price of one	
9. Checked out a discount Cadbury's Dairy Milk	21. Zipped through while browsing
10. Checked out chocolates again	22. Spent a 'lifetime' choosing a soap
11. Conversed with the salesgirl	23. Checked out Perk on discount (picked up 3)
12. Zipped through and picked up batteries on the way	24. Picked up a pizza base
13. Picked up Pepsodent toothpaste	25. Paid and checked out

TABLE CS10.4(c)   Customer Movement 3—Girl with Driver; Entry: 6:36 p.m., Exit: 6:55 p.m.

1. Picked up bread, chips (Lays)	10. Picked up Cobra tile acid
2. Picked up cold drink	11. Picked up tooth brush
3. Picked up biscuit—Good Day Treat	12. Picked up Close Up toothpaste
4. Picked up pulse—*arhar* pulse and Kurkure	13. Picked up *maida*
5. Asked salesgirl for sugar	14. Picked up hair care oil
6. Picked up Rin soap	15. Asked for body oil
7. Picked up Harpic	16. Picked up Rexona deodorant
8. Picked up Ala	17. Picked up a lipstick
9. Picked up Ezee	

TABLE CS10.4(d)   Customer Movement 4—Couple; Entry: 7:05 p.m., Exit: 7.45 p.m.

1. Looked at juice (large pack Real)	12. Picked up merchandise
2. Picked up big packet of *namkeen*	13. Examined curry powder from lowest shelf
3. Picked up big bottle of sauce	14. Examined cashew packet for price
4. Examined a pack of Assam tea	15. Picked up cardamom packet
5. Looked for her husband	16. Picked up sugar
6. Summoned husband, brought him back, and picked up Darjeeling tea	17. Picked up Sundrop oil jar from top shelf and put on the floor and compared price. Touched Fortune jar. Contacted salesperson. Finally picked up Sundrop oil.
7. Looked at biscuits, touched Britannia cream biscuits in 3rd row	18. Picked up frozen peas
8. Put cream biscuits in a basket	19. Examined the new stock
9. Evaluated more biscuits	20. Came to check out bakery items
10. Took a packet of Cheetos	21. Went to bakery and asked for something
11. Picked up merchandise	22. Came back without buying

TABLE CS10.4(e)   Customer Movement 5—Mother and Child; Entry: 6:37 p.m., Exit: 7:05 p.m.

1. Woman entered with basket	12. Examined medicinal soap
2. Picked up Knorr soup, picked up Kissan bottle, put it in basket, and then returned it	13. Picked up canned food
	14. Picked up Harpic
3. Put *papad* in the basket	15. Examined Whisper sanitary napkins
4. Picked up pickles, son also picked up pickles, spends about a minute	16. Picked up Camay soap (smelt it and put it in basket)
5. Picked up pulses	17. Picked up Stayfree sanitary napkins
6. Returned them and picked up other pulses	18. Picked up butter
7. Made way for a cart	19. Left bakery section without buying
8. Son took her to shelf with Maggi noodles, picked up 4 packets and put it in a basket	20. Picked up 2 chocolates
	21. Picked up coupons
9. Picked up a toothpaste	22. Salesman showed her casseroles as a free gift
10. Picked up Dettol	23. Examined Cera glasses. Picked up casserole and glasses
11. Picked up 2 packets of Rin	24. Entered name in register
	25. Paid by card

TABLE CS10.4(f) Customer Movement 6—Well-dressed Executive; Entry: 7:28 p.m., Exit: 7:52 p.m.

1. Picked up Real juice	9. Examined cheese slices, tomato soup packets
2. Examined tea packet, asked salesgirl for details	10. Browsed the merchandise
3. Left trolley and examined Knorr soup while salesperson explained. Picked up 3 packets of Knorr soup and put in the trolley.	11. Picked up a packet of Maggi
	12. Examined the bottle of soya sauce for price
4. Picked up brown bread	13. Examined baby powder
5. Picked up rice packet	14. Browsed the merchandise
6. Picked up packet of pulses	15. Browsed the merchandise
7. Browsed the merchandise	16. Examined table cloth and picked dusters
8. Examined soup dishes	17. Observed people walking around
	18. Examined gourmet cooking book

TABLE CS10.4(g) Customer Movement 7—Lady in a Saree; Entry: 8:05 p.m., Exit: 8:15 p.m.

1. Picked up roasted channa	6. Picked up toothbrush
2. Picked up 'Bagh Bakheri' brand of tea but returned it	7. Picked up pet jars—demanded all blue jars
3. Picked up Good Day biscuit	8. Picked up match box
4. Opened fridge and took out Amul butter	9. Picked up soaps (set of 4 Breeze soaps)
5. Picked up Colgate Fresh	

TABLE CS10.4(h) Customer Movement 8—Lady in Mid-20s; Entry: 7:36 p.m., Exit: 7:55 p.m.

1. Picked up bakery items	6. Picked up rice from top of racks
2. Picked up some more bakery items	7. Picked up *besan*
3. Picked up potato chips	8. Picked up *dal*
4. Picked up mixture	9. Paid at the counter
5. Picked up Chivada	

TABLE CS10.4(i) Customer Movement 9—Middle-aged Couple; Entry: 6:50 p.m., Exit: 7:28 p.m.

1. Picked up Snax	4. Touched naphthalene balls but did not buy any
2. Picked up *hing* (asafoetida)	5. Walked to the bill counter
3. Picked up Saffola oil	

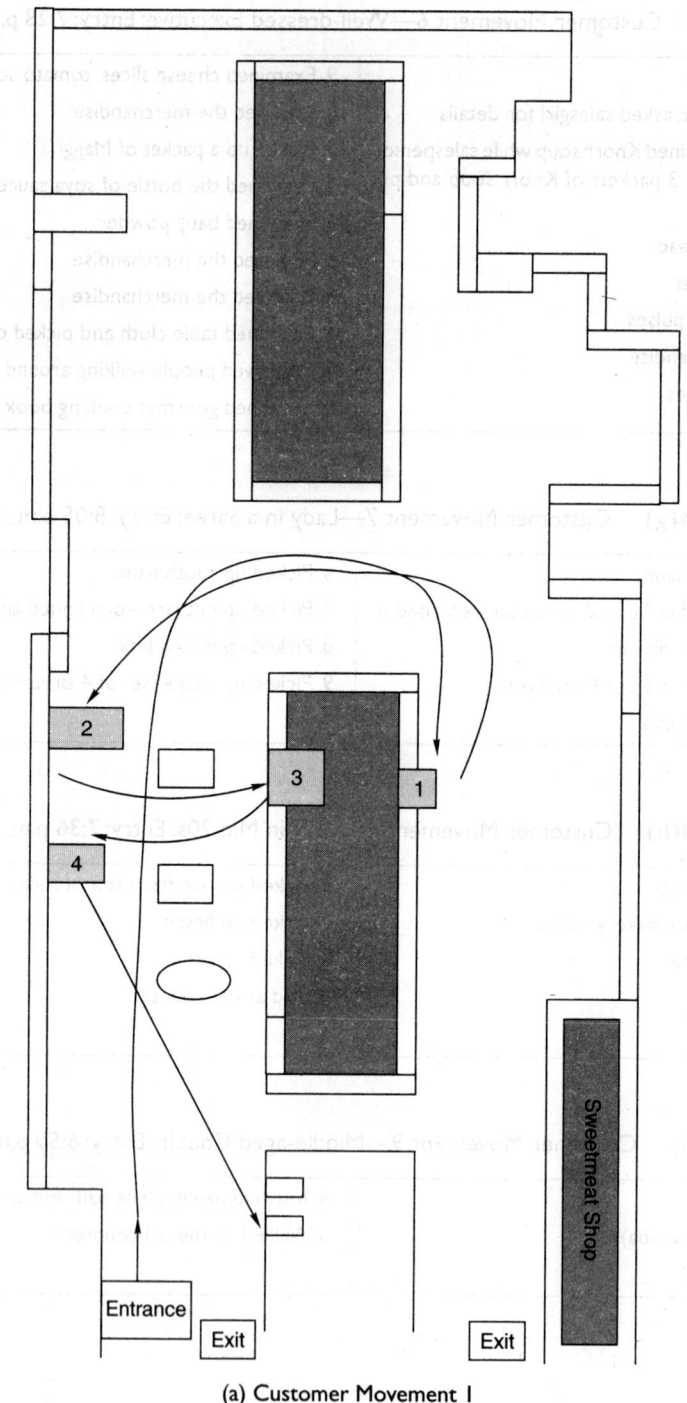

(a) Customer Movement 1

FIG. CS10.5   Customer Movement at Sector 34 Store (contd)

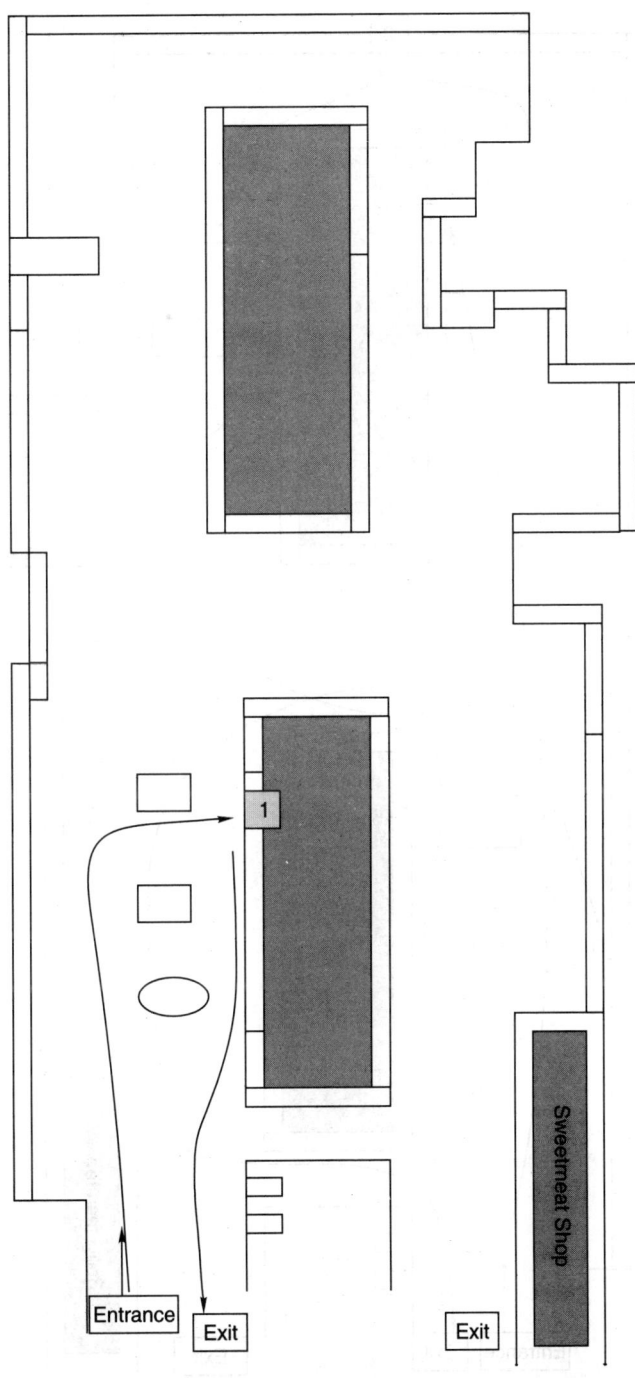

(b) Customer Movement 2

FIG. CS10.5 (Contd)

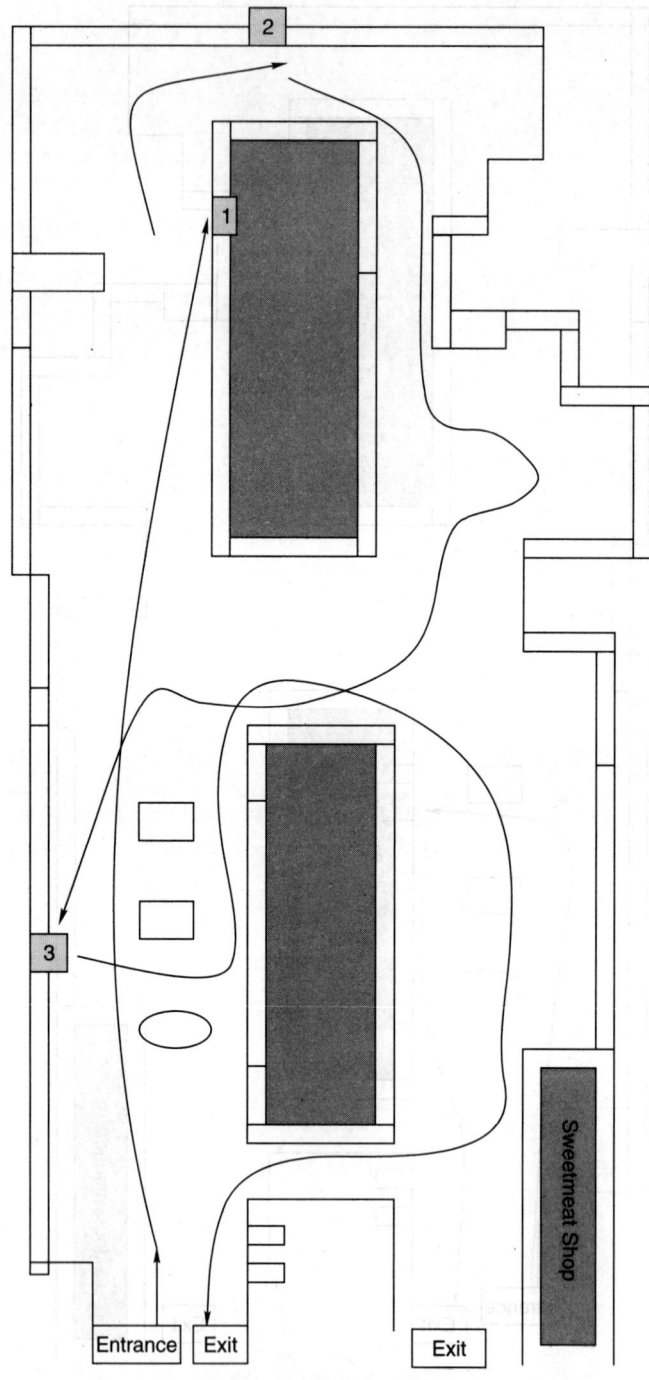

(c) Customer Movement 3

FIG. CS10.5 (Contd)

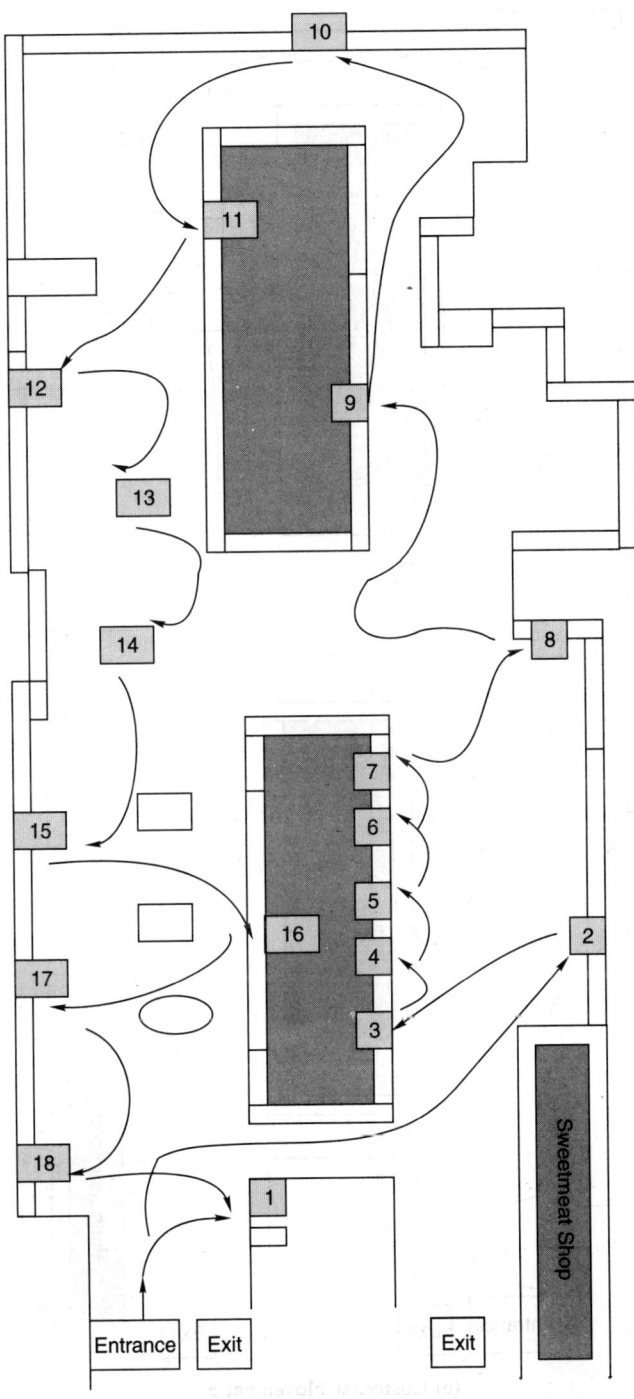

(d) Customer Movement 4

FIG. CS10.5 (Contd)

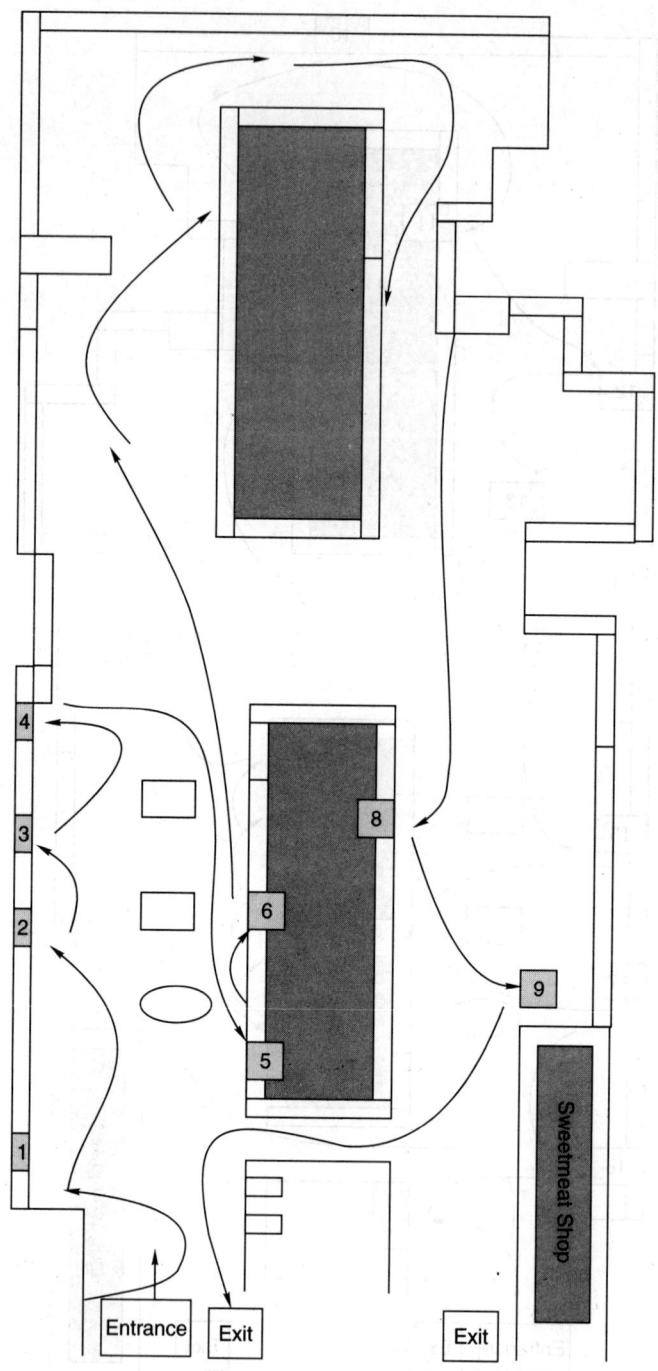

(e) Customer Movement 5

FIG. CS10.5 (Contd)

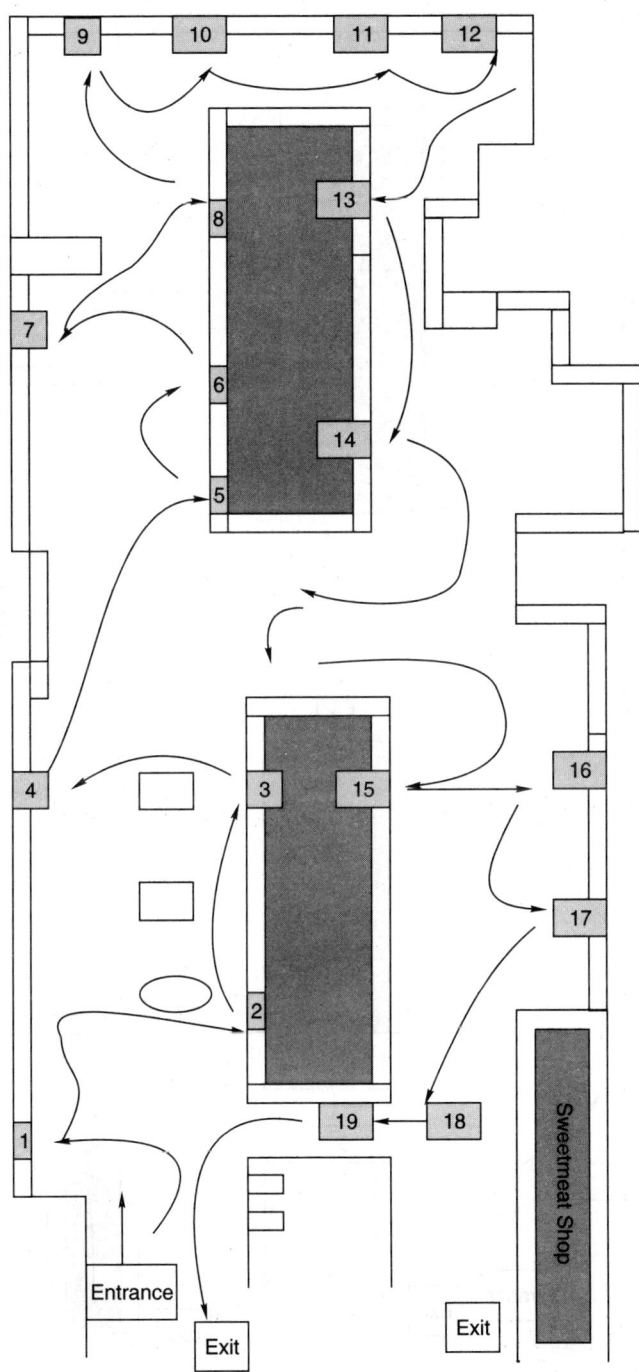

(f) Customer Movement 6

FIG. CS10.5 (Contd)

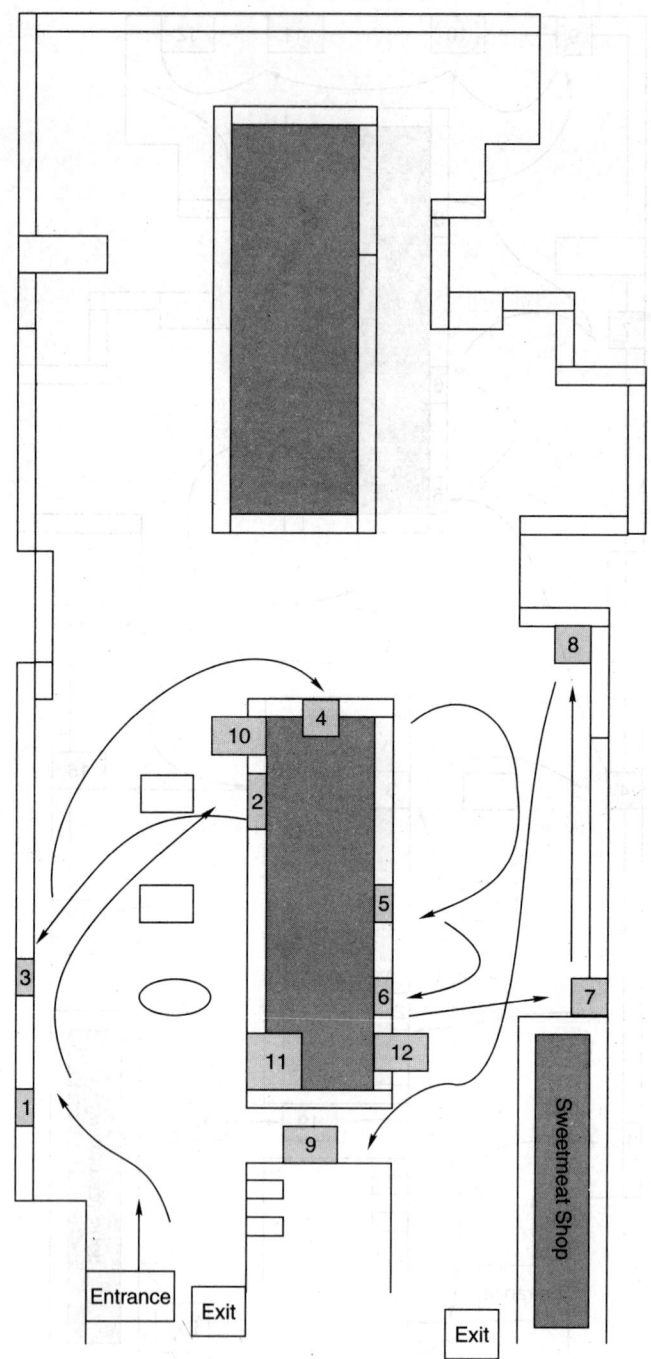

(g) Customer Movement 7

FIG. CS10.5 (Contd)

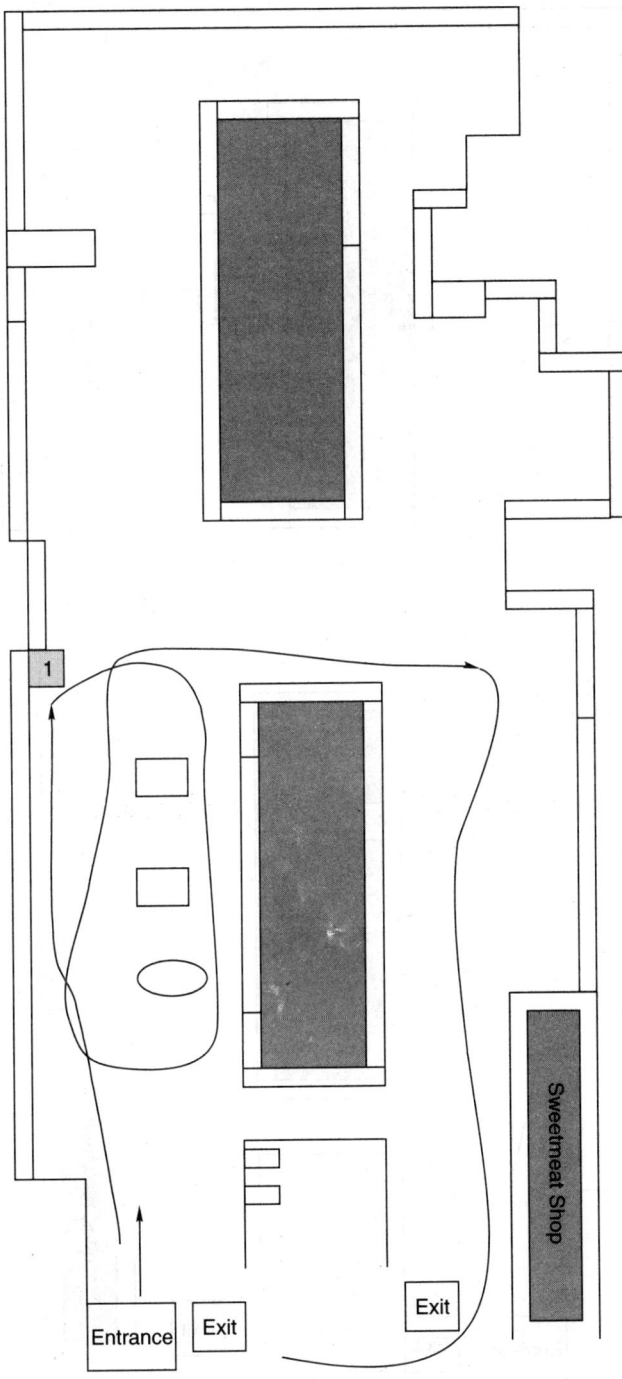

1

Sweetmeat Shop

Entrance   Exit   Exit

(h) Customer Movement 8

FIG. CS10.5 (Contd)

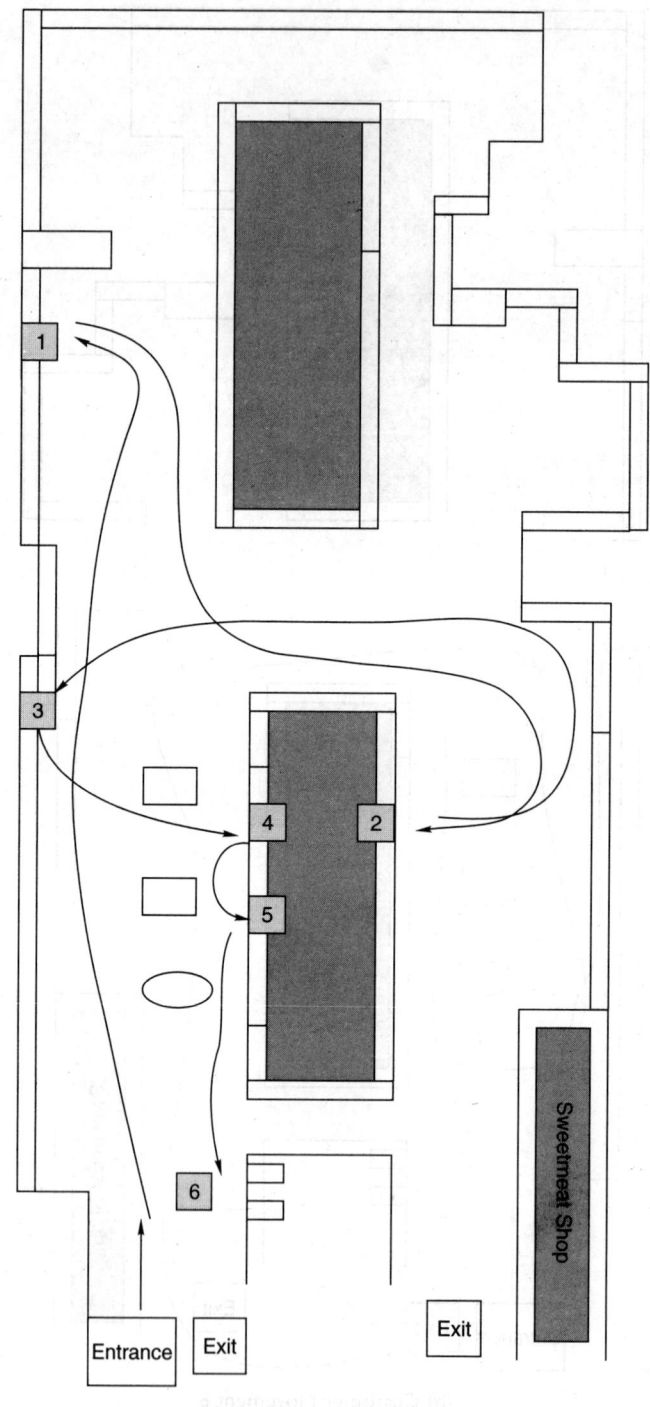

(i) Customer Movement 9

FIG. CS10.5 (Contd)

TABLE CS10.5(a)   Customer Movement 1—Grandma (55 yrs) and Grandson (5 yrs);
Entry: 7:00 p.m., Exit: 7:05 p.m.

1. Picked up pulses	3. Picked up banana chips
2. Picked up biscuits	4. Picked up Marie biscuits

TABLE CS10.5(b)   Customer Movement 2—Male in 30s; Entry: 7:10 p.m., Exit: 7:12 p.m.

1. Entry	3. Exit
2. Picked up Gujarati snacks (*khakhra*)	

TABLE CS10.5(c)   Customer Movement 3—Man Around 50 (Alone); Entry: 6:40 p.m., Exit: 7:02 p.m.

1. Picked up soap	3. Picked up Horlicks
2. Picked up washing powder	

TABLE CS10.5(d)   Customer Movement 4—Couple (Around 45 years); Entry: 7:06 p.m., Exit: 7:25 p.m.

1. Picked up cups	10. Picked up toothpaste
2. Picked up Maggi noodles	11. Picked up surface cleaner
3. Picked up Everest Masala	12. Picked up soap
4. Picked up *hing* (asafoetida)	13. Picked up common medicine
5. Picked up grocery items	14. Picked up Whisper
6. Picked up packaged peas	15. Picked up Peppy chips and biscuits
7. Picked up *chevada* and pulses	16. Picked up banana and other wafers
8. Picked up chilli sauce	17. Picked up jam
9. Picked up wafers	18. Picked up cornflakes

TABLE CS10.5(e)   Customer Movement 5—Two Ladies in Mid-30s; Entry: 7:14 p.m., Exit: 7:24 p.m.

1. Picked up rusks	6. Picked up snacks
2. Picked up biscuits	7. Picked up dry fruits
3. Picked up biscuits	8. Picked up dal
4. Picked up biscuits	9. Picked up custard mix
5. Picked up snacks	

TABLE CS10.5(f)   Customer Movement 6—Young Couple Male 35 yrs, Female 30 yrs; Entry: 7:26 p.m., Exit: 8:00 p.m.

1. Picked up tea	11. Picked up Vim bar, naphthalene balls
2. Picked up *namkeen*	12. Picked up Good Knight mats
3. Picked up salt	13. Picked up *agarbatti*
4. Picked up biscuits	14. Picked up toothpaste
5. Picked up deodorant	15. Picked up poha/groundnut
6. Picked up shampoo	16. Picked up homemade paste
7. Picked up Moov	17. Picked up instant popcorn
8. Picked up soap	18. Picked up *dhaniya* masala
9. Picked up Rin soap	19. Picked up *papad*
10. Picked up Domex	

TABLE CS10.5(g)   Customer Movement 7—Lady 55 yrs and Grandson 12 yrs; Entry: 6:51 p.m., Exit: 7:05 p.m.

1. Picked up Horlicks/tea sachets	7. Grandson picked up Maggi
2. Picked up snacks	8. Picked up sugar
3. Picked up biscuits	9. Picked up chocolate
4. Picked up salt	10. Grandson picked up dry fruit
5. Picked up *dall/poha*	11. Grandson picked up mouth freshner
6. Picked up masala	12. Picked up *papad*

TABLE CS10.5(h)   Customer Movement 8—Entry: 6:38 p.m., Exit: 6:45 p.m.

1. Picked up Amul Mithai Mate

TABLE CS10.5(i)   Customer Movement 9—Mother-in-law and Daughter-in-law; Entry: 7:05 p.m., Exit: 7:20 p.m.

1. Picked up Lactogen milk powder	4. Picked up Haldiram products
2. Picked up pulses and rice	5. Picked up Samrat Namkin
3. Picked up biscuits	6. Requisitioned and got *atta*

Questions

1. Analyse the performance of the two stores.
2. Using Figs CS10.4 and CS10.5, describe shopper behaviour in the two stores.
3. What are the implications of the layout of the two stores? With the help of suitable diagrams, suggest modification in the layouts, if required.

11 Retail Marketing Strategy

LEARNING OBJECTIVES

After studying this chapter, you will be able to
- know how retail brands are built
- understand the role of a business intelligence system in retailing
- learn about building a better customer experience
- understand the use of social media marketing in retail

INTRODUCTION

A retail store banks on being relevant to the customers for its success. This is the primary task of marketing, which consists of the three components of sensing customer value, designing offers based on these values, and delivering these values consistently, as also being distinct in relation to the competition the store faces in every trading area. It is commonly understood that the store has to sell itself. The communication mix can only create awareness and arouse interest. The final decision to shop, put into the cart, and then pay for the merchandise or service depends mostly on how much the shopper liked the store and whether he/she enjoyed buying from the store.

In this chapter, we will look at the processes and tools required for building long-term relations with customers. We will first examine the interrelationship among affect, cognition, and conation (mental process that makes one want/decide to do something), and the significance of this relationship for consumer's evaluation of a retail store format. We will then consider a framework for developing sales enhancement strategies and selling tactics. Thereafter, we will learn how retailers can use business intelligence to deliver good results for their business. We will then examine the balanced scorecard approach for better consumer experience and shall finally move on to social media marketing, and how retailers can use this upcoming medium to their advantage.

BUILDING A RETAIL BRAND

Brands are built; they are not born. They are made on hard work, sincerity, persistence, and also a lot of luck. Retailers have a dual task of not only building the brand of the store, but also help build and sell product brands.

Brands are defined as a set of experiences delivered consistently over time, market segments, formats, and geographies. Consumers need time to form an attitude towards a store. Most retailers work with a time frame of about two years before they consider a store stabilized. A stabilized store understands its customer needs very well; and customers, based on their experiences, feel that they relate to the store.

Brand building can also be considered a journey of thinking in a logical, rational, analytical, and objective way to thinking in an intuitive, holistic, and subjective way. Once a brand is built and accepted, customers do not evaluate, but make their store choices based on their overall impression rather than on the dimensions of the store. In a study conducted to understand format choices among consumers, it was found that even for very high involvement purchases, the choice of grocery stores is made based on overall impression.

Affect, Cognition, and Conation[1]

In this section, we will explore the interrelationship among affect, cognition, and conation in the context of the theory of planned behaviour[2] in store format choice, which is the most accepted work among the theoretical foundations linking attitude and behaviour.

Several recent advances in neurosciences indicate that emotional decision-making is faster than rational processing. Affect may precede cognition or the two may operate independently in certain kinds of decisions. Zajonc's experiments demonstrated that reliable affective distinctions (like–dislike ratings) can be made without any interpolation of recognition memory (old–new judgements). This was called the *affective primacy hypothesis*. He concluded that affect and cognition are under the control of separate and partially independent systems that could impact each other in several ways. Other researchers have also demonstrated that affect and cognition are distinct components of attitude with differential impact on conation.

Affective components have been found to be significantly better predictors of global attitude than cognitive components. The significance of affect or cognition to an individual determines the attitude change process or its operationalization. Attitudes rooted in emotions are more susceptible to cognitive persuasion attempts, while cognition-rooted attitudes are more susceptible to emotional attempts. A subject's pre-persuasion conative responses are primarily affect-driven, while the post-persuasion responses tend to be mainly related to thoughts.

Both affect and evaluation have strong correlations with the global measure of attitude and are two distinct constructs with low correlation between them. Affect is more strongly associated with the global measure of attitude or behavioural tendencies than beliefs. For example, affective persuasion tends to produce significantly more positive attitudes towards blood donation than cognitive stimuli. However, it has also been found that affect, cognition, global attitude, and behavioural intentions are significantly correlated, suggesting a convergent validity of the measures of attitude components. Affective evaluations also tend to be faster than cognitive evaluations because of easier accessibility of attitudes formed through affective processes. Recent neuroscientific work and psychological research when considered in unison describe attitude as a *dual locus construct* comprising affect and cognition, which need to be treated independently.

There is merit in building a favourable consumer attitude towards the format, as attitude is a strong antecedent of behaviour and their relationship is well mediated through intention. The affective and cognitive components of attitude tend to have differential impact on the store format choice. The affective component, in general, is a stronger predictor of intention than the cognitive component, indicating that the consumers primarily do a global assessment of the format proposed, rather than a detailed evaluative assessment. It may be indicative of the stage of format evaluation and consumers' familiarity with it, as the recent format such as the hypermarket has shown the highest cognitive evaluation, while the oldest format such as the *kirana* has shown the highest affective component. It may, therefore, be possible to conjecture that the basis of a consumer's format evaluation undergoes a transition from cognitive to affective with increased familiarity and evolution of the format. As a result, it becomes important for the store formats to determine the attitude profiles of their target

TABLE 11.1   Cross-sectional View of the Target Group Composition across Store Formats (An Illustrative Example)

Store Formats Studied (in Ascending Order of Emergence in Indian Retail)	Target Group Composition		
	Affective	*Cognitive*	*Composite*
Hypermarket (Most recent)	++	++++	++
Internet	+++	++	++++
Discounters	++++	++	+++
Supermarket	++++	+	++
Kirana (Oldest)	+++++	-	-

group from time to time as it may form the basis of the retail format's communication decisions and business proposition changes.

A largely affective target group may be approached primarily with affective cues, while cognitive cues may be communicated sporadically. On the other hand, a cognitive profile heavy target group, as in the case of hypermarkets, may be targeted primarily with evaluative or utilitarian cues such as value for money positioning, discounts, savings made in a shopping trip, or a loyalty promotion.

An illustrative example is presented in Table 11.1 and Fig. 11.1 to highlight the role of different attitude components and their possible transition over time. This may be attributed to shopper 'literacy'. Shoppers gradually learn about the format and the formula and develop more understanding of what the retailer is doing with promotions, layout, and product range.

The role of the affective components seems to be very critical in determining intention, and hence, the marketers will require to study the affect formation and reinforcement process among, say, grocery customers to be able to impact their store format choice process. The marketing stimuli that influence both affect and cognition components are likely to be the most rewarding from the marketing point of view.

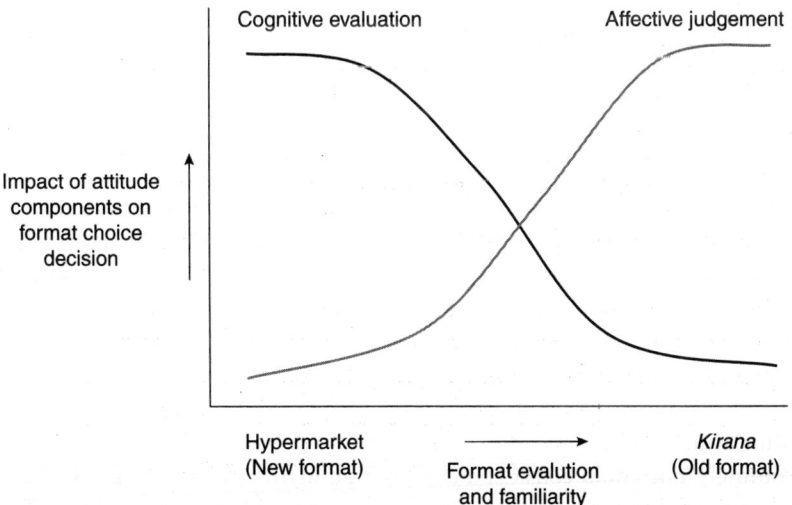

FIG. 11.1   Possible Temporal Transition among Attitude Components Used by Consumers for Format Choice Decision

Building brands in retail is difficult as customers tend to evaluate a store frequently and every transaction needs to reinforce the value that the brand stands for. This becomes a challenge as the delivery of value happens in different environments. Every trading area has a different terrain in terms of customer composition, competition, adjacencies, traffic patterns, and back-end support.

SALES ENHANCEMENT STRATEGIES

Retailers need to continuously try to enhance sales performance. This is achieved through increased footfall, increased conversion rates, increased bill and list sizes. The role of merchandising, category management, better displays, and promotion strategies has been discussed in Chapter 7. In this chapter, we will examine the role that a salesperson can play in converting prospective buyers into customers as also cross-sell or upsell. We propose a framework here for determining the role of a salesperson.

The performance of a retail outlet can be attributed to two broad sets of factors—structural and operational. The former includes the aspects of location, trading area, fixed asset investment (building, architecture, interiors, and technology) in the outlet, traffic patterns, competitive scenario, and the geographical terrain. The latter includes merchandise, atmospherics, people, systems, processes, marketing programmes, and customer service. As the market evolves and matures, the structural factors in a given trading area quickly become similar for retailers. A continued flow of customers and their retention depends on how the store consistently provides a good experience. This becomes possible only when the operational factors are managed well. Sales enhancement plans would need to be developed for each of these factors in the light of the strategy for the store. A framework for developing these strategies and plans will be described here.

Framework for Developing Strategies[3]

The sales of a store have been found to be dependent on the operations of the store. However, it has also been found that this relationship is not always linear. There have been instances where stores do phenomenally well despite the service or operations not being that good. In such situations, sales are driven largely by structural factors such as location, or a monopolistic situation, where this would be the only store keeping particular merchandise. In either case, customers are buying out of compulsion which means that this is a very vulnerable position for the store. On the other hand, a very well designed store with excellent operations may not do well simply because the trading area or the location chosen is not appropriate. Such a phenomenon is being seen in many places, where, for example, the anchor store does not gel with the other stores in the mall.

In a study conducted across a large retail chain, it was found that a high selling outlet did not have a high operational efficiency, and that a low operational efficiency did not mean that the store was a low selling outlet. The operational efficiency did not correlate directly to the ownership type (owned, leased, or franchised) and location. It was also found that while operational efficiencies relate to internal processes, their impact is on the external stakeholders too; first the customers and then the competitors. A good effort would not only help in retaining customers, it would impact the competition as the outlet would start attracting more customers based on the word-of-mouth spread by the customers. The sales enhancement plans need to be developed vis-à-vis competition and trading area.

Accordingly, one could consider a classification matrix developed based on an internal and an external measure of performance. This classification would help in developing a general strategy for all outlets falling in each of the quadrants of the matrix, as given in Fig. 11.2. A portfolio of outlets would also help regional managers in focusing their resources and time in bringing perceptible change among customers, franchisees, and their employees.

		Operational efficiency	
		High	*Low*
Market leader (sales higher than competitors)	*Yes*	**Q1** Enhance market share	**Q2** Defend the market
	No	**Q3** Leverage the outlet	**Q4** Put the house in order

FIG. 11.2 Outlet Classification and Strategy Matrix

Quadrant 1 Outlets

These stores are the flagship outlets of a company. They have garnered the largest share of the trading area potential. In addition, they are putting their best foot forward and have put in all necessary and desired measures to ensure customer and employee satisfaction. These outlets can very easily expand their trading areas (an account in marketing means a customer and his/her purchase). A retailer must leverage these outlets in propagating best practices across the network. These stores and franchisees need to be portrayed as icons or champions and must be showcased. They can also be utilized as trainers or speakers at training, workshops, customer meets, and franchisee meets or as leaders in managing the stores. New ideas in processes, technology, and marketing practices can be experimented at these outlets. For the innovation to be successful, necessary capacity building should be ensured by sending the store managers/franchisees for higher level trainings. All these measures would enhance the emotional quotient of these franchisees leading to their increased involvement in business. These outlets must keep redefining and setting higher benchmarks for the industry, resulting in leadership for the retailer.

Quadrant 2 Outlets

Dealers falling in this quadrant are the most vulnerable and would tend to lose customers with any small competitive activity. Being the highest selling outlets, they are the prime targets of competitors. Defending the current customers is the main and only objective of these stores. These outlets perform well due to structural reasons, such as location, modernization, traffic rules, and credit. Store managers/franchisees would typically not be involved in day-to-day operations, even though in many cases they would be living out of the outlet. They are on an auto-pilot mode. High sales, large repeat customer base, and no major perceptible threat from other outlets make them complacent. They also feel that any extra effort would contribute only incrementally. Consequently, they spend more time in other activities. In many cases, the outlet facilities are being utilized for this purpose. Motivating these franchisees to implement any initiative would be a challenge since they also would not be willing to invest. Retailers would need to commit themselves much more in implementing the action plans at these outlets. Any improvement in the operations would go a long way in establishing leadership as it would affect the largest base of customers in the trading area and reduce their trade-offs and compulsions.

Quadrant 3 Outlets

These dealers are poised to take the leap and become trading area leaders, barring those where the gap between the outlet and the leader is very significant. The franchisees in this quadrant are involved and committed. They are ready to invest and are open to new ideas. At these outlets, customer solicitation is the primary activity which may entail enhanced facilities or sales activities. Attracting more customers helps as they would enjoy a high level of experience that is already being rendered by the dealer. This may also help in expanding the trading area. These dealers must pick their competitors one by one and deploy plans to win over customers from them.

Quadrant 4 Outlets

These outlets have a long way to go. They may be high selling but are lower than the leader of the trading area. These dealers need to put their house in order immediately. Retailers would need to commit upfront in case of these outlets for bringing the change. They require overhauling in terms of modernization, upkeep of the outlet, employee behaviour, and more importantly lower customer perceptions. These outlets are hazardous to the brand.

Selling Tactics

A retailer needs to define the role to be played by its salespeople in converting walk-ins into customers. The roles and the tactics would depend on the selling situations. A framework for understanding those situations is given in Fig. 11.3. The role is envisaged based on the type of categories at the store and the format of the store. The former is an indication of the extent of involvement of the customer with regard to the category. For the latter, formats have been classified primarily based on cognition and affect, indicating the use of logic and emotions in store format choices.

	Traditional Store Formats	Modern Store Formats	
	Primarily Affect Set	*Cognition Set (Evaluative)*	*Affect Set (Feel-based)*
Low Involvement Categories, e.g., groceries, fuel	**WL:** Social congruity, in-store experience **SC:** Store manager's role, flexibility, and proximity **SE:** Leverage personalization, establish more reasons for engaging with format	**WL:** Less scientific pre-purchase cues lead to non-incremental footfalls; lack of understanding of basket composition impairs in-store experience **SC:** Perception of savings in pre-purchase processes **SE:** Leveraging knowledge on destination categories KVIs, innovative campaigns, loyalty programmes	**WL:** More reasons to shop than the price advantage or base experience alone **SC:** Relaxed and urbane shopping experience **SE:** Specialized focus through connoisseur's day in a week, dedicated sections for catalogue browsing, category explorations
High Involvement Categories, e.g., mobiles and accessories, automobiles, apparels, cosmetics	**WL:** Purchase process low on experiencing the product/brand **SC:** Patronage, complaint redressal **SE:** Limited modernization, creating room for experiencing the product or its surrogates	**WL:** Variety in ways of experiencing the product/brand **SC:** Perception of savings in pre-purchase processes **SE:** Comparison charts (e.g., compareindia.in), shelf life experiments, skin clinics	**WL:** Variety in ways of experiencing the product/brand **SC:** Relaxed and urbane shopping experience **SE:** Display aesthetics, feel the product opportunities, what others say catalogue, new introductions newsletter
	WL: Weak link	SC: Strong connect	SE: Sales effort

FIG. 11.3 Selling Situations

BUSINESS INTELLIGENCE

A business intelligence (BI) system is an integrated set of tools, technologies, and programmed products that are used to collect, integrate, analyse, and make data available.[4] The main tasks of a BI system include intelligent exploration, integration, aggregation, and a multidimensional analysis of data originating from various information resources.[5] Here, data is treated as a highly valuable corporate resource, and is transformed from quantity to quality.[6] As a result, massive data from many different sources of a large enterprise can be integrated into a coherent body of information to provide a holistic view of its business.[7] Hence, meaningful information can be delivered at the right time, at the right location, and in the right form.[8] This would assist individuals, departments, divisions, or even larger units to facilitate improved decision-making.[9]

Retailers rely on business analytics to deliver good results for their retail business. Business intelligence helps in consolidating, tracking, analysing, and reporting on relevant data. Financial performance and strategy management software provides planning, budgeting, and consolidation for linking a strategy to the dynamic plans and targets. Advanced analytics software gives the insight to anticipate trends and predict future outcomes.[10] It also helps quick start with a particular issue or domain (reduce start-up time for a system).

Aid of Business Analytics

Following are some of the important aspects of retailing that can derive value from business analytics.

Shopping Experience

1. Identify, report on, and analyse trends to respond to consumer buying needs and behaviour.
2. Use predictive models and association rules to determine which group of products work best for which customers.
3. Gain insight into customer perceptions of service, store, products and merchandising, and integrate results across the business.
4. Create flexible seasons for basics, seasons, and 'waves'.

Promotion Planning, Merchandise Planning, and Market Basket Analysis

1. Optimize merchandise levels, minimize out-of-stocks, and manage inventory costs.
2. Conduct market basket analysis to anticipate customer response and improve promotions.
3. Develop plans for key financial indicators including returns, cost of goods, supply chain costs, and gross profit.
4. Plan for the impact of markdowns and promotions on inventory value and margin.

Smarter Operations

1. Align corporate and store operations around critical revenue and profitability targets; and quickly adjust plans and resource allocations to achieve profitable growth.
2. Set, measure, and monitor key performance metrics based on standard financial statements.
3. Use predictive models to improve recruitment and optimize staffing decisions.
4. Increase cost savings by comparing and benchmarking performance across stores, channels, regions, and divisions.
5. Gain visibility into key metrics across the chain—sales, labour, inventory, and promotions.
6. Monitor turnover and employee productivity.

In the context of customer relationship management (CRM), business intelligence means the analytical processing of information about customers and their behaviour with the goal of optimizing the management of relationships with customers by maximizing their satisfaction and enhancing their loyalty and in turn, profitability. Integrated strategies for implementing business intelligence enable companies to develop excellence in their CRM, thereby achieving a significant competitive advantage.

One of the largest speciality retailers of big and tall men's apparel with nearly 500 stores in the US upgraded its IT infrastructure and replaced the old systems. It wanted better reporting capabilities for its direct catalogue and web sales. It wanted to host a warehouse that integrated data from different applications and source systems via a night batch upload. The warehouse also conducted data quality checks and appended incomplete fields or flagged data with discrepancies. The company was able to access the reporting and key performance indicators (KPIs) through the Internet. Before implementing the BI system, executives would have to go through 150 different reports that did not have what they needed. Now the company creates only 23 reports that run the company successfully. The system created a feature that allows authorized users to create purchase orders through the system while looking at current inventory, buying patterns, and other useful information. Order information is then sent to the vendor as well as the finance system. This has improved the profit margins by 3.5 per cent over the course of two years.

Business intelligence also helps other members of values chains. It can help a wholesaler to identify data integration adapters to cure data inaccuracies. For instance, a wholesaler supplying meat produce and other groceries to about 2,400 independent groceries and coordinating advertisements and product specials, has used BI to improve reporting and ad-hoc query analysis. The company's advertising planning system allows the wholesaler to get daily reports (as opposed to the weekly reports it used to get). The migration also allows the running of ad-hoc reports on demand to manage inventory better against scheduled advertising circulars that clients plan to run. Earlier retailers would end up getting the wrong items that did not match with the advertisements, but the data and systems integration implemented now allows smaller, independent stores to compete with larger food chains by creating their own advertisements to help draw customers and new business.

Key Success Factors

Business intelligence systems use analytics and performance management concepts to leverage enterprise system databases and provide core management control system (MCS) capability. It has been observed that organizational absorptive capacity (i.e., the ability to gather, absorb, and strategically leverage new external information) is critical to establishing appropriate technology infrastructure and assimilating BI systems for organizational benefit. Further, findings show that while top management plays a significant role in effective deployment of BI systems, their impact is indirect and a function of operational managers' absorptive capacity. In particular, this indirect effect suggests that leveraging BI systems is driven from the bottom–up as opposed to the top–down. This differentiates BI from other isolated strategic MCS innovations that have traditionally been viewed as top management driven.[11] Some of the key success factors include the following:[12]

- Committed management support and sponsorship
- Clear vision
- Well-established business case
- Business-centric championship
- Balanced team composition

- User-oriented change management
- Business-driven, scalable, and flexible technical framework
- Sustainable data quality and integrity

Findings suggest that when managers envision information systems as a resource that provides opportunities for competitive actions rather than viewing it in a service role, competitive advantages will evolve. Furthermore, practitioners will be better able to leverage investments in information systems, if they recognize its embedded role within the competitive actions or responses a firm undertakes to maintain or improve relative performance.[13]

Investment Decision

Every planned BI solution must be justified by the potential benefits (such as increased profit or greater efficiency) it can bring to the organization. Following are four components of the justification of an investment in BI.

Business Factors It is essential to identify the business reasons for implementing BI, the strategic goals of the company, and the application goals of the planned solution. The goals of the BI solution must be in line with the strategic goals of the company.

Requirements of Business Analyses The information needed for achieving strategic goals and for decision-making must be defined. This information is intended for higher management.

Cost and Benefit Analysis This is an evaluation of the costs of implementation and maintenance of the BI system and a definition of the expected benefits. The tangible and measurable benefits of BI must be financially evaluated, while intangible benefits and their positive effects for the entire organization must be defined in a qualitative way.

Risk Assessment This is a definition of risks regarding the technology, the complexity of the system, integration into the business and existing information systems, the project team, and financial investment.

Companies benefit as BI brings[14]

- faster and more accurate reporting;
- an improved decision-making process;
- improved customer satisfaction;
- increased revenues;
- savings in IT; and
- savings in other areas (in addition to information technology).

It also helps in[15]

- lowering costs;
- increasing revenue;
- improving customer satisfaction; and
- improving communication within the company.

Some other benefits of business intelligence are increase in profit and increase in market share.[16]

It is also necessary to take into account the following costs involved in BI:[17]

Determining the Total Cost of Investment   It is necessary to identify all costs associated with an investment in information technology (including, e.g., the costs of external services, auxiliary materials, the corresponding part of the salaries of employees involved in the project, etc.). This task is not always easy because it is often difficult to distinguish the costs associated with the investment from those which are not.

Determining the Current Costs   These are the costs of maintenance, upgrades, and repair services, etc., in order to obtain an answer to the question of how much the system costs in one year.

Determining the Boundaries of the System and the Project   In theory, the limits of each project should be clearly defined, but in practice, this is often not the case. Among other things, for example, various projects may share the same resources (people, equipment, etc.), related to different departments. It may be very difficult to clearly identify the costs in such cases.

Preliminary Costs   These are the costs incurred before the decision as to whether the investment will be realized or not has been made, namely the costs associated with project preparation, data collection, feasibility study, etc.

Opportunity Costs   By definition, these costs never appear in traditional bookkeeping accounts, as they are not actual costs, but rather the costs of alternatives which have not been pursued (the costs of opportunities not taken up). Managers often ask how much it would have cost had a different investment been chosen instead of the actual one. Opportunity costs are often a tool through which we compare various investment projects with each other, based on which, the one with the lowest cost is chosen.

Reduced Benefits   These are the costs that come due to a poorly designed system, errors due to the inadequate training of users, declinatory reactions of users of the new system, slow system responsiveness, an inability to work due to system malfunctions, and so on.

Cost of Risk   Risk, for instance, is connected with the decision as to whether to opt for a more expensive solution from a renowned provider or for a cheaper solution from an unknown provider. The latter possibility is more likely to cause significant unforeseen costs in the future because of poor quality, yet one cannot actually know for sure. The price difference can also be interpreted as a premium for insurance against such risks—the question is simply whether we are willing to bear this cost.

Measuring the benefits of BI, however, represents an even bigger problem than measuring the costs. Many effects assumed to be created by BI consist mainly of non-financial and even intangible benefits such as the improved quality and timeliness of information. Although such non-financial effects should lead to financial outcomes (e.g., cost savings), there may be a time lag between the acquisition of information from BI and the related financial gain. Further, BI often has an influence on the quality of CRM, customer satisfaction, and the search for new market opportunities, areas to which we often cannot attribute any specific financial value.[18] Therefore, measuring BI benefits can be extremely difficult in practice.[19]

CUSTOMER SERVICE

Retailing strategy for creating competitive advantage is invariably the delivery of high quality of service. It helps in creating the right kind of experience for shoppers. Customer service has also been found a strong driver of not only customer loyalty but also brand building for a retailer. Services are intangible, inconsistent, and inseparable. They are produced in the presence of the customer. A shop is a place for stocking products until a customer walks into it and interacts with the elements of the store. What the customer takes away is not just the merchandise but also a shopping experience that becomes the pivot for brand building.

Due to its basic nature, it is difficult to measure service quality objectively. Over the years, many approaches have been proposed. Among these models, SERVQUAL is the most prominent and the most widely used.[20] They proposed that the consumer's opinion of quality is formed by comparison of performance with expectations. Good service quality means that there are no gaps between performance and expectations, and customers' perceptions of service performance should meet or exceed their expectations. Five determinants of service quality have been identified, which include tangibility, reliability, responsiveness, assurance, and empathy.

Using the SERVQUAL model, Dabholkar et al. (1996) proposed an instrument called RSQS, which measures service quality in a retailing environment.[21] This instrument uses the common dimensions of pure service environments and retail environments and complements them with specific dimensions of service quality relevant to retailing (Exhibit 11.1 and Fig. 11.4).

In a study conducted in India, it was found that the customers found lack of retailers in all aspects of service quality.[22] The largest gap existed with regard to parking and other policies. The low gaps existed with regard to service promises. The study also brought out the relative importance of each of the dimensions, the relevance, and applicability of the RSQS scale.

Retailers must keep all these dimensions in mind since they are interrelated. All of them have very high correlation values. These are also called the components of a retail mix. A retailer would find the best combination based on the value being delivered to the customers. The components tend to work in tandem and the resultant service to the customer is far better than that can be provided by any of the dimensions independently. It is very interesting to note that price does not find a place in this set of variables. Therefore, even price formats, such as discount stores, category killers, hypermarkets, and mass-merchandisers would need to pay attention to these. For retailers positioned in non-price dimensions, attention to these factors becomes mandatory to survive and grow.

HR–Marketing Interface for Customer Service

The five dimensions of service quality in retail indicate the role of interface of frontline employees in rendering high levels of service. Except the physical aspects, the other four dimensions reflect the internal processes, policies, people, and systems of the retailer. It has to do more with the human capital than just the money invested in the business, even though the latter may amount to a larger sum. The satisfaction of the customers depends largely on how satisfied the employees are in discharging their responsibilities. It can be achieved only when the marketing function works in tandem with the human resources department. One of the best ways to describe this interface has been portrayed by the *service profit chain*.[23]

The service profit chain establishes the links among profitability, customer loyalty and employee satisfaction, and loyalty and productivity. The profit and growth of a company are stimulated by customer loyalty. Loyalty is a direct result of satisfaction. Customer satisfaction is largely influenced by the value delivered to the customers. These values are created by motivated and satisfied employees. Employee satisfaction is primarily a result of high quality support services and policies that enable employees to deliver results to customers. Each of these links need to be measured as given below:

1. Profit and growth
   - How do we define our loyal customers?
   - Do measurements of customer profitability include profits from referrals?

EXHIBIT 11.1   Dimensions and items used in the RSQS model

Dimension	Items
Physical aspects	This store has modern-looking equipment and fixtures.
	The physical facilities at this store are visually appealing.
	Materials associated with this store's service (such as shopping bags, catalogues, or statements) are visually appealing.
	This store has clean, attractive, and convenient public areas (e.g., restrooms).
	The store layout at this store makes it easy for customers to find what they need.
	The store layout at this store makes it easy for customers to move around in the store.
Reliability	When this store promises to do something by a certain time, it will do so.
	This store provides its services at the time it promises to do so.
	This store performs the service right the first time.
	This store has merchandise available when the customers want it.
	This store insists on error-free sales transactions and records.
Personal interaction	Employees in this store have the knowledge to answer customers' questions.
	The behaviour of employees in this store instils confidence in customers.
	Customers feel safe in their transactions with this store.
	Employees in this store give prompt service to customers.
	Employees in this store tell customers exactly when services will be performed.
	Employees in this store are never too busy to respond to customers' requests.
	This store gives customers individual attention.
	Employees in this store are consistently courteous with customers.
Problem solving	Employees in this store treat customers courteously on the telephone.
	This store willingly handles returns and exchanges.
	When a customer has a problem, this store shows a sincere interest in solving it.
	Employees in this store are able to handle customer complaints directly and immediately.
Policy	This store offers high quality merchandise.
	This store provides plenty of convenient parking for customers.
	This store has operating hours convenient for all its customers.
	This store accepts most major credit cards.
	This store offers its own credit cards.

- What proportion of business development expenditures and incentives are directed towards retention of existing customers?
- Why do customers defect?

2. Customer satisfaction
   - Is customer satisfaction data collected in objective, consistent, and periodic fashion?
   - What are the listening posts for obtaining customer feedback in your organization?
   - How is information concerning customer satisfaction used to solve customer problems?

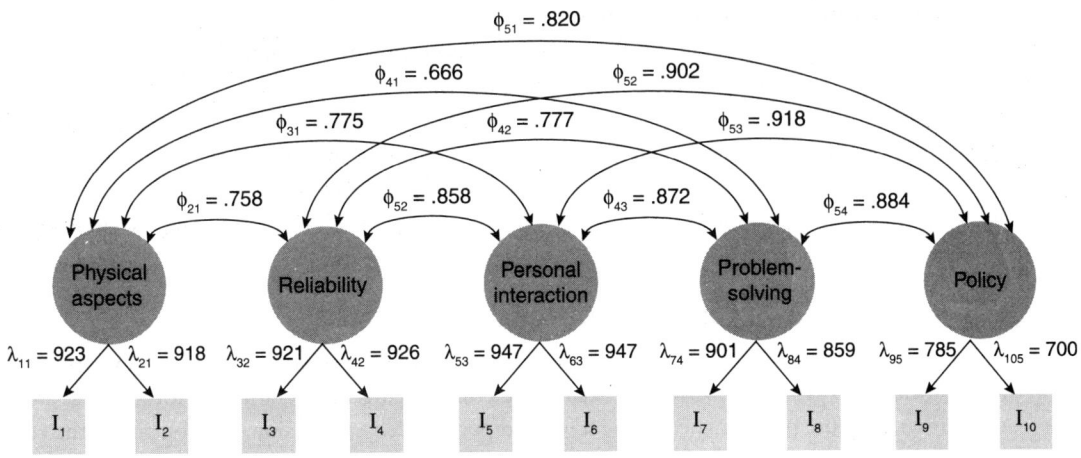

FIG. 11.4 Interrelations among the Dimensions of RSQS

3. External service value
   - How do we measure service value?
   - How is the information concerning customers' perceptions shared with those responsible for designing of service?
   - To what extent are the measures taken of differences between customer perception of quality delivered and their expectations before delivery?
   - Do our organizations' efforts to improve external service emphasize effective recovery from service errors in additions to providing a service right the first time?
4. Employee productivity
   - How do you measure employee productivity?
   - To what extent do the measures of productivity identify changes in quality as well as quantity of service produced per unit of input?
5. Employee loyalty
   - How do you create employee loyalty?
   - Have we made an effort to determine the right level of employee retention?
6. Employee satisfaction
   - Is employee satisfaction measured in the ways that can be linked to similar measures of customer satisfaction with sufficient frequency and consistency to establish trends for management?
   - Are employee satisfaction measurement criteria and methods geared to what customers and the managers believe are important?
   - To what extent are the measures of customer satisfaction, customer loyalty, or the quality and quantity of service output used in recognizing and rewarding employees?
7. Internal service quality
   - Do employees know who their customers are?
   - Are the employees satisfied with the technological and personal support they receive on the job?
8. Leadership
   - To what extent is the leadership
     creative, creative versus stately, or conservative?

Participatory, caring versus removed, elitist

Listening, coaching, and teaching versus supervising and managing?

Motivating by mission versus motivating by fear?

Leading by personally demonstrating values versus institutionalized policies?

- How much time is spent by the leadership personally developing and maintaining a corporate culture centered on service to customers and fellow employees?

9. What are the most important relationships in your service-profit chain? To what extent does each of the measures correlate with profit and growth at the front line?

Balanced Scorecard for Better Customer Experience

The balanced scorecard (BSC), with four perspectives—financial, customer, internal business processes, and learning and growth—provides a balanced picture of current operating performance as well as the drivers of future performance.[24] The scorecard puts strategy and vision, not control, at the centre (Fig. 11.5). It establishes goals and assumes that people will adopt behaviours and actions necessary to arrive at those goals. The measures are designed to lead the company towards the overall vision.

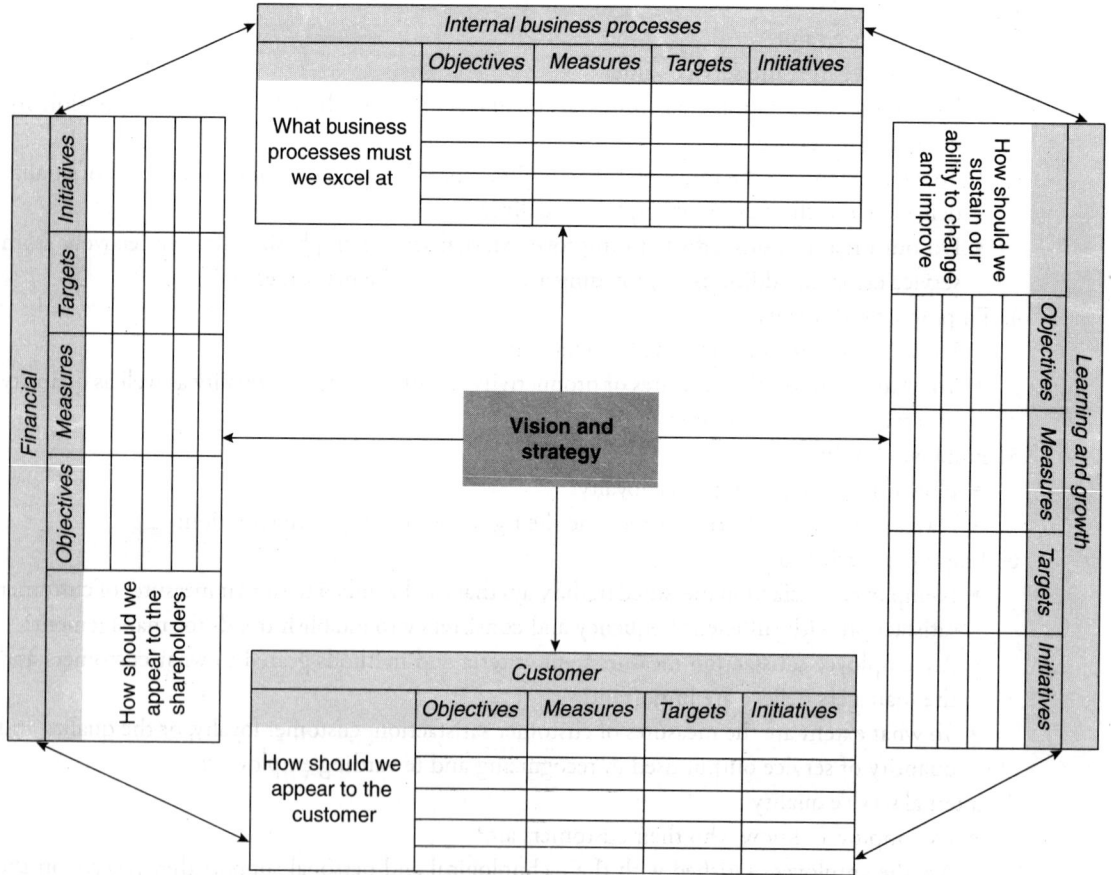

FIG. 11.5 Balanced Scorecard—Vision and Strategy

Since most traditional measurement systems have originated from the finance function, they tend to have a control bias. Traditional performance measurement systems specify the particular actions they want employees to take and then measure to see whether the employees have, in fact, taken those actions. In a consistently changing environment, a control focus must give way to planning focus that leads the retailers to better results than simply tell how they performed in the past. The balanced scorecard is well suited to such organizations where managers may know the end result but cannot tell the teams exactly how to achieve that result.

Perspective 1: Financials

The financial performance measures define the long-run objectives of the business unit. Most businesses will emphasize profitability objectives. However, this should change based on the stage of market development. Retailers in the early stage of their life cycle can stress rapid growth objectives, whereas in the maturity stage they may maximize cash flows. The framework to select these objectives based on these dimensions is given in Table 11.2.

Perspective 2: Customers

In the customer perspective of the BSC, the customer and market segments in which the business unit will compete are identified. The retailer's performance measurement parameters are set in line with the targeted segments. The customer perspective typically includes several generic measures such as customer satisfaction, customer retention, new customer acquisition, customer profitability, and market and account share in the targeted segments. These measures should be customized to the targeted customer groups from whom growth and profitability are derived. These customizations would be based largely on value propositions of the company and would be built on products or services, image and perceptions, and relationships with its customers.

Perspective 3: Internal Business Processes

The critical internal business processes enable retailers to deliver on the value propositions chosen for the targeted market segments as also satisfy shareholder expectations of excellent financial returns. A retailer would identify the critical internal processes in which the organization must excel. The measures chosen would have the greatest impact on customer satisfaction and financial objectives of the retailer.

TABLE 11.2 Customizing Measures for Business Strategies and Financial Terms

		Revenue Growth and Mix	Improvement	Asset Utilization
Business unit strategy	Growth	Sales growth rate by segment		Investment (percentage of sales)
		Percentage revenue from new products, services, and customers		R&D (percentage of sales)
	Sustain	Share of targeted customers and accounts	Cost vs Competitors	Working capital ratios (cash-to-cash cycle)
		Cross-selling	Cost reduction rates	ROCE by key asset categories
		Percentage revenues from new applications	Indirect expenses (percentage of sales)	Asset utilization rates
		Customer and product line profitability		
	Harvest	Customer and product line profitability	Unit costs (per unit of output, per transaction)	Payback
		Percentage unprofitable cutomers		Thoughput

Two fundamental differences exist between traditional approaches to performance measurement and the BSC. While the traditional approaches attempt to monitor and improve existing business processes, the BSC approach would usually identify new processes also in line with the desired objectives.

Perspective 4: Learning and Growth

There are three sources of organizational learning and growth—people, systems, and organizational procedures. The objectives in this regard are set based on the financial, customer, and internal business process objectives on the BSC. Once all four are put together, directions for building capabilities emerge. The focus areas in this regard tend to be people, systems, and procedures. To close these gaps in capabilities, retailers need to invest in re-skilling employees, enhancing information technology and systems, and aligning organizational procedures and routines.

Research has proved that BSC can be applied to retailers with good result. It is a tool that needs to be built for every business separately. The scores and the weights attached as well as the dimensions for each of the perspectives need to be decided by the people in the organization, and would also change with time to be in consonance with the changing requirement of the retailers over time. Illustrative BSCs for two retailers are shown in Figs 11.6 and 11.7(a)–(f).[25]

SOCIAL MEDIA MARKETING[26]

Companies are increasingly looking towards leveraging the power of online media, especially with the boom in the number of active online users in India. As part of their integrated marketing strategy, social networking sites and community blogs are being used for promotional and brand building activities. People of similar interests can effectively use a social networking site to come together and share their likes and preferences. *Social networking* could be defined as the process of sharing information by connecting with individuals with similar interests. Messages (related to a company or brand) in social networking sites usually spread fast because such messages are perceived to be true and absolutely trustworthy as they apparently come from a trusted source rather than the company, organization, or the brand itself. Social media marketing to a large extent is done on a huge platform of social networking sites. Marketers use various tools such as

- live blogging and tweets to announce promotional campaigns and product offers;
- social networks, such as wall posts or fan pages;
- viral marketing through YouTube and other similar service providers; and
- link sharing on sites such as LinkedIn, Facebook, and Twitter.

Often online community groups are considered synonymous to social networking sites. However, there is an essential difference between the two. Social networking is individual-centric where the user can share his/her ideas, activities, events, links, and interests within their individual network, whereas online community is group-centric. Some of the well known online communities include Yahoo e-groups and Google groups. These are essentially newsgroups where discussions on common interests occur in the form of a threaded forum. Community blogs technically come under the category of social networking sites because the activity is still individual-centric with the only difference being that the networking is limited to a community instead of being global as in Facebook or LinkedIn. Interactive blogs do not fall under the category of social networking sites as their interface is developed in such a way that the user interacts in an interactive way, and thus involvement is better. There are also niche social networking sites such as LinkedIn, which is a professional networking service, or in other words, is a business-oriented social networking service.

	Elements	Goals	Measurements	Final score
Financial	Pre-opening membership	Achieve BEP memberships prior to opening	Number of memberships	25
	BEP sales	Achieve break-even sales in $ value within 3 months of commencement	$ value within 3 months	25
	Capex	Maintain within budget	Completed within budget	20
	Revenue growth from brands/ advertising	Meeting the target set in $ value	Achieved expected $ value	5
	On target opening	To avoid time overrun	To open within target date	20
	Revenue per trainer	For each trainer to have 15 clients at any point in time	Signing up the required members	5
	Subtotal	**40**		**100**
Customer	Number of new members	To reach BEP sales and potential profit	Signed required membership to earn BEP sales and profit	30
	Customer satisfaction	Maximize customer satisfaction	Mystery shopping	30
	Understand customer decision-making matrix	Maximize number of customers	Number of customers	20
	Customers' complaints	Minimize number of complaints	Number of complaints posted and Average time to respond and reach satisfactory solutions to a complaint	20
	Subtotal	**30**		**100**
Internal processes	Loyalty programme	To retain customers	Total number of renewals every month	15
	All facilities being operational	All facilities being operational on day of opening	Physical checks	10
	Optimal use of facilities	Identify facilities which are used less frequently	Frequent checks, visits, and customer surveys	10
	Time utilization per trainer	Maximum efficiency per trainer	Idle time per trainer	10
	Membership fees and sponsorship deals	Timely collection	Outstanding membership fees and sponsorship deals	15
	Timing of introduction of new offers: packages/services/ classes	To set the market trend	Time from conception to operational implementation: maintaining market leadership	15
	User friendly	Simplify access to gym and machines	Customer survey	15
	Subtotal	**20**		**100**
Learning and growth	Keeping up to speed with new technology/packages/services/ classes	To set the market trend	Time from conception to operational implementation: maintaining market leadership	45
	Amount spent on employee training	$ value per employee and designation	Cost of training per employee and increase in revenue per trainer	35
	Employee satisfaction and retention	Lowest employee turnover	Attrition rate	20
	Subtotal	**10**		**100**
Total score		**100**		

FIG. 11.6 Balanced Scorecard of a Fitness Centre

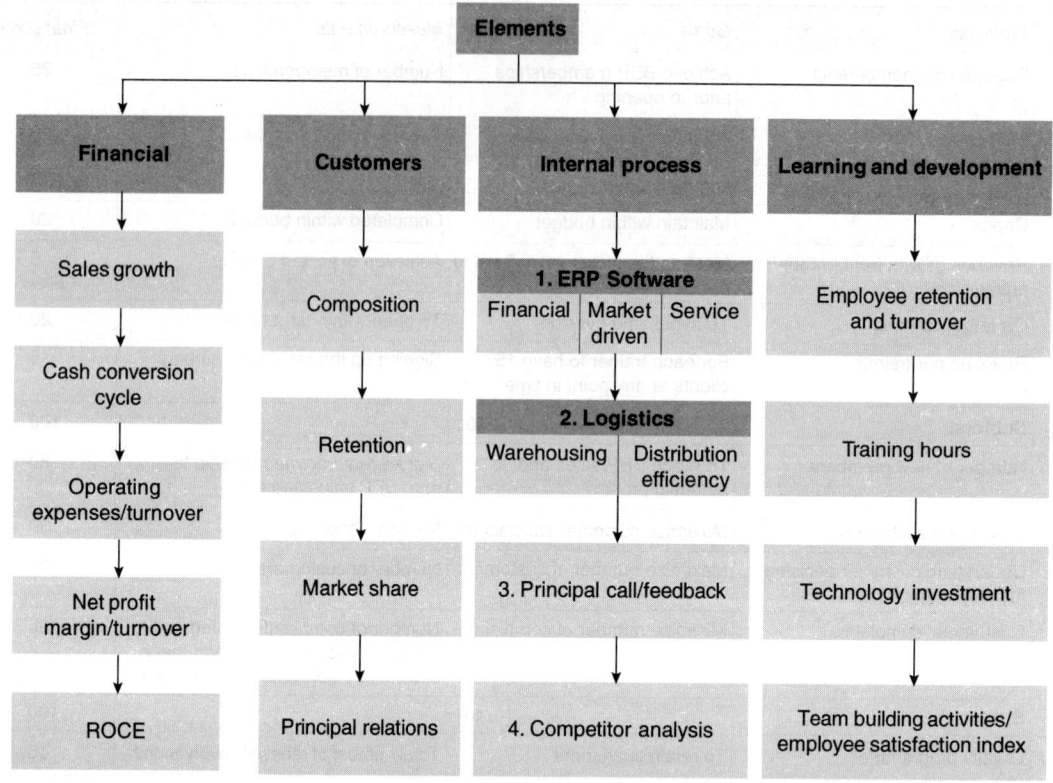

(a) Elements under the Four Perspectives

Perspective		Elements	Goals		Weight % (internal)	Measurements	Total weight	Final score
			Subjective	Objective				
Finance	1	Sales growth					35	
	2	Cash conversion cycle					25	
	3	Operating expenses/turnover					20	
	4	Net profit margin/turnover					10	
	5	ROCE					10	
Subtotal					**40%**		**100**	
Customer	1	Customer composition					20	
	2	Retention					25	
	3	Market share					30	
	4	Principal relations					25	
Subtotal					**30%**		**100**	

(b) Weights Assigned to Each Element (contd)

FIG. 11.7   Balanced Scorecard of a Consumer Durable Retailer (contd)

Perspective		Elements	Goals		Weight % (internal)	Measurements	Total weight	Final score
			Subjective	Objective				
Internal process	1	ERP software					50	
	2	Logistics					30	
	3	Principal call/feedback					10	
	4	Competitor analysis					10	
Subtotal					**15%**		**100**	
Learning and growth	1	Employee retention: turnaround					30	
	2	Training hours					40	
	3	Technology investment					20	
	4	Employee satisfaction index					10	
Subtotal					**15%**		**100**	

(b) Weights Assigned to Each Element

Financial								
S. No.	Elements	Goals			Measurements		Total weight	Final score
		Subjective	Objective	Weight % (Internal)	Actuals to budgeted			
1	Annual sales (up by 10% over last year)		2,900,311,000		MOM measurement by annexure 1 and 2		35%	
2	Cash conversion cycle (increased to improve wholesale business)		35 days		Actuals to budgeted		25%	
			Stores: 20 days		Actuals to budgeted			
			Debtors: 70 days		Actuals to budgeted			
			Creditors: 55 days		Actuals to budgeted			
3	Operating expenses/ turnover 5.5%		159,517,105		Actuals to budgeted		20%	
4	Net profit margin/ turnover 3%		87,009,330		MOM comparison to annexure 1 and 2		10%	
5	ROCE		25.00%		Actuals to budgeted		10%	
Subtotal							**40.00%**	**100%**

(c) Financial Perspective—Goals and Measurements

FIG. 11.7 (Contd)

				Customer				
S. No.	**Elements**	**Goals**				**Measurements**	**Total weight**	**Final score**
		Subjective	*Objective*	**Weight % (Internal)**				
1	Customer composition		Achieve wholesale: Retail 75:25			Ratio composition attained	30%	
1.1	Wholesale		2,175,233,250	50				
1.1.1	Institutions		1,413,901,612.50					
1.1.2	Power retailer and others		1,413,901,612.50	50				
1.2	Retail		725,077,750					
2	Retention						25%	
2.1	Retail	**a.** Customer satisfaction **b.** Improve cross-sell		35		**a.** After sales quality call **b.** Customer satisfaction index **c.** Response days **d.** Cost control		
2.2	Wholesale			65				
2.2.1	Timely delivery	Dealer satisfaction				Order requisition to delivery 5 days		
2.2.2	Credit period	Attain quality				**a.** < 45 days, **b.** 45–90 days, **c.** > 90 days		
2.2.3	Provisions of bad debt/sales			2,088,3223.92		**a.** < 072%, **b.** = 072%, **c.** > 072%		
3	Market share		Maintain and improve				30%	
3.1	Product			50				
3.1.1	UAE							
3.1.1.i	Electronics		Improve M.S. from 21% to 25%			**a.** < 25%, **b.** = 25%, **c.** > 25%		
3.1.1.j	IT		Improve M.S. from 24% to 28%			**a.** < 28%, **b.** = 28%, **c.** > 28%		
3.1.2	MENA							
3.1.2.i	Electronics		Improve M.S. from 12% to 15%			**a.** < 15%, **b.** = 15%, **c.** > 15%		
3.1.2.j	IT		Improve M.S. from 14% to 18%			**a.** < 18%, **b.** = 18%, **c.** >18%		
3.2	Geographical share			50				
3.2.1	UAE		20,030,217,700					
3.2.2	MENA		870,093,300					
4	Principal relations	Maintain and improve					15%	
Subtotal				**30%**			**100%**	

(d) Customer Perspective—Goals and Measurements

FIG. 11.7 (Contd)

S. No.	Elements	Goals			Measurements	Total weight	Final score
		Subjective	Objective	Weight % (Internal)			
1	ERP software		100% accuracy			40%	
1.1	Financial			40			
1.1.1	Monthly administrative cost Variance (5.2% of sales)		Maintain costs at 5.2% of sales		**a.** < Budget, **b.** Equal to budget **c.** Exceeds budget		
1.1.2	Monthly turnover/Net working capital variance (10% sales)		Maintain ratio at 10% of sales		**a.** < Budget **b.** Equal to budget **c.** Exceeds budget		
1.1.3	Weekly overdue receivables		Efficient debtor recovery		**a.** < Credit period **b.** = Credit period **c.** > Credit period		
1.2	Market driven			40			
1.2.1	Sales and margin report each product location-wise		**a.** Optimal product mix		**a.** Stock report slow moving **b.** Actual to budget		
1.2.2	Sales and margin report each location product-wise		Demographic efficiency		**a.** Stock report slow moving **b.** Actual to budget		
1.2.3	Sales and margin report Each customer location/ product wise		Optimized segmentation strategy		Actuals to budgeted		
1.3	Service			20			
1.3.1	Quality control query		Improve customer satisfaction, improve loyalty customer base		Improve customer satisfaction, improve loyalty customer base		
2	Logistics					30%	
2.1	Warehousing (Wholesale and retail)		Encourage effective buying and diminishing stock days	60			
2.1.1	Quarterly freight forwarder evaluation		Efficient utilization of provider		**a.** Reduction in delivery days **b.** Current overhead cost to past, **c.** Current credit period provided by company to past **d.** Compliance with material storage standards		
2.1.2	Monthly review re-order levels for all products		**a.** Efficient buying forecast, **b.** Cost optimization		**a.** Manufacture time **b.** Delivery days **c.** Credit terms		
2.1.3	Quarterly physical stock verification		Achieve 100 % quantitative stock accuracy		**a.** Matching physical quantity with system report **b.** Safety standards met		
2.2	Distribution efficiency (Wholesale and retail)			40			
2.2.1	Delivery to customers and retail outlets from order date		**a.** Customer satisfaction, **b.** Increase market share **c.** Improve loyalty programme efficiency **d.** Diminish administrative cost		**a.** < 3 days, **b.** = 3 days, **c.** > 3 days		
2.2.2	Collection of damaged/ defective equipment from complaint date				**a.** < 2 days, **b.** = 2 days, **c.** > 2 days		
2.2.3	Delivery of repaired/ replacement equipment from repair date				**a.** < 3 days, **b.** = 3 days, **c.** > 3 days		

(e) Internal Business Process—Goals and Measurements (contd)

FIG. 11.7 (Contd)

S. No.	Elements	Goals			Measurements (%)	Total weight	Final score
		Subjective	*Objective*	*Weight % (Internal)*			
3	Principal call/ feedback					10%	
3.1	Half-yearly vendor evaluation	Maintain or scrap vendor agreements that positively improve sales while maximizing cost optimization			**a.** Change in sales YOY, **b.** Review of credit period, if applicable **c.** Advertising and other marketing budget allocations **d.** Store mapping **e.** Sales forecasting effectiveness		
3.2	Monthly customer complaint/Feedback report extracts				**a.** Customer satisfaction index **b.** Loyalty programme feedback		
3.3	New product launch—catalogue and training from supplier	**a.** Principal relations **b.** Franchise agreements			**a.** Customer satisfaction index **b.** Training effectiveness evaluation **c.** Change in sales		
4	Loyalty programme	Improve customer retention and market share			**a.** Specific discounts and offers with RBS cards **b.** Review % of sales through RBS CC by quarter **c.** Number of customers signing up10%	10%	
5	Competitor analysis					10%	
5.1	Monthly report of competitor wise product pricing	**a.** Improve strategy deployment **b.** Reduce reaction time			**a.** Half-yearly review of market share **b.** Sales to margin variances **c.** Net working capital and administrative cost to sales variance **d.** Customer satisfaction index		
5.2	Quarterly report of competitor wise product market share						
5.3	Half-yearly new product launches report by competitors to principal suppliers						
Subtotal				**15%**		**100%**	

(e) Internal business process—Goals and Measurements

FIG. 11.7 (Contd)

Learning and Growth						
S. No.	*Elements*	*Goals*			*Measurements*	*Final score*	*Total score*
		Subjective	*Objective*	*Weight % (Internal)*	*Total Weight*		
1	Retention: Turnaround	Beat industry norm for employee retention			**a.** Department wise—logistics, top management, finance, etc. **b.** Incentive and bonus scheme introduction and review	30%	
2	Training hours (.025% of sales)	Efficient utilization of training staff and reducing process attrition			**a.** 60 hrs/year, **b.** Course effectiveness evaluation **c.** Cost within budget	40%	
	b. Coverage						
	c. Efficacy						
3	Technology investment		Follow ERP, audit, and principal recommendations		**a.** Quarterly internal audit findings **b.** Achievement of ISO certifications	20%	
4	Team building activities/Employee satisfaction index	Quarterly/ annually			**a.** Peer acceptance **b.** Employee involvement surveys **c.** No. of complaints raised and management response time	10%	
Subtotal				**15.00%**		**100%**	

(f) Learning and growth—Goals and Measurements

FIG. 11.7 (Contd)

Shoppers Stop's Facebook Tweet 20 Campaign

Evolution of Social Networking Sites

It was around 1995 when online communities such as Geocities, Tripod, and Theglobe had started bringing people together through chat rooms and encouraged users to share personal information on web pages. These sites provided an inexpensive online space and easy-to-use publishing tools for the users to design and develop their own pages. Social networking began quite early in the online space, but gathered steam only with the emergence of Friendster in 2002. The major breakthrough in social networking came with the advent of MySpace in August 2003. Many other companies also started their services in the same period. While LinkedIn and Xing were pure business/professional networking sites, last.fm was a music sharing site. MySpace attracted many old Friendster customers by providing customized services and reducing the

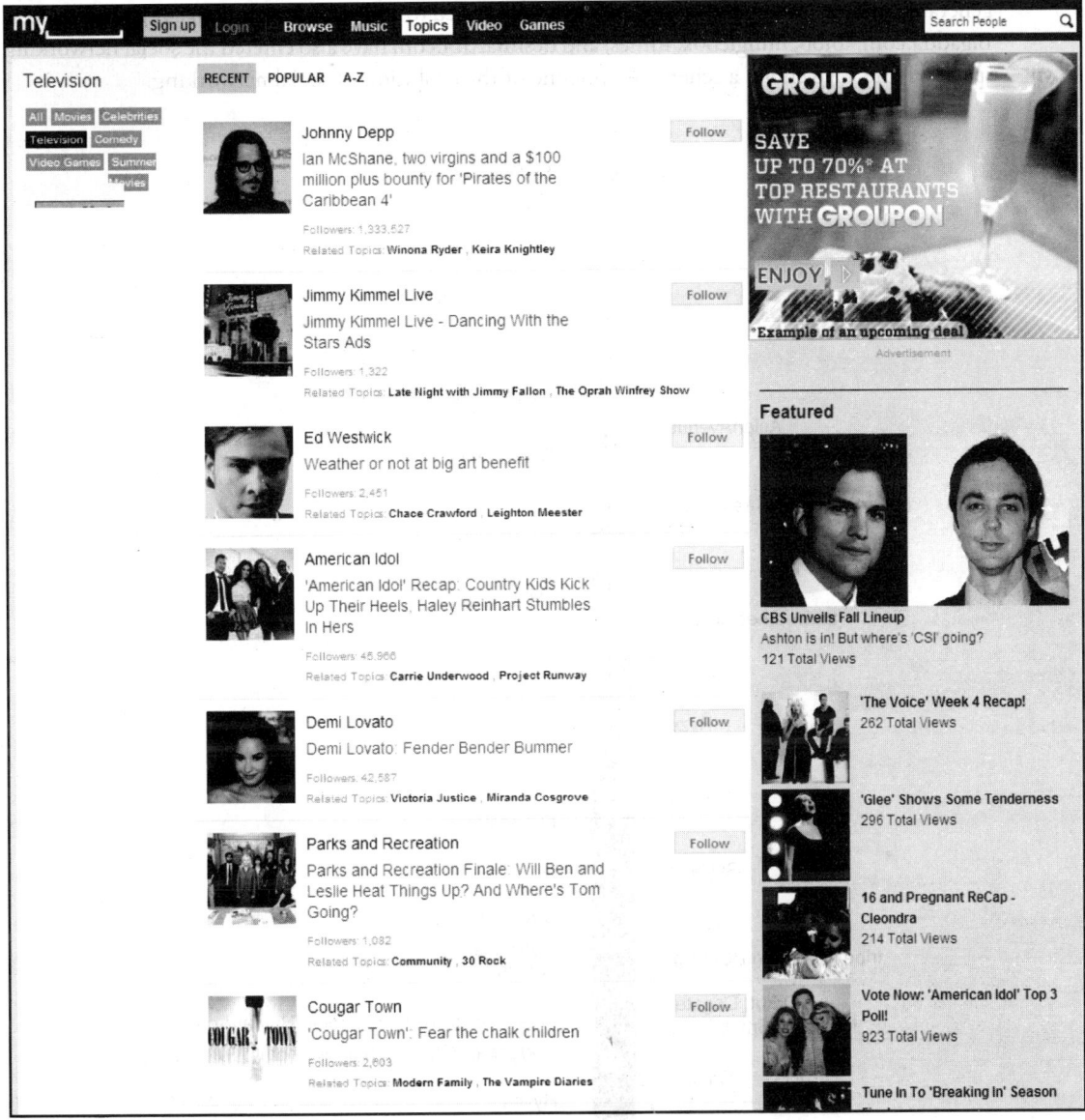

A Screenshot of MySpace

restrictions. Music companies, bands, celebrities, and other advertisers used MySpace for their promotions and this attracted many teenagers who could post their status and express their feelings.

In India, social media evolution started late in 2005. Hi5 was the first social networking site in India which became popular due to its ability to make new friends and other features which gave its users the freedom of speech. In 2006, Orkut became popular due to its multiple features, simple user interface, and exclusivity where people can share information easily and make/find friends easily through its communities. Though Facebook was introduced in 2006 worldwide, it gained popularity in late 2007 in India. In 2009, Twitter became popular as cricketers, bollywood celebrities, and other prominent personalities started sharing their thoughts and opinions, including their updates which generated interest among the fans who largely subscribed to Twitter. Many Indian companies such as Bigadda.com, ibibo, minglebox, itimes, and desimartini.com have also entered the social networking space. Figure 11.8 shows a schematic timeline of the evolution of social networking.

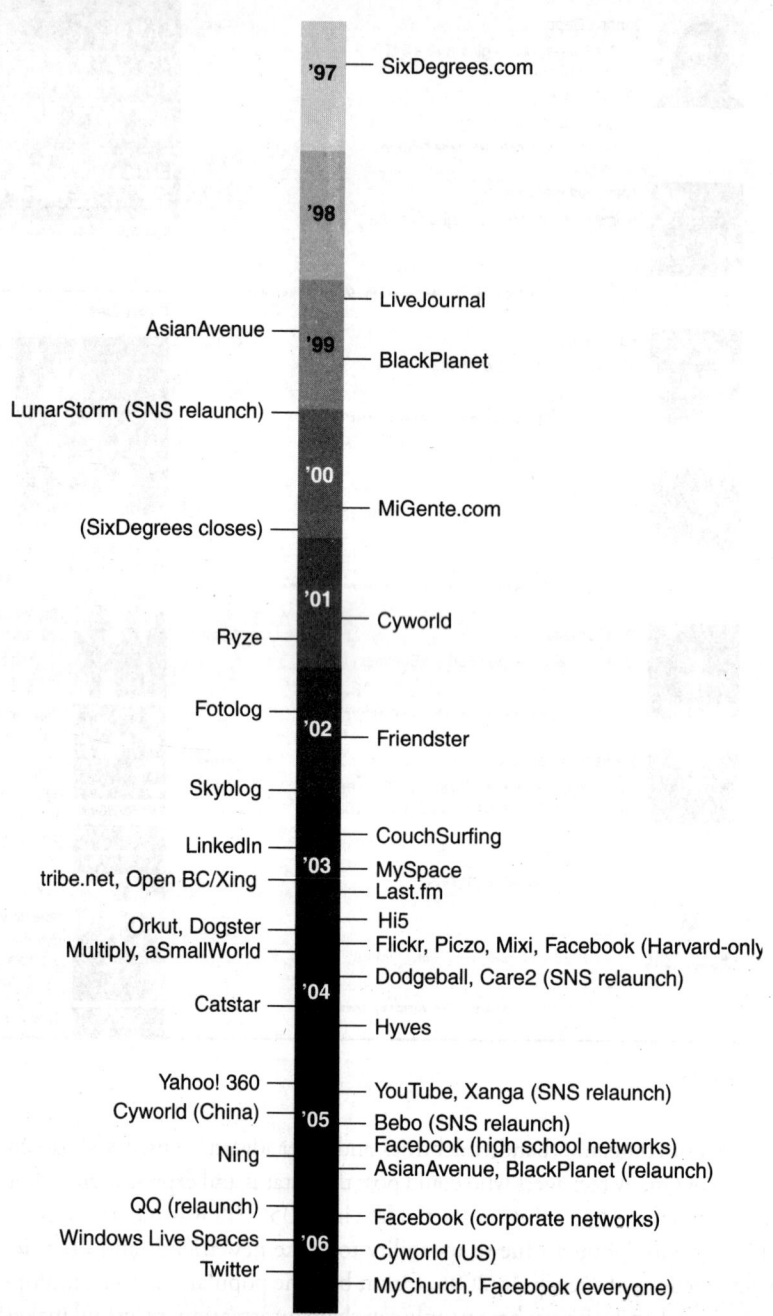

FIG. 11.8 Schematic Timeline Showing the Evolution of Social Networking (Chronology of Social Networking Sites)

Source: http://jcmc.indiana.edu/vol13/issue1/boyd.ellison.html, accessed on 5 November 2010.

Benefits and Limitations of Social Networking

The main purpose of using social networking sites is to keep in touch with friends. People also use social networking sites to kill boredom and enjoy the fun of trivial communication. Physical distances are no more barriers. Messages are perceived to be true and trustworthy as they come from friends and known sources. In the context of marketing, this helps in faster spread of information and purchase decisions. Further, the incremental cost of social media advertising is very low.

Social media marketing is more like a conversation with the consumer, whereas traditional marketing is like broadcasting and basically involves push strategy at work. Retailers must keep this distinction in mind. Target launched their Facebook campaign a few years ago. The page has many applications to ensure interactions amongst the members. This has helped increase brand awareness and loyalty. Walmart also launched a Facebook campaign along the same lines. However, it did not have a similar range and focus in applications.

Some of the critical success factors for a successful social networking campaign are as follows:

- Exciting and entertaining features/applications to various customer communities/segments
- Privacy of customers and offering customized services
- Rich user interface and good/flexible features and applications
- Efficient technology and robust design, yet simple to use
- Understanding people behaviour and providing good experience
- Strong marketing and technical teams
- Building trust among its users
- Proactive thinking
- Risk mitigation plans in case of cyber threats
- Strong defence mechanisms in times of unwanted negative publicity

Usage Trends in India

More than 90 per cent users log into Facebook and follow by ibibo and Twitter. Some of the trends as reported by ViziSense are as follows:

1. Majority of the users of social networking sites are in the age group 15–24.
2. LinkedIn is a business social networking site that has the highest concentration of users within the age group 25–34.
3. Graduates form the majority of the user base amd are followed by those pursuing graduation.
4. The male–female breakup of the total online user base of social networking sites is 80:20.
5. Photos have higher page views than applications; however, the time spent (52% of the total time spent in Facebook) on applications is more than that on photos.
6. Both graduates and undergraduates form about 70 per cent of the total users who use applications.
7. Applications attract about 64 per cent users who are from metros and have a higher proportion of unique users who are students.

Social Marketing in Retail

Social networks enjoyed 22.49 per cent of the total page views of the Indian audience, whereas portals managed to get only 3.86 per cent of the total page views in 2010. Visits to social networking sites have already overtaken visits to email sites. Moreover, now the most popular reason for people to visit a social network is not just to make acquaintances and friends but also to find out about promotional offers and sales (Exhibit 11.2).

EXHIBIT 11.2   Croma's Facebook Page and Shoppers Stop's Twitter Page

Word of mouth is the prime focus of Croma when it updates its Facebook fan page. The discussion boards also act as a prime source to obtain the feedback about the quality of the products and the services being offered in the retail stores. Moreover, Facebook users who have bought products on offer in Croma also recommend to other people who then like Croma's fan page. Croma also puts up offers on display in the Facebook fan pages and Twitter, but it ensures that the offers are not pushed. Croma has a blog where it releases the monthly catalogues and product informational brochures with relevant photographs. This catalogue is the largest of its kind till now in India. It makes sure

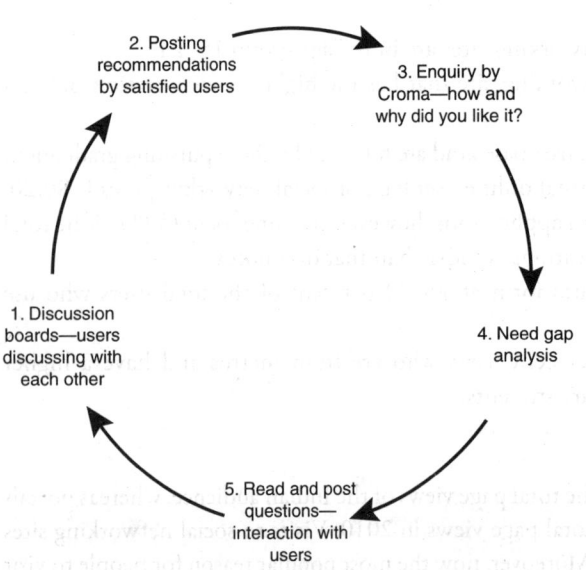

that either the blog or the Facebook fan page does not turn into a forum.

The result is that Croma knows that its primary target segment is the urban male in the age group of 18–25 years. The multiplier effect has helped it earn goodwill amongst its customer base and has reduced the need for TV commercials, which would have otherwise been used for increasing the brand awareness at a higher cost. Figure 11.9 shows the social media cycle at Croma.

Shoppers Stop has also been using Facebook to achieve the same objective as that of Croma. It is also trying to integrate Facebook and Twitter with its e-commerce portal. Its IT team is working on creating a pop-up on the home page to increase the conversion rates, whenever a user visits its e-commerce portal. It has a large product catalogue where it is now integrating a 'like' button with each and every product listed in the catalogue. Shoppers Stop has already piloted a widget which enhances the experience with the customers who are members of its strong loyalty programme. It is also creating applications that will be compatible with the WAP platform. This is to leverage the growth in mobile Internet owing to the introduction of 3G.

Croma's Facebook Fan Page

FIG. 11.9   Social Media Cycle at Croma

Shoppers Stop's Twitter Page

Major retailers in India now have multiple retail channels including brick and mortar, catalogue, and Internet formats. Consumers use different channels at different stages of buying. Retailers now need more information on their target market profiles and shopping behaviours. They can use social media to closely interact with the customer and in the process gather more insights on the shopping behaviour and the associated target market profiles. One of the ways through which retailers can achieve this is by using the analytics data that Facebook and Twitter provide it. Facebook already provides analytics to marketers and now Twitter is also set to provide such valuable information to marketers. Retailers in India are still to develop a strategy for using social media. Some of them such as Big Bazaar, Shoppers Stop, and Croma have used it to improve its sales successfully. Analytics serve three key purposes for retailers, thus furthering business growth.

Studying Customers This refers to tracking prime customers, their locations, socio-economic background, lifestyle habits, and their maturity levels while making the purchase decisions.

Analysis of Transactional Data Analysis based on customers' buying behaviour, tastes, and preferences would help the retailer immensely, for instance, in better layout planning and adjacencies inside the retail store.

Predictive Modelling This type of modelling involves processing the insights obtained from the customers' buying behaviour, predicting how customers in future would upgrade their buying behaviour, and the categories in which they might be interested in future. Depending thus on the future lifestyle habits of the customer, the retail store can make further expansion plans.

Current Retail Use of Social Media in India

Retailers in India currently use social media for the following purposes (Fig. 11.10):

Brand Engagement Brand engagement is done through contests, surveys, promotional communications, and offering discount vouchers/coupons.

E-commerce This is done through the online portal where, by integrating Facebook and Twitter, it is easy for the retailers to track traffic and also obtain demographic analytics, and thus delve deeper into consumer insights.

Listening Post This ensures listening to customer feedback about product and service quality and at the same time helping them have an excellent experience with the brand or retail store. This increases brand loyalty and patronage. Listening also helps retailers deal with reputation management and sustain favourable customer relationships.

Limited Application of Social Media in Retail

Until the recession hit the market, marketers were using mass media as a marketing and communication medium. Later on, marketers started looking for alternative media for advertising. Moreover, with the increasing need to break the clutter in a cost effective manner, marketers began to realize the importance of various social media, such as viral videos, social networking sites, and community blogs. A viral video is one that becomes popular through the process of Internet sharing, typically through video sharing websites, social media, and email. Despite the benefits discussed, social media has not yet been adopted in a big way by retailers. This is so due to the following reasons:

1. Retailers are accustomed to working with pre-defined metrics and always look at the returns made on investments. So, in the case of spending on marketing promotions, retailers are

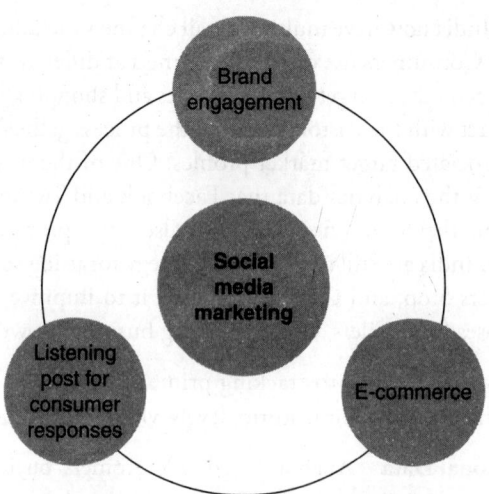

FIG. 11.10 Uses of Social Media Marketing in Indian Retail

always stressing on a set ROI while communicating the creative brief to the advertising agencies. Mass media like the television are still being preferred as there are metrics such as 'effective reach' or 'frequency' through which the impact and effectiveness of the advertising and promotional campaigns can be precisely measured (and hence the ROI). However, for social media such as Facebook and Twitter, the same does not apply. Retailers are apprehensive as they do not know or cannot determine how much their campaigns have been generating sales, and hence the measurement of ROI becomes difficult.

2. Many retailers still do not consider social media as something which can be complementary to mass media. In the latter, broadcasting is done and this helps the retailers attract more footfalls. But are the footfalls actually converting to sales? Traditionally, the conversion rates are very low and hence social media should be seen as a tool to interact with the customer, know about their likes and dislikes, build excitement around the retail store through promotions in the social media, and thus increase loyalty that will automatically increase the conversion rates, which means converting more number of footfalls to sales.

3. Retailers not only in India but also in other countries are yet to favourably look at social media as complementary to mass media in their marketing and advertising plans. As an example, Courts which is a prime electronics, furniture, and IT retailer in Singapore does have a fan page in Facebook, but it is not much active with only 35+ members till date.

4. There is lack of awareness amongst many marketers about the various advertising tools that Facebook and Twitter offer. There is also a perception that social media marketing is an expensive proposition when in reality it is not the case.

5. Marketers are primarily risk averse and hence are apprehensive of the speed at which negative publicity spreads in social networking sites through word of mouth.

6. Advertising agencies do not have the incentive to try out social media as an alternative to mass media because the latter still has a greater reach and the money made by advertising through this is greater than that for social media.

7. For retailers, the offline brick and mortar model is still successful and they try to replicate this same model online which often proves to be irrelevant and results in a failure. Discouraged

by this failure, retailers prefer to maintain a state of inertia where they are happy to earn profits with the existing brick and mortar model.

SUMMARY

Retailers need to connect to their customers on a continuous basis. They also need to provide excellent experience every time a customer walks into the store. Stores need to sell themselves, and advertising and promotions are a very expensive way to market and build brands.

Retail is a service business and like any other service business, retailers need to build their brand based on consistent customer expertise that is not only invigorating but also differentiating. Over time, through a sustained effort, retailers need to move from an evaluative cognitive choice behaviour to an affect-based choice. This can be possible only when the store delivers good customer service using all the five dimensions, namely physical aspects, reliability, personal interaction, problem solving, and policy. The role of the front-line employee thus becomes very crucial. Retailers must remember that while they may sell merchandise, they are actually processing customers which can be possible only through good people policies. To this end, with a little insight and planning, they can use social media to their advantage.

NOTES

1. Anand, Kamaljit Singh and Piyush Kumar Sinha 2009, 'Store Format Choice in an Evolving Market: Role of Affect, Cognition, and Involvement', *The International Review of Retail, Distribution and Consumer Research*, 19: 5, pp. 505–34.

2. Ajzen, I. 1985, *From Intentions to Actions: A Theory of Planned Behavior*, J. Kuhl and J.Beckman (Eds), *Action-control: From Cognition to Behavior*, Springer, Heidelberg, pp. 11–39.

3. Based on unpublished study conducted by Prof. Piyush Kumar Sinha, Prof. Rajendra Patel, and Kamaljit Singh Anand, IIMA, 2009.

4. Reinschmidt, J. and A. Francoise 2000, *Business Intelligence Certification Guide*, IBM International Technical Support Organization, San Jose.

5. Olszak, C and E. Ziemba 2007, 'Approach to Building and Implementing Business Intelligence Systems', *Interdisciplinary Journal of Information, Knowledge, and Management*, Vol. 2, pp. 135–48.

6. Wang, H. and S. Wang 2008, 'A Knowledge Management Approach to Data Mining Process for Business Intelligence', *Industrial Management and Data Systems*, pp. 622–34.

7. Bose, R. 2009, 'Advanced Analytics: Opportunities and Challenges', *Industrial Management and Data Systems*, pp. 155–72.

8. Negash, S. 2004, 'Business Intelligence', *Communications of the Association for Information Systems*, Vol. 13, pp. 177–95.

9. Jagielska, I., P. Darke, and G. Zagari 2003, 'Business Intelligence Systems for Decision Support: Concepts, Processes and Practice', *Proceedings of the 7th International Conference of the International Society for Decision Support Systems*.

10. www.ibm.com, accessed on 07 July 2010.

11. Elbashir, Mohamed Z. Philip A. Collier, Steve G. Sutton, 'The Role of Organizational Absorptive Capacity in Strategic Use of Business Intelligence to Support Integrated Management Control Systems', *Accounting Review*, January 2011, Vol. 86, Issue 1, pp. 155–84.

12. Yeoh, William and Andy Koronios 2010, 'Critical Succces Factors For Busines Inteligence Systems', *Journal of Computer Information Systems*, Spring, Vol. 50, Issue 3, pp. 23-32.

13. Vannoy, Sandra A., and A.F. Salam 2010, 'Managerial Interpretations of the Role of Information Systems in Competitive Actions and Firm Performance: A Grounded Theory Investigation', *Information Systems Research*, September, Vol. 21, Issue 3, pp. 496–515.

14. Thompson, O. 2006. Business Intelligence Success, Lessons Learned, Process ERP Partners, LLC, http://www.sydmart.com/artic/bi_success.pdf, accessed on 2 March 2009.

15. Carver, A. and M. Ritacco 2006, 'The Business Value of Business Intelligence: A Framework for

Measuring the Benefits of Business Intelligence', *Business Objects,* p. 6.

16. Atre, S. and L.T. Moss 2003, 'Business Intelligence Roadmap: The Complete Project Lifecycle for Decision–Support Applications', Boston, Addison–Wesley.

17. Remenyi, D., F. Bannister and A. Money 2007, *The Effective Measurement and Management of ICT Costs and Benefits,* 3rd Edn, Oxford CIMA Publishing.

18. B. Hočevar and J. Jaklič 2010, 'Assessing Benefits of Business Intelligence Systems—A Case Study', *Management,* Vol. 15, pp. 87–119.

19. Lönnqvist, A. and V. Pirttimäki 2006, 'The Measurement of Business Intelligence', *Information Systems Management Journal,* pp. 32–40.

20 Parasuraman, A, V.A. Zeithaml, and L.L. Berry (1988), 'SERVQUAL: A Multiple-item Scale for Measuring Consumer Perceptions of Service Quality', *Journal of Retailing,* 64(1), 12–40.

21. Dabholkar Pratibha A, Dayle I. Thorpe, and Joseph O. Rentz, 1996, 'A Measure of Service Quality in Retail Stores: Scale Development and Validation', *Journal of the Academy of Marketing Science,* Vol. 21(1), pp. 3–16.

22. Parikh, Darshan 2006, 'Measuring Retail Service Quality: An Empirical Assessment of the Instrument', *Vikalpa,* Vol. 31(2), pp. 45–55.

23. Heskett J.L., O.J. Thomas, Gary Loveman, W. Earl Sasser Jr., and Leonard L. Schlesinger, 'Putting the Service Profit Chain to Work', *Harvard Business Review.*

24. Robert S. Kaplan and David P. Norton 1996, 'Linking the Balanced Scorecard to Strategy', *California Management Review,* Vol. 39, No. 1, Fall, pp. 53–79.

25. Authors acknowledge the support of Prof. Rajendra D. Patel, IIMA, for these examples.

26. Pathi, Abhinav and Kothapalli Sandeep 2011, 'Business Growth Opportunities for Retail Stores Using Social Networking', Report on the Project Carried out under the Supervision of Prof. Piyush Kumar Sinha, IIMA.

CONCEPT REVIEW QUESTIONS

1. Explain the role of affect and cognition in building a retail brand.
2. How does time become an important factor in the brand building of a retail store?
3. Explain the role of operational efficiency in developing store sales strategies.
4. Explain the role of involvement in planning sales tactics in the store.
5. Enumerate the roles of business analytics for retail.
6. What factors determine the success of business intelligence for a retailer? How would you measure its benefits?
7. How can a retailer make use of social media to further its objectives?

CRITICAL THINKING QUESTIONS

1. How should a retailer go about developing a BSC for its business which is flexible enough to suit its plans?
2. How should one go about planning a good social marketing campaign for a chain of stores?

PROJECTS

1. Meet ten customers in front of three similar stores. Ask them to describe the store brand. Describe the differences across customers and stores. Meet the store manager/owner and ask the same question to him/her. Assess any gap between the store managers' and customers' descriptions.
2. Meet some of the store managers and executives from communication agencies. Gather information on any social marketing campaign that they would have undertaken for a retail brand. Develop a framework.

CASE STUDY

Infibeam*

Vishal Mehta, Founder and Chairman, Infibeam was jubilant. He was returning from Gandhinagar after a successful meeting with the officials of the Government of Gujarat for powering shopping at all e-Gram centres in the state of Gujarat. The government would make its network available to Infibeam which would provide access to 14,000 villages of the state of Gujarat with products not available easily. 'This is a big step for us. We would become one of the first online retailers to harness these untapped rural markets,' said Vishal. 'I know. This would help in adding a large set of customers, especially with a very large number of families in Gujarat having their members living outside India. But it will also mean that we need to look at different strategies for acquiring new customers, which may increase the cost of acquisition substantially,' concurred Manu, VP, Planning and Strategy. On not getting any response from Vishal for a while, he turned and found him lost deep into thought. Vishal was thinking of what may be a completely new direction and strategy for marketing communication.

Company Background

After working for six years at Amazon, Vishal Mehta, teamed up with 4 of his colleagues, and came back to India in 2007 to do an Amazon for India. They conceptualised Infibeam.com, a platform where customers could browse through products including books, mobile phones, gifts, and apparel, place orders and have the same delivered within India within a matter of days. Vishal knew that it would not be easy setting up something like Amazon in India as the payment and physical infrastructure was not as developed as in the US market. However, within three years, Infibeam had become a significant player and had gained about 1.5% share of the Indian online retailing market. Vishal made sure that Infibeam had the widest selection, right pricing and provided the best possible experience to its customers (Exhibit CS11.1).

Around 2009, many brands and brick-and-mortar retailers started Internet retailing in order to offer another channel to their customers and increase sales. Infibeam approached a few of these companies to power their online stores and provide related e-commerce services including fulfilment and customer service.

Over the next 2 years they entered into successful partnerships with Shoppers Stop, FutureGroup, Prestige TTK, Indian Premier League, Hidesign, NDTV, Dainik Jagran, Anand Bazaar Patrika and many others. Currently, it has approximately 100 such partner stores. In June 2011, Infibeam launched its novel 'Do-It-Yourself' e-commerce store platform called BuildaBazaar.com to allow retailers, brands, and individuals to set up an e-commerce store on the fly. The Buildabazaar platform provides a gamut of services to these retailers like product presentation, merchandising, shopping cart, and checkout; web store management tools for web store administration; product catalogue content and reporting and analytics services; web infrastructure and managed hosting; order management and processing. Infibeam plans to provide associated services like warehousing, last mile delivery, search and social media marketing to the same set of Buildabazaar retailers.

Retailers could not only sell their own set of products through their Buildabazaar store but could also sell Infibeam products on this; where the sourcing and fulfilment would be done by Infibeam retail for its set of products. Store owners in turn would be required to pay a transaction fee for every product of their own and receive a commission for every Infibeam product that they sold from their website. Unlike international players like vendder.com and Yahoo! Small Business, this was the only portal where the sellers would be able to choose their own product portfolio.

Infibeam, through Buildabazaar, did not charge its clients a huge upfront cost as compared to its traditional competitors like Martjack, ATG, and Novator. A minimal monthly fee was modelled to distinguish between serious and non-serious players (between ₹500 and ₹2,500 per month). It further charged its clients on every transaction that occurred on their portal. Clients accepted the offer as they did not need to invest upfront. Further Infibeam's development lead time was considerably lesser than its competition to an extent that it could possibly get an e-commerce company up and running within a matter of days. In a unique arrangement, the products sold by the clients would also show up on Infibeam. It not only

---

*Professor Piyush Kumar Sinha prepared this case with co-authors Nupur Gupta, PGP student class of 2012, and Varsha Verma, FPM student class of 2014. Cases are meant solely to form the basis for class discussion. Cases are not intended to serve as endorsements, sources of primary data, or illustrations of effective or ineffective management.

provided the clients a technology platform for their own e-commerce portal but also provided a demand generator. Infibeam had grown more than thrice in revenue every year between 2008 and 2011 with a major proportion of this revenue coming from its sales to retail consumers.

All this while Infibeam kept innovating on payments and expanded into newer formats. Infibeam also acquired other businesses like Picsquare.com, a photo printing website, and a remote cataloguing company in Delhi to give it a head start in each of these horizontals and/or verticals. To target the US NRI population, in August 2010, Infibeam launched a US facing website www.Infibeam.us where non resident Indians could order gifts for their friends and relatives in India. By the end of 2010, Infibeam had 250 employees with offices in Bangalore, Delhi, Mumbai, Kolkata, and Ahmedabad, Vishal's hometown and the company's head office.

A new concept, the Vishwagram Bazaar, planned in close association with the Government of Gujarat to target the rural population in the state was being looked at. The Gujarat Government was expected to implement an Internet connected network of approximately 18,000 e-Gram centers each of its villages. Infibeam would invest ₹2,000 crore in technology, supply chain infrastructure, and inventory and was expected to provide employment to around 20,000 people over a period of 5 years. The rural customer would be offered various products including FMCG, apparel, books, mobile phones, and electronics by Infibeam. Also, villagers would be allowed to sell their produce on the same platform, and thus, create a cooperative sellers' market. Infibeam planned to partner with India Post to provide last mile delivery and the option of 'cash on delivery' payment mechanism for their purchases. The rural customers could browse the products online on the local e-gram online store, order products and pay cash when the product was delivered to them. To facilitate transactions, Infibeam would launch the platform in Gujarati. The revenue model was based upon product sales to end customers and commission third party sales made over its Vishwagram platform.

Online Retailing in India

During 2007, the year Infibeam started, e-commerce in India was still in its infancy. This could largely be attributed to the fact that not many people were comfortable transacting for products online as well as not many compelling offerings were there in the market. This was also the time when online travel ticketing took off with offerings like IRCTC, makemytrip.com, and cleartrip.com doing significant business. Non-travel e-commerce or Internet retail grew in tandem with Internet accessibility and penetration of payment options. The Indian e-commerce industry was still in the nascent phase with only 42 million Internet users (2007) at 3.7% penetration growing at 30% year over year. Compared to the US market, where e-commerce had existed for more than a decade with 212 million Internet users that accounted for 70.2% of the total population and growing at about 4%, and China (Exhibit CS11.2), where the market was less than 5 years old with 162 million users that accounted for 12.3% of total population and growing at over 50%.[1] Despite the economic slowdown, Internet retailing in India grew by 38% (2007-09), reaching ₹26 billion in 2009.

Internet retailing offered several advantages to the customer, mainly pricing, selection, and convenience. Better prices as compared to physical retail were offered owing to lower fixed costs and overheads, direct and bulk sourcing. The buyers also had the additional benefit of comparing prices across brands and referring to user reviews before making his purchase decision. It provided wider selection than physical retail given the fact that all products on display on a portal need not be in inventory with the Internet retailer. It therefore offered virtualisation of inventory. Moreover, users need not make their way through heavy traffic to the closest mall; the products were delivered at the customer's doorstep within a couple of days. Despite these benefits, e-commerce in India was still small (accounting for <1% of total retail market). The key reason could be possibly the low penetration of credit and debit cards (31% of the Internet users had credit cards in 2008)[2] along with low penetration of high quality broadband Internet. Also, the Indian customer was still adapting to the idea of purchasing online and many people were still wary of making online payments.

The Internet subscription rate was expected to grow by 17% over 2008–13. This increase would in turn lead to a rise in Internet access at home. Mobile commerce, which had led to significant growth of e-commerce in the US, though nascent in India, was expected to pick

1. Miniwatts Marketing Group (2010), Internet Usage Stats and Population Report, Retrieved 28 May 2011, from http://www.internetworldstats.com/: http://www.internetworldstats.com/asia/cn.htm
2. JuxtConsult (2009), JuxtConsult India Online 2008, JuxtConsult.

up in the next decade as only 23% of total mobile users currently had access to Internet on their phones. Besides accessibility, a number of factors were attributed to the relatively slow adoption of electronic commerce in India between the years 2000 and 2007. While many e-commerce companies were launched, lacklustre execution and poor customer service didn't help win the trust of the customers. Also, since customers had other choices available to them, adoption rates were drastically low. The few sites which managed to build trust and long-time customer loyalty by offering a clear value proposition, succeeded. Among the first e-commerce sites that were able to make an impact in India were online ticket booking portals, which had a clearly defined customer segment—time pressed corporate travellers as well as upper and middle class customers who were English literate and had Internet access. E-commerce soon grew to include hotel and tour packages, and lastly sale of products like books and music (Exhibit CS11.3).

Around 2006–07, Internet retail faced several challenges in India. One of the biggest challenges was to manage supply chain of products from the manufacturer to the end consumer. There needed to be seamless co-ordination between e-commerce companies and last mile delivery agents so as to deliver the right product as per the promised time and provide accurate delivery information to the customer. This would require strong back-end support and faster delivery times for providing acceptable service levels to end customers. Another problem e-commerce companies were facing was the complex system of taxation on goods being sold from one state into another. The system of paying taxes and claiming credits was hard to manage for e-commerce companies at scale.

In the early 2000s, the e-commerce in India was dominated by marketplaces like Bazeee (now eBay), Rediff, and Indiatimes shopping. eBay acquired Baazee for $50 million in 2004 and renamed it ebay.in. They had more than 12,800 sellers registered and were purely a C2C marketplace. Later, many domestic retailers like Rediff.com started picking up by customising their services to suit the price conscious Indian customer.

They offered discounts and promotions during festivals when Indians tend to shop the most. In 2009, media products Internet retail showed a huge growth of 40%. Media products, especially books and music, were the most popular items of purchase due to their low cost and standardized quality.

Competitors

Flipkart

Flipkart was an Indian e-commerce portal set up in October 2007 by Sachin Bansal and Binny Bansal, who had earlier worked for Amazon India Development Center. The online store started by selling books and later expanded to other categories like CDs, DVDs, mobile phones and computers. With initial private funding, Flipkart employed social networking websites and word of mouth advertising to create awareness.[3] 50% of their orders come from the metros: Mumbai, Bangalore, Delhi, Chennai, Kolkata, and Hyderabad. The remaining buyers were from other parts of the country. The most saleable categories were fiction, trade paperbacks, and Indian writers.[4] The company broke even in March 2008 and claimed to have shown 100% growth each quarter. In 2009–10, the company raised to the tune of US$10 million from venture capital funds Accel India and Tiger Global Management. It reported sales of ₹250 million for the year 2009–10.

By 2010 the company had expanded to eight categories of books, mobiles, movies, music, games, cameras, computers, and other electronic gadgets. In the same year they invested heavily in a television advertising campaign. As of October 2010 the company had 500,000 users. Books were their top selling product category. The company reported revenues of ₹75 crores for 2010–2011. The management projected revenue of ₹400 crores in 2012–13 and planned to be a billion rupee company by 2014–15.[5] Hailed as India's Amazon.com, Flipkart is close to raising $150 million in a PE round of funding from General Atlantic Partners in one of the biggest ever deals for an Indian Internet firm, making it the first Indian Internet company to sport a billion dollar valuation.[6]

---

3. Flipkart (2007–11), http://www.flipkart.com/s/about, retrieved 24 May 2011, from http://www.flipkart.com/: http://www.flipkart.com/s/about
4. Livemint.com (26 May 2011). Binny Bansal The Flipside of an E-Venture, Bangalore, Karnataka, India.
5. Livemint.com (6 March 2011). Flipkart Eyes ₹4500 crore, Mumbai, Maharashtra, India.
6. http://thenextweb.com/in/2011/07/29/flipkart-may-have-just-become-the-first-indian-billion-dollar-internet-company/, retrieved on 10 November 2011

eBay India[7]

In 1995, eBay Inc. launched its website eBay.com which became the first and the largest global online marketplace where practically anyone could trade anything. eBay offered a platform for the sale of goods and services by a diverse community of individuals and businesses. The website offered both auction and 'Buy it Now' option for purchase of articles. eBay owed its popularity to the fact that it offered honest user feedback and reviews and allowed direct communication between buyers and sellers. This in turn encouraged honest dealings as higher user ratings increased the seller's business. User response was also considered critical in website design and category planning. As of 2011, the eBay community included more than 90 million active users from all around the world. At any given time, eBay worldwide hosted almost 200 million listings, with new listings being added at a rate of approximately 6.6 million listings per day. The categories on eBay, in excess of 50,000, included articles ranging from collectibles, antiques and sports memorabilia to computers, IT and even stamps. Other popular categories were glass, photography, electronics, jewellery, and gemstones.

Company operations were localized in about 30 countries with US being the largest market. eBay India was launched in 2004 and soon became one of the most popular online shopping websites. By 2010 it had 2.5 million registered users including about 12,800 sellers in 2471 cities. Worldwide eBay advertised through different media and also employed social and viral marketing. In India print and television were the main channels used.

Indiaplaza[8]

Indiaplaza, launched in the year 1999, was one of the first e-commerce portals in India targeting the NRI segment with Indian products. In 2007, Indian e-commerce venture Fabmall.com acquired Indiaplaza and continued the operations under the name Indiaplaza. It offered over 7 million products to its users which included books, music, videos, cameras, mobile phones, appliances, apparel, flowers, cakes, toys and many more categories. To increase customer satisfaction, it provided 24 hour customer service and also ran promotions like rewards and loyalty programs for banks, airlines, and IT companies. In addition to their e-commerce portal, they were also involved in powering shopping portals of other companies. This was similar to Infibeam's infrastructure business model. Indiaplaza was known for its low prices and reliable operations. It recorded a turnover of around ₹20 crore in the year 2007.

Rediff[9]

Rediff.com, which in 1996 started primarily as a news and information site soon provided a plethora of services from online shopping to travel planning to news and chat sites over and above free email and search engines. The company was headquartered in Mumbai, India with offices in New Delhi, India and New York, USA. Shopping. rediff.com was one of the first e-commerce portals in India and attracted 15 million visitors every month. The website offered products ranging from books, car accessories, hardware, health and beauty, jewellery, kitchenware, apparel, electronics, and toys. Its revenues were 14.6 million in 2009–2010 and 17.94 million in 2010–2011. In 2010, the company started a new initiative 'Deal Ho Jaye!' where they provided attractive deals on new consumer services available in their city through postings on the website. This facility was available in metros across 70 categories with discounts in the range of 30–60 per cent.

Indiatimes shopping[10]

Ranked No. 158 worldwide among the top 1000 most popular websites, shopping.indiatimes.com supported by the Times Group, was primarily known for its wide range of consumer electronic items (contributing 20% of the revenues) at competitive prices in addition to other categories like branded apparels, accessories like watches and bags, jewellery items and gift items like flowers, chocolates, and cakes. Leveraging on the parent company's brand image, Indiatimes shopping was able

7. ebay.in (1995–2011), Company Overview, retrieved 26 May 2011, from http://www.ebay.in/
8. Digital Inspiration (3 June 2007), *Online Shopping Portals—Are Valuations Enriching?* Retrieved from http://www.labnol. org: http://www.labnol.org/india/knowledge/online-shopping-portals-are-valuations-enriching/214/
9. Rediff.com (24 May 2011), *Rediff.Com Reports Results for the 4th Quarter and Fiscal Year Ended March 31, 2011*, retrieved from http://investor.rediff.com: http://investor.rediff.com/earreleasesDt.asp?path=2011%5C5%5Cer245201119335. html&y=2010
10. Statshow (n.d.), *Summary of shopping.indiatimes.com*, retrieved from http://www.statshow.com: http://www.statshow. com/shopping.indiatimes.com

to reach a wide base of customers. Good distribution network and different payment options to customers had also contributed to the popularity of the portal. Indiatimes used latest encryption technology and strict privacy rules to protect credit card information in order to build customer trust. In 2010, it reached 47 million users and recorded 199 million page views per month. Its estimated monthly revenues were ₹26 million.

Infibeam.com Online Store

Infibeam.com was designed with a viewer friendly interface. The left navigation allowed potential customers to narrow down their search of products by city, price, brand, colour and other product specific features. In year 2008 Infibeam added eleven new categories of mobiles, health equipment, mobile accessories, cameras, and photographic imaging. In July 2008, the Gifts Store was added where people could order cakes, flowers and other gift items for special occasions to be delivered to their friends and family. Separate stores were launched for popular festivals like Diwali and Christmas. Nine more categories were added to the website in between 2008 and 2010. In March 2011, Infibeam launched the Magic Box, where customers were offered one specific product every day at a very heavily discounted price. In continuation Infibeam launched the personalised version of the Magic Box, where people could add specific products to their Magic Box and Infibeam promised to surprise them within 72 hours with the best deal on that product.

Between 2008 and 2011, the number of visits to the site grew by over 300% year over year between 2008 and 2011. This was with minimal marketing efforts and no advertising. In the same period the number of customers increased by over 400%. With consistent additions to the product portfolio, Infibeam was able to increase customer satisfaction resulting in increase in number of transactions occurring on its portals. Infibeam also had higher than industry repeat customer purchases and among the highest conversion rates.

Consumer Profile

Infibeam targeted the community of Internet users who were currently online. Demographically, online retailers appealed to customers who had easy access to the internet. Internet shopping penetration rates, as a percentage of online population, increased from 47% in 2007 to 59.2% in 2010. Most Indian online shoppers were in the age group 18–49 years, with the dominant group being college going students (30%) and young men (28%)[11] (Exhibit CS11.4). They had an average annual income of USD 22,977.[12] An increase in income levels would increase personal consumption and in turn also increase online purchasing.

Situation segmentation also affected Internet shopping. A recently conducted study in the US found that most online shoppers used Internet to make purchases because they found Internet convenient to use. The survey also found that 30 per cent of online shoppers liked the ability of shopping in their own homes and that 25 per cent liked the fact of being able to shop at any time of the day. Popular e-commerce sites provide a satisfying experience to the consumers that encourage them to return. For Internet retail to be successful, it is important to appeal to customer values by building trust. A survey of bank account holding Internet users between ages 18 and 49 in India indicated that secure payment (87%), price (84%), and convenient payment methods (83%) were the most important factors during online purchase. Other important factors were speedy transactions, website reputation, and customer care and delivery charges.

Pricing

Across categories, Infibeam tried to maintain low prices for its products throughout the year. This was one of the key value propositions, that the same product would be available for the lowest possible price throughout the year. Prices across competition websites were monitored regularly and target purchase prices were set accordingly. Like Amazon, Infibeam's strength lay in supply chain of the tail products which was not easily available elsewhere offline.

Merchandising

Infibeam offered a wide variety of products across many categories to its customers (Table CS11.1)

Customer Service

Infibeam provided customer care through 24 hour phone support, email and detailed information through its help page on the website. It gave full refund or replacement

---

11. I-CUBE 2009-2010 Report (2010), *I-CUBE 2009-2010 Internet in India*, IAMAI, IMRB.
12. Master Card Worldwide (2008), *Master Card Worldwide Insights*, Master Card Worldwide.

TABLE CS11.1   Product Categories with % Share of Orders

Product Categories	% Share of Orders
1. Books and Magazines	50
2. Electronics	25
Home entertainment and appliances	38
Computers, cameras and peripherals	34
Mobiles and peripherals	28
3. Lifestyle	25
Apparel and accessories	49
Home lifestyle	32
Gifts	12
Others	7

for all damaged or incorrect deliveries. Incidences of such cases were less than 1% on delivered orders. This rate was the lowest in the industry. Most complaints received were resolved within a day.

Supply Chain Management

Infibeam had invested substantially in expanding its supply chain. The company's distribution network consisted of five warehouses across Delhi, Bangalore, Ahmedabad, Mumbai, and Calcutta. Starting with only a few hundred SKUs being sourced from less than 50 suppliers, it was sourcing more than 12 million SKUs from around 700 suppliers for its own portal by 2011. The average lead-time was less than one day for most suppliers. Items purchased by the consumers were delivered through multiple courier agencies including Fedex, BlueDart, Aramex, FirstFlight and many local courier agencies. The average delivery time taken by these last mile delivery companies was close to two days.

Inventory Management

Infibeam manages its inventory in each of its warehouses based on the following parameters:

1. Probability of sale
2. Expected demand volume
3. Vendor lead time in to the nearest Infibeam warehouse

4. Supplier terms
5. Obsolescence factor of the product category

Based on these parameters, products were either stocked at the Infibeam warehouse or were sourced as and when demand for these products came in. The two ways of sourcing were called 'Predictive' and 'Reactive' sourcing. In all cases Infibeam tried to optimize on the overall customer experience and minimize on the amount of obsolete inventory sitting on the company's books. Infibeam also had liquidation channels like the Magic Box and Hot Deals section where it could liquidate its excess inventory at regular intervals of time.

Delhi was the main centre of operations. A new 20,000 sq. ft warehouse was set up to cater to the increasing demand. Mumbai was also an important hub for both sourcing, shipments, and marketing. Infibeam's technical team was located out of Bangalore, Ahmedabad, and New Delhi. New offices were planned set up in Hyderabad and Chennai.

Marketing

Infibeam had not done any major marketing campaign so far. In April 2010, it offered its Social Connect feature. Users could now use their Facebook, Twitter, Yahoo, Google, Flicker, Blogger, or OpenID accounts, to access the website. It sponsored Confluence, the Annual International Business School Summit organized by the Indian Institute of Management, Ahmedabad, a top management business school of the country.

Infibeam often did joint promotions with large corporate like Banking and Airlines where it offered special discounts to customers and employees of those banks and airlines. A bulk of marketing efforts of Infibeam were focused on its present registered users by direct emailers containing information about latest deals and promotional offers.

Customer Acquisition Pattern

Infibeam had almost equal share of orders coming from North (29%), West (30%) and South (31%). Eastern states had a share of 10% of the total orders received. Table CS11.2 lists the states ranked according to share of the overall traffic received on the website:

The traffic on the website had increased 100% over 2010 and the portal received more than 4 million unique visits per month. Exhibit CS11.5 shared pattern

TABLE CS11.2 Top States with % Share of Overall Traffic

State	% share of overall traffic
Maharashtra	19
NCR	15
Karnataka	14
Tamil Nadu	10
Andhra Pradesh	8
Uttar Pradesh	6
Gujarat	5
Others	23

of customer visits to Infibeam and its competitors. Also average time spent on the website, called browsing time, increased by 50% during 2010 indicating more page views per user. The number of registered users increased 360% CAGR over 2007–11.

Buying Patterns

Infibeam received more than 4 million visits to its site Infibeam.com per month with number of visits peaking in the mid-week and relatively lesser traffic over the weekends. This was in contrast to brick-and-mortar shopping patterns. The average transaction value was between ₹1,000 and 1,500 during FY2010. This varied across time and across categories.

Customer Acquisition Strategies

Since its inception, Infibeam had relied solely on word of mouth advertising and promotions on its websites. It ran several blogs about its new offers on other websites that targeted the internet savvy 20–35 year olds. Unlike other companies that were spending between ₹1500–2000 per customer as acquisition costs, Infibeam spent less than ₹100. The portal's most popular promotion was Magic Box. One deal was put up every day, which was decided using 10 parameters including new launches, aspired products, and deals being offered by sellers. User reviews and the number of visitors looking at a particular product were also factored in. Infibeam used data from the Wish List (Shopping Cart) to decide on the success rate of the deal. Other than Magic Box, the portal carried a Hot Deals section that offered attractive discounts on a number of products across categories.

Back at Nehrunagar, Ahmedabad Office

'We have gained customer very quickly due to our partners. We got to find a way to maintain our 360% YOY growth in customer acquisition,' said Vishal as he and Manu entered their office situated by the Nehrunagar Road, Ahmedabad. 'The most important task ahead for us is to acquire customers by converting them from the offline mode to online mode and increase its market share and profitability. We have acquired a significant base of innovators. We need to create more awareness to generate a wider stream of adaptors. For this we may need to advertise. But this will push our customer acquisition cost very significantly. Currently we spend about ₹100 per customer as against the industry average of approximately ₹1,000,' replied Manu.

'Good point Manu, we are relatively less known in the offline customer marketplace. However is it the right time to make an investment to capture this market when there is still a lot of scope to capture the online buyers?' asked Vishal. 'We need to target both, but in a phased manner. Customers currently online would help building sales through more repeat orders, while, new offline customers will drive future growth by switching to online buying in the future. It is important that we start creating awareness and build trust among the Indian shoppers,' replied Manu.

After this conversation and many more brainstorming sessions, Vishal and his team decided to invest ₹5 crores in advertising across different avenues over the next year (Exhibit CS11.6). 'Call up some of the leading ad agencies. I need a plan with clear objectives and a course of action that outperforms and not outshout others. Although we are among the first two retailers on Google and we perform almost a good as Flipkart in terms of unique visitors, our off-line awareness needs to be worked on. Also we must keep in mind that we have to raise ₹2,000 crores and marketing communication tends to have a critical role in India towards this purpose. eGram for us is an apple,' Vishal concluded.

EXHIBIT CS11.1   Infibeam History

Date	Initiative
Feb 2008	Infibeam offer Rent-a-car service. Service currently available in all major cities namely Ahmedabad, Bangalore, Chennai, Delhi, Hyderabad, Mumbai and for all locations in Gujarat, Rajasthan, and Maharashtra
March 2008	Infibeam out of Beta mode
	Infibeam launches Mobile Store
May 2008	Watches, health equipment, mobile accessories categories launched
June 2008	Infibeam.com opens cameras and photographic imaging products showcase
July 2008	Infibeam.com launches apparel, jewellery, beauty, and perfume products
	Gifts store launched
Aug 2008	Apparel accessory and furnishings stores launched
Sept 2008	Deal of the day offer launched
	Gift certificates available on Infibeam.com
Oct 2008	Diwali Store launched
	International Shipping made available
Nov 2008	Home appliances, toys and games stores launched
	Acquisition of picsquare.com
Dec 2008	Christmas and New Years gifts store launched
	Launch of Presentsir.com
Jan 2009	Religion and spirituality and Valentine gifts store launched
	'Hot Deals' with discounts and 'Free Offers' on specific purchases
Feb 2009	FutureBazaar Books Store powered by Infibeam.com
	Camera accessories store launched
March 2009	Kitchenware and home entertainment store launched
April 2009	Picsquare.com launches designs from leading designers, to print on t-shirts, mugs, calendar, posters, key-chains etc.
	in.com co-brands its bookstore with Infibeam.com
17th April 2009	Infibeam.com joins the Nano fever by collating Tata dealers spread across India, in a bid to provide hassle free online booking to customers
May 2009	Travel Store launched
	New features added to Automobile store like information on dealers across India, latest used car value, car insurance calculator, etc.
June 2009	Magazine, movie, and music stores launched
Sept 2009	Infibeam's Executive Gift Voucher launched
Oct 2009	New user interface of Infibeam.com site
Jan 2010	Prestige TTK website powered by Infibeam
	Unified Search option made available on Infibeam.com
	eBook Store launched
	Pi launched (India's first eBook reader)

(Contd)

Date	Initiative
March 2010	Official IPL store powered by Infibeam
April 2010	Launch of the social connect feature
	Users may now use their Facebook, Twitter, Yahoo, Google, Flickr, Blogger, or OpenID accounts, to access the website.
May 2010	Hidesign.com powered by Infibeam
12th May 2010	Infibeam Launches Books Digitization Services, Print On Demand
	The digital books would initially be sold through Infibeam.com's eBooks store, and it would also act as a digital distribution channel for other websites, as well as print on demand functionality
	Available as both free and paid services: the free digitization service would involve Infibeam getting exclusive online and physical distribution rights of the books, which would be sold on a revenue share basis
June 2010	NDTVshopping powered by Infibeam
June 2010	Android 2.2 Powered Pi Launched in answer to Amazon.com's Kindle
	Official FIFA merchandise made available in Infibeam.com
	Strategic alliance to manufacture mobile phones
Aug 2010	Infibeam.us launched
Oct 2010	Infibeam.com becomes India's largest bookstore with 10 million titles
Dec 2010	Cash on delivery option made available on Infibeam.com
Jan 2011	Enters in MOU with Gujarat Govt. to power Vishwagram
Jan 2011	Pi-square launched
Feb 2011	ICC World Cup products launched
March 2011	Infibeam launched a Daily Deal section called Magic Box
Apr 2011	KKR store powered by Infibeam:
	KKR was one of the 10 franchises of the Indian Premier League. Infibeam partnered with KKR to launch a wide range of KKR merchandise

EXHIBIT CS11.2   E-commerce in US—Amazon.com

Launched in 1995, Amazon.com initially offered its web customers the convenience of browsing a selection of millions of books in a single sitting. During the first 30 days of business, Amazon.com fulfilled orders for customers in 50 states and 45 countries in the US—all shipped from his Seattle-area garage. With technological innovations, Amazon grew to offer more product categories like DVDs, CDs, MP3 downloads, computer software, video games, electronics, apparel, furniture, food, and toys. Amazon.com operated retail websites and offered programs that enabled third parties to sell products on its websites. They also provided services for third-party retailers, marketing and promotional services, and web services for developers. In addition, Amazon operated other websites, including www.a9.com and www.alexa.com that enabled search and navigation and www.imdb.com which was a comprehensive movie database.[13]

Amazon had also started offering e-commerce platforms to other retailers and individual sellers enabling them to leverage the Amazon.com platform. In the year

---

13. Amazon.com (Feburary 2011), *Mediakits: Overview*, retrieved 20 May 2011, from http://www.amazon.com: http://phx.corporate-ir.net/phoenix.zhtml?c=176060&p=irol-Mediakit

2010, Amazon recorded revenue of USD 34.204 billion with a net income of USD 1.152 billion.[14]

E-commerce in China[15]

Founded in 1999 in Eastern China, Alibaba group had over 60 million registered users in all its marketplaces across 70 cities and regions, including China, Hong Kong, India, Japan, Korea, Taiwan, the United Kingdom, and United States. Taobao, launched by Alibaba, reported more than 370 million registered users as of 2010 and hosted more than 800 million product listings.

In 2003, only 5.3% of China population was using Internet. Ebay entered China in the year 2004 and planned to dominate the China market. Alibaba group was a local privately owned internet based business, offering services like business-to-business international trade, online retail and payment platforms, and data-centric cloud computing services. The company helped small- and medium-sized enterprises to conduct their business online.

Alibaba launched a new website named Taobao—meaning 'digging for treasure' in 2003 in Chinese language for online auction and online shopping offering a similar proposition as eBay and Amazon. The offering was to provide a platform for business retailer and individual entrepreneurs and help them to open online retail stores that would mainly cater to customers in mainland China, Hong Kong, Macau, and Taiwan. Unlike eBay, which charged its sellers for listing and transaction fees, Taobao was free to use and attracted a lot attention among the local Chinese population because of its name causing more and more users to switch from eBay to Taobao.

Taobao understood its customers well, and thus, reached higher satisfaction levels as compared to its competitor Ebay. Taobao's listings were more customer-centric while eBay's listings were more product-centric. At that time, China had about three hundred million cell phone users versus ninety million Internet users. Taobao offered instant messaging and voice mail to mobile phones for buyers and sellers because Chinese users were cell-phone savvy rather than computer savvy. By March 2006, Taobao had outpaced eBay and became the leader in China's consumer-to-consumer (C2C) market, with 67% market share in terms of users, while eBay had only 29% market share.

There were three prime reasons for the globally renowned eBay's failure to dominate China and for the local business company Taobao to become the market leader. First, eBay failed to recognize that the Chinese market and the business environment are very different from that of the West. Second, because the top management team didn't understand the local market, they spent a lot of money doing the wrong things, such as advertising on the Internet in a country where small businesses didn't use the Internet. The fact that eBay had a strong brand in the United States didn't mean it would be a strong brand in China. Third, rather than adapt products and services to local customers, eBay stuck to its 'global platform', which again did not fit local customers' tastes and preferences.

China Internet Usage[16]			
Year	Users	Population	% Penetration
2000	22,500,000	1,288,307,100	1.7
2001	33,700,000	1,288,307,100	2.6
2002	59,100,000	1,288,307,100	4.6
2003	69,000,000	1,288,307,100	5.4
2004	94,000,000	1,288,307,100	7.3
2005	103,000,000	1,289,664,808	7.9
2006	137,000,000	1,317,431,495	10.4
2007	162,000,000	1,317,431,495	12.3
2008	253,000,000	1,330,044,605	19.0
2009	384,000,000	1,338,612,968	28.7
2010	420,000,000	1,330,141,295	31.6

14. United States Securities And Exchange Commission, (27 January 2010), *Amazon.com, inc.*, retrieved 18 May 2011, from http://www.sec.gov/: http://www.sec.gov/Archives/edgar/data/1018724/000119312511016253/d10k.htm
15. Forbes.com (12 September 2010), *How Ebay Failed in China*, retrieved 28 May 2011, from http://www.forbes.com/: http://blogs.forbes.com/china/2010/09/12/how-ebay-failed-in-china/
16. Miniwatts Marketing Group (26 March 2011), http://www.internetworldstats.com, retrieved 22 May 2011, from http://www.internetworldstats.com/stats3.htm

EXHIBIT CS11.3

Most preferred online shopping websites (other than travel)[17]

Website	% Use on Preferred Basis (2007)	Increase over 2006
Ebay	34	–4
Rediff	25	–4
Google	8	5
Yahoo	7	–0.5
Indiatimes	7	–4
Futurebazaar	6	6
Sify	2	0.6
Shopping	2	0.4
Amazon	1	–0.1
Indiaplaza	1	0.6

Total Online Shoppers in 2007: 19.1 million

2008 Top 10 most preferred online shopping websites (other than travel)[18]

Website	% Users
Ebay	33
Rediff	19
Google	17
Indiatimes	8
Futurebazaar	8
Yahoo	6
Indiaplaza	4
Sify	3
Homeshop 18	2
Amazon	0.9

Total Online Shoppers in 2008: 28 million

2009 Most preferred online shopping websites (other than travel)[19]

Website	% Users	Change Over Previous Year
Google	24	–9.9
Ebay	21	–0.6
Rediff	15	–2.3
Yahoo	13	–0.4
Indiatimes	6	2
Homeshop 18	3	2
Indiaplaza	2	0.7
Sify	2	0.2
In.com	1	
Futurebazaar	1	–2.9
Amazon	0.5	–0.5
Bookmyshow	0.5	
NDTV	0.1	
Others	10	

Total Online Shoppers in 2009: 34.5 million

17. JuxtConsult, (2007), *The Online Marketplace*, JuxtConsult.
18. JuxtConsult, (2008), *India Online 2008 Main Report*, JuxtConsult.
19. JuxtConsult, (2009), *India Online 2009*, JuxtConsult.

EXHIBIT CS11.4   Profile of Internet Users in India[20]

Age Group	Active Internet Users	E-mail	Chat	Information	Entertainment	E-commerce	Others
School going kids	14	20	10	45	20	3	2
College going	30	30	9	37	12	5	7
Young men	28	52	8	16	8	5	11
Older men	13	52	3	25	4	7	9
Working women	8	46	5	26	3	9	11
Non-working women	7	43	8	21	10	8	10
Total	100	40	8	29	11	4	8

Survey conducted in 31 cities on Active Internet users (01-09-2009 data)
Total Claimed internet users—81 million
Active internet users—60 million

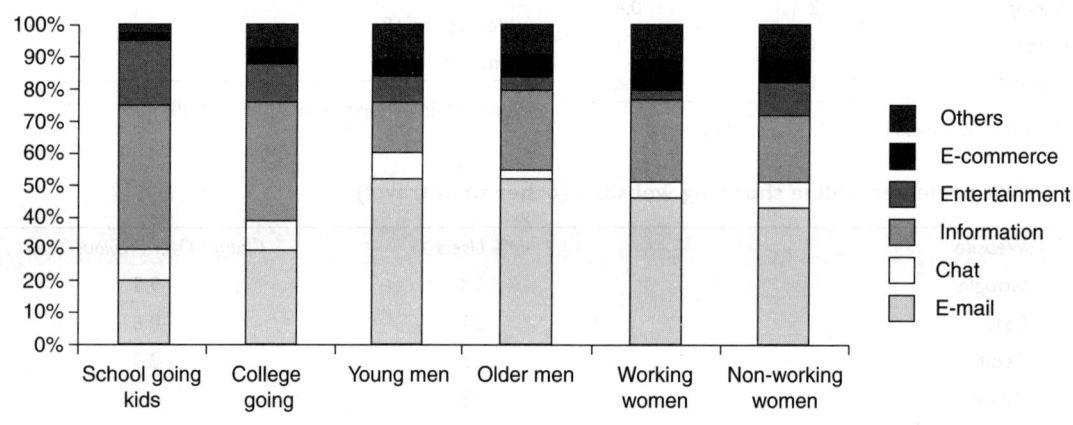

EXHIBIT CS11.5   User Visits Patterns

Infibeam.com

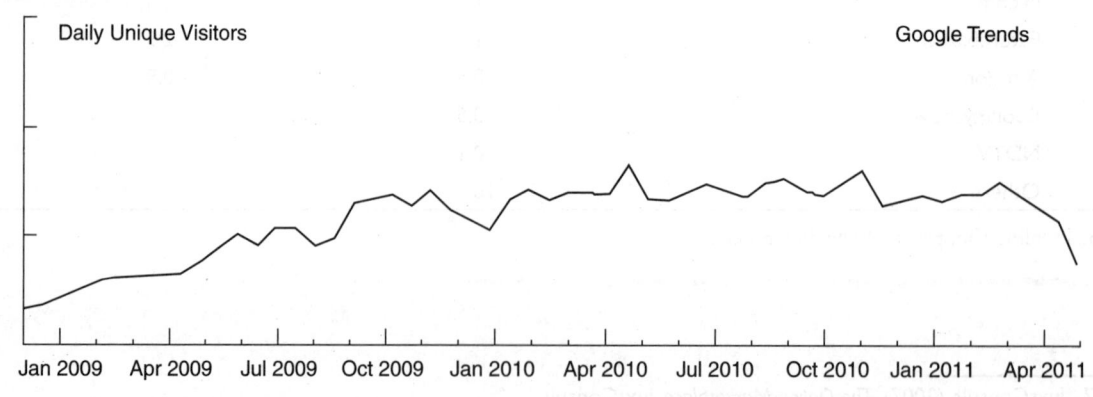

(Contd)

20. IAMAI, (2009), *IAMAI Report 2009*, IAMAI.

Flipkart.com

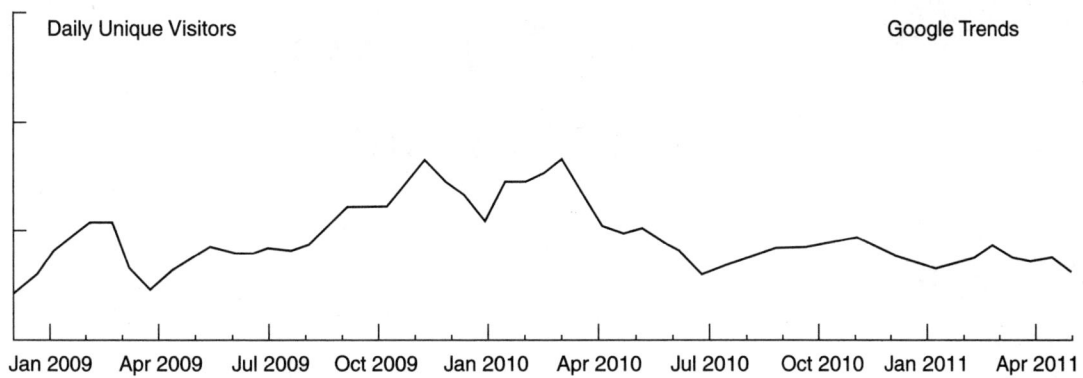

eBay.in

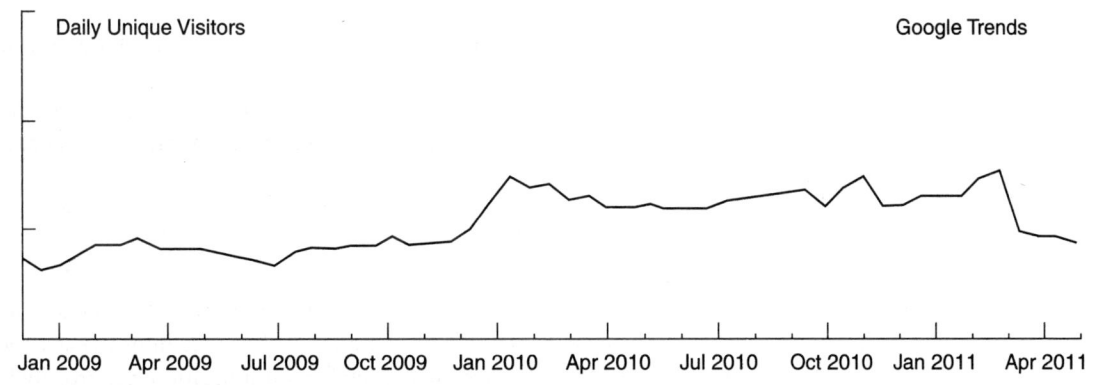

EXHIBIT CS11.6   Advertising Conversion Rates

Media Channel	Reach/₹100,000	Conversion Rate
Television/Direct mail	1,000,000	.01
Internet	100,000	.05
Email	100,000	.07
SMS	50,000	.06

Source: Company Records

Questions

1. Assess the potential of Internet retailing in India in comparison to other countries.
2. Estimate the customer acquisition cost and its implications for customer life time value.
3. Determine the marketing communication objectives for Infibeam.

12 Point of Purchase Communication

LEARNING OBJECTIVES

After studying this chapter, you will be able to

- understand the importance and role of communication in retailing
- discuss the various tools of external and internal communication, with emphasis on point of purchase communication
- understand how point of purchase communication can be effectively used by retailers to increase the sales of merchandise
- gain an insight into the elements and role of packaging in retail communication
- develop a strategy and plan for point of purchase communication on the basis of customer expectations

INTRODUCTION

Retailers use several tools to communicate with their customers. The retail communication programme helps generate sales from the retailer's target market. Retailers use a mix of tools to inform, persuade, and remind customers about their presence. The elements of retail communication can broadly be segregated into two groups: *out of store* or *divergent communication* and *in-store* or *point of purchase* (PoP) *communication*.

In external or divergent communication, the retailer uses mass media vehicles, such as television, newspaper, and radio to attract customers to the store and generate store traffic. External communication is also used to build and manage the store image so that it becomes a destination for its customers. Retailers can choose from mass media advertising, direct marketing, sales promotions, and public relations policies for achieving the desired communication objective. Table 12.1 lists some external communication media commonly used by retailers and provides a glimpse of the advantages and limitations of each medium.

Point of purchase communication reinforces the store image by ensuring that there is no dissonance in the minds of the customers. It also reminds the customers of items that they may have missed. This genre of communication aims to generate impulse as well as unplanned purchases. It also informs the customers of various offers and promotional schemes that connect with the divergent communication. Point of purchase communication is a very potent tool in case of selective category or shelf-specific communication. Stores use tools such as visual merchandising, signage and graphics, and other forms of PoP communication to achieve their desired objectives.

An effective retail communication strategy would combine the two sets of communication—external and internal—to create a synergic impact.[1] With the advent of new format stores that allow self-purchase, the role of PoP has increased tremendously in Indian retailing. At these stores, companies are formulating separate strategies for PoP that are very different from the communication

TABLE 12.1 Comparison of Various External Communication Media

Medium	Advantages	Limitations
Newspaper	• Permits product illustration, frequent publication • Some flexibility in responding to sudden change • Regularly used as shopping guide • Geographical selectivity to a limited extent • Immediacy • One of the traditional advertising media	• Poor colour reproduction • Short life span • Poor qualitative selectivity as everyone reads the newspaper • Many competing advertisements
Radio	• Personal—a human voice can be more persuasive than print • Flexible—permits sudden change in message • Particular stations may appeal to selective audiences because of typical programming content • Relatively inexpensive	• Audio only—may cause lesser impact than visual media • Cannot use illustrations • Short life of message • Needs consistent use to be most valuable in achieving recognition
Television	• Combines sound, light, and motion to convey the message • Greater impact • Some flexibility in responding to sudden change • Gives a sense of immediacy • Has wide reach and thus can be used to build a new retail brand	• Expensive for small or medium-sized retailers • Message is shortlived • Suffers from catchment area principle • Time and production costs are high • Media costs are very high • Complexity of production
Outdoor Media	• Costs are low per person reached • Low cost per impression delivered • Frequent repetition of the message • Good reinforcement media • Good geographical selectivity	• Poor qualitative selectivity • Extreme copy limitations • Message has to be simple
Direct Mail	• Reaches a select market with precision • Can be used on a limited budget • Flexible in timing and message • Allows a personal touch	• High cost per person per message • 'Junk mail' possibilities
Inserts	• Allows specific geographic market coverage • Easily prepared • Low cost • Easy distribution • Allows immediate response	• High non-readership • Lots of wastage as people do not take them seriously

Source: Sapru, Prem 2003, 'For Consumer Space of Mind', *Retail Biz*, October, p. 38.

at the traditional stores. PoP communication is no longer a peripheral and supporting communication. In many cases, it is now the primary tool of communication. Retail advertising or divergent communication is similar to brand advertising, but PoP is very specific to retailing. There is a strong need to establish PoP communication as an area as important as any other form of mainline advertising. This chapter deals with PoP communication in detail.

CONVERGENT OR INTERNAL COMMUNICATION

Convergent, internal, or PoP communication, as stated earlier, is that aspect of retail communication that comes into play once the customer is within the precincts of the store. Customers interpret the communication according to their respective cognitive and affective predisposition. Retailers need to ensure that all the elements of internal communication work in synchronicity so that a large degree of consistency is maintained in the communication.

Before we go on to discuss the importance of PoP, it is important to note that it is different from advertising. First, it happens at the point of action. Second, PoP is dependent on the retailer and the store to a great extent. Third, the usage depends on the kind of product bought and the customer's frequency of visit to the shop. It is therefore required that this effort should be seen as fundamentally different from mainline advertising. It plays a very important role in influencing the consumer decision-making process. For the retailer, with the increasing decline in sales support at the retail outlet, PoP acts as a surrogate salesperson. When PoP is well designed, it adds to the overall attractiveness of the shop.

Role of PoP

For the manufacturer, PoP material is far more cost effective than mass media advertising. This is primarily because exposure to the intended target audience is assured at the retail outlet. It has been observed that, often, the retailers keep many of the discounts that the company offers for themselves. Thus, communication of these benefits or discounts ensures that they reach the consumers. PoP materials also ensure precise marketing. In order to ensure that the PoP material addresses the target market, different PoP material is used in *kirana* stores and supermarkets. Many retailers take little initiative for pushing the company's goods. PoP counters this and acts as a surrogate salesperson. Attractive and informative PoP can effectively occupy the minds of the consumers and reduce dissonance during waiting time. It can help consumers by making shopping interesting, thus removing some of the frustration involved in the shopping exercise. PoP communication is especially useful when consumers are shopping with children as well-designed PoP can effectively engage them while the parents are making purchases.

Point of purchase communication reminds the consumer of the brand presence of any premium that the consumer may have witnessed through the mass media. This premise is based on the encoding specificity principle. According to this principle, recall or retrieval of a certain piece of stored information is enhanced when the context in which the information was encoded is similar or the same. In other words, the likelihood of recall improves when the features present in the environment when the memory was encoded match those present in the retrieval environment. Retailers can thus provide PoP cues to increase the probability of recall of the product advertised in the mass media. Thus, a poster at a store containing a frame from a TV commercial or a print advertisement about a brand of chocolate as an answer to a mid-meal hunger pang would cause the shopper to remember the brand while browsing at the store.

Frontage of a *Kirana* Store—Note the Use of Walls for PoP Communication

Source: http://www.bandhavgarh.net

PoP Material

Source: www.produceforkids.org

It has been found that a high level of brand awareness does not always translate into sales. Shoppers take into consideration the information they acquire in stores, in addition to relying on out-of-store communication.[2] PoP communication plays an important role in such a situation. Advertising attracts customers, but the success of all communication efforts in many cases depends on the last 5 per cent of the effort which manifests itself at the point of purchase, just before the consumer chooses to buy, rather than the 95 per cent that preceded it.[3] At the retail outlet, PoP communication provides the marketer the last opportunity to communicate with the shopper before a purchase is made. This communication at the shop can play several roles. These include informing, reminding, encouraging, creating excitement or interactivity, and building store image. As discussed earlier, information recall is enhanced when the context in which people attempt to retrieve information is the same as the context in which they originally coded the information.[4] PoP information activates consumers' memories pertaining to a brand and its features, and helps the consumer to make a purchase decision in favour of the displayed brand. It also induces shoppers to stay at the retail outlet for a longer duration, leading to increased spending.[5]

In some cases, PoP is found to lead to patronizing the shop.[6] It also helps in bringing congruence between self-image and store image. A higher store loyalty is shown by shoppers who perceive congruence between their self-image and the image of the store.[7] The store image is created by several factors, especially quality and assortment of merchandise, salespeople, and store atmosphere.[8] PoP communication helps facilitate a store to perform on all three factors. For instance, displays and layout have been found to have a more significant role in stores with high-fashion appeal than in stores that appeal to the masses.[9] Similarly, a lifestyle store uses PoP more extensively to create an atmosphere that is in consonance with the brand and the store image.[10] PoP communication is an effective communication tool for not only lifestyle stores but also small neighbourhood stores. The face change brought at the *paan* (betel leaf)/cigarette shops in India is due to the planned efforts of the cigarette and *gutka* companies. Denied the use of mainline media, cigarette companies had no choice but to use the outlet as their main communication media for continued communication. It is interesting to note that the changes at the *paan* shops have been brought about without changing the assortment, salespeople, or even the layout in many cases.

Point of purchase communication has to work in an environment where many other stimuli are fighting for the consumers' attention. Consumers' shopping behaviour cannot be fully understood outside the context in which it occurs—neither consumers nor brands exist in isolation. A shopper goes through a process of 'see–touch–sense–select' in order to buy a product. The degree to which the consumer follows the whole or part of this process varies with brand, product category, and other elements of the marketing mix.[11]

Point of purchase communication is a critical element of integrated marketing communication, where the other elements of communication in the mass media are dovetailed to draw an overall plan for retail communication. Retailers try to enhance the recall of products by using PoP materials that convey messages that are consistent with those present in the mass media. Thus, many PoP materials use pictures of celebrities endorsing the brand or the mnemonic for endorsement to remind consumers about products so promoted. This phenomenon is also seen in packaging where the mass media communication shows pack shots. This is based on the assumption that, when the consumer sees the package at the retail outlet, it would generate recall. PoP communication can be used as an effective merchandising tool that enables the retailer to effectively utilize floor space and boost sales by assisting consumers in making product and brand selection. Among the various factors that affect the purchase behaviour of the consumer, retail communication manifests itself in the form of packaging and PoP communication.

Tester Unit

Product Display

Displays Units for Aisles or as Gondolas
Source: www.popaiindia.org.in

Product Display Units Used by Retailers

ROLE OF PACKAGING

The primary function of packaging is to ensure that the product is safe. The packaging should be done keeping in mind the shipping, transportation, and warehousing requirements of the merchandise. The pack should also ensure the safety of the product at the retail outlet. In addition, the pack provides brand and product identification, which will be recognized by the consumer and will encourage trial and repeat purchases. It presents the product in an attractive and appealing manner. Packaging gives important product information that could influence the purchase decision. It also carries mandatory information, such as the date of manufacture and the expiry date. It helps in identifying the variety, size, and flavour of the product. It enhances the product by making the pack easy to open, close, dispense, and carry in the store.[12] A product pack usually contains the following elements.

Pack Structure The pack structure helps the retailer in stocking as well as building brand equity. It can influence the perceptions of the product. A well-known example of this is the Coke bottle, which strikes an emotional chord with the customer. People of all ages appreciate its grip, feel, and aesthetic value. This has been one of the main reasons for giving primacy to the shape of the Coke bottle in all its communication.[13]

Graphics Graphics are capable of communicating both informative and emotional messages. The specific information that is communicated by graphics include brand identity, product name, product description, flavour or variety identification, attribute description, benefit statement, usage directions, nutritional information, warning or caution statements, and illustrations. The emotional aspects are subliminal. These are communicated through logo styling, copy, symbols, icons, textures, photography, and illustrations.

Brand Identity The purpose of brand identity is to build brand recognition, and create memorability and loyalty. The styling of the brand name is the signature that brings instant recognition from customers and enhances familiarity with the brand. The logo, which is another important part of the brand identity, can take the form of the brand name or an abstract shape.

Copy This communicates specific product information on the product, its usage, and attributes.

Colour This is the most emotional and subjective part of packaging. The colour of the pack performs many functions. It identifies the brand. It can set the mood, such as fun, elegance, playfulness, or warmth. Customers can identify the colour of the product inside the pack. It can assist in differentiating products, product varieties, and flavours. A more utilitarian use of colour applies to product categorization and differentiation. Consumers have become so accustomed to colour cues that identify certain product categories, flavours, quality associations, and so on that they respond to these cues automatically. This is especially applicable to food packaging. When customers cannot see the actual product, they make judgements based on the package and the appearance of the pack. Hence, when new products are launched, they have graphics and colours that best bring out the association with the product inside.

Colour is a vitally important element of food; it is a highly visual element to which human emotions, minds, and palates are extremely sensitive. Food packaging is governed by two main principles. First, the pack should look 'good enough to eat'. This entails an appeal to the emotional and the subconscious psychological factors that are common to the great majority of people. Second, the pack should have a visual appeal per se and should contribute to the selling process. Studies on the impact of packaging on appetite show that people most strongly respond to red and orange.

With special reference to confectionery, factors affecting the colour selection of the food pack include the following:[14]

- *Product* The nature of the product would have a considerable influence on the nature of the package. A plastic bag is suitable for peanuts but not for a pack of chocolates.
- *Nature of sale* Most sales of confectionery products are of an impulse nature. It is for this reason that heavy emphasis is placed on attractive packaging. Most of the packs for confectionery are designed keeping this aspect in mind.
- *Selling features* These include taste, flavour, and quality, all of which can be emphasized by using suitable colours. Colour can convey appropriate associations, for example, Diwali packaging of confectionery is communicated through the use of red and yellow colours.
- *Product associations* Certain colours are associated with certain product types. This is especially seen in the case of confectionery. For example, Cadbury's Dairy Milk uses the colour purple, which is normally not recommended for food packaging. However, the long presence of the brand in this category has ensured that the association with the category is maintained.
- *Age of the consumer* Here again, it is observed that bright colours are especially appealing to children. This is the reason that most products that are aimed at young children have bright and attractive packaging.
- *Purchasing habits* The main factor that is associated with purchasing habits of confectionery is that it is often bought as a gift purchase. Impulse buying is also a strong consumer behaviour that is associated with confectionery purchase.
- *Selling conditions* This is of special significance to the *kirana* store environment, where there is often not enough proper lighting or space and hence the task of ensuring visibility is a greater challenge.

The pack of any product needs to be evaluated on the basis of a model called the VIEW model.[15] VIEW refers to (a) visibility, or the ability of the pack to stand out on a shelf; (b) information, or provision of relevant information such as product usage instructions, claimed benefits, and supplementary information; (c) emotional appeal, or the ability of the pack to evoke the desired feeling and mood; and (d) workability, which addresses the following issues: How does the pack function? Does it protect the goods? Does it facilitate easy storage? Does it have the instructions for use?[16]

Other display materials are evaluated on the basis of their ability to attract and hold attention through (a) contrast, which can be created by using different colours, lighting, form, letters, and textures; (b) repetition, which attracts the consumer's attention by duplicating an object and strengthening the impression; (c) size—when a huge display is kept next to small displays, the larger display, due to its dominance, has a greater chance of being noticed;[17] and (d) physical motion, which is a powerful attention getter. Using motorized or electrical supply to create movement, PoP can catch the attention of shoppers and involve them.

DESIGNING POINT OF PURCHASE COMMUNICATION

The approaches to PoP entail looking at it from several directions. However, it is difficult for a retailer, or a company that wants to communicate with its customers at the retail outlet, to differentiate shoppers on the basis of their purchase behaviour or the impact of the feature advertising. Further, stores deal in many products and brands that have different positioning and appeal. A store needs to balance the communication expectations of all its shoppers. In India, due to the unique problems of small retail outlets, cluttered merchandise, low visibility, and lack of proper communication plans at the store front, PoP communication needs to be developed very differently.

Studies on the Impact of PoP

In the field of retail communication, there is limited work on the impact of PoP and packaging on consumer behaviour. One study observed the sale of juices and cereals in four conditions: (i) product without an advertisement or PoP display, (ii) product with PoP display but no advertisement, (iii) product with mass media advertising but no PoP display, and (iv) product with both display and advertising. It was found that the sale of juices increased significantly in the last case. The sale of cereals remained more or less stable across the test conditions.[18] In another study conducted by the Point of Purchase Advertising International (POPAI), it was found that cash counter products account for the highest in-store decisions.[19] In India, the findings of a study that looked at the impact of PoP from the consumers' and retailers' perspectives[20] are listed below.

Consumers' Perspective

The impact of PoP from the consumers' perspective was as follows:

1. Products supported by PoP material were noticed and consumed more by brand conscious consumers. The visual merchandising at the retail outlet would find favour and relevance for the consumer when the consumer has a high exposure to mass media communication.
2. PoP was not seen as an extension of mainline advertising. This is a definite cause for concern. When the visual stimulus at the retail outlet does not effectively bring forth the key selling proposition of the mass media communication, its effectiveness is suspected.
3. Ninety five per cent of respondents could not link any PoP with any promotion. This again calls for the need to design retail communication that has a greater impact.
4. Posters and glow signs are the most recalled PoP materials. This shows the impact of light and size on the recall of the visual stimulus.
5. The colour of the PoP material was noticed most by consumers.

Retailers' Perspective

The impact of PoP from the retailers' perspective was as follows:

1. Glow signs were seen as more effective PoP tools. Retailers wanted PoP material that would add value to their shop.
2. More PoP was seen with new launches and events. This shows the retailers' understanding of the consumers' need for excitement, which is then linked to promotions.
3. Racks, glow signs, and shelves were the permanent types of PoP used by retailers.
4. The retailers wanted few but effective PoPs to avoid clutter.
5. Retailers preferred PoP that fits with the overall store display and ambience. This shows retailers' dislike for any cue that gives the appearance of an aberration.

The study showed that purchasing behaviour is linked to shopping behaviour and the demographics of the consumer. The more frequent the visit, the less the recall of PoP, and the more involved the purchase, the more the use of PoP. Retail communication must play two main functions—the rational function, where the consumer is a conscious decision-maker and looks for as much information as possible before making the decision, and the emotional function where the customer seeks an experience. The emotional function is very relevant in the case of children, for whom the visit to the retail outlet is an expedition. They crave for excitement and seek this at the outlet. Thus, effective retail communication is that which can not only attract the attention of the child but also offer a visual treat. However, younger children usually do not visit stores unaccompanied. Thus, the communication must address the concern of the parent as well as the child.[21]

Familiarity and Involvement

The study mentioned in the previous section found that neither retailers nor customers used PoP communication while deciding about merchandise purchasing.[22] However, some patterns do emerge that may be used to develop parameters to understand shopper expectations of required information. It was found that, with an increase in the frequency of visits to the store, the use of PoP decreases. Frequent buyers did not find PoP helpful for making buying decisions. On the other hand, occasional buyers and inquirers found PoP helpful. First timers relied more on sales personnel for their information search. We can, therefore, infer that the extent of purchase involvement will influence the use of PoP material directly. It was noticed that the information search, which manifested in higher consumption of PoP at the store, is associated with purchase involvement.

In the case of durable, lifestyle, and hi-tech products, involvement with the product is high, and hence information search is high. Customers of these segments found PoP helpful in their buying decisions. It reminded and attracted them, as contrasted with FMCG store customers, who found PoP to be of little consequence. It can therefore be assumed that information search is directly proportional to purchase involvement. Research also showed that frequent buyers are more familiar with their favourite stores, the information search is less, and, hence, there is very low reliance on PoP material for product knowledge. Hence, the use of PoP material reduces with the level of familiarity with the store.

Mode of Shopping

Point of purchase communication needs to be designed to facilitate purchase at the store. It has to keep in mind the information seeking behaviour of customers, who can be classified as those being in 'blinkered', 'magpie', and 'browser' modes.[23] The *blinkered shopping mode* is very mechanical. In this instance, the shopper confidently walks into the shop and then demands the desired product. Hence, the aim of communication is to enable easy brand recognition and to help consumers to identify what they want. The consumers are seeking a visual stimulus of instant recognition, where they just need to see the brand of their pre-decided choice. This is the mode found in case of low involvement categories. The *magpie shopping mode* is one where the consumer allows him/herself to be distracted and attracted by different brands on the fixture. This is a situation where the consumer is looking for a treat. This behaviour is typical of children at the retail outlet. Children actively seek a visual sensation. This could well be in the hope of more similar tangible benefits in the immediate future. Hence, the communication aim is to persuade the consumer. The consumer at this point is actively seeking a 'touch and sense' emotion. Finally, the *browser mode* finds the consumer behaving more rationally, reading the details of the packs and comparing prices. Consumers in this mode are great perceivers of risk. In this situation, the aim of retail communication is to inform. Here, the consumer is in an information-seeking mode and is mainly interested in the facts behind the offering. The purchase involves a selection function. The act of see, touch, and sense is minimal.

Levels of Information Search and Involvement

It is also worth clarifying the different levels of information search that customers get involved in. These are generally classified as planned, unplanned, and impulse purchases. The Point of Purchase Advertising International (POPAI) uses the following categorization to define the different kinds of shopping behaviour:[24]

- *Specifically planned*   A specific brand or item that was planned prior to the visit to the shop and purchased as planned.
- *Generally planned*   A pre-store decision to purchase a product category, but not the specific item.
- *Substitute*   A change from a generally or specifically planned item to a functional substitute.
- *Unplanned*   An item bought that the shopper did not have in mind on entering the shop.
- *Impulse*   The dictionary defines *impulse* as a compelling force, whim, or an inspiration. Impulse purchases are made in a store that are different from those the consumer planned to make before entering the store.[25] Impulse purchase is the *raison d'etre* of most visual communication at the retail outlet. However, the word 'impulse' is subject to many interpretations in the context of shopping behaviour. These are (a) pure impulse, which is a novelty or an escape that breaks the normal buying pattern; (b) reminder impulse, which occurs when shoppers see an item and remember that their stock is low; (c) suggestion impulse, in which purchases occur when a shopper sees the product for the first time and then visualizes a need for it; and (d) planned impulse, when purchasing takes place when the shopper makes specific purchase decisions based on special coupons.[26]

The rate of unplanned purchasing appears to depend on the type of stimulation technique, the product that is being promoted, and the customer, who selectively exposes himself/herself to, and selectively perceives the promotional stimuli. Thus, there is a need to be aware of the kind of shopping trip and the impulse behaviour the particular stimulus generates.[27]

It can be assumed that purchasing entails customer involvement, which is essentially a process of information search. The amount of information search depends on the value customers feel they will gain from searching versus the cost of searching.[28] The value of the search is in how it improves the customers' purchase decision. The amount of information search is influenced by the nature and use of the product being purchased, characteristics of the individual customer, and aspects of the market and buying situation in which the purchase is made. The degree of relevance or 'involvement' determines the consumer's level of motivation to search for knowledge or information about a product or service.[29] A large number of studies have indicated that involved consumers are more active processors of information and they attend to and comprehend more elaborate meaning and inferences.[30] Involvement has also been defined as a multifaceted construct. These dimensions are combined and used to arrive at an overall involvement profile of consumers applicable to any product class. The dimensions of consumer involvement are as follows:

- (a) The perceived importance and risk of the product class, its personal meaning and relevance, and the perceived importance of the consequences of a mis-purchase
- (b) The subjective probability of making a mis-purchase, or the probability of a poor brand choice
- (c) The symbolic or sign value attributed by the consumer to a product class, its purchase, or its consumption that differentiates functional risk from psychological risk
- (d) The hedonic value of the product class or its ability to provide pleasures and affect[31]

TABLE 12.2 Classification of Stores Based on Benefits Sought

Performance Benefit of the Store	Type of Store		
	Convenience	Variety	Speciality/experiential
Convenience	High	Medium	Low
Assortment/variety	Low	High	Medium
Shopping experience	Medium	Low	High

Store Benefits

Customers see a store as a collection of characteristics and benefits. These can be a good basis for classifying stores as convenience, variety, and experiential.[32] Each store offers specific benefits to its customers, which become the compelling reason to patronize it. These benefits are derived out of several variables such as price, discounts offered, travel time, assortment range, quality, atmospherics/ambience, and service. The customers process information about each store and form an impression of the benefits the store provides. Table 12.2 shows a classification of stores based on the benefits sought.

Expectation-based PoP Communication Model

This expectation of store benefit may have an impact on the extent of information search by the customers and hence may impact the level of involvement. Shopper expectation can be described as the combination of the level of involvement with purchasing and the benefit a customer seeks from that particular store. This yields a matrix, as given in the shopper expectation model (Table 12.3), which can be utilized to determine the strategies and tools for an effective PoP communication, as provided in Table 12.4. Each of the nine situations of the shopper expectation model, shown in Table 12.3, is discussed here.

Low Involvement Purchase—Convenient Stores   The first box depicts a buying situation where the involvement of the shopper is very low and the effort he/she expends is also low. The shopper comes to the store asking for the product by the category name. The store choice is based on the convenience of location. The PoP communication in such a situation is very helpful in affecting brand switch. Packaging would be the most potent communication tool. A prominent display of the product would give the 'touch and feel' confidence. In such cases, retailers would keep the product at eye level and near the counter. Confectionery and bakery products are found most commonly on the counters. Posters, danglers, and attractive packaging would be the PoP tools to grab the attention of the shopper.

Low Involvement Purchase—Variety Store   In this case, although the shopper's involvement is low, the store provides variety. The shopper wants to have more variety and thus looks for a store that provides more options and is also conveniently located. In this situation, the shopper asks for a brand but does not mind switching if the preferred brand is not available. The idea is to buy from the same store and not take the trouble to go to other stores. Only after the brand set is exhausted, would the shopper think of another store. The retailer has to rise above the clutter and stand out among stores selling similar products. Since involvement is low, it is a challenge for the retailer to differentiate sufficiently to attract shoppers' attention. Store location, better frontage, and glow signboards, kiosks, and window dressing play a major role in attracting shoppers and inducing them to come inside the store.

Low Involvement Purchase—Experience Centric Store   In this situation, the shopper is store loyal, and due to low involvement with the product, does not want to exert any extra effort to buy a brand.

TABLE 12.3 Shopper Expectation Model for PoP Communication

		Store Benefit		
		Convenience	*Variety*	*Experiential*
Involvement in Buying	Low	• Least effort in shopping • Convenient location *Example:* • Corner shops	• Least effort • Store location and appearance *Example:* • A neighbourhood store with better frontage	• Least effort • Familiarity *Example:* • Patronized neighbourhood stores
	Medium	• Brand comparison • Convenient location • Limited assortment *Example:* • Personal care products at medical stores	• Brand comparison • Large assortment • Clear communication of offers and schemes *Example:* • Medium-size stores • Department stores • Clothes stores • Home and kitchen appliance stores • Cosmetics	• Brand comparison • Large assortment • Visual merchandising *Example:* • FMCG/durable superstores • Office products—consumables and peripherals
	High	• Availability of preferred brands • Convenient location *Examples:* • Cigarettes • Personal care products • Music albums	• Availability of preferred brands • Store that gives best bargain for the brand *Example:* • Premium cosmetics • Music stores • Shoppers Stop	• Availability of preferred brands • Store that best identifies with the self-image of the shopper *Example:* • Planet M for music • Crossword for books • Exclusive brand showrooms

Such shoppers are more prone to impulse buying and, with a little persuasion, will buy more products. Shoppers in such stores seek benefits such as store association, easy purchase process, familiarity with the place, and friendly salespeople. Book, music, and card shops, fast food joints, and computer peripheral stores are some typical examples. The retailer must stimulate shoppers to try more products. The store needs to keep the shopper informed of new products through salespeople and interactive kiosks to effectively communicate about store brands, new schemes, and bargains. The retailer should try to retain the shoppers for the longest possible time for increased purchases.

Medium Involvement Purchase—Convenient Store   In this case, the shopper is more involved than in the previous case, but would prefer to buy from a store that is conveniently located. The shopper seeks variety and, thus, apart from store location, assortment of products also becomes important. The shopper wants optimization of shopping time and effort. The retailer has to help the shopper choose a brand through eye-catching posters and attractive packaging. Apart from the convenient location of the store, the retailer must plan the product assortment as per the requirements of the loyal customers.

TABLE 12.4 Communication Challenges and Strategies

		Store Benefit		
		Convenience	*Variety*	*Experiential*
Involvement in Buying	Low	*Purpose:* • Minimize transaction time *Communication Challenge:* • Grabbing attention *Strategy:* • Immediate sighting • Touch and feel *Tools:* • Eye-catching posters and danglers • Attractive packaging • Display at eye level or at the counter	*Purpose:* • Minimize store search *Communication Challenge:* • Attracting shopper to the store *Strategy:* • Differentiate from similar stores *Tools:* • Better frontage • Glow sign boards • Better lighting inside the store • Kiosks	*Purpose:* • Reinforce store loyalty *Communication Challenge:* • Building a one-to-one relationship with the shopper *Strategy:* • Personalized attention • Induce unplanned purchase *Tools:* • Friendly and suggestive salespeople • Display near the waiting line • Interactive kiosks
	Medium	*Purpose:* • Optimization of time and effort *Communication Challenge:* • Help choose a brand *Strategy:* • Provide information about various brands • Touch and feel *Tools:* • Eye-catching posters and danglers • Attractive packaging • Display at eye level or at the counter • Testing sample	*Purpose:* • Provide limited choices *Communication Challenge:* • How to get shopper's mind as well as wallet share *Strategy:* • Leverage on own strengths • Stress on functional and rational purchase • Offer schemes • Bundle offers *Tools:* • Provide comparison leaflets highlighting product features prominently • Price discounts • Posters/banners offering schemes	*Purpose:* • Induce shopper to indulge *Communication Challenge:* • Make buying more personal and involving *Strategy:* • Offer better services • Provide intangible benefits *Tools:* • Better showroom management • Put impulse products near cash counters • Place seating near waiting line • Special attention to ladies and children • TV for engaging shoppers

(Contd)

Table 12.4 (Contd)

		Store Benefit		
		Convenience	*Variety*	*Experiential*
Involvement in Buying	High	*Purpose:* • Enhance brand salience *Communication Challenge:* • Reinforce brand image *Strategy:* • Integrate with main communication *Tools:* • Large and creative displays • Attractive packaging • Window displays	*Purpose:* • Allow comparison *Communication Challenge:* • Score over competition *Strategy:* • Provide tangible information to project strengths *Tools:* • Use the salesperson • Product demonstrations • Information brochures • Interactive kiosks • Shop-in-shop	*Purpose:* • Make the shop a destination *Communication Challenge:* • Making shopping enjoyable and memorable *Strategy:* • Personalized attention • Induce longer stay *Tools:* • Atmospherics • Spatials • Visual merchandising • Interactive kiosks

Medium Involvement Purchase—Variety Store   In this type of shopping, the shopper has a medium level of involvement in buying and is looking for options in terms of benefits derived from the store. The basic behaviour is variety seeking. The shopper seeks variety not just in products but also amongst stores. Store location is of importance and so is the external appearance of the store. The retailer must induce the shopper to come inside the store and look around for various options. Apart from that, the retailer has to make sure that the shopper is engaged. The shopper would prefer a brand that offers a better bargain. Since the shopper is in a comparison mode, communication in this line, such as leaflets that provide necessary information, will be sought. The challenge is to get the mind as well as wallet share by leveraging on tangible benefits such as schemes and price discounts. Category management is an important function in such stores.

Medium Involvement Purchase—Experience Store   In this case, the shopper has already decided upon the store and aims to seek variety within the chosen store. The communication challenge is to provide the required information and reduce dissonance by making the buying process more personal and involving. The shopper will spend more time in the store. Shopping in such cases is a planned process and not just an activity. This provides the retailers an opportunity to push their own retail brands. The strategy here is to offer better service, and provide add-on intangible benefits. Large format food stores such as FoodWorld fall into this category.

High Involvement Purchase—Convenient Store   In this type of shopping, the shopper is seeking a particular brand and is also ready to expend effort to buy it. A store that is conveniently located and stocks the required brand will gain the patronage of such shoppers. Stores near or on the way to the workplace would often fall in this category. Due to easy availability and high visibility, the communication at the shop reinforces the shopper's belief in the brand and enhances brand salience. The communication strategy would be to integrate PoP with the main advertising campaign through creative displays and attractive packaging.

High Involvement Purchase—Variety Store   Shoppers visiting such stores have already decided on the brand they wish to buy. However, they would like to reassure themselves by collecting information about competing brands. Thus, the retailer has to provide information for comparison and let the shopper re-evaluate the decision. In this case, the shopper would stick to the original brand choice unless the other brand offers specific value enhancement. The strategy would be to provide tangible information to project strengths through salespeople, product demonstrations, information brochures, and interactive kiosks. Stores dealing in premium cosmetics, high-end durable goods, and lifestyle stores dealing in branded products would fall in this category.

High Involvement Purchase—Experience Store   Here, both the store and brand are pre-decided and there is high loyalty towards them. The shopper prefers stores that give the best identification with the self-image of the shopper. Exclusive branded showrooms, and stores such as Planet M and Crossword would fall in this category. Here, the retailer has to project the store as a destination. Shopping at such stores has greater entertainment and social value. The communication challenge would be to make shopping more enjoyable and memorable. The retailer should give personal attention to shoppers and should know the likes and dislikes of individual shoppers. Atmospherics and spatial and visual merchandising should be used to induce longer stays by shoppers.

SUMMARY

Retail communication consists of two broad categories—external and in-store communication. While the former is utilized for the purpose of building traffic and creating an image for the store, the latter is concerned with delivering the experience, as promised. Customers process the two sets of communication differently and, hence, they need to be treated differently in terms of strategies and tool selection. External communication is carried out principally through mass media.

In-store communication is achieved through the display of products and other PoP material. Most PoP material is placed in positions that are highly visible. These are generally the attraction points in the retail outlet, which would invariably catch the attention of the consumer. Thus, the first important function that is performed by PoP is that of informing the consumer of the presence of the brand or any premium that the company may be offering to the customer. Display material is evaluated on its ability to attract and hold attention through contrast, repetition, physical motion, and size.

Point of purchase communication needs to be measured differently and, hence, the resource allocation also needs to be re-evaluated. Today, most of the communication is one-way and passive. It has to be made active and, wherever possible, interactive. The exercise of PoP communication will have to be looked at from the perspective of involvement and store benefit to arrive at the customer's communication requirements. This communication expectation has to be utilized to develop strategies and tools for different situations.

NOTES

1. Allenby, G.M. and J.L. Ginter 1995, 'The Effects of In-Store Displays and Feature Advertising on Consideration Sets', *International Journal of Research in Marketing*, Vol. 12, pp. 67–80.

2. Underhill, P. 1998, *Why We Buy—The Science of Shopping*, Simon & Schuster Co., New York.

3. Quelch, J. and K. Cannon-Bonventre 1983, 'Better Marketing at the Point of Purchase', *Harvard Business Review*, November–December, pp. 1–8.

4. Connolly, A. and D. Firth 1999, 'Visual Planning—the Power of Thinking Visually', *Journal of Brand Management*, Vol. 6, No. 5, pp. 161–73.

5. Donovar, R.J., J.R. Rossiter, G. Marcollin, and A. Nesdale 1994, 'Store Atmosphere and Purchasing Behaviour', *Journal of Retailing*, Vol. 70 (3), pp. 283–94.

6. Wakefield, K. and J. Baker 1998, 'Excitement at the Mall: Determinants and Effects on Shopping

Response', *Journal of Retailing*, Vol. 74 (4), pp. 515–39.

7. Bellenger, D.N., E. Steinberg, and W. Stanton 1976, 'The Congruence of Store Image and Self Image', *Journal of Retailing*, Vol. 52 (1), pp. 17–32.

8. Berry, L.L. 1969, 'The Component of Department Store Image: A Theoretical and Empirical Analysis', *Journal of Retailing*, Vol. 45 (1), pp. 3–18; Pierre Martineau 1958, 'The Personality of the Retail Store', *Harvard Business Review*, Vol. 36, January–February, pp. 47–55.

9. Rich, S. and B. Portis 1964, 'The Imageries of Department Stores', *Journal of Marketing*, Vol. 28, pp. 10–5.

10. Sinha, P.K. and D.P. Uniyal 2000, 'Communication @ Point of Purchase', Unpublished Working Paper, Mudra Institute of Communications, Ahmedabad.

11. Connolly, A. and D. Firth 1999, 'Visual Planning—The Power of Thinking Visually', *Journal of Brand Management*, Vol. 6, No. 5, pp. 161–73.

12. Meyers, Herbert M. and Lubliner, Murray J. 1998, *The Marketer's Guide to Successful Package Design*, Lincolnwood, USA.

13. Davison, Lucy and David Redhill 1998, 'Structural Packaging Design: Building and Protecting Brand Value', *Journal of Brand Management*, Vol. 6, No. 1, pp. 13–21, Henry Stewart Publications.

14. Meyers, Herbert M. and Lubliner, Murray J. 1998, *The Marketer's Guide to Successful Package Design*, Lincolnwood, USA.

15. Twedt, W.D. 1968 'How Much Value can be Added through Packaging', *Journal of Marketing*, 32, pp. 61–5.

16. Shimp, T.A. 1997, 'Advertising, Promotion and Supplemental Aspects of Integrated Marketing Communications', 4th edn, The Dryden Press, Harcourt Brace College Publishers, Orlando, Florida, USA.

17. Marquardt, Ray 1983, 'Merchandising Displays are Most Effective when Marketing Artistic Factors Combine', *Marketing News*, Vol. 19, August.

18. POPAI 1995, 'Consumer Buying Habits Study: Measuring the In Store Decision Making of Supermarket and Mass Merchandise Store Shoppers', New Jersey, 66, North Van Brunt Street, USA.

19. POPAI 1995, 'Establishing PoP Advertising as a Measured Medium', Pilot Survey Report, ARF and Prime Consulting Group Inc, Washington D.C.

20. Sinha, P.K. and D.P. Uniyal 2000, 'Communication @ Point of Purchase', Unpublished Working Paper, Mudra Institute of Communications, Ahmedabad.

21. Anuradha, M.K., P.K. Sinha, and R. Krishna 2003, 'Children in a Kirana Store: Building a Case for Retail Communication', *Journal of Brand Management*, Vol. 10 (3), February, pp. 219–32.

22. Sinha, P.K. and D.P. Uniyal 2000, 'Communication @ Point of Purchase', Unpublished Working Paper, Mudra Institute of Communications, Ahmedabad.

23. Connolly, A. and D. Firth 1999, 'Visual Planning—The Power of Thinking Visually', *Journal of Brand Management*, Vol. 6, No. 5, pp. 161–73.

24. POPAI 1995, 'Establishing PoP Advertising as a Measured Medium', Pilot Survey Report, ARF and Prime Consulting Group Inc., Washington, D.C.

25. Hawkins, Del I., Roger J. Best, and Kenneth A. Coney 1995, *Consumer Behaviour: Implications for Marketing Strategy*, 6th ed, Chicago, Irwin, USA.

26. Hawkins, Del I., Roger J. Best, and Kenneth A. Coney 1995, *Consumer Behaviour: Implications for Marketing Strategy*, 6th ed, Chicago, Irwin, USA.

27. Kollat, D.T. and R.P. Willet 1967, 'Customer Impulse Purchase Behaviour', *Journal of Marketing Research*, Vol. 4, February, pp. 21–31.

28. Punj, G.N. and R. Staelin 1983, 'A Model of Consumer Information Search Behaviour for New Automobiles', *Journal of Consumer Research*, Vol. 9, March, pp. 366–80; Srinivasan, N. and B.T. Ratchford 1991, 'An Empirical Test of a Model of External Search for Automobile', *Journal of Consumer Research*, Vol. 18, September, pp. 233–42.

29. Schiffman, L.G. and L.L. Kanuk 2000, *Consumer Behaviour*, 7th edn, Prentice-Hall of India Private Limited, M-79, Connaught Circus, New Delhi, India.

30. Swinyard, W.R. 1993, 'The Effect of Mood, Involvement, and Quality of Store Experience on Shopping Intentions', *Journal of Consumer Research*, 20, September, pp. 71–80.

31. Kapferer, J. and G. Laurent 1985, 'Measuring Consumer Involvement Profiles', *Journal of Marketing Research*, Vol. 22, February, pp. 41–53.

32. Levy, M. and B. Weitz 2003, *Retailing Management*, 5th ed, Tata McGraw-Hill Publishing Company Limited, New Delhi, India.

CONCEPT REVIEW QUESTIONS

1. What is the role of communication in enhancing sales as well as brand experience at the retail point?
2. Differentiate divergent and convergent communication. Explain the types of divergent communication used by retailers and their benefits and limitations.
3. Describe the role of packaging in retail communication with the help of examples.

4. What are the different modes of shopping? How do these have an impact on the communication plan?
5. Explain the role of involvement in retail communication.
6. Explain the shopper expectation model of PoP communication. Pick any three boxes and indicate the communication objectives and plans for each of them.

CRITICAL THINKING QUESTIONS

1. How would you enhance the performance of PoP communication in a variety store?

2. When would you use a combination of PoP display and feature advertisements?

PROJECTS

1. Visit a store and find out the different types of PoP communication tools used. Discuss the rationale and utility of each of them with the store manager or the merchandiser.

2. Meet a merchandiser and find out how their key performance areas are identified and evaluated.

CASE STUDY

Stores and Shoppers

I. *Discussed here are two caselets—that of a* kirana *store and fashion jewellery store. The focus here is on the description of the store and the shoppers who frequent the stores. Analyse the information provided in the caselets and answer the question at the end of this section.*

1. Khodiyar *Kirana* Store[1]

The store was started 20 years ago, as the only *kirana* store in Bopal (Ahmedabad), at a time when Bopal was a rural area with barely two or three stores in the vicinity. Even the areas surrounding it were very underdeveloped. It was started by the present shop owner's father. It was a flourishing business then as it was a novelty to have such a store with various items, especially essentials that were frequently required. Although it had a much smaller set-up, customers would flock to it simply because it was convenient and also because there was no competition. Customers came to the store even from close by villages. In the last decade, however, quite a few *kirana* stores had mushroomed, and the area had also developed. Over the past few years, almost 30 stores had opened in Bopal, making it a far more commercial place than before. With

the region growing and moving away from a rural set-up, two things started to happen. First, the initial customers from the village moved away to other villages as Bopal started to develop, and second, people from Ahmedabad city moved into Bopal. These people were city dwellers who were prepared to travel even for everyday groceries to stores they felt were bigger and better. Till four years ago, the sales of Khodiyar was about ₹150,000 per month and the store earned a profit margin of 10 per cent, but now the sales had decreased to ₹80,000 per month and the profit margin was round 6 per cent.

More than 50 per cent of Bopal residents were double income no kids (DINK) families and bought their essentials from Ahmedabad. Of the remaining, about 10 per

---

1. Case written by Prof. Piyush Kumar Sinha, Indian Institute of Management Ahmedabad, and Dwarika Prasad Uniyal, Mudra Institute of Communications Ahmedabad, based on a course project carried out by the students of PGDM(C), MICA.

cent had moved to other *kirana* stores that were either closer or offered better service. Some 20 per cent of them preferred to get their groceries delivered at their homes.

Description and Ambience of the Store

The store name was written in the local language (Gujarati) with blue and white paint sparingly. The store was not distinctly visible. This, however, was no different from most of the *kirana* stores. Even the shopping complex where the store was located was quite unassuming.

The entrance was made of mud and was not paved. It was not very clean either. The entrance appeared to be an extension of a house. The shop was small and did not have much space for customers to move in. The shopkeeper felt offended whenever anybody tried to get into the store. He preferred the transaction to get over at the counter. However, sometimes, when the consumers wanted to check out the quality of rice or type of *dal* (pulses), they would step into the store and move around very uncomfortably. The shopkeeper did not seem to mind this intrusion in case of regular customers. There was no place for any customer to sit. There were two concrete extensions of the store where only the shop owner sat occasionally.

The shelves were partially filled at the time of the study. Things were not kept in order, they were arranged haphazardly. Although each product had a specific shelf space, it was invariably covered with dust and not kept in any orderly manner. Many sachets and other items were dangling from the top right in the middle of the store, which made the store look extremely cluttered. The counter was in order but appeared quite unappealing, with the weighing machine right in front. The polythene packs were dumped just behind the counter and pulled out randomly whenever asked for by customers. The sacks containing rice and pulses were all kept on the floor, adding to the disorderly look of the store.

The suppliers came at their own leisure time and arranged their products in accordance to their

Front View

Left-hand Shelf

Right-hand Shelf

Front View (Close up)

Views of Shelves at the Khodiyar *Kirana* Store

convenience. The shop owner did not seem to mind this and let the supplier arrange the items in any fashion.

Observations of customers at the store indicated the following:

- The customers primarily comprised labourers. They often purchased small quantities of essentials (e.g., *dal*, rice, cooking oil) on their way back home.
- Another set of customers were the housewives from neighbouring localities who did their daily or weekly shopping there.
- The store offered home delivery to its old customers. Often, customers came and gave the storekeeper a list.

- The interaction and involvement of customers was restricted to the product. The neighbouring shop owners would occasionally buy merchandise on credit.
- Some of the women exchanged pleasantries. Only a few were very chatty.
- Rarely did any customer enquire about discounts and schemes.
- The labourers made cash purchases and most of them carried the amount in their hand whereas the regular customers had credit accounts.
- A lot of children came to read the comic strip in the local newspaper kept beside the counter.

2. Lady Grace

Lady Grace was established in the year 1992. It was one of the first few shops exclusively dedicated to fashion jewellery. It had five franchisees in Ahmedabad. This shop was located on CG Road, the main shopping street of the city. Although the store did not face the road, it had done well to build a good customer base over the years. The following is the list of merchandise the store offered:

- Earrings
- Bracelets
- Necklaces
- Armlets and anklets
- Finger rings
- Revlon cosmetics
- Estelle jewellery
- Belts
- Hair accessories
- Key rings
- Bangles
- Scarves
- Bindis
- Heavy jewellery sets
- Children's accessories

The owner managed the shop with a manager, eight salesgirls, and one helper. The shop was divided into two floors—ground and upper. The total area of the shop was about 900 sq. ft.

The frontage of the store was 17 ft and had glass window displays. Figures CS12.1 and CS12.2 show the map of the two shop floors.

Common patterns of shopping behaviour were as follows:

- Rarely did people come alone.

- Groups of two or three were most common.
- Shoppers were women.
- They were mainly from SEC A1 and SEC A2.
- The language in which the shopper conversed with the accompanying person as well as the saleswomen was Hindi and Gujarati. English was rarely spoken.
- The average time spent in the shop was around twenty minutes.
- Largely, the shoppers were familiar with the shop; those who were not enquired at the counter near the door.
- The shoppers moved directly to a specific counter and then browsed around, and ended up buying something extra.
- The shoppers were highly involved with the accompanying person while making a purchase decision.
- The conversion rate was more than 80 per cent.
- There were hardly any shoppers who went upstairs.
- There were hardly any men who came to shop, and, if at all they came, they shopped for the women who accompanied them, and not for themselves.
- Shoppers browsed and shifted between racks and counters.
- Young girls and women, in most cases, bought accessories for themselves, not for gifting.
- The earrings section was the most sought after category.

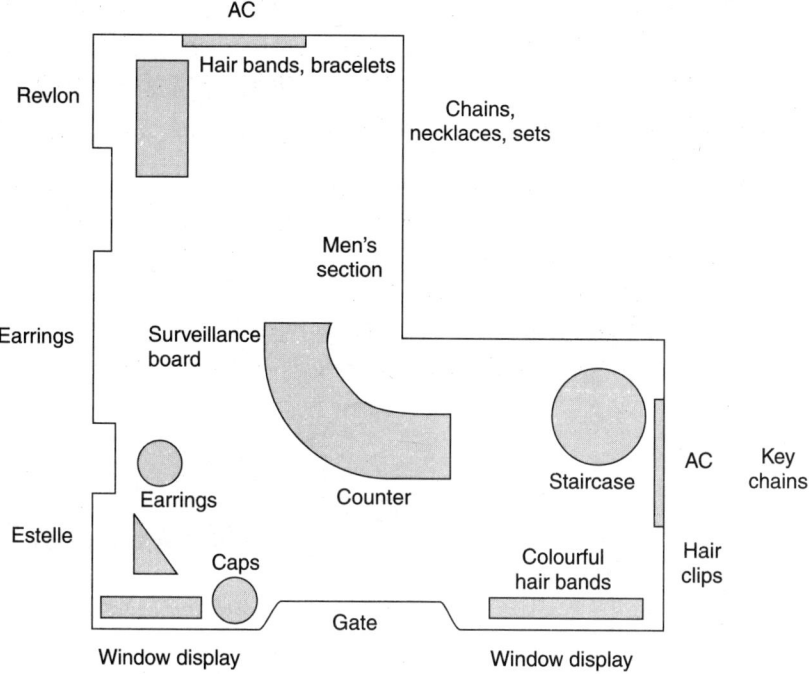

FIG. CS12.1   Map of the Ground Floor

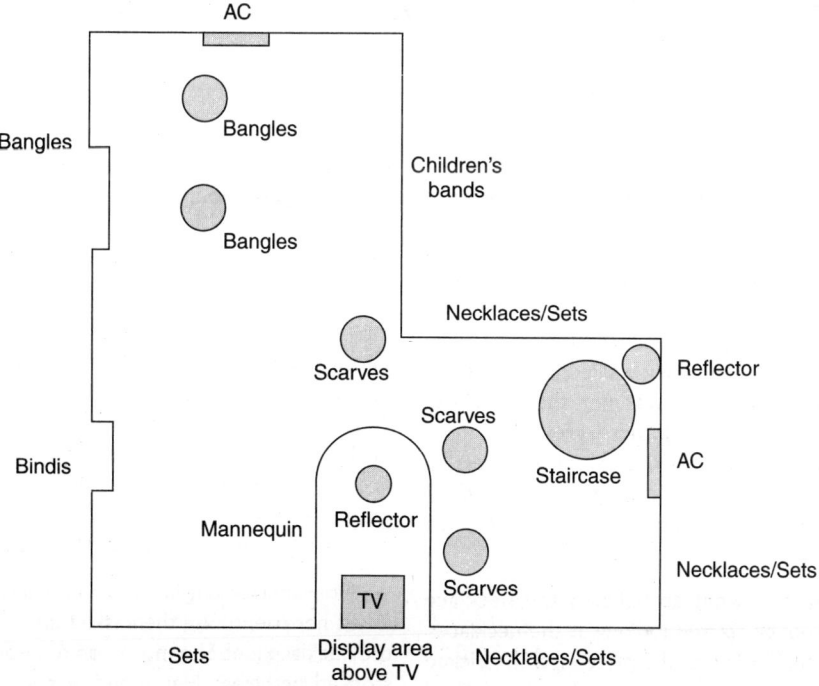

FIG. CS12.2   Map of the First Floor

Product Display at Lady Grace

II. *Given here are descriptions of some shoppers at a variety store and a book store. Go through these shopper descriptions and answer the questions at the end of the section.*

1. Variety Shop

Shopper I

Two young college going girls entered the store. They were talking to each other. They walked in confidently, and looked for neither the door nor the knob. The shopper was wearing casual clothes—grey jeans and a black shirt—and the accompanying person was wearing semi-formals—white trousers and a grey shirt. Both of them were wearing thin-stripped sandals and carried purses.

The two women went straight to the necklace counter. The shopper started looking at the necklaces, touched them, and looked at the price tags. She picked up one after five minutes, held it in her hands, and consulted her friend. Her friend did not quite like it. The shopper then called the saleswoman, showed her the chain which she herself was wearing, and probably asked for a similar one. Their conversation was in Gujarati. The saleswoman helped her and directed her to the desired rack. The shopper looked confused and was unable to decide. She wore one of the necklaces with the help of the saleswoman. Her friend was still looking at the necklace rack. The shopper looked at herself in the mirror, adjusted the necklace, and smiled. She then asked her friend's opinion, who gave her a look of approval.

'How am I looking in this? *Achha hai kya?,*' the shopper asked her friend. She then asked for a basket and kept the necklace in it. She moved on to another rack which stocked bracelets. Her friend was still looking at the necklaces. The shopper then saw the anklets and armlets and stopped at the earrings section. She conversed with her friend in English while fiddling with the earrings. She then moved on to the counter for making the payment, paid in cash, and took the receipt. Even after paying the bill, the shopper was unsure about leaving the shop. She looked at the hair accessories on the racks facing the counter. Then suddenly her friend told her what the time was and both of them pulled the door and walked out.

Shopper 2

Two young girls, aged around 22 years, walked into the store. They climbed the stairs and went straight to the bangles counter. Both of them were wearing cotton *salwar kameez*. One of them spoke to the saleswoman in Gujarati and told her that she was looking forward to attending a marriage and wanted bangles for the same. This lady was identified as the shopper. Both the women started looking at bangles of different hues and sizes, speaking to each other at the same time. For five minutes, the shopper just kept looking at them, did not touch or take out even a single bangle. It was apparent from her facial expression that she liked the variety but was confused about what to pick. Then the saleswoman approached them. She had figured out that the shopper needed help. She took out a pair of silver-coloured glass bangles. The shopper wanted to try them on but the size did not fit her. She then asked for a bigger size. Her friend took out some metal bangles and fiddled with

them. The shopper also took out the same and tried them. The shopper took another ten minutes to decide on what to purchase.

'*Kya loon, kuchh samajh mein nahin aa raha. Bahut achhi variety hai,*' she said. (I can't decide what do pick. There's a lot of variety.) She kept on touching, trying, and fiddling with different bangles. At last she bought four bronze-coloured metal bangles. She kept looking at the saleswoman while she was taking out the bangles for her and indicated something about the required size. After this, the shopper walked up to the rack where metal necklaces were kept (where the stairs to the first floor end). She touched one and fiddled with it, her eyes kept looking at the watch. She asked for its price and left it after hearing it. Her expression reflected that it was exorbitant. She went back to the bangles section again. Her friend had picked up one bangle set for herself in the meantime. The shopper also took out the same for herself and asked the saleswoman to pack them. They then went down and looked at the bill processing. The shopper took out money from her purse and took the receipt. She talked to her friend and they exchanged money. Finally, she took the packet and walked out of the store. They spent 35–40 minutes in the shop and made purchases worth five hundred and twenty rupees.

2. Book Store

Two men from L'Oreal walked in, dressed in executive formal clothing with ties. Both were in their mid-thirties. Both the gentlemen walked in straight to the CD section without stopping at the bestseller or discounted books rack. One person started browsing the CDs and flipped it to see the contents and price tags, the other person was just observing the merchandise, with hands in his pockets. Finally, the latter, finding the browsing gentleman at a loss, picked up a Harry Potter CD and stated, 'This is very nice; the kid will like it, buy this!' The shopper heeded his advice and kept the CD in his shopping cart. After that, both went further ahead in the English movies section and browsed through the movies.

The shopper picked up the 'Godfather' collection but kept it down after looking at the price tag of ₹990. The other person again recommended that it is a nice collection as it contains all 3 parts of the movie, which has won several Oscars. Again, the shopper picked it up and read through the laurels that the movie had won on the back side and added this also to his cart. After browsing for some more time in the movies section, both went to the cashier and purchased the selected CDs. The approximate time spent by them in the store was 20 minutes.

Questions

1. From the observation details given in this section, assign a suitable grid (from the shopper expectations model) to each shop.

2. What do you infer from the shopper behaviour mentioned in each case and what are the implications for retailers?

13 Establishing a Pricing Strategy

LEARNING OBJECTIVES

After studying this chapter, you will be able to
- develop an understanding of the pricing process and gain insight into the various factors that influence a retailer's pricing decision
- discuss how retailers set their pricing objectives and understand the different strategies and bases of pricing
- understand the process of price modifications by a retailer
- discuss the phenomenon of reference price and understand how it can be utilized by retailers

INTRODUCTION

Prices are one of the most tangible means of creating differentiation and, hence, building the image of the store. Price differentiation has, in fact, given rise to new store formats, referred to as 'price formats'. Price formats include discount stores, off-price retailers, and every-day low price (EDLP) retailers. Pricing is one of the most important variables in retail decision-making. From the customer's point of view, price is frequently a major reason for shopping in a particular store. The customer is often interested in the best value for a particular price. From the retailer's viewpoint, pricing decision has an impact on its image. Therefore, pricing decisions are made keeping in mind the retailer's mission statement, goals and objectives, strategy, and product mix and management.

FACTORS AFFECTING PRICING DECISIONS

The decision to price an item at a certain level is the outcome of the interaction of the retailer's pricing objectives with its decisions on the merchandise carried, location, promotion, credit, and customer services; the store image the retailer wishes to convey; and the legal constraints involved, as illustrated in Fig. 13.1.[1]

Merchandise   Retailers set prices by carefully analysing the attributes of the merchandise and the value the customer attaches to these attributes. The range of merchandise selection presents the retailer with an opportunity to provide different levels of prices to consumers. The retailer controls prices through either the cost of goods sold or the gross margin that is added to the cost. So, a retailer can either buy the merchandise at a lower cost or charge a higher markup to sell at a specified price. It can also buy merchandise that costs more, but sell these at a lower margin to maintain its price line.

Location   The location of the retail store in terms of proximity to its competitors and customers has a significant effect on the prices that can be charged. A store located among competitors with comparable

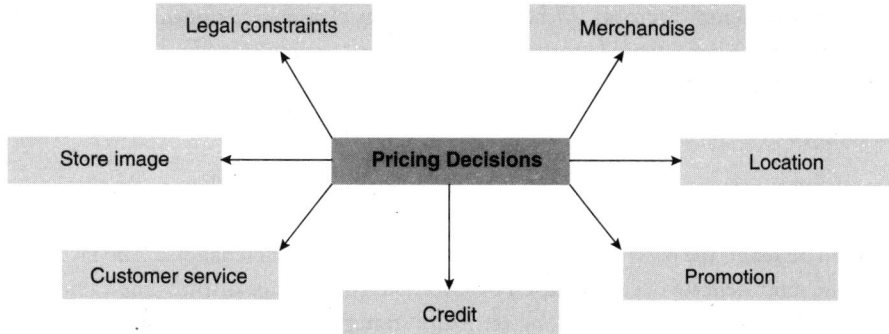

FIG. 13.1   Factors Affecting Pricing Decisions

merchandise and customer service has less pricing flexibility. The distance between the store and its customers also has an impact on its pricing decisions. When this distance is more, the store may have to either increase its promotional efforts or reduce the prices of its merchandise in order to attract customers.

Promotion   Promotion and pricing decisions are usually interrelated. When a retailer brings a change in its prices and offers discounts or other modifications, it may choose to attract customers through promotions in order to build awareness. A retailer who promotes heavily and is also price-competitive may increase sales more than a retailer who uses high promotion or low-price strategies independently.

Credit   For a given price level, retailers selling merchandise on credit are often able to generate greater demand than retailers offering special discounts for cash-paying customers. Many stores, such as Sears and Tesco, generate good business out of their store cards. It helps them to not only sell merchandise but also earn from financing the transaction. It is also observed that customers tend to buy more than their 'list' when using credit, leading to a multiplier effect on the revenue of the store.

Customer Services   Retailers who offer many customer services (e.g., delivery, gift wrapping, alterations, more pleasant surroundings, and sales assistance) have the option of charging higher prices. This may also result in higher profits. A retailer can exercise the option of either charging separately for these services or adding the charges into the product prices. A separate charge provides a choice to the customers. Some retailers do not impose any charges on these services. Rather, they provide these services free of cost to enhance value to the customers.

Store Image   The customer consciously or unconsciously links the retailer's prices with its image. The pricing policies and strategies interact with store image policies and strategies. For example, if a store selling designer apparel starts to discount its merchandise regularly, it may lose the image of being an exclusive store.

Legal Constraints   Pricing decisions must be made after examining the impact of the legal environment, especially the retail laws of the land where the retailer is operating. For example, in the US, reducing prices is easy. However, it can be controversial in Japan, which has a vertical monopoly of market distribution used by large manufacturers to suppress competition and keep fixed prices high. Similarly, most packaged products in India list a mandatory maximum retail price (MRP). No retailer can sell its merchandise above the MRP.

Other Environmental Factors   Other factors such as channel relationships, demand patterns, and seasonality are also considered in formulating the overall pricing strategy.

PRICE SETTING

Price setting is a crucial decision for retailers. In a market situation where price cuts are rampant and promotional schemes fill the marketplace, one gets the impression that price is the only way to compete. Prices can be set on the basis of competitive forces and cost of merchandise. The fact is that pricing is one of the most delicate decisions taken by a retailer. Any change disturbs the value equation of the customers. Leading retailers take a long-term and strategic view of pricing and use it well to keep the customer association valuable. The major components of a pricing system are depicted in Fig. 13.2.

Pricing Objectives

A retailer's pricing objectives reflect its overall goals. They are consistent with the retailer's overall image and positioning, sales, profit, and return on investment goals.[2] The pricing objectives may be stated in terms of three goals: (i) sales and profits, (ii) return on investments, and (iii) early recovery of cash. Sales and profit goals are reflected in terms of units sold and revenue generated. The profit goals are set either to earn more profit per unit or a smaller margin per unit. In both cases, the amount of profit may remain the same, though the volume sold would be very different. A retailer sets its pricing objectives in light of its overall objective, target market, and the composition of its retail mix. The objectives of a retailer may be achieved through three price options:

1. *Build volume by playing a price game*   This is a policy that has given birth to a distinct format of retailing called price formats. Such retailers offer the merchandise at the lowest possible price. This can be achieved by buying in large quantities and passing the benefits of

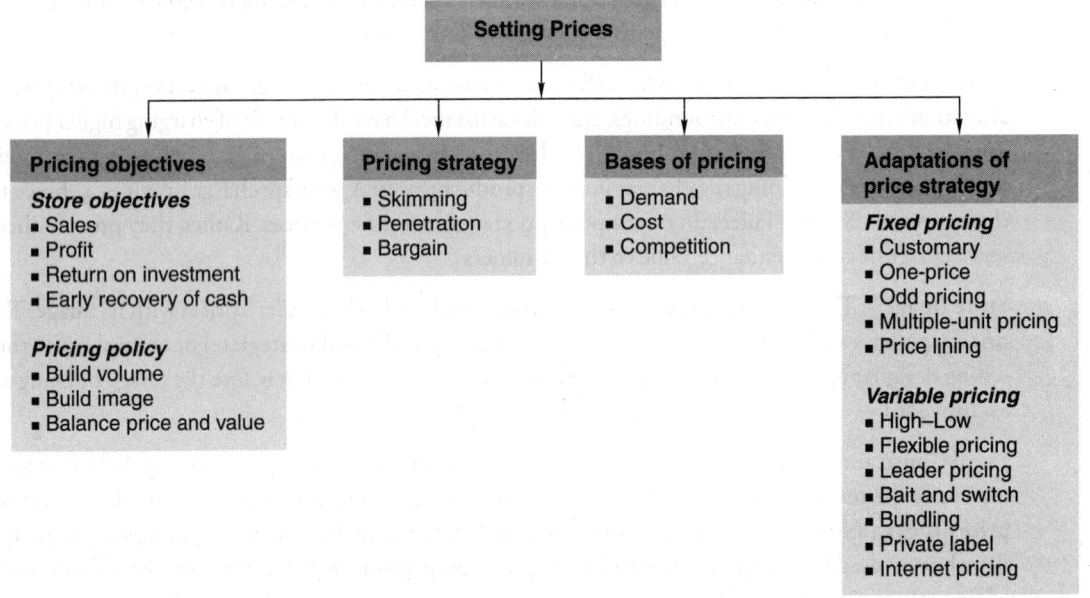

FIG. 13.2   Components of Pricing System

low cost purchase to the customer, as practised by Walmart. Wholesale clubs such as Sam's Club and Metro link this benefit to the quantity of merchandise bought by the customers. Such retailers do not sell less than a given number of units of an item of merchandise.

2. *Establish a distinctively high value image* Retailers that follow a policy of setting up a premium image through prices deal in merchandise that is generally exclusive or designer in nature. A distinctively superior in-store and out-of-store service also forms a major part of the value delivery. These retailers cater to a niche market—usually to customers in the higher socio-economic strata. The effort is to earn a higher margin per unit sold. The value is designated by either the quality and features of the merchandise or the exclusivity that creates an aura around the merchandise sold. Such stores also offer allied services and, in many cases, unconditional guarantees.

3. *Become a price–value optimizer* Low price policy is also followed by focusing on a category and driving volume through assortment and price, as in the case of Toys"R"Us. Low pricing policy is fairly common among stores that sell out-of-fashion or outdated products. Flea markets also follow such pricing policy. A large number of retailers, such as department stores, tend to optimize on the price and quality vectors. They practise a policy of moderate prices. They compete with low-price retailers on other assortment and in-store services. On the other hand, they fight the competition with high-end retailers on the basis of competitive prices and a wider choice of merchandise.

The retailer needs to set more than one set of pricing objectives. These would be prioritized and indicated as short-term and long-term pricing objectives. Besides these broad objectives, retailers choose from other secondary objectives listed in Exhibit 13.1.

EXHIBIT CS13.1   Pricing Objectives of a Retailer

Primary Pricing Objectives
- Build volume
- Establish a distinctive image
- Optimize price–value relationships

Secondary Pricing Objectives
- Maintain a proper image
- Discourage customers from becoming overly price-conscious
- Be perceived as fair by all parties (including suppliers, employees, and customers)
- Be consistent in setting prices
- Increase customer traffic during slow periods
- Clear out seasonal merchandise
- Match competitors' prices without starting a price war
- Promote a 'we-will-not be-undersold' philosophy
- Be regarded as a price leader in the market by consumers
- Provide ample customer service
- Minimize the chance of government actions relating to price advertising and anti-trust matters
- Discourage potential competitors from entering the marketplace
- Create and maintain customer interest
- Encourage repeat business

Pricing Strategy

The pricing strategy of a retailer must be consistent with its positioning, overall image, target market, composition of retail mix, and pricing policy. A retailer can use pricing strategies to attract particular market segments to the store. Higher prices and expensive brands encourage customers from higher socio-economic groups to buy at the store. In order to maintain the right merchandise mix, retailers can use price to clear stocks for faster replenishments. The location of the retailer's store also has a strong influence on price. In some circumstances, location may even be the major determinant of price. Stores located in a mall use a pricing strategy that is different from that of remotely located hypermarkets. In a low-income locality, a store may be forced to stock only certain SKUs with lower prices and may have to adopt a particular store layout and design. Lack of competition in an area may also allow retailers to charge a different price. Retailers at airports and railway stations capitalize on the 'captive customer'. The overall objectives of the pricing and business of the retailer will also influence the decision on strategy.

Different store formats require different pricing strategies. Department stores and drugstores offer average prices with margins between moderate to good. Their target market is middle-class shoppers desiring average to above-average products, good atmosphere, and service. Discount-orientated retailers use low prices as a major competitive advantage. Off-price retailers and discount departments operate in this category with a low status image and fewer shopping frills. These retailers have low profit margins per unit, serve a large, price-conscious target market, and have low operating costs and high inventory turnover. Speciality stores and upscale department stores have high per unit margins serving a smaller target market with high customer loyalty, offering distinctive services and product ranges.

Return on investments (ROI) and early recovery of cash are the two profit-based strategic options used by retailers. The ROI approach is followed when a firm stipulates that it must generate a given percentage return on the investments. Early recovery of cash is used by retailers who may be short of funds, wish to expand, or are uncertain about the future. For example, a small independent retailer can rapidly increase sales and quickly generate the needed cash by raising or lowering prices. A market skimming strategy is often applied by retailers with early ROI and early recovery of cash, whereas an aggressive pricing strategy is used when the retailer wants to grow faster.

Some retailers choose an aggressive pricing strategy known as market penetration or predatory prices. A retailer can achieve higher revenues by setting low prices and selling large quantities. This practice is followed by retailers targeting price-sensitive customers or product categories. The low prices tend to discourage competition. This strategy is used when retail costs do not increase at the same rate as sales volumes. Some retailers concentrate on total profit. With a market skimming strategy, a retailer charges premium prices and achieves high profit. This is possible in markets that are insensitive to price in relation to service, assortment, and status, and when new competitors are unlikely to enter the market. This strategy is also adopted by retailers who achieve additional sales at a higher retail cost.

Bases of Pricing

A retailer has to assess several factors before setting its prices. Broadly, it needs to understand its customers, competition, and costs and achieve a good balance amongst these factors while implementing its strategies. In practice, retailers integrate demand, cost, and competitive price orientations in formulating a price strategy. For instance, when a retailer finds that its prices have to be reduced due to moves by other retailers (competition orientation), it needs to evaluate the impact on revenues and determine whether the given price level will allow a traditional markup to be maintained (cost orientation) and what its impact would be on the positioning of the store as well as the role of the category in the business (demand orientation).

Demand-oriented Pricing

In demand-oriented pricing, a retailer sets its prices on the basis of consumer demands. It determines the range of prices acceptable to the target market. The top of this range, that is, the maximum price people will pay for a product/service, is called *demand ceiling*. Demand-oriented pricing takes into account two psychological aspects of pricing—(i) price–quality association and (ii) prestige pricing. According to the *price–quality association* theory, consumers correlate quality with price. Hence, a consumer may feel that high prices connote high quality, and low prices connote low quality. This association is relevant in situations where brand names are insignificant factors in product choice and the competing firms or products are hard to judge on bases other than price.

Prestige pricing is based on the assumption that consumers will not buy goods and services at prices deemed too low as, in their minds, there is a significant price–quality association. Therefore, some retailers may refrain from carrying the least expensive versions of items because their customers may feel these items are inferior. Prestige pricing is not suitable for 'economizers' who always shop for bargains. A retailer thus needs to find out the perceived value of an item for its target markets and segments in order to formulate its pricing strategy. Value maps are tools used for this purpose. These are used to determine the current and desirable pricing of items based on the values perceived by the customers.

Cost-oriented Pricing

Markup pricing is the most widely practised form of cost-oriented pricing. A markup is the gross margin that a retailer charges on its cost of merchandise. It is determined so as to cover all the operating expenses incurred in the sale of the product and to generate desirable profits. To calculate the selling price (or retail price), a retailer uses the following equation:

$$\text{Retail Price} = \text{Cost} + \text{Markup}$$

Markup is generally expressed as a percentage of the retail price or cost. It can also be expressed in value terms. Markup as a percentage of retail price is expressed as

$$\text{Markup on Retail Price} = (\text{Retail Price} - \text{Cost}) \div \text{Retail Price}$$
$$= \text{Markup} \div \text{Retail Price}$$

Markup as a percentage of cost is expressed as

$$\text{Markup on Cost} = (\text{Retail Price} - \text{Cost}) \div \text{Cost} = \text{Markup} \div \text{Cost}$$

Illustration 1: Markup
A retailer purchases a merchandise for ₹1,000 and sells it for ₹1,450. The difference between the price and the cost, which is the markup, is ₹450. This markup can be expressed as a percentage of the price, which is 31.03% (₹450 ÷ ₹1,450). It can also be expressed as a percentage of cost, which is 45% (₹450 ÷ ₹1,000).

In many cases, the retailer prefers to fix the markup on the cost of purchase of the merchandise. In such cases, the following equation can be use to find the markup percentage on selling price:

$$\text{Markup on Retail Price} = \text{Percentage Markup on Cost} \div$$
$$(100\% + \text{Percentage Markup on Cost})$$

Likewise, when we know the markup on the retail price, we can easily find the percentage markup on cost:

Markup on Cost = Percentage Markup on Retail Price ÷
(100% – Percentage Markup on Retail Price)

Illustration 2: Markup on Retail Price and Cost
In Illustration 1, the retailer earned 45% markup on its merchandise cost. This should be the same as 31.03% markup on the selling price:

Markup on Retail Price = 45% ÷ (100% + 45%)
= 31.03%

Likewise, with 31.03% markup on the selling price, the markup on cost can be calculated to be 45%:

Markup on Cost = 31.03% ÷ (100% – 31.03%)
= 45%

Initial Markup   Planned or initial markup is determined by deducting the cost of the merchandise from the original retail value assigned to the merchandise. Actual or maintained markup is based on the actual prices received for merchandise sold during a period of time less the merchandise cost. The difference between initial and maintained markups reflects adjustments from the original retail values caused by markdowns, added markups, shortages, and discounts. When a retailer does not plan any reduction, the initial markup percentage is equal to the planned retail operating expenses and profit divided by planned net sales. This is similar to the basic markup percentage formula. The initial markup percentage depends on planned retail operating expenses, profit, reductions, and net sales:

$$
\begin{array}{l}\text{Initial Markup}\\\text{Percentage on}\\\text{Retail Price}\end{array} = \begin{bmatrix}\text{Planned Retail}\\\text{Operating Expenses +}\\\text{Planned Profit +}\\\text{Planned Retail Reductions}\end{bmatrix} \div \begin{bmatrix}\text{Planned Net Sales}\\\text{Planned Retail}\\\text{Reductions}\end{bmatrix}
$$

The initial markup can be also determined from any of the variations of the above formula as given below:

$$
\begin{array}{l}\text{Initial Markup}\\\text{Percentage on}\\\text{Retail Price}\end{array} = \begin{bmatrix}\text{Operating Expenses +}\\\text{Net Profit + Markdowns +}\\\text{Shrinkages + Employee and}\\\text{Customer Discounts +}\\\text{Alternative costs -}\\\text{Cash discounts}\end{bmatrix} \div \begin{bmatrix}\text{Net Sales + Markdowns +}\\\text{Shrinkages + Employee}\\\text{and Customer Discounts}\end{bmatrix}
$$

or

$$
\begin{array}{l}\text{Initial Markup}\\\text{Percentage on}\\\text{Retail Price}\end{array} = \begin{bmatrix}\text{Gross Margin +}\\\text{Alteration Costs -}\\\text{Cash Discounts +}\\\text{Reductions}\end{bmatrix} \div \begin{bmatrix}\text{Net Sales + Markdowns +}\\\text{Shrinkages + Employee and}\\\text{Customer Discounts}\end{bmatrix}
$$

or

$$\text{Initial Markup Percentage on Retail Price} = \begin{bmatrix} \text{Gross Marging + Alteration Costs -} \\ \text{Cash Discounts + Reductions} \end{bmatrix} \div \begin{bmatrix} \text{Net Sales +} \\ \text{Reductions} \end{bmatrix}$$

Illustration 3: Initial Markup

For one of its stores, a retailer has planned net sales of ₹1,000,000 for a given category for the first quarter. Its operating expenses are ₹300,000. It is targeting a net profit ₹50,000. The reductions for the period are planned as follows:

	(₹)
Markdowns	75,000
Shrinkages	20,000
Discounts (Customer)	5,000
Discounts (Employee)	5,000
Alteration costs	20,000
Cash discounts (From suppliers)	10,000

The initial markup on retail prices for the category can be computed as

$$[300,000 + 50,000 + 75,000 + 20,000 + 5,000 + 5,000 + 20,000 - 10,000] \div$$
$$[1,000,000 + (75,000 + 20,000 + 5,000 + 5,000)]$$
$$= 42.08\%$$

The initial markup on cost for the category can also be computed. For this purpose, the cost of merchandise needs to be calculated. We know that

Gross Margin (Markup) = Net Sales – Total Cost of Merchandise

where,

Gross Margin (Markup) = Operating Expenses + Net Profit

and

Total Cost of Merchandise = Cost of Merchandise + Alteration Cost – Cash Discount

Thus,

Gross Margin = 1,000,000 – [Cost of Merchandise + 20,000 – 10,000]
300,000 + 50,000 = 990,000 – Cost of Merchandise
Cost of Merchandise = 990,000 – 350,000 = 640,000
Markup (on Cost) = 350,000 ÷ 640,000 = 54.65%

Maintained Markup   The markup may not always provide the desired profitability. This may be due to price modifications during the planning period. A retailer calculates the initial or planned markup at the beginning of the plan period. The actual or maintained markup needs to be arrived at during the period or at the end of it. This helps to determine the actual gross margin earned by the retailer. The maintained markup percentage is determined on the actual expenses and costs during the period using the following equation:

$$\text{Maintained Markup Percentage on Retail Price} = \begin{bmatrix} \text{Actual Retail Operating Expenses +} \\ \text{Actual Profit + Planned Retail} \\ \text{Reductions} \end{bmatrix} \div [\text{Actual Net Sales}]$$

or

$$\text{Maintained Markup Percentage on Retail Price} = \begin{bmatrix} \text{Average Selling Price -} \\ \text{Average Merchandise Cost} \end{bmatrix} \div [\text{Actual Selling Price}]$$

The markups for categories of merchandise or even individual products tend to be different over time and buying cycles. In certain products, markups can vary dramatically. For instance, at many full-line discount stores, the maintained markup as a percentage of sales ranges from under 20 per cent for one merchandiser to more than 40 per cent for others. In such cases, retailers adopt a variable markup policy and adjust markups by merchandise category to achieve their sales and pricing objectives. Depending on the variation in the cost of the merchandise, the retailer manages its markups to generate customer traffic by offering certain products at especially attractive prices. The variable markup policy recognizes that costs associated with separate goods/service categories may fluctuate widely. It allows for differences in product investments. Some retailers use direct product profitability as a method for planning variable markups. In this method, a retailer determines the profitability of each category or unit of merchandise by computing the adjusted per unit gross margin and assigning direct product costs for expenses such as warehousing, transportation, handling, and selling. The use of this method is limited as it requires assigning costs that may not be easy to allocate.

Illustration 4: Maintained Markup

A retailer purchased 50 units of pens for ₹50 each. The selling price of each pen was fixed at ₹75. This provided the retailer with an initial markup of 50%. The retailer planned to sell all the units in a month. However, it was able to sell only 40 units at the intended price. The remaining 10 units had to be sold at ₹60 each. The maintained markup in this case can be computed as given below:

Maintained Markup = (Average Selling Price − Merchandise Cost) ÷ Average Selling Price
= [{(75 × 40 + 60 × 10) ÷ 50} − 50] ÷ [(75 × 40 + 60 × 10) ÷ 50]
= [(3,600 ÷ 50) − 50] ÷ [3600 ÷ 50]
= 22 ÷ 72
= 30.55%

The maintained markup percentage as a percentage of the initial markup can also be calculated with the help of the following equation:

(Initial Markup Percentage − Maintained Markup Percentage) ÷ Initial Markup Percentage
= [(50% − 30.55%) ÷ (50%)]
= 19.45% ÷ 50% = 38.90%

Markups need to be planned at the sub-category level, if not at the item or SKU level. Some sub-categories yield a higher profit, while, in many other cases, retailers have to charge a low markup. Because of changes in market conditions, the initial markup is seldom equal to the maintained markup. Most retailers use some kind of reduction to ensure the planned stock turnaround. The reductions could be in the form of markdowns, customer discounts, shrinkages, shortages, employee discounts, and alterations. Some large retailers consider cash discounts in calculating the initial markup while many do not include it as the buyer may not have a direct role in cash discounts. Retailers also like to price the mix of merchandise lines in such a fashion that it obtains a desired storewide markup percentage.

Markdowns usually occur due to errors in buying, pricing, merchandising, or promotion. Buying errors occur on the supply side of the pricing equation when too large a quantity may have been purchased due to a faulty demand estimation. It may also happen due to unforeseen factors, such as unpredicted competitor action, unforeseen recession, or a sudden shift in customer preferences. Unforeseen changes in season or climatic conditions could also result in excess stock. Consequently, the retailer has to reduce the price to move the merchandise. Pricing errors occur when the price of the item is too high to move the product at the speed and in the quantity desired. The goods may have been bought in the right styles, at the right time, in the right quantities, but the price of the item may have been set at a higher level. This is generally the case when retailers try to take advantage of a fad or a fashion that fails to click.

Merchandising errors occur when there is a lack of clear communication in the sales department about the current stocks. It may also be caused when there is a lack of clarity about the relationship of the new merchandise with the current stock, the store's image, or the needs of the store's target market. Promotion errors occur when the retailer fails to provide proper information to customers through advertising, sales promotion activities, or in-store displays. Improper handling of merchandise by the sales staff and, sometimes, ineffective visual presentation of merchandise may also lead to excess stocks that may have to be sold at a price that is lower than the original price.

In order to guard against these errors, retailers may develop a markdown policy that guides the store about the amount and the timing of markdowns. Early markdowns accelerate the movement of merchandise and allow the retailer to dispose of the merchandise at a lesser markdown per unit. Late markdowns avoid disrupting the sale of regular merchandise by frequent markdowns. In case of early markdown, the magnitude is planned to be large enough to provide the sales stimulant. Late markdown amounts need to be high enough to ensure that the remaining merchandise is sold off as early as possible. The choice depends on the type of merchandise, time of season, competition, and the requirement of a particular situation. As a rule of thumb, prices should be marked down by at least 25 per cent for customers to notice a difference in pricing.

Competition-oriented Pricing

Competition-oriented pricing is similar to demand-oriented pricing in the sense that it is also based on an external variable—competition. A competition-oriented pricing strategy is popular because of its sheer simplicity and assumption that the market price is fair for both the consumer and the retailer. Pricing at the market level does not disrupt competition and, therefore, does not lead to retaliation.

A retailer following a competition-oriented pricing strategy uses competitors' prices, rather than demand or cost considerations, as a benchmark. A retailer might thus change its prices when competitors do, even if demand or cost factors remain the same. Table 13.1 outlines the choices a retailer has in setting its prices in accordance with its competitors' prices. The role of the elements of a retail mix is also outlined. While following a competition-oriented pricing strategy, the retailer must ensure that its pricing is in line with its overall strategy mix. For instance, a store with a good location, favourable image, superior service, good assortment, and exclusive brands can afford to set higher prices compared to its competitors'.

On the other hand, a store located away from shop clusters may have to use low prices to turn it into a destination store, given that other variables remain comparable. Also, a store that follows rather than leads a fashion, style, or trend would not be in a position to charge better prices. One of the reasons that hypermarkets and category killers can charge lower prices is that these stores do not provide personalized services to their customers. Most of them are self-service stores. Therefore, although competition-based pricing may seem to be as simple as matching prices, the pricing decision needs to be based on the competitive positioning and the internal operations of the retailer.

TABLE 13.1 Competition-oriented Pricing

Retail Mix Variable	Pricing below the Market	Pricing at the Market	Pricing above the Market
Location	Poor, inconvenient site, low rent	Close to competitors, no locational advantage	Absence of strong competitor, convenient to consumers
Customer service	Self-service, little product knowledge on part of sales personnel, no displays	Moderate assistance by sales personnel	High levels of personal selling, delivery, and exchange
Product assortment	More emphasis on bestsellers	Medium or large assortment	Selected or large assortment
Atmosphere	Inexpensive fixtures, little or no carpeting or panelling, racks for merchandise	Moderate atmosphere	Attractive, pleasant decor with many displays
Role of fashion in assortment	Fashion follower, conservative	Concentration on accepted bestsellers	Fashion leader
Special services	Not available	Not available, or available at extra charges	Included in price
Merchandise lines carried	Some brands, private labels, closeouts, items by small manufacturers	Selection of brands, private labels	Exclusive brands and private labels

Adapting the Pricing Strategy

Retailers need to adapt their pricing strategies in order to achieve their pricing objectives effectively. These adaptations help in building the revenue streams as well as in differentiating the stores in a competitive market.

Pricing strategies can be classified into fixed pricing and variable pricing. Retailers following a fixed pricing strategy can choose customary pricing, odd pricing, multiple-unit pricing, price lining, or a one-price policy. Fixed prices are usually followed by high-end department stores. Many choices are available to retailers who follow variable pricing. These are high–low pricing, flexible pricing, loss leading, bait and switch pricing, price bundling, private label pricing, and multi-channel pricing.

Customary Pricing

Customary pricing is used when a retailer sets certain prices for goods and services and seeks to maintain those prices over an extended period of time. The pricing of newspapers, movie tickets, vending machine products, and pay phone services are some common examples of customary pricing. In each of these cases, the retailer seeks to maintain the price over periods long enough to tell the customers that the services or merchandise are fairly priced. In many cases, stores that follow customary pricing become references or benchmarks for determining the 'priciness' of other stores.

Retailers who follow customary pricing need to choose the merchandise and customer segments carefully. Since the price to the customer does not change, the variations in costs have to be borne by the retailer. When selling to a price-insensitive segment, the retailer can always build the loss into its markup. In case a retailer strives to sell its goods and services at consistently low prices throughout the selling season, as in the case of EDLP, it needs to be established that the costs and demands will not vary, and, in case they do, the variation will be marginal. Such retailers stress on buying the merchandise efficiently. They need to be very good at forecasting the demand for the goods they sell. The major savings come from the lowered advertising and product costs of the retailer and the decreased production and shipping costs of the manufacturers, brought about by stable sales levels. Such pricing practices also increase the credibility of the retailer's prices to the consumer. A retailer should not use customary pricing when costs are rising or when customer demand varies a lot.

One-price Policy

Under the one-price policy, a retailer charges the same price from the customer. It may be used in conjunction with fixed or variable pricing. For example, with variable pricing, all customers interested in a particular section of theatre seats would pay the same price. The advantage of this policy is that the system is easy to manage, does not require skilled salespeople, makes shopping quicker, permits self-service, puts the consumer under less pressure, and is tied to the firm's price goals. Dollar Stores, where all products are sold at $1 or a similar fixed value, follow a one-price policy. Bargaining is usually not permitted in such stores.

Odd Pricing

The practice of setting retail prices that end in digits such as 5, 8, or 9—for example, ₹99.99, ₹49.98, or ₹59.95—is referred to as odd pricing. Bata is a classical example of a store that uses odd pricing. Odd pricing is a form of psychological pricing based on the assumption that odd prices are perceived to be the lowest possible prices, thus encouraging the customer to purchase more units.

Multiple-unit Pricing

In the case of multiple-unit pricing, the price of the complete package is less than the price of each unit in the package, if sold individually. Grocery retailers use multiple-unit pricing for items that are consumed rapidly or used together, such as cigarettes, candy bars, and beverages. Retailers use multiple-unit pricing to encourage additional sales and to increase profits. It can also help sell slow moving and end-of-season merchandise.

Price Lining

Retailers often employ price lining and sell merchandise at a limited range of price points, with each point representing a distinct level of quality, rather than stock merchandise at several different price levels.[3] For example, a retailer who stocks 150 units of an item and has 5 price lines would have an assortment of only 30 units in each line. On the other hand, if the 150 units were divided among only 3 price lines, there would be 50 units in each line. For price lining, retailers first determine their price floors and ceilings in each product category. They then set a limited number of price points within the range. Such a policy benefits both the customer and the retailer. Price lining aids retailers in merchandise planning. They can disregard products not fitting within price lines and thereby reduce inventory levels. Price lining also results in the stock turnover going up when the number of SKUs carried is limited, resulting in increased sales and fewer markdowns. Sometimes, retailers become specialists in these product lines. This enables them to concentrate all their merchandising and promotional efforts on these lines and clearly define their store image. From the shoppers' perspective, it is easy to shop when price lining is used because it enables them to compare different price levels. Moreover, a set of products is available with small price differences to cover the range of prices.

Price lining has its limitations too.[4] First, depending on the price points selected, price lining may leave gaps between prices that are perceived as too high by consumers. Second, cost variations can make it difficult to maintain price points and price ranges. When costs rise, retailers tend to eliminate lower priced items or those with reduced markups. Third, markdowns or special sales may disrupt the balance in a price line unless the prices of all items in that line are reduced proportionately. Fourth, price lines must be coordinated for complementary product categories such as shirts, skirts, and shoes.

High–Low Pricing

High–low pricing involves the use of initial high prices and lower special promotion prices on featured items. This pricing strategy is used mostly by fashion retailers. Initial high prices ride on the novelty and exclusivity of the product and the retailer is able to mark up the prices substantially. Since fashion products are prone to high rate of obsolescence and fashion retailers need to bring in new merchandise on a regular basis, the existing stocks have to be cleared within a given period. For instance, fashion retailers usually follow a three-to-four month cycle. During this cycle, for about eight weeks, the merchandise is sold at its original price. For the rest of the time, it is sold at a lower price before it is offered at a markdown or liquidated. Retailers practising high–low pricing often schedule regular sales. Off-price retailers base their business on the pricing practices of fashion retailers.

Flexible Pricing

Under flexible or variable pricing, a retailer alters its prices to coincide with fluctuations in costs or consumer demand. For example, movie tickets are priced lower on weekdays compared to weekends. Restaurants advertise 'happy hour' meals at a discounted price during weekdays to increase demand. Prices are kept at a lower level during periods of low demand to boost sales. Flexible pricing is a strategy in which the same products and quantities are offered to different customers at different prices. It is also used in situations calling for personal selling. Many jewellery stores, auto dealers, house painters, online auctions, and consumer electronic retailers use flexible pricing. Retailers following a flexible pricing strategy encourage shoppers to spend more time in shopping and give them the impression that they are being offered a higher value. This way, the retailers generate high margins from shoppers. It requires high initial prices and good salespeople. The advantage of flexible pricing is that the salesperson can make price adjustments based on a competitor's price or the consumer's interest, bargaining ability, or past relationship with the retailer. The limitation of flexible pricing is that it can increase costs as customers begin to bargain for everything or feel dissatisfied on finding that another person has paid less for the same product.

A special form of flexible pricing is *contingency pricing*, where the retailer is not paid until the service is performed and payment is contingent on the services being satisfactory. For example, in the case of service retailing, customers prefer to pay after the service has been rendered, provided that they are satisfied with it. This presents some risk to the retailer since considerable time and effort may be spent without payment. A retailer should use variable pricing when fluctuations in demand and cost force the retailer to change prices. This also gives an impression that the retailer is conscious of customers' requirements. The customers feel that the value rendered is commensurate to the price charged. One more form of flexible pricing is *multi-channel pricing*. The same merchandise can be priced differently when made available through a different channel. This is achieved when customers are fully aware that the value delivered by each channel is different. Hence, similar merchandise can be priced differently for supermarkets, airports, and non-store formats.

Bundle Pricing

Bundling generally involves selling distinct multiple items offered together at a special price.[5] It is based on the assumption that there are perceived savings in cost or time for the bundle, justifying the purchase. A popular example of bundling is tie-in promotions, wherein, on a purchase of one product, the other product is offered at a lower price. This is generally done for complementary products, such as tea and snacks. Bundling is a very common practice for introducing trials of new products. Many a times, it is used for clearing slow moving products. Bundle pricing is also used to tie up a service with a product. For example, a bookstore with an attached café can offer a cup of free coffee beyond a particular value of purchase, or a store can have a arrangement with a movie theatre for free tickets to a new release on the purchase of a particular item.

Leader Pricing

In leader pricing, a retailer advertises and sells selected items in its goods/service assortment at less than the usual profit margins.[6] The goal is to increase customer traffic for the retailer so as to sell regularly priced goods and services in addition to the specially priced items. Leader pricing often involves frequently purchased, nationally branded, high turnover goods and services because it is easy for customers to detect low prices, thereby generating high customer patronage. Supermarkets, home improvement centres, discount department stores, toy stores, drugstores, and fast-food restaurants are some retailers that utilize leader shopping to draw shoppers.

Bait and Switch Pricing

The practice of advertising a low priced model of shopping goods such as a television or a computer to lure shoppers into a store is called bait and switch pricing.[7] Once the shoppers are in the store, a salesperson tries to persuade them to purchase a higher priced model. Very often, retailers incur a loss on a particular category or SKU to gain from the total purchase by the customers.

Coupons and Rebates

These are some of the most commonly used practices for offering a price variation. They help in discriminating the value delivered to different sets of customers. Coupons are given to customers either before purchase or after purchase. In the latter case, the customer gets the benefit in the next purchase. This is aimed at increasing the chances of repeat purchase by customers. In the former case, the coupons are provided to the customers through newspapers, inserts, or direct mailers they get before coming to the store. In many cases, these coupons are also made available at the store. They can be given at the entry, aisles, shelves, or even while purchasing. While most of the coupons tend to provide benefit to all the customers, some variations of these exist in the form of lottery-based coupons. In such cases, the reward is large but dependent on whether the customer wins the lottery. Sometimes, stores draw winners for each day or even for every three hours. The aim in all such cases is to initiate purchases of the promoted products by inducing the customer to decide on a purchase immediately.

Rebates are direct price offs based on the purchase by the customers. They are generally provided for the next purchase. In a competitive market, coupons and rebates have become very commonplace and retailers need to be careful regarding the response to them. Unless they have been designed and communicated well, the redemption rate of coupons and rebates may be very low. They appeal most to deal-prone customers. The number of such customers vary based on the product category and the value proposition of the retailer.

Private-label Pricing

Private label brands can be purchased by retailers at a cheaper price, have a higher markup percentage, and still be priced lower than a comparable national brand. It is believed that consumers find it difficult to make exact comparisons between private brands and national brands of similar goods. Some retailers use their store image as an advantage by developing their own exclusive private labels. The most common perception is that private label brands are cheaper. Value retailers such as Tesco use private brands to not only provide products at better price levels but also to fill gaps not fulfilled by national brands.

Pricing on the Internet

The Internet has come as an exciting new channel of retailing. Since most products were initially offered at a low price to attract customers, it came to be perceived as a low-cost channel. The truth, however, may not be so. High-priced products are also being retailed through the Internet. The Internet provides two distinct advantages. It enables the retailer to offer its customers a lower price and a wider assortment due to disintermediation and a lag in ordering and delivery. Also, retailers using the Internet as a medium do not have to pay sales tax. Internet retailing is advantageous to customers too as it enables them to compare prices. The most interesting pricing strategy on the Internet is auctioning as epitomized by eBay.com. Instead of retailers, the customers compete among themselves for the best price. E-tailers such as priceline.com also allow their customers the choice of offering a price and then finding a seller who can match the requested price the best. In such cases, customers would have to trade off the choice on the route and the airlines and may not get the desired route/airlines. In most cases, price determination on the Internet seems to have moved from the sellers' domain to the customers' domain.

REFERENCE PRICE

A customer's price perception of a product is determined by not only the retail price of the product but also other factors such as the price image of a brand,[8] perceived price,[9] evoked price,[10] price belief,[11] advertised/comparative price,[12] and reservation price.* Shoppers evaluate offers on the basis of a benchmark called *reference price*. Several studies have been conducted to understand the phenomenon of reference price, define it, identify its determinants, develop benchmarks, and study its impact and its communication.

Defining Reference Price

Shoppers use a benchmark or a reference point in assessing the value of particular offers. This phenomenon of reference price, wherein shoppers compare the price of an offer with a benchmark, has been studied for a long time.[13] The comparison is carried out by customers to estimate the gain or loss from a purchase. Reference price has been defined as the shopper's perceived current price of a brand, and can also be termed as anticipated price.[14] It could also be a weighted or smoothened average of past prices.[15] Another definition suggests that it is the current price of the last brand purchased.[16] Reference price may also include information on past price trends and the market performance of a brand.[17] It has also been included in the expected price construct.[18] Studies suggest that the value of a transaction is determined on the basis of the reference price and the selling price, and a purchase is made only when the deal is found acceptable.[19]

Reference price is studied as a psychological construct that asserts that judgements are proportional to deviations from a comparison standard.[20, 21] In such a case, the customer uses the price of a representative product or item from a category to represent the price levels of a category or a store.[22] This comparison generally leads to the setting of a range of values or prices for a given

---

* For definitions, students may refer to the glossary provided at the end of the book.

product or category.[23] The range of prices is decided on the basis of the context of the stimuli, such as the store image or location or time of purchase.[24] This distribution is also formed due to normal price perceptions, lowest price perceptions, and the latitude of price acceptance.[25] Shoppers using the central route, that is, shoppers who show a more cognitive or rational basis for deciding their purchases, tend to use internal reference price, whereas those using the peripheral route or affective/ conative and emotional bases use external reference price.[26]

Benchmarks for Reference Price

It has been found that a large majority of shoppers hold some sort of price information when they come to a store.[27] These may not always be accurate prices but are estimations. Shoppers tend to use two types of benchmarks for creating reference price: internal and external.

Internal reference price is memory based, and previously encountered prices are used to compare current prices. Shoppers use three types of memory-based reference prices: (i) prices of previously chosen brands,[28] (ii) brand-specific past prices, and (iii) past prices and other information.[29] Internal reference price can be classified into three overlapping categories: aspirational prices, market prices, and historical prices. Aspirational prices are the prices that the shopper would aim to pay, whereas market prices are based on the perceived price levels in the market. Historical prices are determined on the basis of the shopper's purchase experiences.

The *external reference price* is created in accordance with stimuli present in the external environment. These could be announcements at the point of sale[30] through advertisements[31] or catalogues.[32] Shoppers tend to check and remember prices while shopping, though the extent may be subject to cultural context. A study conducted on supermarket shoppers in the US showed that only about 21 per cent of shoppers in the US did not remember prices,[33] whereas, in a similar study conducted in Europe, this figure stood at about 40 per cent.[34] The two studies also differed in terms of the accuracy of recall—the shoppers in the US tended to remember prices more accurately than their European counterparts. Though not very clear, such memories have also been found to differ across product categories.[35] The rationale for external reference price is in line with a study which suggests that price expectations are formed on the basis of the past prices of the brand.[36] The concept of stimulus-based reference price is based on the assumption that shoppers enter a store without prior knowledge of prices. The reference price is formed in comparison with a reference brand's current price or a randomly chosen brand's current price. In the latter case, the reference price is used to compare all other brands, resulting in gains or losses for these brands.[37]

Impact of Reference Price

Reference price is studied for its impact on shopper perception, purchase behaviour, and price search. Customers usually evaluate deals in relation to the reference price. The difference between the actual price and the reference price creates transaction utility.[38] The pharmaceutical industry in Europe utilizes reference prices to categorize drugs so as to manage medical costs by encouraging the purchase of less expensive drugs that are fully reimbursable by the government.[39] Reference price affects deal proneness and purchase intentions of shoppers depending on the uncertainty of prices.[40] Reference price is found to influence shopper response significantly and consistently across aggregate markets or households.[41] This aspect has been studied extensively.[42]

Both internal and external reference price influence brand choice. Pricing policies can be framed on the basis of the reference price mechanism used by the shoppers.[43] It is suggested that EDLP is a good pricing strategy since in this case only memory-based reference price is used, whereas in the case of a high–low strategy, a shopper would use both internal and external reference price. A change in the price of one brand affects the choice probabilities of other brands.

Reference price is also used for segmenting shoppers and understanding their price behaviour. When the prices of products are set to compare favourably with the brand's price history, they stimulate demand for customers who base their purchase decisions on internal reference prices.[44] Conversely, external reference price driven shoppers are targeted by identifying the set of brands the segment typically considers, setting a price that is lower than the other brands in the set, and using store promotion to communicate the low prices. Based on reference price, shoppers have been segmented as loss and gain sensitive.[45] The loss sensitive segment is found to be less sensitive to past brand use and shows stronger reaction to price, feature, and display than average shoppers.

By rotating promotions across brands, a retailer is able to reduce the effect of individual brand reference prices. High reference price reduces shopper search intentions and, when announced with a low price guarantee, it helps reduce shopper scepticism.[46] In normal price estimation tasks, shoppers rely more on price claims at the time of shopping than on prior price beliefs.[47] This tendency increases when the prices are below price expectations and diminishes when the prices are above expectations. In an experiment that compared advertisements with and without plausible reference prices, it was found that a high plausible reference price improved the perception of the advertised offer, and an exaggerated reference price improved even sceptical shoppers' perception and reduced search in case of higher sale price advertisements.[48]

A reference price based model is able to predict the purchase probability of customers better than standard demand models that incorporate only the current observed brand prices.[49] A reference price has a significant impact on shopper response and these effects are asymmetric.[50] It has been found that shoppers are two and a half times more responsive to an increase in excess of the reference price than to a comparable decrease. Reference prices also help in planning promotions.[51] They provide the retailers with a measurement to judge the effectiveness and worth of the promotion for their customers.

Reference Price Controversy

Reference price is a subject of controversy as it creates a comparison of the prices of competing brands. Although it is misleading and hence has been subject to controversy for quite a long time,[52] it helps shoppers in shopping and is commonly used by a large majority.[53] The controversy arises out of the perception that advertised reference prices suggest to shoppers that they will save money and get a good deal. An extensive review of literature regarding comparative price advertising has been carried out.[54] In a meta-analysis of 38 articles from several peer-reviewed journals, it has been found that comparative advertisements are effective. Also, the potential for deception is rife because of the strong influence of external reference prices even when they are exaggerated, and the adverse effects of reference prices may not be as severe as had been suggested in earlier studies. The presence of external reference prices increases the shoppers' internal reference prices and, thus, their perceptions of value and purchase intention, and thereby reduces search.

Empirical Generalizations Regarding Reference Price

Based on a survey of literature on reference price, three generalizations have been drawn.[55] First, reference price has a consistent and significant impact on shopper demand. This generalization assumes that comparison between the current reference price and the current observed prices exists. The same is extended to a comparison with the expected future price, especially in case of consumer durables.

Second, internal reference price utilizes past prices as part of the shoppers' information set. Third, shoppers react differently to price increases and price decreases relative to reference price. They react more strongly to price increases than price decreases. This generalization is derived from studies on shoppers' perception of gain and loss and their tendency for loss aversion.

The perception of reference prices is context and time specific. The context is largely defined as the category of the product,[56] brand preference, frequency of purchase, use experience,[57] shopper segment,[58] loyalty, asymmetric switching based on perceived quality,[59] stockout and deal proneness,[60] and prior knowledge.[61]

The following conclusions can be drawn from the various studies on reference price:

(a) **Reference price exists along a continuum, which is referred to as the shopper's reference range.** The reference range is visualized as an internalized psychological scale that provides a basis for price comparison and appraisal. New externally provided prices are compared to internal price levels stored in memory. The outcome of this comparison establishes the acceptability of new price information to the user. Figure 13.3 shows the reference price continuum.

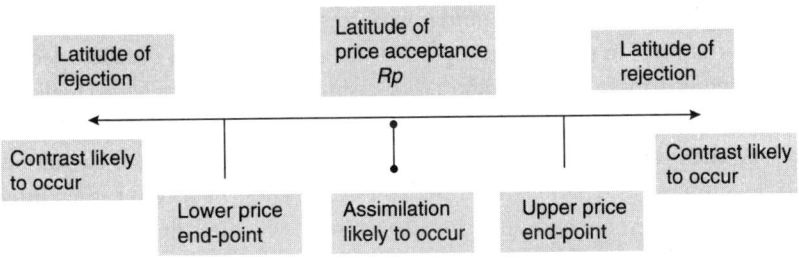

FIG. 13.3 Reference Price Continuum

The latitude of acceptance depends on the following factors:

- *Level of knowledge* The level of knowledge affects both the reference price level and the breadth of price acceptability. Shoppers with a better knowledge of price distributions are more likely to notice any deviations from their reference price level. Better price knowledge therefore results in a narrower latitude of price acceptance.
- *Frequency of purchase* It is understood that shoppers with a high purchase frequency have a better knowledge of prices and, therefore, have a narrower latitude of acceptance.
- *Brand loyalty* Brand loyalty will further affect the latitude of price acceptance. Shoppers who are more brand loyal are likely to have a wider latitude of price acceptance for that specific product or service. When shoppers are more brand loyal, they are more likely to focus on the benefits of the brand than on the price. Deviation from the reference price level must be fairly significant before the shopper even takes notice of the price. Shoppers who are less brand loyal are more focused on price than on benefits. As a result, their deviation from the reference price level is smaller.
- *Quality perceptions* Many shoppers believe that a higher price results in higher quality and are therefore willing to pay more. This is particularly true of those who know little about the product. Therefore, the level of acceptable price is higher for shoppers who believe that price and quality are positively related.

(b) **Reference price formation depends on previous price knowledge and contextual variables.** Past prices are an important component in reference price formation. However, users may purchase products or services with which they have had no previous price experience and therefore have no previous price knowledge. In such a case, they may use contextual variables found in the external environment with reference to price formation. Two contextual variables have been found to affect the formation of reference price: promotional pricing strategies and external reference price.

(c) **Reaction to price is a function of price expectations and individual idiosyncrasies.** There are generally two extreme reactions with respect to price: acceptance or rejection. If a price falls within the latitude of price acceptance, assimilation is likely to occur. *Assimilation* is the movement toward shoppers' reference price and *contrast* is the movement away from shoppers' reference price. Assimilation increases the likelihood that a price will be accepted because it is seen as being closer to a shopper's reference price position than it may actually be. Contrast causes the price to be seen as being farther from a shopper's reference price than it may actually be and therefore increases the likelihood of rejection. As a result, the greater the distance between the reference price and the actual price, the more likely a shopper is to contrast it with the actual price, thus causing a negative reaction.

Studies suggest that the level of cognitive resources or the effort people use in making a judgement plays an important role in reference price formation and subsequent purchase decisions. It is known that contrast requires more cognitive effort than assimilation. Subjects with a high need for cognition tend to exhibit the contrast effect and those with a low need for cognition more often engage in assimilation. The proposed reasoning is that people with a high need for cognition exert the effort necessary to suppress associations with the contextual cues. As a result, they interpret the target object in terms of alternate and opposite associations, which results in contrast. Shoppers with a low need for cognition display assimilation, which requires less energy. For assimilation to occur, shoppers are understood to use contextual cues to aid their judgement.

(d) **User reference price serves as an anchor and can be affected by cues in the external environment.** New prices when encountered are placed in relation to reference price on a reference range. Prices that are found in the external environment can affect the reference price. The introduction of prices considerably below or above the reference range restricts the judgement within the reference range to only a certain area located farthest from the external price. The shopper reference price may then shift in the opposite direction from the external price.

Research findings from a study in India on reference prices yielded the following inferences:[62]

1. Shoppers buying frequently purchased products use stimulus-based reference prices more often. The manner in which shoppers assess purchase price, that is, whether they use stimulus-based or memory-based reference price constructs, varies with the product category. Majority of shoppers in the frequently purchased product category use stimulus-based reference price constructs as compared to memory-based reference price constructs, while in an infrequently purchased product category, more shoppers use memory-based stimuli. The categories also differ in terms of variables that influence the construction of reference price. In case of frequently purchased products, shoppers were found to use bases that relate to the act of shopping at the store, leading to stimulus-based reference price.

2. Brand loyal shoppers use past prices as reference points. Across the two product categories, shoppers using memory-based reference price constructs show a high level of brand loyalty. This implies that a highly brand loyal shopper is more likely to compare the price of a

purchase with a past purchase price. On the other hand, shoppers employing stimulus-based reference price constructs are essentially brand switchers. Such shoppers are more inclined to seek external stimuli. The difference also lies in the order of these bases. In case of the infrequently purchased category, shoppers use the price of the specific brand as against a set of brands, as in the case of frequently purchased products.

3. Frequent shoppers use current prices as reference price points. Shoppers using stimulus-based reference price constructs shop considerably more frequently compared to shoppers using memory-based reference price constructs. Frequent shoppers are more willing to experiment with brands and thereby seek current prices of alternative offerings. Memory-based shoppers, in contrast, have a much longer inter-purchase period. In effect, infrequent shoppers primarily assess the price of a brand against the prices they have paid in the past for a similar purchase.

4. Shoppers having high purchase involvement use stimulus-based reference price constructs. Most of the shoppers using stimulus-based reference price constructs exhibit high purchase involvement. Involvement among such shoppers is uniform across the two product categories. In contrast, shoppers using memory-based reference price constructs, in both product categories, have low purchase involvement. Thus, shoppers who are highly involved in purchasing seek information on all offerings.

5. Shoppers using stimulus-based reference prices do not depend on the recall of past purchases. There is a very high correlation between the type of reference price construct used and the shoppers' recall of past purchase. Shoppers using memory-based reference price constructs would, by definition, have high recall of past purchase. In addition, shoppers using stimulus-based reference price constructs have very low recall of past purchase.

6. Willingness to expend search efforts supports stimulus-based reference price. Shoppers using stimulus-based reference price constructs show high willingness and inclination to seek information on product offerings across stores. They are particular about browsing in shops that provide adequate information on all brand offerings. These shoppers use stimulus-based reference price constructs not by default (i.e., using external stimuli only when they are available in a shop) but by choice. They seek stores that stock all brands and provide point of purchase communication.

Implications of Reference Prices

Based on the inferences discussed in the previous section, the study drew the following implications from the perspective of the retailer and the marketer.

Segmenting Shoppers   Reference prices could be an additional basis for segmenting shoppers on their price perception. This can be easily done by retailers in India as, unlike stores in developed economies, most stores in India deal in a particular product category. The store can then plan different marketing strategies for the identified segments. Stores that deal in a variety of categories would have to segment their shoppers according to the category being bought.

Formulating Pricing Strategies   Once the shoppers are profiled and it is determined that the majority of shoppers at a particular store use memory-based reference price constructs to assess the current purchase price, it would not be enough to price a brand lower than its competing brands. The price would also have to compare favourably with what has been charged in the past. To assess the relative effect of these two types of price comparisons (i.e., prices of other brands and the prices of the same brand), the brand manager should examine the price effect (i.e., the price parameter) as well as the reference price effects (i.e., the gain and loss parameters).

Designing Appropriate Promotions   Incorporating reference price effects has also been shown to be important in developing optimal promotion strategies in the retail environment. In case of shoppers who are sensitive to reference price and use experience to evaluate current prices, marketers should be concerned that shoppers who buy their brands repeatedly are the ones who are most likely to use past price information in their brand-choice decisions. If so, price promotions may be an ineffective way of targeting other brands' loyal shoppers. Further, if the majority of shoppers are found to be memory-based reference price shoppers, 'price-offs' may not be the right promotional strategy.

Identifying Relevant Value Propositions at the Retail Point   If a retailer determines that most of its shoppers use memory-based reference price constructs, then emphasis may be placed on making shopping a memorable experience (since such shoppers have high purchase recall), which would strengthen loyalty. Alternatively, if the shoppers use stimulus-based reference price constructs, they would seek extensive information on available market offerings. In such cases, the retailer would need to carry a broad assortment of brands and provide very good in-store communication.

FAIRNESS IN PRICING[63]

Fairness seems to matter greatly to consumers. It is an important source of satisfaction with purchases, and consumers seem to react quite negatively to perceived unfairness. In marketing, much of the research on fairness has focused on prices. Thaler first asserted that consumers derive utility from the fairness of a price (transaction utility) and maintained that this was judged by a comparison of the actual price with some reference price. Such reference prices appear to be influenced by a variety of factors including past prices, prices in comparable stores, perceptions of the cost of the product to the seller, etc. Recent work has broadened the perspective on price fairness to include judgements based on social comparisons between different customers' inputs and outcomes, consistent with equity theory. Overall, the existing research on price fairness fits into the broad framework of *distributive justice*, which assumes that judgements of fairness are based on the allocation of material outcomes.

It is also found that when buyers encounter price discrepancy, perceived price unfairness is affected by reference price as well as the magnitude of price discrepancy.[64]

In addition, they moderate the effect of pre-trust on perceived price unfairness. It is interesting to note that a low pre-trust is better than a high pre-trust under certain conditions. Pre-trust has a significant effect on post-trust and this effect is moderated by the magnitude of price discrepancy. However, the magnitude of price discrepancy does not have a significant effect on post-trust. Prior or pre-trust not only has a direct effect on future purchase intention but also has indirect effects through subsequent (post) trust.

IMPACT OF PRICING STRATEGY ON FORMATS

Retail formats are designed as a combination of merchandise, display, service, and price. Each of the formats uses one of these to differentiate themselves. However, over the years, as competition intensified, price became one of the most used variables to increase sales. This led to a price war among retailers of all kinds. Everyone used price and its different modifications. Discounts became almost a permanent feature in every store and in every format. This started erasing the difference between discount stores and department stores. The pressure to increase sales led to reduction in profitability and many stores faced very difficult times, entering into downward spirals. The impact of this could be felt as customers started classifying store formats based on pricing strategies such as discount, high–low, EDLP, or dollar stores. In such a scenario, a new price-based classification of store format has emerged, as shown in Fig. 13.4.

	Price	Non-price
Generalist	• Hypermarkets • Discount stores • Dollar stores	• Department stores • *Kirana*/general stores
Specialist	• Category killers • Multi-brand outlets	• Supermarkets • Boutiques • Exclusive outlets • Mutli-brand outlets

FIG. 13.4   Price-based Classification of Store Formats

SOLVED PROBLEMS

Markup

Question: A buyer for a women's department needs ₹120,000 worth of merchandise. She has already purchased 200 dresses that cost ₹180 each and has decided to retail these for ₹300 each. What markup per cent must she obtain on the remaining purchases in order to average a 54 per cent markup for the month?

Solution:

(a) Find total needs at cost

Cost = Retail price × Cost %
= 120,000 × (100 − 54%)
= 120,000 × 46% = 55,200

(b) Find retail value of the purchases
Retail = 200 × 300 = 60,000

(c) Find cost value of the purchases
Cost = 200 × 180 = 36,000

(d) Find balance on retail
Retail balance = Total retail
− Retail value of dress purchases
= 120,000 − 60,000 = 60,000

(e) Find balance at cost
Retail balance = Total cost
− Cost of dresses purchased
= 55,200 − 36,000 = 19,200

(f) Final markup per cent needed on balance
Markup % balance = (Retail balance
− Cost balance)/Retail
balance
= 60,000 − 19,200/60,000
= 40,800/60,000 = 68%

Markdown

Question: A buyer for a book and music store bought 200 CDs and priced them at ₹159.50 each. The shop sold 50 CDs at this price. The remaining CDs were marked down to ₹119.50 for a special sales event. During the sale, 85 CDs were sold. After the sale, the store re-priced the remaining CDs at ₹149.5 and sold all of them.

Determine the following:
(a) Total markdown
(b) Markdown cancellations
(c) Net rupee markdown
(d) Net markdown per cent

Solution:

(a) Total markdown (prior to sale) 150 CDs reduced from ₹159.50 to ₹119.50

Total markdown = 150 × (159.50 − 119.50)
= 150 × 40
= 6,000

(b) Markdown cancellations (after the sale) 65 CDs were re-priced to 149.50

Markdown cancellations = 65 × (119.5 − 149.5)
= 65 × 30
= 1,950

(c) Net markdown = Total markdown
− Markdown cancellations
= 6,000 − 1,950
= 4,050

(d) Markdown %

Total sales prior to sale period
= 50 CDs × 159.50 each = 7,975

Sales during the sale
= 85 CDs × 119.50 each = 10,157.50

Sales after the sale period
= 65 CDs × 149.50 each = 9,717.50

Total sales = 27,850

Net markdown %
= Net markdown/Total sales
= 4,050/27,850
= 14.54%

Effect of Markdown on Profitability

Question: For a shipment of shoes, a store had planned an initial markup of 54 per cent. The transportation cost for the shoes was 2.30 per cent. Towards the end of the month, the operating expenses are estimated to be 34.25 per cent. Loss or shrinkage is usually about 2.50 per cent for the department. No employee discounts are taken during the month. Reductions were planned to be 12.50 per cent, but the merchandise did not sell well and the buyer would like to take the additional reductions. Cash discounts are not taken either. What happens to profit if reductions are increased to 20 per cent from the initially planned 12.50 per cent?

Solution:

Value of the planned profit:

Initial markup % = Operating expense %
+ Transportation %
+ Profit % + Reductions %

Profit % = Initial markup %
− (Operating expense %
+ Transport % + Reductions %)

Reductions = Stock shortage (SS)
+ Employee discount (ED)
+ Markdowns (MD)

So

Profit % = 54% − (34.25% + 2.30% + 2.50%
+ 0% + 12.50%)
= 54% − 51.82% = 2.18%

But when actual reductions become 20%,

Actual profit % = 54% − 59.32%
= −5.32% (Loss occurs).

SUMMARY

Price is the most tangible factor based on which the customer determines the value derived from a purchase. A retailer decides on its objectives on the lines of merchandise carried, location, promotion, credit, customer services, the store image it wishes to convey, and the relevant legal constraints. Its pricing strategy must be consistent with its overall image, selection of target market, composition of retail mix, and selection of price policy. A good pricing strategy is based on the understanding of demand, cost, and competition.

Each of these orientations—demand orientation, cost orientation, and competition orientation—must be understood individually as well as jointly. Psychological pricing, markup pricing, alternative ways of computing markups, gross margins, direct product profitability, and pricing at or above the market are among the key aspects of strategy planning. When implementing a price strategy, several specific tools can be used to supplement the broad base of the strategy. Retailers should know when to use customary and variable pricing, one-price policies and flexible pricing, odd pricing, leader pricing, multiple-unit pricing, and price lining.

Retailers may be required to adjust prices to various internal and external conditions. Price adjustments include markdowns, additional markups, and employee discounts. Shoppers also use a benchmark or a reference point in assessing the value of the offers. Reference price is found to influence shopper response significantly and consistently across aggregate markets or households. Both internal and external reference price influence brand choice. Pricing policies can be framed on the basis of the reference price mechanism used by the shoppers.

NOTES

1. Dunne, Patrick M., F. Robert Lusch, and David A. Griffith 2002, *Retailing*, 4th edn, Thomson South-Western Publication, pp. 368–72.

2. Berman, Barry and Joel R. Evans 2002, *Retail Management: A Strategic Approach*, 8th edn, Prentice Hall of India, p. 169.

3. Dunne, Patrick M., F. Robert Lusch, and David A. Griffith 2002, *Retailing*, 4th edn, Thomson South-Western Publication, p. 382.

4. Berman, Barry and Joel R. Evans 2002, *Retail Management: A Strategic Approach*, 8th edn, Prentice Hall of India, p. 580.

5. Dunne, Patrick M., F. Robert Lusch, and David A. Griffith 2002, *Retailing*, 4th edn, Thomson South-Western Publication, p. 384.

6. Dunne, Patrick M., F. Robert Lusch, and David A. Griffith 2002, *Retailing*, 4th edn, Thomson South-Western Publication, p. 384.

7. Dunne, Patrick M., F. Robert Lusch, and David A. Griffith 2002, *Retailing*, 4th edn, Thomson South-Western Publication, p. 384.

8. Gabor, A. and C. Granger 1964, 'Price Sensitivity of Shoppers', *Journal of Advertising Research*, Vol. 4, December, pp. 40–4.

9. Monroe, Kent B. 1973, 'Buyers' Subjective Perception of Prices', *Journal of Marketing Research*, Vol. 10, February, pp. 70–80.

10. Rao, V. and D. Gautschi 1982, 'The Role of Price in Individual Utility Judgements: Development and Empirical Validation of Alternate Models', in McAlister L. (ed.) *Research in Marketing*, Jai Press, Greenwich.

11. Erickson, G.M. and J.K. Johansson 1985, 'The Role of Price in Multi-attribute Product Evaluation', *Journal of Shopper Research*, Vol. 12, September, pp. 195–9.

12. Compeau, L.D. and D. Grewal 1998, 'Comparative Price Advertisements: An Integrative Review', *Journal of Public Policy and Marketing*, Vol. 17, Fall, pp. 257–73.

13. Emery, F.E. 1970, 'Some Psychological Aspects of Price', in B. Taylor and G. Willis (eds) *Pricing Strategy*, Brandon System, Princeton, NJ, pp. 89–97; Monroe, Kent B. 1973, 'Buyers' Subjective Perception of Prices', *Journal of Marketing Research*, Vol. 10, February, pp. 70–80.

14. Winer, R.S. 1989, 'A Multi-Stage Model of Choice Incorporating Reference Price', *Marketing Letters*, Vol. 1, pp. 27–36.

15. Lattin, J.E. and R.E. Bucklin 1989, 'Reference Effect of Price and Promotion on Brand Choice Behaviour', *Journal of Marketing Research*, Vol. 26, August, pp. 299–310; Kalwani, M.U., C.K. Yim, H.J. Rinne, and Y. Sujita 1990, 'A Price Expectation Model of Shopper Brand Choice', *Journal of Marketing Research*, Vol. 27, August, pp. 251–61; Putler, D.S. 1992, 'Incorporating Reference Price Effects into a Theory of Shopper Choice', *Marketing Science*, Vol. 11, Summer, pp. 287–309; Kalyanraman, G. and J.D.C. Little 1994, 'An Empirical Analysis of Latitude of Price Acceptance in Shopper Packaged Goods', *Journal of Marketing Research*, Vol. 21, December, pp. 408–18.

16. Hardie, B.G.S., E.J. Johnson, and P.S. Fader 1993, 'Modelling Loss Aversion and Reference Dependence Effects on Brand Choice', *Marketing Science*, Vol. 12, Fall, pp. 378–94.

17. Winer, R.S. 1986, 'A Reference Price Model of Brand Choice for Frequently Purchased Products', *Journal of Shopper Research*, Vol. 13, September, pp. 250–6.

18. Kalwani, M.U., C.K. Yim, H.J. Rinne, and Y. Sujita 1990, 'A Price Expectation Model of Shopper Brand Choice', *Journal of Marketing Research*, Vol. 27, August, pp. 251–61.

19. Thaler, R. 1985, 'Mental Accounting and Shopper Choice', *Marketing Science*, Vol. 4, No. 3, pp. 199–214.

20. Helson, H. 1947, 'Adaptation-Level as Frame of Reference for Prediction of Psychophysical Data', *American Journal of Psychology*, Vol. 60, January, pp. 1–29.

21. Sherif, C.W. 1963, 'Social Categorisation as a Function of Latitude of Acceptance and Series Range', *Journal of Abnormal Psychology*, Vol. 67, August, pp. 148–56.

22. Medlin, D.L., M.W. Altom, and T.D. Murphy 1984, 'Given versus Induced Category Representation: Use of Prototype and Exemplar Information in Classification', *Journal of Experimental Psychology: Learning, Memory, and Cognition*, Vol. 10, July, pp. 333–52.

23. Volkmann, John 1951, 'Scales of Judgement and Their Implications for Social Psychology', in John Rohrer and Muzafer Sherif (eds), *Social Psychology at Crossroads*, Harper and Row, New York, pp. 273–94.

24. Parducci, A. 1965, 'Category Judgement: A Range-frequency Model', *Psychological Review*, Vol. 72, November, pp. 407–18.

25. Lichtenstien, D.R. and W.O. Bearden 1989, 'Contextual Influences on Perceptions of Merchant-Supplied Reference Price', *Journal of Shopper Research*, Vol. 16, June, pp. 55–66.

26. Compeau, L.D. and D. Grewal 1998, 'Comparative Price Advertisements: An Integrative Review', *Journal of Public Policy and Marketing*, Vol. 17, Fall, pp. 257–73.

27. Vanheule, M. and X. Dreze 2002, 'Measuring the Price Knowledge Shoppers Bring to the Store', *Journal of Marketing*, Vol. 66, October, pp. 72–85.

28. Biehal, G. and D. Chakravarti 1983, 'Information Accessibility as a Moderator of Shopper Choice', *Journal of Shopper Research*, Vol. 10, June, pp. 1–14.

29. Mayhew, G.E. and R.S. Winer 1992, 'An Empirical Analysis of Internal and External Reference Price Using Scanner Data', *Journal of Shopper Research*,
Vol. 19, June, pp. 62–70; Rajendaran, K.N. and G.J. Tellis 1994, 'Contextual and Temporal Components of Reference Price', *Journal of Marketing*, Vol. 58, January, pp. 22–34; Mazumdar, T. and P. Papatla 1995, 'Loyalty Differences in the Use of Internal and External Reference Prices', *Marketing Letters*, April, Vol. 6, Issue 2, pp. 111–22; Lattin, J.E. and R.E. Bucklin 1989, 'Reference Effect of Price and Promotion on Brand Choice Behaviour', *Journal of Marketing Research*, Vol. 26, August, pp. 299–310.

30. Klien, N.M. and J.E. Oglethorpe 1987, 'Cognitive Reference Points in Shopper Decision Making', in M. Wallendrof and P. Anderson (eds), *Advances in Shopper Research*, Vol. 14, Association for Shopper Research, Provo, Utah, pp. 183–7; Winer, R.S. 1986, 'A Reference Price Model of Brand Choice for Frequently Purchased Products', *Journal of Shopper Research*, Vol. 13, September, pp. 250–6.

31. Biswas, A., E.J. Wilson, and J.W. Licata 1999, 'Reference Pricing Studies in Marketing: A Synthesis of Research Results', *Journal of Business Research*, Vol. 27, No. 3, pp. 239–56; Compeau, L.D. and D. Grewal 1998, 'Comparative Price Advertisements: An Integrative Review', *Journal of Public Policy and Marketing*, Vol. 17, Fall, pp. 257–73.

32. Seawall, M.A. and M.H. Goldstein 1979, 'The Comparative Price Controversy: Shopper Perception of Catalogue Showroom Reference Price', *Journal of Marketing*, Vol. 43, Summer, pp. 85–92.

33. Sawyer, A.G. and P.H. Dickson 1990, 'The Price Knowledge and Search of Supermarket Shoppers', *Journal of Marketing*, Vol. 54, July, pp. 42–53.

34. Vanheule, M. and X. Dreze 2002, 'Measuring the Price Knowledge Shoppers Bring to the Store', *Journal of Marketing*, Vol. 66, October, pp. 72–85.

35. Conover, J.N. 1986, 'The Accuracy of Price Knowledge: Issues in Research Methodology', in Richard Lutz (ed.), *Advances in Shopper Research*, Vol. 13, Association for Shopper Research, Provo, Utah, pp. 589–93.

36. Jacobson, R. and C. Obermiller 1990, 'The Formation of Expected Future Price: A Reference Price for Forward Looking Shoppers', *Journal of Shopper Research*, Vol. 16, March, pp. 420–32.

37. Briesch, R.A., L. Krishnamurthi, T. Mazumdar, and S.P. Raj 1997, 'A Comparative Analysis of Reference

Price Model', *Journal of Shopper Research*, Vol. 24, November, pp. 202–14.

38. Thaler, R. 1985, 'Mental Accounting and Shopper Choice', *Marketing Science*, Vol. 4, No. 3, pp. 199–214; Monroe, K.B. and J.D. Chapman 1987, 'Framing Effects on Buyers' Subjective Product Evaluations', in M. Wallendrof and P. Anderson (eds), *Advances in Shopper Research*, Vol. 14, Association for Shopper Research, Provo, Utah, pp. 193–7; Monroe, K.B. 1990, 'Pricing: Making Profitable Decisions', McGraw-Hill, New York.

39. Ioannides-Demos, L.L., J.E. Ibrahim, and J.L. McNeil 2002, 'Reference Based Pricing Schemes', *Pharmaeconomics*, Vol. 20, No. 9, pp. 577–91.

40. Vaidyanathan, R., P. Aggarwal, D.R. Stem, D.D. Muehling, and U.N. Umesh 2000, 'Deal Evaluation and Purchase Intentions: The Impact of Aspirational and Market Based Internal Reference Price', *Journal of Product and Brand Management*, Vol. 9, No. 3, pp. 179–92.

41. Kalyanraman, G. and R.S. Winer 1995, 'Empirical Generalisation for Reference Price Research', *Marketing Science*, Vol. 14, Summer, pp. 161–9.

42. Biswas, A., E.J. Wilson, and J.W. Licata 1993, 'Reference Pricing Studies in Marketing: A Synthesis of Research Results', *Journal of Business Research*, Vol. 27, No. 3, pp. 239–56.

43. Kumar, V., K. Karnade, and W. Reinartz 1998, 'The Impact of Internal and External Reference Price on Brand Choices: The Moderating Role of Contextual Variables', *Journal of Retailing*, Vol. 74, No. 3, pp. 401–26.

44. Mazumdar, T. and P. Papatla 2000, 'An Investigation of Reference Price Segments', *Journal of Marketing*, Vol. 31, May, pp. 246–58.

45. Erdem, T., G. Mayhew, and B. Sun 2001, 'Understanding Reference Price Shoppers: A Within and Cross-Category Analysis', *Journal of Marketing Research*, Vol. 38, November, pp. 445–57.

46. Biswas, Pullig C., M.I. Yagci, and D.H. Dean 2002, 'Shopper Evaluation of Low Price Guarantees: The Moderating Role of Reference Price and Store Image', *Journal of Shopper Psychology*, Vol. 12, No. 2, pp. 107–18.

47. Yadav, M.S. and K. Seiders 1998, 'Is the Price Right? Understanding Contingent Processing in Reference Price Formation', *Journal of Retailing*, Vol. 74, No. 3, pp. 311–29.

48. Urbany, J.E., W.O. Bearden, and D.C. Weilbaker 1988, 'The Effect of Plausible and Exaggerated Reference Price on Shopper Perceptions and Price Research', *Journal of Shopper Research*, Vol. 15, pp. 95–110.

49. Winer, R.S. 1986, 'A Reference Price Model of Brand Choice for Frequently Purchased Products', *Journal of Shopper Research*, Vol. 13, September, pp. 250–6.

50. Putler, D.S. 1992, 'Incorporating Reference Price Effects into a Theory of Shopper Choice', *Marketing Science*, Vol. 11, Summer, pp. 287–309.

51. Greenleaf, E.A. 1995, 'The Impact of Reference Price Effects on the Profitability of Price Promotions', *Marketing Science*, Vol. 14, Winter, pp. 82–104.

52. Hollander, S.C. 1960, 'The Wheel of Retailing', *Journal of Marketing*, Vol. 25, July, pp. 37–42; Jung, A.F. 1961, 'Price Variations among Discount Houses and Other Retailers', *Journal of Retailing*, Vol. 37, Spring, pp. 13–16; Davidson, W.R. and A.F. Doody 1963, 'The Future of Discounting', *Journal of Marketing*, Vol. 27, January, pp. 36–9; Dardis, R. and L. Skow 1969, 'Price Variation for Soft Goods in Discount and Department Stores', *Journal of Marketing*, Vol. 33, April, pp. 45–9.

53. Seawall, M.A. and M.H. Goldstein 1979, 'The Comparative Price Controversy: Shopper Perception of Catalogue Showroom Reference Price', *Journal of Marketing*, Vol. 43, Summer, pp. 85–92.

54. Compeau, L.D. and D. Grewal 1998, 'Comparative Price Advertisements: An Integrative Review', *Journal of Public Policy and Marketing*, Vol. 17, Fall, pp. 257–73.

55. Kalyanraman, G. and R.S. Winer 1995, 'Empirical Generalisation for Reference Price Research', *Marketing Science*, Vol. 14, Summer, pp. 161–9.

56. Winer, R.S. 1986, 'A Reference Price Model of Brand Choice for Frequently Purchased Products', *Journal of Shopper Research*, Vol. 13, September, pp. 250–6; Greenleaf, E.A. 1995, 'The Impact of Reference Price Effects on the Profitability of Price Promotions', *Marketing Science*, Vol. 14, Winter, pp. 82–104.

57. Rajendaran, K.N. and G.J. Tellis 1994, 'Contextual and Temporal Components of Reference Price', *Journal of Marketing*, Vol. 58, January, pp. 22–34.

58. Mazumdar, T. and P. Papatla 2000, 'An Investigation of Reference Price Segments', *Journal of Marketing*,

Vol. 31, May, pp. 246–158; Erdem, T., G. Mayhew, and B. Sun 2001, 'Understanding Reference Price Shoppers: A Within and Cross-Category Analysis', *Journal of Marketing Research*, Vol. 38, November, pp. 445–57.

59. Allenby, G.M. and P.E. Rossy, 'Quality Perception and Asymmetric Switching between Brands', *Marketing Science*, Vol. 10, Summer, pp. 185–204.

60. Kumar, V., K. Karnade, and W. Reinartz 1998, 'The Impact of Internal and External Reference Price on Brand Choices: The Moderating Role of Contextual Variables', *Journal of Retailing*, Vol. 74, No. 3, pp. 401–26.

61. Vanheule, M. and X. Dreze 2002, 'Measuring the Price Knowledge Shoppers Bring to the Store', *Journal of Marketing*, Vol. 66, October, pp. 72–85.

62. Sinha, Piyush Kumar and P.V. Prasad 2004, 'Reference Price: Impact of Shopper's Behaviour at the Store', *Decision*, Vol. 31, No. 1, pp. 19–50.

63. Ashworth, Laurence and Peter R. Darke 2006, 'The Principle Matters: Antecedents and Consequences of Procedural Justice in the Context of Pricing'. *Advances in Consumer Research*, Vol. 33, Issue 1, p. 236.

64. Tripathi, Sanjeev 2010, 'Effects of Price Discrepancies, Referents for Comparison and Prior Trust in Sellers on Buyers' Perceptions of Price Unfairness, Subsequent Trust and Purchase Intention', Unpublished Thesis, Indian Institute of Management, Ahmedabad.

CONCEPT REVIEW QUESTIONS

1. What are the components of a pricing system? Explain each of them briefly.
2. What are the different pricing strategies that a retailer can use? How does a retailer decide which strategy to use?
3. Describe different bases of pricing. Enumerate the factors that would influence the decision about the most appropriate basis.
4. How is markup determined? Illustrate with an example.
5. With the help of an example, show how a markdown can be calculated.
6. What are the several ways of modifying prices? How does a retailer select them?
7. What is reference price? How does the customer form a reference price? What should the retailer do to utilize this concept?

CRITICAL THINKING QUESTIONS

1. What determines the price modification decision of a fashion retailer and a base stock retailer?
2. When can price itself be the strategy and not just an element of the retail mix?
3. How does price help position a store?
4. How can the reference price concept be used for products such as batteries, toys, menswear, children's wear, and grocery items?

PROJECTS

1. Choose a grocery store, a branded store, and a women's fashion store and visit each store thrice in a month with a gap of one week. Observe the price changes in each store.
2. Find out stores that do not exhibit prices overtly. Understand the reasons thereof.
3. Visit a store and speak to customers to find out whether they find the prices too high or low. Understand the dynamics.

14 Building Store Loyalty

LEARNING OBJECTIVES

After studying this chapter, you will be able to
- discuss the concept of loyalty and its attitudinal and behavioural dimensions
- understand store choice and patronage behaviour of customers
- delineate the drivers of loyalty and patronage
- gain an insight into the strategies used for managing loyalty programmes

INTRODUCTION

The concept of store loyalty is derived from the concept of brand loyalty, which refers to the tendency to make repeat purchases of products of the same brand. *Store loyalty* refers to the tendency to repeatedly shop at the same store for similar or other products.[1]

The concepts of loyalty and commitment are borrowed from the field of organizational behaviour (OB). There is inherently a large affective component in loyalty. Amongst other factors, loyalty has elements of trust which is built over a period of time with repeated experiences at a store and is likely to be relatively stable over a long period of time. A loyal customer would give preference to a specific store and would tend to be far more forgiving of errors of the store. There would also be a tendency to resolve any dissonance that arises from dissatisfaction by increasing the value of other attributes where the store is better or by downplaying the importance of the store's weaknesses. Loyalty can be dislodged only if there is a major dissonance.[2] Such dissonance can arise from a significant decrease in store performance or a large mismatch between changing customer expectations and store offerings. Dissonance will be tolerated only to a certain extent or threshold. Beyond that threshold, loyalty is eroded, usually in favour of another store.[3] This chapter will describe loyalty from the perspective of store choice by shoppers and will then discuss their patronage behaviour. It shall also discuss how a robust loyalty programme can be developed.

STORE CHOICE BEHAVIOUR OF SHOPPERS

Store choice is recognized as a cognitive process. It is as much an information processing behaviour as any other purchase decision. Many similarities have been found between store choice behaviour of shoppers and brand choice. The only difference is the importance of the spatial dimension. While brand choice is devoid of any geography, the choice of a store is very much influenced by location.[4]

In a study of store choice behaviour among audio equipment shoppers, it was found that the amount of pre-purchase information regarding the brand determined the type of store chosen.[5] Shoppers who had higher levels of pre-purchase information generally shopped at speciality stores, whereas shoppers with low pre-purchase information bought at department stores. This is mainly attributed to the tendency of customers to adopt a risk reduction policy with regard to their impending purchase. A store is chosen on the basis of the confidence that the customer has in the nature and quality of product and service that would be received at the store. The importance placed on the customer's familiarity with the store will depend upon the perceived risk in making an erroneous purchase and the importance of the product category to the shopper.

As an extension of the above study, the store choice problem has also been studied using the framework of diffusion of innovation propounded by Cunningham.[6] This application highlights that the perceived risk attached to a product is transferred to the store and such transfer is more likely for product categories that are not dominated by strong brands. In such cases, the store becomes a product of sorts and apparently is susceptible to the same kind of risk handling analysis technique accorded to products.

Another dimension that has been found to influence the store choice decision is the type of shopping task. A task is defined as the goal set by the shopper to resolve the needs derived out of a specific situation. Store choice is differentiated by the nature of the task.[7] The store choice is considered a decision across various tasks as described by respondents, such as 'urgent purchase', 'large quantities', 'difficult job', 'regular purchase', and 'get ideas'. In the study, the chosen stores differed in their salience rating depending on the task the shopper intended to perform.

The salience of the stores has also been found to be affected by situational factors. In one study, it was found that situational attributes such as time pressure and gift versus self-shopping can influence store choice and attribute salience.[8] It is also indicated that the situational influence needs to be evaluated for every visit and hence some shoppers may change their choice because of situation-specific drivers. These situational influences may be classified as the competitive setting, the individual's situational set, and the shopping occasion. The shopper may also evaluate each of the situations in light of the cost incurred and the utilities derived out of shopping. The study suggests that these costs can be classified as fixed and variable costs of shopping.[9] *Variable costs* are related to the basket size or the list and hence are likely to change with every trip. *Fixed costs*, such as the location of the store or the price format, would remain unchanged regardless of list size. These costs can be converted into utilities for each shopper by the store.

In a study of the two price formats—every day low price (EDLP) and high–low (HILO)—it has been found that a store can influence the choice of shoppers by enhancing the perceived utilities.[10] A concept of preference threshold has been propounded, which suggests that shoppers tend to show preference for a store depending on the threshold value allotted by the shopper.[11] It is assumed that if the perceived value is less than the threshold, the shopper may not choose the store. The threshold value for an individual customer is affected to a large extent by the image characteristics of the store.

Store choice has also been found to be dependent on the socio-economic background of consumers and their personality and past purchase experience.[12] As compared to young shoppers, elderly shoppers tend to be less price conscious and proximity of residence to store is not an important factor for them. They consider shopping as a recreational activity and thus choose a store that is perceived to be high on 'entertainment' value.[13]

The concept of positioning of stores has been captured in marketing literature over the last decade.[14] Shoppers look for and develop 'hot buttons' that help in choosing among stores. Shoppers quickly name the store that provides them with these buttons, such as 'most convenient' or 'lowest prices', hence reducing the cognitive dimension in the decision problem. Shoppers also use a combination of 'quality of staff' and 'occurrence of low prices and the frequency of promotions' in choosing a store.[15]

The role of ambience in store choice has also been found to be significant. Atmospherics play an important part in the development of retail marketing strategy.[16] Shoppers determine the value of merchandise based on monetary as well as non-monetary costs.[17] It has been found that recreation (a non-monetary value) is the major reason for visiting a regional shopping centre.[18] The shopping experience, as created by the store environment, has been found to play an important role in building store patronage. Along with the merchandise, it triggers affective reaction among shoppers.[19] It also contributes to creating store patronage intentions.[20]

Store choice is considered a dynamic decision and can be conceptualized as a problem of deciding when and where to shop.[21] The decision regarding where to shop is the traditional store location choice problem, and the one regarding when to shop is the shopping trip incidence problem relating to the timing of shopping trips. The two decision processes are correlated. Store choice has also been found to be dependent on the timing of shopping trips as consumers may go to a local store for short 'fill-in' trips and may visit a more distant grocery store for regular shopping trips.[22] Both these decisions are influenced by shopper characteristics and consumption patterns.[23]

Store Choice Behaviour of Indian Consumers

Given the Indian retailing scenario, which seems to be driven more by euphoria, there is a growing need to evaluate the true drivers of shopping behaviour in the Indian context. A large section of customers feel that the new formats add insufficient additional value, except for novelty. The key observations of a study conducted in India are as follows:[24]

1. The primary reasons for choosing a store were convenience and merchandise. Store ambience and service were subsidiary reasons.
2. Shoppers would like to minimize the effort of shopping by reducing either travel time or the time spent in the shop.
3. The gender and age of the shoppers greatly influenced the choice of store. Monthly household income did come out as a significant factor, but it was reflected more in terms of the type of products bought.
4. Shoppers in the age group of 30–50 had the highest expectations from a store and hence used many more dimensions in making choices.
5. Men gave more importance to proximity. Women tended to trade this off with the merchandise offered by the store. They were also more regular buyers of the store.
6. Ambience and facilities were more important when the shoppers spent more time in the store.
7. Brand spread in the merchandise was given greater importance in stores that not only carried the preferred brand but also gave an opportunity to compare other brands.
8. Many stores, such as cigarette and tobacco product outlets, were visited for reasons other than the product.

Table 14.1, developed on the basis of the above study, matches the identified drivers of choice across various kinds of stores with the important characteristics of the store that respondents remember after their visit. Across all categories of stores, it can be generalized that the drivers of store choice seem to be more basic in nature and tend to be utilitarian compared to the general impression about the significant features of the stores visited by the respondents. For instance, the major drivers for choosing a grocery store seem to be proximity to place of residence and the comfort level that the respondent experiences in dealing with the store owner, as measured in terms of their

TABLE 14.1   Store Choice Drivers across Stores

	What Brought You to This Store?	What Did You Observe about the Store?
Grocery Store	1. Proximity to my house 2. Have been visiting for many years 3. Personal relationship with shopkeeper	1. Variety of brands 2. Convenient timings 3. Proximity to residence
Durables	1. Quality of merchandise 2. Variety	1. In-store services were delightful 2. Trustworthiness of the store
Chemist	1. Availability of the prescription	1. Proximity 2. Service was delightful
Books, Music, Lifestyle Products	1. Ambience	1. Entertainment 2. Ambience
Apparel	1. Quality and variety of merchandise 2. Ambience	1. Store format/design 2. Ambience

Source: Sinha, Piyush Kumar, Arindam Banerjee, and Dwarika Uniyal 2002, 'Deciding Where to Buy: Store Choice Behaviour of Indian Shoppers', *Vikalpa*, No. 2, pp. 13–27.

personal relationship with the shopkeeper. However, product variety and convenient timings seem to be the primary impressions about the stores that respondents remember after visiting them. Similar variance in store choice drivers and post visit impressions were noted among other categories of stores. This comparison indicates that the stores visited by the respondents in the study were generally providing service characteristics that were not considered important by the respondents while making a choice decision. In general, dimensions such as in-store service, trustworthiness, entertainment value, and store design did not have any impact on store choice. In-store ambience was the only store environment parameter that influenced store choice in certain product categories, while all the other dimensions were associated with utilitarian benefits.

STORE LOYALTY AND PATRONAGE*

Loyalty is the prime objective that every retailer aims to achieve through its retail strategy and mix elements. Loyalty ensures patronage for a retailer. It not only provides constancy and longevity to the business but also creates an effective competitive advantage. Loyalty has two facets—attitudinal and behavioural. The attitudinal dimension demonstrates the tendency of the customer to look at the store favourably and, in many cases, to recommend it to others. The behavioural manifestation of loyalty is reflected in patronage. A consumer could display patronage behaviour and yet not be loyal. This 'spurious' loyalty is indistinguishable from intended loyalty in the short term and occurs due to price offers and heavy promotions. Deal-prone consumers usually shift to a store that offers the best price/discounts and, over a short period of time, they may exhibit the same shopping patterns as loyal customers.[25]

Store patronage is defined and measured in behavioural terms. There are five ways of looking at patronage. These are not mutually exclusive.

---

* This section is largely based on a working paper by Subhashini Kaul, titled 'A Conceptual Note on Influencing Store Loyalty: Implications for Indian Retailers', No. 2006–10–06, IIMA. (Prepared for a project under the supervision of Prof. Piyush Kumar Sinha.)

1. Do the consumers shop exclusively at a certain store?
2. Do they spend a 'larger' percentage of their total expenditure at a certain store?
3. Does a 'larger' percentage of total shopping trips to similar stores happen at a certain store?
4. Do the customers buy a 'larger' percentage of quantity/items at a certain store?
5. Are the consecutive trips made to a certain store 'significantly' more than consecutive runs made to other similar competing stores?

Loyal shoppers, as per the first definition, are so rare as to be practically negligible. One of the earliest studies in this area was conducted by Cunningham.[26] The rarity of loyal customers has been confirmed in subsequent studies.[27] Most consumers are multiple-store shoppers though differences exist across store types. Exclusive shopping at a single store is rare. In the second definition, patronage is usually measured by comparing a consumer's total weekly/monthly purchase (in monetary terms) from the store with the normal family consumption in a month. The third definition recognizes the multiple-store shopping behaviour and measures patronage as the proportion of trips made to a particular store given the average number of trips made in a given time period. The fourth definition, more applicable in studies related to frequently purchased, low-value items such as groceries, looks at the number of items purchased and not their value as an indication of patronage behaviour. The last definition presupposes that loyalty erodes fast. This idea has found application in situations where competitiveness is high, promotions and deals are constantly offered to lure shoppers, and retaining a customer is difficult given the numerous alternatives. The second, third, and fourth definitions of patronage are most commonly applied in patronage-related studies and would be more pertinent to the present Indian context.

Understanding Loyalty

The framework given in Fig. 14.1 can be used to understand and build loyalty and patronage among shoppers. Patronage has been indicated as the ultimate output. Being a behavioural dimension, this may be more relevant to retailers. The figure indicates that both intended and spurious loyalty build patronage. A store needs to identify these since the strategies to build patronage in each case would be different. Three main sets of variables have been found to have an impact on loyalty. These are store-related variables, shopper-related variables, and situation-related variables. Although there is also a possibility of interplay among these three variables, for the sake of simplicity, this interaction has been ignored in this framework.

Store-related Variables

Loyalty has been found to be affected by variables that are related to the store. Some of these variables are discussed in this section.

Trade Area and Location   Most of the work in this area stems from a model proposed by Huff.[28] Huff's model states that customer patronage is directly proportional to the utility factors given by square feet and inversely proportional to dis-utility factors given by physical distance. The limit to enhancing loyalty is essentially dependent on the limited centripetal pull of a store/shopping centre.[29] Convenience comes out as the main motive and is proposed as the primary reason for loyalty. Location-related variables are given importance in analysing both trade areas and retail patronage behaviour.[30] Studies focusing on these variables most often count the benefits of locating a store in a shopping centre/mall to increase the store's 'destination' traffic rather than just stay with the convenience pull. Many of

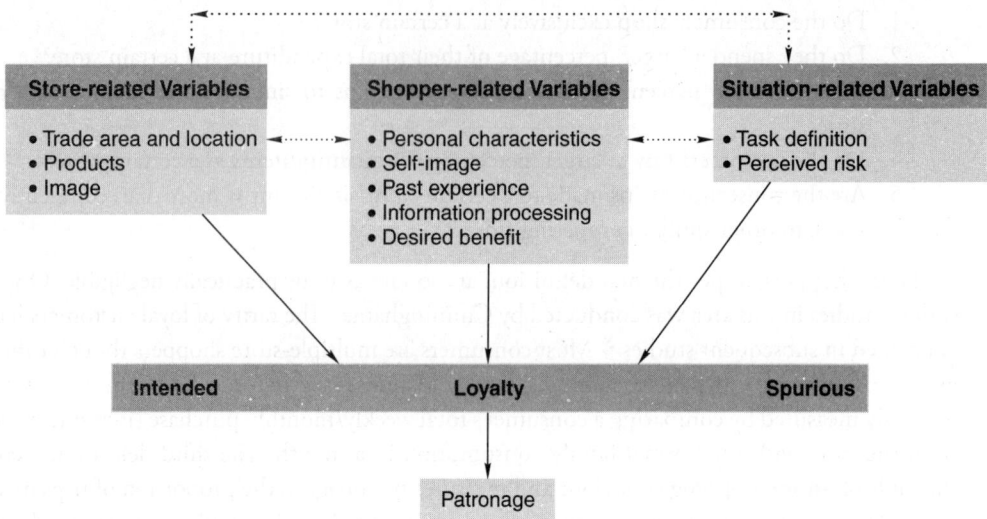

FIG. 14.1   Framework for Store Loyalty and Patronage

these studies determine shopping centre traffic more accurately than single store traffic.[31] Huff's model has subsequently been modified by introducing trade overlap areas for effects on store patronage.[32] Generically speaking, these studies have resulted in the formation of the theory of gravitational pull in the field of retailing patronage studies.

Products   Within a given trade area, the 'uniqueness of assortment' has been emphasized as a way of influencing store loyalty and patronage. In consumer priorities, assortment and variety come after convenience and price.[33] Given that consumers are favourably inclined to revisit a store where they have had positive shopping experiences (i.e., when they found something they could not find anywhere else), these studies suggest that competing stores need to differentiate themselves on the basis of the type and quality of assortment offered. The emphasis here is on tailoring the environmental cues using retail mix elements to foster loyalty.

One of the commonly used strategies in this regard has been to develop store or private labels. Consumers have distinct perceptions of national and local brands vis-à-vis the retail private store brands. Categories such as paper, plastic and wraps, and food products have high penetration of private brands. The lowest share is observed in the case of cosmetics and baby foods. In India, private brands are found in more than 50 per cent of the stores. Categories such as grocery and washing products show a higher presence of such brands.[34] It has been observed that the impact of store brands on consumer loyalty is lower in product categories where the 'quality believability' of national brands is stronger.

In some categories, brand names become more important online, whereas in some others this does not play a significant role, depending on the extent of information available to consumers. Brand names are more valuable when information on fewer attributes is available online. Sensory search attributes, particularly visual cues about the product (e.g., paper towel design), have a lower impact and factual information (i.e., non-sensory attributes, such as the fat content of margarine) has a higher impact on the online choices. Price sensitivity is higher online, but this is due to online promotions being stronger signals of price discounts. The combined effect of price and promotion on choice is weaker online than offline.[35]

Store Image   The image of a store has been found to drive loyalty. The more positive the store image, the greater is the degree of loyalty. Several studies report direct linkages between store image and intensity of store loyalty.[36] Store image reflects shoppers' perception of a store in terms of functional and psychological attributes. These can also be classified as tangible and intangible attributes. The tangible attributes of a store, such as merchandise, location, salespeople, and displays, are explicit and observable. The intangible aspects, such as ambience, co-shoppers, and other psycho-social factors, are difficult to measure and hence manage.[37] Retail literature also discusses the congruence between self-image and store image. Studies show that this congruence leads to loyalty. Shoppers select cues from the store environment and draw inferences about the characteristics of a typical shopper of the store. They then compare this image inference with their own self-image and build an attitude towards the store.[38]

Store image is also affected by the tenant mix. Malls with anchor stores tend to absorb the image of the anchor stores. A mall with a department store as an anchor reflects an image of high quality merchandise and customer service. A mall with a price format store as an anchor has an image of a lower price low service mall.[39] It has also been found that shopping at an upscale mall is more likely to create high level of self-congruity. Shoppers belonging to high economic strata are more likely to perceive stores housed in a downscale mall to have a lower quality image.[40] The study propounds that store image should be seen as a result of an interaction between the mall image, socio-economic status of shoppers, and store type.

Shopper-related Variables

Several factors, such as the age, income, and social class of the shopper, have been found to influence retail patronage decisions.[41] The orientation of the shopper also impacts the preference of a store. Several studies have found a correlation between shopping orientations and lifestyle with store loyalty and preference for stores. It has been found that shoppers seeking more hedonic gratification from shopping tend to patronize 'new' format stores that focus on experiential marketing and offer better ambience and service.[42] Shopping orientation correlates differently with the information mix elements, varying with source, source credibility, and preference for a source by some consumers and usage of such information.[43]

The aspect of congruity between the retail mix elements as designed by the retailer and the self-image/self-concept of the consumer has received much attention. Research has shown that the greater the congruence between self-image and store image, the greater is the probability that the customer is loyal.[44] It has also been found that if retail mix elements are in congruence with the desired benefits, it results in customer loyalty.[45] There is a direct linkage between personal values and desired consumer benefits. Past experience with the outlet has also emerged as one of the major drivers of loyalty. It acts as an influencer in forming expectations about desired benefits from purchasing at a store.[46] A consumer's selection of a store is not completely random. The more recent the purchase experience and the more frequent the visits to the store, the more is the likelihood of repurchasing that product in that store.[47]

Several theories can be applied to study information processing by consumers. One set of theories assumes that evaluation criteria are considered simultaneously. This theory states that consumers do not distinguish between objective and subjective evaluation criteria. They tend to use both simultaneously when arriving at a decision.[48] Another set of theories holds that the processing happens sequentially—first there are certain factors used to make a choice among clusters and then, within the chosen cluster, other parameters are used for decision-making.[49] It is generally agreed that as dimensions of comparison among stores increase, and the consumer has to process vast amounts of information before making a choice, the hierarchical process becomes more relevant.[50]

The third set of theories states that consumers use a limited set of evaluative criteria when making a choice and that this varies depending on personality, context, and product. To assess store perception on attributes that are meaningless to consumers could be misleading to a retailer. These theories draw significantly from automatic cognitive information processing models and the threshold model of consumer behaviour and examine how attitude leads to consumer behaviour/patronage.[51]

Situation-related Variables

Another set of variables that has been found to have an impact on loyalty consists of situational factors. These factors include task definition, level of involvement, shopping orientation, and usage of information. These are manifested in the task definition by the shopper and the involvement with shopping. These indicate the intensity of need and the comfort of the shopper in taking a purchase decision. The store choice has been found to depend on buying situations that differ with the level of involvement. Shopping orientation correlates differently with the information mix elements varying with source, source credibility, and preference for a source by some consumers, and usage of such information. The usage of information and attitude change depending on the product and the context.[52] The relative importance of information sources differs by level of product-specific buying experiences. Thus, a consumer segment identified as using a highly complex cognitive process of decision-making for a product could exhibit significant deviations for the same product at a different store.[53]

Managing Shopper Loyalty

Most retailers initiate loyalty programmes. These programmes aim at delivering higher value to members as compared to non-member shoppers. Exhibit 14.1 shows an example of a loyalty programme provided by Shoppers Stop. It has been established that it is cheaper to retain existing customers as compared to acquiring new ones. It is assumed that existing shoppers are satisfied with the store and contribute a higher share to the store's revenues. Unfortunately, this is not true in all cases. In a study of a loyalty programme of a particular retailer, it was found that more than half of its members were not satisfied with the store and most of its business came from a handful of members.

There is also a debate on the proportion of revenue that a store should accrue out of its members of the loyalty programme. A drugstore found that about two-thirds of its sales were coming from its loyalty programme members as compared to other stores where the share stood at one-third of revenues. Although the figure is heartening, it raises a question as to whether the store is lagging in acquiring new shoppers.

It should also be kept in mind that customer relationship management (CRM) and loyalty programmes are not synonymous. A good CRM practice does not always require a loyalty programme. A retailer needs to assess its loyalty programme based on the objectives it wants to achieve. Similarly, a loyalty programme is not a guarantee for good CRM practices by a store.

A retailer should ask the following questions before embarking on a loyalty programme to make sure that its members are satisfied and they contribute to the store's revenues.

Is a Loyalty Programme Needed for My Store?   It is not necessary that every retailer should run a loyalty programme. It is dependent on the company's approach to customer relationship, the importance of retaining customers, and the operational issues related to the programme. A retailer can plan to have different levels of relationships with its customers. Each of these levels, as depicted in Table 14.2,[54] defines

EXHIBIT 14.1   Example of a Loyalty Programme

Shoppers Stop—First Citizen

Benefits	Classic Moments	Silver Edge	Golden Glow
First Citizenship Membership ₹150	₹150	–	–
First Citizen Points (or net purchase)	1 Reward point for every ₹100 purchased	1 Reward point for every ₹50 purchased	1 Reward point for every ₹34 purchased
Extra Reward Points on Stop!, Life, and Kashish (Private Brands)	–	1%	2%
Programme Partners Reward Points	0.25%	0.50%	1%
Associate Card	₹100	Upto 2: ₹100	2 Free; 3rd ₹100
Regular Updates	Yes	Yes	Yes
Free Parking*	Yes#	Yes#	Yes
Reserved Parking*	–	–	Yes
Valet Parking*	Yes	Yes	Yes
Exclusive Cash Counters	Yes	Yes	Yes
Home Delivery of Alterations*	–	–	Yes
Exclusive Previews of Merchandise and Sale	Yes	Yes	Yes
Free First Update	–	–	**Yes**
Out-store Offers	Yes	Yes	Yes
In-store Offers	Yes	Yes	Yes
Exclusive In-store and Out-store Offers	–	–	Yes

* Conditions apply. Subject to availability.
\# Parking charges reimbursable against purchases at Shoppers Stop only.
Source: http://www.shoppersstop.com

the kind of association the retailer would have with its customers and hence the need and expanse of the loyalty programme. The first level of the relationship is totally based on transaction—every time such customers visit the store, they are treated as new customers. A store whose major customer segment consists of such a type would hardly benefit from loyalty programmes. Loyalty programmes should be considered only when both the customers and the store want to have a higher level of relationship. Similarly, stores which depend on transient customers would find that the cost of acquiring new

TABLE 14.2 Levels of Relationships

Level	Bond	Orientation	Primary Marketing Element	Sustained Competitive Advantage
One	Financial	Customer	Price	Low
Two	Financial and social	Client	Personalized communication	Medium
Three	Financial, social, and structural	Advocate	Service delivery	High

customers is lower than that of retaining them. Online consumers tend to exhibit a higher degree of state dependence compared to the effects of current marketing activities.[55] In other words, past purchase outcomes appear to have a greater impact on online consumers than the impact of current promotions. This is likely due to some of the features available in online stores, such as personal shopping lists and records of previous orders, which may train consumers to be more reliant on past purchases when making current purchase decisions and thus make them more state dependent. This is the key reason behind the finding that loyalty promotions are more profitable online than offline; whereas competitive promotions are more profitable offline than online. Conversely, if the impact of past purchases is held constant, online consumers can be more or less responsive to current price promotions depending on the product category. Hence, they would not find loyalty programmes beneficial. Stores must also recognize that loyalty programmes do not just translate into creating a database of customers. They involve major investments in infrastructure and operations. While a store can manage with a limited infrastructure base, the operation requires continuous attention to keep the programme relevant.

Is the Programme Related to Corporate Strategy?　Unless the loyalty programme is integral to the store's strategy, the store would simply go through the motion without achieving the fullest benefits while adding to its operational costs. There is a need to link the programme to the achievement of the corporate objective and to define the role it plays in shaping the corporate strategy. A loyalty programme is more useful in situations where it is possible to generate more value out of existing customers. This would depend upon the potential that exists with each store customer and the share that the store has been able to garner. It can be argued that since a store mostly operates within a limited catchment area, success would depend on extracting more value out of the shoppers in the restricted area, and the purchase volume and frequency would have a very important role to play. For instance, when a household purchases grains or cereals for its yearly requirements, every purchase is new and past knowledge about a store might not play a dominant role in decision-making. The store may be visited, but largely for gathering information, before a final decision is made. The repeat as well as referral sale in case of such purchases would not come out of the efforts of the loyalty programme but by delivering the desired value.

What are the Objectives of the Programme?　A large number of retailers simply join the bandwagon and start a loyalty programme. Some find it fanciful and many start these programmes because the competitors or most large retailers follow such practices. When a loyalty programme is sought by its members for the discounts and price-offs that are also available to non-members, it stops being a strategic tool. Like any marketing programme, it is essential for the store to set objectives that are simple, measurable, achievable, reviewable, and transparent (SMART).

Two sets of objectives are available to the stores—sales-linked and attitude-linked. In order to achieve the sales-linked objectives, the store would set a target of sales to be achieved from the members of the programme. This would be operationalized in terms of (i) the share of requirement of individual member customers and (ii) the contribution of the programme to the total store sales.

While, in the former situation, the marketing effort is targeted at individual customers, in the latter case, the store would strike a balance between acquiring new customers and marketing to the existing customers. Achieving a balance between acquiring new customers and retaining existing ones is crucial even when existing customers contribute a large share of the store's revenues. For instance, when the loyalty programme contributes a major share of the total sales of the store, it is a remarkable performance, as most programmes do not usually contribute more than forty per cent of sales. However, it also raises a few concerns—the store may not be acquiring new customers, or, worse, its competitors may be weaning away new customers, especially in a growing market such as India.

The other set of objectives relates to the change that the programme would bring about in the attitude of the member customers. There are certain fallacies in the assumptions about loyalty programme customers: (a) that members of loyalty programmes are always satisfied customers, and (b) that they would definitely increase their purchase with the passage of time or bring referrals. A store needs to work continuously on these customers—they cannot just be taken for granted. It has to develop strategies to ensure that the store members have a favourable attitude towards the store and that they recommend the store to others. A continuous tracking of attitudes would be required in order to elevate the shoppers from buyers to advocates.

When a first-time customer show a high probability of being a customer again, it would be profitable for the retailer to take different positions in the market, where one firm may offer the loyalty programme and another may resort to low price as the competitive strategy. This asymmetric equilibrium enables the firms to create segmentation across the purchase occasions and thereby earn higher profits for both.[56]

Do I Have the Required Resources? Loyalty management is a resource-heavy effort. Unfortunately, the most commonly used connotation of 'resource' is information technology. This has given such programmes a technology rather than a marketing perspective. A store must build the competence of managing relationships to make them relevant and fruitful, besides building the infrastructure for maintaining customer information. The competence has to be built in terms of understanding relationships, giving them meaning, making them mutually beneficial, and determining when to terminate the relationships. This requires resources in terms of people, communication, and systems for evaluation. Stores also need to create the necessary organizational structure and processes to escalate and link the information from the programme to the top management for decision-making.

How am I Going to Communicate with Shoppers? A store needs to decide on the basic objective of communicating with its customers. It has to decide whether its communication plan would simply update customer information or strive to make customers more aware about upcoming offers, thereby making their shopping experience more rewarding. There can be no better alternative than loyalty programmes where the communication is focused in terms of objectives as well as targets. This requires two processes that have to operate continuously—(i) updating of customer information and (ii) communication with the shoppers. The former process would generate information to determine the status of shoppers and the second would help in developing the communication plans. Many loyalty programmes are launched with much fanfare but soon they lose their charm and are relegated to a junk mail generation exercise. A store has to develop a long-term perspective and draw up communication plans for the foreseeable future. A crucial role in this regard is played by customer feedback systems. It has been proven that successful feedback systems do not operate by their mere existence; stores need to elicit responses, act on them, and complete the communication loop by informing members and non-members of the actions taken and results achieved.

Would My Programme be Relevant in the Longer Term? It is a challenge to keep customers intrigued as they become progressively more demanding. A store needs to continuously analyse the data of members to understand trends and predict the behaviour of shoppers. The behavioural patterns need to be linked to the strategies undertaken by the store and its competitors to understand causal relationships. This information can then be utilized by the store to develop strategies for delivering enhanced value to members by segmenting them into groups with different attitudes and behaviour regarding purchases from the store. It is also necessary to develop a process that creates new offers that add value to the store as well as the members. Although most offers are sales-linked, stores should also make an effort to study consumer behaviour, preferences, and the associations with the store. Exclusivity is the key to loyalty programme success. Members must derive value that is continually higher and more useful than that available to non-members.

Observations on Consumer Loyalty Behaviour

It is observed that customers who spend heavily or are more frequent enroll in a store's loyalty programme earlier, buying behaviour changes only slightly after buyers join the programme, and small changes in loyalty appear to erode 6–9 months after buyers join.[57]

Non-redeemers, compared to redeemers, visit stores less often and spend less, suggesting lower involvement with, and lower value to, the retailer. Individual redemption behaviour and the use of points to obtain different products indicate different aspects of redemption, implying that it would appear to have different meanings to different consumers or even the same consumer at different times. The most valuable customers tend to balance the value of redemption events against the frequency of events; they seem to be highly engaged in the scheme and maximize this by trading off value and frequency based on a variety of reasons and drivers. Customers who use the scheme in a more traditional way 'harvest' high-value items, involving a form of 'saving' for high-value items in a manner consistent with windfall gains. The high spenders do not tend to serially redeem the highest value items. Consumers tend to use the aspects of the scheme design to create their own redemption behaviour. Planned behaviour focused on hedonic items tends to be interrupted by impulse redemption on items both for utilitarian and hedonic purposes. The mood of the consumer is important both before and after redemption. Aspects of positive feelings towards the retailer are encouraged by the scheme and redemption, and there is some evidence of behaviour change to enhance collection of points and thus rewards.[58]

SUMMARY

Customer loyalty is crucial to the success of a store since the catchment area of a store is limited and the business can survive only when more value is derived out of every customer. This entails understanding the store choice and loyalty behaviour of customers.

Store choice has been found to be a risk and effort minimization strategy on the part of the customer. This makes a store subject to a catchment area from which most of its customers would come. In order that a store is chosen by the customers on a regular basis, it is necessary for the store to identify the drivers of choice. The three main drivers are merchandise, location, and price. However, there are retailers that have become destination stores due to some parameters in which they excel and get to be known for. Price and hedonic experience are two factors that help a store draw its customers from a longer distance.

It has been found that loyalty and patronage behaviour are affected mostly by store characteristics, shopper characteristics, and situational variables. It is necessary to understand that loyalty has two dimensions—attitudinal and behavioural. Patronage is the behavioural manifestation. Loyalty may be intended or spurious. Shoppers need to be classified on these two dimensions so that their loyalty status can be determined and appropriate strategies can be developed to ensure sustained patronage. A store would

have to assess these on a continuous basis and ensure that the attitude and behaviour of its customers are favourable.

A successful loyalty programme aims at serving the needs of each of the customer segments differently. Using a mass marketing programme, as is generally done for acquiring customers, can be fatal. Retailers need to make the loyalty programme integral to their business strategy and devote resources for it. It cannot be taken as just another marketing communication exercise. A retailer needs to assess its loyalty programme based on the objectives it wants to achieve.

NOTES

1. Osman, M.Z. 1993, 'A Conceptual Model of Retail Image Influences on Loyalty Patronage Behaviour', *International Review of Retail Distribution and Consumer Research*, Vol. 2, pp. 133–48.

2. Reynolds, F.D., W.R. Darden, and W.S. Martin 1974, 'Developing an Image of the Store Loyal Customer', *Journal of Retailing*, Vol. 50, pp. 73–84.

3. Anderson, R.E. 1973, 'Consumer Dissatisfaction: The Effect of Disconfirmed Expectancy of Perceived Product Performance', *Journal of Marketing Research*, Vol. 10, February, pp. 38–44.

4. Fotheringham, A. Stewart 1988, 'Consumer Store Choice and Choice Set Definition', *Marketing Science*, Summer, Vol. 7, No. 3, pp. 299–310; Meyer, J. Robert and Thomas C. Eagle 1982, 'Context-Induced Parameter Instability in a Disaggregate-Stochastic Model of Store Choice', *Journal of Marketing Research*, February, Vol. 19, pp. 62–71.

5. Dash, Joseph F., Leon G. Schiffman, and Conrad Berenson 1976, 'Risk and Personality-related Dimensions of Store Choice', *Journal of Marketing*, Vol. 40, January, pp. 32–9.

6. Hisrich, Robert D., Ronald J. Dornoff, and Jerome B. Kernan 1972, 'Perceived Risk in Store Selection', *Journal of Marketing Research*, November, Vol. 9, pp. 435–9.

7. Kenhove, Patrick Van, Kristof De. Wulf, and Walter Van Waterschoot 1999, 'The Impact of Task Definition on Store-Attribute Saliences and Store Choice', *Journal of Retailing*, Vol. 75, No. 1, pp. 125–37.

8. Mattson, Bruce E. 1982, 'Situational Influences on Store Choice', *Journal of Retailing*, Fall, Vol. 58, No. 3, pp. 46–58.

9. Bell, David R., Teck-Hua Ho, and C.S. Tang 1998, 'Determining Where to Shop: Fixed and Variable Cost of Shopping', *Journal of Marketing Research*, Vol. 35, August, pp. 352–69.

10. Tang, C.S., David R. Bell, and Teck-Hua Ho 2001, 'Store Choice and Shopping Behaviour: How Price Format Works', *California Management Review*, Winter, Vol. 43, No. 2, pp. 56–74.

11. Malhotra, Naresh K. 1983, 'A Threshold Model of Store Choice', *Journal of Retailing*, Summer, Vol. 59, No. 2, pp. 3–21.

12. Dodge, H. Robert and Harry H. Summer 1969, 'Choosing between Retail Stores', *Journal of Retailing*, Fall, Vol. 45, No. 3, pp. 11–21.

13. Lumpkin, James R., Barnett A. Greenberg, and Jac. L. Goldstucker 1985, 'Marketplace Needs of the Elderly: Determinant Attributes and Store Choice', *Journal of Retailing*, Summer, Vol. 61, No. 2, pp. 75–105.

14. Woodside, Arch G., Trappey, III, and J. Randolph 1992, 'Finding out Why Customers Shop Your Store and Buy Your Brand: Automatic Cognitive Processing Models of Primary Choice', *Journal of Advertising Research*, November–December, pp. 59–78.

15. Hutcheson, Graeme D. and L. Mutinho 1998, 'Measuring Preferred Store Satisfaction Using Consumer Choice Criteria as a Mediating Factor',

Journal of Marketing Management, Vol. 14, pp. 705–19.

16. Kotler, Philip 1973, 'Atmospherics as a Marketing Tool', *Journal of Retailing*, Vol. 49, Winter, pp. 48–64.

17. Zeithaml, V. 1988, 'Consumer Perception of Price, Quality and Value: A Means-End Model and Synthesis of Evidence', *Journal of Marketing*, Vol. 52, July, pp. 2–22.

18. Treblanche, Nic S. 1999, 'The Perceived Benefit Derived from Visits to a Super Regional Shopping Centre', *South African Journal of Business*, Vol. 30, No. 4, pp. 141–6.

19. Baker, J., D. Grewal, and Levy 1992, 'An Experimental Approach to Making Retail Store Environmental Decisions', *Journal of Retailing*, Vol. 68, Winter, pp. 445–60.

20. Baker, J., D. Grewal, A. Parasuraman, and B. Glenn 2002, 'The Influence of Multi-Store Environmental Clues on Perceived Merchandise Value and Patronage Intentions', *Journal of Marketing*, Vol. 66, April, pp. 120–41.

21. Leszczyc, Peter, T.L. Popkowski, and Ashish Sinha 2000, 'Consumer Store Choice Dynamics: An Analysis of the Competitive Market Structure for Grocery Stores', *Journal of Retailing*, Vol. 76, No. 3, pp. 323–45.

22. Kahn, B. and D.D. Schmittlein 1989, 'Shopping Trip Behaviour: An Empirical Study', *Marketing Letters*, Vol. 1, No. 1, pp. 55–69.

23. Leszczyc, Peter and J.P. Harry, Timmermans, 1979, 'Store Switching Behaiviour', Marketing Letter, Vol. 8, No. 2, pp. 193–204; Kim, B. and Kyungdo Park 1997, 'Studying Patterns of Grocery Shopping Trips', *Journal of Retailing*, Vol. 73, No. 4, pp. 501–17.

24. Sinha, Piyush Kumar, Arindam Banerjee, and Dwarika Uniyal 2002, 'Deciding Where to Buy: Store Choice Behaviour of Indian Shoppers', *Vikalpa*, No. 2, pp. 13–27.

25. Lichtenstein, Donald R., Scot Burton, and Richard G. Netemeyer 1997, 'An Examination of Deal-Proneness across Sales Promotion Types: A Consumer Segmentation Perspective', *Journal of Retailing*, Vol. 73, No. 2, pp. 282–97.

26. Cunningham, R.M. 1961, 'Customer Loyalty to Store and Brand', *Harvard Business Review*, Vol. 39, pp. 127–37.

27. Keng, Kau Ah and A.S.C. Ehrenberg 1984, 'Patterns of Store Choice', *Journal of Marketing Research*, Vol. 21, November, pp. 399–409.

28. Huff, David L. 1964, 'Defining and Estimating a Trade Area', *Journal of Marketing*, Vol. 18, July, pp. 34–8.

29. Applebaum, William 1966, 'Methods for Determining Store Trade Areas, Market Penetration and Potential Sales', *Journal of Marketing Research*, Vol. 3, May, pp. 127–41.

30. Hubbard, Raymond 1978, 'A Review of Selected Factors Conditioning Consumer Travel Behaviour', *Journal of Consumer Research*, 5 June, pp. 1–21.

31. Gautschi, David A. 1981, 'Specification of Patronage Models for Retail Centre Choice', *Journal of Marketing Research*, 18 May, pp. 162–74.

32. Bucklin, Louis P. 1971, 'Trade Area Boundaries: Some Issues in Theory and Methodology', *Journal of Marketing Research*, Vol. VIII, February, pp. 30–7.

33. Arnold, Stephen J., Tae H. Ourn, Tigert, and J. Douglas 1983, 'Determining Attributes in Retail Patronage: Seasonal, Temporal, Regional and International Comparisons', *Journal of Marketing Research*, Vol. 20, May, pp. 149–57; Craig, Samuel C., Avijit Ghosh, and Sara McLafferty 1984, 'Models of Retail Location Process: A Review', *Journal of Retailing*, Vol. 60, Spring, pp. 5–26; Louviere, Jordan J. and Gary J. Gaeth 1987, 'Decomposing the Determinants of Retail Facility Choice Using the Method of Hierarchical Information Integration: A Supermarket Illustration', *Journal of Retailing*, Vol. 63, Spring, pp. 25–48.

34. *Business Today*, 26 October 2003, 'Retail: The Power of Private Label', An ACNielsen Survey.

35. Degeratu, Alexandru M., Arvind Rangaswamy, and Jianan Wu 2000, 'Consumer Choice Behaviour in Online and Traditional Supermarkets: The Effects of Brand Name, Price, and Other Search Attributes', *International Journal of Research in Marketing*, Vol. 17, Issue 1, pp. 55–78.

36. Kunkel, John H. and Leonard L. Berry 1968, 'A Behavioural Conception of Retail Image', *Journal of Marketing*, Vol. 32, October, pp. 21–7; Korgaonkar, P.K., D. Lund, and B. Price 1985, 'A Structural Equations Approach toward Examination of Store Attitude and Store Patronage Behaviour', *Journal of Retailing*, Vol. 61, Summer, pp. 39–60; Reynolds F.D., W.R. Darden, and W.S. Martin 1974,

'Developing an Image of the Store Loyal Customer', *Journal of Retailing*, Vol. 50, pp. 73–84.

37. Martineau Pierre 1958, 'The Personality of Retail Store', *Harvard Business Review*, Vol. 26, pp. 47–55.

38. Joseph, Sirgy M., Dhruv Grewal, and Tamara Mangleburg 2000, 'Retail Environment, Self-image Congruence and Retail Patronage—An Integrated Model and a Research Agenda', *Journal of Business Research*, Vol. 49(2), pp. 127–38.

39. Kirkup, M.H. and Rafiq Mohammad 1994, 'Managing Tenant Mix in New Shopping Centres', *International Journal of Retail and Distribution Management*, Vol. 22(6), pp. 29–37.

40. Chebal, J., M.J. Sirgy, and V. St-James 2006, 'Upscale Image Transfer from Malls to Store: A Self-image Congruence Explanation', *Journal of Business Research*, Vol. 59, pp. 12, 88–96.

41. Moore, Charles Thomas and Joseph Barry Mason 1969, 'A Research Note on Major Retail Centre Patronage', *Journal of Marketing*, July, p. 61.

42. Sinha, Piyush Kumar 2003, 'Shopping Orientation in the Evolving Indian Market', *Vikalpa*, Vol. 28, No. 2, April–June, pp. 13–22.

43. Moschis, George P. 1976, 'Shopping Orientations and Consumer Uses of Information', *Journal of Retailing*, Vol. 52, No. 2, Summer, pp. 61–70.

44. Pathak, D.S., W.J.E. Crissy, and R.W. Sweitzer 1974, 'Customer Image versus the Retailers' Anticipated Image', *Journal of Retailing*, Vol. 50, Winter, pp. 21–8, 116; McClure, P.J. and J.K. Ryans Jr. 1968, 'Differences between retailers' and consumers' perceptions', *Journal of Marketing Research*, 5 February, pp. 35–40; Dornoff, Ronald J. and Ronald L. Tatham 972, 'Congruence Between Personal Image and Store Image', *Journal of the Market Research Society*, Vol. 14, pp. 45–52.

45. Osman, M.Z. 1993, 'A Conceptual Model of Retail Image Influences on Loyalty Patronage Behaviour', *International Review of Retail Distribution and Consumer Research*, Vol. 2, pp. 133–48.

46. Guttman, J. 1990, 'Adding Meaning to Values by Directly Assessing Value-benefit Relationships', *Journal of Business Research*, No. 20, March, pp. 153–60.

47. Aaker, David A. and J. Morgan Jones 1971, 'Modeling Store Choice Behaviour', *Journal of Marketing Research*, Vol. VIII, February, pp. 38–42.

48. Hirschman, Elizabeth C., and S. Krishnan 1981, 'Subjective and Objective Criteria in Consumer Choice: An Examination of Retail Patronage Criteria', *Journal of Consumer Affairs*, Summer, Vol. 15, No. 1, pp. 115–27.

49. Fotheringham, Stewart A. 1988, 'Consumer Store Choice and Choice Set Definition', *Marketing Science*, Vol. 7, No. 3, Summer, pp. 299–310.

50. Black, William C. 1984, 'Choice-set Definition in Patronage Modeling', *Journal of Retailing*, Vol. 60, No. 2, Summer, pp. 63–85.

51. Kau, Paul and Lowell Hill 1972, 'A Threshold Model of Purchasing Decisions', *Journal of Marketing Research*, Vol. 9, August, pp. 264–70; Malhotra, Naresh K. 1983, 'A Threshold Model of Store Choice', *Journal of Retailing*, Vol. 59, No. 2, pp. 3–21; Pokowski, L., Timmermans, and J.P. Harry 1997, 'Store Switching Behaviour', *Marketing Letters*, Vol. 8, No. 2, pp. 193–204.

52. Moschis, G.P. 1976, 'Shopping Orientations and Consumer Uses of Information', *Journal of Retailing*, Vol. 52, No. 2, pp. 61–70, 93.

53. Kline, Barbara and Wagner, Janet 1994, 'Information Sources and Retail Buyer Decision-making: The Effect of Product-specific Buying Experience', *Journal of Retailing*, Vol. 70, No. 1, Winter, pp. 75–88.

54. Berry, L.L. and A. Parasuraman 1991, 'Marketing Services: Competing through Quality', p. 137.

55. Zhang, Jie and Michel Wedel 2009, 'The Effectiveness of Customized Promotions in Online and Offline Stores', *Journal of Marketing Research*, Vol. XLVI, pp. 190–206.

56. Singh, Siddharth S., Dipak C. Jain, and Trichy V. Krishnan, 'Customer Loyalty Programs: Are They Profitable', *Management Science*, Vol. 54, No. 6, June 2008, pp. 1205–11.

57. Meyer-Waarden, Lars and Christophe Benavent 2009, 'Grocery Retail Loyalty Program Effects: Self-selection or Purchase Behaviour Change?', *Academy of Marketing Science*, Vol. 37, pp. 345–58.

58. Smith, Andrew and Leigh Sparks 2009, 'Reward Redemption Behaviour in Retail Loyalty Schemes', *British Journal of Management*, Vol. 20, pp. 204–18.

CONCEPT REVIEW QUESTIONS

1. Define loyalty and explain how it is related to patronage. Describe the drivers of both.
2. Describe a model of store choice and its impact on loyalty.
3. What constitutes a good loyalty programme? What steps are needed to make it successful?
4. How can a customer be loyal and still not patronize a store? How would you increase purchases by such customers?

CRITICAL THINKING QUESTION

Loyalty

	High	Low
Patronage High		
Low		

Look at the matrix given here. Suggest strategies to manage customers in each of the quadrants.

PROJECTS

1. Meet about ten customers each at a *kirana* store, supermarket, hypermarket, lifestyle store, and an exclusive branded store. Identify loyalty patterns and their drivers.
2. Talk to ten customers and find out whether they have shifted their purchases across different stores, especially with the advent of new formats. Discuss the reasons for doing so.
3. Visit a store that has redesigned or repositioned recently. Check whether the customer profile has changed. If it has not changed, find out why this exercise was taken up by the store.

CASE STUDY

Crossword—Customer Relationship Management[1]

In the morning of 15 January 2005, Sriram sat in his office in Mumbai awaiting Aniyan and Balaji. Aniyan had joined Crossword about nine months ago and was in charge of its operations. Balaji looked after the Book Rewards Programme (BRP)—the customer loyalty programme of the store chain. Sriram had received the customer relationship assessment survey report that was conducted three months ago. While waiting for his colleagues, his thoughts started drifting and his face broke into a smile as he thought about the past few years. It seemed like yesterday, when he and his wife Anita, along with a young team for India Book House Limited, founded Crossword with the vision of revolutionizing the concept of book retailing in India. The first Crossword store was opened in October 1992 at Mahalaxmi,[2] Mumbai. The chain was later bought by K. Raheja Corporation, which also owned Shoppers Stop, India's leading lifestyle department store chain. Within two years of starting, Crossword had featured in *Advertising Age International*, USA, as one of the marketing superstars, and *The Bookseller*, UK, had described it as being on the cutting edge of retailing in India. He was

---

1. Case prepared by Prof. Piyush Kumar Sinha and Ms Vandana Sood, Indian Institute of Management Ahmedabad. The case is prepared as a basis for class discussion rather than to illustrate either effective or ineffective handling of an administrative situation. Copyright © 2005 by the Indian Institute of Management Ahmedabad.

2. An upper strata locality

happy with the report that Crossword was perceived as the country's leading bookstore with a better image than all other book retailers on all parameters. However, the BRP was an area of concern. The programme had more than 60,000 members, but the number of active BRP members was only 25,000. A re-activation was urgently required for the survival of the BRP programme. He had asked Aniyan and Balaji to assess the factors causing this and to suggest measures for improving the BRP programme. His reverie was interrupted with a knock on the door. Aniyan and Balaji entered the office with the much awaited plan.

The Company

In 2005, Crossword had a turnover of about ₹590 million.[3] Its nearest rival was a Chennai-based retailer with stores in Chennai, Kolkata, and Bangalore. It projected a sale of ₹750 million in 2004–05.[4] The other competitor, by contrast, had about ₹1 crore of business annually.[5] Crossword was one of India's fastest growing bookstores. It had twenty stores in Mumbai, Bangalore, Ahmedabad, Gurgaon, Pune, Vadodara, Kolkata, Chennai, and Hyderabad. Twelve of these stores were franchised. Crossword had been able to change the way customers bought books by designing large, spacious, well laid out stores with bright cheerful interiors that encouraged people to stay and browse. The stores were located centrally for the customers to reach easily. They were part of shopping centres or malls, mostly on the high streets. Besides these large stores (5,000–10,000 sq. ft), Crossword also used smaller format stores (750–1,000 sq. ft) called Crossword Corners (CC), which were opened to provide better accessibility to customers. They were mostly a part of larger stores that were proximous and attracted a large number of shoppers from the vicinity. It was trying to tie up with large lifestyle stores such as Westside and Pantaloons, which also offered multiple shopping choices. A few of the CCs were operating at some Shoppers Stop and Piramyd outlets. It was planning to set up CCs at railway stations and airports. CCs had been a successful concept that achieved 100 per cent return on capital employed in the first year of its operation.

Crossword was designed as a centre for the community. It aimed to be a place of cultural and social interaction where shoppers gravitated to be informed, entertained, and enlightened. This was the core philosophy that would determine the way business would be carried out at the store. This was reflected in Crossword's vision, mission, and pledge (Fig. CS14.1). It organized book reading sessions, discussions, and debates on varied subjects from literature and art and other general interest topics such as child sexual abuse, war and peace, business and management, travel, parenting, and health. Among the numerous writers who had visited the store were Arundhati Roy, Vikram Chandra, Vikram Seth, Tara Deshpande, Kiran Nagarkar, Andrew Motion, Michele Roberts, Sashi Tharoor, Shobha De, Charles Handy, Tarla Dalal, and Jack Canfield. Promotional events included pictionary contests, quizzes, slide shows, and the annual affair with Santa and his elves. Ian Anderson of Jethro Tull had also performed at Crossword. 'While we do crossword puzzles for fun, they are also a learning experience. The name "Crossword" was chosen to reflect the fun and learning experience of a visit to the store. The name embodies our vision as a place and space for people who seek information, knowledge, or just the pleasure of reading,' replied Sriram on being asked about the choice of the store name. Many families who normally would not think of visiting bookstores had started visiting Crossword on a regular basis.

Merchandise and Store Layout

Over the years, Crossword had become a destination store for books, magazines, music, CD-ROMS, toys, and stationery. It not only offered a wide range of products but also created an ambience that would get the customer to spend more time and money at the store. It believed in the wallet and watch (WW) concept that when the store made customers spend more time, the likelihood of a sale increased. It encouraged the customers to enjoy a relaxing atmosphere, or simply to unwind during a break from work or just browse through its collection. The store created value through a model in which the customer was the focal point (Fig. CS14.2).

The merchandise mix was standardized across all stores, and was decided by the corporate team in Mumbai. Every outlet had five mandatory categories—books, music, CDs, toys, and magazines. The other categories common to all stores were toys, stationery, gifts, magazines, and CDs. The mix with respect to the titles and albums were ascertained on the basis of sales and demand. The floor plan was decided in consultation with the in-house interior decorator. Books were allocated

---

3. 1 million = 0.1 crore

4. The Chennai-based store dealt in many other product categories besides the categories dealt by Crossword.

5. Aditi De, 'Book Store Boom', *The Hindu Businessline*, Internet Edition, 29 March 2004.

CROSSWORD

Our Vision

To be a dominant network of profitable community
centre, where people gravitate
to be informed, to be entertained, and to be enlightened,
led by books and related products.

Our Mission

- To fulfill the information, knowledge and leisure needs of the community profitably through the retailing of books and related products. To be the dominant retailer in our category with at least 30% market share in the markets we operate in.

- To be customer focused in every aspect of the business. To build life-long relationships with customers.

- To build the reading habit, and to promote books, to nurture and reward the best of Indian writing.

- To create retail environments that are cases in the urban jungle—friendly, fun, relaxing and rewarding.

- To provide a platform for the cultural and social interaction of the community—to be a community center.

Our Pledge

Today and every day
I'll help make at least
One person's day.
For them to say
Thank God for Crossword

Our Values

1. *Fun*: We will build stores that are fun, enjoyable spaces to be in. We will build an organisation that people enjoy being with and working in.
2. *Learning*: We will create stores and an organisation that enable continuous learning.
3. *Excellence*: We will constantly strive for excellence in everything we do.
4. *Fairness*: We will always act fairly, with respect for all people, and with a win-win attitude.
5. *Integrity*: We will always conduct ourselves and act with integrity.
6. *Social Responsibility*: We will be socially responsible.
7. *Make a Difference*: We will work to make a difference to our customers, our stakeholders, our community and ourselves.

FIG. CS14.1 Vision, Mission, and Pledge of Crossword

60 per cent of the floor space. The remaining 40 per cent of the space was occupied by other categories that were city-specific. For instance, in Ahmedabad, the music section occupied 50 per cent of the non-book space. Each store had a store manager, department owner, and customer service executive. The department owners took care of the departments and reported to the store manager. They were assisted by respective buyers and merchandisers. While the buyers were product specialists, the merchandisers were responsible for the sales targets. For a target of ₹1 million[6] per year for a particular category, the category managers at any given time had to stock merchandise worth ₹0.25 million.[7]

---

6. 1 lakh = 0.10 million
7. http://www.etstrategicmarketing.com/smjuly-aug3/art9.html

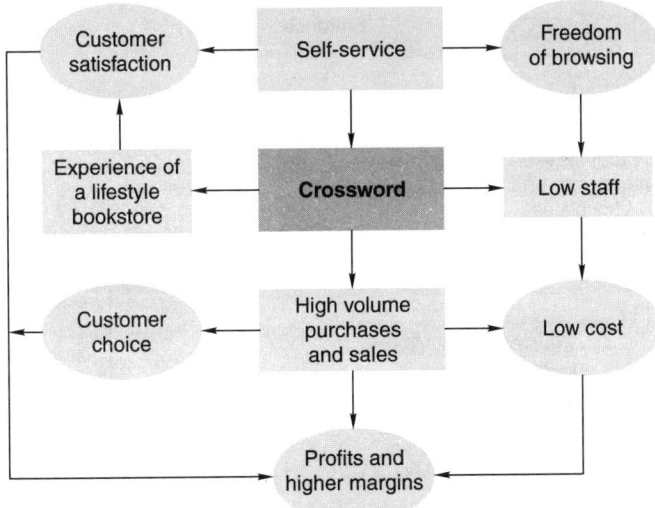

FIG. CS14.2 Crossword Value Delivery Model

Crossword stores were designed to encourage free and leisurely shopping. On arrival, the shopper was exposed to the displays of the latest offerings on the bestsellers/new releases of books and music. Following this, in the same aisle continued the other popular fare that included novels by Indian authors, crime thrillers, and romance novels along with non-fiction work like self-improvement books, management books, and CD ROMs. This section was followed by more serious subjects such as philosophy, history, politics, and books in local languages. The third section featured speciality books on culinary skills, gardening, beauty, and fitness. The gifts section, with its wide array of stationery and greeting cards among other trinkets, was kept between the two sections. The arrangement of merchandise in one of the stores is shown in Fig. CS14.3. More than 90 per cent of the shoppers were aware that Crossword was more than a bookstore and sold other merchandise as well.

The children's section was at the end of the store. It ensured that the shoppers traversed the entire length of the store and had a good look browsing at whatever the store had to offer. The books were juxtaposed to the toys and puzzles that were displayed to attract children. The music section ran along the book section. The cash counter near the entrance signified the end of purchase. Impulse purchase merchandise such as chocolates, magazines, newspapers, and teabags were displayed prominently near the counter. The traffic flow could take three directions: one led from the books to

the stationery and then to the children's books/toys section; the other followed the path from the entry to the music section towards the stationery and then to the children's books/toys section. The third, less frequented flow of traffic went into the magazine and CD-ROM section. All routes ended at the children's section and made the customer walk through the entire length of the store. At the same time, this section was away from serious readers.

Store Ambience

Crossword provided a comfortable and pleasant ambience to its shoppers. The stores were brightly lit and clear signs defined the racks. Tables and chairs were provided to encourage browsing. The shelves in the middle of the store were not more than three to four feet in height. This made it convenient for all customers to access the merchandise. Also, shoppers could see across the store from the entrance. This gave a feeling of spaciousness to the store. The colours within the store were an extension of the basic Crossword theme colours. In the beginning, the store followed a combination of yellow and black. The new stores had a softer colour combination. The spacing and utilization of colours was well balanced and it merged unobtrusively into the fixtures and other elements of the interiors. The lighting of the store was mild and unobtrusive. It allowed for no hidden dark spaces and was conducive for reading and browsing the merchandise. Separate lights in the aisles gave the impact of a larger space. There were also adjustable reading

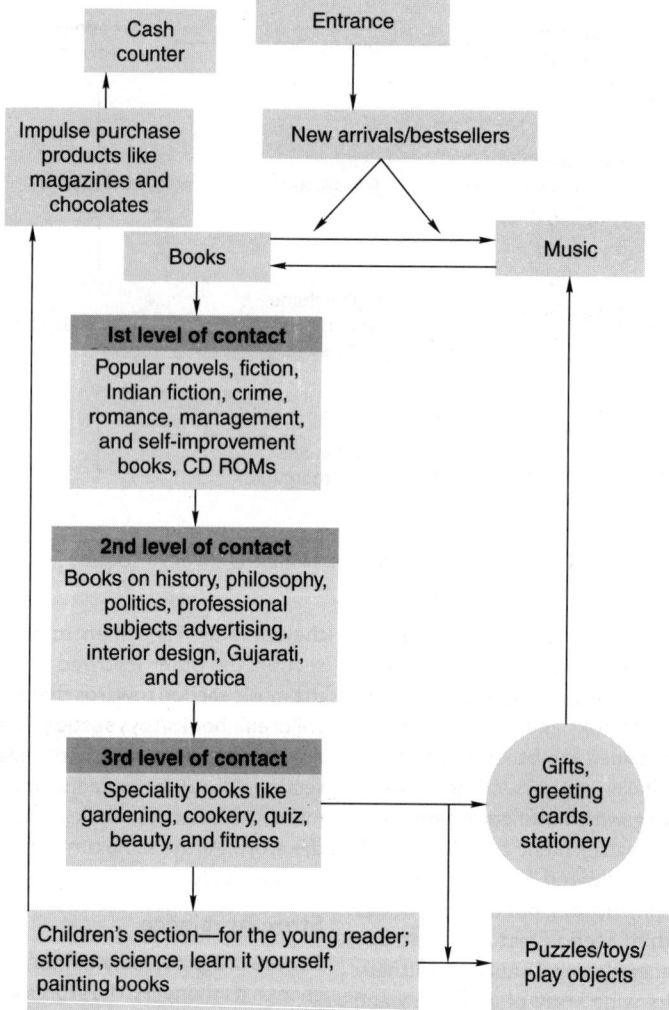

FIG. CS14.3   Merchandise Display

lights above the racks that could be tilted to allow the reader to focus the light better. Light instrumental music was played in the store. There was no apparent attempt at creating a deliberate olfactory experience for the visitor in terms of fragrances and scents. The only scent that sometimes pervaded into the surroundings was the fragrance of the brews being prepared at the coffee shop in the store. The fixtures were aimed at enhancing the interactive experience of the shopper at the store. These interaction points included listening posts, TVs, and pay phones. The wall had a white texture that did not have a differentiating finish. The flooring in older stores was a pleasant cream and brown. The floor tiles were shiny and well polished. Some shoppers found it

uncomfortable for walking and standing for long. In the new stores, the floor was carpeted. The spacing between the bookstands and the wall shelves was adequate for two shoppers to stand back to back without contact. The spacing between the aisles was also adequate for walking unhindered by any fixtures unless the crowd was particularly heavy. Several books were kept at lower levels. The staff was alert and assisted those browsing and picking books from these shelves.

Crossword had uniquely designed carry bags and pushcarts. These were placed strategically throughout the store for easy accessibility when the shoppers decided to take them for carrying their purchases. The visibility of all the signs and displays was ensured through careful placement based on space, height, and lighting considerations. There were various posters and portraits placed at strategic locations all over store. The posters guided the customers. They were witty ('SHOUT for help. This isn't a library'). The portraits of legends from the fields of art, literature, and politics were placed on the walls. Signs informing the latest sales figures of popular books were kept near the particular rack throughout the store. These were changed frequently, depending upon the sales trend during that particular period. On many shelves the customers could find books recommended by Sriram. They carried a strip with his signature and promise of return of the book and refund if the reader did not find it worthy (Fig. CS14.4).

FIG. CS14.4   A Strip with Sriram's Signature

Sales Strategy

The sales strategy was designed to enable the shoppers to enjoy buying at the store. It strongly believed that sales was a definite output when the correct support was provided to the shoppers. The key result areas for the store personnel, called customer support executives, included 5 'S': service, sales, stock, section, and support to the team. The team leaders and the store in-charge were also evaluated for the 6th 'S', that is, statutories. The store personnel were instructed to refrain from interfering with the shopping process unless they were approached. They were responsible for the sections allocated to them for maintenance as well as for ensuring a pleasant shopping experience. Help desks were kept at several places. The personnel at the desks were staff who could access the information regarding the availability and location of the merchandise on the computer. Every desk had a computer that was connected to the main database. Customers could also register a request when the desired merchandise was not available. They were later informed when the merchandise arrived at the store.

Services

Crossword offered several services to the customers. Services such as dial-a-book, fax-a-book, and email-a-book enabled customers to shop from their homes. The unobtrusively helpful staff assisted them in finding the right book, the right CD, or the right gift for the occasion. Crossword gift vouchers were popular. The store had a 'return, exchange, and refunds' policy. The customer could return merchandise within fifteen days. Although conditions applied, in most cases, the replacements were made unconditionally. The store offered to exchange even those products that were bought and then gifted. The receiver of the gift could also ask for an exchange. The cafe within the stores and the unique store experience made it easy and enjoyable for customers to shop at Crossword. The study brought out that the awareness of the additional services provided by Crossword was low. On an average, only about one fourth of the customers are aware of these additional services.

Book Retailing: The Indian Scenario

In India, the book retailing business was going through a major revolution. The current market size of the industry was estimated to be around ₹30–60 billion. It was expected to grow by 15 per cent per annum. The store operated on a 40 per cent gross margin. Consumers had started favouring stores that delivered experiences that appealed to their senses, hearts, and minds. Three trends that supported this belief were individualism, globalization, and symbolic experience.[8]
From tiny bookstores around the corner, the industry was witnessing stores with enticing layouts and service. Traditionally, shopping for books was restricted only to book lovers. Thus, browsing through these bookstores was seen as a book lover's hobby. New bookstores were adopting experiential marketing techniques in order to offer a holistic book-buying experience to the readers. Besides books, these bookstores provided value-added services that created a harmonious atmosphere. They offered comfortable seating, cheerful interiors, relaxing atmosphere, air-conditioned comfort, better layout, more space, zero 'brush factor', and little baskets and trolleys to hold books. They also offered their customers a café, reading tables and chairs, comfortable corners, and toilet facilities. All of these ensured that the customers

---

8. http://www.etretailbiz.com/sept04/booksmart.htm

were able to browse in comfort for hours. Positioned as lifestyle bookstores, they aimed to give their consumers a complete 'experience', encouraging them to stay and browse. However, the share of the new format stores was estimated to be no more than 15 per cent. They operated with a net income of less than 5 per cent.

Although mom-and-pop stores dealing in merchandise other than books did provide a high level of personalized service, book retailers had done very little in terms of customizing products or adding to their offering. Customer relationship management (CRM) was at a nascent stage. Most of the retailers who had CRM initiatives did not collect or analyse customer data on a regular basis. In many cases, the data was either just the un-updated address of the customers or purchase data that was seldom used for developing strategies. They were aware that customer information and intelligent and rigorous warehousing and mining of transaction behaviour was a critical success factor in retailing. They had launched several programmes, based on the concept of rewarding customers for continuing patronage through a combination of priority services, price-offs or discounts, product previews, and so on. Most such schemes involved both an entry fee and points system, with the number of points earned depending on the value of the purchase. Shoppers Stop's First Citizen Club, Ebony's Ebony Programme, Vivek's Akshya, and Bharat Petroleum's Petro Card and Fleet Card were some of the successful loyalty programmes. However, most loyalty programmes did not go beyond offering discounts on purchases. They seldom used them to build long lasting relationships with customers.

Book Rewards Programme

The Book Rewards Programme (BRP) was started by Crossword in 1999. The programme offered rewards to encourage people to read more through exclusive events, benefits, offers, and discounts at all its stores around the country. Discounts were offered only during promotions or sales and not the year round. Members were invited for sales before they were opened to other customers. It was the only programme that gave an accumulated points statement on the bill with every purchase. The members were sent 'eWords', a monthly newsletter that included over 50 reviews of new books, events, and best-seller lists. The marketing team had the task of coming up with a certain number of events at every store for the year. Innovative initiatives encouraged customers to frequent the store more often and even take part in activities. They continuously collected feedback from the customer, resulting in return, 'the customers voting with their feet'.

Information from the Book Rewards Programme was shared with franchisees. The benefits and terms and conditions of BRP are given in Exhibit CS14.1.

The basic qualifications for becoming a book rewards member were 'knowing the alphabet' and a payment of an enrolment fee of ₹150. The customer was required to fill up a book rewards customer profile and hand it over at the cash counter. A temporary card was issued immediately. The form was then processed within a time period of two weeks. The customer was then sent a book rewards kit which includes a welcome letter, a membership booklet, and the book rewards card. The card operated on the principle of 'the more you read, the more you gain'. For every ₹40 spent at any Crossword outlet, a book rewards member earned one point. So, for example, when a customer spent ₹100 at the store, two points were added. The extra sum of ₹20 was carried forward and added to reflect in the total points tally. The card could be used only after the customer had accumulated a minimum of 100 points. The card could be presented at any Crossword outlet to get an update on points accumulated. Each point had a redemption value of ₹1. Customers started collecting points the moment they enrolled. The points could be redeemed against Crossword gift vouchers and could be used to buy books, CD-ROMs, music, or any other item available at the stores. These vouchers could also be gifted. The members also received exclusive offers, discounts, and benefits such as special tie-ups with various companies and their brands for better deals. As an original member, the customer became a principal cardholder, but the benefits of this programme could be passed on to others as well. This could be done by enrolling the immediate family as associate members. A processing fee of ₹100 for each additional member was charged. The membership could also be gifted to friends. For this, the book rewards customer profile of the nominee had to be filled along with an enrolment fee of ₹150. The nominee received a separate book rewards card and became a principal cardholder. The associate members were entitled to the same offers and privileges as principal cardholders. However, all points earned accrued to the principal cardholder. The members could also check their points tally by visiting the company website by entering their 16 digit card number and their date of birth. The cash memo issued on each purchase stated the current points accrued so far. The membership was valued for two-years. It was extended automatically when the member made a purchase at least once every two years. The programme was operational at all Crossword outlets. Purchases made at any Crossword outlet were added to the book rewards balance of the customers.

Exhibit CS14.1 The Book Rewards Programme

Benefits

- Reward points on purchases—1 point for every ₹40 spent
- Information on in-store offers and promotions
- Online checking of points balance
- Priority in buying/ordering new releases as well as events at the store
- Free subscription to 'eWords'
- Exclusive offers
- Associate membership cards
- Gift-a-membership

Terms and Conditions

- Benefits and offers available through programme partners may change or be withdrawn without prior intimation. Crossword will not be responsible for any liability arising from such situations or from the use of such offers.
- No two offers or discounts can be clubbed unless specified otherwise.
- A BRP membership number can be entered against an institutional sale transaction only if full rates are paid against merchandise purchased. In other words, if any discount is afforded on an institutional sales order, you will not get Book Rewards points against it.
- The Book Rewards Membership is for individuals only—it is not a corporate card.
- A membership can be revoked or refused if a member/customer is involved in any act of fraud, shoplifting, or cheating.
- Crossword reserves the right to revise terms and conditions governing the Book Rewards Membership without prior notice.
- Crossword reserves the right to modify or terminate the Book Rewards Programme at any given time. It may also decide to terminate membership for a period of time as decided by the management.
- Any dispute arising would fall under the Mumbai jurisdiction.

Source: http://www.crosswordbookstores.com/html/brp-how%20brp%20operates%20page1.asp

---

BRP Member Profile

The BRP consisted of 60,000 members. A large number of the members were well-educated. Post-graduates and MBAs constituted the largest segment. There were more males than female members (1000:555). This was largely because the primary membership was usually in the name of male members of the family. The number of married members was the same as unmarried members (999:1000). The store attracted a wide variety of customers. The top ten occupations of BRP members were executives (11.80%), top and middle level management (8.87%), IT professionals (8.54%), students (8.16%), homemakers (7.42%), self-employed persons (7.39%), engineers (6.84%), doctors (6.62%), consultants (5.47%), and academicians (4.25%). A large number (22%–40%) of members came from outside the cities where the stores were located.

About 65% of the members made purchases on Friday, Saturday, and Sunday. November (20%) and August (12%) witnessed higher sales. February and March were lean months, contributing just about 2 per cent of the total sales. It was noticed that these months were generally lean months in book retailing. Other months showed equal proportion (9%) of sales. Although there was no established rationale, it was thought that the visiting NRIs contributed to higher sales in November.

The BRP members contributed 32 per cent to the total sales of Crossword. It ranged from 28 per cent to 55 per cent at different stores. Franchised stores contributed 40 per cent of the total BRP sales. Among them, the two leading stores were Ahmedabad (15%) and Bangalore (11%). The largest contribution (35%) came from one its own stores in Mumbai. Of the total BRP sales in 2004, 74 per cent came from products priced within ₹500. Products priced between ₹225 and ₹350 contributed 25 per cent of the total BRP sales. About 10 per cent of the members bought products valued at more than ₹1,000, some of them (1% of total) spending as much as ₹4,000 in the year.

Books contributed 68 per cent of the total BRP sales. Books related to children and education (18%), fiction (15%), audio-visual aids (13%), management/business books (10%), CD-ROMs (7%), and family, home, and practical interest books (7%) were leading categories of items. It was observed that 60 per cent of the sales came from books priced upto ₹350 or lower. The fiction books priced at ₹350 and below accounted for 75 per cent of the total fiction book sales to BRP members.

The average purchase value of the BRP members was ₹2,500. This value was 2.6 times higher than the average bill value of other customers (Fig. CS14.5). Based on the bill value, BRP members were classified into five segments:

Crossword Tribes (10%): They represented customers who made a large number of purchase visits. They had high cumulative annual bills as well as a high average bill amount of ₹400 per visit or ₹1,000 in case of 2 visits

to the store. They contributed 48 per cent of the total BRP sales.

Crossword Core (12%): These customers made frequent visits to the store. They also purchased a lot. Their average bill value ranged between ₹200 and ₹400 per visit. They contributed 17 per cent of the total BRP sales.

Crossword Wannabes (19%): They represented customers with a cumulative bill of less than ₹4,000 for the year, with an average bill value ranging between ₹100 and ₹200. They contributed 4 per cent of the total BRP sales.

Crossword Eager Beavers (14%): They represented customers who purchased less than 10 items, with a cumulative bill of ₹500–1,000 for the year. They contributed 5 per cent of the total BRP sales.

Crossword Climbers (45%): These customers had a cumulative bill value of less than ₹500 for the year. They purchased less than 5 items and contributed 26 per cent of the total BRP sales.

Customer Perception of Crossword and BRP

Customers visited many stores to buy books. Different stores posed as competition in different cities. Oxford Bookstore was the only major chain of stores present in the cities where Crossword operated. The major

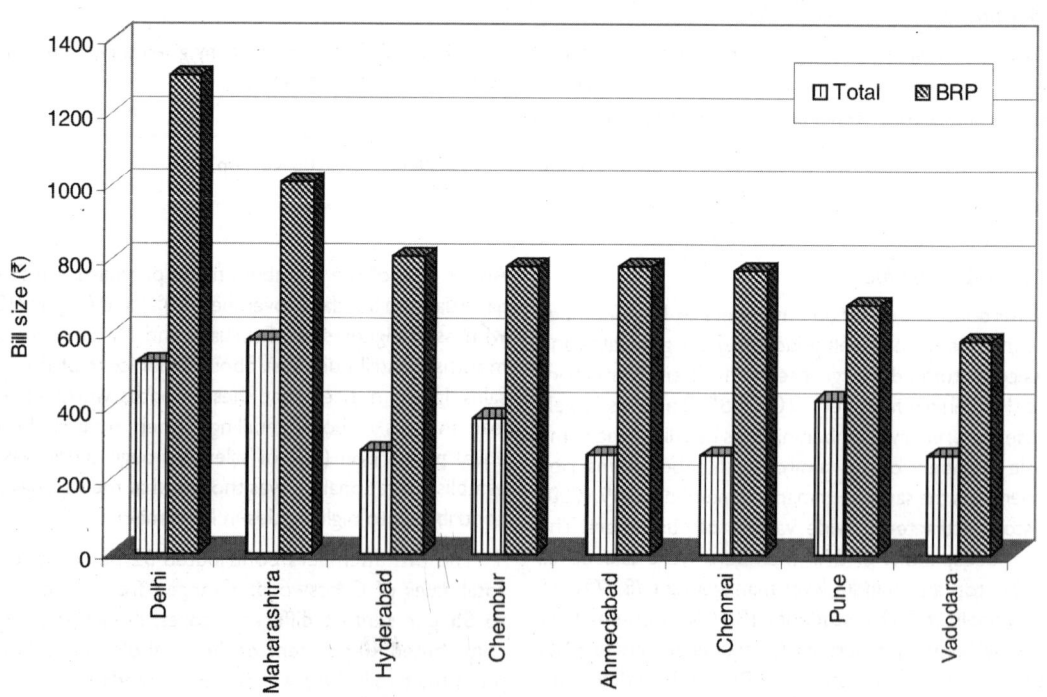

FIG. CS14.5   Average Bill Size of BRP Members vis-à-vis Total Customers

Mumbai	
A	33%
B	20%
C	8%
D	5%
E	3%

Pune	
A	25%
B	13%
C	12%
D	11%
E	6%

Ahmedabad	
A	22%
B	14%
C	9%
D	3%

Baroda	
A	30%
B	14%
C	6%

FIG. CS14.6   Percentage of Crossword Customers who Visited Competing Bookstores

Note: A, B, C, D, and E are competing bookstores.

competitors in each of the cities are given in Fig. CS14.6. Almost 70 per cent of the customers bought from other stores, whereas 5 per cent of the customers had also bought from international stores, mainly Borders and Barnes & Noble. Crossword was perceived as a leading store well ahead of the local competitors, though it scored lower than international competitors. Customers found the store wanting in terms of prices and the arrangement of merchandise. Although it scored very high on the overall experience, even those who had rated the store as excellent expressed concern about value for money and price (Table CS14.1a and b). BRP members rated the store higher than walk-in customers on all parameters. In terms of loyalty measures, Crossword scored higher than even international retailers in all aspects. These measures indicated that 26 per cent of the customers were committed, 56 per cent would recommend it to others, 60 per cent would continue to buy, and 41 per cent intended to increase the purchase from the store. About 80 per cent of the customers indicated that they were truly loyal (high commitment and strong urge to continue). Only 17 per cent felt trapped (low commitment but strong urge to continue).

Where are the Worms in Our Books?

Sriram was puzzled. 'We have one of the largest loyalty programmes in the industry. Members yield much higher returns than the walk-in customers. They also rate the store higher. We score well in terms of loyalty measures. Still we have just 40 per cent of members who are active (purchased in one year) and contributing. Where is the worm?,' he asked Aniyan and Balaji. 'I can see two reasons for this,' replied Aniyan, 'One, if you look at the overall importance attached to factors that lead to store loyalty, BRP plays a marginal role. Customers seem to come to us and even register for the programme because we do not seem to have any competition. The store, its overall quality, is the most important driver. Communication

seems to be the next factor. BRP is not found to be a significant driver.' At this point of time he presented one of the slides of the findings of the survey (Fig. CS14.7). Balaji was not convinced. 'I am not sure if this is due to lack of competition', he argued, 'because when you look at the distribution of scores on the scale, while only 11 per cent customers have found it excellent, about 75 per cent of them have found it good (Fig. CS14.8). It could also be because many of them did not have enough experience of the store. We must remember that only 22 per cent of our customers are frequent buyers.'

'Let's look at the rating scores on the BRP in more detail. I am sure we would find some clues there. Balaji, could you show those slides that talk specifically of the BRP programme?,' requested Sriram. The study showed that BRP members, among all processes, had rated two processes, billing and cashiering, and communication, lower than walk-in customers (Tables CS14.2 a–f). They also rated the store lower in almost all aspects of merchandise range and quality. They found the sales personnel very helpful, except in their ability to respond to queries. The aspect of display of books was not a major concern, though the members had indicated a desire for a better visibility of bestsellers and new arrivals. The store feature appealed to them. 'I think the major area for concern is the communication with BRP members within the store as well as away from it,' opined Balaji. 'We have a low score on communication on the whole as well as on its adequacy. More importantly, the members have rated us lower than the walk-ins in terms of the relevance of our communication. They are not finding value in our communication. You may be right here. But I would say that we need to have a much more strategic view of our BRP programme. It has been five years since the programme began. This is the first real review of the programme. In the mean time customer expectations have undergone a sea change,' said Aniyan.

TABLE CS14.1(a)   Image Perceptions

Top Box % (Excellent Rating)	Total	Walk-in	BRP Members
Is a leading bookstore	51	47	69↑
Is run by professionals	35	32	52↑
Cares about its customers	34	31	50↑
Is a store I can trust	34	30	52↑
Provides an enjoyable shopping experience	39	37	54↑
Is the centre of social and culture interaction	30	30	33
Has a good variety of different types of books	37	35	51↑
Is a comfortable place to browse	36	32	60↑
Is hassle-free and time efficient	34	32	48↑
Prices recently released books competitively	30	29	35
Is uncluttered and well laid out	29	28	32
Has a welcoming and pleasing atmosphere	35	34	36
Provides responsive and personalized service	30	28	36
Understands interests of people and stocks books accordingly	31	30	37

↓↑ Loyalty significantly lower/ahead than walk-in customers

TABLE CS14.1(b)   Image Perceptions

Top Box % (Strongly Agree)	Crossword	National Benchmark	Borders, Barnes & Noble Benchmark
Is a leading bookstore	51	27↓	63
Is run by professionals	35	25↓	53↑
Cares about its customers	34	20↓	55↑
Is a store I can trust	34	21↓	59↑
Provides an enjoyable shopping experience	39	20↓	53
Is the centre of social and culture interaction	30	15↓	28
Has a good variety of different types of books	37	19↓	59↑
Is a comfortable place to browse	36	19↓	44
Is hassle-free and time efficient	34	19↓	37
Prices recently released books competitively	30	22↓	41
Is uncluttered and well laid out	29	16↓	50↑
Has a welcoming and pleasing atmosphere	35	19↓	38
Provides responsive and personalized service	30	15↓	47↑
Understands interests and stocks books accordingly	31	17↓	50↑

↓↑ Benchmark significantly lower than/ahead of Crossword

Figures represent % rating 'strongly agree' on a 5-point scale of agree–disagree.

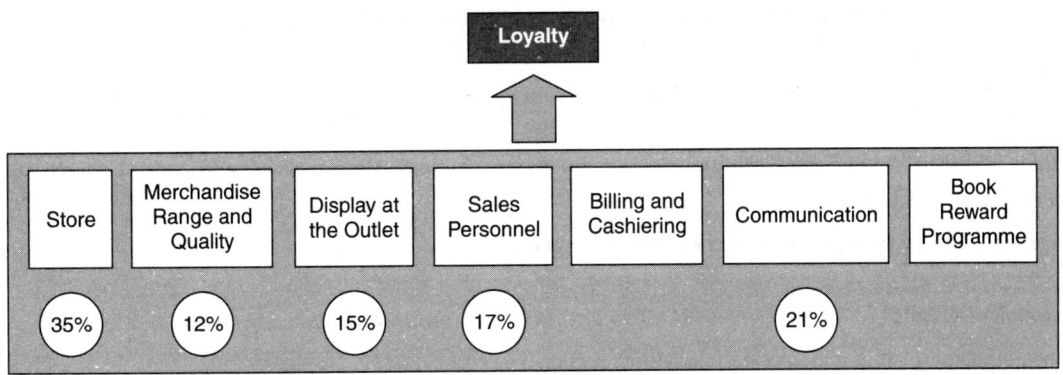

FIG. CS14.7 What Drives Loyalty at Crossword

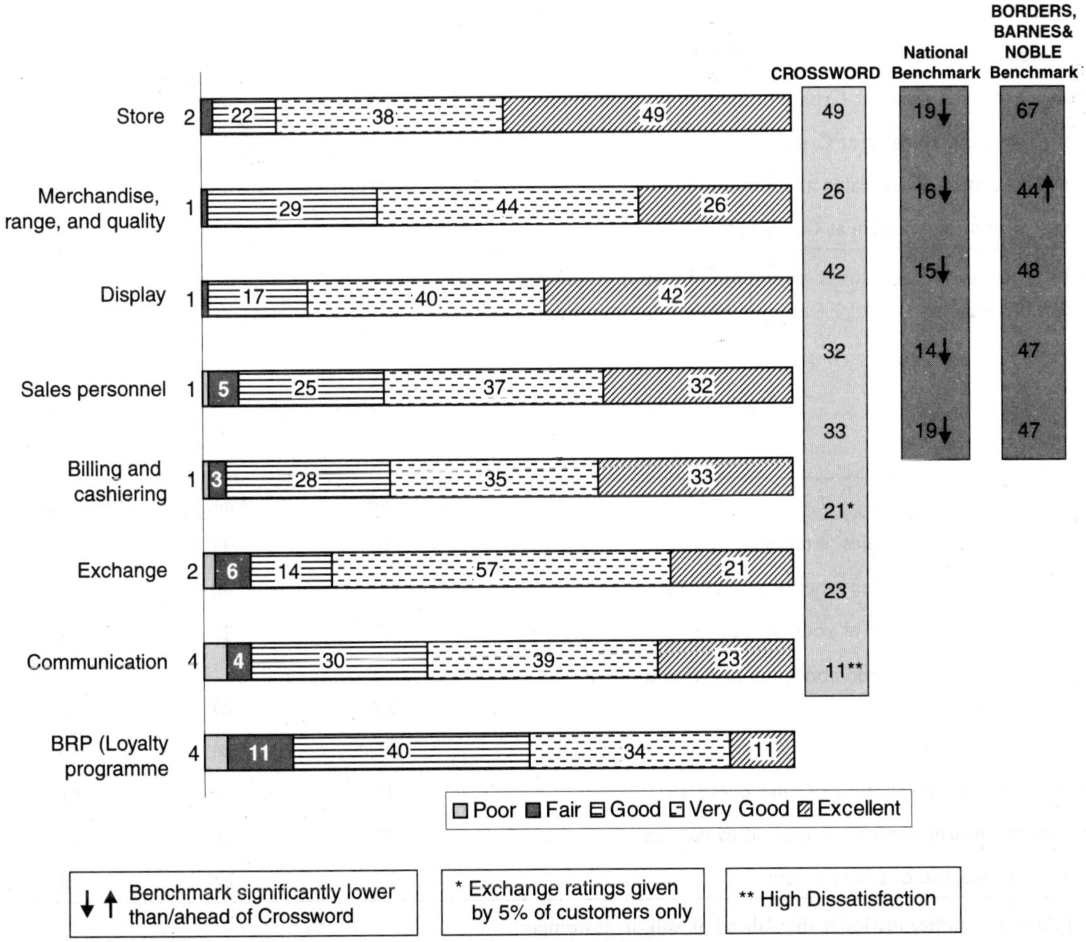

	CROSSWORD	National Benchmark	BORDERS, BARNES & NOBLE Benchmark
Store 2 ▤22▤ ⋯38⋯ ⟋49⟋	49	19↓	67
Merchandise, range, and quality 1 ▤29▤ ⋯44⋯ ⟋26⟋	26	16↓	44↑
Display 1 ▤17▤ ⋯40⋯ ⟋42⟋	42	15↓	48
Sales personnel 1 ■5 ▤25▤ ⋯37⋯ ⟋32⟋	32	14↓	47
Billing and cashiering 1 ■3 ▤28▤ ⋯35⋯ ⟋33⟋	33	19↓	47
Exchange 2 ■6 ▤14▤ ⋯57⋯ ⟋21⟋	21*		
Communication 4 ■4 ▤30▤ ⋯39⋯ ⟋23⟋	23		
BRP (Loyalty programme 4 ■11 ▤40▤ ⋯34⋯ ⟋11⟋	11**		

☐ Poor ■ Fair ▤ Good ⋯ Very Good ⟋ Excellent

↓↑ Benchmark significantly lower than/ahead of Crossword

* Exchange ratings given by 5% of customers only

** High Dissatisfaction

FIG. CS14.8 Overall Processes

TABLE CS14.2 (a)   Attributes—Merchandise Range and Quality

Top Box Score

	Total	Walk-in	BRP Members
Overall merchandise range and quality	26	25	32
Range of topics/sections	34	36	22*
Selection of titles within each topic/section in books in the adult section	29	29	25
Selection of authors	24	26	13*
Range of topics/sections in books in the children's section	31	32	24
Selection of titles within each topic/section in the children's section	29	28	29
Selection of authors in the children's section	20	21	15
Availability of new arrivals in books	22	23	20
Availability of best sellers	23	24	21
Range of toys available at Crossword	24	26	16*
Range of music available at Crossword	21	20	22
Range of stationery available at Crossword	19	19	21
Range of movies available at Crossword	17	17	19

↓↑ Loyalty significantly lower than/ahead of walk-in customers
* High dissatisfaction, i.e., 15% or more given Fair/Poor ratings

TABLE CS14.2 (b)   Attributes—Sales Personnel

Top Box Score

	Total	Walk-in	BRP Members
Overall quality of the sales personnel	32	31	37
Availability of salesperson when you need them	40	40	39
Allowing you to browse at your own pace	37	35	48↑
Knowledge of salesperson about the books and other merchandise	29	29	30*
Politeness and courtesy	35	34	40
Friendliness and helpfulness of sales personnel	35	34	41
Ability of the salesperson to respond to queries	28	28	27
Speed of response of sales personnel	27	27	28

↓↑ Loyalty significantly lower than/ahead of walk-in customers
* (High dissatisfaction), i.e., 15% or more given Fair/Poor ratings

TABLE CS14.2(c) Attributes—Store

Top Box Score

	Total	Walk-in	BRP Members
Overall quality of store	49	47	61↑
Adequacy of space in the store to allow browsing amongst various sections	45	44	53
Comfort of air conditioning/temperature in the store	35	35	38
Ability to provide adequate lighting in the store to allow for comfortable reading/browsing	32	31	37↑
Seating/book reading space inside the store	27*	26*	37*↑
Seating arrangements to sit and browse through books	29*	28*	36*
Ability to provide cheerful and warm ambience of the store	32	31	37
Parking arrangements outside the store	18*	18*	18*↑
Location of the store	28	27	37

↓↑ Loyalty significantly lower than/ahead of walk-in customers
* High dissatisfaction, i.e., 15% or more given fair/poor ratings

TABLE CS14.2 (d) Attributes—Display of Books (Storewise)

Top Box Score

	Total	Walk-in	BRP Members
Overall quality of display of books	42	40	58↑
Convenience of arrangement/display of books	43	42	53↑
Neatness of arrangement of books	37	35	47↑
Shelf planning and layout	26	26	27
Visibility of new arrivals/best sellers	27	28	21
Visibility of recommendations	25	25	26
Attractiveness of display in the store	28	28	29
Overall quality of display of music and movies CDs/cassettes	28	28	30
Overall quality of display of toys and stationery	26	26	26

↓↑ Loyalty significantly lower than/ahead of walk-in customers

TABLE CS14.2(e) Attributes—Billing and Cashiering

Top Box Score

	Total	Walk-in	BRP Members
Billing and cashiering	33	34	29
Efficiency and helpfulness of the cashier	39	38	45
Accuracy of billing	35	34	43↑
Adequacy of billing counters	32	32	32
Ability of cashier to deal with your queries on LBR programme, etc.	28	28	29

↓↑ Loyalty significantly lower than/ahead of walk-in customers

TABLE CS14.2 (f) Attributes—Communications

	Total	Walk-in	BRP Members
			Top Box Score
Adequacy of communication	20	14	23
Relevance of communication	14	16	13

↓↑ Loyalty significantly lower than/ahead of walk-in customers

Sriram felt as if Aniyan was reading his mind. He said, 'I would go by what you are saying, Aniyan. We have so far focused on growth and opening new stores. While we may be doing pretty well as a chain, the time may have come to also look at consolidating each of our stores. In my opinion, our BRP should become the engine of our next phase of growth and cementing our leadership. We have the annual planning meeting scheduled in February. Let us present our strategy and plan for the BRP to the Board. I would like to review the report by the end of this month and, Balaji, you would have to take the lead in this.'

Questions

1. Analyse the performance of Crossword's Book Reward Programme.
2. Identify the key issues faced by Sriram and his team. What is the root cause behind the fact that, in spite of the fact that the programme had over 60,000 members, only 25,000 of them were active members? Explain the low contribution of BRP to the performance of the store.
3. Develop strategies to improve the performance of the Book Reward Programme so that more members can be activated and the value delivered to each customer can be enhanced.

15 The Shop as a Social Entity*

LEARNING OBJECTIVES

After studying this chapter, you will be able to
- look at a shop as a social entity
- gain an insight into the tangible and intangible aspects of the world within a retail shop
- understand how a store needs to design its policies keeping in mind the fact that the various aspects within a store influence shoppers' perceptions about the store

INTRODUCTION

Shoppers change their behaviour when they shop from different retail outlets, even when the product or the brand bought is the same. In a study, it was found that when shoppers buy something from a smaller store, they speak in their mother tongue or the local language, but when they buy from a large format, well laid out store, they start speaking in English. In the former case, they are relaxed and casual while in the latter they become formal. In stores that they visit frequently, they are found to be demanding and 'brave', and in newer stores, timid and patient. In many cases, the study found that people take on a very different role inside a store. For instance, men, who may behave very differently when out of the store, were seen to behave like 'zombies' in the stores pushing carts. All this happens because, as human beings, shoppers' behaviour is likely to be modified by stimuli in the external environment. This chapter attempts to understand how the store influences and modifies the behaviour of shoppers. It also illustrates shoppers' perception of the store and its various aspects with the help of extracts of what people have reported about their perceptions.

SHOP AS A 'SOCIETY'

A shop is a world of its own. It is a society defined as

- the sum of human conditions and activities regarded as a whole and functioning interdependently;
- the customs and organization of an ordered community;
- composed of companionship, company, and social interaction; and
- an association of people united by a common interest or aim.

* Based on research conducted by the authors in Ahmedabad and Brown, Stephen and Darach Turley (eds) 1997, 'Shoppers on the Verge of a Nervous Breakdown', *Consumer Research, Postcards from the Edge*, Routledge.

A shop is all of these. It is an entity different from the outside world. No two shops are similar. Each has its own 'language' and code of conduct. A lot of people come to a shop with common interests and move like an ordered group. This indicates that a shop is a different environment or society. The constituents of this society may take two broad forms—tangible and intangible. The tangible constituents consist of all those things present in the shop that can be seen and touched. The intangibles consist of aspects that are felt, sensed, and experienced.

Tangible Aspects

The shop, as a society, is composed of the following tangible aspects.

The Larger Social System

Every shop is a part of a larger social system called the market. Shops tend to get clustered around the place where there is traffic and, in the process, get located on a 'main road'. Such roads are the 'spines' of the city. Typically, these roads emerge from either the bus stand or the railway station and encourage growth concentrically. These tend to be the busiest areas where shoppers from in and around the town gather to shop. In India, usually the roads where the shops are clustered are narrow, and there is heavy traffic and congestion. There is often a problem of parking on such roads. There are all kinds of vehicular and pedestrian traffic—including animal and human drawn transport and stray animals—on the roads, with the vast majority of vehicles being self-driven. These roads are also used by mobile vendors. Shop owners use them for priority parking. Because of the chaotic and disorganized nature of the market, it is very difficult to differentiate one shop from the other. The shopkeepers rely only on small signs hanging above their shops for people to spot their shops. These numerous signs add to the clutter and congestion.

The link between these external elements and shopper behaviour becomes clear in the shopper's emotional reaction to retail environments. This emotional reaction may be influenced by the individual's personality, the amount of stimulus screening, shopper's mood, and mood inducing capabilities of the shopping experience.[1] Situational variables are as important as individual consumer characteristics in explaining consumer behaviour. It is also suggested that physical and social surroundings such as location, decor, noise, aromas, lighting intensity, physical layout, and other persons present may affect a consumer's purchasing behaviour.[2] The following are the commonly used five groups of situational factors:

1. *Physical surroundings* are the most readily apparent features of a situation. These features include geographical and institutional location, decor, sounds, aromas, lighting, weather, and visible configurations of merchandise or other material surrounding the stimulus object.
2. *Social surroundings* provide additional depth to the description of a situation. Other persons present, their characteristics, their apparent roles, and interpersonal interactions are relevant examples.
3. *Temporal perspective* is a dimension of situations that may be specified in units ranging from the time of the day to the season of the year. Time may also be measured relative to some past or future event for the situational participant. This allows conceptions such as time since last purchase, time since or until meals or payday, and time constraints imposed by prior or standing commitments.
4. *Task definition* features of a situation include an intent or requirement to select, shop for, or obtain information about a general or specific purchase. In addition, it may reflect different

buyer and user roles anticipated by the individual. For instance, a person shopping for a small appliance as a wedding gift for a friend is in a different situation than he/she would be in shopping for a small appliance for personal use.

5. *Antecedent states* make up a final group of features that characterize a situation. These are momentary moods (such as acute anxiety, pleasantness, hostility, and excitation) or momentary conditions (such as cash on hand, fatigue, and illness) rather than chronic individual traits. These conditions are further stipulated to be immediately antecedent (prior) to the current situation, in order to distinguish between the states that the individual brings to the situation and the states of the individual which result from the situation.

A crowded, cluttered environment fosters a low price image. However, crowding does have negative connotations.[3] In crowded stores, respondents said that they

- spent less time shopping in the store;
- did less impulsive shopping;
- purchased fewer items per trip (lower priority needs are deleted);
- were less likely to socialize or seek contact with store personnel;
- were less receptive to new store layouts (too hard to find things in the crowd or clutter); and
- were more nervous, tense, and confused and thus less confident about their purchases.

These findings were especially true for time-constrained shoppers. Task-oriented shoppers, who make fewer unplanned purchases and spend less time per shopping trip, may also be more sensitive to crowded conditions. Asian shoppers have been found to be more tolerant of crowding than southern Europeans. The British are the least tolerant of all three groups.[4]

Warm colours such as red and yellow attract people to a store, while cool colours such as blue and green encourage more contemplation and less avoidance of the environment. Interestingly, the two types of colours were not related to price or quality perceptions of the store.[5] Noise, like crowding, is also detrimental to human performance. It seems to have a negative impact on helping behaviour, people being less helpful in noisy environments.[6] For retail settings, the implication is that shoppers will avoid or quickly leave a noisy environment.

Similarly, temperature also pays a role. Subjects who feel uncomfortably hot tend to react less positively to other people than subjects who are comfortable with the ambient temperature.[7] The implication seems to be that consumers would avoid shopping environments that have temperature outside of their comfort range. Of course, this range may vary according to person, season, setting, and shopping purpose.

Format of the Shop

The format of the shop is determined by a number of factors, such as size, layout, merchandise, and access provided to the shopper. The Indian retail scenario is proliferated with small shops. These have narrow frontage and often extend their merchandise on to the footpath, forcing pedestrians into the road. Consequently, the *dukaans* (shops) flow into one another and become inseparable as distinct stores. Even when their size is small, these shops stock most of the brands in the category. Brands and their extensions have littered the retail outlets, leaving no space for anything but the merchandise. In several instances, there is insufficient space in the shop for the retailer, leave alone for shoppers, to stand or move. 'The store is a store and hence should be used for storing' seems to be the mantra for most small retailers.

The business is totally product-centric. The shopper has no place in the whole exercise. There is very little room for shoppers. Even when they can go inside the shop, in most instances, they can only order from a distance. The most important person—the shopper—therefore becomes an external entity and is kept firmly at arm's length. As a result, shoppers are so conditioned that even in a self-service store they tend to browse visually and do not touch or feel the products.

Type of Merchandise

Shopping is an information search process. The process depends on the planning of the purchase by the shopper before arriving at the store. The planning is, in turn, dependent on the involvement that the shopper has with the product/brand being bought. This level of involvement determines the benefit that shoppers would seek from the store. As the involvement increases, the expectation from the shop increases and moves from a tangible transaction level to an intangible experience level, as depicted in Fig. 15.1.

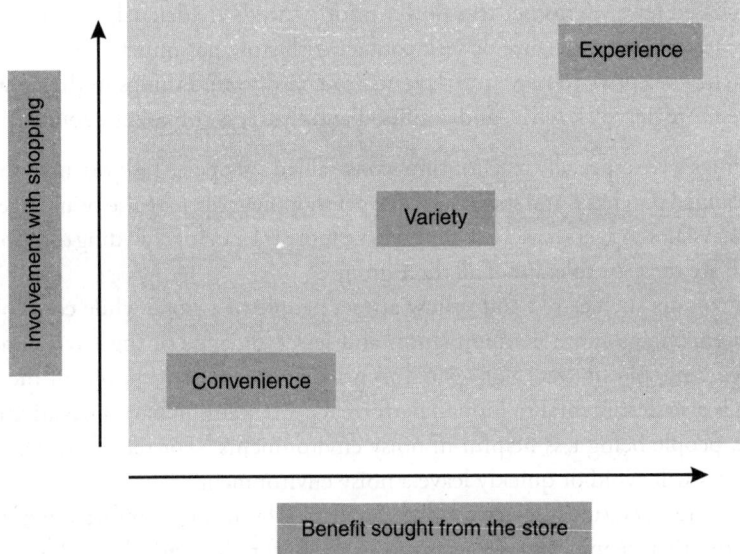

FIG. 15.1   Levels of Customer Expectations

Visual Merchandising and PoP Communication

Visual merchandising and point of purchase (PoP) communication play an important part in retailing. The practice that started in the fashion and clothing industry has now become vital even for low-value merchandise. Research has shown that effective visual merchandising and PoP communication can push sales up by as much as 64 per cent. Deploying these modes of communication very strategically, one company experienced an increase of almost 40 per cent in chocolate sales. Visual merchandising and PoP communication help in setting the mood for shopping. These can not only enhance the shopping experience, but also alter the flow of traffic within a store. Nike, Titan, and large format organized retailers, such as Shoppers Stop and FoodWorld, are good examples of organizations that have successfully implemented visual merchandising and PoP communication. In many stores, visual merchandising decisions are reviewed very frequently, sometimes several times a day.

EXHIBIT 15.1   Perceptions of Store Environment

Shopper 1

I made my way through the crammed maze to the portable CD section, in a small section of the store, and looked at the selection they had on offer. This on the whole was very limited and, to be honest, it looked as if it had just been thrown onto the chipboard shelves. Straightaway, I knew I wasn't going to purchase anything here.

Shopper 2

Walking through the doors of this shop was really like stepping out onto a building site ... I glanced at the barren rails and quickly realized that I was wasting my time here.

Exhibit 15.1 shows the perceptions of two shoppers about the store environment and its communication and merchandise (or the lack of it).

Salespeople

Salespeople can affect purchase decisions to a large extent. They can make or break the sale as well as the store. Observational research on salespeople's behaviour brought out four general typologies of salespeople.

Information Kiosks   These are individuals who behave like kiosks. They are passive providers. Like kiosks, they deliver information only when it is specifically requested for by shoppers.

Box Pushers   These salespeople sell without knowing the shoppers' requirements. They are bent upon selling whatever merchandise is available in the store.

Warriors   These salespeople consider the shopper as the 'enemy' to be conquered. For them, the shopper is the 'other party'. It is an 'us vs them' situation. The shopping experience is quickly converted into a grim battle.

Shopper-friendly Salespeople   Liked by shoppers, shopper-friendly salespeople consider and ask for the requirements of shoppers and make shopping a rewarding endeavour. Regrettably, this type is not found in large numbers.

These findings point towards the amount of training provided to salespeople. They are too sales-centric and display limited knowledge about the details of the products they are selling. Shopper orientation is a long way off. The new self-service department stores pose peculiar problems for salespeople. Most of the staff in these stores do not know when to help out. They become part of the 'visual merchandise' in the shop. Exhibit 15.2 provides extracts of consumers' perceptions about the kind of salespeople encountered by them.

Other Shoppers

The presence of other shoppers in the store generates interactions that work both ways. Both empty and crowded stores send positive and negative signals simultaneously. Usually, a crowded shop is perceived as successful and hence preferred. For shoppers who perceive a crowded store as a successful one, elbowroom may represent a negative signal. Shoppers with similar taste tend to visit similar shops. Such mirrored profiles create a sense of familiarity and belongingness.

Exhibit 15.3 illustrates shoppers' perceptions about other shoppers in the store.

EXHIBIT 15.2   Perceptions about Salepeople

Shopper 1

I wanted to buy a microwave oven. As my wife and I entered the store we were nicely escorted to the section where ovens were stacked. We were handed over to the lady in that section. She led us straight to one of the brands and explained all the features in detail. The presentation was nice and well structured: a good sales talk. But, we were not shown any other brand, nor was there any comparison extended, until we started looking around on our own. Did she know exactly what my profile was and that the brand shown was the right brand and model for us? If she did, she must be a mind reader, as the store did not have my details. (As such, I doubt if it has details of its shoppers, except on the bill book.)

Shopper 2

I am always dismayed when I visit a cosmetics shop. Why are women's cosmetics and lingerie stores 'MANNED'?

EXHIBIT 15.3   Perceptions about Other Shoppers

Shopper 1

They say good things come in small packages, but when you find yourself in what feels like a herd of cattle and behaves in a similar fashion, somehow those words of wisdom lose their value and provide no consolation whatsoever. However, I've discovered a wonderful defence mechanism when I find myself in a situation where crowds are inevitable. I define it as the art of shoving, and find it very effective indeed!

Shopper 2

As the store had only opened at the start of the week, it appeared to be still suffering from what I would call the 'curious shopper syndrome'. No!, let's be honest!, You know the sort, the shoppers with no intention of, perish the thought, actually buying anything. No! they're there to further infuriate those of us trying to make purposeful progress through the store.

EXHIBIT 15.4   Perceptions about Store Facilities

Shopper

I love going to clothes shops. The one fault all clothes shops have is that when I am trying on clothes, the changing rooms are too warm and stuffy and it is very unpleasant. I break out in a sweat and feel trapped. I always end up saying, 'Why did I do that when I know what will happen?' I just keep forgetting. I get into a fluster and that makes it worse.

Other Facilities

In addition to the format of the shop, its merchandise, communication strategies, salespeople, and the other shoppers present in the store, the facilities available in the store—changing rooms, shopping trolleys, carry bags, and parking facilities—also affect shoppers' perceptions of the store. These facilities also help shoppers to differentiate between stores. Thus, shoppers may prefer shops that offer these conveniences. The quality of these facilities would also influence shoppers. Exhibit 15.4 describes a shopper's discomfort with the quality of changing rooms in most apparel stores.

Intangible Aspects

There are several intangible aspects in every shop. These include the processes in the store, language and conduct of the staff, and the 'atmospherics', that is, the ambience of the store. These aspects are discussed in this section.

EXHIBIT 15.5   Shopper Perception of Codes of Conduct

Shopper

How else do we explain the change in the language we speak when we shop at different stores? We tend to talk softly, walk slowly, and control our children more in lifestyle or branded stores. We tend to check at such stores if smoking is allowed, while at a *kirana* store we feel offended if we are refrained. Why do we feel embarrassed when, in a lifestyle store, we do not realize that the cash we are carrying may be insufficient? The same feeling does not arise in a convenience store. Nobody told us to behave this way, but we do.

Processes in the Store

Caring stores design processes around the shopper. The hospitality provided to the shopper does not end with a soft drink or temperature-control alone—that is merely the beginning. Shopping is a pleasurable experience only when shoppers do not feel that they are being 'processed'. All processes within the store—the merchandise choice process, delivery process, billing process, and payment process—interact with the shopper one way or the other. It is up to the store to make sure that these processes create an enjoyable shopping experience. However, most of the time, processes seem to be geared to store requirements such as operations, staff movement, security, and economy. The logic behind most of the process design is control and not facilitation.

Language and Code of Conduct

Every store has a distinct language and code of conduct. These are sets of unwritten rules that are never communicated explicitly by the retailer. Nor are they actively sought by shoppers. Still, they are communicated very well by most retailers.

Exhibit 15.5 displays a shopper's opinion about the presence of unwritten codes of conduct in different stores.

Atmospherics

This is the most intangible aspect of the structure of the store as a society. The atmospherics or the ambience creates an aura about the store that is not only felt inside the store but lingers with the shoppers. It is not easy to express. Shops are often differentiated by this 'there-is-something-in-the-air' parameter. This aura appeals to the senses of sight, smell, and hearing. Imagine a music shop without any 'air display', or Barista without the smell of coffee. Lighting, music, colour, and aesthetics are used to create this aura. Research on the expectation of shoppers towards atmospherics highlighted that the store ambience should (a) stimulate and motivate them to buy, and (b) invigorate them so that they feel charged/relaxed after shopping.

SUMMARY

A shop can be defined as a whole and functioning social unit with a distinct set of customs, organization, interaction patterns, and association of people united by a common interest/aim. A shop is a composite of several tangible and intangible ingredients. The store format, merchandise on offer, communication tools, facilities, salespeople, and other shoppers in a store comprise the tangible aspects. The intangible aspects include the various processes within the store, its code of conduct, and most importantly, its atmospherics. Each of these components is important and individually potent. Their interaction creates a result that makes every store different. Thus, even when a store is part of a chain, each store is different simply because the shoppers in each store are different. Further, they may not be different demographically, but they would differ in their socio-cultural make up, leading to different behavioural patterns.

We must remember that shopping is a personal activity performed as a social conduct and that the behaviour of shoppers outside the store may not be similar to the behaviour exhibited inside the store. This is due to the variables present inside the store. A store thus needs to design its policies in these areas keeping in mind all the tangible and intangible factors inside the store.

NOTES

1. Langrehr, Frederick W. 1991, 'Retail Shopping Mall Semiotics and Hedonic Consumption', *Advances in Consumer Research*, Vol. 18, Issue 1, pp. 428–33.
2. Belk, Russell W. 1975, 'Situational Variables and Consumer Behavior', *Journal of Consumer Research*, 2 December, pp. 157–64.
3. Langrehr, Frederick W 1991, 'Retail Shopping Mall Semiotics and Hedonic Consumption', *Advances in Consumer Research*, Vol. 18, Issue 1, pp. 428–33.
4. Gillis, A.R., Madeline A. Richard, and John Hagan 1986, 'Ethnic Susceptibility to Crowding—An Empirical Analysis', *Environment and Behavior*, 18 November, pp. 683–706.
5. Bellizzi, Joseph A., Ayn E. Crowley, and Ronald W. Hasty 1983, 'The Effects of Color in Store Design', *Journal of Retailing*, 59 (Spring), pp. 21–45.
6. Page, Richard A. 1977, 'Noise and Helping Behavior', *Environment and Behavior*, September, pp. 311–34.
7. Griffith, William 1970, 'Environmental Effects on Interpersonal Affective Behavior: Ambient Effective Temperature and Attraction', *Journal of Personality and Social Psychology*, 15 (July), pp. 240–4.

CONCEPT REVIEW QUESTIONS

1. How is a retail outlet a social system? What are its tangible and intangible parts? What do customers expect in this system?

2. How do salespeople shape the perception of customers about them?

CRITICAL THINKING QUESTIONS

1. If you were to go to a petrol station and find that blaring music is being played and salespeople are humming along, what would you make of it? Should this behaviour be allowed? In what kind of stores could such a practice be allowed?

2. Are crowds desirable or undesirable in a store? Think of a store where crowds would be desirable and one where they would be bad for the store. Explain the rationale behind your answer.

PROJECT

Meet a person dealing in semiotics—the study of signs and symbols and their use or interpretation. Develop an understanding of how signs and symbols used in the interior designing of the store can affect customer experience.

16 Technology in Retailing

LEARNING OBJECTIVES

After studying this chapter, you will be able to
- understand the role of technology in enhancing customer experience
- discuss the latest developments in the use of retail technology inside the store and on the Internet
- understand the applications of various technologies in retailing
- gain an insight into the recent trends and challenges in the use of technology in retailing

INTRODUCTION

Today the consumer is in charge. Providing value to customers has become a challenge for retailers. Consumers now have a wider choice of merchandise available. They also have access to a large amount of information that they use to arrive at the buying decision. Consequently, competition for customers is fierce. Customers want 'value' in terms of not only price, ambience and appearance, quality, and information but also selection, convenience, service, and entertainment.[1] Stores are finding it difficult to attract enough footfall. Customer loyalty is being challenged every day. Retailers have to be satisfied with low profit margins of 3–5 per cent. Many retailers are finding it difficult to survive.[2] Information technology (IT) helps retailers to manage costs and deliver better value to customers. Technology is used across the value chain, and more so in the supply chain. This chapter, however, focuses on the use of technology that interacts with the customers directly.

Technology is being considered as an important tool in building and maintaining relationships. It is being used to learn about the needs, preferences, and shopping habits of individual consumers. Technology enables retailers to identify consumers at the point of purchase. This helps them to tailor their offers to meet the needs of individual shoppers. Retailers are using sophisticated software tools that help them develop mathematical models to understand the effectiveness of their marketing efforts. These models also help in deciding about the retail mix elements and arrive at optimum solutions. They help retailers in faster decision-making and implementation across stores. The use of technology enhances the shopping experiences by providing convenience, better service, speed, and value to the customer. It aids retailers in helping customers with product information and selection without much increase in costs. The use of technology makes the shopping experience more fun. The use of technology helps protect consumers' privacy.

Consumers are increasingly using technology-driven tools when they shop. In a study conducted in the US, it was found that 18 per cent of consumers searched for product information on the Internet and 13 per cent used it to make purchases. Fifteen per cent used in-store kiosks, 14 per cent used self-scanning or checkout systems, and over 50 per cent of consumers used loyalty cards. These percentages, however, are still low when compared to the usage of traditional paper-based tools such as store circulars (87 %), coupons (85 %), and shopping lists (82 %).[3] Another consumer research study indicated that consumers are willing to accept technology solutions in retail, especially those that address their most pressing issues of long lines at the checkout counters, lack of product information in the store, lack of employee knowledge, difficulties identifying where products are located in the store, and out-of-stock situations.

TYPES OF TECHNOLOGIES USED IN RETAILING

Retailers use two main types of technologies: (i) in-store technologies and (ii) online technologies. These technologies are used for information, display and identification, checkouts, point-of-sale (POS) signage, and hand-held shopping assistance and body scanning, especially for physical stores.

In-store Technologies

In-store technologies may be used in the form of kiosks, virtual display cases, radio frequency identification device (RFID) tags, electronic POS signage, hand-held assistance devices, body scanning systems, and self-scanning and self-checkout systems.

Interactive Kiosks

Interactive kiosks are computers with touch-screen displays that provide shoppers with information about products in the store. With the help of these kiosks, customers can identify and select products without moving around the store. Kiosks help retailers in offering an expanded selection of items. Video kiosks may also provide and print a map of the store and indicate the location of the chosen merchandise. This reduces and controls the movement of the shopper, which is beneficial for both the retailer and the shopper. Frequent shopper kiosks that are located near the entrance of retail stores are modifications of interactive kiosks. When a consumer inserts a frequent shopper card into the kiosk, it displays a customized set of products and promotions based on the shopper's past purchases. It may also display recipes, special offers, samples, and sweepstake opportunities. The system automatically detects electronic coupons at checkout. At music stores, customers can use the interactive kiosks to hear selections from any CD or view a trailer from any DVD by scanning the bar code. Customers can also get more information on other albums an artist has recorded. By swiping their loyalty cards, they can receive recommendations for music they might like. It was estimated that that by 2007 more than $7.5 billion in goods and services would be sold via kiosks, up from $200 million in 2001.[4]

Kiosks are becoming very useful to some types of retailers. For instance, mom-and-pop stores can now match the range of many large stores without investing in space. Customers can order their merchandise through the kiosks and can collect it after some time, or ask for home delivery.[5] A store can choose to provide this service for merchandise that is bought infrequently and in small quantities, thereby reducing its inventory costs. Kiosks are finding favour in emerging economies, where real estate is costly and supply chain infrastructure is not so well developed. They are providing self-employment with low investments.[6] Interactive, self-service kiosks are finding many uses in retailing. They allow for automatic delivery of RFID key fobs activated at the kiosk for payment and loyalty applications for retailers. Kiosks fulfil the purpose of registry creation, retrieval, updating, and uploading registrant's product selections from a palm-type scanning device. They give their customers the ability to enjoy self-service and create, update, and print out registries using a single

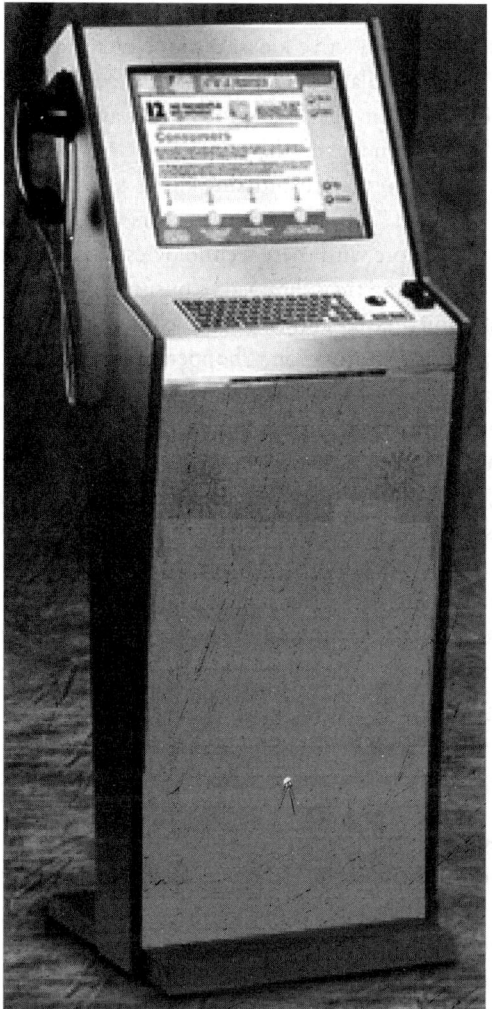

Interactive Kiosk

Self-checkout System

Self-scanning Device

In-store Technology

touch-screen application, simplifying these processes significantly. Kiosks are also used for gift card dispensing for loyalty programmes. Kiosk technology easily allows customers to collect points, redeem awards for discounts and savings, or to receive special offers. Loyalty kiosks are also helpful in tracking and collecting information about customers. For physical retailers, it is almost impossible to have every single product option physically located in the store. Interactive kiosks can help these retailers by allowing the customer access to their extended product lines. DaimlerChrysler's dealers, for example, use interactive kiosks that provide access to an extended list of vehicle options including interior/exterior colour selections, standard equipment, and optional features and equipment. Similarly, BMW started using interactive kiosks for an online gaming experience known as BMW X3 Adventure, featuring three different in-car driving experiences and outdoor sporting activities, including mountain biking, snowboarding, and kayaking. Retailers dealing in paints use kiosks so that customers can browse through a collection of inspirational palettes, preview colours in virtual rooms, and receive instant colour coordination tips. These interactive kiosks also include practical tips for painting projects and provide users with a paint calculator and supplies lists. Self-service checkout kiosks are the easiest way for retailers to expedite the checkout process and avoid lines. Airlines have started using check-in kiosks, especially for frequent travellers.

Studies have revealed that consumers find both product information/ordering kiosks and frequent shopper kiosks useful. A study indicated that, on an average, 76 per cent of customers rated kiosks as an advantage, 60 per cent were more likely to shop at a store with these technologies, and 80 per cent expected to use the technologies at least some of the time they shopped. Consumers felt that product information/ordering kiosks would make shopping faster and easier by helping them find what they wanted and providing detailed/current product information. Shoppers liked frequent shopper kiosks because these highlight items that have special deals, schemes, or offers attached to them and eliminate the need to clip and carry coupons, thus saving them money.

Virtual display cases received lower scores because the products shown on the screen cannot be physically examined and purchased in the store, and in some cases, special glasses are required to view the images. In all three cases, consumers disliked the prospect of waiting in line to use the machines and recommended that several kiosks be installed in each store to accommodate demand.[7] Another study indicated that the opinion about the benefits of kiosks is mixed. Some feel that it is still experimental and retailers have not been able to determine the return on their investments on kiosks.[8] Others feel that kiosks have the power to influence the value chain by controlling the ultimate stage of point of purchase.[9] Understanding the profile of the customers using kiosks and their usage pattern determines the role of kiosks in influencing the value chain.[10]

Virtual Display Case

A 'virtual display case' is a large-screen, rear projection video display and computer graphics system which shows three-dimensional images of shelves and the merchandise on them. These are generally located near store entrances. These cases allow customers to scan and purchase items without going around the store. Consumers are provided with a pair of 3-D glasses to view the images. A hand-held controller and joystick allows consumers to select product categories, zoom in on shelf displays, and pick up products and examine them from any angle. When products are selected from the virtual shelf, they appear to float in space. To select a product for purchase, consumers have to simply drop it into a simulated shopping basket.

Radio Frequency Identification Tags

Radio frequency identification (RFID) tags are electronic devices used for storing information about the merchandise as well as for tracking them. As large as a pinhead, consisting of an antenna and a chip that contains an electronic product code, these tags can store more information about a product than bar codes. Besides the information about the merchandise, an RFID tag can store information about when and where the product was made, where its components came from, and what its shelf and physical life is. The tags signal their presence over a radio frequency when they pass within the range of a special scanner. These tags have long been in use in high-cost applications, such as automated tolling systems and security identification badges. Recent innovations have caused the price of the tags to plummet and their performance to improve. In 2000, RFID tags cost $1 each. They cost 25 to 40 cents in 2003, and are widely expected to cost no more than 5 cents a piece in a few years.[11]

Retailers can derive several advantages from the use of RFID. They can improve customer service and manage pilferage losses. This technology can be used to locate mislaid products, deter theft, and even to offer customers personalized sales pitches through displays mounted in dressing rooms. These tags and readers can also replace bar codes and reduce checkout efforts. Radio frequency identification tags have utility in the supply chain also. Unlike bar codes, the unique electronic product codes (EPC) enable products tagged in factories to be tracked as they move along the supply chain to the consumers. It is estimated that a retailer or consumer goods manufacturer using RFID can bring down the total warehouse labour costs by nearly 3 per cent. It is a very good tool for companies that practise vendor managed inventory. The information in RFID readers can be shared on the Internet. This exchange of information may save both parties 20–40 per cent or more in inventory and out-of-stock costs.

Retailers and suppliers need to be careful in using this technology. Consumers may not see the benefit, except in case of more in-stock items. A larger benefit is expected to come from supply chain applications. The main value of RFID is the elimination of the need for individual handling of merchandise.[12] An October 2002 pilot study by the Auto-ID Centre found that RFID-tagged pallets failed 3 per cent of the time even when double-tagged, and only 78 per cent of the individually tagged pallets were read accurately. This requires a robust technology, which is yet to come by. This technology is evolving but would take some time.[13]

Electronic Point-of-sale Signage

Electronic POS signs are liquid crystal displays (LCDs) that show the names and prices of merchandise. In large stores, these may also display currency conversions. These signs are attached to store shelves, peg hooks, or products. They replace the conventional price tags and printed shelf labels. Consumers have shown a liking for e-POS as it provides them with accurate price information on the shelf. By enabling easy comparisons without the need to read the packs, they help customers make product decisions faster and avoid errors. Electronic POS signs help in faster checkout as manual price checks are not required. However, many customers feel that the costs of these systems may lead to higher prices at the store.

Hand-held Shopping Assistant

The hand-held shopping assistant is a device consisting of a touch-sensitive screen and a bar-code reader. As soon as the customers scan the bar code of the chosen product, the device provides them product information, such as specifications, operating instructions, usage suggestions, and warranty information. When a product is chosen, the assistant downloads the information through a wireless modem that connects it to the manufacturer's database. Shoppers who have used this device were happy as they had access to accurate, detailed, and current product information. They found that this was a good replacement of salespeople, especially those who may not have much product knowledge. However, they were concerned that shopping may take more time due to delays in download process.

Body Scanning

Body scanning is a computerized system for taking body measurements. It helps apparel retailers in finding the exact size of clothing that customers need. It is more useful in the case of custom-made products and for altering clothes that have been bought. This system uses video cameras that are attached to a computer. The body measurements are taken from several angles and a 3-D model of the shopper is generated. They can then select the clothes they wish to purchase. The computer shows an image of the body wearing the clothing. When a consumer chooses and orders the clothes, the information is transferred for manufacturing the clothes as per the unique measurements. These measurements are stored in a 'smart card' that can be used at any time in the store.

Self-scanning and Self-checkout Systems

The self-scanning system is a hand-held bar code reader used by shoppers to scan and tally their purchases while shopping. The scanner displays the price of the chosen item. Shoppers can then match it with the shelf price. The system also keeps a running total of selected purchases as the shopper adds or deletes items in the list. After shopping, the scanner prints out a ticket that the shopper can take to an express checkout counter. The self-checkout system helps consumers in checking out on their own. Using the system, they scan their purchases and keep them in their bags. They then make the payment through their cards. The system includes an automated teller machine (ATM), a bar code scanner, a weighing scale, and check stand. An overhead camera keeps watch on the purchases. Customers like both self-scanning and self-checkout systems as they help them avoid long lines and speed up the checkout process. However, consumers seem to like self-scanning more because an attendant can accept payments and bag their purchases when a self-checkout system is not used.

Electronic Retailing

Retailers use the electronic medium to provide information about their store and the available merchandise. They use information technology to design websites that can provide store information, act as virtual showrooms, and enable customers to shop online. These online sites differ in two ways: (i) the way in which products are displayed on the screen—in a two- or three-dimensional format (ii) whether the site allows consumers to actually purchase products online or just retrieve information about the store, product, and promotional offers.

Consumers have shown a positive attitude towards all three types of online sites, that is, sites providing store information, virtual information sites, and sites that enable customers to shop online. In a study, it was found that 57 per cent of shoppers rate online technologies as an advantage, 50 per cent indicate that they would be more likely to shop at a store selling or promoting their wares online, and 63 per cent indicate that they would use these technologies at least some of the time they shop. Consumers saw the greatest advantage in online technologies that were directly tied to the in-store shopping experience. Fifty-six per cent believed that it would be beneficial to show three-dimensional images of products and store aisles, and 61 per cent would like to access local store information. People cited the convenience of shopping from home at any hour and the ability to search for product and pricing information as the most appealing features. Their greatest concerns were the inability to touch and feel products when shopping online, the security of their credit card information, and their lack of or difficulty in using computers.[14]

ECR AND TECHNOLOGY

Efficient consumer response (ECR) involves re-engineering, re-designing, and computerizing of the supply chain and aims to provide greater value to the consumer. Technology plays a crucial role in making the supply chain more efficient and helps in implementing ECR. The results of a study on the concerns, status, and benefits of ECR in Japan showed that the business environment was ripe for large-scale ECR implementation. In addition to the general benefits of ECR, channel members also valued the specific benefits related to efficient replenishment. Companies that had already implemented

ECR and those that had not differed significantly in their perceptions of the barriers to ECR adoption. Financial barriers were big factors for those who had not implemented ECR. For companies that had implemented ECR, lack of both skill- and technology-related capabilities and the attitudes of channel members were the main barriers to implementation.[15]

Technology finds use across the value chain. Supply chain and inventory management are the areas that have been amenable to technology adoption for long. It can be used for determining and managing prices. Pricing software can be used to map a highly detailed path toward achieving retailers' goals. It can also assess the sales impact of price changes within and across categories. The software can also suggest when a store in one area can charge higher prices on certain products than a nearby store that is in a slightly less affluent area. Similarly, by tracking seasonal demands, it helps in framing discounting policies. Some retailers use wireless scanners to record people's purchases on a card. On reaching the checkout counter, customers hand over their cards and make their payments. In some cases, sales associates use these devices to handle sales. A salesperson scans an item's bar code, which sends a signal to the stockroom. The item is kept ready for the customer to pick up at a designated loading area. When customers arrive there, they pass the bar code under a reader that signals the salesperson in the stockroom to bring out the item.

Technologies like electronic POS signage are found to be applicable to every category, especially in the frequently purchased categories. Technologies that provide information, like hand-held assistants, are found to be more suitable in product categories such as music and books, consumer electronics, and toys because they offer a wide selection of items and the product is either complex or the features are not necessarily apparent. Consumers in such cases need sufficient and accurate product information. Product information/ordering kiosks and hand-held shopping assistants score higher than online shopping sites in all product categories. Consumers are more likely to use the hand-held shopping assistant than the product information/ordering kiosk when shopping for small appliances and consumer electronics since it is easier to carry. These technologies can also be used for home furnishing product categories as these categories require high information search and a time consuming shopping process. The self-scanning device may be particularly useful for product categories that the customers are familiar with and buy frequently and in smaller quantities, such as groceries, office supplies, and seasonal merchandise. Body-scanning devices can be used by apparel and jewellery shoppers for a perfect match.

ADOPTION OF TECHNOLOGY—TRENDS AND CHALLENGES

Gartner Inc. predicts that as more 'toys', that is, technical devices, are brought to bear on retailing, it might be possible to make shoppers more interested in going to the store.[16] Two trends—the drive for differentiation and the clamour for collaboration among intermediaries—are seen as major influencers of technology usage in the current retailing scenario. Differentiation by large manufacturers and retailers will encourage more direct marketing. Although differentiation by manufacturers creates entry barriers for small firms, differentiation by retailers may open opportunities. Some collaboration initiatives will increase the supply chain efficiency up to the retailer, but the adoption rate of collaborative technologies by stores is likely to be slow. With more differentiation, consumers will have greater choice.

Retailers may face certain challenges in the use of technology. Some technologies that could boost the efficiency of the system may be resisted by consumers.[17] In a study on the influence of technology anxiety on the use of self-service technologies, it was found that respondents with higher levels of technology anxiety use fewer self-service technologies. Technology anxiety was found to be a better, more consistent predictor of self-service technology usage than demographic variables. Technology anxiety was also found to influence overall levels of satisfaction, intentions to use self-service technologies again, and the likelihood of participating in positive word-of-mouth recommendations of consumers who had an initially satisfying experience.[18]

Organizational innovativeness also offers a significant explanation of technology adoption. Organizations need to develop technological opportunism by taking specific actions, such as focusing on the future, having the top management advocate new technologies, and by becoming more of an adhocracy culture and less of a hierarchy culture. Organizations need to decide on the relative emphasis on internal (research and development) versus external (buying, licensing) technology development. It should be kept in mind that technology orientation and market orientation are complementary aspects that are essential for the firm to function efficiently.[19] Organizations that possess not only the technical capabilities for automation but also the ability to learn and share information are most likely to automate their supply chain processes.[20]

Technology needs to be seen as an investment, not an expense. It is an enabler for strategies that can change the retail paradigm and propel retailers ahead of competition.[21] There are expenses associated with acquiring and installing new technologies and integrating them with existing systems. The store personnel and customers need to be educated so that they can make better use of the available technology. To help minimize the risk of failure, it is suggested that retailers take the following precautions:[22]

- Experiment with new technologies in the product categories where they deliver the greatest value
- Deploy in-store technologies in communities with a relatively high percentage of 'technology adopters'
- Make technology easy to use and provide support and training
- Promote technology benefits that consumers have rated as most important
- Minimize or eliminate those aspects of technology that consumers dislike
- Track consumer usage of and satisfaction with technologies and make refinements

Retailers need to take into consideration the likes, dislikes, and orientation of customers while deciding to use new technologies. They also need to develop the processes within the organization in order to make good use of these technologies.

Technology–Human Interface

The advent of technology in retail has allowed retailers to bring about drastic changes in their business operations at an unprecedented rate. The usage of technological applications has become a must for retailers, without which they would have to struggle to survive. Particularly in retail, the product delivered to, or carried by, the customer to his or her place, is a blend of merchandise and service. The service provided by the retailer is delivered through the human interface between the employee and the customer.

Studies have shown that with the application of technology, 70 per cent of the ordering time will be reduced, which can translate to improvement of the interface between the customers and sales.[23] The retailers can increase their efficiency through new technology in terms of the speed of checkouts, effective pricing mechanism, and ordering system. This would help them focus on more important tasks for improving the overall profitability.

Today's retailers think about investing in latest technology as a crucial component of their business strategy, resulting in efficiency and profitability to gain a competitive edge. With labour, property, and supply chain costs increasing manifold, there is a drastic change in the way the retail business is handled. Moreover, customers' shopping behaviour is also transforming in a dynamic way, which is compelling retailers to look beyond the normal boundaries and embrace new trends in technology for surviving the cut-throat competition.

Retailers have to invest a huge amount of money on new technology and thereby expect the benefits to materialize rapidly for them in terms of store performance and productivity. Some issues faced by the retailer in this process of implementation of the new technology are as follows:[24]

- Too complicated for customers' usage
- End user complication
- Poorly designed keystrokes
- Not accessible to everyone
- Generation of unbudgeted tasks
- Difficulty faced by store engineers in maintenance
- No effective training
- Wrong location of the device
- Not much time savings in staff hours due to undefined roles

As a retailer, it is easier to measure profits, store performance, and level of investments. However, it is a challenge to concentrate on areas such as technology and human interface, which are difficult to measure. The retailer has to undeniably take into account the amount of lost sales due to the inefficiencies in the applied technologies.

It is important to keep a track of the customers' overall shopping experience in a physical store, which will help in making the whole shopping trip fruitful. Similarly, when it comes to online retailers, an important issue is managing the effectiveness of the web applications installed by them. It is a great challenge to reduce the ever-increasing gap between new technology and customer awareness.[25] For instance, despite increase in bandwidth, a common problem for all web application servers is that they remain overloaded during peak hours. The management of security and integrity of data is also proving to be a big challenge for marketers. Retailers have to be cautious while using new technology because consumers make spontaneous judgements in seconds and, if not satisfied, would gradually turn to competitors' websites.

The Information Age has rapidly progressed and customers are managing information on their fingertips. Advancements in information and communication technology have changed the way retail operations are carried out. The key areas of the business are definitely in focus, but as a retailer it is very important to understand that the human warmth and sociability factor differs across different types of products or services, and perhaps that is the reason why many online stores have little emotional or social appeal and lack the human touch.[26] Many customers find that online stores, when compared to the offline stores, are impersonal and automated.

The usage of technology has in some aspects failed to realize its actual potential for a retailer. Retailer have to definitely embrace the benefits derived from the use of new technology but also take precautionary steps to ensure that they do not distance themselves from the customers.

SUMMARY

Retailers have access to a large number of technological innovations. While information technology is used extensively for managing back-end processes, some devices have also been developed to enhance the customer shopping experience at the store. These technologies can be classified as in-store technologies and electronic retailing. These help customers in choosing the merchandise, comparing it, and knowing the prices and promotions for the basket of products bought by them. These devices help improve the shopping process by reducing the time and effort spent by the shoppers. Many of these help in shopping without the help of salespeople. In some cases, the devices connect to the website of the store, where the customers can order even that merchandise which is not available at the store and get it delivered at home.

The adoption of these technologies has been slow due to high costs. The slow rate of adoption is also attributed to the orientation of customers towards technology. Some customers are wary of using technology. Retailers need to segment their customers accordingly and make an effort to communicate with their customers through a programme that helps them use the technology and find out the benefits of the same.

NOTES

1. Williams, Theresa and Mark J. Larson 1999, 'Retail Technology in the Next Century: What's "In Store" for Consumers', Indiana University, KPMG Study, p. 1.
2. Hopkins, Pegeen, 'Better Times in Store', www.contextmag.com/archives/2000206/Feature1 BetterTimes.asp, accessed on 15 April 2004.
3. Williams, Theresa and Mark J. Larson 1999, 'Retail Technology in the Next Century: What's "In Store" for Consumers', Indiana University, KPMG Study, p. 6.
4. Hopkins, Pegeen, 'Better Times in Store', www.contextmag.com/archives/2000206/Feature1 BetterTimes.asp, accessed on 15 April 2004.
5. Metters, R., M. Ketzenberg, and G. Gilden 2000, 'Welcome Back, Mom and POP', *Harvard Business Review*, May–June, pp. 24–5.
6. Robinson, Terry M. 1997, 'Retailing in Eastern Siberia and the Russian Far East', *International Journal of Retail and Distribution Management*, Vol. 25, No. 9, pp. 301–08.
7. Williams, Theresa and Mark J. Larson 1999, 'Retail Technology in the Next Century: What's "In Store" for Consumers', Indiana University, KPMG Study, p. 1.
8. Fox, B. 1993, 'Still Experimental: Kiosks ROI Remain Unproven', *Chain Store Age Executive*, Vol. 69, No. 6, pp. 57–8.
9. Norris, S. 1994, 'Flash Point', *Marketing Week*, Vol. 1, July, pp. 47–8.
10. Rowley, J. 1995, 'Multimedia Kiosks in Retailing', *International Journal of Retail and Distribution Management*, Vol. 23, No. 5, pp. 32–40.
11. Niemeyer, Alex, Minsok H. Pak, and Sanjay E. Ramaswamy 2003, *The McKinsey Quarterly*, No. 4.
12. Chartered Institute of Logistics and Transport 2004, 'RFID—Could it Spell the End of the Super-store Checkout', *CILT World*, Issue 10, p. 23.
13. Doyale, Shaun 2004, 'Auto-ID Technology in Retail and its Application in Marketing', *Database Marketing and Customer Strategy Management*, Vol. 11, No. 3, pp. 274–9.
14. Williams, Theresa and Mark J. Larson 1999, 'Retail Technology in the Next Century: What's "In Store" for Consumers', Indiana University, KPMG Study, p. 24.
15. Lohtia, Ritu, 'Frank' Tian Xie, and Ramesh Subramaniam 2004, 'Efficient Consumer Response in Japan: Industry Concerns, Current Status, Benefits, and Barriers to Implementation', *Journal of Business Research*, Mar., Vol. 57, No. 3, pp. 306–11.
16. Hopkins, Pegeen, 'Better times in store', www.contextmag.com/archives/2000206/Feature1 BetterTimes.asp, accessed on 15 April 2004.

17. Larson, Ronald B. 2003, 'Emerging Trends in the Food Distribution System', *Journal of Food Products Marketing*, Vol. 9, No. 2, pp. 53–68.
18. Meuter, Matthew L., Amy L. Ostrom, Mary Jo Bitner, and Robert Roundtree 2003, 'The Influence of Technology Anxiety on Consumer Use and Experiences with Self-service Technologies', *Journal of Business Research*, November, Vol. 56, No. 11, pp. 899–906.
19. Srinivasan, Raji, Gary L. Lilien, and Arvind Rangaswamy 2002, 'Technological Opportunism and Radical Technology Adoption: An Application to E-Business', *Journal of Marketing*, Jul., Vol. 66, No. 3, pp. 47–60.
20. Zahay, Debra L. and Robert B. Handfield 2004, 'The Role of Learning and Technical Capabilities in Predicting Adoption of B2B Technologies', *Industrial Marketing Management*, October, Vol. 33, No. 7, pp. 627–41.
21. The Canadian Retail Technology Survey 2001.
22. Williams, Theresa and Larson, Mark J. (1999), 'Retail Technology in the Next Century: What's "In Store" for Consumers', Indiana University, KPMG Study, p. 24.
23. Oliver, Hilary 2006, 'Evolve with Retail Technology', *Natural Foods Merchandiser*, December, Vol. 27 Issue 12.
24. http://www.retailhumanfactors.com, accessed on 5 January 2011.
25. 'Achieving Success in Retail', *Enterprise Innovation*, June 2008, Vol. 4, Issue 3.
26. Hassanein, Khaled 2005–6, 'The Impact of Infusing Social Presence in the Web Interface: An Investigation Across Product Types', *International Journal of Electronic Commerce*, Vol. 10.

CONCEPT REVIEW QUESTIONS

1. What roles can technology play in enhancing customer experiences?
2. What are the main in-store technologies used in retailing? What are the usual opinions of customers regarding these technologies?
3. What factors should be kept in mind while identifying appropriate technology in retailing?

CRITICAL THINKING QUESTION

When customers have comfortably adopted complicated devices such as mobile phones and computers, what deters them from adopting retail technologies? What should a *kirana* store do to get its customers to use some of the technologies mentioned in the chapter?

PROJECT

Visit a store and find out the extent of technology used in interfacing with the customers. Discuss the technologies used and the reasons thereof with the store manager.

CASE STUDY

Evolution of Business Models in B2C E-commerce: The Case of Fabmall[1]

K. Kumar and B. Mahadevan

Online and Physical Retail: Some Facts

Fabmall today has two businesses—online and physical retail. The online business is expected to grow from transaction volumes of ₹7.5 million per month to a volume of ₹20 million per month in 18 months. At this level, it will generate a profit before tax of ₹1 million per month. As the volumes scale further, the expenses will not scale at the same level and therefore the profit margin on sales will grow at a much faster pace.

The physical retail business will grow exponentially. From revenues of ₹4 million per month in April 2003, it is already at ₹15 million per month in November 2003—a sales growth of 250 per cent in seven months! The explosive pace of growth is expected to continue at least for the next three years. Beyond a critical mass, the profit margin on sales will probably settle at 3–4 per cent of sales and may not rise with further sales.

The two businesses fulfil two business needs—one can scale significantly and while the profit margin will not grow, the absolute profits can explode. The other business may not become a huge business but as the volumes grow, the profits can grow asymmetrically. It is important to understand the needs of each business and fuel its growth.

The meteoric rise of business-to-customer (B2C) e-commerce firms during the late 90s and the subsequent bursting of the dotcom bubble have left level several questions unanswered in the minds of practitioners about the viability of Internet ventures and the need for appropriate business models. What are we to learn from the Internet firms that have survived this transition? What are the transformations these firms have gone through in their business models? Professors K. Kumar[2] and B. Mahadevan[3] discuss these issues in conversation with V.S. Sudhakar, Managing Director, Fabmall.

Fabmart, a pureplay Internet retail platform, was set up in 1999 at the height of the dotcom boom. Four years later, the startup transformed itself into Fabmall, a multi-channel retail business, with six physical stores and a significant presence in cyber space. During the course of the conversation, Sudhakar shows how the transition of a pureplay Internet firm into a multi-channel retailing organization signals the importance of changing the business model in line with market developments.

The experience of Sudhakar and his team in bringing about this transition has many distinctive features that other organizations could learn from. Having substantial clarity on the role of the Internet could well be an important element of success. Further, the ability to select and focus unambiguously on customer segments could differentiate an e-tailer and influence several elements of the business model. A successful business requires that there is a willingness on the part of the management to change several operational features of the business model from time to time. Moreover, evolution of business models requires the management to be passionate and yet objectively review the business assumptions periodically.

KK: *In entrepreneurial literature, one clear categorization is between evolutionary and revolutionary ventures. A revolutionary venture typically attempts to change the way the world lives. In my opinion Fabmall falls under this category because you are trying to change the way people buy. There aren't many examples of such ventures in India. So, from an entrepreneurial perspective, your business model is of particular interest. Could you describe the key principles behind the launch of Fabmart in September 1999?*

VSS: When I was the CEO of Planetasia, in the early days of the Internet, we used to advise corporates on how to leverage the Internet as a communication platform. We built a website for Shoppers Stop and wanted them to extend it to shopping online; we were having discussions

---

1. Now Indiaplaza.

2. K. Kumar is visiting faculty, Corporate Strategy and Policy, IIM Bangalore. (email id: kumark@iimb.ernet.in)

3. B. Mahadevan is Professor, Production and Operations Management, IIM Bangalore and Chief Editor, IIMB Management Review. (email id: mahadev@iimb.ernet.in)

with Citibank to build an online payment gateway. The issue in those days was, once you built the gateway, who was going to use it? Without the gateway, transactions through the Internet would not be possible, and without transactions, the gateway did not make much sense. So somebody had to break that chain. We suggested to Citibank to set up an e-mall, where all their merchants could set up shop and create a transactions platform using the gateway. While they were comfortable with the idea of the payment gateway, the mall was not their core business. Planetasia, an Internet services company, too was not interested in setting up the mall. Consequently, a group of six promoters, five from an IT background, set up Fabmart as an online retail platform in June 1999. We decided on a few basic parameters of establishing the business.

First, we decided not to get lost in the Internet technology: we were very clear that the primary nature of our business was retailing, and the Internet was merely a channel. So from day one we decided to focus on the core success factors of a retail company. The challenges involved in creating a new channel excited us.

Second, we were clear that our competition was not just other online retailers. Our competition was the physical world, because when customers are looking at the value proposition that a retailer is offering, it doesn't matter whether they buy online or in a physical store. Being an Internet-based retail business meant that we could get orders from anywhere in the country. Therefore the competition was any retailer anywhere in the country.

Third, we decided to do it category by category, as though we were setting up a physical store. We started with the music store, then we added books. Later, we decided to do jewellery. It is possibly the most difficult product to sell online. The jewellery store did fairly well and we realized the importance of building credibility and trust. The fact that we delivered exactly as promised was something that delighted customers.

Fourth, we were clear that in the first phase of online business all customer order would be sourced, processed, and shipped by us, not by the vendors. This would enable us to retain control and guarantee service quality to the customer.

Finally, we wanted to establish online retail as a sensible alternative to physical retail. We knew that it could never be a 100 per cent replacement because there is an element of criticality about physical retail. In fact I had a simple formula—in any online business, I will be able to get only x% of all customers. Within that x I will get only y% of their share. So the product of x and y is ultimately the market share that an online business could have. If xy could grow to about 5–10 per cent in five years, we were talking very big business.

BM: *How did the customers respond to your venture initially?*

VSS: Initially we were surprised by the positive response from the customers. Perhaps, when we started the business, there were practically no expectations on the part of the customers. The mere fact that customers were able to order online and have it delivered was significant. But this success started to build expectations. Customers began to expect quicker delivery, wider range, more features, and so on. I think that was a positive change—it indicated that people can feel secure ordering online, and start looking for better features and convenience.

BM: *Your point about expectations—that good performances become qualifiers—is indeed interesting. What impact did this have on the business? What changes did you make in your business operations?*

VSS: One of the first things we did was a major change in the software in September 2000. We realized that, for various reasons, we needed to source items from multiple cities. For instance, it is better to source Carnatic music from Chennai than from Mumbai. So we started shipping out of four locations—Bangalore, Chennai, Hyderabad, and Mumbai. Moreover, as the business grew, we needed to source and ship from the closest point to the customer. This required major changes in the software and we ended up building a strong supply chain focus into the solution itself.

With the new multi-location, multiple-payment (MLMP) feature built into the software, we added sufficient flexibility for payment and customer service in several locations. We improvized as we went along, adding features when we faced problems. In this process, we were constantly striking the right trade-off between the features and the software complexity in order to ensure reliability of the software.

The second major change was the introduction of grocery, where ideally orders have to be shipped the same day. One way of achieving this is to stock the goods yourself, and the second is to work off the premises of a retailer (the Tesco model). We chose the latter model.

Working on a partnership basis provided new learning opportunities for us and it initially worked well. We started with Bangalore, then added Chennai, and later Hyderabad. By this time, the Bangalore business had grown to about ₹0.7 million per month of sales out of a partner whose business from the retail store was about ₹1.4–1.5 million. As a result, the service quality and stocking levels dropped and space constraints became evident. For the partner it was a question of focus. If he/she continued to give up space, the business stood to suffer. Moreover, these were individual retailers for whom working capital was an issue.

The other alternative was to look for multiple partners within a city, who were forward looking and had good systems—a difficult proposition. So we decided to have our own warehouse in Bangalore. It was a huge change for us because, for the first time, we actually had to buy, stock, and do the entire inventory management for our business.

BM: *What were the distinctive elements in the first version of your business model? For example, I remember that you never looked at advertising as a revenue stream although, at that time, it was considered to be an important revenue stream by most B2C sites.*

VSS: Any banner advertisement is typically a link to go elsewhere. We were very clear that we would avoid anything that drew the customer away from the store. Secondly, we were also clear that we would like a customer to come only to shop—or to window shop.

There are two distinct segments in online shopping: one focuses on the serious shopper and the other on impulsive buyers. A portal like Indiatimes or Rediff is in the business of offering people different activities such as mail services, news, chat, and shopping, converting all of them into revenue. We were clear from the beginning that we were not a portal. What happens there is an impulse-driven buying model.

Ours is a need-driven buying model. It was a tricky call because, clearly, the number of visits generated would come down substantially in a need-driven buying model. But we decided that it was hopefully a surer path and would clarify our positioning in the minds of the customer. We have seen it evolve in the last three years. Today if you look at Indiatimes or Rediff, perhaps 70–80 per cent of the business comes from 30–50 impulse-driven products. While the number of visitors

is much lower in our case, our average order value is much higher, with a much larger range. Moreover, repeat purchase is also much higher.

BM: *This is very interesting. I think you have actually replicated a B2B* model. In B2B visitors do not browse a site the second time unless they are serious customers.*

VSS: Basically, we believe in depth. We don't want to have ten of this and thirty of that. We decided that in any particular category, our online store must compare favourably with a physical store. Although we couldn't build a range as huge as Amazon.com's, if we had access to the inventory of ten physical stores, we could be bigger than any single physical store. In the category of books that we sell, for instance, we carry 2.5 million titles, of which around 750,000 are available on any given day. This is far greater depth for a reader than any other retailer selling books.

KK: *On the subject of grocery, you mentioned that before you decided to set up your own warehouses, you had tied up with individual supermarkets. Did you consider looking at a more resourceful chain than individual stores?*

VSS: In 2000 there were not many grocery chains in India. We spoke to FoodWorld and later to Nilgiris in Bangalore. But FoodWorld had ideas of starting their own online grocery. While Nilgiris initially appeared keen, they could not move forward on this initiative for various internal reasons. So we had no choice but to set up our own. We decided to go in for a warehouse rather than setting up a physical store. Initially, we switched over to the warehouse model in Bangalore, but continued with our Chennai and Hyderabad partnerships. Later on we realized there was a consistent pattern of partnership limitations once we hit a business of ₹0.7 million per month.

BM: *When you started Fabmart in 1999 (with grocery added in 2000), there was enough experience from alternative models such as Netgrocer, Webvan, and Tesco. Going by the processes you described earlier, you seem to have reinvented the wheel. What were the business considerations that made it inevitable? Were there other contextual reasons?*

VSS: Tesco had not really come into the public eye then—it caught public attention as a success story sometime during 2001. Early to mid 2000 were the days of Webvan, and what really proved to be disastrous to Webvan was a billion dollar investment in a warehouse.

---

* Business-to-business

So we believed that the key differentiator of the online models was avoidance of stocking and inventory management. The beauty of this model is that it enables a strong outward business focus—in the first eight to nine months of Fabmart, most of our time was spent on customer issues, attending to customer requests and so on, and not on internal issues like inventory management.

Another factor, which I still believe is very critical, especially for start-ups, is a significant degree of outsourcing. This reduces the size of the organization and increases the time available for market development, customer relations, etc. For instance, in Planetasia about 40 per cent of my time was spent on people management, but in the first year of Fabmart, this took less than 10 per cent.

BM: *Your transformation seems to signal that brick and mortar aspects are important components of a business model. What exactly triggered this move?*

VSS: By the end of 2001, we realized that international retailers were embracing the concept of multi-channel retailing. We also realized that in order to build a retail brand we needed to access the customer in multiple ways. Two of our colleagues came from a physical retail background and had considerable experience with franchising, having worked for Disney. They believed that our strong focus on customer service could be leveraged gainfully by engaging in physical retail chains as well.

BM: *What are the key elements of this transformation to a multi-channel operation? Why did you not have the same range of products in your brick and mortar setup as well?*

VSS: In order to make this transformation, we had to make two choices: this mode of physical operation and the product category. Between investing in a physical retail chain of our own and doing it on a franchise mode, we were in favour of the latter at that point.

Secondly, we had to choose our product category. When we did an analysis to understand what was needed to succeed in each category, we realized that, except for grocery, the products that we were selling online required specialized knowledge of what to stock and how much. In apparel or jewellery you needed to understand the trends in fashion, in books you had to estimate the volume of sale of each title, whereas the grocery business is not subject to such significant swings. By and large, what matters is building technology to efficiently move your good across the supply chain.

In this sense, it is far more technology-driven than merchandising skill-driven.

Moreover, by then we also had some experience in the field, with the online grocery business and the warehouse. We had the necessary merchandising skills—buying, managing supplies, warehousing, and stock taking—and infrastructure in place, and had developed systems and relationships with suppliers. In our online business we were able to turn over our inventory 15–16 times a year, which was better than most retail stores. The only thing we needed to learn was how to sell in the physical store. So if we were going into physical retail, the obvious choice was grocery.

KK: *What are the advantages of a franchise mode of operation in your business?*

VSS: The big advantage of a franchise network is that you can scale up investment substantially. Your investment into the stores comes from multiple people. Another critical difference is having an owner sitting in the store, rather than an employee. However, the difficulty initially lay in finding the right kind of franchisees and convincing them. It was difficult because we had nothing to show except the online business, the warehouse, and how we moved the stock. We gradually got them interested and set up two stores in Bangalore.

By this time, we realized that the physical grocery business was going to be massive, and if you could make it to the top ten grocery retailers in India, you could get significant volumes and make profits even though the margins in retail are low. Everything depends on how well you control your costs and how efficiently you move the merchandise across the supply chain.

KK: *You have two businesses under one banner: online and offline. How do you manage both simultaneously? What issues crop up in such a multi-channel operation?*

VSS: By the end of 2002 we actually started looking at these two stores as two businesses within the legal entity called Fabmall. In fact, in terms of people, I am possibly the only common link between the two businesses today. At some point we may even look at splitting it into two separate organizations. Of course, we believe that the brand name is very critical irrespective of whether they are two organizations or one, but I think we are yet to exploit the synergy between the two. The dynamics of cost and operations are different for online and physical organizations. So even if the brands, the management, and the commitment to the customer are the same, the pricing could be different.

One characteristic of the online business is that interaction with the customer is significant compared to the physical store, which comes as a surprise to most people. Similarly, though popular perception is otherwise, I believe there is a strong brand loyalty in the grocery business. If your quality, your range of products, and pricing are within the parameters of what the customer is used to and what the competition is offering, there is no real reason for the customer to shift. Although the competitor is just a click away, the customer will certainly check, but continue to stay unless there is a huge disparity in the price.

KK: *You seem to be investing considerably less in the second phase, where you are building inventory, stores, and physical infrastructure. How does that match with the overall plan?*

VSS: We have the legacy of a strong brand, which we are carrying forward, so we are not spending significantly on brand building. Our brand value and our good track record ensure that our business partners are willing to work with us. The going will be tough but challenging because the focus is to see how to get the business cash positive and still invest in growth. Our creativity will obviously be put to test in newer and alternative areas. We have now focused on the operating cost at a line item level, which has brought in a significant budgeting focus. The budgeting is now done at a micro level. Gross margin is a key focus area, far more critical than the top line. Today people at every level of the organization are involved with the budget at the line item, expense level. The don't talk top line, they talk only bottom line.

As far as the physical business is concerned, we are driving it through the franchisee route, with the store investments coming through the franchisees. The inventory is the only investment we have and the focus is on managing it well using technology. We have four big stores and two small stores where we do about ₹12 million worth of business per month. We run on a total inventory base of about ₹7.5 million. So we are able to leverage it reasonably well and we are stretching the money to go much farther.

BM: *So, in the first phase of the business model the emphasis is on customer acquisition and trust building, and in the second phase, you seem to be looking at costs and bottom lines and making them more viable ...*

VSS: I agree. The focus is on leveraging the brand value built in the first phase of the business and scaling it in the second phase.

BM: *With 50 per cent of the total turnover now expected from the physical infrastructure, how will you leverage the online strengths in the offline version of your business?*

VSS: To begin with, our track record gives us the strength to look into the second phase of the business. If the first phase of the business had not existed, it would possibly not have been easy for us to do what we are doing now. As I said earlier, there is significant focus on the viability of the business. We were always careful with money, even in the dotcom boom days, but there is a huge difference between being careful with your money and creating a strong bottomline focus. Creating a viable business is not easy, since we are still to reach critical mass. We have gained significant learning and maturity from the first phase, which is driving the second phase.

From the merchandising perspective, we are no longer seen as a predominantly IT-oriented team. Our retailing skills are not questioned now. A lot of the learning on customer service applies to the physical business as well. From a technology point of view too, the learning of the first three and a half years is definitely useful.

BM: *Changing the focus of the business, getting a new set of investors on board, and parting amicably with your existing investors can be turbulent events in the life of any company. But the way you have described it, it all seems to have gone smoothly. Can you tell us how all these fell into place?*

VSS: There are two parts to it. The last transition was somewhat turbulent. There were no battles, but it was high pressure, with the outcome being uncertain at some stages. It was a tough period for us. At various points we kept asking ourselves what we were willing to live with, and what we were willing to give away. Moreover, we made the transition despite being close to break point many times, which itself was a big thing. Many companies would have succumbed at that stage. We did it with our business, our people, and our vision intact.

BM: *Many B2C sites continue to have serious fulfilment problems. How important is fulfilment in a B2C online business?*

VSS: Fulfilment, support, and genuinely caring customer service are very important. One of the biggest lessons we have learnt is that, however difficult it is, you stretch your last muscle to get the fulfilment right—as close to 100 per cent correct as possible! Only then can you keep customers happy. I think we have survived primarily because of our efforts in that direction.

Another critical thing is that we have trusted people and that has paid off. For instance, when we offered a no-questions-asked return guarantee on all goods including jewellery, people told us we were being foolish. But wherever we have had returns, it has always been for a good reason, and most of the time they have taken a replacement rather than cash. Our return rate is extremely low. This I think also reflects the kind of customers we have—serious shoppers, not impulse buyers.

BM: *Your observations on the customer segments in B2C are indeed interesting. It appears that differentiating and clarifying the target customer segments can make a significant difference to the success of the business.*

VSS: I agree. In the first phase of our business, we focused only on serious shoppers. We are now trying to leverage impulse business that can both serve to introduce the brand, and build volumes and margins on the same platform. We are in the process of coming to a mutually beneficial arrangement with MSN India. So far, MSN India has stayed away from shopping because they wanted to either do it well or not at all. If MSN brings traffic to the impulse driven business, and we are able to induce at least 20 per cent of the traffic to move to serious buying at a later point, we will be on to a good thing.

BM: *That probably also signals the credibility and positioning you have reached for MSN to enter into such an agreement with you.... How did you shut off some of the revenue streams, which are tempting to a new Internet pureplay firm? What were the implications of your decisions, with regard to venture capital (VC) funding, considering that in the initial stages, money is the life-blood of a B2C venture?*

VSS: You have to be clear about who you are. We were very clear with our VCs from day one that our core interest was in retailing, using Internet as the platform, and therefore we would not engage in anything that would take us away from our core interest. So we never had too much pressure from them about advertisements or other revenue streams.

KK: *What other mistakes do people often commit when they start an Internet retailing venture?*

VSS: An Internet business requires significant and sustained investment till you reach critical mass, after which it will hopefully become a very profitable business. Unfortunately, people did not realize this in the early days. They assumed that anybody with some amount of

Internet knowledge and technology experience could get into Internet retailing, but it requires a lot of investment to build a brand, relationships, logistic networks, and the stability required on an ongoing basis. Amazon. com is a classic case, a success story. They continue to invest in acquiring customers even today, when they could be a very profitable company without the acquisition investment. Bezos took big risks. I used to keep wondering why he wasn't showing profits in the year 2000, when the company could have cut back on the investment into customer acquisition and declared profits. On hindsight, maybe it was a deliberate strategy on his part to make investments dry up and discourage competition. Today, he is the king, the game is over. The entry barriers are so high that nobody can get in and he is laughing all the way to the bank.

BM: *How does an entrepreneur sense when it is time for the next edition of the business model?*

VSS: I see a business model essentially as a route to a goal. If you have stuck to your goal and your path for some time and you do not see the results, it's time for you to check whether your goal and your path are right. If you have realized that your goal itself is wrong, it is critical to be able to acknowledge it unemotionally and move on. The key is for an entrepreneur to be able to be passionate about a business and still be unattached to the extent of taking a tough call if it needs to be taken.

We have been reviewing our business dispassionately to see whether it will be profitable in the long term, whether we have the sustenance to reach critical mass, and what we need to create that sustenance. I am sure that if, at some point, we believed that it was not viable, we would have taken a tough call. Fortunately, we have passed this phase and we now are within striking distance of making the business break even. For us, it is always passion guided by objectivity. We are willing to relook at the goal and the path every six months and take calls as necessary.

Our current business plan is like straddling two horses—one which can give us a short-term boost both in terms of volumes and profitability, and the other which is going to be a long distance runner, which can become very profitable. In the online business, the problem really is that profitability may still be two or three years away. But we believe that if we stay on, fight this battle, keep a strong bottomline focus, find creative ways of taking this business forward, and get to the critical mass, like Amazon has done, then it will be an extremely profitable business. Meanwhile, with the new physical presence, we are getting the benefit of higher volumes and a short-term boost.

KK: *So, in your assessment, for the pureplay online business to reach a stage of viability, it will take some time. In the meanwhile, to ensure profitability, you have shifted to the hybrid model.*

VSS: That's partly true. The multi-channel retailing model also makes sense because it gives the customers the option to buy whenever and wherever they want, and is therefore more likely to succeed. We believe that there is a synergy between the two.

KK: *Clearly there are two strategies for multi-channel offering. You may start in a pureplay Internet form and then add the physical channels, or you may start off as a physical player and then go online. What are the pros and cons of these two approaches?*

VSS: In terms of focus from the management, if it goes from the Internet to the physical, there will be focus on both, whereas when it moves the other way, most likely the Internet will be inadequately focused upon. When a physical retailer moves to the Internet, the Internet venture often never gets the respect, the energy, and the time that it deserves. In order to succeed in it, the CEO should see the Internet as an integral part of the business. If you are already involved in the business on the Internet, and if the physical channel promises larger volumes, there is a greater chance that you would focus on that as well. Moreover, there are fewer chances of channel conflict if the transition is from the Internet to the physical. The other way round, with the price differentials, the chances are that the Internet would be viewed as a competing channel.

KK: *Businesses always look at benchmarks in their desire to be at the top. So who is your competitor now, given this transition from online to hybrid?*

VSS: Today we have two businesses. So we have to benchmark against competition in both of them. In the physical retail business, in grocery, our prime competitor is FoodWorld—they are the largest and the oldest and have definitely done a good job of building from scratch. There are the new hypermarkets like Giant which are coming up and you also have new format *kiranas* like Subhiksha in Chennai—and there are other supermarkets like ourselves. I don't think that value propositions from the different format of retailing have got frozen in the minds of customers as yet. So, in the next two years, there is going to be a huge power play between all these entities and formats.

Regarding the online business, there are two customer profiles that are evolving—the serious customer and the impulse customer. With the serious customer, I don't think we have any real competition today. Whereas, with the impulse customer, there is Indiatimes, and to a lesser extent, Rediff. We have realized that the community of impulse customers also needs to be courted, which is the reason for our alliance with MSN. Moreover, even though you dispense with customer acquisition spending, you still need to be visible to your existing customers through modes other than your email newsletters for them to remember you.

KK: *That would be a significant change in thinking between 1999 and now.*

VSS: Yes. For instance, the way you do merchandising for the impulse category is different. The class of vendors you go to is different. In fact, we are planning to dedicate one person to merchandise for the impulse shelf, because the way you think has to be different. But here we have to guard against inferior quality. Sometimes, the serious shopper too can be impulse driven and we have to have products which straddle both.

In conclusion, I must say that between running an IT business and being a retailer, retailing is more exciting and much more fun. It is tough, it is challenging, but one thing I can say is that it is never boring!

Questions

1. What are the main concerns in using technology for customer service?
2. Describe the major customer segments for an online retailer like Fabmall.
3. List the key success factors for an online business. Describe how Fabmall has managed some of these factors to achieve success.

Glossary

Advertised/Comparative Price	Price advertised by the retailer as compared to the prices offered by competitors or any other benchmark.
AIO Framework	A framework that is used to classify shoppers into various segments on the basis of their activities, interests, and opinions (AIO).
Analogue Model	A computerized site selection tool in which potential sales for a new store are estimated on the basis of sales of similar stores in existing areas, competition at a prospective location, the new store's expected market share at that location, and the size and density of a location's primary trading area.
Assortment Plans	Plans that break down the merchandise budgets into specific units of merchandise to be purchased in terms of SKUs for each style, colour, or size.
Assortment Tactics	Assortment is one of the most tangible variables for creating differentiation. It helps customers classify retailers on the basis of the products and services offered by them. The purpose of assortment tactics is to offer an assortment that balances the needs of consumers with the business objectives of the retailer and suppliers.
Atmospherics	A term popularized by Philip Kotler, used to refer to the ambience of a store.
Bait and Switch Pricing	The practice of advertising a low-priced model of shopping goods to lure shoppers into the store. Once the shoppers are in the store, a salesperson tries to persuade them to purchase a higher-priced model.
Balanced Scorecard	An instrument that provides a balanced picture of current operating performance as well as the drivers of future performance.
Bermuda Triangle Effect	A phenomenon where mid-sized firms are the most vulnerable as they have neither the low operation cost of a small firm, nor the economies of scale of a large firm.
Blinkered Mode	A mode in which shopping is very automatic. It is characterized by shoppers zooming in on familiar brands, with no time spent on reading labels or studying product attributes.
Body Scanning	A computerized system for taking body measurements. It helps apparel retailers in finding the exact size of clothing the customers need.
Box (Limited-line) Stores	Food-based discounters that focus on a small selection of items, moderate hours of operation (as compared to other supermarkets), few additional services, and limited manufacturer brands.
Brand	A set of experiences delivered consistently over time, market segments, formats, and geographies.
Browser Mode	A mode in which the shopper behaves more rationally, reading the 'back of pack' copy, comparing prices and ingredients, seeking more information about product attributes, and making piece-value comparisons across various brands.
Bundling	A practice whre distinct multiple items are offered together at a special price.

Business Intelligence (BI) System	An integrated set of tools, technologies, and programmed products that are used to collect, integrate, analyse, and make data available.
Buyer Responsibilities	The responsibilities of retail buyers can be broadly classified into three groups: (a) selection, feasibility, and monitoring of merchandise, (b) selection and appraisal of suppliers and negotiations with them, and (c) pricing-related decisions of merchandise.
Car Boot Sale	A form of retailing in which a vehicle is modified for the sale of merchandise such as books, magazines, clothes, music cassettes, export surplus and/or rejects, and fast food items.
Category Business District (CBD)	The hub of retailing in a city; synonymous with the term *downtown*, and has high vehicular and pedestrian traffic.
Category Killers	A discount store that offers a narrow variety but deep assortment of merchandise.
Category Management	A merchandising technique that improves productivity. It focuses on product category results rather than the performance of individual brands. The category management process produces enhanced business results by focusing on delivering value to the customer.
Category Tactics	A set of store variables used by a retailer to keep the store and its offer suitable for its target customers. Category tactics are grouped into assortment, pricing, display, and promotion tactics.
Chain Retailer	A retailer operating multiple outlets (store units) under a common ownership and name.
Circulation Graphics	Graphics such as signages and circulation store directories are used as directional tools to guide customers. In larger stores, graphics help customers know exactly where they are in a store and how to get to each floor.
Circulation Plans	There is a limited number of ways for shoppers to move within the store. Planning the circulation of the store involves both facilitating and determining these movements, based on the expected pattern of customer behaviour.
Closeout Retailers	Off-price retailers that sell a broad but consistent assortment of general merchandise, apparel, and soft home goods.
Combination Stores/ Supercentres	Food-based retailers that unite supermarket and general merchandise sales in one facility, with the latter typically accounting for 25 to 40 per cent of total sales.
Competition-oriented Pricing	A practice where the retailer uses the competitors' price, rather than demand or cost considerations, as a guide for price setting.
Consumer Cooperative	A retail firm where consumers invest in the enterprise. The officers are elected. Consumer-members share the profits or savings that accrue.
Contract Management	A course of action wherein the parties to a contract come together to meet their obligations.
Convenience Category	A category that is assigned the role of adding the value of convenience in shopping.
Convenience Stores	Also referred to as 'mom-and-pop stores', these are well-located stores that stay open for long hours and provide an average atmosphere and customer service.

Conventional Supermarket	A self-service food store offering groceries and a limited range of non-food items, such as health and beauty aids, and general merchandise.
Convergent or Internal Communication	That aspect of retail communication which comes into play once the customer is within the precincts of the store.
Curved Plans	Plans that encourage circulation since curved walls suggest more movements than straight ones.
Demand-oriented Pricing	The practice of setting prices on the basis of what consumers desire. The retailer determines the range of prices acceptable to the target market in order to decide on price.
Department Store	A large retail unit with an extensive assortment of goods and services that are organized into separate departments.
Destination Category	A category that consists of products and services for which the retailer is the primary provider. Categories with a destination role have the responsibility of creating a clear competitive advantage for the store.
Diagonal Path	A circulation plan that immediately creates movement by defying the normal rectilinear grid of a store.
Distribution Service Output	Utilities and disutilities created by distribution services. These can be seen as positive and negative customer values, which can be classified as economic (in perceived terms, functional), emotional, epistemic, and conditional values.
Distributive Justice	Judgments of fairness based on the allocation of material outcomes.
Do-it-yourself (DIY) Store	A category specialist offering equipment/material used by 'do-it-yourselfers'.
Drugstores	Speciality stores that concentrate on health and personal grooming merchandise. Pharmaceuticals represent over 50 per cent of drugstore sales and an even greater percentage of their profits.
Economic Order Quantity (EOQ)	The process of determining the inventory level by minimizing carrying costs and ordering costs.
Efficient Consumer Response (ECR)	A process for providing consumers with the best possible value, service, and variety.
Electronic Data Interchange (EDI)	Computer-to-computer exchange of data between trading partners.
Electronic Point-of-sale (POS) Signage	Liquid-crystal displays (LCDs) that show the names and prices of merchandise. In large stores, they may also provide the customers with currency conversions. These signs are attached to store shelves, peg hooks, or products.
Electronic Retailing	Also referred to as e-tailing or Internet retailing, it is a retail format in which the retailer and customer communicate with each other through an interactive electronic network. The customer can order merchandise directly and the merchandise is then delivered to the customer's address.
Everyday Low Pricing (EDLP)	A pricing strategy in which a retailer strives to sell its goods and services at consistently low prices throughout the selling season.
Evoked Price	The price evoked at the mention of a product or brand.
Extended Problem-solving	A form of purchase decision in which shoppers devote considerable time and effort to analysing alternatives.

External or Divergent Communication	In this mode of communication, the retailer reaches out to a large section of the target audience through mass media vehicles, such as television, newspaper, and radio.
Factory Outlet	A manufacturer-owned store selling manufacturer closeouts, discontinued merchandise, irregulars, cancelled orders, and sometimes, in season, first quality merchandise.
Flea Market	A market characterized by many retail vendors offering a range of products at discount prices in plain surroundings. Flea markets follow the tradition of street selling and shoppers sample and haggle over prices.
Flexible Pricing	The practice of offering the same products and quantities to different customers at different prices.
Food-based Superstores	Very large supermarkets ranging from 20,000 to 50,000 square feet. They cater to consumers' grocery needs and offer them the ability to buy fill-in general merchandise.
Franchising	A contractual agreement between a franchiser and a franchisee that allows the franchisee to operate a retail outlet using a name and format developed and supported by the franchiser.
Full-line Discount Store	A store selling a broad merchandise assortment for less than conventional prices.
Generally Planned Purchase	A pre-store decision to purchase a product category, but not the specific item.
Gross Margin Return on Floor Space (GMROF)	A measure of the productivity of space. It determines the sales generated from the investment in space.
Gross Margin Return on Investment (GMROI)	Measures the gross earnings of the retailers for the investment in merchandise.
Habitual Decision-making	A purchase decision process involving little or no conscious effort. This process is followed mainly in cases of repeat purchase.
Hand-held Shopping Assistant	A device consisting of a touch-sensitive screen and a bar-code reader. As soon as the customers scan the bar-code of the chosen product, the device provides them product information such as specifications, operating instructions, usage suggestions, and warranty information.
High–low Pricing	A pricing strategy that involves the use of high everyday prices and low leader specials on featured items.
Huff's Gravity Model	A model based on the premise that the probability that a given customer will shop in a particular store or shopping centre increases with the size of the store or centre and reduces with distance or travel time.
Hypermarket	A very large retail store offering low prices. It combines a discount store and superstore food retailer in one building.
Impulse Purchase	Purchase of an item due to a compelling force, whim, or an inspiration inside the store.
Independent Retailer	A retailer who owns a single retail unit.
Interactive Kiosks	Computers with touch-screen displays that provide shoppers with information about products in the store.

Inventory Management	The process of efficiently handling merchandise assortment while keeping the ordering, shipping, and other related costs under control.
Leader Pricing	A practice in which the retailer advertises and sells selected items in its goods/service assortment at less than the usual profit margins.
Leased Department	A department in a retail store rented generally by a manufacturer. The lessee is responsible for all aspects of business and pays the store a rent.
Limited Problem-solving	A purchase decision process involving a moderate amount of effort and time.
Liquidator	A retail format that comes in and liquidates leftover merchandise when an established retailer shuts down or downsizes.
Logistics Management	The process of managing transportation and associated areas to attain an efficient and effective distribution system.
Magpie Mode	A shopping mode in which the shopper allows himself/herself to be distracted by different brands on display. This mode is associated with situations where the shopper is seeking a change or a treat.
Markdown Management	Any reduction in the price of an item from its initially established price. The markdown percentage is the amount of reduction divided by the original selling price.
Mediagraphics	A method in which demographic characteristics, product ownership, and media data are used to build segments that can be addressed differently by varying product offerings and media plans.
Merchandise Plan	A forecast of specific merchandise purchased and its value, typically for a period of six months or a year.
Mobile Vans	Modified vehicles that usually sell poultry and meat products and books. They move from location to location, for fixed periods of time, thus providing convenience by coming closer to customers.
Morning Stars	Categories that contribute significantly to the retailer's business. They account for a high share of the retailer's sales; however, the rate of growth has either stabilized or is witnessing a decline.
Multiple Regression Model	A computerized site selection tool that uses equations showing the association between potential store sales and several independent variables at each location under consideration.
Multiple-unit Pricing	A practice where the pricing of a mutiple-unit package is set in such a way that the price of the complete package is less than the price of each unit if sold individually.
Negotiation	A discussion between two or more parties to bring out a solution.
Negotiation Dilemma	The tension between cooperation and competition.
Non-store-based Retailing	A form of retailing in which sales are made to consumers without using physical stores. Non-store retailers are known by the media they use to communicate with their customers, such as direct marketing, vending machines, or e-tailing.
Occasional/Seasonal Category	Categories that are provided by retailers to cater to the seasonal or occasional needs of customers.

Odd Pricing	The practice of setting retail prices that end in the digits 5 or 9, such as ₹99.99 and ₹59.95.
Off-price Stores	Stores offering brand names and designer labels at a low price in an efficient, limited service environment.
One Price Policy	A pricing practice where retailers charge the same price from the customer.
Open-to-buy Planning	The difference between planned purchases and the purchase commitments already made by a buyer for a given time period. It represents the amount the buyer has left to spend for that period and is reduced each time a purchase is made.
Overstored Trade Area	An area that has so many stores selling a specific good or service that several stores are on the brink of closure.
Perceived Price	The perception of the product and the price associated with it.
Planned BOM Inventory	= Planned Sales × Stock-to-sales Ratio
Planned EOM Inventory	The end of month (EOM) stock for any month is the planned beginning of month (BOM) stock for the following month.
Planned Reductions	These are reductions required due to markdowns, employee discounts, shrinkages, employee theft, or shoplifting.
Point of Purchase (PoP) Communication	Internal communication that reinforces the store image by ensuring that there is no dissonance in the minds of the customers. Stores use tools, such as visual merchandising, signage and graphics, and other forms of PoP communication, to achieve their desired objectives. PoP communication plays various roles, such as informing, reminding, encouraging, creating excitement or interactivity, and building store image.
Preferred Category	A category that provides competitive value to the target consumer. Categories with this role are used to induce customers to prefer the store to its competitors.
Prestige Pricing	Pricing based on the assumption that consumers will not buy goods and services at prices deemed too low as they associate quality with price.
Price Belief	Belief that the customer has towards prices in general.
Price Image	The image of the price that a particular brand may carry.
Price Lining	A practice in which the retailer sells merchandise at a limited range of price points, with each point representing a distinct level of quality, rather than stocking merchandise at various price levels.
Pricing Tactics	Price is a strong differentiator for retailers. Pricing tactics help retailers in managing their price on the basis of the requirements of the category. The prices of categories are set primarily on the basis of their roles. Retailers use price to create image, build traffic, and to keep the value delivered to customers competitive.
Primary Zone	The geographic area from which the store or shopping centre derives 50 to 80 per cent of its customers.
Promotional Tactics	These are the sources of creative selling ideas. Promotional tactics enable retailers and manufacturers to meet objectives when brand substitution occurs.
Pure Play	Retailers who have a presence only on the Internet and do not have any physical store.

Questionables	Categories that do not fit with the store strategies and plans.
Race Track Walkway or Pathway Plan	A plan that is common in larger stores, and consists of a distinct circulation path that moves shoppers through the store. The pathway may be defined by differing floor materials, changes in the ceiling treatment, or even just a clearing of display units.
Radio Frequency Identification (RFID) Tags	Electronic devices for storing information about merchandise as well as for tracking them. As large as a pinhead, consisting of an antenna and a chip that contains an electronic product code, these tags can store more information about a product than bar codes.
Recycled Merchandise Retailers	These sell cast-off clothes, furniture, sporting goods, and computers. This category includes pawnshops, thrift shops, consignment shops, and even flea markets.
Reference Price	A shopper's perceived current price of a brand. Reference price could also be termed as anticipated price.
Reservation Price	The price reserved by customers for a particular product or category of products.
Retail Format	A sytem through which retailers deliver the value promised to their customers.
Retailing	An activity that ensures that customers derive maximum value from the buying process. This involves activities and steps needed to place the merchandise made elsewhere into the hands of customers or to provide services to the customers.
Retail Service Quality Scale (RSQS)	An instrument used for measuring retail service quality.
Saturated Trade Area	A geographic area with an adequate amount of retail facilities to satisfy the needs of its population. It offers customers a good opportunity of selection.
Secondary Zone	A geographic area of secondary importance in terms of customer sales, generating about 20 per cent of a store's sales.
Self-scanning and Self-checkout System	A hand-held bar-code reader used by shoppers to scan and tally their purchases while shopping. The scanner displays the price of the chosen item.
Service Profit Chain	Linking of activities for connecting customer loyalty and profitability.
SERVQUAL	An instrument used for measuring service quality.
Shelf Presentation Tactics	Position-sensitive tactics that have a significant impact on sales. The position of the shelf, number of facings, and the pack size affect the sales of merchandise. Tactics in this area determine how the category will be presented to consumers at the point of sale. Some of the key decisions made at this stage are vis-à-vis the criteria used for managing shelf space, category location, category layout, on-shelf service levels, and specific sub-category/segment and SKU space allocation.
Single Price Retailers	Closeout stores that sell all their merchandise at a single price.
Sleepers	Consist of categories and products that do not move fast.
Social Marketing	Communication and marketing to consumers through online communities.
Social Networking	The process of sharing information by connecting with individuals with similar interests.
Socio Economic Classification (SEC)	Provides an indication of socio-economic position, based on occupation.

Speciality Store	A small-sized store that concentrates on a limited number of complementary merchandise categories and provides a high level of service.
Specifically Planned Purchase	The purchase of a specific brand or item that was planned prior to the visit to the shop and purchased as planned.
Store Loyalty	Loyalty is the prime objective that every retailer aims to achieve through its retail strategy and mix elements. It has two facets: attitudinal and behavioural. The attitudinal dimension demonstrates the tendency of the customer to look at the store favourably, and, in many cases, to recommend it to others. The behavioural manifestation of loyalty is reflected in patronage.
Store Patronage	The behavioural manifestation of loyalty is reflected in patronage.
Straight Plan	A circulation plan that provides for shoppers to cover the store with direct access from the front to the back.
String	An unplanned shopping area comprising a group of retail stores, often with similar or compatible product lines, located along a street or highway. There is little extension onto perpendicular streets.
Substitute Purchase	A change from a generally or specifically planned item to a functional substitute.
Supercentre	A one-stop combination of a supermarket and discount department store that offers from 80,000 to over 1,00,000 products.
Supply Chain Business Processes	A network of activities designed with a focus on customers and with a purpose of dynamic management of flows of products, information, cash, knowledge, and ideas in the chain.
Supply Chain Management (SCM)	The integration of key business processes from the end user through to the original supplier that provides products, services, and information that add value for customers and stockholders.
Tertiary Zone	A zone that includes customers who occasionally shop at the store or shopping centre.
Trading Area	A geographical area containing the customers of a particular store or group of stores for specified goods or services.
Understored Trade Area	An area that has too few stores selling a specific good or service to satisfy the needs of the population.
Unplanned Purchase	A purchased item that the shopper did not have in mind on entering the shop.
Value and Lifestyle (VALS) Segmentation	Refers to the classification of shoppers into different types, based on their unique style of living.
Variable Pricing	The practice of altering prices to coincide with fluctuations in costs or consumer demand.
Variety Store	A store that handles a wide assortment of inexpensive and popularly priced goods and services, such as stationery, gift items, women's accessories, health and beauty aids, light hardware, toys, houseware, and confectionery items.
Vending Machine	A retailing format involving the coin- or card-operated dispensing of goods (such as beverages) and services.

Vertical Marketing System	A system consisting of all levels of independently owned businesses along a channel of distribution.
Video Kiosk	A freestanding, interactive, electronic computer terminal that displays products and related information on a video screen. It often uses a touch screen for consumers to make selections.
Virtual Display Case	A large-screen, rear projection video display and computer graphics system that shows three-dimensional images of shelves and the merchandise on them.
Warehouse Club	A retailer that offers a limited assortment of food and general merchandise, with limited services, at low prices to small businesses.
Winners	Categories and items which are the cash generators for the store. They are highly profitable and are big draws for the customers.

Subject Index

Company and Brand Index

About the Authors

Piyush Kumar Sinha, Professor, Marketing, and Chairperson, Centre for Retailing, Indian Institute of Management Ahmedabad (IIMA), has over 30 years of academic and industry experience. He has also served as Dean, Mudra Institute of Communications Ahmedabad (MICA), and has taught at leading business schools in India.

Dr Sinha is active in research in the areas of retailing and consumer behaviour. He is involved in qualitative research in the area of marketing and has presented and published numerous papers in national and international journals of repute.

Dwarika Prasad Uniyal is currently Associate Professor (Marketing), Indian Institute of Management (IIM) Kashipur. Earlier, he was the Founding Dean (Academic) of Jindal Global Business School (JGBS), O.P. Jindal Global University. He has held professorial positions in premier business schools, such as S.P. Jain Institute of Management and Research (SPJIMR), Mumbai, S.P. Jain Centre of Management (SPJCM), Dubai-Singapore, and MICA, and is still a visiting faculty at some of the institutes mentioned above.

Dr Uniyal has published several research papers and articles in national and international journals as well as leading magazines and newspapers.

Related Titles

SALES AND DISTRIBUTION MANAGEMENT
Second Edition
[9780198077046]

Tapan K. Panda, *Director-PGPM, Great Lakes Institute of Management Studies, Chennai* and **Sunil Sahadev**, *Faculty at University of Sheffield, UK*

The second edition of *Sales and Distribution Management* is a comprehensive textbook, which has been updated and enlarged with new chapters. Specially designed to meet the requirements of management students specializing in sales and marketing, it gives a balanced presentation of the concepts of sales and distribution through examples and cases. Readers will find this textbook highly useful for its application of theoretical concepts explained through illustrative corporate examples and cases.

MARKETING RESEARCH
Concepts, Practices, and Cases
[9780195676969]

Sunanda Easwaran, *IBS-Mumbai* and **Sharmila J. Singh**, *National Qualitative Head, GFK Mode India*

Marketing Research: Concepts, Practices, and Cases is a comprehensive textbook specially designed to meet the needs of management students. It combines the quantitative and qualitative aspects of marketing research, and addresses its utility for both the researcher and the end-user. It provides in-depth coverage of the key elements of the subject: its theoretical foundations, techniques of planning and design, research methodology for the implementation of quantitative and qualitative techniques, presentation and interpretation of findings through reports, and the use of marketing research techniques for developing and evaluating marketing strategies.

SERVICES
Marketing, Operations, and Management
[9780195689082]

Vinnie Jauhari, *Director, IIMT, Gurgaon* and **Kirti Dutta**, *Assistant Professor, BULMIM, Delhi*

Services: Marketing, Operations, and Management explores the core concepts of the service industry and uses numerous examples, exhibits, flow charts, formats, and illustrations to explain them. Management students will find this book highly useful for its explanation of the key concepts through industry-related examples. The book will also be useful to professionals in the service industry due to its practice-oriented approach.

BRAND MANAGEMENT
(with CD)
Principles and Practices
[9780198069867]

Kirti Dutta, *Bhartiya Vidya Bhavan's Usha & Lakshmi Mittal Institute of Management, New Delhi*

Brand Management: Principles and Practices is a comprehensive textbook that has been written in a simple and lucid language in the Indian context. The text and theory is suitably illustrated with numerous examples, exhibits, and case studies. Each chapter is linked with the accompanying CD that contains presentations, television commercials, and videos that explain the key concepts. The CD also includes exercises for enhancing decision-making abilities.

Other Related Titles

9780198063308	Baines et al.: *Marketing*	9780198072027	Mallik: *Sales Management*
9780195671230	Joshi: *International Marketing (Includes CD)*	9780198074120	Jethwaney & Jain: *Advertising Management, 2e*
9780198061151	Bajaj et al.: *Retail Management, 2e*	9780195667585	Apte: *Services Marketing*
		9780195677942	Ghosh: *Industrial Marketing*